The Sociometry Reader

THE
Sociometry Reader

EDITED BY

J. L. Moreno, with Helen H. Jennings, Joan H. Criswell,
Leo Katz, Robert R. Blake, Jane S. Mouton, Merl E. Bonney,
Mary L. Northway, Charles P. Loomis, Charles Proctor,
Renato Tagiuri, and Jiri Nehnevajsa

PREFACE BY
J. L. Moreno

THE FREE PRESS
OF GLENCOE, ILLINOIS

PREFACE

In the last hundred and fifty years, three main currents of social thought developed—sociology, scientific socialism, and sociometry—each related to a different geographic and cultural area: sociology to France, socialism to Germany-Russia, and sociometry to the United States. Each of the three disciplines is defined broadly. The focus of sociology was to develop a rigorous system that embraces all social sciences. The focus of socialist doctrine was to prepare and produce proletarian revolutions. The focus of sociometry was to comprehend and measure the socius. This is a heuristic hypothesis, designed to arrange the productivity of social science around these three points of reference.

The first part of the hypothesis, that is, that sociology owes its origin to France, is probably most easy to accept, as it is primarily to the French revolution between 1789 and 1795, and French writers like Claude Saint Simon, Auguste Comte, Pierre Proudhon, and Emile Durkheim that sociology owes its name and existence. The productivity of the French revolution consisted of the emancipation of the bourgeois class—that is as far as it went or was able to go; it spent itself in doing it—and inspired the emergence and consolidation of sociology as a scientific system. The total configuration of social forces during the nineteenth century in France—and also in England—did not permit the victory of a proletarian revolution to cluster, although it was the battleground of at least two major efforts. As already said, its revolutionary energy had spent itself in the emancipation of the bourgeois and its theoretical energy in the development of sociology.

The second part of the hypothesis, that scientific socialism owes its origin to the German-Russian combine, is also plausible. No one denies that many seeds of thought that entered into the doctrine of Karl Marx came from French and English writers, but on the other hand, no one can deny that it is in Germany and Russia where its most feverish theories developed and that it is there where the most violent proletarian revolutions culminated in victory. Scientific socialism became, in the hands of Marx, Engels, and Lenin, as rigorous a system of revolutionary social science and interpretation of history as did sociology in the hands of Comte and Durkheim.

This hypothesis is, of course, an oversimplification, and this it is meant to be. Its merit would lie in helping to bring the speed, development, and direction which the social sciences have had in the last two centuries in line with the powerful political currents of our time. The first consequence would then be to consider Marx exclusively as the founder of scientific socialism and not to claim him, as it is often the case, along with Comte and Proudhon as one of the founders of sociology, an honor which he would most likely have refused. This also gives proper consideration to the deep cleavage and divergence which exists between sociology and revolutionary socialism. By classifying Marx as a "sociologist" one dilutes and sentimentalizes the theoretical and practical clash between the two historical movements. This hypothesis makes more understandable the tight resistance against sociology in Soviet Russia and in the countries dominated by its influence and, in turn, the tight resistance against revolutionary socialism in the western democracies. One may assume that this sharp demarcation of boundaries is not only due to political reasons but to genuine differences of thoughtways which hinder the infiltration of sociology and western cultural concepts into the Soviet world.

The third part of the hypothesis, that sociometry owes its origin to the U.S.A. is more difficult to explain; indeed, it needs more elaborate explanation. First, one would have to prove that it is a "main current" of thought; it smacks of arrogance to single it out among other significant trends in the USA. Second, it does not explain the rich development of sociology in the U.S.A. *before* the advent of sociometry. Before I go into the discussion of these two arguments let me define clearly the position I am taking. *All the excellence of American sociology, I claim, has found its climax in sociometry and its allied developments. It is for the first time, in sociometry, that the social sciences in the U.S.A. showed "collective originality."* By this I mean that sociometry is not so much the work of a single individual, but a collective effort within a "favorable" social climate.

It may be helpful here to differentiate between sociometry and the sociometric movement, sociometry being the most systematic and the furthest developed crystallization of the trend towards group measurement in the social sciences in the last two decades, sociometric movement being the influence beyond its pales, upon all branches of social sciences, anthropology, sociology, psychology, psychiatry, etc. This does also not mean that sociometric measurement is an exclusive property of the U.S.A.; it is known that some seeds of social measurement existed already in France, England, and Germany in the work of forerunners as Adolphe Quetelet, John Graunt, and Johann Sussmilch, but their efforts did not take root—they did not develop beyond the "demo-metric" variety—the historical situation was not ready, and the social climate not favorable.

The first argument, that sociometry has become a main current of thought, can easily be verified by referring to the many thousands of quantitative studies of group structure which have been carried out in the last thirty years, in the great majority of cases under the term "sociometric." Perhaps even more striking is the fact that sociometric terms and techniques are becoming increasingly anonymous, universally applied, and frequently used as the basic reference for studies which are in themselves non-sociometric.

An analysis of American sociology before sociometry entered the field could easily show that my second argument is also reasonable, as it was largely under foreign influence, particularly that of Comte, Spencer, and Darwin. This influence can be especially noted in the two great leaders of American sociology, Ward and Giddings. This does not reduce their genius as "individuals," but their work did not develop a collective productivity, an American school of thought; it was colored by the cultural determinants which were French and English. On the other hand, one can already discern a tendency towards sociometry in the work of Cooley, Mead, and others, which substantiates the historic continuity of sociometric thought in the U.S. It is in the spirit of my hypothesis that, although certain aspects of sociometry and microsociology had already been conceptualized by Simmel, Von Wiese, Gurvitch, and myself in Europe, it is still a genuine American movement because it would have died there, whereas it flowered here to great productivity. More than any other living variety of the human species, the American man loves to express status in figures, he is the *"homo metrum."*

When I speak of the sociometric movement, I mean sociometry in its broadest sense and the direct and indirect influence it has exercised upon all branches of social science in the last thirty years; sociometry as it has marched on under various labels, guises, and in various modifications as group dynamics, action research, process and interaction analysis, etc.; (a) spontaneity theory and evaluation of spontaneity; (b) theory of interpersonal relations and theory of action; (c) the revision of the experimental method in the social sciences; (d) the measurement of interpersonal relations and the measurement of groups; (e) the empirical and experimental study of small groups; (f) the emergence of social microscopy and microsociology; (g) initiation and development of social interaction research; the study of social networks and communication; (h) the gradual emergence of an experimental sociology; (i) the experimental approach to role theory known as role-playing, psychodrama and sociodrama; (j) experimental research and creativity research.

There has been considerable consensus among leading social scientists in giving sociometry a broad definition, as a point of confluence of many individual contributions:

F. Stuart Chapin:

"Sociometry is the mathematical study of psychological properties of populations, the experimental technique of and the results obtained by application of quantitative methods," so reads the definition of the subject given by J. L. Moreno,[1] who has chiefly popularized the term among students of human behavior. My inclination is to go to the etymology of the word which shows it to be a combination of the Latin *socius,* meaning social, and the Latin *metrum,* meaning measure, or the Greek *metron,* meaning measure. Thus the term would mean "social measurement."[2]

Read Bain:

"Sociometry is and probably will remain a generic term to describe *all* measurements of societal and interpersonal data."[3]

George A. Lundberg:

"There is no doubt that to the general public the word 'sociometric' means today having to do with the measurement of social phenomena."[4]

Florian Znaniecky:

"Sociometry seems to have solved this age-old methodical difficulty in a more satisfactory way than any other attempts to introduce quantitative methods into social science; for in Moreno's pregnant terms, it does not sacrifice the 'socius' to the 'metrum,' empirical content to formal technique."[5]

"In the social field mathematics was applied first to demographic statistics, whose original assumption was that the human individual is an ultimate 'indivisible' entity and that consequently every collective phe-

---

[1] J. L. Moreno, "Psychological Organization of Groups in the Community," *Proceedings of the 57th Annual Session of the American Association on Mental Deficiency,* Boston, June, 1933; read at the joint meeting of the American Psychiatric Association and the American Association on Mental Deficiency.

[2] F. Stuart Chapin, *Sociometry,* III (1940), 245.

[3] Read Bain, *Sociometry,* VI (1943), 212.

[4] George A. Lundberg, *Sociometry,* VI (1943), 219.

[5] Florian Znaniecki, *Sociometry,* VI (1943), 227.

nomenon is a mere sum of individual phenomena. The majority of sociologists, however, are by now fully aware that the human individual as member of a collectivity is not an independent unit but a participant in collective systems and processes and that the main task of mathematical methods in sociology is the quantitative analysis of such systems and processes. A step toward the final elimination of this old source of confusion is the recent development of sociometry—a method of research with important though as yet only partially realized, possibilities."[6]

Georges Gurvitch:

"That which constitutes all the originality of sociometry is that the measure (metrum) is only a technical, very limited means of obtaining better understanding of purely qualitative relationships with the *socius;* these relationships are characterized by their *spontaneity,* their *creative element,* their link with the *moment,* their integration into concrete and unique configurations."[7]

Leopold von Wiese:

"We consider sociometry as a method, which if it is applied consequently and in the most comprehensive way possible would raise our science from the position of social scientific astrology to astronomy."[8]

E. W. Burgess:

"If statistics deal with measurement, why is there any necessity for a separate field of sociometry which also is concerned with measurement? The superficial answer might be that statistics is concerned with measurement in general and that sociometry is confined to social phenomena. But there would be no point in creating a new discipline unless there were something in the nature of social phenomena that required the devising of special methods of measurement. If society is conceived as an aggregate of individual organisms, as in population studies, there would be no need of sociometry. But if we take as our subject-matter the person and groups of persons, then the analysis of interpersonal relations and the devising of instruments for their measurement become important. Sociometry is to be further differentiated from statistics in the fact that the former deals with all types of measurement significant for understanding

---

6 Florian Znaniecki, *American Journal of Sociology,* Vol. L, No. 6 (1945).
7 Georges Gurvitch, *Sociometry in France and the United States* (1949), p. 2.
8 Leopold von Wiese, *Sociometry in France and the United States* (1949), p. 214.

human behavior and not exclusively with those requiring statistical form-ulae."[9]

Before I elaborate further on the historical and political significance of the sociometric movement, several questions should be answered: (1) What, precisely, is sociometry? (2) Why did sociometry emerge in the United States and why could it not emerge elsewhere, for instance, in France, Germany, or Soviet Russia? (3) Why did it succeed in the United States?

1) What, precisely, is sociometry? The cornerstone of sociometry is its "Doctrine of Spontaneity and Creativity." It has created an experimental methodology which is applicable to all social sciences. It is the sociometric revision of the scientific method of the social sciences that will gradually make such a thing as a science of society possible. It gives its subjects research status by changing them from subjects into participating and evaluating actors; a social science becomes sociometric to the degree in which it gives the members of the group research status and to the degree in which it is able to measure their activities; it goes to work with actual or prospective groups and develops procedures which can be used in actual situations. It puts an equally strong emphasis upon group dynamics and group action as upon measurement and evaluation. In the early phases of sociometry, measurement was mere counting, for instance, counting of words, of acts, of roles, of choices and rejections, of steps in walking or of mouthfuls and pauses in eating; these naive, rough forms of measurement were an indispensable first step before standardized units of universal validity could be established.

2) When sociometry entered the field three powerful currents of ideas existed in the United States: pragmatism, progressive education and social engineering (to have things "done"). But more important, perhaps, is that the United States of America is a commonwealth in which *small* groups enjoy (or at least enjoyed at the time when sociometry emerged) a greater degree of independence of action than in France, Germany, and Soviet Russia, and are therefore more easily amenable to open experiments with small groups and genuine small groups research—and negatively, the absence of an over-all religious or cultural ideology as Marxism, Catholicism, or Nationalism which might have been so overpowering as to hinder the growth and outbursts of small-group "spontaneity." Its supreme political position after World War I made it into an enormous sociological island, open to everything novel—people, ideas—and almost carelessly embracing and permitting every form of social experimentation. If we could chart the nation's social structure, a socio-

---

[9] E. W. Burgess, *Sociometry*, VI (1943), 223.

gram of its human relations, positive and negative, of its sympathies and antagonisms, we will probably see millions of small groups, each gravitating around its own center, the connections between them being weak or distorted in the majority of cases. It may have been due to the continuous influx of new groups of pioneering migrants and the comparative independence of the small group to start and take off, left unharnessed by a rigid, central idea of government, or culture, that it became the natural soil for the ever-changing and pliable sociometric action experiments and methods. The low social cohesion of the American nation as a whole had to be offset by a high autonomy and cohesion of its small groups.[10] In contrast to the United States, some of the cultural *centers* on the European continent, for instance, Germany and Soviet Russia, could not consolidate themselves except on extreme levels of high cohesion of social structure which were parallel with a low degree of freedom—their only alternative was social anarchy and chaos—they could not integrate their social forces on a median level (between the two extremes) which would permit the spontaneous and natural movement of their small groups.

3) Sociometry succeeded rapidly in the U.S.A. because it fulfilled an important need for its gradual integration into a united, national culture; its three major forms, the sociometric experiment, group psychotherapy, and psychodrama, provide a binder to tie the parts together. They promise to transform areas of low cohesion into areas of high cohesion without sacrificing, however, the spontaneity and the freedom of small groups. Cohesion of the group is measured by the degree of co-operativess and collaborative interaction forthcoming from as many sub-groups and members as possible on behalf of the purpose for which the group is formed. There is great probability that in a spontaneously growing society the cohesion rises and declines in proportion to the number of small, independent groups within it and with the number of independent goals (criteria) around which they revolve. As a free, democratic society is more inclined to permit the production of a large number of independent small groups with a large number of different and independent goals, its cohesion will tend to be low.[11]

The historic significance of sociometry rests with the medial position which it has between sociology and scientific socialism. If one would like to play with the Hegelian formula of dialectic development one could say that

---

[10] See "The Function of a 'Department of Human Relations' within the Structure of the Government of the United States," *Sociometry, Experimental Method and the Science of Society*, p. III.

[11] For factual evidence in support of the above hypotheses, see *Sociometry*, Vol. I–XV (1937–1952).

sociology presented the thesis; socialistic doctrine, the antithesis; and sociometry, the synthesis; every step, however, being somewhat more than the previous step. Sociology is historically defined by the two or three great systems it has developed. Scientific socialism is defined by the two or three great proletarian revolutions it has incited. Sociometry is defined by its operations; it is immaterial whether they are called sociometric or by any other name. Sociometry is recognized by what it does, stirring to action and keeping action open but using scientific precision and experimental methods to keep action in bounds. Sociology, for instance, becomes a science in proportion to becoming sociometric, but the same is true about revolutionary socialism; it, too, becomes a science in proportion to becoming sociometric. It is bound to happen sooner or later that sociology, with its dependent social sciences, and revolutionary socialism will converge and meet on a new level of social insight—the sociometric. The methodical development of sociometry is the dynamic link which should bring sociology and scientific socialism to increased convergence and, finally, to unity. Universally accepted standards of social measurement will also aid to resolve the international tension between the communistic and democratic societies. There are two principles pregnant in sociometry, one of which it shares with sociology, but not with revolutionary socialism and vice versa. It shares with classic sociology the tendency towards elaborated social systems, a tendency which is not shared by scientific socialism in equal measure. Sociometry shares with revolutionary socialism the idea of planned social action, with the fundamental modification, however, that it must be experimentally devised and controlled, that it must be applied to small groups first and applied to larger groups as the knowledge derived from small systems increases. It is thus the sociometric action experiment which links sociometry with scientific socialism and separates them both from sociology. *It is in the sense of the dialectic theory of sociometry that the analysis made here will become increasingly "less" true the more scientific socialism will permit its Marxian hypotheses to be tested within sociometric settings (this may sound Utopian, but ideas have a way of boring from within) and the more sociology will include into its operations actual experiments.* Indeed, this analysis is less portent and correct today than thirty years ago when sociology was entirely engrossed in general systems which, however ingenious in prospect and vision, never actually stepped from the libraries and classrooms into social reality of the "Ding an sich" and never became a "sociology of the people, by the people and for the people."

Sociometry did not develop in a vacuum; many generations of social philosophers have anticipated and formulated a number of the hypotheses which I have brought to a clearer formulation and empirical test. However, I do not have any illusions as to my importance. I am fully aware that sociometry might have come into existence without me, just as sociology would have come into existence in France without Comte, and Marxism in Germany and Russia without Marx.

J. L. Moreno

ACKNOWLEDGMENTS

The editors and The Free Press acknowledge, with thanks, the permissions granted by publishers and copyright holders to reprint papers included in this volume. Specifically, acknowledgment is due the following:

Beacon House, Inc., publishers of *Sociometry*, for permission to reprint the following articles: "Statistics of Social Configurations," by J. L. Moreno and H. H. Jennings, I (1938), 342–74; "A Method for Depicting Social Relationships Obtained by Sociometric Testing," by Mary L. Northway, III (1940), 144–50; "Informal Groupings in a Spanish-American Village," by Charles P. Loomis, IV (1941), 36–55; "Status: Its Measurement and Control in Education," by Leslie D. Zeleny, IV (1941), 193–204; "Discussion of Papers on Sociometry," by E. W. Burgess, VI (1943), 223–24; "Outsiders," by Mary L. Northway, VII (1944), 10–25; "A Rationale for Weighting First, Second, and Third Sociometric Choices," by D. T. Campbell, XVII (1945), 242–43; "Foundations of Sociometric Measurement," by Joan H. Criswell, IX (1946), 7–13; "The Constant Frame of Reference Problem in Sociometry," by Daisy S. Edwards, XI (1948), 372–79; "A Matrix Approach to the Analysis of Sociometric Data: Preliminary Report," by Elaine Forsythe and Leo Katz, IX (1946), 340–47; "Sociogram and Sociomatrix," by J. L. Moreno, IX (1946), 348–49; "Measurement of Reciprocation under Multiple Criteria of Choice," by Joan H. Criswell, IX (1946), 126–27; "Leadership and Sociometric Choice," by H. H. Jennings, X (1947), 32–49; "The Social Atom and Death," by J. L. Moreno, X (1947), 80–84; "Sociometric Status and Personal Problems of Adolescents," by R. G. Kuhlen and H. S. Bretsch, X (1947), 122–32; "The Measurement of Group Integration," by Joan H. Criswell, X (1947), 259–67; "Organization of the Social Atom," by J. L. Moreno, X (1947), 287–93; "Some Relationships between Interpersonal Judgments and Sociometric Status in a College Group," by R. L. French and I. N. Mensh, XI (1948), 335–45; "Buddy Ratings: Popularity Contest or Leadership Criteria?" by R. J. Wherry and D. H. Fryer, XII (1949), 170–90; "Sociometric Concepts in Personnel Administration," by Joan H. Criswell, XII (1949), 287–300; "The Accuracy of Teachers' Judgments Concerning the Sociometric Status of Sixth-grade Pupils," by Norman E. Gronlund, XIII (1950), 197–225; "The Use of a Sociometric Test as a Predictor of Combat Unit Effectiveness," by Daniel M. Goodacre, III, XIV (1951), 148–52; "An Analysis of Social Rejection in a College Men's Residence Hall," by J. W. Kidd, XVI (1951), 225–34; "A Note on the Use of Target Sociograms," by Mary L. Northway, XIV (1951), 235–36; "Distance and Friendships as Factors in the Gross Interaction Matrix," by John T. Gullahorn, XV (1952), 123–34; "Sociometric Choice and Organizational Effectiveness: A Multi-relational Approach," by F. Massarik, R. Tannenbaum, M. Kahane, and I. R. Weschler, XVI (1953), 211–38; "Analysis of Social Interaction and Sociometric Perception," by Edgar F. Borgatta, XVII (1954), 7–32; "Judgmental Response Sets in the Perception of Sociometric Status," by Herbert M. Schiff, XVII (1954), 207–27; "A Plan for Sociometric Studies in a Longitudinal Programme of Research in Child Development," by Mary L. Northway, VII (1954), 272–81; "The Reliability of Sociometric Measures," by Jane Srygley Mouton, Robert R. Blake, and Benjamin Fruchter, XVIII (1955), 7–48; "Job Satisfaction and Interpersonal Desirability Values," by B. J. Speroff, XVIII (1955), 69–72; "The Sociometric System," by J. L. Moreno, XXVIII (1955), 88–89; "Creativity-spontaneity-cultural Conserves," by J. L. Moreno, XVIII (1955), 108–13; "The Validity of Sociometric Responses," by Jane Srygley Mouton, Robert R. Blake, and Benjamin Fruchter, XVIII (1955), 181–206; "Sociometry: Decades of Growth," by Jiri Nehnevajsa, XVIII (1955), 304–51; "The Transparency of Interpersonal Choice," by Renato Tagiuri, Nathan Kogan, and Jerome S. Bruner, XVIII (1955), 368–79.

Beacon House, Inc., publishers of "Principle of Encounter," "Psychological Currents," "Role," "Social and Organic Unity of Mankind," "Sociometry, Sociology and Scientific Socialism," "The Social Atom: A Definition," and "Tele: A Definition," from *Who Shall Survive?* by J. L. Moreno (New York, 1953); and "Three Dimensions of Society—the External Society, the Sociometric Matrix and the Social Reality," from *Sociometry, Experimental Method and the Science of Society,* by J. L. Moreno (New York, 1951).

Tavistock Publications, Ltd., publishers of *Human Relations,* for permission to reprint the following articles: "The Analysis of Sociograms Using Matrix Algebra," by Leon Festinger, II (1949), 153–58; "The Three-dimensional Basis of Emotional Interactions in Small Groups, Part I," by F. Kräupl Taylor, VII (1954), 441–71; "The Three-dimensional Basis of Emotional Interactions in Small Groups, Part II," by F. Kräupl Taylor, VIII (1955), 3–28; "Awareness of One's Social Appeal," by F. Kräupl Taylor, IX (1956), 47–56.

The American Sociological Society, publishers of the *American Sociological Review,* for permission to reprint "The Sociography of Some Community

Relations," by George A. Lundberg and Margaret Lawsing, II (1937), 326–28; and "A Method for the Analysis of the Structure of Complex Organizations," by Robert S. Weiss and Eugene Jacobson, (1955), 661–68.

The Institute of Mathematical Statistics, publishers of the *Annals of Mathematical Statistics,* for permission to reprint "The Distribution of the Number of Isolates in a Social Group," by Leo Katz, XXIII (1952), 271–76; and "Probability Distributions of Random Variables Associated with a Structure of the Sample Space of Sociometric Investigations," by Leo Katz and James H. Powell, XXVIII (1957), 442–48.

Psychometrika, Inc., publishers of *Psychometrika,* for permission to reprint "A New Status Index Derived from Sociometric Analysis," by Leo Katz XVIII (1953), 39–43; and "A Proposed Index of the Conformity of One Sociometric Measurement to Another," by Leo Katz and James H. Powell, XVIII (1953), 249–58.

Adult Education Association of the United States, publishers of *Adult Leadership,* for permission to reprint "Tapping Human Power Lines," by Charles P. Loomis, I (1953), 12–14.

The University of Chicago Press, publishers of the *American Journal of Sociology,* for permission to reprint "Selection of Compatible Flying Partners," by Leslie D. Zeleny, LII (1947), 424–31.

Beacon House, Inc., publishers of *Group Psychotherapy,* for permission to reprint "Role Playing Skill and Sociometric Peer Status," by Jane Srygley Mouton, Robert L. Bell, Jr., and Robert R. Blake, I (1956), 7–17.

Harper and Brothers, publishers of "Sociometric Choice Process in Personality and Group Formation," by H. H. Jennings, from *Group Relations at the Crossroads,* edited by Muzafer Sherif and M. O. Wilson (New York, 1953).

The American Psychological Association, publishers of the *Journal of Abnormal and Social Psychology,* for permission to reprint "Leadership Behavior and Combat Performance of Airplane Commanders," by Andrew Halpin, XLIX (1954), 19–22.

The Aero Medical Association, publishers of the *Journal of Aviation Medicine,* for permission to reprint "Nominating Technique as a Method of Evaluating Air Group Morale," by J. G. Jenkins, XIX (1954), 12–19.

The Journal Press, publishers of the *Journal of Social Psychology,* for permission to reprint "Some Intrapersonal and Interpersonal Determinants of Individual Differences in Socioempathic Ability among Adolescents," by David P. Ausubel and Herbert M. Schiff, XLI (1955), 39–56.

Contents

xix

Contents

xxi

Contents

Part III—MAJOR AREAS OF EXPLORATION

Contents

Contents

Part IV—HISTORY

Editor: Jiri Nehnevajsa

PART I

Foundations

SOCIAL AND ORGANIC UNITY OF MANKIND

By J. L. MORENO

A truly therapeutic procedure cannot have less an objective than the whole of mankind. But no adequate therapy can be prescribed as long as mankind is not a unity in some fashion and as long as its organization remains unknown. It helped us in the beginning to think, although we had no definite proof for it, that mankind is a social and organic unity. Once we had chosen this principle as our guide another idea developed of necessity. If this whole of mankind is a unity, then tendencies must emerge between the different parts of this unity drawing them at one time apart and drawing them at another time together. These tendencies may be sometimes advantageous for the parts and disadvantageous for the whole, or advantageous for some parts and disadvantageous for other parts. These tendencies may become apparent on the surface in the relation of individuals or of groups of individuals as affinities or disaffinities, as attractions and repulsions. These attractions and repulsions must be related to an index of biological, social, and psychological facts, and this index must be detectable. These attractions and repulsions or their derivatives may have a near or distant effect not only upon the immediate participants in the relation but also upon all other parts of that unity which we call mankind. The relations which exist between the different parts may disclose an order of relationships as highly differentiated as any order found in the rest of the universe. A number of scant proofs have been uncovered which indicate that such a unity of mankind does exist. Its organization develops and distributes itself in space apparently according to a *law of social gravity* which seems to be valid for every kind of grouping irrespective of the membership.

Once the unity of mankind had come within the possibility of proof the next question which by necessity arose was how this unity originated. A closer relationship must have existed between individuals in the earlier stages of the development; in the absence of social organs, such as language, the interactions between the members of a group were physically more intimate than in levels of a later date. A predominantly psycho-organic level of society must have preceded the predominantly psychosocial level in which we live. A process of increased individualization must have gone parallel with increased differentiation of the groups the individuals formed, a gradual evolution from simpler to more complex patterns according to a *sociogenetic law*. Something must have happened which drew individuals more and more apart than they

3

were before—the source of differentiation may have been one time a new climate, another time the crossing of different racial groups—but however far apart they were drawn by these differences, something evidently was left to fill the gap between them, like a remainder from more primitive days, a certain mold of interrelations into which their social impulses craved to be fitted and upon which social organs as language were drafted. We are used to reckoning with a strict determination of our physical organism. We are gradually learning that our mental organism also develops as a unit step by step. However, we are not yet used to reckoning with the idea that also the whole of mankind develops in accord with definite laws. But if such laws exist and can be ascertained, then the adjustment of man to them is a logical consequence and therapeutic procedures have to be constructed accordingly.

Christianity can be looked at as the greatest and most ingenious psychotherapeutic procedure man has ever invented, compared with which medical psychotherapy has been of practically negligible effect. It can be said that the goal of Christianity was from its very beginnings the treatment of the whole of mankind and not of this or that individual and not of this or that group of people. An attack against its foundations has been attempted many times during its existence but none has been so persuasive and aggressive as the concentrated efforts against it during the last hundred years. The one line of attack, as led by Marx, asserted that Christianity is a tool in the hand of the capitalistic class, a narcosis of the people to keep them under suppression. The other line of attack, as led by Nietzsche, asserted that Christianity has brought into the world a subtle technique of sublimation with which it tried to keep the instinctual drives of man in submission, but that this process of sublimation has never changed more than the surface and that the human beast breaks out of these chains whenever it has an occasion. Marx thought little of psychotherapeutics of any sort. He thought the psyche a private matter and expected a solution from economics. But Nietzsche suggested (as Freud later did in fuller measure), a form of negative sublimation, a reversal of the active form of Christian sublimation, attained through analysis of psychological development, unaware that he didn't do else but continue on a side line the very doctrine of Christianity he thought to have overcome.

In considering this, we began to speculate over the possibility of a therapeutic procedure which does not center primarily in the idea of sublimation, but which leaves man in the state in which he is spontaneously inclined to be and to join the groups he is spontaneously inclined to join; which does not appeal to man either through suggestion or through confessional analysis, but which encourages him to stay on the level towards which he naturally tends;

which does not forcibly transgress the development of individuals and groups beyond their spontaneous striving as has often been attempted by sublimating agencies. We were developing a therapeutic procedure which leaves the individuals on an unsublimated level, that is, on a level which is as near as possible to the level of their natural growth and as free as possible from indoctrination. It is based upon the affinities among them and the patterns resulting from their spontaneous interactions. The patterns are used as a guide in the classification, the construction, and, when necessary, for the reconstruction of groupings. This concept carried us away from such forms of psychotherapy as center in the idea of changing the individual or of restoring him to normalcy through direct attack, and towards a therapy which centers in the idea of leaving the individual unchanged, changed only so far as this is bound to occur through the reorganization of groupings. But it appeared to us in a final conclusion that if an individual had once found his place in the community in accord with laws which appear to control the psychological properties of population, the laws of sociogenetics, of sociodynamics and of social gravitation, he would be safeguarded against trespassing the limits of his natural growth and expansion and that sublimation in a modified form could then be called back to function again as agent. It is a form of *active* sublimation, productive as well as curative, productive of individuality, a form of sublimation which does not arise through analysis backward towards the past trauma but through the training of the individual's spontaneity based on the analysis of present performance.

The Problem of Natural Selection within the Framework of Sociometry

After a community was analyzed throughout, down to its "social atoms," more general questions arose in face of the imbalances found within its entire structure. (1) Do we have to retreat to a less differentiated form of society in order to reach a stage from which a fresh start can be made, and, if this is so, how far back do we have to go? (2) Or can we overcome the imbalances as we advance without halting the present flow of progress? (3) What type of society can, then, and which shall survive?

Darwin's hypothesis of natural selection contends that the organisms best adapted to the environment survive; variations favorable to adaptation tend to be preserved, those unfavorable to adaptation tend to be destroyed. "Who shall survive?" is a question which has been asked thus far from the point of view of the biologist. We are raising this question again, but it is from the point of view of the sociologist, more precisely, that of the sociometrist. Which are the "social" laws of natural selection? Who shall survive? The question could be asked only in a society which is, as sociometry has proven with overwhelming evidence, satisfied with wasting a very considerable part of its human element. In contrast, it would lose meaning in a sociometric society where no one would be cast out and all be given an opportunity to participate to the best of their abilities, in other words, to survive.

For the gross manifestations of natural selection of the species which Darwin described, direct evidence is impossible or difficult to obtain, whereas by means of sociometric methods we are able to gain direct evidence as to how natural selection takes place continuously in the very society of which we are a part, every second, in millions of places. Individuals and groups are pushed out from the anchorages in social aggregates to which they belong, from material resources which they need, from love and reproduction, from jobs and homes. It is in billions of small groups, therefore, in which the process of natural, social selection comes to the awareness of the sociometrist. It is in sociograms that these minute processes are brought to visibility. How the microscopic social laws which we have discovered may correlate with the gross evolutionary laws of the biologist is secondary at this point. However, one cannot help but think that if these minute social forces are given long and continuous range of influence into the remote recesses of the past and future, the gross developments which evolutionary theory postulates might result from them.

Therefore, it is important to know whether the construction of a community is possible, in which each of its members is to the utmost degree a free agent in the making of the collectives of which he is a part, and in which the different groups of which it consists are so organized and fitted to each other that an enduring and harmonious commonwealth is the result. But when we began to let loose each individual and each group against one another, each in full pursuit of his happiness, each striving to see his particular wishes or the wishes of his group fulfilled, then we recognize the origin of different psychological currents that pervade the population of the community and divide it into different sections. In the face of the clash of the spontaneous forces we reconsidered the problem of freedom.

Looking for a solution, we turned our mind back to a similar dilemma in which we found ourselves when we attempted years ago to adjust men's mental and nervous equipment to impromptu situations. The occasion was the organization of play groups to whose participants nothing but spontaneous expression was permitted. However brilliant the spontaneous, creative ability of an individual appeared as long as he acted alone, as soon as he had to act together with a group of individuals who had to release also only spontaneous expression the product often lacked in unity and harmony. In the face of this difficulty we refused to turn back to the dogmatic patterns in play. We decided to stick by all means to the *principle of spontaneity* for the individuals participating in the group training. To meet it we devised a technique to support individuals in the attempt at spontaneous group production.

When we faced a community we realized the similarity of the problem. We had only to substitute for the play groups social groups. As in the one case we wanted to keep the principle of spontaneity pure, in this case we wanted by all means to keep the principle of freedom, for the individual and for the collective, as far as possible unrestrained and uncensored; and just as in the first instance every participant takes direct part in the authorship, direction, and performance of the production, in the second instance every individual is permitted to impress his intentions upon every activity of which he is a part. And in the face of the contradicting and combating psychological currents, which are the more powerful and complicated the larger the populations are, again we did not turn back to dogmatic, out-lived forms. We sought a *"technique of freedom,"* a technique of balancing the spontaneous social forces to the greatest possible harmony and unity of all.

Freud and Nietzsche were essentially historians. Nietzsche, the philosopher, circled around morals and cultures of the past that he tried to surpass. Freud, the physician, circled around the traumatic origins of mental disturbance. They were both psychoanalysts, they recommended this returning, remembering and analyzing as a therapy in itself. To them the *"now and here"* seemed superficial. They did not know what to do with the *moment.* They did not take the moment in earnest, they did not think it through. It seemed to them that the only thing to do with the moment and its conflicts was to explain them, that is, to uncover the associations back to their causes. The other alternative would have appeared an absurdity to them: to live, to act out in the moment, to act unanalyzed. It would have seemed to be the end of psychology and of the psychologist. Spontaneity and spontaneous acting would have been refused by them because it appeared to be an affirmation of immaturity, of childhood, of unconscious living, a dangerous disregard for just that which the psychoanalyst tried to illumine. But *there is an alternative: to step into life itself, as a producer, to develop a technique from the moment upward in the direction of spontaneous-creative evolution of society, in the direction of life and time.*

7

CREATIVITY-SPONTANEITY-CULTURAL CONSERVES

By J. L. Moreno

A. Spontaneity

Spontaneity is the variable degree of adequate response to a situation of a variable degree of novelty. Novelty of behavior by itself is not the measure of spontaneity. Novelty has to be qualified against its adequacy in situ. Adequacy of behavior by itself is also not the measure of spontaneity. Adequacy has to be qualified against its novelty. The novelty, for instance, of extreme psychotic behavior may be to such a degree incoherent that the actor is unable to solve any concrete problem, to plan an act of suicide, to cut a piece of bread or to solve a thought problem. We speak then of pathological spontaneity. The adequacy of behavior may be unnovel to a degree which results in strict, rigid or automatic conformity to a cultural conserve. Such adherence may gradually obliterate the ability of the organism and the talent of the actor to change. Spontaneity operates in the here and now. The novelty of a moment demands a past which does not contain this particular novelty. Spontaneity research has enabled us to recognize the various phases and degrees of spontaneity as one continuous process, the reduction and loss of spontaneity, impulsive abreactions and the pathological excesses as well as adequate and disciplined spontaneity, productive and creative spontaneity. It recognized also that spontaneity does not operate in a vacuum but in relation to already structured phenomena, cultural and social conserves.

The questions are: What value has a novel response and when is a response adequate? A novel response like two plus two is seven or a horse has 15 eyes and 25 legs may have, within certain contexts of artistic creation, more creativity than the stereotype response two and two is four or a horse has two eyes and four legs; in other words a logically correct response is not always the indication of creative behavior, and, of course, inadequate responses are not necessarily indications of non-creativity. There are all kinds of mixtures possible of near-adequacy and near-novelty which may pass as comparatively creative. Each performance has to be evaluated within its own context. We should not give a higher creativity rating to an individual who says automatically "Two and two is four" although it may be more adequate and useful than a mental patient who says in a manic state at one moment "Two and two is seven", and at another moment "Two and two are five billion", etc. The freedom in association of words and gestures may

8

have at times the merit of preparing the ground for a creativity state, whereas the one who insists that "two and two is four" may be the hopeless case of an individual who is always right.

An "adequate" response is *appropriateness, competency* and *skill* in dealing with a situation, however small or great the challenge of its novelty. A man can be creative, original, dramatic, but not always have spontaneously an appropriate response in new situations. On the other hand, if he would have only stereotype responses available, however much dramatized and alarming, he would fall within the domain of inadequacy of response. For instance, if a woman is married to a man whose rate of creativity is superior to hers, his competency and skill in social relations, a larger number of significant roles for the setting in which he functions, she is threatened with falling out of the relationship unless she is able to approximate his range and depth of creativity towards herself and others. Another illustration is the creation of new organisms, at the time when animal life was confined to the sea. A new animal organism would arise when it would undergo through the evolutional process, anatomical and physical changes. These changes would be a novel response to the old situation of the sea.

It appeared, therefore, useful to differentiate three types of spontaneity:

1. Whenever a *novel* response occurs without adequacy, that is undisciplined or pathological spontaneity.
2. Whenever an *adequate* response occurs without significant characteristics of novelty and creativity.
3. Whenever an adequate response occurs *with* characteristics of novelty and creativity.

B. CREATIVITY

Creativity manifests itself in any series of creativity states or creative acts. Spontaneity and creativity are not identical or similar processes. They are different categories, although strategically linked. In the case of Man, his spontaneity may be diametrically opposite to his creativity; an individual may have a high degree of spontaneity but be entirely uncreative, a spontaneous idiot. Creativity belongs to the categories of the substance—the arch substance. It is the elementary X without any specialized connotation, the X which may be recognized by its acts. In order to become effective, it (the sleeping beauty) needs a catalyzer. The catalyzer of creativity is spontaneity.

Creativity is related to the "act" itself; spontaneity is related to the "readiness" of the act. The finished product of a creative process, the cul-

9

tural conserve, has its roots in a spontaneous creative matrix, the original manifestation of creativity. The difference between a cultural conserve and the spontaneous creative matrix of this conserve at the moment when it is springing into existence is fundamental. Let us imagine the music of the Ninth Symphony at the moment it was being created by Beethoven, and let us also imagine the same music as a work of art—a finished product—separated from the composer himself. On the surface, it may appear as if the creative units which went into the Ninth Symphony—its musical themes, its climaxes, its harmonies, etc.—must also have been in its original matrix, and that no difference exists between the one in its state in Beethoven's mind and the other in its conserved state—except only that of locus. It might seem as if it were merely a transposition of the same material—the same sum total of creative units—from one locus in time (the mind of Beethoven) to another (the musical score). Closer inspection, however, will show that this is not true. As Beethoven was walking through his garden trying intensively to warm up to his musical ideas, his whole personality was in an uproar. He made use of every possible physical and mental starter he could muster in order to get going in the right direction. These visions, images, thoughts and action-patterns—both musical and non-musical inspirations—were the indispensable background out of which the music of the Ninth Symphony grew. But all this background (which cannot truthfully be divorced from the state in which Beethoven was when he was truly being a creator) is not to be found in the finished product—the musical score or its performance by a noted orchestra. Only the result is there. The fact that this background has been deleted from our present-day idea of Beethoven is the result of an intellectual trick which is played upon us by millenia of being indoctrinated by cultural conserves. If we look upon the initial spontaneous-creative phase in Beethoven's composition of the Ninth Symphony as a positive phase and not as a transition in the direction of an end-product, we can see in Beethoven's musical compositions, his concepts of God, the universe and the destiny of humanity, in the loves, joys and griefs of his private life and—especially—in the gestures and movements of his body a united pattern from which a *surface* layer (the cultural conserve) can be lifted to satisfy certain pragmatic demands. At the moment of composition, Beethoven's mind experienced these concepts, visions and images in conjunction with the developing symphony. They were integral parts of a creative act—of a series of creative acts. He made a cross-section through them in such a way that only the material which could be fitted into the prospective conserve was included; the direction of the cross-section was determined by its frame. In this particular instance, the frame was that of musical notation; in another case it might have been the frame of language notation; at still another, it might have been a mechanical invention; at still another, it might have been a human relationship, a matrimonial relationship or a working crew.

We should guard ourselves to diagnose a state of creativity from the signs of easy overt warm-up. We should not depreciate a state of creativity because it has a slow and difficult onset. We should not over-rate overt and overheated activity and under-rate inflexibility and passivity. We should not over-rate unconserved response and under-rate conserved response. We should not be biased in favor of novelty and originality and in disfavor of "traditional" but adequate response. On the other hand, we should not be biased in favor of slow and difficult onset, inflexibility or traditional response; only careful analysis of the objective facts should decide whether it is high, average or low creativity. We usually over-rate the finished product of the cultural conserve, the finished poem, the great music, the balanced interpersonal relation, and the organized behavior of a group as to their actual, present dynamic creativity. We are deceived by the comparative perfection and smoothness of a cultural conserve and evaluate it as if it would be the immediate delivery of a creative act. We underestimate the "spontaneous creative matrix" of a poem, of a symphony, of a love relation, of an initial group formation because of their frequent inferiority as to perfection and smoothness. The sermon on the mount was first a "burning" spontaneous creative matrix long before it became a cultural conserve which every minister can repeat fervently ad infinitum. We are to such an extent enraptured with the high grade conserves of a culture that we forget their origin from poorly structured but spontaneous-creative matrices. It is that spontaneous creative state which we try to bring to a test and all the stages leading up to the cultural conserve, not only the finished product.

C. The Warming-Up Process

The warming-up process, the operational manifestation of spontaneity is a general condition existing before and in the course of any creative act—before and during an act of sleeping, eating, sexual intercourse, walking, artistic creation or any act of self realization. Spontaneity is generated in action whenever an organism is found in the process of warming-up. Whether spontaneity generates warming-up or warming-up generates spontaneity is similar to the question: "Which is first—the chicken or the egg?"

It is useful to differentiate several types of warming-up: (a) *Undirected warming-up*, individual or group—vague, chaotic, confused, moving towards several goals on several tracks simultaneously. (b) *Directed warming-up*, individual or group—moving without any deviation clearly and powerfully towards a creative act, its exclusive, specific goal. Midway between undirected and directed warming-up, there are many perceptual cues emerging. In the course of getting ready to make a response, the individual may try to get oriented—to get out of the fog when driving a car or to find the melody which fits into his musical composition or to find a mathematical formula for a hypothetical question or to find an ending for a poem or an answer to his wife's quarrels. As soon as he is sure what to do, he has sudden flashes of perception, then he acts quickly—registers the ending of the poem in his mind, rushes to the piano and tries the melody, writes a letter resigning from his job or talks to his wife, etc. Often perceptual spontaneity, however, is indistinguishable from readiness to act. (c) *A general state of warming-up*—The individual is aware that a novel response will be required from him in the situation in which he is, for instance: A girl who is taken out on a blind date for the first time, or a doctor who makes his first call in medical practice or a pastor who renders his first sermon. The individual is excited in various degrees of intensity, the organism gets ready for an unexpected event—his heart rate may be increased, pulse may be more rapid, his respiration rate increased, etc. (d) *Immediate warming-up* in an emergency situation. (e) *Chain warm-up*—an idea or feeling being augmented by traveling from one actor to another and returning to the initiating actor.

D. CULTURAL CONSERVES

Cultural conserves are products of creativity; they are antipodal to the spontaneous creative matrices which emerge every time a creative process is in the making, in the intensive heat of status nascendi. They aim at being the finished products of a creative process and, as such, have assumed an almost sacred quality. The cultural conserve renders to the individual a service similar to that which it renders as a historical category to culture at large—continuity of heritage—securing for him the preservation and the continuity of his creative ego. But spontaneity and creativity never cease entirely to affect cultural conserves, some "amount" of them enters into every one of its renderings, in a greater or lesser degree. By "amount" of spontaneity, we do not mean amounts which are stored up or conserved. Even the greatest possible amount of stored-up spontaneity and creativity could not make a butterfly anything more than a butterfly. Yet even the smallest amount of "free" spontaneity, summoned and created by a being on the spur of the moment—a product, in other words, of the moment—is of greater value than all the treasures of the past, of past "moments". Spontaneous creativity—however supreme it may be in itself—once conserved is, by definition, no longer spontaneity; it has lost its actuality in the universe. What "conserved" creativity truly represents, at best, is power, a means of expressing superiority when actual superiority has ceased to be available.

HYPOTHESES

1. Everything that is *negative* presupposes something that is *positive*. Anxiety, fear and defense are negative categories, they presuppose a positive category, spontaneity. Frustration, projection, substitution and sublimation are negative categories, they presuppose a positive category, creativity. Energy, matter, sexuality, tele are sub-forms of creativity. 2. All men are endowed with spontaneity and creativity although there may be considerable differences in degree of endowment. 3. They exist sui generis. 4. They are not identical with intelligence or memory and not derivative of conditional reflexes or sexual automatic responses.

In order to make experiments feasible, we must be ready to "compromise" and try to simulate a nearly lifelike setting. If the investigator is not willing to compromise but limits himself to the study of spontaneity and creativity on very high levels, he may never be able to get creativity into his test tube and measure and observe it there from close distance. It is the small, average and minute types of creativity which are important in the daily life of human beings, in their work relations, family relations, business relations, etc., and not the great creativity of exceptional individuals. If the concepts of spontaneity and creativity are central to human behavior, they must be traceable in every human act and co-act, on all levels of human performance from the most trivial to the highest. In the application of the scientific method to such high level concepts as spontaneity and creativity, we must make heartbreaking compromises in order to get an experimental contact with them. But we will not compromise to the other extreme, diluting and pushing spontaneity and creativity out of the experiment; they must be continuously considered before an experiment is set up and during its ongoing. We should not sell them "down the river" out of fear that they may complicate the experiment.

If spontaneity and creativity are of central importance in human behavior then there must be some *constancy*, frequency and regularity of appearance. If there is constancy, then there should be also predictability. We have been inclined in the past to relate spontaneity and creativity only to artistic productions. Sociometrists have tried to point out and I believe successfully, the great amount of spontaneity and creativity operating in interpersonal relations. They were among the first to bring them from the philosophical heaven down to earth.

Spontaneity and Creativity Tests

Optimal conditions created by the actors and for the actors in order to make "tests" feasible are: (a) total extemporaneity of production to (b) extreme realism of the production (not pretending or as if, fictitious), complete carrying out of episodes as they are felt and experienced by the subjects. If they have experiences beyond realization, in situ, in ordinary life, they are given on the stage laboratory opportunity to be realized, "surplus" realization and "surplus" reality.

Optimal conditions created by the experiments for the actor: (a) minimally structured situations alien to the private roles of the actor, and (b) various stages of structured situations up to entirely planned.

The tests, as far as they have been used in our psychodramatic institutes, have tried to probe spontaneity and creativity (a) in interpersonal situations, (b) in person-object relations. It was found that some people have more spontaneity and creativity towards people than towards objects; that some people have more spontaneity and creativity towards objects than towards people; and that some people have low or high spontaneity and creativity towards both. The question whether a life situation can be approximated on the stage so as significantly to correlate an individual's behavior in a stage situation to his behavior in the real world can be answered in the positive; but regardless of success in approximating outside behavior, the crucial material of the psychodramatic laboratory is *the production emerging in the Here and Now*. If total spontaneity and creativity is permitted to the actor as far as they are available to him, his past, present and future will enter the production anyway. It is the immediate frame of reference for evaluation.

THE PRINCIPLE OF ENCOUNTER

By J. L. Moreno

The principle underlying all forms of interpersonal and social experience is *Begegnung* (the encounter). *Begegnung* is a German word, difficult to translate, like *Gestalt* (configuration), *Einfühlung* (empathy) and *Stegreif* (spontaneity). It has attained many connotations that no single Anglo-Saxon word conveys; several English words have to be used to express its atmosphere. It means meeting, contact of bodies, confronting each other, facing each other, countering and battling, seeing and perceiving, touching and entering into each other, sharing and loving, communicating with each other in a primary, intuitive manner by speech or gesture, by kiss and embrace, becoming one—*una cum uno*. The word *Begegnung* contains the root for the word *gegen*, which means "against." It thus encompasses not only loving, but also hostile and threatening relationships. Encounter which derives from the French *rencontre* is the nearest translation of *Begegnung*.

The German *zwischen-menschlich* and the English "interpersonal" or "interactional" are anemic notions compared to the living concept of encounter. *Begegnung* conveys the notion that two or more persons meet not only to face one another, but to live and experience one another as actors, each in his own right. It is not only an emotional rapport, like the professional meeting of a physician or therapist and patient; or an intellectual rapport, like teacher and student; or a scientific rapport, like a participant observer with his subject. It is a meeting on the most intensive level of communication. The participants are not put there by any external authority; they are there because they want to be, representing the supreme authority of the self-chosen path.

The persons are there in space; they may meet for the first time with all their strengths and weaknesses—human actors seething with spontaneity and zest. It is not *Einfühlung*, it is *Zweifühlung*—togetherness, sharing life. It is an intuitive reversal of roles, a realization of the self through the other; it is identity, the rare, unforgotten experience of total reciprocity.

The visible definition of encounter is two persons exchanging eyes to comprehend and know each other. "A meeting of two: eye to eye, face to face. And when you are near I will tear your eyes out and place them instead of mine, and you will tear my eyes out and will place them instead of yours, then I will look at you with your eyes and you will look at me with mine."

The encounter is extemporaneous, unstructured, unplanned, unrehearsed.

15

It occurs on the spur of the moment. It is "in the moment" and "in the here," "in the now" and "in becoming."

Encounter is also the real basis of the psychotherapeutic process and not the transference of psychoanalysis. Transference, counter-transference, projections, and distorted perceptions are secondarily superimposed upon it. A number of observations had led the author to the critique of transference, the development of the theory of interpersonal relations and interpersonal therapy in the sense in which they are now used and accepted.

TELE: A DEFINITION

By J. L. Moreno

The scientific counterpart of encounter is *tele*. (Gr., far, influence into distance. For the experimental, mathematical, and statistical verification of tele see Bibliography references.) It is considered the cement that holds individuals and groups together. Group cohesiveness, reciprocity of relationships, communication, and shared experiences are functions of tele. Tele is the constant frame of reference for *all* forms and methods of psychotherapy, including not only professional methods of psychotherapy like psychoanalysis, psychodrama, or group psychotherapy, but also nonprofessional methods like faith healing, or methods which have apparently no relation to psychotherapy, like Chinese thought reform.

Gordon Allport says:

> Moreno defines tele as "insight into," "appreciation of" and "feeling for" the "actual make up" of the other person. Thus defined it is indeed the foundation of all sound therapy, as it is of all wholesome human relationships. Occasionally it may grow out of a previous transference situation, but I suspect that normally tele is present from the outset and increases as sessions continue. Only at certain periods it is obscured by an onrush of transference (or rarely, counter-transference), and it may occasionally break down altogether with the result that the therapeutic relationship depends on the presence of tele, and thereby differs in this respect only because the patient's distress thrusts his inner needs forward with the result that projections and transference and hostility sometimes obscure for the time being the basic telic relationship.[1]

Neither transference nor empathy could explain in a satisfactory way the emergent cohesion of a social configuration. Social configurations consist of two or multiple ways of interaction. They are social wholes, not from the point of view of one particular person A, or B, or C, although they are included in it. I hypothesized that empathy and transference are parts of a more elementary and more inclusive process, *tele*. It is an objective social process functioning with transference as a psychopathological outgrowth and empathy as esthetic outgrowth. The process of *reciprocation* does not enter into the meaning of empathy—and transference is considered the factor responsible for

---

[1] Gordon W. Allport, "Comments on: J. L. Moreno, Transference, Counter-Transference and Tele: Their Relation to Group Research and Group Psychotherapy," *Group Psychotherapy*, VII (1954), 307–308.

dissociation and disintegration in social groups. Tele is the factor responsible for the increased mutuality of choices surpassing chance possibility and for the increased rate of interaction between members of a group.

Tele operates on the wish level, the social desire level, the choice level, and the behavioral level of a relationship. It has, besides a *conative*, also a *cognitive* aspect. Choice sociometry and perceptual sociometry supplement one another.

It can be hypothesized that the greater the sociometric distance between an individual and others in their common social space, the more inaccurate will be his social evaluation of their relationship to him and to each other; he may guess accurately how A, B, and C whom he chooses feels towards him, but he may have a vague perception how A feels about B, A feels about C, B feels about C, B feels about A, etc. The day may come when, through cultivation and training of many generations in the conation and cognition of tele, in role enactment and role perception, we will be able to penetrate the social universe by standing still, without moving into it, and communicate with individuals at a distance without meeting them physically, attaining the effects of extrasensory perception without an extrasensory function.

STATISTICS OF SOCIAL CONFIGURATIONS

By J. L. Moreno and Helen H. Jennings

I. The Problem of Sociometric Statistics

This paper presents a technique for the measurement of social configurations. It discusses the validity of sociometric procedure. Deviations from chance are taken as a reference base in the measurements. Quantitative analysis of choices is used as a method of studying the frequency distributions of choices. Statistics of configurations are found to be fundamental to the measurement of social organization. Statistical calculations confirm the evidence for the sociodynamic effect and the network. Constructs of sociometric scales are given as suggestive schemes.

Sociometry deals with social configurations, aggregates of individuals. Owing to its specific characteristics, this field demands a new appropriate treatment. It was evident from the start that existing statistical techniques could not be automatically transferred from other fields to this new field. The problem is therefore what kind of statistical methods can be constructed for the purpose. A critique of sociometric procedures is first advisable to clarify the direction in which to search.

II. Critique of Sociometric Procedure

Experimental procedures are often set up and put into operation without a careful, epistemological critique of their meaning in relationship to the phenomena studied. An experimental procedure may be accepted by its originator, who, fascinated by its apparent usefulness, may blindly go through the statistical treatment of the data anxious to find that the experiment is a reliable approach. We begin with a critical analysis of the experimental procedures which have elicited the facts here treated.

The most general critique of sociometric procedure one can imagine is that it is an *invention* fashioned to fit certain social phenomena. The data may be therefore to a large extent determined by the frame of the procedure used in fact-finding. To this frame of testing, the tested individuals submit themselves for various reasons. As the individuals submit themselves freely to the procedures, the tester knows, a *priori*, the theoretical distribution and possibilities of relationships. The materials to be correlated are the responses of the individuals within the frame of the procedure which has been invented. The single elements of which the configurations can consist are as theoretical possibilities familiar in advance. The resulting configurations can be treated statistically and rationally because there is already knowledge of the single elements of which they are composed.

These sociometric configurations are *not* what is usually called a Gestalt. They have characteristics which might be attributable to Gestalt. One part of the structure is interdependent with another part; a change in position of one individual may affect the whole structure. But it is known with analytical exactitude how the whole configuration is built up by its single elements. It has some characteristics of a Gestalt but not the crucial one. The atomic elements of a sociogram are determinable analytically.

The sociometrist, as a student of group dynamics and of social configurations is in a different situation from the Gestalt theorist. He does not approach something given, a Gestalt; he is himself the framer of a Gestalt and therefore the inventor of the framework. And it is within these frameworks that he approaches the social phenomena he studies and not outside of them. The creator of a Gestalt may know the single elements which he manipulated in the original framework and he alone may understand why the configurations resulting look as they do. A later observer who did not know the original creation might have reasons to develop a Gestalt theory, but the originators of a frame are in a different position. For the original maker and inventor of music, for instance, if we may visualize such a supreme mind, the melody may not be a Gestalt. He would know about the units which go into its formation. The units of which he would know, however, may be totally different from the parts into which *we* divide melody, the single tones. Sociometric structures like musical notations, are languages, symbolic references, not the process itself. They are analogous to the frames of time and space in the sense of Kant. The conceptual mind uses them to align the phenomena.

III. Sociometric Procedure

There are two forms of experimental procedure which may be considered here. One is a procedure which is carried out in a laboratory. The potentialities of life are in this case reconstructed in a comparatively artificial situation. The effect is to bring the participating individuals with maximum closeness to the experimental situation. The other type is entirely different. *The experimental procedure is so constructed that it is able to become the life pattern itself, the one in which the individuals are.*

The laboratory is gone. This procedure is continuously molded and re-molded through critical evaluation and thus brought nearer and nearer to an identity with the life setting. Finally, only the historian of the procedure may be aware that the frame of the setting and the life pattern have ever been two different things. The experimental setting has become a social institution.

The closer a procedure is to the life setting the more accurate and com-prehensive will the fact-finding become. Studies can be carried out at different distances from the life setting and from the point of view of comparative research each may have a special value. There are methods in which the investigator elicits from the subjects verbal or non-verbal responses in regard to their inter-personal relations or can use observational methods for their study. In these instances, the test groups, that is, the sum of individuals composing them, remain in a research status. Such methods fall under the general category of a *research sociometry*.[1] They have to be differentiated from other methods in which the subjects' re-sponses and desires are made active and put into operation. Because of the fact that the individuals forming the group know in advance the meaning of the procedure and accept it, they can make it their plan of action, they are identical with it. *They are in full consciousness operators in their own behalf.* Such methods fall under the general category of *operational sociometry*.[2] In addition to operational sociometry which is often carried out for pure research objectives, procedures have been de-veloped which have therapeutic aims exclusively. *Assignment therapy*[3] in which the factor of spontaneous choice is merely one contributory factor illustrates the therapeutic aspect of sociometry.

The most characteristic feature of sociometric procedure in its opera-tional form is that it tries to warm up the individuals to the experimental setting, until the experimental setting and the life pattern of the individuals have become one and the same thing. The experimental setting is a con-struct of our mind, its frame is known and its propensities can be visual-ized, but the life pattern in which these individuals interact is unknown. With the sociometric device we succeed in penetrating a domain which otherwise would remain incomprehensible.

---

[1]Research Sociometry and "Near Sociometric" procedures are not identical notions. Near sociometry is an evaluation of procedure and results. Research sociometry is a classification of method. See references 1, 5, 9, 13, 15, 16, 17 for examples of the research type.

[2]See references 4, 6, 13, 14 for examples of this type.

[3]See references 13, pp. 269-331 and 5, pp. 402-421 for examples of this type.

21

When operational techniques are applied, something happens not figured on at the start. The procedure used in time changes the position of individuals and the structures which we are trying to measure and thus what we try to measure escapes our test. The longer the sociometric procedure is applied, the better we understand the changes of the structure, and the more accurate and complete our knowledge becomes.

To classify operational apart from research methods is an aid in considering more specifically the distance which the frame of an experiment has from the life pattern. Such distance may account for the great difference in results obtained. The nearer to the life scene the frame is constructed, so that it may reach into all manifest and fantasy levels of inter-personal relations, the better will be the opportunity to get the data required. The greater the distance of the construct from the life pattern, and the more rigid it is as such, the less adequate and complete will be the data.

It is evident that a simple procedure setup and the complex inter-personal pattern which it attempts to reach are by no means always congruent. A "choice" may never emerge in the activities of an individual, or the warming-up to a clear and decided feeling of preference may emerge only in a limited number of cases, and where it emerges it may remain inconsequential because of a lack of decisive action towards the person desired. The choices may often be half-conscious, often mere wishes. A person may not know towards whom he is "drawn." Sociometric tests therefore, ought to be constructed more and more in such fashion that they are able to embrace as far as possible the full complexity of the actual interrelations existing in the population. The more flexible the procedure is made, the more it becomes capable of tapping these concrete actualities.

When, however, the complexities of a social aggregate reach the most comprehensive patterns of living, with all the implications of the fully mature mental processes, statistical treatment may tend to over-simplify the procedure and the data to such a degree that the resulting statistical findings become impermissible and unscientific. This is why techniques of presentation derived from the arts, such as the psychodrama[4] seem sometimes more appropriate than statistics.

IV. General Frames of Reference

There is some confusion in sociometric work in regard to appropriate frames of reference. The experiences, feelings and decisions of the individuals

---

[4]See references 10, 11.

forming a certain social aggregate are one class of facts to which we refer. They are a psychological frame of reference. The social situations—families, churches, industrial units, or whole cultures,—in which these social aggregates take part are another class of facts to which we refer. They are a sociological frame of reference. Similarly a biological frame of reference, an ecological frame of reference, and others can be discerned as affecting social structure. Methodical scrutiny shows that none of these classes of facts is separable from another. The facts that belong to these realms are raw, preparatory materials, but not the frame of sociometric reference itself. The reference which is sociometrically valid is the composite of individual and symbolic responses which represents the living social aggregates, into the weaving of which many factors have contributed.

It is undeniable that the social configurations as portrayed in our sociograms are elementary and rough in texture compared with the complex relationships, rhythms and tempos operating within a living social aggregate. With the devising of new sociometric techniques and with the improvement of the present instruments, the more subtle and more mature processes— the economic milieu, the religious milieu, the cultural milieu, which operates within social aggregates—will be made increasingly comprehensible. It is our contention that these entities, economy, religion, or culture, whatever the logic of their existence may be, cannot be so impersonal as to exist independent of the societies in which the persons actually think, live and act. These processes must express themselves within living social aggregates although their interaction may be more difficult to trace. It is to the comprehension of these richly textured, integrated and fully matured configurations that sociometric work aspires.

As the object of sociometric study is not a single series of data, a series of psychological data, a series of sociological data, of cultural or biological data, but the whole configuration in which they are interwoven, the ultimate sociometric frame of reference could be neither of these series of data exclusively, but the social configurations in which they are interwoven as a whole. Therefore, a pertinent form of statistical treatment would be one which deals with social configurations as wholes, and not with single series of facts, more or less artificially separated from the total picture.

V. Chance Experiments

A population of 26 was taken as a convenient unit to use in comparison with a chance distribution of a group of 26 fictitious individuals, and three choices were made by each member. For our analysis any size of population, large or small, would have been satisfactory, but use of 26 persons happened to permit an unselected sampling of groups already tested.[5] Without including the same group more than once, seven groups of 26 individuals were selected from among those which happened to have this size population. The test choices had been taken on the criterion of table-partners, and none of the choices could go outside the group, thus making comparison possible.

The chance experiments were set up as follows: Fictitious individuals—Mr. 1, Mr. 2, Mr. 3, etc. to Mr. 26,—were written on ballots. The chance ballots, except that for Mr. 1, were placed in a shuffling apparatus and three drawings were made for Mr. 1's choosing—the first drawing being called his 1st choice, the second drawing being called his 2nd choice, and the third drawing, his 3rd choice. The three ballots were then replaced in the shuffling apparatus and drawings similarly made for Mr. 2, Mr. 3, etc. The 26 fictitious individuals, each having three choices, produce 78 blind choices. Seven such chance tests were made, using a total of 546 choices, the same number as in the sampling of actual sociometric tests. An analysis of the chance choices is recorded in Table 1. Analysis of the chance structures is recorded in Table 3. An analysis of the choices resulting from the sampling of seven cottage groups is given in Table 2. An analysis of the actual structures is recorded in Table 4.

TABLE 1
Chance Experiments with the Sociometric Test
Statistical Analysis of the Choices

No. of Choices	0	1	2	3	4	5	6	7	8	9
Chance Balloting 1	2	4	4	4	8	2	2	..	..	..
Chance Balloting 2	2	3	6	3	8	3	..	1	..	..
Chance Balloting 3	1	1	10	5	4	4	1	..	..	..
Chance Balloting 4	..	3	10	5	2	4	2	..	..	..
Chance Balloting 5	3	5	2	9	2	3	2	1	..	..
Chance Balloting 6	1	3	8	5	5	1	2	1	..	..
Chance Balloting 7	2	2	5	8	5	2	2	..	..	..
Total	11	21	45	39	34	19	11	3		..
Average	1.6	3.0	6.3	5.6	4.9	2.7	1.6	.4	..	..

[5]At the New York State Training School for Girls, periodical sociometric testing for dining-table partners at meals is made at intervals of 8 weeks, and three choices are allowed, a 1st, 2nd, and 3rd, to each girl. Only 10 cottage groups happened to have a population of 26 at the time table choices were made and 3 of these were omitted in order not to include the same group more than once. Thus the sampling covers seven different cottage groups. See Sociometric Control Studies of Grouping and Regrouping, Sociometry Monograph No. 7, Beacon House, New York, 1945.

24

TABLE 2

Actual Sociometric Test
Statistical Analysis of the Choices

No. of Choices	0	1	2	3	4	5	6	7	8	9	10	11
Test 1	4	7	4	3	..	2	2	2	1	..	1	..
Test 2	6	3	4	3	2	4	1	1	1	1	..	..
Test 3	5	4	3	4	4	1	2	1	2	..	..	..
Test 4	3	5	4	6	3	1	..	3	..	1	..	..
Test 5	7	3	5	1	2	4	..	2	..	1	..	1
Test 6	3	2	5	8	3	2	2	..	1	..	..	..
Test 7	7	5	5	1	2	.	1	1	1	1	..	2
Total	35	29	30	26	16	14	8	10	6	4	1	3
Average	5.0	4.1	4.3	3.7	2.3	2.0	1.1	1.4	.9	.6	.1	.4

TABLE 3

Statistical Analysis of Configurations Occurring in Chance

	Isolated	Unreciprocated	Mutual	Chain Relations	Closed Structures (triangles, etc.)	Leader Structures
Chance Balloting 1	2	68	5	..	..	4
Chance Balloting 2	2	74	2	..	..	4
Chance Balloting 3	1	64	7	2	..	5
Chance Balloting 4	..	72	3	..	..	6
Chance Balloting 5	2	68	5	2	..	6
Chance Balloting 6	1	70	4	1	..	4
Chance Balloting 7	2	70	4	1	..	4
Total	10	486	30	6	0	33
Average	1.4	69.4	4.3	0.9	0	4.7

Study of the findings of sociometric tests showed that the resulting configurations, in order to be compared with one another, were in need of some common reference base from which to measure the deviations. It appeared that the most logical ground for establishing such a reference could be secured by ascertaining the characteristics of typical configurations produced by chance balloting for a similar size population with a like number of choices. It became possible to chart the respective sociograms of each experiment, so that each fictitious person was seen in respect to all other fictitious persons in the same group; it was also possible to show the range in types of structures within each chance configuration of a group.

TABLE 4

Statistical Analysis of Configurations Occurring in Actual Sociometric Tests

	Isolated	Unreciprocated	Mutual	Chain Relations	Closed Structures (triangles, etc.)	Leader Structures
Test 1	4	54	12	4	1	8
Test 2	6	48	15	1	1	8
Test 3	5	56	11	4	..	6
Test 4	3	46	16	2	2	5
Test 5	7	48	15	1	2	8
Test 6	3	44	17	2	1	5
Test 7	7	62	8	2	..	6
Total	35	358	94	16	7	46
Average	5	51.1	13.4	2.3	1	6.6

As soon as the results of chance balloting were secured, the problem of the theoretical computation of the data arose.[6]

"Under the conditions of this study the probability of a certain child's being selected by any other child is $p = \frac{3}{25}$

The probability of not being chosen is:

$$q = 1 - p = \frac{22}{25}$$

The two values, p and q, are basic for the whole analysis.

The *first* question to be answered reads: What is the probable number of children who, by mere chance selection, would be picked out by their fellows, not at all, once, twice, and so on? The corresponding probabilities can be derived from the binominal formula (III, chapter 9).

The first ten members of the series $\left(\frac{22}{25} + \frac{3}{25}\right)^{25}$ have been computed and give the following values:

$$\left(\frac{22}{25}\right)^{25} = .0409$$

$$53130 \left(\frac{22}{25}\right)^{20} \left(\frac{3}{25}\right)^{5} = .1023$$

$$25 \left(\frac{22}{25}\right)^{24} \frac{3}{25}^{7} = .1395$$

$$177100 \left(\frac{22}{25}\right)^{19} \left(\frac{3}{25}\right)^{6} = .0465$$

$$300 \left(\frac{22}{25}\right)^{23} \left(\frac{3}{25}\right)^{2} = .2281$$

$$480700 \left(\frac{22}{25}\right)^{18} \left(\frac{3}{25}\right)^{7} = .0172$$

$$2300 \left(\frac{22}{25}\right)^{22} \left(\frac{3}{25}\right)^{3} = .2383$$

$$1081575 \left(\frac{22}{25}\right)^{17} \left(\frac{3}{25}\right)^{8} = .0053$$

---

[6] The quotation here is in Lazarsfeld's own wording of the analysis.

$$12650 \left(\frac{22}{25}\right)^{21} \left(\frac{3}{25}\right)^{4} = .1787 \qquad 2042975 \left(\frac{22}{25}\right)^{16} \left(\frac{3}{25}\right)^{9} = .0014$$

The general formula for n children, each child being permitted a choices, reads:

$$(p + q)^{n-1}$$

$$p = \frac{a}{n-1} \qquad q = 1 - p$$

The *second* question to be answered reads: How many mutuals are likely to occur; mutuals being two children who select one another.

The chance that two specific children choose one another is:

$$p^2 = \left(\frac{3}{25}\right)^{2}$$

That one child is "mutually" chosen by any other child is 25 times as probable. With 26 children in the group, the number of mutuals will be:

$$m = \frac{26 \times 25}{2} \left(\frac{3}{25}\right)^{2}$$

as the mutual choice of A by B, and B by A, give the same "mutual." Under the condition of this experiment the probable frequency of "mutuals" originating by chance is then: m=4.68.

The general formula for "n" children, each making a choices by chance, is:

$$m = \frac{n(n-1) \cdot p^2}{2} \qquad p = \frac{a}{n-1} \qquad a = \text{no. of choices}$$

The *third* question to be answered reads: "How many unreciprocated choices can be expected on a mere chance basis?" An "unreciprocated" between two specific children has the probability:

$$p = \left(\frac{3}{25}\right) \cdot \left(\frac{22}{25}\right)$$

By the same reasoning we used in the previous problems, we derive therefrom the probable frequency or "unreciprocated" among 26 children as:

$$u = 26 \times 25 \times \frac{3}{25} \times \frac{22}{25} = 68.64$$

(The fraction, 2, is to be omitted here because an unreciprocated choice of A by B is to be counted separately from an unreciprocated choice of B by A.)

The general formula for the probable frequency of unreciprocated choices originating by mere chance is:

27

$$u = n(n - 1)pq$$

$$p = \frac{a}{n - 1} \qquad q = 1 - p$$

The Chi-Square test was applied in comparing how much the computed chance values and the experimental chance values (E) differ. For the purpose of the test the computed chance values were figured for the case that there were 7 repetitions, as in the original chance experiments. The test value (see II, chapter 4) is:

$$\chi^2 = \frac{(E - C)^2}{C}$$

For this table the chi-square value is 4.055, which corresponds to a probability of 85%. That means that in five out of six chance experiments we are likely to get a distribution which deviates even more from the computed one than the one obtained in the chance tests. As a result of the close fit of the chance experiment with the theoretical distribution we have, of course, an equally close matching when it comes to the figures for "mutuals" and for "unreciprocated" choices.

By an extension of the considerations carried through in the foregoing examples, we could get the probable values for any other choices, for instance three or more children forming a ring, or one child being selected by a great number of children, but selecting none of them on her part, and so on."

Theoretical analysis, secured by carrying out the binomial expansion $\left(\frac{22}{25} + \frac{3}{25}\right)^{25}$ and multiplying by the number of persons, 26, gives the following findings:

No. of Times Chosen	0	1	2	3	4	5	6	7	8 or more
No. of Persons	1.1	3.6	5.9	6.2	4.6	2.7	1.2	0.5	0.2

The average number of mutuals in the chance experiments is 4.3; see Table 3. The theoretical findings show 4.68 under these conditions of 3 choices within a population of 26 persons. The number of unreciprocated structures in the chance experiments is 69.4; see Table 3. The theoretical results show 68.64 under the same conditions. The experimental chance findings so closely follow the theoretical chance probabilities that only the experimental findings will be used for comparison with actual sociometric findings.

VI. Comparison of Actual Sociometric Findings With Chance Experiments

Study of the actual frequency distribution of the seven different social configurations shows that the two extremes are more excessively developed than in chance. See Diagram I. The number of isolates and others at the lower end of the distribution are many more than they are in chance. There are fewer in the middle portions of the distribution who are moderately well-chosen than there are in the chance experiments. But the number who are over-chosen are many more than in chance, not only in number but in their volume of choices received. Whereas in chance one can seldom be

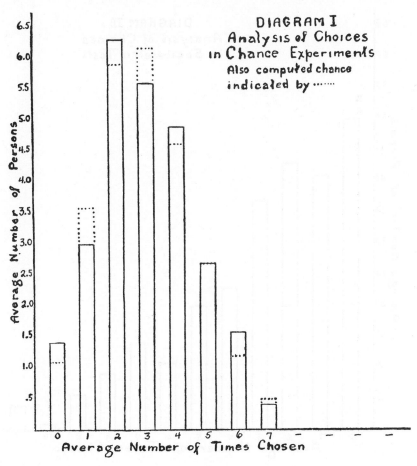

DIAGRAM I
Analysis of Choices
in Chance Experiments
Also computed chance
indicated by ·······

chosen more than six times, the actual tests show persons chosen 7, 8, 9, 10, and 11 times. In fact, the range is practically 5 points greater in the actual distribution than in the experimental chance distribution. On the other hand, the probability to receive no choice at all is much greater than in chance. See Diagrams II and III.

A greater concentration of many choices upon few individuals and of a weak concentration of few choices upon many individuals skews the distribution of the sampling still further than takes place in the chance experiments, and in a direction it need not necessarily take by chance. This feature of the distribution is an expression of the phenomenon which

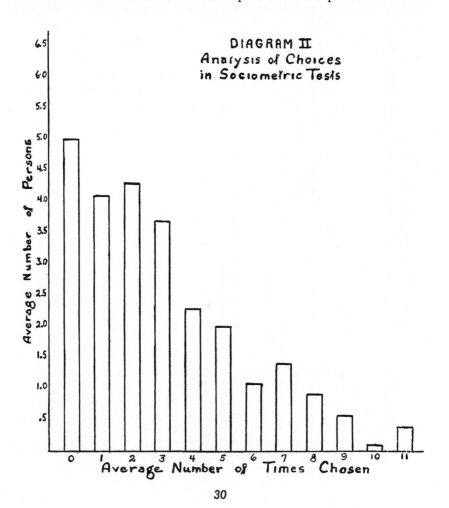

DIAGRAM II
Analysis of Choices
in Sociometric Tests

has been called the *sociodynamic effect*. The chance distribution seen as a whole is also normally skewed, but the middle portions are higher and the extremes less pronounced. The actual frequency distribution compared with the chance frequency distribution shows the quantity of isolates to be 250% greater. The quantity of overchosen individuals (receiving 5 or more choices) is 39% greater, while the volume of their choices is 73% greater. Such statistical findings suggest that if the size of the population increases and the number of choices remains constant, the gap between

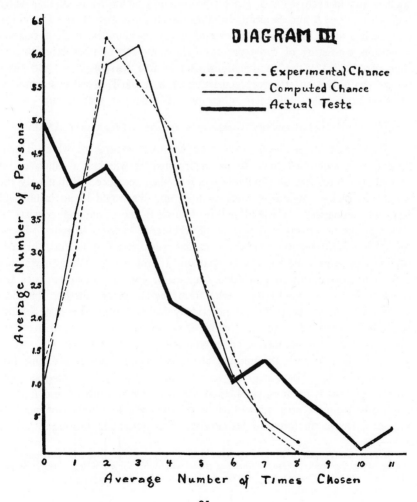

the chance frequency distribution and the actual distribution would increase immensely[7].

Comparison of the chance sociograms with the actual sociograms shows other differences. The probability of mutual structures is 213% greater in the actual configurations than in the chance and the number of unreciprocated structures is 35.8% greater by chance than actually. The more complex structures, such as triangles, squares, and other closed patterns, of which there are seven in the actual sociograms, are lacking in the chance sociograms. Even structures of chain-relations are found only in six instances and in each instance the reciprocations connect no more than three individuals (i.e. A and B mutually choose each other and B and C reciprocate each other). In the actual configurations, the number of chain-relation structures consisting of three persons each is 9; the number consisting of four persons is 2; the number consisting of five persons is 4; and there is one chain-relation structure consisting of 8. Linked to various members of these chains here and there other mutual structures branch out.

VII. CONTRAST BETWEEN QUANTITATIVE AND STRUCTURAL ANALYSIS

The question has been raised whether all structures of which a configuration is composed have to be determined or whether a minimum of crucial structures can be a reliable index of their measure. But if only the isolates in each configuration were counted up, this would be an insufficient basis of comparison. It would not be known if the remainder consists of choosing but unreciprocated persons or whether it consists of pairs. If, on the other hand, only the number of mutual pairs were counted up, this also would be an unreliable basis of comparison. It would not be known whether the remainder of the configuration consists of entirely unchosen ones because their choices go to those who form the pairs, or whether the individuals who form the pairs are practically isolated from the rest because they choose each other but are cut off from others. As discussed in "Who Shall Survive?" the number of chain-relations, squares, triangles, etc., seems to depend largely upon the number of mutual pairs. This needs some further explanation. There may be many mutual pairs in a sociogram and no chain-relations or more complex structures. On the other hand if there are many complex structures, then a relatively large number of pairs is present. Hence, in order to be adequate this statistical technique has to

---

[7] If 500 individuals with five choices each were compared with the corresponding chance structure under these conditions, there would be shown a gap vastly greater than the one here reported for 26 individuals with three choices.

treat social configurations as a whole. Statistics of single structures apart from the configuration as a whole may offer a distorted view of the whole.

If we select from Table 1 and Table 2 two populations which have almost identical quantitative results, the selection of Choice Ballot No. 7 and Sociometric Test No. 6 is suggested. They have the *same* number of persons who receive 1 choice, the same number receiving 2 choices, the same number receiving 3 choices, a like number receiving 5 choices, and a like number receiving 6 choices. There is only one more person receiving no choice in the Sociometric Test No. 6; only 2 more receiving 4 choices than in Chance Ballot No. 7; and the only other difference is that the range of receiving stops at 6 in the Chance Ballot No. 7, while one person receives 8 in Sociometric Test No. 6.

The structural analysis of the configurations produced by the choices shows a fundamental contrast, a contrast which is not heralded by mere choice analysis. Chance Ballot No. 7 produces the following structures: 2 isolated, 70 unreciprocated, 4 mutual relations, 1 chain-relation, no closed structures, and 4 leader structures (persons receiving 5 or more choices). Sociometric Test No. 6 produces 3 isolated, 44 unreciprocated, 17 mutual relations, 2 chain-relations, 1 closed structure, and 5 leader structures.

Just as the tabulation of structures is superior to the tabulation of choices, sociogram reading is able to add new information to the tabulation of structures. It aids in uncovering still farther-reaching differences. Examining the sociograms of these configurations (see Sociograms I and II), we find that the chain-relation structure build by the Chance Ballot No. 7 consists of 3 persons (Person 4 and Person 13 and Person 12), while the chain-relation structures produced by the Sociometric Test No. 6 in one instance consists of 3 persons (Hazel, Hilda, Betty), and in the other of 8 persons (Maxine, Eva, Martha, Marion, Adele, Mary, Jane, and Ruth), with other mutual-relations linked to members of this structure (Marion and Mary are mutual respectively with Frances and Edna). The closed structure is found to involve none of these individuals but to be a closed triangle of three different persons (Helen, Robin, and Jean). Only two of the leader individuals in the Chance Ballot No. 7 configuration have a mutual-relation structure with anyone (Person 5 and Person 12 have one each), whereas in the sociogram of Sociometric Test No. 6 two· leader individuals (Mary and Marion) are seen to have three mutual structures (the maximum possible since only three choices are allowed), two other leader individuals (Adele and Eva) have two each, and the other leader (Edna) has one.

This is a significant illustration of the value of the sociogram in socio-

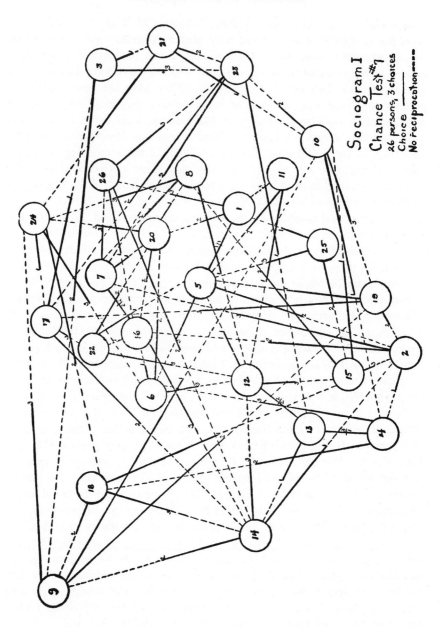

Sociogram I
Chance Test #7
26 persons, 3 choices
Choice —————
No reciprocation ------

metric work. It proves to be not merely another means of schematic representation of data, but an invention for exploratory aims. It is an accurate reproduction of the results of a sociometric test on the level of inquiry and can be well compared with the constructs in the geometry of spaces. It accomplishes our original search for a spatial science[8] which would do for ideas, things, and persons what the geometry of spaces accomplishes for geometrical figures.[9] From the early beginnings of sociometric work, chart-

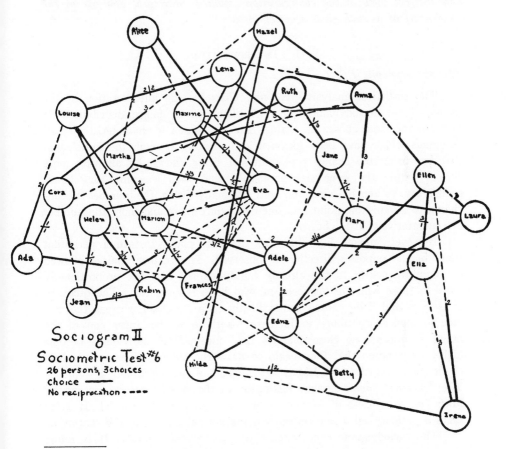

Sociogram II
Sociometric Test #6
26 persons, 3 choices
choice ———
No reciprocation - - - -

---

[8] See reference 10, page 3-5.

[9] A construction problem in geometry when formulated analytically is found to be equivalent to that of a system of simultaneous equations. A construction problem in sociometry when presented as a sociogram, is also found to be analogous to a system of simultaneous equations. Geometry deals with the properties of physical space, sociometry deals with the properties of social space.

ing the data in the form of a sociogram and following the sociogram as a trail has led from one discovery to another, to the tele, to the social atom, the network, and in this paper to a method of its own statistics.

The comparisons given above illustrate that it is necessary to approach sociometric material in its intrinsic form, that is, in the form of the social configurations themselves and not in the form of their single elements. *Quantitative analysis of choices is of limited value: it appears as an artificial and abstract view of the configurations studied. Structural analysis of the configurations as such gives a better picture.*[10]

VIII. INTERPRETATION

The Sociodynamic Effect

The statistical analysis gives new clues for the interpretation of the theory of the sociodynamic effect. A distortion of choice distribution in favor of the more chosen as against the less chosen is characteristic of all groupings which have been sociometrically tested. It might be anticipated that increasing the chance probability of being chosen by allowing more choices within the same size population and thus lessening the chance probability to remain unchosen will gradually bring the number of unchosen to a vanishing point and likewise reduce more and more the number of comparatively little chosen.

However, in actuality, this does not take place. Instead a persistent trend in the opposite direction is observed. The further choices allowed go more frequently to the already highly chosen and not proportionally more to those who are unchosen or who have few choices. The quantity of isolates and little chosen comes finally to a standstill whereas the volume of choices continues to increase for those at the upper end of the range. It appears on close analysis that once certain individuals become highly over-chosen that they begin to draw the choices of many members of the community less and less as individuals and more and more as symbols. The *"surplus" choice* become analogous to the *surplus value* observed by Marx in the process of production and accumulation of capital. It is at times a pathological distortion beyond the normal process of differentiation.

The sociodynamic effect apparently has general validity. It is found in some degree in all social aggregates, whatever their kind, whether the criterion is search for mates, search for employment, or in socio-cultural

---

[10]Such statistical treatment is applicable also to other types of configurations, for instance, to aesthetic configurations, configurations of musical tones, of colors, etc.

relations. It is found in populations of children as soon as they begin to develop societies of their own, as well as in adult populations, in groups of various levels of chronological age and mental age and in populations of different races and nationalities. Its effect may change in degree, but it is universally present, appearing like a halo effect inherent in every social structure. It may be pronounced where differences of any sort are intensely felt by the participants, whether these are aesthetic differences, racial differences, sexual differences, economic differences, cultural differences, or differences between old and young.

An example of the degree of distortion which the sociodynamic effect has contributed within the seven cottages of 26 individuals each (182 persons) is the following: 20% of the population have to be satisfied with no choice at all; 35% of the population have to be satisfied with 5% of the choices; on the other hand, 2% of the population control 8% of the choices, 8% control 23%, and 25% control 58%. (See Table 2.)

The frequency distribution of choices shown by sociometric data is comparable to the frequency distribution of wealth in a capitalistic society.[11] (See Diagram IV). In this case also the extremes of distribution are accentuated. The exceedingly wealthy are few; the exceedingly poor are many. The question can be raised whether the similar characteristics of the economic and sociometric curves are accidental occurrences or whether they are both expressions of the same law, a law of sociodynamics.

Network Theory

There are certain structural processes observable in the groups studied which are best explained if it is assumed that networks exist. One of these structural phenomena is the chain-relation. Chain-relations are rarely found in structures formed by children of kindergarten and First or Second grade age, but develop at times gradually with an increased number of mutual pairs. Increase in pair structures does not force the formation of chain-relations. In young children's groups, for instance, pair-structures appear frequently without connection with any other pair-structures. However, among the individuals who develop a pair-structure there are some who as they mature in this capacity develop a special characteristic. After they have developed the ability to click with one partner, this partnership does not remain a singular case, but similarly they develop the sense to click with other persons who like themselves have developed a simliar *sense* for inter-personal choice. And thus chain-relations emerge and extend. This

---

[11]See reference 8, p. 54 or 7, p. 145.

phenomenon appears hand in hand with the maturation and differentiation of social organization. It is a process of structural growth.

The occurrence of these chain structures cannot be explained solely as a reflection of sociodynamic effects. Outside of a particular chain formation not only isolated or little chosen individuals but also pair structures

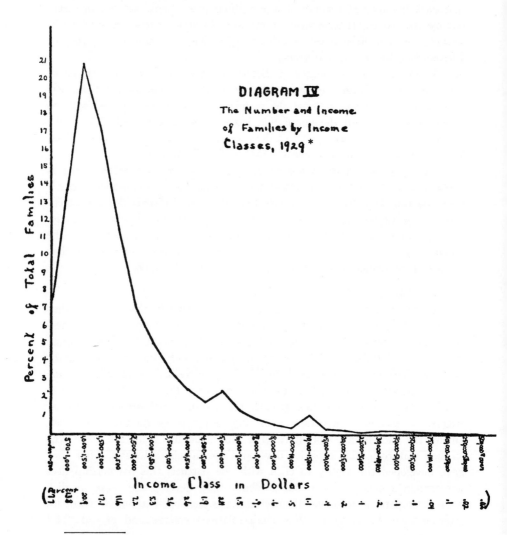

DIAGRAM IV

The Number and Income of Families by Income Classes, 1929*

*See Reference 7.

or even leaders may remain left out. Another group dynamic process must therefore stimulate chain formation.

It had been seen that the individuals, who in the sociometric study of a whole community, form a social aggregate around one criterion form other social aggregates around other criteria and that the individuals who produce structures of chain-relations in one aggregate may produce them in other aggregates. If these chain-relations are traced as they cross through the boundaries of each particular aggregate, a new and larger configuration is seen developing,—a psychological network. The simple fact that individuals are more attracted to some individuals and not to others has many consequences. It leaves out those with whom reciprocal relations have not been established and even within the same group there may be formed different networks which do not cross or break through one another.

The dynamic meaning of chain-relations in social structure is better understood in view of a network hypothesis. The chain-relations in each aggregate are often not only contributing to network formation but are themselves a network effect. As chain-relations develop between different social aggregates, existing networks stimulate and increase the development of chain-relations in each single structure.

The relationship between sociodynamic effect and the development of networks appears to be complex. Sometimes its effect is simply negative. The greater the sociodynamic effect the larger the number of isolates and the larger the number and volume of most chosen, the less choices are free for chain-relations and network formation.

This analysis increases understanding of an obscure phenomenon, the beginnings of social organization. Marx has described the possible conditions under which the state withers. A minimum of both sociodynamic effects and networks is necessary for social organization to function with a reasonable degree of differentiation. Without them, not only the state but society[12] itself withers.

Tele

The study of the cohesion of forces within a group can be made through an analysis of choices made and choices received, the choices going to individuals inside and to individuals outside of this constellation. A dif-

---

[12]We mean society as we find it at the present stage of evolution. But types of society, free of sociodynamic effect, can be constructed in which several individuals *share* in a choice, several individuals sharing a single individual. This is not paradoxical, at least not to some of our most characteristic feelings. In our chief religions, millions of people are sharing in the love of a single person, God.

ferent study of cohesion is based upon the configurational aspect. It considers, instead of single elements, choices, the inter-personal structures and the degree of cohesion produced by them. Cohesion would be very low, for instance, if a large number of choices going to the individuals of a group were unreciprocated. There would be a surplus of choices within the constellation but a *loss* of tele.

Tele has been defined as "an inter-personal experience growing out of person-to-person and person-to-object contacts from the birth level on and gradually developing the *sense* for inter-personal relations," also as a sociometric structure: "that some real process in one person's life situation is sensitive and corresponds to some real process in another person's life situation and that there are numerous degrees, positive and negative, of these inter-personal sensitivities."[13] The tele process is "an objective system of interpersonal relations."

That the tele process represents an objective system can be deduced indirectly through quantitative calculations.[14] A study of the two sociograms on pages 18 and 19, shows that the number of clickings between the actual individuals forming Sociogram 2, is very much higher than the number of clickings between the individuals forming Chance Sociogram 1. The factor responsible for the increased trend towards mutuality of choice far surpassing chance possibility is called tele. A close analysis of the two sociograms indicates still further the forms in which this factor, tele, operates. Not only that the number of pairs formed in actuality are higher than in chance, but in actuality the trend is stronger for a first choice to draw a first choice; for a second or third choice to draw a second or third choice. Whereas in chance, even where pair relations happen they are incongruous. These findings gain support from our studies of the evolution of children groups, from a simple level to a higher level of differentiation. In the kindergarten and early grades of a public school, the quantity of unreciprocated choices is higher than found in the 4th, 5th or 6th grade levels—but far closer to what is found in chance. Correspondingly the number of clickings or pair-relations is far smaller in these early grade levels than found later on and therefore far closer to chance probability. On the basis of the quantitative aspect of the tele factor discussed above, one may conclude that when the

---

[13]See reference 11, p. 16; p. 215; p. 74.

[14]It would be important as a contribution at the present time if derivatives of the tele process, as the sociodynamic effect and networks, were traced through other measurements than the sociometric methods used here. These phenomena must influence the findings of any kind of social phenomena studied, whether studied through public opinion polls, social distance tests, or attitude questionnaires, etc.

DIAGRAM V

Tele Chart I

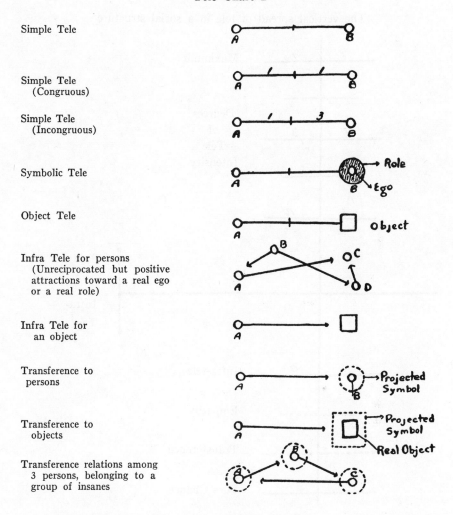

Simple Tele

Simple Tele
(Congruous)

Simple Tele
(Incongruous)

Symbolic Tele

Object Tele

Infra Tele for persons
(Unreciprocated but positive
attractions toward a real ego
or a real role)

Infra Tele for
an object

Transference to
persons

Transference to
objects

Transference relations among
3 persons, belonging to a
group of insanes

The tele process may show many varieties of tele. Some of them are illustrated in the diagrams above. The attraction of A for B is responded to by an attraction of B for A in the same life situation. This is *simple tele*.

If the attraction between two persons occurs on the same level of preference, then the simple tele can be called *congruous*. A chooses B first; B chooses A first. If the attraction between two persons occurs on different levels of preference then the simple tele can be called incongruous. A chooses B first; B chooses A third.

DIAGRAM VI

Tele Chart II

The vertical spread of tele in a social structure

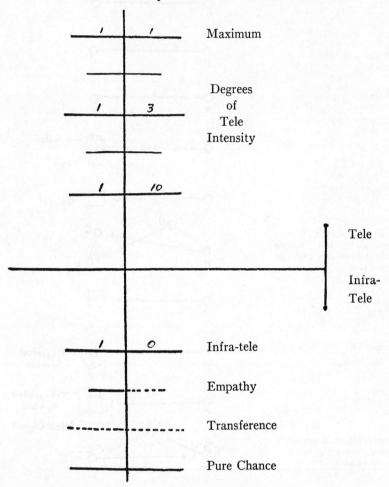

Diagram VI shows a scale ranging from maximum tele to pure chance.

The attraction of A for B may not be for B's real ego, but for his alter ego, for some role or symbol which he represents—the role of the physician, the priest, the judge, etc. B, in turn, may not be attracted to A's real ego, but to a role he represents, for instance, the role of the scientist. This is *symbolic or role* tele.

A is attracted towards an object which, in turn, is useful to him, for instance, any food towards which A reaches spontaneously and which, in turn, satisfies his needs and benefits his health. This is *object* tele.

In all these three cases, the attraction is *positive* from both sides whether the sides are the two egos of two persons, two roles of these two persons, or a person and an object.

A form of attraction can take place which is *positive* for the one person but not shared by the other person. It is unreciprocated. A chooses B. B does not choose A. A chooses B in a certain role. B does not choose A either as an ego or in any role. This is *infra-tele* for persons and roles. There can also be an infra-tele for objects. Developments in the tele process which can be classified as aesthetic formations are, for instance, the *Einfuhlung* (empathy) of an actor into his part, the assimilation of an object, as a portrait. Empathy is positive but the process of reciprocation does not enter into its meaning.

There are developments in the tele process which can be classified as psychopathological formations, for instance, a person A, when in relation to a person B, sees B in a role which B does not actually experience, a role which A *projects* into B. It is a delusion of A, a projected symbol. This is *transference*.

A person A may be attracted to an object, for instance, a food, but not for what it actually is and not for what effect it may have upon his body, but as a symbol. He may attach to it a certain mystical significance which is entirely subjective, a delusion. It is a pathological attraction and may be definitely harmful to him. This is an *object transference*.

The quantitative study of transference effect upon social structure is possible through comparing a group of insane persons with a group of normal persons under the same conditions. Studies of groups of insanes reveal that the sociogram produced by them is neither all transference nor all tele. It is a mixture of both. The structure of an insane group will probably appear below the tele level but above the chance level. As far as it was above chance, it would account for the degree to which true tele processes are mixed in processes of transference and delusions.

tele factor is very weak as in early infancy and childhood, the factor of chance is far more responsible for the inter-personal sociogram resulting. The stronger the tele factor becomes in later childhood and adolescence, the more it affects and shapes the structure and the weaker is in turn the influence which pure chance has upon it.

If the tele process were a *subjective* system, as transference, hit-or-miss guessing or vague intuitions, the amount of clicking and of chain and network formation in the configurations studied would not develop beyond chance. The increasing number of pair and chain relations with increasing maturity of the participants and the age of the configuration in which they are, suggest that an objective social process is functioning, with transference as psychopathological outgrowth and empathy as aesthetic outgrowth. (See Diagram V and VI.)

IX. DISCUSSION OF SOCIOMETRIC SCALES

In the course of configurational statistics, the idea of comparing one social aggregate with another from the point of view of the degree of integration, the comparative strength of cohesion which holds individual members together, arose as soon as the first sociometric studies were made.[15] Rough rankings of different groups studied were made according to degree of integration.

(a)   Scales on the Basis of Choice Analysis[16]

A sociometric scale can be worked out on the basis of the quantitative analysis of the choices made by the participating individuals. The general formula for the concentration of *inside* choices (Ratio of Interest) for any population[17] is

$$\frac{Y}{N \times X}$$

in which N equals size of population in the group; X, the number of choices per individual, and Y, the number of choices sent inside the group by its members. (See Diagram VII.)

The general formula for the concentration of *outside* choices upon a given group (Ratio of Attraction) within a larger population[18] is

$$\frac{Y'}{(N' - N) \times X}$$

in which N' equals size of the total population and Y' equals the number of choices sent inside the group by members of the outside population.

Next, the total concentration of choices in a group from its own members *and* outside population members can be expressed by the formula

---

[15]See reference 13, pp. 98-103.

[16]We express our appreciation to Professor Henry E. Garrett for critical review of the following statistics.

[17]This technique was first introduced in the study of the Hudson community. Every group in the community was to greater or smaller degree the focus of choices coming from members *inside* a particular group or from members *outside* of that group. The degree of the concentration of the choices varied from group to group and a scale was worked out showing how the different groups rank. For a group, Cottage 8, with 26 members each having five choices, 100% concentration of the in-group members would have been 130 choices, but the actual concentration found as contributed by its members was 43 choices, i.e. 33%, the Ratio of their Interest. For Cottage 1, for instance, the concentration was but 29%, for Cottage 13, 66%, etc. (Ref. 13.)

[18]This group of 26 being placed in a large field of 435 individuals which was broken up into 16 specific constellations could have become the center of the focus of the choices of all these members from all these groups. The degree of concentration of choices relative to this larger field was calculated for Cottage 8 as follows. The total population of 435 minus Cottage 8's population of 26 was 409. The number of available outside choices was hence 409 times five, or 2,045 choices. If the 26 members of Cottage 8 were to receive 2,045 choices, the degree of concentration of incoming choices from outside members would be 100 per cent. The number of choices received by the members of Cottage 8 was 35. This figure can be used to calculate the Ratio of Attraction members of Cottage 8 have for outside members. (Ref. 13.)

DIAGRAM VII

A Sociometric Scale of a Closed Group
(criterion is limited to members of this group)
Direction and Concentration of Choices as Basis

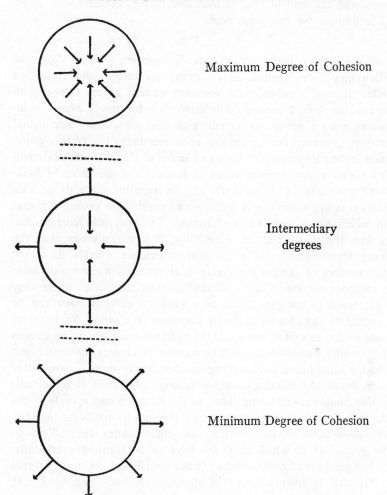

Maximum Degree of Cohesion

Intermediary
degrees

Minimum Degree of Cohesion

Between the top and bottom sociograms, numerous intermediary levels can be found for degree of choice concentration; as described on page 30 the various levels of the above scale can be readily determined. These can, of course, be compared wtih the degree of concentration found by *chance*.

45

$$\frac{Y + Y'}{(N' + N) \times X}$$

See Diagram VIII.

As a hypothetical norm for the concentration of choices within a group can be considered the sum of choices available to the members of a given group.[19] The formula for this norm reads

$$N \times X = Y + Y'$$

The direction taken by choices of outside members and the degree of concentration they show upon a certain group are inconclusive in regard to what effect it may have upon the members of that group. It opens up many potentialities but it cannot be inferred that because a higher number of choices enter a group the members of that group are more bound to one another. Concentration of choices upon members of a certain group and cohesion among these members are two *different* things. Statistical comparisons have shown "between the Ratio of Interest and the Index of Relative Popularity (Ratio of Attraction) . . . a negative correlation. This inverse relation is appreciable and indicates a considerable probability that any group which has a high Ratio of Interest for itself will have a comparatively low Index of Relative Popularity."[20] This indicates that the choices going from members of a group to individuals outside it, or the reverse, the number of choices coming to a group from members of other groups is an index for the *diffusion* of choices from the places where they originate in regard to the population as a whole. A different view can be taken in regard to the choices made by members of a group for members of that *same* group, especially drastic if the criterion upon which the choices rest is of a socially intimate nature. The number of choices the individuals who live in the same house have for one another can be more appropriately called an index of the existing cohesion among them than if individuals living in *other* houses are choosing them, as the latter choices operate at the time of the test outside of the house in which the persons are living together.

However, even these cohesive forces, the forces holding the individuals within the groupings in which they are have to be considered critically. They may not produce all *true* cohesion. It has been found, for example, that "a high Ratio of Interest was not in all instances correlated to a high

---

[19]Thus for the given group, Cottage 8, the number would be 26 times five, or 130 choices. To satisfy this norm it is required that if only 43 choices come from inside members, 87 choices should come from outside members.

[20]See reference 5, p. 424.

DIAGRAM VIII

A Sociometric Scale of an Open Group
(criterion allows the inclusion of other individuals than
the members of this group)
Direction and Concentration of Choices as Basis

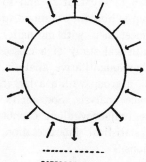

From inside, a minimum of cohesion

From outside a maximum of attraction

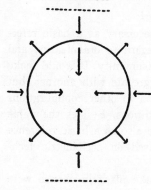

An equilibrium in attraction
and cohesion

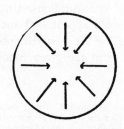

From inside, a maximum of cohesion
From outside, a minimum of attraction

Between the top and bottom sociograms, numerous intermediary levels can be found for degrees of choice concentration and attraction.

standard of conduct if other factors existed in the organization of the group to counter-affect this. . . . In a certain case a high Ratio of Interest shown for its own group was a disadvantage. The members did not look for other outlets and at the same time there were numerous rejections among themselves."[21]

Quantitative analysis of choices is *one* aspect in the study of cohesiveness, but it gives a comparatively artificial picture of the actual events within a social configuration. Far more crucial than to say that so and so many choices come in to members of a certain group is how they respond to these choices, how they reciprocate, whether they meet them with mutuality or not. Just as we have found in regard to the statistical study of a closed group that structural analysis is more inclusive than quantitative analysis, also in statistical evaluation of an open group, i.e., a group within a larger population, structural analysis is superior to choice analysis. Sociometric scales of groups in a community based on choice frequency alone cannot stand by themselves. They need for adequate statistical interpretation, scales which are based on configurational calculations.

(b) Scales on the Basis of Configurational Analysis

A more precise and comprehensive scale is necessary as a basic reference for all possible types of configurations in regard to organization and degree of cohesion as they may be found in the community. It would make possible not only the comparison of one social aggregate with another, but the determination of its precise position in relation to other configurations of the same size population under the same conditions. Besides the value of such a scale for research, it would have a value also as a basic reference for operational and therapeutic experiments[22] based on sociometric techniques.

If the deviations in a configuration which take place in chance were taken as the normal points on a scale, we have a reference base from which to measure the deviations which take place in actual configurations. Until norms can be established for actual populations, it would appear that such a chance reference base provides a useful measuring rod. It is understood that each chance level must be computed on the basis of the given conditions for that population.

---

[21]See reference 13, pp. 99-100.

[22]In control studies presented elsewhere, structural developments were compared as they happened when placements were made as indicated by the sociometric test as against chance placements. See reference 4. The reliability of the placements made could accordingly be studied with greater accuracy if not only position developments of individuals were compared but configurations as wholes.

If a population of a given size with a given number of choices were to produce a configuration in which every choice going out from a person is reciprocated by another person of that population, the sociodynamic effect would be zero. If that same population were to produce a configuration in which every choice going out from a person remains unreciprocated, the socio-dynamic effect would likewise be zero. These two theoretical possibilities represent respectively the maximum degree of cohesion and the minimum degree of cohesion. For these two levels, chance probability in the distribution of choices does not provide. Nevertheless, it is within this wide range that actual configurations must fall in one or another intermediary stage. Although the mathematical working out of these intermediary stages is complex, it can be done with precision. A theoretical construct of a sociometric scale simplified for the purpose of illustration is given in Diagram IX.

A series of configurations, as indicated in the construct, differs in the essential respect from a series of single elements in that it is multi-dimensional. On one point of the scale there is not only one solution but many. Also on each level of the scale there can be many sociotropic[23] varieties (factorial n) all having the same level of integration.

In the example used for the construct on page 34, five persons can produce 120 sociotropic varieties by a shift of position. The scale opens the way of learning whether the maximum degree of integration is also the best therapeutic level of a social aggregate. It may well be that they vary considerably.

As in statistics of single elements, it appears possible that, after a sufficiently large number of different populations have been tested and their configurations determined, the field worker will be able to predict the position of a group on a sociometric scale when approaching a new community before testing it. He will become able to predict approximately the range within which the configuration of this community will fall. Yet, however large the sampling of configurations taken from a given population is, and however accurate the prediction of the possible configuration of the untested part of this population may become, the rest of the population has nevertheless to be actually tested if a transaction of useful treatment of this part should be contemplated. The slightest variation in the untested part of this population may concern a number of individuals, however few. Types of sampling can become useful for prediction purposes from

---

[23]Two sociograms are sociotropic if they are formed by the same persons and have the same sociometric properties, seen as total configurations. They may differ in the position one or the other individual may have within them.

a tested to an untested part, but it is not permissible to assume this automatically for treatment purposes.

DIAGRAM IX

Theoretical Construct of a Sociometric Scale
(On Configurational Basis)

Five Persons, Two Choices   Analysis of the Scale

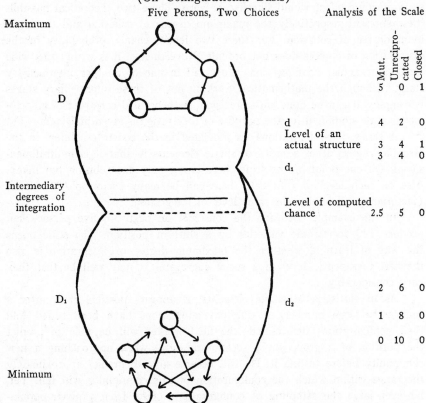

	Mut.	Unrecipro-cated	Closed
Maximum	5	0	1
d	4	2	0
Level of an actual structure	3	4	1
	3	4	0
d_1			
Level of computed chance	2.5	5	0
	2	6	0
d_2	1	8	0
	0	10	0

D
Intermediary degrees of integration
D_1
Minimum

The Scale is illustrated by configurations produced by 5 persons with 2 choices each. Six main levels of integration are indicated in the diagram. Only the top or maximum level of integration and the bottom or minimum level of integration are drawn. The intermediary degrees are indicated by a straight line. The composition of each degree however, is presented in the analysis to the right of the Scale.

Each of the six levels has, due to the possible shifting of the 5 persons and 2 choices, 120 sociotropic varieties. Sociotropic varieties are of the same level of integration although the position of the individual members may differ.

D —Deviation of maximum from chance.
D_1—Deviation of chance from minimum.
d —Deviation of maximum from average actual.
d_1 —Deviation of average actual from chance.
d_2 —Deviation of average actual from minimum.

REFERENCES

1. Criswell, Joan H., Racial Cleavage in Negro-White Groups, *Sociometry*, 1937, Vol. 1, pp. 81-89.
2. Fisher, R. A., *Statistical Methods for Research Workers*, 1936.
3. Forsith, C. H., *An Introduction to the Mathematical Analysis of Statistics*.
4. Jennings, H. H., Control Study of Sociometric Assignment, *Sociometric Review*, New York State Training School for Girls, Hudson, N. Y., 1936. Now available in *Sociometric Control Studies of Grouping and Regrouping*, Sociometry Monographs No. 7, Beacon House, New York, 1945.
5. ————, Sociometric Studies, a supplement in *Who Shall Survive?*, Beacon House, New York, 1934, pp. 373-423.
6. ————, Structure of Leadership, Development and Sphere of Influence, *Sociometry*, 1937, Vol. 1, pp. 99-143.
7. Leven, Maurice, *The Income Structure of the United States*, Brookings Institution, Washington, D. C., 1938.
8. Leven, Maurice; Moulton, Harold G.; and Warburton Clark, *America's Capacity to Consume*, Brookings Institution, Washington, D. C., 1934.
9. Lundberg, George A.; and Steele, Mary, Social Attraction-Patterns in a Village, *Sociometry*, 1938, Vol. 1, pp. 375-419.
10. Moreno, J. L., *Das Stegreiftheater*, Gustav Kiepenheuer, Berlin, 1923.
11. ————, Inter-Personal Therapy and the Psychopathology of Inter-Personal Relations, *Sociometry*, 1937, Vol. 1, pp. 9-76. Now available as *Psychodrama and the Psychopathology of Inter-Personal Relations*, Psychodrama Monographs, No. 16, Beacon House, New York, 1945.
12. ————, Sociometry in Relation to Other Social Sciences, *Sociometry*, 1937, Vol. 1, pp. 206-219.
13. ————, *Who Shall Survive?*, A New Approach to the Problem of Human Interrelations, Beacon House, New York, 1934.
14. Moreno, J. L., and Jennings, H. H., Advances in Sociometric Technique, *Sociometric Review*, New York State Training School for Girls, Hudson, N. Y., 1936. Now available as *Sociometric Control Studies of Grouping and Regrouping*, Sociometry Monographs, No. 7, Beacon House, New York, 1945.
15. Murphy, Lois Barclay, *Social Behavior and Child Personality*, Columbia University Press, New York, 1937.
16. Newstetter, Wilber I.; Feldstein, Marc J.; and Newcomb, Theodore M., *Group Adjustment, A Study in Experimental Sociology*, see Chapter XIII, Western Reserve University, Cleveland, Ohio, 1938.
17. Stockton, Richard, *Sociometric Survey of Riverdale Country Day School*, 1932. Unpublished.

THE SOCIAL ATOM: A DEFINITION

By J. L. Moreno

1) The social atom is the nucleus of all individuals towards whom a person is related in a significant manner or who are related to him at the same time; the relationship may be emotional, social, or cultural.

2) The sum of interpersonal structures resulting from choices and rejection centered about a given individual is his social atom.

3) It is the smallest nucleus of individuals in the social universe who are "emotionally" intorwoven. We say "emotional" because even the highest spiritual or intellectual relationships are meaningless without some feeling.

4) The social atoms are the centers of attraction, rejection, or indifference. We say attraction or rejection because the interweaving of emotional, social, or cultural factors eventually takes the form of attraction, rejection or indifference on the surface of human contact.

5) The social atom is the ultimate universal "common denominator" of all social forms, it is not "normative" like the family or an abstraction from the group like the individual.

6) By emotions, we do not mean this or that emotion, but *all* emotions that bind or separate people, like love and hate, pity and compassion, jealousy and envy, gaiety and joy, anger and hate; attractions and repulsions are not emotions, they are their *end* products. By social relations, we mean *all* social relation, from mere acquaintances to professional and industrial relations. By cultural relations we mean *all* cultural relations from simple sharing of ideas to esthetic, ethical, and religious relations.

7) Social atoms are the "smallest" unit of social relationships. This is so by no means in a numerical and absolute sense. For two strangers meeting on the street corner or two occasional lovers the number of participants are two. For a powerful individual attractive and attracted to thousands of individuals the number of participants forming an immediate network of emotions may be thousands, but the pattern of relationship is still also in this case the smallest imaginable under the circumstances.

8) Social atoms and physical atoms are contrary in origin and meaning. The social atom is an existential category, it consists of individuals; once brought to cognizance it is *in immediate evidence and cannot be further reduced.* Contrary to it, the physical atom is not in immediate evidence and can be further reduced. It is not a reality but a construct. The term *atomos* is a misnomer, for the physical atom is not the smallest and simplest elementary par-

ticle of matter. Electrons, neutrons, protons, etc. are smaller, and in the course of time still smaller particles may be found. But it cannot be imagined that at any time a smaller social structure than the social atom will be found, as it is nothing else but the *most immediate social coexistence of individuals.*

9) The formation of social atoms may be due to a variety of contingencies of contact: chance, proximity, and choice; but choice produces the most enduring form of contact, the social expression of spontaneity, par excellence.

10) Atom is derived from a Greek word, *atomos,* meaning "any very small thing." The term was introduced into scientific language by Democritus. He used it to indicate the smallest particles in the physical universe. But physicists have no priority on the term; many words introduced by early philosophers describing physical phenomena, such as gravitation, atom, attraction, saturation, have a poetic-symbolic character; they are metaphors for psychosocial experiences and belong rightly in our social vocabulary, whence they have been taken. We may learn more about the meaning of "atomic structure" of the universe from sociometric studies than we ever learned from physics.

There are two significant microscopic formations of the atom, the social atom and the cultural atom. Their existence has been brought to empirical test by means of microsociology and social microscopy. A pattern of attractions, repulsions, and indifferences can be discerned on the threshold between individual and group. This pattern is called the "social atom." It is the smallest functional unit within the social group. Every person is positively or negatively related to an indefinite number of socii, who in turn may be related to him positively or negatively. Besides these two-way relations there are one-way relations observable. Some socii are related to the central person and unknown to him, and he may be related to some socii unknown to them. It is the total configuration which comprises the social atom. An individual has from birth a structure of relationships around him—mother, father, grandmother and other members of his early environment. The volume of the social atom is in continuous expansion as we grow up; it is within it that we live most concretely.

Every individual, just as he is the focus of numerous attractions and repulsions, also appears as the focus of numerous roles which are related to the roles of other individuals. Just as he has at all times a set of friends and a set of enemies, he also has a range of roles and a range of counter-roles. They are in various stages of development. The tangible aspects of what is known as "ego or self" are the roles in which he operates. The focal pattern of role-relations around an individual is called his *cultural atom.* The term is selected as an analogue to the term "social atom." The use of the word "atom" here can be justified if we consider a cultural atom as the smallest functional unit within a cultural pattern. The adjective "cultural" can be justified when we consider roles and relationships between roles as the most significant development within any specific culture. The socio-atomic organization of a group cannot be separated from its cultural-atomic organization. The social and cultural atom are manifestations of the *same* social reality.

ORGANIZATION OF THE SOCIAL ATOM

By J. L. Moreno

The number of acquaintances which an individual has at the time of testing has been called by me his "acquaintance volume". A person may remember about many of these individuals only that he has met them or talked with them. Most of them, however, do not matter to him, do not mean anything personal to him. And he doesn't matter to them; he doesn't mean anything to them, at least at the moment. But among these acquaintances there is a small group who mean something personal to him, in some degree and in respect to some criterion; he is attracted to them or he rejects them. There may be in this group, whether he knows it or not, individuals to whom he means something, who are attracted to him or who reject him. If we compare with the physiological cell this acquaintance volume, we may say that the general pattern of acquaintances which are without individual meaning for him is like the cytoplasm, and the meaningful acquaintances like the nucleus of the cell. Often the boundary between the outer mass and the nucleus of acquaintances may not be absolute. There may be some individual about whom it cannot be said with finality whether he is a mere acquaintance or already an emotional partner. But the general demarcation line between the nucleus of emotionally related individuals which I termed the "social atom" and the rest of the acquaintance volume will be very clear.

The point of transition from being a mere acquaintance to becoming an emotional partner in a social atom is theoretically significant. A study of numerous social atoms reveals a definite line of demarcation between the acquaintance volume and the social nucleus proper, the "social threshold". We can say that the moment that I wish a certain acquaintance—an individual whom I have just met or whom I may have known for some time— to become closer to me, to enter into a relationship with me, more or less permanent in respect to some criterion, work, love, or whatever, this person has passed the social threshold of my social atom. The same can be said about individuals who wish to enter into a relationship with me, whether I reciprocate their desire or not. They also have passed the threshold of my social atom. To my social atom evidently would belong all individuals to whom I am bound by an invisible desire which may be little or not at all manifest; also those individuals to whom I am tied in actual overt relationships. Indeed, we here see the social atom itself further subdivided into two parts: the outer part of the nucleus formed by the "wished" relationships and the inner part of the nucleus formed by the actualized ones.

The emotional currents which, so to speak, pervade a social atom are of varying intensity. There are many levels of preference. We made a study of the factors contributing to this uneven distribution of preferences, or better said, the uneven intensity of feeling preferences. For a certain social situation (choosing of house-members), the majority of the subjects made full use of their choices. Some did not have enough with five preferences. But a considerable number did not use the full five choices, and a very few chose but one or none at all.

In our usual procedure the individuals tested expressed five degrees of preference, but they did not suggest how many individuals they liked *equally* well. Therefore a series of tests was subsequently made in which the emphasis was slightly differently placed. The subjects were instructed: "As you choose, weigh carefully whether you would like two or three individuals to live with you equally well. You may like two or three persons 'first choice,' or two or three persons 'second choice'; or all the persons to whom you are attracted may be the same degree of choice; or there may be just one 'first choice' and the rest in other degrees, perhaps each at a different degree of preference." The results showed again several levels of preference but often several individuals at the same level of preference. In regard to work a certain young woman named one person first, a man; three persons second, two women and a man; in regard to living in the same house she named no one, preferring to live alone; in regard to love she named one man first and four men second; in regard to social and cultural contact she named ten persons with whom she liked to associate equally well.

II.

RELATIONS TOWARD THINGS VS. RELATIONS TOWARD PERSONS

Evidently there are individuals whose feelings of preference are more articulate than those of others. Also, some may have more articulate preferences in respect to one criterion, for instance, work. However, it seemed to us that the wide differences of preferential feeling which individuals reveal who are of similar intelligence and under similar environmental influences cannot be explained satisfactorily by simply calling them more or less articulate. There must be other factors of persistent influence.

Now there are besides the preferences for individuals the preferences for things, objects, values, and objectives, like sex, food, money, ideas, etc. A sociometric test was constructed in which the subjects spontaneously reveal in order of preference the things to which they are attracted: for instance,

ACQUAINTANCE VOLUME—Acquaintances which are without emotional meaning for
the subject.

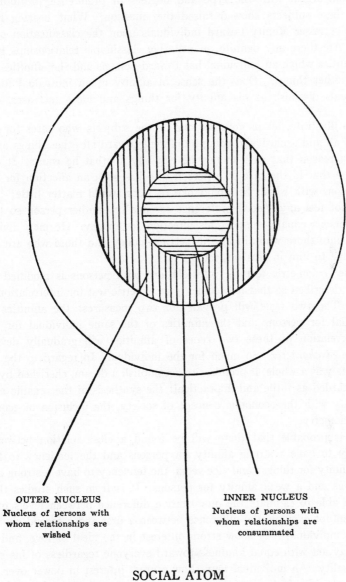

OUTER NUCLEUS

Nucleus of persons with
whom relationships are
wished

INNER NUCLEUS

Nucleus of persons with
whom relationships are
consummated

SOCIAL ATOM
Nucleus of persons emotionally related to the subject
(outer and inner nucleus)

money, sex, clothes, automobiles, books, etc. An analysis of the results and their comparison with the type and degrees of preference for individuals which these subjects showed raised the question: What bearing has the greater or lesser affinity toward individuals upon the classification of character? Are there any definite quantitative classifiable relationships between the affinities which an individual has toward persons and the affinities he has toward other things? Does the sense of affinity of an individual for other individuals diminish as his affinity for things and ideas increases, or vice versa?

To illustrate, let us consider one of the subjects who cares for money most of all and exclusively, being indifferent toward all other things and giving as a reason that with money he can buy all that he wants. It can be well seen that in the case of a person who has such an affection for money the persons with whom he would like to work would matter little; that he would not feel any special preference for one or another person so long as these persons equally support his affection for money. He may divide the persons into those who aid him in getting money and those who are of disadvantage to him in this respect.

The sociometric test for interrelations with persons is modified in the manner described so that it becomes a sociometric test for interrelations with things. The two tests will provide for two measures: the affinities of an individual for persons and the affinities of the same individual for things. The correlation of these two types of affinities will gradually develop a measure of *character*. So much for the individual. In regard to the group, and society as a whole, it promises to accomplish a dream, cherished by many but discarded as futile and impractical: the synthesis of the organic concept of society with the economic concept of society, the inclusion of economics into sociometry.

It is probable that there will be found a close relation between the tendency to have a strong affinity for persons and the tendency to have a weak affinity for things; and vice versa, the tendency to have a strong affinity for things and a weak affinity for persons. It is from such studies that we shall be able to estimate the quantitative difference between levels of preference, as for example the difference between a first and a second choice.

An individual may show strong interest in the ideal of love, and urged by it may act with equal kindness toward everyone regardless of his specific individuality. An individual may show a great interest in power over things and people—for instance, for money as conferring the power to buy—and he may act with equal eagerness to gain money for himself regardless of the specific individualities of the people from whom he has to wrest it. An individual may show a great interest in sensuous pleasures, for instance, sex, and a slight interest in the specific individuals involved. What is, sociometrically speaking, the affinity, the positive or negative "tele"[1] for each of these things as compared with the tele for the persons whom one meets in pursuing life's goals?

We find that individuals who have a slight interest in *specific* individuals in regard to sex are far from being disinterested in personal characteristics; they may have a great interest in certain *group characteristics* in regard to sex. Such individuals develop little attachment to a specific individual, but may be intensely drawn toward individuals possessing certain physical and mental attributes regardless of their individuality. Such a person craves a certain complex of attributes and little, or not at all, the individual carrying them. He uses the individuals; he is not in love with them. He can emancipate, free, separate himself from a specific individual in regard to sex because he was attached to a *combination of attributes* which exist and grow elsewhere also. His sexual impulse is independent of individual persons. Therefore he may be free of attachment to a pattern of individual traits. The more universally distributed these attributes are or these combinations of attributes, the larger will be the number of persons belonging to the group toward which he is drawn. His "freedom" from a specific individual will be relatively greater, the larger the number of individuals who belong to this group.

In the sociometric tests we may find the dominating preference for sex as an impersonal thing suddenly interrupted if a person of group S complex competes with a person of group Non-S. And in general, the feeling-preferences for various things, values, ideas, objects or objectives may at certain points be interrupted, distorted, and complicated by feeling-preferences for individuals. In regard to money, or the equivalents of money, an individual may proceed to accumulate it undisturbed by the individual differences between its owners until he hits upon an individual or individuals to whom he is sensitive (persons whose association he craves because of their social, intellectual, or "racial" superiority, etc.). Then his emotional energy, hitherto directed toward money, may be interfered with and slowed up by personal elements which are wrongly called subjective. This energy may even be transformed and turned in the opposite direction, into the losing of money, the desire to buy with money the association with this person or these persons

---

[1]See *Who Shall Survive?* pp. 158-164.

who have social standing, political influence, sexual appeal, etc. In regard to race as a thing, an individual may find a dominating preference for individuals of a certain race not because of their specific individuality but because of their "race", suddenly interrupted if a person of the group to which he is sensitive competes. This person may not belong to the race required and demanded by him in principle. A monk, subscribing to a certain idea of conduct, may act toward everyone he meets with the same "equalized" affection until this attitude is suddenly interrupted by an individual to whom he is sensitive. It may be useful to differentiate between attraction to individuals for their exclusive individual characteristics—which cannot be "replaced" at least in the thought of the person attracted—and attractions for their group characteristics.

III.

GENERAL SOCIOLOGICAL IMPLICATIONS

The imbalances arising can be harmonized, to some extent at least, through constructive rearrangement of people and of things. But this is only a palliative measure. The true solution would be a spontaneous balancing of all these factors. The question is what is the next stage in the evolution of human society, what kind of society will finally crystallize, perhaps aided in finding its destiny by sociometric guides? Theoretically I can visualize three solutions.

The first possibility is a human society in which the preferences for things entirely dominate the preferences for persons; a society in which attachments to persons are extinguished. Attachments exist only to things independent of persons, and to persons only so far as they carry certain things, since the optimum of satisfaction will depend only upon things and things can be indefinitely "replaced" by other things. The individual being may reach a degree of happiness and balance he has never known heretofore. It would be a technological panacea. The emotional currents between persons would be reduced to zero. A certain kind of love would still matter, but not whom one loves; work would matter but not with whom one works; food would matter but not with whom one eats; ideas would matter, too, but not who embodies them. A society would arise in which individuals become symbols and things the only reality. It may bring an optimum of happiness with the extinction of the interrelation strains. The solitaire, the saint, and the schizophrenic are psychological pioneers in this direction. Feeling-for-things would replace feeling-for-persons.

A second outcome would be a human society in which the preferences for individuals would entirely dominate the preferences for things; a society in which attachments to things in themselves would be extinguished; attachments would exist only to individuals and to things only as they are an expression of individuals, an emotional or personality panacea.

A third resultant would be a human society in which the preferences for individuals and the preferences for things would be extinguished; it would not matter whom you love or what you eat. All attachments are extinguished: the Buddhistic panacea.

THE SOCIAL ATOM AND DEATH

By J. L. Moreno

The gods and immortals which men have cherished for millennia have lost a great deal of the dignity and value which they were supposed to have. Is the idea of immortality entirely a figment of the human mind? I believe that in the future it will become fashionable again and find new attraction for the philosopher and the dreamer. We have been thrown down from the heavens and have a hard time to keep midway between heaven and hell.

You all know that one of the basic concepts which sociometry has developed is that of the social atom. Atom is derived from a Greek word "atomos" which means the smallest thing. The term has been introduced by Democrites into scientific language. He used it to indicate the smallest particles in the physical universe. However, the physicists have no priority on the word; many words introduced by early philosophers describing physical phenomena as gravitation, atom, attraction, saturation, have a poetic-symbolic character; they are metaphors for psycho-social experiences and belong rightly in our social vocabulary, whence they have been taken.

Sociologists have used the term socius in a vague way for a long time. It has never meant anything specific until sociometry discovered and defined it as the social atom. People usually thought of the individual as the center of the social universe, of the family as the next larger unit, then the neighborhood, the village, etc.; from the point of view of surface experience sociologists accepted tacitly a scale starting with the individual and ending with the entire universe. We sociometrists challenged this view. The social atom is the smallest social unit, not the individual.[1] The social atom is simply an individual *and* the people (near or distant) to whom he is significantly related at the time. We have shown that these configurations function as if they would be one unit. They may not be the same people with whom a person is officially related and who are in turn officially related to him, but they are always people to whom he has a feeling relationship. It is like an *aura* of attractions and rejections, radiating from him and towards him. These social atoms change from time to

---

[1]See "Psychodramatic Shock Therapy," Psychodrama Monograph No. 5, Beacon House, New York, p. 29. From a philogenetic point of view "the individual" appears to be a more recent development than an aggregate of individuals.

time in their membership, but there is a consistency about their structure, the way our bone structure has a certain consistency. I predicted this would be found true of the social atom in 1931 when I first "saw" a psychological geography of a whole community. Jennings' findings confirmed this prediction. An individual has from birth on already a structure of relationships around him, mother, father, grandmother, and so forth. The volume of the social atom is in continuous expansion as we grow up; it is within it that we live most concretely.

I am now coming to the topic which I intended to discuss in this paper: the consistency of these social atoms changes as we get old, especially the ability to replace loss of membership. Although the social atom is changing intermittently as long as we are young and more resourceful, when one individual member goes out of it another individual fulfilling a similar role takes his place. As one friend steps out, the old friend is rapidly replaced by a new one; social repair seems to take place almost automatically. But when an individual fulfilling one function is lost rarely more than one steps in to replace him. It is as if the central individual cannot sustain two or three of the same kind. There is, simultaneously, a continuous pull from millions of other social atoms, equally craving for replacements. The total effect is as if the dynamic economy of the social is operating in accord with an unconscious postulate—to keep the social atoms in equilibrium, what I have also called their "sociostasis." Thus a certain range of telic contacts always exists and remains fairly constant. Their frequency of emotional exchange tends towards balance. This is the reason why what I have called the "emotional expansiveness"[2] of an individual can be measured.

But as we grow older replacements of lost members in significant roles take place with greater difficulty; similar as repairs are more difficult to our physical organism in the course of aging. It is the phenomenon of "social" death, not from the point of view of the body, not in the individual sense of the psyche, not how we die from within but how we die from *without*. A man or woman of sixty may be related to twelve or fifteen individuals, so many women and so many men, of various age levels representing various interests, in such roles and in such counter-roles. Social death throws its shadow upon him long before physical or mental death. An individual may begin to lose in the cohesion of his social atom for various reasons: a) loss of affection, b) replace-

---

[2] Who Shall Survive?, p. 73 and 134.

ment by another individual not as well suited, and c) death. The death of an individual member is usually a more permanent loss, the shock coming from it is rarely considered in its full significance. If we happen to survice the ones we love or hate, we die a bit with them as we feel the shadow of death marching from one person of our social atom to another. The people who move in to replace them do not always substitute the lost ones, even the very fact of substitution represents a certain loss. Therefore we feel from childhood on through the networks of our social atom, the meaning of death long before it actually comes with the signs of physical and mental disability. Maybe that we sociometrists will find the predeterminants for social death, a syndrome quite different from the one pointed out by the physician and psychiatrist. We were warming up to the death of the people whom we loved or hated or who loved or hated us. It should be possible to find remedies against the social death shock.

It is probable that the minute shocks coming from social death experience paves the way to premature aging, old sickness and physical death. Old people should learn not to give in to this curse, they should find friends, someone to love again. They should first try to restore the youth of their social atom. It is probably easier to treat the social atom disorders by sociatric devices than to treat their physical and mental complaints. The idea that love and spontaneity is for the young only, that old people should prepare themselves for death, is an antiquated cruelty. A new breath of hope should come to geriatrics, the science of old age, from the recognition that we do not live only within ourselves, but that there is a "without" of the self which is highly structured, and responsive to growth and decay. Death is a live function, it has a social reality. The death of one person is connected with the death of many others. The people towards whose death you are sensitive and who are sensitive towards yours make up the last social atom you have. We are all surrounded continuously by people with whom we die. Physical death is something negative, we don't experience it, the other fellow does, the fellow who is a member of our social atom. Social death is a *positive* force. Death is among us, like birth. Just as the infant—to an extent —pushes himself into birth, we push ourselves into death, *and each other*, often prematurely. As the s (spontaneity) factor operates throughout pregnancy towards birth, it warms up the sparks of fear in the social atoms and pushes its members towards death. We see how birth pro-

64

gresses during pregnancy, from conception on. Similarly we see how death progresses, from its conceptions in the social atom, the first people whom we have experienced as dying, and the little shocks we received from it. When we will know more about the processes going on in the social atom of individuals we may invent means of repairing its disorders. Maybe a new profession will develop in time, the sociatrists, who among other matters will treat socio-atomic disorders.

I recall the case of twelve individuals who were sensitive for each other's death expectancy and so infected each other. They belonged to the same profession, they were all physicians, and their respective social atoms crossed and overlapped each other's. One pioneered with a coronary thrombosis. Five of the group succumbed to the same ailment, the other six of the group lived in fear of it. At this writing two of them have died from it, three have recovered from an actual attack, the balance of the group are increasingly worried, the first thing they read in the newspapers are the death notices and they are frequently going for physical check ups. We sociometrists are aware that more important than printed matter are the psychosocial networks. News travels through them, but also death news. If you don't have a coronary thrombosis, or any other physical or mental ailment which appeals to you because it has appealed to your socio-atomic associates, you may pass without a mental attack of it. But another may be sensitized by such news and hasten the onset of such an attack if, of course, there are some somatic conditions inviting it. I had an opportunity to put on the psychodrama stage people who were chained to one another by mutual love and death fears. Some of the individuals knew one another only through a link but they had high regard for each other. To their surprise they found out during their work on the stage that what happened to one meant a great deal to the other. The work out on the stage seemed to bring them relief, a sort of death catharsis. Mirroring each other's death awareness awakened their sense of humor. Another case concerns eight air pilots. The subject was the ninth. As he was enacting on the stage shocks from death experience a scene suddenly occurred to him which he had felt more keenly than the death of his grandfather and of a younger brother: with eight other candidates for air service, he was undergoing a physical checkup. They were all accepted except himself, he did not pass. He saw them there for the first time in the examination room. Before he left they arranged to keep in touch with each other. He wrote them and they wrote back, but after a while, from every one of them in succession his own letters returned, stamped "Missing in action." These new and rather incidental members of his social atom were apparently dead. As he was re-enacting the situation on the stage he said: "There but by the grace of God, so I."

The eight men were not quite dead yet, they were beckoning him to follow. The life of men extends beyond their physical death through their social atoms. A man dies when his social atom dies. Physical and individual death are not the end of life, they can be viewed as functions of an older unit, of the socio-atomic processes[3] in which they are both embedded.

---

[3]The following formulation of the socio-atomic process fifteen years ago has been fully corroborated by research in social microscopy. "They are a study of the *inner* structures of groups and can be compared with studies concerning the nuclear nature of the atom or the physiological structure of the cell." See "Group Method and Group Psychotherapy," Sociometry Monograph, No. 5, page 102, Beacon House, New York, 1931.

THEORY OF INTERPERSONAL NETWORKS

By J. L. Moreno

The psychogeographic mapping of the community shows, first, the relationship of local geography to psychological processes; second, the community as a psychological whole and the interrelations of its parts—families, industrial units, etc.; third, the existence of psychological currents which break group lines, as racial, economic, social, sexual, and cultural currents. But these bonds are not the deepest level of the structure which we have tried to raise. There are still deeper layers. We had suspected that beneath the ever flowing and ever changing currents there must be a permanent structure, a container, a bed which carries and mingles its currents, however different their goals may be. The clue to this hypothesis was furnished by the structural analysis of groups; certain forms, as pairs, chains, triangles, etc., recur regularly and are definitely related to the degree of differentiation a group has attained. The other is the trend of individuals to break group lines as if mysteriously drawn by certain psychological currents. We have found that these currents which break group lines, and even community lines, are not lawless. They are related to more or less permanent structures which bind individuals together into complex lines of transportation and communication, large "networks."

PROOFS THAT NETWORKS EXIST

In the fall of 1932 an epidemic of runaways occurred in Hudson. Within fourteen days, fourteen girls ran away. This high incidence was unusual for the community. In the preceding seven months only ten girls had run away. The rush appeared to be without adequate motivation: the motivations, however convincing for the individual cases, failed to explain the *chain*, the fact that so many felt themselves motivated to run away just at this particular time and within so short a period. To say that it was caused by mass suggestion is not a satisfactory explanation either. Another clue comes from the sociometric classifications and sociograms; they indicate that a far larger number of individuals than those who participated in this chain have shown a sociometric position within the community predisposing them to run away as much as these fourteen girls who did. A better hypothesis was that these fourteen girls were a part of some *hidden existing networks* and that the rest, who were equally predisposed, were not.

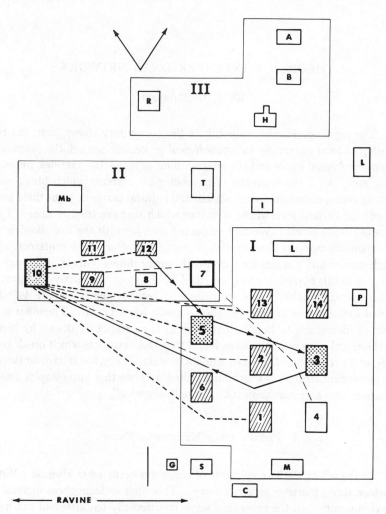

PSYCHOLOGICAL GEOGRAPHY—MAP I

The map illustrates the topographical outlay of Hudson and the psychological status of each region in relation to *runaways produced and to inter-racial trends.*

The community has three different sections, each of which form a kind of neighborhood: Neighborhood I, formed by C1 (now C3),* C2 (now C4), C13 (now C15), C14 (now C16), C3 (now C5), C4 (now C6), C5 (now C7), and C6 (now C8); Neighborhood II, formed by C7 (now C9), C8 (now C10), C9 (now C11), C10 (now C12), C11 (now C13), and C12 (now C14); Neighborhood III, formed by CA (now C1) and CB (now C2). The two colored cottages border on the ends of Neighborhood II and are distinguished by heavier black contours.

* The numbering of the cottages was originally A, B, 1, 2, 3, etc. In a later renumbering Cottages A and B were changed to 1 and 2, Cottages 1, 2, 3, etc., became 3, 4, 5, and so forth. The reader should take this into consideration when comparing Map I with Map II which was based on the new numbering.

Two girls, LS and SR, ran away on October 31, from Cottage (C) 14. The next day, November 1, five girls from C7 ran away: RT, LC, DD, HN, and FL. Four days later, November 5, four girls from C5 followed: HC, HL, ZR, and HIL. A week later, November 13, three girls from the colored C12 followed: LW, HL, and JN. Thereafter no runaway incident occurred until January 8, 1933. In the corresponding period for 1931 there were only three runaways.

The fourteen girls came from four specific cottages, C14, C7, C5, and C12. That they belonged together in *a chain within a network* is supported by the following: Only two of the fourteen girls, FL and HN, both from C7, had made an attempt to run away before. Chronic centers for running away were thus only in this one set. The other three sets were free of them. HN had made her attempt about fifteen months previously when she was in another group. FL had run away from C7 on August 27, about nine weeks before her second attempt. The question arises: why did the chain of fourteen just described not start at that time? An analysis of the position of the four sets at that period offers an explanation. FL was then in an isolated, insignificant position within C7. It was another girl, CE, who had for weeks contemplated a runaway. She looked for a companion for the venture. On the twenty-seventh she confided in FL, who in an impromptu fashion decided to go with her. CE, the source of the inspiration in August, did not belong to the network which we have described above, but to a different one; apparently she did not succeed in inspiring those within it to similar actions. FL herself was not an inspiring center and no current was initiated by her sufficient to sway others to emulate her action. To say it figuratively, *the best road, here a network, cannot make a car run through it. The driver must contribute.* The position of FL in the network was not yet crystallized or established.

We traced the positions of these fourteen on the Psychological Geography maps and found that interrelations existed among the girls who belonged to the same cottage and also between individuals of each of the four runaway sets. The positions of the sets are seen to be as follows: Set in C14, SR and LS are an isolated pair; set in C7, RT chooses HN; DD chooses HN and DD also chooses LC; FL is isolated and rejects HN, but forms a mutual pair with CE with whom she made an earlier runaway attempt; RT forms mutual pairs with four members of her group; set in C5, ZR is the center of attraction of 6 individuals in her group; ZR forms a mutual pair with HIL and is attractive to HC and HL; set in C12, LW, HL and JN are all isolated but interrelated by indirection. The interrelations *between* the sets are seen to be as follows: LS

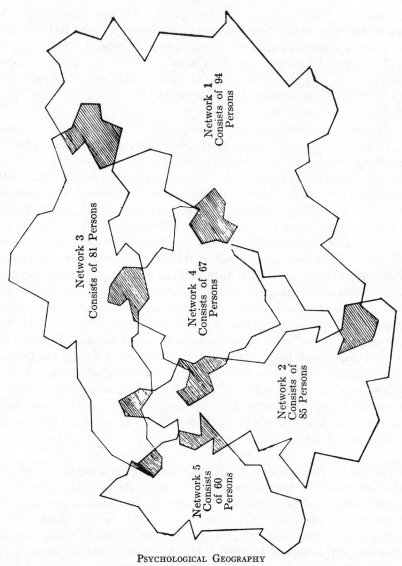

PSYCHOLOGICAL GEOGRAPHY

NETWORKS IN A COMMUNITY—MAP II

The chart illustrates the subdivisions of the whole community into five more or less distinct bundles, each comprising a specific number of individuals. The individuals who belong to each of these networks were found to be so interlocked, directly or by indirection, that emotional states could travel to the members of the respective network with the least possible delay.

70

These networks are invisible. They were traced by means of a microscopic technique as follows: Each line (tele) which went out from a member of any group to a member of any other group, and from this person on to a member of a third group and from this person on to a member of a fourth group, etc., as long as the chain continued. Only such persons are counted who are interlocked as belonging to the same network, irrespective of the cottage in which they lived. We began the counting with a certain individual in Cottage 4, following the line which went to an individual in Cottage 1, and from this individual to another individual in Cottage 6, to find that this last individual had a line going to another individual in Cottage 7, to find that this individual in Cottage 7 had no line going out to any individual in another cottage. At this point the network broke up. We returned to Cottage 4 and proceeded in a similar manner with every individual in the cottage who showed connections to individuals in other cottages, until again we arrived with each of them to the point where the net broke up. In this manner we were enabled to construct what we called the *main communication line* of the network.

Once the members of the main communication line of the network were ascertained, we began to trace from each of its members those individuals within her own group who were *directly* related to her. These branches formed the side lines of the network. It is understood that again each individual of a side line was followed up to determine her contacts to members of other cottages and if such new members were found in other cottages, for them also.

On this basis we ascertained in Hudson complicated networks: in the same cottage, for instance, Cottage 4, a number of individuals belong to one network, Network 1; another number of individuals unrelated directly to the former belong to another network, Network 2. The individuals belonging to it are in general different from the ones involved in Network 1. But they are by no means fully cut off from them. As as example, in Cottage 1 some of the same individuals share in four different networks. But not every group is so promiscuous.

Except for small bridges crossing between these networks, which we have indicated by lines in the sections which are overlapping, we could distinguish within the community five more or less distinct bundles: Network 1 consisting of 94 individuals, Network 2 consisting of 85 individuals, Network 3 consisting of 81 individuals, Network 4 consisting of 67 individuals and Network 5 consisting of 50 individuals. The total number of people participating in the Networks is thus 387. Therefore, 48 individuals out of the population of 435 did not participate in them; this number is still smaller than the number of unchosen ones. Some of the unchosen individuals chose themselves into chain-producing contacts. The question which arises is: what effect has the being left out of the main communication of networks on the development of social roles, social perceptions, social symbols, in these neglected individuals, and how does all this affect their behavior in the social groups in which they live?

The networks represent the oldest form of social communication. Traces of them are already in subhuman societies. They are collective formations, the individual participants are unconscious of all the networks in which they partake, although they may be aware of one or another link between some of the individuals, or realize that such networks exist. An individual cannot move out of networks, just as he cannot move outside of his skin. Networks pre-exist him and pre-exist the official groups of which he is a part.

in C14 forms a mutual pair with LC from C7; DD in C7 is interrelated to ZR in C5; HC in C5 is interrelated to LW in C12; further, LS in C14 is interrelated with SN in C12, who, while not a participant in the runaway, is in a chain relation to JN of C12; also, DD from C7 forms a pair with HL of C12. The main line of the network seems to go from SR to LS in C14, to LC and DD in C7, hence to ZR and HC in C5, and from there to LW in C12.

The broken lines indicate the inter-racial choice between colored members of C7 and white members of C4, C9, and C5, and between colored members of C10 and white members of C1, C12, C8, C2, C13 ,C9, and C5.

The runaway-status of each cottage from June 1, 1931, to September 1, 1933, is indicated as follows: Cottages which had no runaways during this period are left blank, CA C*B*, C4, C7, and C8. Cottages which yielded most of the runaways (6 or more) are indicated by small black squares, C3, C5, and C10. Cottages which had up to 5 runaways are indicated by large black squares: C1, C2, C6, C13, C14, C9, C11, and C12.

A continuous line indicates at what point a runaway chain which started October 31, 1932, and lasted until November 13, 1932, was initiated. An arrow indicates the direction which the chain took: from C12 to C5, from C5 to C3, from C3 to C10, where it ended.

Further Explanatory to Chart: G—Gatehouse; S—Storehouse; C—Church; M—Main Building; P—Paint Shop; E—Educational Building; I—Industrial Building; T—Teachers' Cottage; Mb—Mercantile Building; L—Laundry; H—Hospital; R—Receiving Cottage.

These relations had been uncovered through the sociometric test in respect to the criterion of living in proximity. *Only a part of these relations are conscious and intentional for every individual in this chain.* For instance, SR is fully aware of her relation to LS and of all the detailed planning developed step by step, up to the goal of running away. But she was, as we ascertained, unaware of the processes going on within the other three sets. LS in turn was conscious of the part she played with SR and as she was related to LC in C7, she was aware that LC was discontented and had ideas about escaping. However, she had never become intimate with LC in reference to running away. LC had also kept it secret from LS that she was entangled with DD and through the latter with HN and RT. Therefore, LS was entirely unaware of the processes between DD and the others; in fact, she was unacquainted with any of them and unconscious of the further entanglements of the set in C7 with that in C5, whose intermediary agent was ZR with whom she was also unacquainted. Similarly, as the set in C14 was unaware of the set in C7 and C5, the set in C7 was unaware of the set in C14 and C12; in turn, the set in C12 was unaware of the set in C7 and C14, and the set in C5 was unaware of the set in C14 and partially of the set in C7.

The individuals of each of the four sets, although living in different sections of the same community at the time before the episodes took place, were absorbed by a similar idea and yet unaware of the fact that the social current flowing back and forth among them had gradually enveloped them, and that it had developed a number of fixed contacts and produced channels through which emotions and suggestive ideas could pass uncensored from one to the other without the majority in the community having knowledge of them.

But when FL was found and returned to the cottage the situation had changed. The publicity which she had received from her first escape brought her into particular contact with four girls of her cottage who ruminated in a similar direction. Thus the set in C7 consolidated itself more and more between August 27 and November 1. When, on October 31, SR and LS in C14 ran away, the impetus was provided and the suggestive current travelled through the minds of those who belonged to the same network and who were ready to be "touched off" by the action. If the network would not have existed, the chances are that the runaway pair in C14 would have remained isolated actors: the idea would not have spread.

Another factor is in need of discussion. It is rare that a girl runs away alone. When this is the case, as with BN from C12 on August 29, 1932, or with CI from C5 on November 14, 1931, they are fully isolated individuals. They belong to the few who *fall between* networks, either because they are newcomers in the community or because they did not attach themselves in the community to anyone, perhaps never having the intention to stay. In the 27 months' period studied only four run away alone. The overwhelming majority went either in pairs or in groups of three or more.

Further proof that networks exist is shown by the following: a series of runaways which started in C4 with DV, TB, and DN on August 18, 1932, did *not* develop into a chain of runaways. On August 27, CE ran away with FL from C7 and on August 29, BN escaped alone from C12. Then the episode died out. The latter, BN, was unrelated to any network and the others did not develop a chain evidently because *no roads were established through which their suggestion could travel unhindered.*

The described runaway chain broke off on November 14 after 14 girls had run away. As the networks to which they belonged consisted of 94 members, 80 more girls were touched by the current and 13 of them we considered potential runaway cases if the intensity of the current had continued with equal strength and if no resistance had developed. But three instances can be considered to have contributed to stop it. One is the added watchfulness of the officers as the larger the number of escapes grew. Another is that the last set of runaways in the chain came from C12 which is a colored group, and it is just there where the network is *thinnest*. The chances that a new impetus would come from there were poor, as few contacts went from C12 to other parts of the community. Just as an electric current has different densities within a circuit, so a psychological current has various social densities within a network. Finally, the two girls who had started the chain had been returned to the school and to their cottage, C14, on November 4, three days after their escape. Their failure and disappointment associated with it now ran rapidly through the same network and caught the same individuals who had received an impetus before. Thus it produced an anticlimax. It could not stop the running away of the set in C5 who escaped the next day, but it may have cautioned and delayed the set in C12 and stopped many potential developments.

Another proof that networks exist is the spreading of news or gossip into a certain direction of the community and not into others. We cite here the case of TL in C8. She had stolen a few things of little value from the school's store with the intention of giving them away as gifts. But before this could happen it was discovered. We followed up how the news of her conduct spread. We followed the expansion of the spreading in three phases, after 24 hours, after one week, and after six weeks. We found that after 24 hours only such individuals knew about it as belonged to the Network II, but not all individuals of this network. With the exception of a few persons, C16, C11, C7, C1, and C2 (C14, C9, C5, CA, and CB on Map II) were entirely left out, as they did not belong to this network. After a week the story of her action had reached the entire network, consisting of 86 individuals, and it had filtered into large parts of the second and third networks. Six weeks later no further spread could be ascertained. The incident had apparently given way to news of more momentary interest.

Another instance may be mentioned here of proofs that networks exist. It is the spread of the news in detail of the incident in the colored group of C12. It was traced to have spread through large portions of Networks I, III, and IV, but Network II was left completely out. This was so far below expectation that it demands a special explanation. Besides the current of resistance from the side of the officers to keep an event of such unpleasantness as secret as possible, it may be that the fact that it happened during vacation time when the school was closed, blocked it. Certain networks were, figuratively, *temporarily disconnected*.

Before we close the discussion on spontaneous spread of rumors, another experiment is worth reporting in which the rumor was "planted." We were aware that rumors passed continually back and forth from mouth to mouth. *The object of the experiment was to demonstrate that these rumors followed the paths of the networks that we had mapped.* The experimenter entered Group I and approached an individual, M, who, according to the map, belonged to Network A. M was a key individual, that is, he was linked up with 22 other individuals, some of whom belonged to his Group I, and others to

Group II, III, IV, and V. *M was chosen to be the person with whom to start the spread of a rumor which concerned a leading personality in the community's administration.* We had found that, in networks comprising more than 100 individuals, only very few participated in any one other network. It seemed, therefore, that the chances were that the rumor would spread with ease and speed through M's own network, Network A, and then would need a longer time to filter through to the other networks. We assumed that it would take its longest time to reach Network E, into which there was no overlapping from Network A. It was gratifying to see our assumptions verified with great accuracy. Check ups from time to time showed that the rumor was, indeed, following the paths we had expected it to follow.

Causes and Organization of Networks

The network is related to the currents which run through it as a glass is related to the water which fills it except that the network is molded by the currents and the glass is not shaped by the liquid it holds. The psychogeographical network is analogous to the nervous system, whose network is also molded by the currents that run through it. It cannot be compared, however, with a telephone system, as the latter is unrelated to the currents which run through it, it is not molded by these currents. According to the principle of the forming of social atoms, each individual is related to a certain number of individuals; the majority of individuals in his community are "left out," that is, no tele related him to them. This is the sociodynamic cause for the development of networks. The existence of communication tracks such as networks is an indirect proof of the powerful influence which social atom formation exercises upon community organization. Anther cause of their existence is the economic principle of producing the greatest effect with the least effort.

There are still other causes responsible for the organization of a particular network. We have found, for instance, that certain psychological currents produced by certain emotional states and attitudes are, even towards the regular networks, occasionally selective. In general, news, gossip, ideas, all external and factual matter and all intimate matter which does not hurt its reporter pass without resistance through the networks as we have described them. But if it comes to a certain secret activity concerning sexual, racial, or political activity, this does not filter through even the regular and established parts of the networks. We followed up this phenomenon in reference to the love making between colored and white girls and in reference to the secret intention of running away, activities which were severely criticized by the house-mothers and other staff members. Participants in these activities always have to be on guard against a squealer. The housemother tries at all times to find out through a trusted girl which girls of the family intend to run away, and her trusted girls try instinctively to get in touch with the girls who belong to the network in which such ideas are simmering. A careful housemother is also always on the watch to find evidence of sexual interests, as love notes, etc. For these reasons the girls are on guard against getting a bad reputation. In her anxiety to hide her activities, a girl engaged in illicit activities produces an instinctive reaction against the networks as if she senses that networks exist and that they are her greatest enemy; it is as if she dreads the nets which would automatically spread her ideas to individuals who may report the facts to their confidants or to the staff. She cannot eliminate these networks, as they are co-produced by her own emotions. But she may try, in collaboration with her companions, to keep information away from certain untrustworthy individuals in her network. This attempt of hers is, of course, the less easily met with suc-cess the larger the networks. Thus the effort to keep a secret and to limit in-formation to a selected group usually ends in failure. One day it filters into the general networks. However, these finer nets within the networks exist and are an important psychogeographical organization. They are like *private* roads with different labels saying in which direction they lead. One has a label, sex; another has a label, runaway; another has the label, staff versus girls; another has the label drug addiction, communism, fascism, or any ac-tivity considered subversive in the particular community. Ideas in regard to these cannot be conveyed to everybody, not even to friends, or friends of friends. It is like having "private" telephone numbers which are not listed in the telephone directory.

Technique of Determining Networks

We followed, on the psychogeographic maps, each tele that went out from a member of any group to a member of any other and from this person on to a member of a third group, and from this person on to a member of a fourth group, etc., as long as the mutual chain continued. We counted only such persons as belonging to the same network who were interlocked, irrespective of the cottage in which they lived (see Map III). This can be called the *main line* of the network. Then we followed up each member of this main line of the network and counted those individuals within her own cottage who were directly related to the member of the related network. These branches formed the *side lines* of the determined network. It is understood that again each individual of a side line was followed up to determine her contacts to members of other cottages, and if such new members of the network were found in other cottages, the same applied to them.

We began the count with certain individuals in C4 who share tele with a number of individuals in C1, who in turn share one part of their tele with individuals in C6, C7 and C16. These, in turn, send a fraction of their tele into C9 and C11, forming a network which, like a subway, connects many sections of the community. We found several of such networks in Hudson. In C4, the same cottage in which this particular network has members, a number of individuals not directly related to the network participate in a second network with groups of individuals in C3, C6, C9, and C14, forming Network II. The individuals belonging to it are, in general, different from the ones involved in Network I. We say "in general" because they are by no means completely cut off from them; for instance, in C1 some of the same individuals share in four different networks. But not every group is so promiscuous. Except for small bridges crossing between these networks, we are able to subdivide the whole community into five more or less distinct bundles: Network I, consisting of 94 individuals; Network II, 85 individuals; Network III, 81; Network IV, 67; and Network V, 60 individuals.

Unavoidably, the larger a network is the larger becomes the number of *dead links,*—that is, the number of relations which are not reciprocally effective, so to speak: emotions which run without registering in the intended other person. They can be called "resistance links" and their sum of resistance is caused by the intrinsic character of the network. This factor is practically negligible in small networks, but in larger ones it plays a definite rôle. The larger the network is, as in the organization of cities or political parties, the larger may become the influence of this resistance within it.

FUNCTION OF NETWORKS

A certain constancy in the organization of a community is the condition of free and independent life of its members. The mechanism that makes this constancy possible in a community is its networks and the psychological currents which flow through them. This form of free and independent life for the single individuals is the privilege of such communities as have reached the heights of complexity and differentiaton. Therefore, societies lacking in constancy and differentiation are unable to offer its members the privileges of free life, as we have demonstrated in the organization of child societies. These are less constant and less differentiated, especially below the eight-year age level, and therefore the members are unfree and dependent, just as the groups which they form are dependent upon the more highly differentiated ones. The networks also have an architectonic function in the community. By virtue of this they are the controlling factors of its development. The older and the more mature the society is, the more the entire network system becomes a controlling super-organization.

The local district or neighborhood is only physically one unit. This analysis shows that it is broken up, not, however, into small units, but into parts which have their corresponding parts in other districts and neighborhoods. The local districts are, so to speak, transversed by psychological currents which bind large groups of individuals together into units, irrespective of neighborhood, district, or borough distinctions. These networks are the kitchens of public opinion. It is through these channels that people affect, educate, or disintegrate one another. It is through these networks that suggestion is transmitted. In one part of a community a person has the reputation of honesty; in another part, of dishonesty. Whatever the actual facts may be, this reputation is due to two different networks in which travel two different opinions about him. In Hudson the suggestion may go through them to run away; in the world at large the idea of war may spread. These networks are traceable and we may learn to control them.

ARCHITECTURAL PLANNING OF A SOCIOMETRIZED COMMUNITY

The physical setting should be a function of the sociometric and sociopsychological set up of a community. The more criteria a population test covers, the more can the physical structure of the community be organized to reflect it: the location of the public centers, the houses, and so on.

The geographical distribution within the community area provides an avenue which can be directly utilized to provide the most auspicious distribution of the population which has been selected. The problem of neighbor selection cannot be solved by a purely arbitrary distribution of the population, as the family units must reside permanently in relatively close proximity and each family will have certain other families as neighbors with their land adjoining. Through the evidence gathered through the sociometric technique the families can be assigned as immediate neighbors who are mutually attracted *and* mutually beneficial. The family units can be so located geographically that harmonious social relations already existing are stimulated and other less advantageous relations discouraged.

The question arises whether the houses should be arranged in the form of long chains or if they should be grouped in several neighborhoods. Commonly this problem is decided by accident or according to architectural or industrial planning. There is another possibility opened up through the sociometric population test: to reflect into the physical organization of the town the psychosocial and sociometric structure of the population. In this manner, perhaps, the forces of social gravitation which draw the groups together or apart may suggest the grouping of the houses and the distribution of the population within the town.

A study of the psychogeographical charts of the Hudson community suggested a number of pertinent questions: Is there any relationship between the attraction-repulsion patterns linking two houses and the physical distance between them? Is it possible that an excess of nearness retards healthy group formation just as much as an excess of distance? Which type of architectural organizations of a community stimulate group formation and which discourage it? What is the relationship of esthetic factors, such as the unattractiveness of the houses and street patterns in city slums and ghettos, to the development of social contacts and sociometric group formation? *The architect of the future will be a student of sociometry;* the sites of cities, industrial plants, and resort places will be chosen so as to meet the needs of the populations living and working in them.

ROLE

By J. L. Moreno

Definition

Role is a fusion of private and collective elements. It is composed of two parts, its collective denominators and its individual differentials. "Rôle," originally a French word which penetrated into English is derived from the Latin *rotula* (the little wheel, or round log, the diminutive of rota-wheel). In antiquity it was used, originally, only to designate a round (wooden) roll on which sheets of parchment were fastened so as to smoothly roll ("wheel") them around it since otherwise the sheets would break or crumble. From this came the word for an assemblage of such leaves into a scroll or book-like composite. This was used, subsequently, to mean any official volume of papers pertaining to law courts, as in France, or to government, as for instance in England: rolls of Parliament—the minutes or proceedings. Whereas in Greece and also in ancient Rome the parts in the theatre were written on the above-mentioned "rolls" and read by the prompters to the actors (who tried to memorize their part), this fixation of the word appears to have been lost in the more illiterate periods of the early and middle centuries of the Dark Ages, for their public presentation of church plays by laymen. Only towards the sixteenth and seventeenth centuries, with the emergence of the modern stage, the parts of the theatrical characters are read from "roles," paper fascicles. Whence each scenic "part" becomes a role.

Still, we observe here the interesting phenomenon that to the word "role" clings the meaning of being something theatrical; external, so to speak (the role is *"played"*); in contrast to the older word "persona" which now has come to mean the fullness of an individual's character, its wholeness of feelings, thoughts, actions and thus has become more complex, "intransparent."

This definition and analysis makes clear that the term "role" came into the sociological vocabulary via the drama and a technological conserve, the book. According to its etymology, *role is the unit of "conserved" behavior*.

Self vs. Roles

It is useful to differentiate between *role-taking*, the taking of a finished, fully established role which does not permit the individual any variation, any degree of freedom; *role-playing*, which permits the individual some degree of freedom; and *role-creating*, which permits the individual a high degree of freedom, as for instance, the *spontaneity player*. *The tangible aspects of what is known as "ego" or "self" are the roles in which it operates.* Role and relationships between roles are the most significant development within any specific culture. Working with the "role" as a point of reference appears to be a methodological advantage as compared with "personality," "self," or "ego." These are less concrete and wrapped up in metapsychological mystery.

Role-emergence is prior to the emergence of the self. Roles do not emerge from the self, but the self may emerge from roles. The hypothesis upheld by many that the genesis of role-emergence and the genesis of language are one and the same is not tenable according to experimental role research. Long before language-linked roles emerge in the child's world, "psychosomatic roles" operate effectively (for instance, the role of the eater, the sleeper, and the walker). There is considerable psychic resistance against the intrusion of language in infants and even some resistance against gestural infiltration. There is no reason to assume that the language-free areas are nonhuman. There is overwhelming evidence that these "silent" areas are coexistent with the vocal ones on the human level and have great potentialities for independent growth. There may be forms of social communication without gestural involvement. *The tele phenomenon operates in all dimensions of communication;* it is therefore an error to reduce it to a mere reflection and correspondent of the communication process via language.

CATEGORIES OF ROLES

One can differentiate three categories of roles: (a) psychosomatic roles, as the sleeper, the eater, the walker; (b) psychodramatic roles as *a* mother, *a* teacher, *a* Negro, *a* Christian, etc.; and (c) social roles, *the* mother, *the* son, *the* daughter, *the* teacher, *the* Negro, *the* Christian, etc. The genesis of roles goes through two stages, role-perception and role-enactment.

MEASUREMENT

A simple method of measuring roles is to use as a norm permanently established processes that do not permit any change, role conserves like Shakespeare's Hamlet or Othello, Goethe's Faust, or Byron's Don Juan. If a number of performers are given the instruction to use the Hamlet text, either literally as it is given by Shakespeare, or to change it freely in the course of the performance, some will prefer the original text, others may ad lib into the text smaller or major changes. These deviations represent the degrees of freedom of the particular performer which can be ascribed to the operation of an s factor. Their additions or substitutions may be within or far below the Shakespearean level of expression. A scale of Hamlet versions would result, the original Shakespeare version being on one end of the scale, a fully transformed personalized text on the other.

Another method of measurement uses as norms social roles which are rigidly prescribed by social and legalistic customs and forms. Illustrations for this are social roles as the policeman, the judge, the physician, and so forth. They are roles or social stereotypes and differ from role-conserves as the sequence of situations, the text of their speeches, are not rigidly outlined. No Shakespeare has written "their" lines and actions in advance. A varying degree of spontaneity is permitted, indeed, it is expected from them. A policeman, for instance, may be required to represent the authority of the law in every situation into which he enters, but he may be required to act differently in varying situations. In fact, without some degree of spontaneity his words and actions may have fatal consequences for him and his fellow citizens. Placing a number of policemen, therefore, into a number of standard life situations which require their interference would result in a scale. On one end of the scale will be the most adequate policeman performance in a particular situation, on the other end the most inadequate performance in the same kind of situation.

Another method of measurement is to let a subject develop a role *in statu nascendi,* placing him at first in a situation that is little structured, and finally in situations that are highly organized. The productions of different subjects will differ greatly and will provide us with a yardstick for role measurement.

Another method of measurement is to place a number of subjects unacquainted with each other into a situation which they have to meet in common. Illustration: six men of equal military rank are camping. Suddenly they see an enemy parachutist landing in the nearby forest. They have to act on the spur of the moment. A jury watches to see how the group grows in *statu nascendi:* it may descern (a) what relationships develop between the six men; who is taking the initiative in the first phase, in the intermediate phases, in the final phase of their interaction. Who emerges as the "leader?" (b) What action do they take towards the enemy? (c) How is the situation ended and by whom?

Another method is to place a number of subjects in a specific role independently and at different times, opposite the *same* auxiliary ego, whose performance has been carefully prepared and highly objectified. He, the ego, can then be an instrument which measures the variations of response coming from the subjects tested.

Yet another method is the study of the same role, for instance the role of the stranger, in a number of different situations. A subject taking this role is for instance first placed vis à vis a girl who happens to be his neighbor in a train; later accosting her on the street. At a still later stage proposing marriage to a girl of a different ethnic background, and finally being fired from his job after several years of dutiful service because of his race. This series would permit the development of a scale in reference to the same role, for instance, stranger, son, worker, and so forth.

There is a consensus in all studies made that role-taking and role-playing have a common origin. The genesis of role-development shows clearly how one grows out of the other, that role-playing and role-taking are two phases of the same process. It has been found in hundreds of tryouts that the process of role-taking is not only cognitive and that, on the other hand, the process of role-playing is not only behavior or mere acting, but that cognition, perception, behavior, and action are finely interwoven and cannot be neatly separated. There are enactable and unenactable roles; recognized and unrecognized roles; enactment of roles before the level of their recognition; recognition of roles before the level of their enactment; adequate, distorted, partial, and loss of role-perception; adequate, distorted, partial, and inability of role-enactment. There is often a discrepancy between the assessment of role-behavior by observers and the assessment of such roles in action by the actors and co-actors themselves. However much taken and frozen a role has become and however much integrated it is into the perception and behavior of a certain individual, there is a weak spot in its armor; in order to emerge in a certain moment it must pass (a) through a process of warming up, however minimal, in which the whole organism is involved, and (b) through a process of mimetic learning as to how to take the role of the other—however "generalized" this "other" may be. The individual represents every time a slightly different version; this is not possible without some minimal playing towards the role, gradually learning and struggling to approximate it—however fragmentary, rudimentary, and embryonic this role-playing process might be. Role-acting and role-perception, role-playing and role-taking go hand in hand in the primary learning and conditioning process. *In situ* they cannot be separated.

ROLE-PLAYING VS. ROLE-TAKING

The term "role" comes from the language of the stage. *Role-playing may be considered as an experimental procedure, a method of learning to perform roles more adequately.* The present popularity of the terms and concept derives from the value it has proven to have as a training device in various social, occupational, and vocational activities, and has resulted from the initiative that the author has taken in developing them. It is through the study of roles in action that the new knowledge about roles developed. *In contrast with role-playing, role-taking is an attitude already frozen in the behavior of the person.* Role-playing is an act, a spontaneous playing; role-taking is a finished product, a role conserve. The American trend is most adequately presented in G. H. Mead's *Mind, Self and Society* (1934). Ralph Linton and others developed this trend further.

The European trend is marked by Moreno's book *Das Stegreiftheater* (1923), further developed in the first edition of this book (1934) and in his "Psychodrama and the Psychopathology of Interpersonal Relations" (*Sociometry*, 1937). The differences between these two trends are important, one trend developed *the idea of role-taking*, the other *the idea of role-playing*. As the two terms are often used interchangeably a discussion of the origin of each concept and their meaning is necessary. Mead's concept of role-taking and Moreno's concept of role-playing represent two different approaches. Mead's thinking was influenced by social behaviorism of the 1920's. He discovered the role and role-taking, taking the role of the other, a process of taking and interiorating the role unto the self, making it readily accessible in societal situations.

These roles, in order to be socially effective, must be already formed, must be finished products, "role-conserves," available for immediate release.

My view started from a position exactly opposite to this; first of all, the role which Mead had to discover was already given "free of charge" in the dramatic productions of the theatre which I encountered. The ideal representations of role-conserves are found in the written plays of Shakespeare, Goethe, and Molière and in the approximations of role-conserves in life itself. *My role theory began with a critique of the role-conserve which was the sharper the more rigid and unyielding the role-conserves appeared to be.* Entering a legitimate theatre meant to witness the most rigid and unyielding presentations of role-conserves one can imagine. The moment of creation was not free and *spontaneity was forbidden to the role-player*. The exceptions did not change the rule because such were the intentions anyway. It is here where I noticed first the resistance of the role-player against the role-conserve, the resistance of the living actor who resented the playing of roles written by a playwright and imposed upon his spirit. I remember the struggle in Eleanora Duse between herself as a private dramatis persona, and the roles that she had to impersonate; the struggle between the role-concepts created by the playwright and the concepts she had of these characters. Later I observed the resistance of people against some of the roles that society coerces them to play, and particularly against their conserved form. I posited therefore the idea of role-spontaneity vs. role-conserve, playing a role spontaneously, modifying it and warming up to it in ever-novel situations, in contrast with role-taking, the rendering of a role which is already formed and established. *The objective of revolutionary role research became then to study roles in* statu nascendi *and if possible in* locus nascendi. The role was frequently found *alien* to the self, as it is often to the living actor. For this resistance against role conserves and stereotypes one may have several explanations: (1) We live in a changing world, new sets of roles are emerging, trying to push the old ones out of existence. (2) Within a given society one set of roles represents one ethnic group, the other set of roles another ethnic group, both struggling for dominance. (3) As the infant exerts resistance against the assimilation of organized and syntaxed language, he exercises a resistance against the social role-cluster with which he is confronted during childhood and adolescence. This resistance may increase as it moves away beyond or outside of himself. It is minimal when he takes his own role; this is the case in the role of the eater, the soundmaker, the eliminator, the breather, the sleeper and the walker—the psychosomatic roles; it increases as he takes the role of an idea superior to him, ghost, angel, God, etc.—psychodramatic roles. It may reach a maximum when it takes the role of the others in social roles.

Every role-taking must have been, in *statu nascendi*, a form of role-playing. The more the role became a conserve, the less spontaneity was necessary to release it. Whenever we learn new roles we exercise role-playing but there is always the tendency present to learn how to play the role with the minimum of effort. It is significant that psychodrama, sociodrama, and role-playing have developed in a rapidly changing world in which many roles have become worn and have either to perish, to be revitalized, or to be replaced by new emerging roles which need rapid acculturation. Role-playing probably renders its greatest service not only in the improvisation of new roles, but in the revitalizing of role-conserves. Taking the role of the other is a dead end. *The turning point was how to vitalize and change the roles, how to become a "role-changer" and "role-player." This objective needed the discovery of a new method, the technique of role-playing.*

Last but not least, similar efforts of trying to find points of agreement and disagreement between my work and that of others, for instance of Bergson and Freud, can be made, perhaps with the same amount of justification. A Bergsonian could make it plausible that my work provides the clinical foundations for "L'Evolution Créatrice" and the *élan vital*. Psychoanalysts could argue that psychodrama is, on the action level, what psychoanalysis is on the verbal level, that the two methods have similar aims. The real and final question, however, is whether, out of the social psychology of Mead, role-practice and role-training, psychodrama, and sociodrama, sociometry, and group psychotherapy could ever have developed and whether out of Bergson's durée and Freud's libido and transference method my elaborate system of action and training methods could ever have arisen. As the history of these techniques shows, the answer is for all three men in the negative. Their contributions were great and prepared the ground, but it took the theorist and practitioner in one, a theory which grew out of and with practice, a synthesis of actor and observer, to give the new methodologies the peculiar concrete shape they have.

SOCIOMETRIC CHOICE PROCESS IN PERSONALITY AND GROUP FORMATION

By Helen H. Jennings

What does sociometric analysis tell us about choice structure in personality and group formation?

Sociometric study of the choosing process, even at the present stage of research, suggests that it is no less than the process by which the individual becomes what he becomes. However fragmentary the various explorations have been, their findings point steadily and uniformly to one major conclusion: certain relationships of choice are the psychological life blood of the individual psyche and determine what pattern his group formations will take.

Sociometric findings show that individuals tend to form two kinds of groups in which different needs are paramount: (1) groups in which the individual as a person receives sustenance, recognition, approval, and appreciation for just being "*himself*"; (2) groups in which the individual's efforts and ideals are focused towards objectives which are not his alone but represent the fulfilling of goals which a number of individuals agree to seek.

The hypothesis is raised that the individual's creativity and productivity and ability to release these in others *are dependent upon* his ability to acquire and maintain fluid, intimate mutual relationships giving such psychological satisfaction that he can function elsewhere in his life context without preoccupation with "what is the other thinking of me?"

This hypothesis is raised out of consideration of (a) the interlocking nature of the choice process as exhibited by the individual *concurrently* in differing sociometric settings, and (b) the apparent significance of particular sociometric patterns for the individual's ability to meet life problems as inferred from sociodramatic exploration. The sociodramatic material, while based upon very few cases, gives results so pointedly differentiating the individual's behavior in choice relationships compared with his behavior outside such relationships that even a preliminary report appears important enough to offer at this time. The sociometric material is given in great detail elsewhere (15, 16, 17, 18). What is new in the present survey is the drawing together of major sociometric findings with unpublished sociodramatic results to focus their implications for personality and group formation (14).

In the sequence of this report the major sociometric findings are discussed first and then the sociodramatic-sociometric findings.

Sociometric Findings[1]

As the individual invests his affection in others, the extent and quality of these investments appear by early adulthood to be stabilized into what can be called his *emotional repertoire*. The repertoire represents his characteristic range for reacting by choice and rejection to others. At the same time, by early adulthood, he is similarly shown to be characterized by consistency in his *stimulus-value* for arousing choice and rejection from others. These findings do not mean that the individual's interpersonal situation in respect to choice and rejection becomes so definite as to be unchangeable by adulthood; they indicate rather that the individual's intrapsychic organization is not subject to random variation in reaction to changes in interpersonal setting, nor, in turn, is the individual randomly reacted to. These findings mean also that the individual's future is being created as he moves through his past and, in a quite specific sense, even *what pattern* will differentiate his interpersonal reflection is being created.

The first thing to be noted about this pattern is that the individual's consistency in use of the choice process involves both his use of choice *and* rejection as expressions of *one* process, and similarly as the focus of one process directed upon him. It is notable also that the individual who is relatively more or relatively less expansive towards others will react to them independently of the length of time he is in association with them.

The individual's extent of emotional expansiveness towards others is seen to be his *individual* characteristic which finds consistent expression without relation to the environmental factors which may exert pressure for or against its fulfillment.[2] These findings are confirmed in research on other populations (6) disclosing that, while they hold for a stable community, the individual tends to retrench from maintaining his full repertoire and to "drop" others who are unlike himself in religion and race when the community in which he is living undergoes rapid population change. Thus, in a very broad sense, the nature of the social setting of the individual *does* affect his expansiveness— perhaps, in the instance cited, the individual reacting as in shock, fear, or grief, by temporarily emotionally holding back.

The average repertoire of positive expansiveness, as measured by the

[1] References in this section are mainly to the writer's *Leadership and Isolation* (15); as this book has a detailed cross-index giving ready access to the data bearing on any point under discussion in this report, page references will not be given.

[2] It may be postulated that the concept of need comes nearer to describing emotional expansiveness than does the concept of trait, as the individual is actually expressing how many persons he feels *the need for* in his life situation and is not consciously displaying consistency.

number of other individuals the individual includes in his life situation by positive choice for associating with them, is found to be about eight, when common situations are explored (working, etc.), and this number is increased to about four more when the setting of leisure time is explored; but as about one-third of the latter overlaps with the former, the average size of positive repertoire is somewhat less in number than twelve other individuals. Upon retest eights months later, no significant differences are found.

It becomes apparent not only that choice is not distributed by chance (24), but upon anaysis it is found that the whole constellation of relationships centered in and emanating from a given individual, his social atom, shows characteristic pattern. Moreover, the incidence of patterns at one time and a later time in the same community appears as a relatively constant factor in the structure of attractions and rejections which characterize it, and reflects the fact that the choice process operates in particular ways.

The characteristic of an "order" which marks the individual's interpersonal reflection on any aspect of choice and in his social atom as a whole is, in turn, notable in the over-all sociometric structure of the community when it is compared at two distant occasions (eight months apart). The tendency of the total structure to retain its characteristics from one time to another, *even though the respective positions of its carriers* (the members of the population) *alter from time to time,* is one of the highly significant factors to be realized in the understanding of the interpersonal structure of the community and disclosed by comparison of the *same* community with itself at sufficiently distant time points to register its changes. The shifts in the interpersonal network that are recorded in the choice-status of individuals in the population are, so to speak, bound to occur since interaction cannot be static; the surprising finding is that, whatever changes occur for *individuals,* the total strutcure is not significantly different. The psychological structure resulting from choice behavior on the part of the members of the population may be most accurately envisioned as an *equilibrium in flux.* The movements which take place continually within it appear to be compensatory movements which do not disturb the total structure *viewed as a totality.*

While the evidence points to a certain stability in interpersonal relationships of choice, positive and negative, within the "architecture of relative permanence" there is constant movement. The finding that the positions of individuals are continually shifting in an "upward" and "downward" direction (and even remaining on a certain level over a long period) registers the fact that the individual has been replenishing relationships which are severed when some members leave the population of the study. What appears as stability of structure is actually the *slowness* of this continuous movement within the structure, with very gradual redistribution of a significantly similar amount of choice expenditure on the part of members whose own choice repertoires are quantitatively stable.

Obviously, to study this phenomenon requires that the choosers must number over several hundred individuals available for choice to and from one another. This condition is difficult to meet. The only other study to date (1), made at the University of Saskatchewan, confirms the findings just described. Recognizing the nature of the field is also important, because occasionally a sociometric study is made to examine such a phenomenon as differentiation in choice between more or less intimate criteria on a population so small that this phenomenon is not evident and the investigator (e.g., 10) naïvely concludes its nonexistence under any conditions. Such naïvete is so widespread in studies illustrating conclusions based on generalizing the significance of one kind of choice-status separated from others that no review of them needs to be given. In any sociometric structure, each position is interdependent in varying ways with other positions, and this is not apparent, nor can it be disclosed unless certain testing conditions prevail. Necessary to such examination of interrelationship patterns, aside from size of field of choice, are: unlimited choice must be permitted the subjects and concurrent tests made on all sociometric criteria at once (both used for the first time in the present study at the New York State Training School for Girls, at Hudson, which community presented a test-population of 443 individuals at the time of Test I, and 457 individuals, eight months later, at the time of the administration of Test II).

The balance in proportions of sociometric structure of a large community at different time points refers to the *total structure* produced by choice behavior and not simply to constancy in number of certain positions of choice-status (e.g., number of isolated positions, number of reciprocations, etc.). The cause appears to lie in the different interpersonal capacity of individuals to draw choice to themselves, and to expand in choice for others, different capacities *which maintain their* respective differences in this respect *even as the group as a whole develops* in interpersonal capacity.[3]

---

[3] The situation may be visualized as that of a freshman class moving on each year to the next academic year; as it moves to senior status, its members are receiving more reactions of positive and negative choice from the population as a whole than they did as juniors, sophomores, or freshman—yet, as the standards of "how you must behave" to be worthy of choice have also risen, even in the senior year the general outline of the choice-structure significantly resembles that of the same group as freshmen when they were receiving fewer choices from upper-classmen. Community standards rise among the members, but interpersonal effort to keep apace of these rises is *still linked* to individual differences, and the advances are relative to these differences.

CONTRAST BETWEEN FORMAL AND INFORMAL SOCIOMETRIC STRUCTURE

In considering what are some of the foundations underlying this stability and slowness of flux within the choice structure, it is necessary to look separately at the use of choice and other behaviors distinguishing common group situations and leisure-time association situations, both in relation to the individual's respective choice-status in each.

In the present study, choice expressed for leisure time refers to decision to be scheduled so that leisure time could be used to associate freely with given other individuals, according to inclination. Choice expressed for association in common group situations refers to decision to collaborate as a co-worker in various work units, usually comprising seven to fifteen individuals, or as a co-liver in various housing units, usually comprising twenty to twenty-eight individuals.

In the working-living situations, the individuals who are chosen by many others appear as individuals who, in interaction with many others, bring about a releasing effect upon them along those lines of development in which they appreciate such release and apparently experience it favorably. In brief, the much-chosen, in their behavior with others in common group situations, contribute in major ways to a milieu of live-and-let-live, democratic mores, and high *esprit de corps*.

In such group settings, choice appears as an expression which is not only a response of attraction towards an individual, but a response which may, in a sense, be considered "earned" by the person chosen. The isolates are individuals who in a community numbering about 450 persons do not actively "win" the attraction of any other members to them as wanted collaborators in any group enterprise; conversely, the much-chosen individuals in the same community are eminently successful in "winning" the attraction of other members to them for common collaboration.

In such settings, the individuals who are isolated from choice by other members show in the trends of their behavior tendencies to conduct themselves in ways which imply a marked lack of orientation on their part to the elements of the total group situations; frequently they not only fail to contribute constructively to the group, but hinder by their behavior the activities undertaken by other members. Especially by their "externalizing" of private feelings of irritability and the like, they subtract from, rather than add to, the general tone of the social milieu about them.

In the over-all picture of functioning in official groups, individuals who are over-chosen by the expression of choice of other members show, in the trends of their behavior, tendencies to conduct themselves in ways which imply an unusual sensitivity and orientation on their part to the elements of the total group situation; to a very much greater extent than the average-chosen member, they constructively contribute to enlarge the social field for participation of other citizens, to encourage the development of individual members, to make possible a wider, richer common experience for all by their innovations altering the *status quo* as they find it; they are thus creative improvers of others' situations as well as their own, and in exercising such leadership *are at the same* time chosen as the most wanted associates by the members.[4] Especially by their "internalizing" of private worries,[5] anxieties, and the like, and by their public display of high *esprit de corps,* they enhance the general tone of the social milieu about them.

In the sense just reported, sheer quantity of choice "earned" by the individual on the sociometric criterion of being wanted *as a member of the official groups of the community* is found to be an index of the extent to which the individual has shown or is showing, in the opinion of his fellow members, capacity to carry *the group-role in question* which they want from him with the sort of interaction which they consider aids the milieu of the group to become what they want it to be.

Both leadership and isolation in official groups appear as phenomena which arise out of individual differences in interpersonal capacity for participation as phenomena which are indigenous to the specific milieu in which they are produced. The specific avenues of rapport which bring one individual in contact with one "constituency" (selection of other persons) may not resemble those which relate a second individual to the persons who are drawn to him. The superior capacity which one individual may have to recognize and respond to the needs of others does not show itself as a generalized capacity which may relate him to *any* other individuals. It appears in the special sensitivity between the individual and specific other persons, resulting in interaction between

---

[4] It should be noted that "high choice-status" under any conditions is not tantamount to "leadership" necessarily; in this community there is a high correlation but it should be clear that study of the individual's behaviors is necessary to determine such a deduction. For example, under conditions of fear, choice may not be freely exercised and many choices may be expressed for individuals who are themselves dominating those who shall be chosen, as under totalitarian regimes and, on a small scale, in the case of some street gangs. On the other hand, such a role as mainly that of idea-producer should not be confused with that of being wanted mainly to advance and maintain the interests of the people as they, the group members, wish; these two roles may or may not be carried by the same individual.

[5] It should be stressed that adjustment difficulties are also carried by many a well-chosen individual, but his manner of handling them keeps others from suffering consequences in a way which is not true of the average-chosen or of the unchosen individual.

them. Similarly, isolation results as the product of special insensitivity between the individual and specific other persons, but to such extent that he can conveniently be described as relatively "self-bound." In either instance, the outcomes reflect both the interpersonal capacities of the members of the community as well as those of the individuals "lifted" to leadership or "sent" into isolation. Both phenomena appear as extremes on the continuum of interpersonal sensitivity between the members of the community and the individual.

Nevertheless, in the one case, such a quality as freedom from self-concern sufficient to enable the individual to be involved with matters affecting many others than himself, and in the other case, such a quality as inability to observe and care about many elements of a situation, unless outgrown, may continue to act respectively favorably and adversely upon the individual's future relation with persons in other groups.

Thus, in the interpersonal structure related to the criteria of living-working, the choice-status of the individual appears directly attributable to the capacities he shows *in interaction* with colleagues to lessen or augment the satisfactions of the common group life. In this sense, choice is found to be evoked towards him or withheld from him, more or less in proportion to *how he carries* his role *in relation to* other members' roles, or, to state it more precisely, in proportion to how others perceive him to interact with them for the benefit of their common-group regime.

In contrast, no such function and no such "judgment" can be discerned in respect to the sheer quantity of choice "earned" by the individual on the sociometric criterion of leisure-time association. In the latter, not only is sheer quantity of choice received by the individual *not* an index to his role *in the informal milieu* in which he is a member, but the role which *any* individual appears to play within it has very much in common with the roles which other individuals play within it.

No one individual aids many others in the leisure-time milieu, so far as is evidenced in this study, in the ways characteristic of the living-working groups. Likewise, no one individual wins from a great number of other individuals in the population their choice for him as a leisure-time associate.

Likewise, in contrast to the exceptionally great "group service" which is implied in the behaviors of those found to be most chosen in the living-working structure of the community, the interaction of even these same individuals in the informal leisure-choice structure may be said to be a highly *mutual* interindividual expression, emotionally supportive to the individuals as persons rather than as group members and at the same time remarkably reciprocal in its function—rather than reflecting extreme exertion on the part of some members as is found in the official groupings. It may be premised that in so far as "service" enters, it appears to be a service which renders each individual about equally indebted to the other, and not many indebted to the few who show extraordinary effort in their behalf.

Leadership, then, as found in the choice structure of the official groups, is not found in any similar sense in the leisure-choice structure. The question arises whether "leadership" is an appropriate term for any aspect of the dynamics of interchange in the informal groupings. However, if the criterion for leadership is the extent of changes brought about in official group regimes by the influence stemming from one individual to others through the leisure-choice network, many an individual not found in a leader-position in his own official groups is found to hold a "hidden" leadership role (15, 17). Moreover, the influence thus reflected in "raising" the tenor of group life in the respective groups throughout the community may, by inference, be considered also crucial in a different way from the "direct" leadership displayed with a given group: without such spread of cross-fertilization through influence of one person to another in the informal structure throughout the community, instigating innovations and increasing the cosmopolitanism of understanding of different ways of life through motivation to "try them out" rather than simply knowing of them by hearsay, it may be premised that the individual groups within the community (through lack of such vitalizing communication) could very readily become and remain insulated from one another.

The free passing-on of "inside" views of how other people live and work in their groups and the accompanying satisfactions or dissatisfactions attributed by them to the regime of such groups, across the informal choice network from person to person, in an apparent atmosphere of confidence and trust and intimacy, makes the leisure-time structure an avenue for the development of "community" concern, broadly serving the members of the population as a whole. In this sense, a well-developed leisure-time structure *in any community* would appear an indispensable vehicle for preventing "official" groups from becoming insulated from one another, provincial in their regimes, and resistant to change and development by their respective membership.

An understanding of the role of formal and informal interpersonal structure in personality and group formation is clarified when both are subject to analysis concurrently; it then becomes clear that there is an interlocking and interdependence of personality expression in each setting, so sharp that it can be said individuals form highly contrasting interpersonal structures differently oriented.

Only a few of the numerous illustrations of the differentiating use of choice according to the nature of the setting need be cited here.

On the average, the individual chooses four individuals for leisure (mean = 4.08). Of these four, it is usual for about two-thirds to be wanted by him for relationships in leisure time *exclusively* rather than for association also in official groupings of the community. The findings represent the *currently* wanted associates along one or another avenue of group life in the community and should be seen in relation to the particular moment in time when the expressions of choice are given. For example, the subjects had previously had about the same number of former associates in work and in housing available for choice. Yet being formerly an associate in a common living group does not appear to increase appreciably the per cent of persons who will become selected by a chooser for relationships during leisure beyond the per cent of such selection which he concurrently shows. On the other hand, after the individual is no longer working with particular persons, he becomes much more likely to consider them for leisure relationships. It thus appears that working with others acts as a deterrent to the development of informal interpersonal response *during* the period of work association, but that *later*, when the individual is no longer in the same work situation, he "picks up" from among his former work associates a considerable number with whom he becomes inclined to form interpersonal relationships on a very different basis, as spending leisure time together. The individual does not "postpone" the forming of relationships for leisure sharing of time with persons he comes to know in a living-together situation, in the manner he reveals he does towards work associates.

Thus, one difference in choice behavior on the part of the individual towards others appears referable in part to the specific context in which he and they have been exposed to interpersonal contact. Certain contexts for interaction (as work situations) appear to act in a retarding way upon the individual's tendency to develop relationships of an informal, perhaps "personalized" sort; other contexts (as common housing) apparently do not so act to any significant extent.

Examination of the relationship between the subject's expansiveness in choice of others for leisure and for living-working, and similarly, the expansiveness of others for him across the criteria, reveals many concomitant developments. The individual who is relatively more often or less often chosen for leisure will, to a considerable extent, be found similarly located in respect to the extent to which he is chosen for living-working situations. The trend towards correspondence in kind of choice-status is further indicated by the correlation which appears between the number reciprocating the subject for leisure and for living-working. The highest degree of correlation is found between the number reciprocating the subject for leisure and the number choosing him for living-working: $r = .84$ on Test I, and .80 on Test II. In this instance, the correlation is much higher than that between the number reciprocating and the number choosing the subject, for living-working, although here it is also high: $r = .70$ on Test I, and .67 on Test II.

Any explanation of this finding may be tied up with a further finding. While no significant correlations appear between the negative expressions by or towards the subject across the criteria of leisure and living-working, for the aspects just considered, there is found a fairly considerable correlation between the number rejected by the subject for leisure and the number rejecting him for living-working: $r = .42$ on Test I and .49 on Test II.

The results across criteria, both on rejection and on positive choice, may be interdependently based.

It appears that the individual who tends to form mutual positive relationships in leisure with those individuals who seek such response from him is at the same time highly likely to be much wanted (even though mainly by different people) as a member of work or living groups. Thus it may be that his facility for getting the response he wants to himself as a person in informal associating provides (or at least is present possibly to offer) an emotional support to interpersonal security that concomitantly acts as a bulwark to enable him to so behave with others in formal work, or other official groups, that he attracts many members in choice for him as a colleague. On the other hand, it appears that if the individual tends much more than most individuals to reject a great number of people in a context of associating in leisure, he tends to be himself highly rejected as a colleague in the official groups for work or living. Those who reject him, again, are for the most part not the same individuals he has himself rejected for leisure. It is as if something of his "attitude" is sensed by many persons who have little or no first-hand knowledge of it. This finding is the more interesting since no correlation is found between number rejected by the individual for living-working and number rejecting him for living-working. Apparently, then, he is an individual who does not himself perceive, or at any rate, direct the volume of his rejections along the same line of group life that is producing it towards him, i.e., along the same criterion for rejection.

On the other hand, this does not obtain for mutuality of rejection within the living-working context considered as a unit; here there appears a high correlation between the extent to which the individual is rejected and the extent of his reciprocated rejection, but, in this context too, only a slight correlation between his rejection of others and the amount of mutual rejection.

Thus, the gross amounts of rejections which the individual projects towards others, or which others direct to him, do not correlate on the *same* criteria, but do correlate to a fairly considerable extent across the criteria of leisure and living-working.

It is as if an index to being much rejected in work or other official group life is to be found in the individual's own extent of negative projections in his informal life with others. In brief, the individual's performance on one criterion (leisure) is more linked with the performance of others towards him on other criteria (living-working) than are either his or their performance within the given criteria considered singly.

Moreover, it appears that no one criterion singly holds an importance such that from its expression the expression on other criteria can be predicted (e.g., from amount of choices made by the individual for living-working, to amount of choices he will make for leisure situations, the correlation in this instance being slight). It becomes clear that *kind* of interaction, e.g., mutual as compared with unreciprocated, may be a more critical factor than quantity of interaction, for the individual's choice-status and the choice-structure of the community as a whole.

Of the many findings, perhaps the most interesting is the differentiating of the direction of choice expression in the different settings.

It will be recalled that in the context of housing and working situations, the individual's expression in choice favors those who in interaction carry forward societal arrangements or conditions for advancing group life of the sort he feels "should be." And, on the other hand, the individual shows, by withholding of choice or by active expression of rejection, disfavor towards those individuals who block or retard such group life as he apparently considers appropriate for living together or working together in a group regime.

In this sense, the individual may be said to take a "group-view" or "group-role-view" in his giving or withholding of choice, through the considerations which appear to enter into the manner in which choice is won or earned from him. The view of group-role-of-member appears to be the deciding factor in the spread and focus of choice and rejection—depending upon the individual's estimate of how a potential-choice-receiver will (or has or can) affect the conditions of living and working between the individual chooser *and* other members. What might be called a group-reference-base is implicit and often explicit in the operation of the choice process as examined in communal living and working situations in the community under study.

In contrast, the chooser apparently selects in leisure time as nearly as possible other individuals who are found to be located on a level like his own in the interpersonal structure of the official groups. In other words, although he directs a predominant amount of choices towards a relatively few well-chosen individuals for living-working, when he is choosing for spending leisure time with others he seldom selects these very individuals, shifting instead to those who are more nearly within his "sociometric-class" in the official life of the community.

The "why" of these discriminations is in several respects suggested by the differences which can be noted in the motivations the individual gives for his choice behavior on the different criteria.

In the work and living groups, the motivations given for the choice structure almost invariably reflect some degree of helpfulness, improvement, or aspiration, *in addition to* whatever element of enjoyment is suggested. In brief, there is implied an *altering* of how the individual now sees himself, to be achieved by his associating with the chosen person because he can "gain" thereby or because the chosen person assumedly has "qualities" he would like to have, and, to some degree also, out of sheer appeal as "someone *I* could help."

Even the most cursory inspection of the choice motivations for leisure discloses a much more intimate view of the chooser and, indirectly, of the chosen than in the case for living-working. Yet the chooser does little analyzing of his feelings, his tendency being a sort of over-all acceptance centered apparently around a theme no more concrete than "enjoyment." This enjoyment the chooser seems to assume is mutual between him and the other person, and on a very "like" plane.

While a kind of over-all exuberance of feeling appears evident, the chooser does not go into "ecstasies" about how wonderful the chosen person is in a manner similar to that which is noted, in many instances, in motivations given for living-working. Perhaps in the latter setting a greater "social distance" lends a kind of enhancement to relationships as compared with what appears to be a notable "psychological closeness" between the chooser and the chosen for leisure-time association.

In the leisure-time grouping, the subject appears to visualize himself as getting a feeling of being fully significant for his own sake. He appears to seek to establish with others an interrelationship structure where there is a minimum of restriction placed on the kind of exchange he can get and give and, conversely, a maximum of freedom to be "himself" without being urged by others to "improve" or "to be different" from what he is.

Throughout, in the motivations he gives for his choices for leisure association, he tends to develop a philosophy or view of life peculiarly his, as relatively distinct from that of the next individual, and this he appears willing to have surveyed or criticized by but few of the very persons he chooses for work partners. At any rate, it is apparent in the motivations expressed that he discerns it may be inappropriate to exchange with co-workers in a like manner the same content of ideas and attitudes and temperamental expressions which he apparently feels he may entrust to leisure associates of his own choosing.

It is as if the picture of self which has been considered as carried within the individual he seeks to find "received" by another very much as he sees it himself. Then, apparently, he can take roles *in addition to* his "self" one, in a more impersonal, so-called "self-less" manner as though he has had or is having enough "self-" satisfaction somewhere in his life context. At any rate, those individuals who appear to find this in abundance in some of the leisure choices received are able to carry roles that interplay, in a highly sustaining and constructive manner, with those of others and result in the projection of many choices to them for work and living situations.

Or, to put it conversely, those individuals in the community under study who, for whatever reason, do not find a "flesh-and-blood" mirror of themselves (or so perceive themselves as finding) do not apparently carry their group roles with the kind of behaviors which bring them either choices on a group-role basis or on an informal person-to-person basis to any appreciable extent.

The leisure-choice structure appears to be a bedrock for morale and mental hygiene. It is within it that the individual seeks and finds an all-inclusive sort of acceptance of himself, confidence in his own "worthiness," opportunity to work out his problems at a rate more compatible with his stage of development, without the responsibilities, cares, and awarenesses which come with participation in work relationships or common living relationships wherein the same indivdual may be urged to "improve," "raise the standards," and, in general, may feel threatened with guilt the cause of which he is often at a loss to discern.

The foundations of leisure-choice apparently to a greater extent than the choice for work or living together appear based more exclusively on warmth and good feeling, as ends in themselves. The work and housing groups have goals of a more "distant" sort which the individual appears unable to keep out of his awareness and which he seems persistently to recognize and acknowledge by the direction of his choice behavior. The motivations he gives for leisure association show a simplicity of response that seems to defy or make unnecessary a critical analysis by the chooser of the chosen.

It is obvious that in both kinds of choice-structure, the informal, less institutionalized, leisure-time association network and the more formal, more institutionalized, work or living collective's network, there are to be found operating codes, value systems, diversified roles, methods of getting conformity, and in various degrees purposes and objectives. In the one case, however, the individual finds larger "personal" expression; in the other, the group situation, perhaps as much as its individual members, "tells" him what he can express to a much greater extent. The pervading difference is rather in the *kinds* of codes operating and *kinds* of roles the individual can acceptably display and in the *kinds* of conformity expected, sought, or demanded, and last, not least, in the *kinds* of growth afforded. It appears not a question of *which* kind of choice-structure, that underpinned with person-to-person spontaneity of rapport or that centered to a greater extent in inherited or passed along "codes for behavior," but of *how* these two structures *appear interdependent* in the individual's life and the life of the community as a whole.

Moreover, the fact that, in all respects examined in the research, the housing group is found to place somewhere between the work group at the one extreme and the leisure-time association at the other extreme indicates we are dealing with a continuum in the interpersonal structure of groups—that the crucial distinctions in structure come about by the nature of the pressures upon the choice process in the one case, compared with the relative lack of pressures upon it in the other, as an important factor accounting for the differences.

At the one extreme, his work group, the individual finds society facing him, telling him he is a group member, in a situation which is not for him alone to mold (with only persons whom he would choose). This collective, more or less formalized, setting where concerns must be shared and obligations held in common, as distinguished from that more fluid, informal, relatively uninstitutionalized setting where concerns and obligations and life itself are so much more, in a total sense, at the command of the individual's wants and wishes, can appropriately therefore be called, in the one case, *sociogroup,* and in the second case, the *psychegroup*.

As the individuals who are members of sociogroups are, of course, persons as well, there is bound to be a residuum of psychegroup behaviors within the atmosphere that develops in the sociogroup; similarly, individuals tend as psychegroup members to a greater or lesser degree to import into its context ways of behaving which they are currently holding to in sociogroup life (e.g., they may impose upon one another the expectation of punctuality, stressed in work programs, for their leisure-time dates). It is the difference *in emphases* taken by the individual in his exercise of choice and rejection in the two instances which suggests how fundamentally different in meaning for him are the two kinds of groups.

The finding that the sociogroup makes it possible for *more* individuals to find some degree of choice from others, as associates within its context who do not find choice reception outside it, may be the reflection of a "third factor" in it which may serve to mediate the effort of individuals to get into rapport with one another. Since the person-to-person relating exemplified in leisure-choice structure has no such "third factor" (as work or any other official group has in the form of more or less definite group objectives around which a group-role develops *via which* the individual can show his interest and make an effort to contribute), the individual is provided with no specific door into its "belongingness." He faces *on his own,* as it were, the other individual and is, so to speak, "psychologically more naked" in this area where there is least cultural protection in the form of group-role standing between him and others.

In the sociogroup, it may be premised, the group-role is an *insulating* factor between the individuals. On the other hand, the very *lack of insulation* in the psychegroup may cause a speeding up of interaction which evokes more facets of the personality and therefore demands and gets greater mutuality per choice expended, while at the same time causing the individual to be increasingly selective in the sense of welcoming fewer into such relationships with him.

It is as if being chosen within the milieu of the psychegroup provides the individual with the feeling he is considered by the other as totally *his kind*— without reservations of any consequential sort—thus as being approved, as it were, by *a surrogate for all others,* standing (in the individual's mind) as a counterpart for mankind as a whole and answering his own questions or doubts on his concept of himself. While at times a psychegroup may be a "friendship" cluster, it is not necessarily identical or tantamount to it. With friends,[6] the individual is conscious of many behaviors he might show (or confidences he might entrust) but which he does not disclose because these may run counter to their approval of his behavior. With some of his friends, however, he feels no such restrictions: *these may be said to be part of the individual's psyche-*

---

[6] The point here is that the psychegroup is operationally definable and should not be confused with any groupings defined at a phenomenological, descriptive level. Sociometric choice can only roughly "infer" friendliness and no research has as yet devised a sociometric criterion to define, much less to measure it.

group. It may be hypothesized that for any given individual the number of his friends will exceed the number of members of his psychegroup but show some overlap in the latter from among the friends who meet deeper needs than friendship, as ordinarily conceived, can or does.

This does not imply that every choice by the individual for leisure association has equal value in offering him a psychological mirror of himself; on the contrary, in the case of complex personalities (in terms of how many roles they see themselves as able to carry and the intricate relations among these roles), one of the individual's choices may meet, as it were, but one aspect of his own view of himself, another choice, another partial aspect, and so on, so that, in this sense, the individual appears to need his total psychegroup in a way that he does not need his total sociogroups and each of his psychegroup choices carries individualized meaning for him. Thus the psychegroup of a particular individual may be said to comprise *that part* of his social atom of most private and personal concern to his own emotional equilibrium.

By comparison, the individual's finding of choice in his sociogroups may be conceived as his finding "society's" approval which is relative to different conditions in different settings. It would be conceivably possible for any individual to say to himself, regarding his situation in any of his sociogroups, "In some other sociogroup (different society) I would likely find many choices as a co-worker"; and conceivably harder for him to face the fact of not finding choice towards himself, as a person, harder to rationalize and to endure.

It becomes obvious that we never deal with the individual *per se* but with *the individual in relationships* and, similarly, that we never deal with culture *per se* but with *culture as expressed in relationships in an interpersonal and intergroup context.*

SOCIODRAMATIC BEHAVIOR AND SOCIOMETRIC POSITION

It is a common observation as well as a common personal experience that each of us shows somewhat different aspects of personality when in situations involving different people and that this is true even when, in other respects, the situations are similar. The extent to which this is true, the *directions* in which it is true, and the apparent causes for such differences are only beginning to be explored through study of the *same* individual by sociometric and sociodramatic analyses.

Sociodrama offers a method which, in vital ways, aids the individual to mobilize his personality resources for communication; moreover, it can readily be integrated with sociometric method to further understanding of the nature of relating generally. A sociodrama is a process of warming up to, embodying, and portraying of actions by individuals whereby they can disclose their feelings, ideas, attitudes, and frames of mind (1) regarding common situations which they have met or may be about to meet in their societal contexts; (2) when the sociodrama is to be portrayed before a group, the group members must have like concern and interest in the problem; hence, any given problem must also be one which is likely to, or presently may, confront the majority of the members of the group—that is, it is a *common* problem; (3) the problem should connect, to as great a degree as possible, with several broad problems falling into the category of common themes so that *sociodramatic importance is compounded.*

An example illustrating the three main criteria of sociodrama just cited (used in the present study) and suitable in most sixth-grade classrooms is:

You are sent by your mother to the store for two cartons of milk, a loaf of bread, and a half-pound of cheese. It is Thursday night and your father doesn't get paid until Friday. Your mother told you she needed the things for supper and for lunch the next day and that, as she has overspent this week and as your father won't be paid that day, you should be especially careful not to lose the money—three fifty-cent pieces which she gives you—or she will have to tell him she spent too much and has nothing left. You wish to save your mother from this embarrassment. However, you meet a friend on the way to the store and play "who can run faster" and to your sorrow you lose the money and can't find it. Your friend has no money with him and leaves you at the door of the store. You have nowhere to turn except to the storekeeper who has known you for some time. Now, take one minute to figure out what you would do or consider the best thing to do in this situation. The storekeeper also has one minute to feel out how he will handle whatever approach you make to him. (One minute elapses.) *Now,* you enter!

The problem themes underlying this specific situation are: son-and-mother relationship in any culture; boy of about 11 years of age growing into independence in facing society generally, epitomized by the storekeeper in particular, in the culture of the United States; boy of this age growing into desire to be entrusted with greater and greater responsibility toward family unit and, specifically, to be entrusted to handle money efficiently. Hence, more is at issue than a dollar or so and more is at issue than the situation itself, namely, the themes which the situation represents. The sociodramatic cuts across a boy's role in society the world over; a son's role in our society; the role of a growing individual facing certain developmental tasks at his particular age, in the United

States, and, dealing with a situation affecting his mother and about which, unless he handles it well, she may be disappointed.

Sociodramatic analysis is analysis of the individual's behaviors comprising his performance in sociodramas, hence his mimic and verbal expressions, his timing of responses, his movements or lack of movements at particular points in the sequence of interaction, his use of words or lack of such use to carry the major communication effort, his use of mimic articulation separate from or integrated with verbal output, his initiating of different moods or ideas, his following-up upon and/or coördinating with such initiating on the part of a co-player, his diverting the direction of the sociodrama to carry it off independently or "waiting upon" the efforts of a co-player to meet the situation, and so on. In general, all aspects of the individual's behaviors which may bear upon the course of the sociodrama, both sequentially (in what is permitted or elicited from any co-player via such behaviors) and in final outcome (e.g., resolution of the sociodramatic theme, desertion of the theme, or building upon the theme, or whatever).

Such analysis may be as detailed or as general as warranted by the purposes set in the research. The important point is that the significant happenings within the sociodrama, correlated with its taking a given course rather than some other course, not be lost in the analysis.

In the course of working with children in classrooms, it was noted by teachers and the writer that the sociodramatic performance of any given child varied greatly in relation to what other children he had as co-players in given situations. Sociograms of many of these classroom groups were available not only for the current period during which the children's sociodramatic performance was being studied but for two or more previous occasions, taken at eight-week interims. It was thus first possible to examine whether or not sociometric position in a given group bears a relation to quality of the individual's sociodramatic performance; and, secondly, how, if at all, the individual's actions in sociodrama vary when he is portraying a role in interaction with someone he has chosen, as against a role in interaction with someone he has not chosen or who has chosen him unreciprocally or reciprocally. This study has been in process since 1950. As it proceeds, it becomes evident that many of the trends appearing in children's classroom groups hold to a large extent also for adults in university classroom groups; in consequence, data from the latter settings are being treated in the same analysis to ascertain the extent to which there is overlap or lack of overlap.

The detailed analysis is so far from completed that only the main features of method and a statement of general trends are sketched here. It will be at once apparent to investigators in the area of personality expression in inter-action that even such aspects of the work as securing comparable sociodramatic situations, administered under comparable conditions, and using within the same time period appropriate sociometric criteria (having like importance), are enormously complicated tasks; hence the following is a preliminary report of research now in progress. The number of individuals so far studied is only 37, "lifted" with their co-players from 20 groups. It must therefore be stressed that even the statement of trends is subject to revision as more groups are added to the analysis and that any evidence from others' research in progress confirm-ing or refuting or clarifying the trends indicated here would be appreciated by the writer.

In the present study the sociodramatic analysis is being made in two ways: (1) the individual is compared with himself under differing sociometric cir-cumstances; (2) individuals in given sociometric positions are compared *as a group* with individuals in other sociometric positions *as a group,* with the cate-gories employed being; chosen 1 S. D. below the mean; chosen nearly at the mean; chosen 1 S. D. above the mean.

The latter analysis indicates at least six main qualitative aspects of socio-dramatic performance which *quantitatively* differentiate the three groups:

1) number of ideas offered for the solution of a problem;
2) ingeniousness of ideas presented;
3) appropriateness of use of the ideas (effectiveness of sequences of be-havior);
4) persistence in facing the situation and seeing it through;
5) flexibility in winning the co-player to one's point of view (rather than dominating, ordering, or threatening him, or "escaping" from the situation by a ruse);
6) ability to establish *close* rapport ("letting one's hair down" when nec-essary to establish intimate understanding of why one takes a par-ticular point of view).

The former analysis suggests that the individual's behavior has a variety of frames of reference—a variety which reflects how the individual perceives others as well as how he may think of others as perceiving him—and that these perceptions are related appreciably to the kind of behavior exhibited. The in-dividual's productivity as measured by the above-mentioned six aspects of per-formance shows a number of trends which appear affected by his sociometric position *in specific relation* to the co-player. Chief among these are the follow-ing:

In general, the performance of any individual with a partner of his own choosing is more productive as compared with his performance with a partner not of his own choosing. The individual is still more productive if he and his partner have chosen each other, and this productivity is greater the higher the levels of choices involved between them. The unchosen individual is surprisingly more productive with a partner he has chosen than he is with one he has not chosen; and this contrast in his performances is much greater than is the contrast between performances on the part of the individual who is used to being chosen, when he faces a partner he has not chosen compared with when he faces one he has chosen.

The much-chosen individual shows a solicitude for the unchosen individual which is not noted in his performance with either those he has chosen or who are chosen to an average extent. With the latter, he appears to guage what a partner can "take" in the sense that he often challenges and "eggs on" someone who has chosen him or whom he has chosen, attuning his behavior to the response it gets, while he almost never uses other than indulgently gentle and encouraging behavior with unchosen individuals, sometimes even "completely" helping out such an individual (e.g., "I remember you told me once it would be a good idea to . . . ," giving the unchosen opportunity to catch on, "Yes, that's what *I* think we should do now"). The unchosen individual, however, often appears unable to utilize the hints and encouragement offered by the much-chosen partner. It is as if the unchosen individual can not "believe" readily in the other individual, however great the latter's warmth and effort ("You say that to a lot of people").

The clearest picture of tendencies appears upon inspection of the individual's performance with the person he has chosen as his first choice. The latter is found to exhibit towards him a manner of interacting which can be said to aid him to interact more confidently, more assertively, more flexibly, and more constructively. The individual's first choice thus appears as someone who apparently agrees with the positive feelings he has about himself and disagrees with and aids him to combat the negative feelings arising in him. These tendencies are evident only to a much lesser degree in the interaction of the individual with those he has chosen on lower choice levels.

The sharpest contrasts to this picture appear in interaction between individuals between whom no choices are expressed; in such sociodramas each player appears more focused upon making his own performance "stand up," as it were, and is relatively much less sensitive to the other's behavior.

Thus, in summary, to gain increasing comprehension of the role of choice in behavior between individuals it appears necessary at this stage of our insights to study such behavior through at least two kinds of analyses concomitantly—one focused upon the individual *per se* and the other upon individuals as a group, having like sociometric interpersonal situations.

The analysis based upon comparing the individual with himself under varying sociometric circumstances in sociodramatic performance shows certain tendencies to characterize his behavior which have an interpersonal import and particularizes the quality of his behavior. The analysis based on comparing individuals in a given sociometric position, as a group, with individuals in another contrasting sociometric position, as a group, shows certain tendencies which differentiate their behavior as groups, in sociodramatic performance, and which hold import for groups.

These tendencies suggest the hypothesis that sociometric choice of one individual for another can be considered as his recognition (whether fully conscious or fully unconscious or only partly either) that the other is (as compared with other available people) sympathetic and releasing to those aspects of his personality which need expression and/or development. In this respect it is also suggested that *the individual's choice behavior has a general importance for his life and for the life of his group.* These tendencies appear, moreover, to indicate that the underpinning of role performance is to an appreciable, if not critical, extent the psychetele responsiveness between individuals which is rooted in person-to-person affect. When this is highly positive, there is reaching out and drawing out of potential ability—otherwise often hidden from expression of the individual under other sociometric circumstances.

Proctor and Loomis have pointed out that it is important to know how much generality for behavior sociometric choice holds (28). While this preliminary report can not answer this question, it indicates that sociometric choice taps the feeling-thinking-doing universe of the individual and bears a complex relation to how he meets situations or is "met by" others in situations.

Whereas in general it is demonstrated that choice expression represents the individual's selection of facilitating relationships, expanding to his performance, there are two main exceptions experimentally found: (1) Occasional individuals show a sort of held-in, as if mutually agreed upon, spontaneity that keeps a *status quo* in each other's performance, notable for the absence of stimulating interplay and for the presence of a "pleased" and uncritical satisfaction in the reactions of both individuals: a "horizontal" product, as it were, of "horizontal" choosing, apparently keeping each person just as "settled" at his present stage of growth as he seemingly wants to remain. (2) Occasional individuals show a working out of destructively aggressive attacks upon each other's efforts, spontaneity harnessed towards destroying each other's "momentum" as if mutually satisfying to both participants; each "catching" whatever he can to find fault with and divert the other's focusing upon the issues; discouraging to organized performance on either part *yet verbally and mimically* highly productive; notable for the absence of constructive interplay and for the presence of apparent delight on the part of each partner in exciting the other while afterwards stating he was trying to help the other who "wouldn't let" him: a "destructive" product, as it were, of "cellar" choosing, wherein spontaneity appears directed towards destroying the self, its growth possibilities, its expanding needs, in favor of its restricting, hostile needs; these tendencies are found *jointly with* similar everyday action tendencies towards the self. There is some indication, too, that the individual tries first to cling to a horizontal stage rather desperately before he is found to "co-operate" in a full-fledged way with influences from associates to push him into a "downward" stage. By and large, however, most of the individuals found on the horizontal stage seem content with such dynamics.

This appears in sharp contrast to the majority of children and the majority of adults studied in graduate classes (the latter, of course, may be far less representative of adults than the former are of children). They seem, on the whole, to have an intolerance of *status quo* and to feel happy with themselves only as they pursue their respective psychological staircase (16) (18). In this respect they can be said to "resist" acculturation in a forward march which is individually their own, as Maslow (20) points out for the self-actualizing personality. It may be that one cause for the rarity of full flowering of personality found by Maslow is the early development of fear in the exercise of choice on the part of the average individual, stopping him in advance from recognizing and acknowledging the most stimulating interaction available to him. The sociodramatic tendencies suggest that ability to exercise choice-daring or choice-initiative in winning needed relationships is a very early task of the child and one which may readily be permanently thwarted to such extent that by adulthood the number of others whom the individual can include in any sociometric sense is accordingly abnormally few—regardless of what genetic potential may have been his.

THE PSYCHOLOGICAL STAIRCASE PHENOMENON

It may well be that the "orderliness" in the sociodramatic trends and the order apparent in sociometric choice structure are mainly attributable to the phenomenon of the psychological staircase characterizing choice behavior (18). The child does not look *anywhere* in making emotional investment in others.

The psychological staircase fittingly describes the fact that the first choice of a given individual for another individual (with but few exceptions) represents an aspect of maturity which the chooser is currently working upon and which the chosen is able and willing to help him with (and/or is so perceived by the chooser). It does not imply that the chooser is, in *all* respects, less mature than the individual who is first choice: it refers only to the *currently active* needs of the chooser compared with those of the chosen.

This phenomenon would account for the stability of choice and its only gradual flux. Each choice being meaningful in a psychological sense, the most stability (duration) is found where the investment taps the deepest core of personality; hence, the greater duration of first choices over second, third, and lower degrees. This phenomenon would account also for the shorter duration of choice made by very young children (five and six years old) in two ways: their rapidity and irregularity of growth would require them, more frequently than when they are older, to change in the directions they invest choice; and their greater emphasis upon immediate psychological comfort and greater intolerance of stress, compared with when they are older, would similarly cause them to need to change "out of" relationships where incompatibility was developing.

The psychology of the choice process, for any given child as it is studied over a period of time, appears marked by occasional sudden surges (leaps ahead in the level of maturity of others sought after), plateaus now and then, where the individual appears to have "settled" for a given level of stimulation from others, and occasional times of "cellar" choices, in the sense that his choice expression seems to be taking him backwards into relationships of a sort he had outgrown from a maturity standpoint. Among children, plateau choices are very rare and "cellar" choices when shown over a period of several months indicate very deep emotional disturbance.

The route which any individual takes as his particular psychological staircase is apparently in no sense a predetermined gravitation; it seems to require exertion on the part of the choice participants, and in this process it can be aptly called "ego-generating." *At each point* some elements of decision on the part of the individuals are involved. Any hurtful psychological mechanisms active in a given child appear in his choice picture as he seeks via the psychological staircase *to work his way* healthfully out of them. Sociometric research discloses that the social space for growth is structured in a highly particularized fashion (15). Choice behavior in leisure-time expression appears in sociodramatic exploration specifically (14) to be a matter of trying to create *with the chosen* the self one wishes to have.

The frontiers of the choice process are being pushed further and further back at this time by sociometric investigations in Canada (1, 27), England (25), France (19, 21, 32), Japan (unpublished), Sweden (4), and the United States (2, 3, 5, 7, 8, 9, 11, 12, 13, 22, 26, 30, 31). It can be anticipated the next decade will give us important knowledge of how our actions reflect our interpersonal situations and how we can create interaction of greater benefit.

GENERAL CONCLUSIONS

The individual appears to seek persistently for regard and esteem and affection towards himself as a person; while this seeking is meeting with reciprocation he shows himself able to relate well to others in common group oriented settings, i.e., sociogroups (such as work-oriented groups), and towards their goals; when, however, he is blocked from fulfillment on a person-to-person level of relating of the kind he needs, comprising for him his psychegroup, his pattern in group-oriented or common-goal-oriented settings is equally unfulfilling in fundamental satisfactions.

The individual's choice behavior appears as an effort to find expressive outlets, in which respect his choices are "intelligent"; that is, they are actually found to be media of release to him. Because of the potent way in which his choices serve his personality-building-and-expression, so to speak, any one or all of them can be to him eventually important as a "reference group" influence in the sense that he will look favorably upon *whatever group memberships are held* by the individuals he chooses if they regard these favorably, and conversely if they do not. As the closest persons to the individual are those he wants to associate with in a person-to-person way, unrestricted by institutionalized considerations (as work mores, etc.), these particular sociometric choices comprise his personal-reference-group, or psychegroup. It is this group which apparently determines what other reference groups he will want or need to seek.

Sociodramatic exploration supports a theory that choice behavior intrinsically involves and is undergirt with a spontaneity component—the individual chooses others who *facilitate his expression,* aiding him by *stimulating* his spontaneity, and this process shows itself in his greater creativity and productivity and ease of approach to attacking more confidently and effectively problems with which he is confronted when in interaction with those he chooses than when not so situated; only very rarely are individuals found in the general child population (public schools) or adult population (graduate classes) whose choice expression is directed apparently against the best interests of themselves and whose interaction shows satisfaction in strong facilitation of negating behaviors. The findings suggest that sociodramatic performance can be used diagnostically to estimate the healthfulness of choice relationships shown by any given individual.

The statement that the choosing process is no less than the process by which the individual becomes what he becomes is suggested by sociodramatic-sociometric exploration which indicates that the individual's use of the choice process can relate him to those who will foster and facilitate his growth, or can relate him to those with whom he can "settle" comfortably at a given level of development, or can, on occasion, relate him increasingly to those who will agree with and actively reinforce whatever negating and self-defeating propensities are emergent in him at a given time; in any event, any choice expression of the individual is apparently fraught with importance for his intrapsychic dynamics as well as for the interpersonal structure of his groups and their membership. This apparently is so because spontaneity components (only describable at present as factors highly activating of behavior) are resident in choice expression facilitating the making of personality and group structure.

It appears warranted to predict that the *concurrent* use of sociometric and sociodramatic investigation of interpersonal processes can eventually particularize our knowledge of the dynamics of personality and group formation not so accessible to study by any other combination of methods.

REFERENCES

1. Baker, William B. "Sociometric Analysis of a College Community: University of Saskatchewan, Canada." Ms in the University of Saskatchewan Library, Saskatoon, Saskatchewan.
2. Bell, Graham B., and French, Robert L. "Consistency of Individual Leadership Position in Small Groups of Varying Membership," *Journal of Abnormal and Social Psychology,* XLV (1950), 764–67.
3. Bock, R. Darrell, and Husain, Suraya Zahid. "Factors of the Tele: A Preliminary Report," *Sociometry,* XV (1952), 206–19.
4. Bjerstedt, Ake. "A Chess-Board Sociogram for Sociographic Representation of Choice Directions and for the Analysis of Sociometric Locomotions," *Sociometry,* XV (1952), 244–62.
5. Coffey, Hubert Stanley. "Socio and Psyche Group Progress: Integrative Concepts," *Journal of Social Issues,* VIII (1952), 65–74.
6. Deutschberger, Paul. "Interaction Patterns in Changing Neighborhoods: New York and Pittsburgh," *Sociometry,* IX (1946), 303–15.
7. Feinberg, Mortimer. "The Relation of Background Experience to Sociometric Acceptance," *Journal of Abnormal and Social Psychology,* XLV (1953), 719–25.
8. Fiedler, Fred E., Warrington, Willard G., and Blaisdell, Francis J. "Unconscious attitudes as Correlates of Sociometric Choice in a Social Group," *Journal of Abnormal and Social Psychology,* XLVII (1952), 790–96.
9. French, Robert L. Sociometric Status and Individual Adjustment among Naval Recruits," *Journal of Abnormal and Social Psychology,* XLVI (1951), 64–72.

10. Gibb, Cecil A. "The Sociometry of Leadership in Temporary Groups," *Sociometry,* XIII (1950), 226–43.
11. Gibb, Jack R. "The Effects of Group Size and of Threat Reduction upon Creativity in a Problem-solving Situation." Ms on file at the Fels Group Dynamics Center, University of Delaware, Newark, Delaware.
12. Goodacre, Daniel M. "The Use of a Sociometric Test as a Predictor of Combat Unit Effectiveness," *Sociometry,* XIV (1951), 148–52.
13. Halpin, Andrew W. "The Leadership Behavior and Combat Performance of Airplane Commanders," *Journal of Abnormal and Social Psychology* XLIX (1954), 19–22.
14. Jennings, Helen Hall. *Sociometry of Sociodramatic Performance.* In preparation.
15. Jennings, Helen Hall. *Leadership and Isolation.* 2nd ed.; New York: Longmans, Green, 1950.
16. Jennings, Helen Hall. *Sociometry in Group Relations.* Washington, D.C.: American Council on Education, 1948; 2nd ed., 1959.
17. Jennings, Helen Hall. "Sociometry of Leadership," *Sociometry,* X (1947), 32–49, 71–79.
18. Jennings, Helen Hall. "Sociometric Grouping in Relation to Child Development *and* Sociodrama as Educative Process," in Caroline Tryon (ed.), *Fostering Mental Health in Our Schools.* Washington, D.C.: National Education Association (A.S.C.D. Yearbook), 1950
19. Maisonneuve, J., Palmade, G., and Fourment, C. "Selective Choices and Propinquity," *Sociometry,* XV (1952), 135–40.
20. Maslow, A. H. "Self-actualizing People: A Study of Psychological Health," *Personality Symposia,* I (1950), 11–34.
21. Maucorps, Paul H. "A Sociometric Inquiry in the French Army," *Sociometry,* XII (1949), 46–80.
22. Moreno, J. L. *Who Shall Survive?* Boston: Beacon House, 1953.
23. Moreno, J. L. *Psychodrama,* Vol. I. Boston: Beacon House, 1946.
24. Moreno, J. L., and Jennings, Helen Hall. "Statistics of Social Configurations," *Sociometry,* I (1938), 342–74.
25. Murray, Hugh. "Stability of Sociometric Relations among Retarded Children," *Sociometry,* XVI (1953), 113–41.
26. Newburger, Howard. "Sociometric Selection in Group Therapy." Unpublished Ph.D. dissertation, New York University, 1952.
27. Northway, Mary L. *A Primer of Sociometry.* Toronto: University of Toronto Press, 1952.
28. Proctor, Charles H., and Loomis, Charles P. "Analysis of Sociometric Data," in Marie Jahoda, Morton Deutsch, and Stuart W. Cook (eds.), *Research Methods in Social Relations.* New York: Dryden, 1951.
29. Tagiuri, Renato. "Relational Analysis: An Extension of Sociometric Method with Emphasis upon Social Perception," *Sociometry,* XV (1952), 91–104.
30. Thelen, Herbert A., *et al. Methods for Research on Interaction in Groups.* Chicago: University of Chicago Press, 1952.
31. Weschler, Irving R., Tannebaum, Robert, and Talbot, Eugene. "A New Management Tool: The Multi-relational Sociometric Survey," *Personnel,* XXIX (1952), 85–94.
32. Zazzo, Rene. "Sociometry and Psychology," *Sociometry,* XII (1949), 32–45.

SOCIOMETRIC BASE OF GROUP PSYCHOTHERAPY

By J. L. Moreno

The formation of synthetic groups has been the earliest problem of sociometry. The task was to establish a theoretical base for group psychotherapy. I assembled the new members of the group (my experiment, 1921) in a room which was fitted out with a number of couches. Every individual was placed on a couch. The fundamental rule of free association was applied to them. The experiment failed—the free associations of one began to mingle with the free associations of the others. This confused them and produced a chaotic situation. The reasons for the failure was obvious. Free association works significantly only along individual tracks; free associations which have significance along the track of individual A have no significance on the track of B or of C, and vice versa. They have no "common unconscious." When free association was rigorously applied, a number of individuals were being separately psychoanalyzed. There was no bridge between them. It did not develop into a *group* psychoanalysis but into a psychoanalysis of several individuals within a group setting. But my objective was *group* production, *group* therapy and *group* analysis, not individual analysis. As the psychoanalytic method of free association proved unproductive, I developed a new method which was based on the study of the formation of groups *in statu nascendi*. "Individuals who never met before and who from the first meeting on have to be participants in the same group represent a new problem to the therapist; we see them when they enter spontaneously into interrelations which lead them to form a group *sub specie momenti;* we can only study their spontaneous reaction in the initial stage of group formation and the activities developing in the course of such organization . . . we can develop the treatment forward instead of backward; we can begin with the initial attitude one person has for the other and follow up to what fate these interrelations lead, what kind of organizations they develop" (see *Who Shall Survive?* 1934). In support of the existence of such an initial common matrix, sociometric research has shown that "immediate response between strangers differs significantly from chance." Barker in his classic experiment took "twelve university students who were complete strangers to each other and were selected from a larger class for its first meeting. Six of these students were men, six were women. Of thirty-six choices of seat mates upon the first occasion, twenty or 55 per cent were repeated upon the second occasion. Of one-hundred-and-thirty-two responses to other choices upon the first oc-

113

casion, 81 or 63 per cent were repeated upon the second occasion. These per cents are both considered higher than would have been obtained if the subjects had chosen entirely at random.[1] It was an important discovery to know that there is *tele*[2] already operating between the members of the group from the first meeting.

This weak, "primary" cohesiveness can be utilized by the therapist towards the development and sharing of common therapeutic aims. All the interactions between them, abreactions, soliloquies, dialogues, *tele,* and transference relations to therapist, auxiliary egos and each other in the course of therapy will be influenced by this original structure and will in turn modify it. The multiple couch experiment had failed; it showed that free association is unable to carry from one individual to another. But it led to the discovery that, if free spontaneous interaction is permitted, a new operational frame of reference develops from which one can look at the successive stages of a synthetic group.

The first concern of the group therapist is the *immediate* behavior of the group. When the therapist faces his group for the first session he perceives immediately, with his skilled sense for interpersonal relations, some of the interaction between the members, for example, the distribution of love, hate, and indifference. The group is not just a collection of individuals. He notices one or two sitting all by themselves, physically isolated from the rest; two or three clustered together, smiling and gossiping; one or two engaged in an argument or sitting side by side but giving each other the cold shoulder. In other words, the first contours of a sociogram begin to form in his mind. He does not have to give a formal test in order to obtain this knowledge. He takes notice of this "embryonic matrix." It comes to him through his immediate observations. It becomes his empathetic guide for the therapeutic process-in-becoming. The

---

[1] R. G. Barker, "The Social Interrelations of Strangers and Acquaintances," *Sociometry* V (1942), 169–79.

[2] In the therapist-patient relationship two processes can be observed: the one process is transference, the development of fantasies (unconscious) which the patient projects upon the therapist, surrounding him with a certain glamor; but then there is another process still more fundamental, *tele,* (derived from the Greek; projection into distance). It radiates from that part of his ego which is not carried away by auto-suggestion. It sizes up the man across the desk and estimates intuitively what kind of person he is. It assesses his immediate behavior, physical, mental, or otherwise and evaluates him as he actually is, consciously or unconsciously, independent of the transference picture the patient may have of him. Simultaneously, just as the patient assesses the immediate behavior of the therapist, the therapist assesses the patient. It is a two-way process, interweaving two or more individuals relating one to another. It is *Zweifühlung* in contrast to *Einfühlung.* It operates from birth on—already in the mother-infant symbiosis (matrix of identity), prior to transference. It is the cement which is destined to hold the group together (cf. my "Psychopathology of Interpersonal Relations," 1937).

group has, from the first session on, whatever its size, a specific structure of interpersonal relations which, however, does not reveal itself at once on the surface but appears later as an underlying *sociometric or group matrix*.

Natural groupings behave differently from groups of strangers. Mother and child, members of a family, matrimonial partners, two lovers, friends and business partners of long standing, and similar intimate interpersonal ensembles have a common matrix of silent understanding. The members of such groups have a common past, they expect a common future, and they share a life together in their home. When, for instance, husband and wife re-enact in a psychodramatic session an intimate episode in which they have been involved, one appears to know the experience of the other with surprising accuracy; the same clairvoyance is evident in the enactment of present episodes and future projections. It is as if they would have developed in the course of years a long and intricate chain of quasi-unconscious states. If one of the dyad or triad begins to draw from one phase of the common experience, the other one has no difficulty in continuing the same thread supplementing the other, as if they were one person and "as if" they would have a common unconscious life. They appear to share in what I have called "co-conscious" and "co-unconscious" states (cf. my "Interpersonal Therapy and the Function of the Unconscious," 1954). But the insight which one person has about what goes on in the other person's mind is often sketchy. They live simultaneously in different worlds which communicate only at times and even then incompletely. The psyche is not transparent. We see man and wife acting out in a psychodrama, side by side, some feelings and thoughts which they never knew in regard to each other. They were themselves taken by surprise upon hearing and seeing what the other party had felt, hitherto fully unnoticed. The checking, reminding and analyzing of each by the other is carried out by the patients themselves. They added parts which one or the other had left out in the particular scene. At times what seemed important to him did not seem important to her. In consequence they placed emphasis upon different points. Indeed, in the interpretation of free associations of a single individual, the psychoanalyst has no control of validity except the assertion of that particular patient that a certain episode has the meaning the therapist ascribes to it. But in the symbiotic responses of co-unconscious states, one acts like a mirror to the other. There are here two subjectivities concurring on the accuracy of an event (cf. my "Interpersonal Therapy and the Psychopathology of Interpersonal Relations," 1937).

In addition to the subjective dimensions of co-conscious and co-unconscious states the interactions are accompanied by a system of complimentary objective and physical signs. These signs can be operationally explored through psychodramatic methods of enactment. Physical or symbolic signs are guideposts in the process of the mutual recall of crucial episodes. An illustration may be seen, e.g., in a trivial psychodramatic episode between a husband and wife. She remembers definitely that he had an outburst of anger towards her but "there was no reason for it." When he reminded her that it happened because she removed the picture of his mother from the piano, and put it on the bookshelf, the incident began to be dimly recalled by her and they began to re-enact it. When she was removing the picture, and she was asked by the director to soliloquize what she was thinking she said, "Your mother is dead now. It is not necessary that her picture is placed on such a prominent spot in the room." The *signs* which helped her to recall this mutual interaction and understand its significance was her *walking* towards the piano, *taking* the picture from the *piano, walking* from the piano to the bookshelf and *placing* the picture flat on the bookshelf, then *turning* towards him. His counter-signs were that he suddenly *left* the room but *returned* when she called him in. Then his outbursts took place, and he soliloquized that he had *left* the room in order to *avoid* a scene and when she called out saying she was going for an *errand,* he felt neglected and retaliated with anger.

Neither the concept of unconscious states (Freud) nor that of the collective unconscious states (Jung) can be easily applied to these problems without stretching the meaning of the terms. The free associations of A may be a path to the unconscious states of A; the free associations of B may be a path to the unconscious states of B; but can the unconscious material of A ever link naturally and directly with the unconscious material of B unless they share in unconscious states? The concept of individual unconscious states becomes unsatisfactory for explaining both movements, from the present situation of A, and in reverse to the present situation of B. We must look for a concept which is so constructed that the objective indication for the existence of this two-way process does not come from a single psyche but from a still deeper reality in which the unconscious states of two or several individuals are interlocked with a system of "co-unconscious" states. Jung postulated that every individual has, besides a personal, a collective unconscious. Although the distinction may be useful, it does not help in solving the dilemma described. Jung does not apply the collective unconscious to the concrete collectivities in which people live. There is nothing gained in turning from a personal to a "collective unconscious" if by doing this the anchorage to the *concrete*, whether individual or group, is lost. Had he turned to the group by developing techniques like group psychotherapy or sociodrama, he might have gained a concrete position for this theory of the collective unconscious, but as it is, he underplayed the individual anchorage but did not establish a safe "collective anchorage" as a counterposition. The problem here is not the collective images of a given culture or of mankind, but the *specific* relatedness and cohesiveness of a group of individuals. In the system of co-unconscious states, extended into the interpersonal networks of the group (cf. my *Who Shall Survive?*) we have found a *rationale* for the significance and effectiveness of role reversal, double, mirror, and other psychodramatic techniques. Now we understand that they are the natural instruments for exploring, modifying and retraining them. But this still leaves a question open. Phenomena like hallucinations and dreams require elaborate symbolic systems of interpretation as long as we limit our communications with the patients to language and free association of words. It is because they originated in a period of our mental growth when acts have a priority over words, in the "no-man's-land" of physical signs, act-hunger, and spontaneous role playing (cf. my "Spontaneity of Child Development," 1943), that direct operational methods and action techniques like psychodrama are better fitted for exploring them.

The theoretical basis of all varieties of group psychotherapy can be formulated with a greater degree of assurance today than when these experiments were initiated in the early thirties. It has three frames of reference. First, the *common interactional matrix* which the individuals share, of a changing constellation and cohesiveness expressed in multiple emotional tensions. Second, the common *co-conscious* and *co-unconscious* experience of the members. The longer a synthetic group endures the more it begins to resemble a natural group, to develop and share an unconscious life, from which its members draw their strength, knowledge and security. This co-unconscious network reflected in sociograms and role diagrams tying the members together with varying degrees of identity is the river bed to which the individual histories act as contributories, their "stream" of co-consciousness and co-unconsciousness. Third, *the role reversal of any member with every other member.* The more different and especially distant the members are, the more urgent it is that they reverse roles with each other in the course of mutual therapy. Psychodrama is an elaborate form of "encounter," and it is the experience of encounter which was the original force in the development of this method (cf. my *Einladung zu einer Begegnung,* 1914). Role reversal puts the cap on the encounter between "you and I." It is the final touch of giving unity, identity, and universality to the group.

THREE DIMENSIONS OF SOCIETY —
THE EXTERNAL SOCIETY, THE SOCIOMETRIC MATRIX AND THE SOCIAL REALITY

By J. L. Moreno

It is of heuristic value to differentiate the social universe into three tendencies or dimensions, the *external society,* the *sociometric matrix* and the *social reality.* By external society I mean all tangible and visible groupings, large or small, formal or informal, of which human society consists. By the sociometric matrix I mean all sociometric structures invisible to the macroscopic eye but which become visible through the sociometric process of analysis. By social reality I mean the dynamic synthesis and interpenetration of the two. It is obvious that neither the matrix nor the external are real or can exist by themselves, one is a function of the other. As dialectic opposites they must merge in some fashion in order to produce the actual process of social living.

The dynamic reason for this split is the underground existence of innumerable social constellations which impinge continuously upon external society, partly in an effort towards its disintegration, partly in an effort towards their realization and, last not least, because of the resistance which external society puts up against its substitution or change. As the profound and chronic conflict between these two tendencies is never fully resolved, the result is a compromise in the form of what may be called the "social reality".

A position which has become axiomatic for sociometrists until proven otherwise is that the official (external) society and the sociometric (internal) matrix are not identical. The one is visible to the senses, it is macroscopic, the other is invisible, it is microscopic. In the sense of this dichotomy all groupings, whether as rigidly formalized and collectivized as an army or a church, or as casual and transitory as a meeting of people on a streetcorner, they belong, as long as they are visible to the naked macroscopic eye, to the externally structured society. One can not assume in advance that the sociogram of an army platoon, for instance is radically different from the official structure of the platoon, rigidly imposed upon the men, or that the sociogram of a casual gathering on a streetcorner is equal or nearly equal to the actually visible formation. It is easily possible that in certain cultures, widely divergent from our own, the sociogram of a rigid social institution is identical with its actual social structure on the reality level.[1] It is therefore methodically of utmost importance not to *mix* the sociometric position which is *neutral* (or let us say as neutral as possible) with the social order just existing and passing. Sociometry is equally applicable to every type of society which has emerged in the past or which might emerge in the future.

The structure of the external society is comparatively easy to describe. It consists of visible, overt and observable groups; it is made up of all the groups recognized by law as legitimate, of all the groups rejected by law as illegitimate, as well as of all the neutral groups permitted, although unclassified and unorganized. The shortest way to obtain a picture of the legitimate groups is to use the system of law ruling a particular society as a guide. In order to obtain a picture of the illegitimate groupings excursions into the underworld are effective. Illustrations of legitimate groups are: the family, the workshop, the school, the army or the church. Illustrations of informal and illegitimate groups are: the casual encounter of two, the crowd, the mass, the mob, the streetcorner gangs or criminal rackets. The structure of the sociometric matrix is more difficult to recognize. Special techniques called sociometric are necessary to unearth it; as the matrix is in continuous dynamic change the techniques have to be applied at regular intervals so as to determine the newly emerging social constellations. The sociometric matrix consists of various constellations, tele, the atom, the super-atom or molecule (several atoms linked together), the "socioid" which may be defined as a cluster of atoms linked together with other clusters of atoms via inter-personal chains or networks; the socioid is the sociometric counterpart of the external structure of a social group; it is rarely identical with what a social group externally shows because parts of its social atoms and chains may extend into another socioid. On the other hand, some of the external structure of a particular social group may not make sense configurationally as a part of a particular socioid but may belong to a socioid hidden within a different social group. Other constellations which can be traced within a sociometric matrix are psychosocial networks. There are in addition large sociodynamic categories which are frequently mobilized f. i. in political and revolutionary activities; they consist of the interpenetration of numerous socioids and represent the sociometric counterpart of "social class" as bourgeoisie or proletariat; they can

---

[1] See "Some Attraction and Repulsion Patterns among Jibaro Indians", by Bengt Danielsson, Sociometry, Vol. XII, February-August, 1949, No. 1-3.

be defined as sociometric structure of social classes or as *classoids*. The social reality itself is the dynamic interweaving of and interaction of the socio-metric matrix with the outer, external society. The sociometric matrix does not exist by itself, just as the outer society does not exist by itself; the latter is continuously pushed and pulled by the structure underneath. Within a sociometric system we distinguish therefore three processes: the outer reality of society, the internal reality of the sociometric matrix and the social reality itself, the historically growing, dynamic social groupings of which the actual social universe consists. If one knows the structure of the official society and the sociometric matrix he can recognize the bits and pieces which enter from the two dimensions into the compromising forms of social reality. The greater the contrast between official society and the sociometric matrix the more intensive is the social conflict and tension between them. One may venture to formulate the following hypothesis: *social conflict and tension increases in direct proportion to the socio-dynamic difference between official society and sociometric matrix.*

I have given attention to the study of the sociometric matrix because it seemed to be the key for solving many riddles. In the beginning I thought that every legitimate group has a corresponding sociometric structure. But soon I recognized that the illegitimate or informal groups too have a corres-ponding sociometric structure. I quote here from *Who Shall Survive?*, p. 111, "There is evident a trend to differentiate between the choices of the girls in respect to the collective and its function, *i.e.*, between those with whom an individual prefers to live and those with whom she prefers to work." But just as it seemed economical to describe the official society as a single social continuum formed by interdependent groups I preferred to consider the sociometric matrix as a single sociometric continuum with a varying dis-crepancy between the two continua, rarely being entirely apart and rarely being entirely identical. The sociometric matrix of a given work group may thus at times show a greater discrepancy than the one of a home group and more than the one of a play group.

Contrasts in the correlations of choices between criteria of working and living, between working and playing are therefore to be expected. My advice to define the criterion around which the group is to be formed speci-fically and concretely was motivated by the desire to attain specific re-sponses. My assumption was that vaguely defined criteria are bound to evoke vague responses from the subjects. This was the reason in early sociometric work for advising against the use of "friendship" as a criterion, for instance: "Who are your friends in town?" Friendship is actually a cluster of criteria. A sociometric friendship study is possible but it requires a theoretical preparation and analysis of the multiple criteria which enter into the social phenomenon friendship. What is true about friendship is equally true about leisure which Jennings uses in a vague fashion and which may cover innumerable things. Not all leisure activities go hand in hand with maximum spontaneity and minimum of restriction. However informal a grouping may be it is to be differentiated from its sociometric structure. We cannot, therefore, compare generally and vaguely "the inter-individual expression of choice for leisure" with the inter-individual choice for living or working together. Because leisure is a cluster of criteria one must differentiate the hundreds of leisure criteria individually from one another and must compare each separately and concretely with equally specific work and living criteria. To mention a few: blind dating, going fishing, hitch hiking, going out to dinner, dancing, accosting strangers in trains, nightclub parties, meeting strangers in hotels, visiting houses of prostitution. It is obvious that leisure can include many things, like friendship. What perception is evoked in a subject when you tell him "Choose your leisure associates"? What is included in leisure, what is excluded from it? There are many, most informal situations of leisure activity: groups of people bathing together on a beach, or an adventurous hitch-hike of a few boys and girls throughout the country.

Some people think that when a group is formed casually and informally the sociometric test is unnecessary because one can see with his own eyes what the structure of this particular informal group is. The confusion of an informal group with the sociometric structure of a group has been en vogue for some time. Illustrations of this tendency can be found in Roethlisberger and Dixon's "Management and the Worker". The authors give us the impression that they have arrived at the core of the intimate structure of the work group if they compare their formation in the wiring room or in the workshop with their intimate and spontaneous grouping in recess or after work hours, when playing cards or chatting, lunching or going home together. There is no question that it is valuable to watch the interactions of the same individuals in different situations, to watch them how they interact in situations of objective responsibility, to get a specific job done in a certain time and when they act more free of such restraints in the lunch hour. But from the sociometric point of view the informal groupings must be submitted as rigorously to sociometric testing and analysis

121

as the more rigidly structured. The fact that Roethlisberger and Dixon portray their data in a sociometric manner, using the form of the sociogram does not bring them closer to the truth. As a matter of fact, the authors do not deal with the deeper dynamics of social groups but with its external manifestations. All the truly dynamic conflicts between employer and employee, labor unions and the owners of industries, between engineers and foremen, foremen and workers are silently passed over. They are not only passed over ideologically or politically, but, what is from a sociometric point of view worse still, the instruments which are able to bring to the surface the sociodynamic forces which operate in an industrial setting are not used, the sociometric instruments of action research[2] in cooperation with the participants. It all culminates in the leaving out the workers themselves from the research undertaken. They are observed, interviewed, analyzed. But they are not given the freedom to think, choose, decide and act. As the action research is not started by them, it is not carried out and not ended by them. It is a research enterprise void of a clear goal, perhaps for the sake of a platonic-utopian science, perhaps for the benefit of employers, it is certainly not consciously constructed to give the workers themselves full participation in matters which are vital to their life. The two writers were probably in fear that by giving the workers prestige and power in the research enterprise instead of keeping them subordinate, keeping the matter nice, sweet and commonplace—and every worker in his place—might end in a bedlam and turn the factory over to a psychiatrist—or they have the still greater fear that sociometric action research will end in social revolution. They do not realize that social revolution is rather promoted than prevented by half-hearted social researches which do not go the whole way of action and analysis but permit the dynamic forces to operate uninhibitedly underground. It is, on the other hand, only the stubbornly carried out one hundred per cent sociometric process from both sides, employers and workers which may produce a true measure against revolutions and may put into the hands of man *techniques of prevention of social revolutions* in the future. Such techniques and skills are not learned in fear and cowardice but only in the course of carefully prepared experimentation. Sociometry is the only promise visible on the horizon to replace revolutions of dictatorship by *revolutions of cooperation.*

---

[2] As it is out of sociometric research that action research and action methods grew, we should watch everyone who gives lip and "print" service to the terms but avoids the operations of action.

An illustration of a similar type are the streetcorner studies by Whyte. However subtle his observational studies and near-sociometric the results, they are inaccurate as well as ineffective because they do not warm up the tramps, the bums, etc., to any action of their own. His sociograms are impressionistic, put together by empathetic participant-observers but not by the participant-actors themselves.

This fundamental position is not altered by the evidence that in every group formation, besides the official criterion, for instance, living together in a particular house or working together on a special job, many "latent" criteria operate, for instance, the search for making dates with co-workers, the desire to find people of a certain political orientation in the work group, perhaps in order to form a socialistic or a fascistic club, gaining members for the Knights of Columbus or the Communist Party, making friends with those who are interested in fishing or stamp collecting. On the other hand we know from sociometric research that in highly spontaneous groups not determined by coercive social pressures as work groups various latent criteria operate which are highly restraining in character, collectivistic and compulsory. A man may pick out as associates on a fishing trip people who have a higher economic and social status than himself; going fishing may be the official criterion of a particular, informal group, but making good business contacts or increasing one's pull in the ruling political party may be latent collective criteria which may operate just as rigidly here and distort the naivete of the informal relationships, as informal criteria frequently distort the character of the more rigorous groups.

A third illustration of the difficulties which arise if the difference between external society and the sociometric matrix is neglected is a recent article[3] by Helen Jennings. It deals with the phenomenon of leisure activity. But it does not make clear to which the dimension the groups formed by leisure activities belong, to the external society or to the sociometric matrix. To this obscurity it adds a new one—from a sociometric point of view leisure, just like friendship, is a cluster of criteria and not a single criterion. As Jennings defines leisure vaguely in her test instructions the data she obtains from her subjects have little validity, as much or as little as the validity one gets if one asks an in-

---

[3] See Helen H. Jennings, "Sociometric Differentiation of the Psychegroup and the Sociogroup", SOCIOMETRY, Vol. X, No. 1, 1947, p. 71.

dividual "Who are your friends?" As a matter of fact, she is committing here the same error with leisure activity for which we have criticized others—the use of no criterion or vague ones like friendship, which were then classified as near-sociometric researches. It is not more sociometric as ask "Whom do you choose as partner for leisure activities" without specifying the particular activity you, or better the subject, is concerned with at the time of the test. Leisure activity can be playing chess, or playing baseball, driving a car or boxing. These activities, although they may be leisure, are determined by rigid rules of the game which must be just as strictly observed as certain codes in a workshop or within a family setting. However great the spontaneity in the making of a choice of partners, however apparently unlimited by external coercion, it is often limited by the skill and competence of the subject and that of the partner. Engaging in sexual intercourse with casual partners may also fall into the class of leisure activities, however, it is such a singularly specific criterion that it cannot be thrown into the same basket with all the other leisure criteria, merely because they all seem to imply freedom from collective coercion. As a matter of fact, even in the choice of a sexual partner or in the pursuit of one, strictly collective criteria play a great role. A man may go out with a girl because he wants to take her away from his friend, not because he loves her particularly. It is not enjoyment which he looks for, it is revenge. A girl may choose as a sexual partner a man whom she does not love; she chooses him, not because she likes him better than anyone else but because her mother likes him, or because he is wealthy, or because he is the town hero and everyone thinks he is wonderful. Here we see collective factors determining private decisions.

The lack of sensitivity for the social criteria which so many sociometrists indicate in their writings may well be due to the circumstance that most investigations are carried out on a diagnostic level only. Therefore, for them the choices made by the subjects propelled by a specific situation are not resolutions to be turned into immediate action; they are just wishes which are to remain on the wish level, phantasies and social projections which may have induced some commentators to consider the sociometric test as a projection technique. Far be it from me to underestimate the many contributions which diagnostic sociometric research has made, but it should be remembered that classic sociometry started out as an action research on a large scale (read *Who Shall Sur-*

124

vive?). That was its heroic time, when choices were choices, actions were actions. Sociometry was then seen through the "eyes" of the participants. It awakened the social scientist to a new conscience and it paved the way for the revision of the experimental method in social science.

The difference between diagnostic and action procedures has been at the very core of sociometric theory since its early days. However, there is a chronic preference of research men for diagnostic procedure as against action procedures. This preference is rooted in a veritable resistance against giving up certain deeply ingrained perceptions and habits of orderly scientific behavior. The perception of the scientist as an observer of subjects and objects and as an experimenter in the safety of a laboratory milieu seems to contradict the perception of the scientist as an actor, an *"action agent,"* with the subjects as co-actors and co-scientists, the experimental situation moving from the laboratory into life itself. Actually the older perception is not given up, it is well integrated into the newer perception of the *action scientist.* The resistance comes from another source, the confusion of action methods and action research with the old controversy between scientific and applied; to "apply" is considered to give less status to a scientist than to establish basic principles. However, sociometric action theory is not the outcome of an emphasis upon pragmatic and empirical thinking but the result of a *critique of the total methodology of social science.* The conclusion was that a theory of human relations cannot be founded without propelling human groups into action. The great misunderstanding, even among sociometrists comes from a *neglect of studying experimentally the warming up process taking place in the making of a choice, a resolution of performance and of action.* It may be useful to differentiate among sociometric criteria between *diagnostic* and *action* criteria. An illustration of a diagnostic criterion is "whom do you invite to have meals in your house." It is specific but it does not provide the subjects with the opportunity to get into immediate action and it does not justify the sociometric director to prompt the subjects to act; in other words the test provides only for information but not for action. An action criterion involves a different situation. It prompts the subjects to a different warming up process. It requires different instructions than a diagnostic test. The settlers come to a town meeting and they are addressed by the sociometric counselor *as a group:* "You are preparing to move into the new settlement Centerville. Whom do you want there as a neighbor?" This is obviously a situation which is different from the diagnostic case. The people have an immediate goal to which they are warmed up. The choices they make are very real things, they are not only wishes. They are prompted to act at present and in the presence of the group. In the diagnostic case the reference is to the past, however crucial; the diagnostic approach can easily be changed to an actional one. Choices are then decisions for action, not attitudes.

THE SOCIOMETRIC SYSTEM

By J. L. Moreno

There is a notable discrepancy between the sociometric system as outlined in the first edition of *Who Shall Survive?* (1934) and the second, revised edition (1953). In the first edition sociometry is described as a subsystem of socionomy, "That part of socionomy which deals with the mathematical study of psychological properties of populations, the experimental technique of and the results obtained by application of quantitative methods is called *sociometry*." (p. 10) In the second edition sociometry is so defined (p. 48-59) that it appears as the all-encompassing system. It appears as if I have reversed my position as to the relationship between socionomy and sociometry. This is a misunderstanding and may require some explanation.

The sociometric system is not an all-encompassing system of social relations, but itself a sub-system within a larger framework. But I have never spelled this out properly and presented a complete scheme. The over-all top of the system is socionomy; it has three branches, sociodynamics, sociometry and sociatry. Socionomy is the science of social laws (or whatever modern equivalent one would give to "law"). Sociodynamics is a science of the structure of social aggregates, of single groups and of group clusters (it overlaps in part with the area which is often labelled group dynamics). Sociometry is the science of socius measurement, an architectonically structured system of social measurements with sociometric tests at its base (which cannot be bypassed); it is not quantitative sociology but the socius quantified, the emphasis is upon socius first, metrum second. And last in line is sociatry, the science of social healing. However, one depends upon the other. In a practical frame of reference the sequence of order is reversed, the processes of social healing come first and the science of social laws comes last. In contrast with the current custom to call all techniques sociometric techniques, from sociometric tests to roleplaying and sociodrama, this would designate their distribution into a number of categories, sociodynamic, sociometric and sociatric techniques.

The reason why sociometry, although theoretically speaking a sub-system, has been continuously put into the center of presentation and has received the major part of the attention in the course of years, can be explained historically by the conditions in which the social sciences were when sociometry emerged. In the first twenty-five years of the twentieth century all

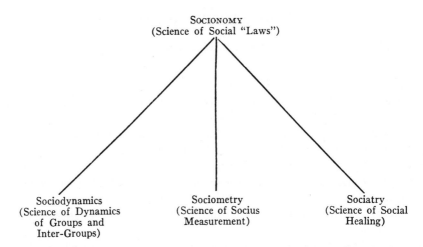

SOCIONOMY
(Science of Social "Laws")

Sociodynamics
(Science of Dynamics
of Groups and
Inter-Groups)

Sociometry
(Science of Socius
Measurement)

Sociatry
(Science of Social
Healing)

social measurement was of a demographic character, it was demometry. It was then of importance to develop sociometric instruments and to demonstrate the possibility that besides the vital statistics of demometry a direct study of the actual structure of groups can be made and measured. The link between the socius and the metrum had then a revolutionary character. It seemed didactic and opportune to focus the attention upon sociometry as a core. This was not only due to my own, but to the great interest which the instrumentalities of sociometry aroused whereas its theoretical implications were overlooked.

The sociometric system throws a new light upon the scientific method. The difference between natural sciences, such as physics and biology, and the human sciences, such as psychology and sociology was already put forth by the classification of Dilthey[1] (1833–1911)—and later by some others, e.g., Rickert[2]—which is based on "comprehension" and "explanation." But the distinction of carrying this thought from the philosophical area into science and from theory into practice, into the area of experimentation, belongs to sociometry.[3]

The physicist who studies the laws of matter, such as of stone, soil, water, fire, examines these phenomena outwardly. Since these matters are deprived of

---

[1] Dilthey, "Einleitung in die Geisteswissenschaften" (1883); French trans., "Introduction à l'étude des sciences humains" (1942).

[2] Heinrich Rickert, "Kulturwissenschaft und Naturwissenschaft" (1899).

[3] See Nurettin Kösemihal, "Sociometry and Cybernetics," *Group Psychotherapy,* XII, No. 1 (1959), 97–101.

life and consciousness, they cannot take "roles" and control themselves. The biologist who studies the organisms of man and animal and the relations between phenomena of life can attain his purpose—as can the physicist—by examining them externally without referring to the consciousness of organisms. In biology what is examined is not the relations of consciousness but only the relations of organisms. Only man, in the sociology of his own world, can take roles and can experiment in an autonomous manner.

Up until now, in the studies of animal and human psychologies, the observer or the investigator has studied the subjects from the outside, as in physics or in biology. But in order to "understand" animal psychology completely we must study consciousness, perceptions, and feelings from the inside. We do not have any common bond that provides the direct relations of consciousness between animals and the observer who is a human being. The knowledge which is obtainable of the psychology, consciousness, and perception of animals is limited to observing the exteriorized movements of the animals, such as mimicry, gestures, behavior, deportment, etc.

It is impossible for the investigator to give roles to animal subjects, as for instance, mice, guinea-pigs, monkeys, and dogs, and to use their feelings and perceptions. Therefore, animal psychology will stay on the surface of animal consciousness and will not penetrate into its depths. The position of the psychologists who study human psychology, and of the social psychologists, sociometrists, sociologists, and social scientists who study human relations is very different from the position of animal psychologists. Here the subjects are not mere mice, guinea-pigs, monkeys, or dogs; they are men. The investigator can use the consciousness of the subjects, each of whom is a human being, if not directly, by means of language and intuition which may throw light on the darkest corners of consciousness. Psychologists and sociologists have studied both human consciousness and the relationship among men from the outside (as a physicist studies stone and soil, or as a biologist studies organisms). The only system that first allowed the subjects to participate fully in the experiment as actors was the sociometric system; it saw them as the persons who participate actively in a common purpose, so that they will be "actors-participators-observers" and a cultural system will be put into operation piece by piece and portrayed in action.

The concepts of "group of organisms" and "organism-environment" can be accepted only by a social observer or a social spectator who looks at the phenomena from the outside. A real social investigator who wants to understand human consciousness and its relations from the inside, intrinsically does not depend on the concepts of "group of organisms" or "organism-environment" but on concepts of "group of actors" or "actors-in-situation."[4]

A "group of actors" is very different from a "group of organisms"; a "group of actors" is a "we," a group of creators, and not a "they" like a "group of organisms."

The first duty of a science, which is based on "actional theory," must be to separate the organism from the actor and behavior from action. Here is Parson's error:[5] for him, organism and actor, behavior and action are one and the same thing. A behavioral science and an actional science are of a different order.

The actor's play can not be considered the same or identical as the things given by the observer. These sometimes can be complementary to each other, but never identical. If "action" marks the living existence of movements and facts, "behavior" marks the *observation* of the movements and facts.

In a science which is based on the theory of "organism-behavior" and which observes the phenomena from the outside, organism comes first and actor second.

A *real* action theory is based on the active interactional concepts of the world of actors, such as "actorial" system, spontaneity, creativity, and warming up.

The system of relations and codes that unite actors and the system of relations that can be observed among organisms constitute two different areas. The actorial system depends upon the consensus that can take place only in an encounter of actors. This secret and imminent consensus is of essential significance in the actualization of the ongoing research. And often even this is not enough. The observers have to participate in the process of production and turn into actors in order to attain an unbroken, integrated social system.

---

[4] J. L. Moreno, *Who Shall Survive?* (New York: Beacon House, Inc., 1934 and 1953); French trans., *Fondements de la Sociometrie,* "Preface," pp. xxv–xxx.
[5] T. Parsons, *The Social System* (Glencoe, Ill.: The Free Press, 1951).

PART II

Methods

A. Sociometric Measurement

INTRODUCTION

By Joan H. Criswell

In the analysis of sociometric data, special problems are posed by the fact that an individual score represents a focus of forces originating in the subject himself and in other group members. Thus, each member provides one view of the group in terms of the relationships between him and each other individual. Ideally, a complete picture of the group would be obtained if all significant intermember relations were determined, and the resulting group structures were combined in some suitable manner.

One problem of scoring is, therefore, to arrive at a mathematically manageable and general expression for each individual with the least possible sacrifice of the relational nature of the measure. It is desirable also that several such scores be obtained by choosing criteria that cover all significant aspects of the group's activity. Besides individual scores, measures must be developed expressing attributes of the group as a whole. Scores representing the status, attitude, or other characteristic, of a group or subgroup should, like individual scores, retain as far as possible the relational character of the data on which they are based. Although the preceding considerations are perhaps peculiarly sociometric, problems shared with scoring methods in general include attainment of scales that are unidimensional and characterized by equal intervals and a zero point.

Development of measurement methods cannot follow a logical series of stages, since it must depend on the interest and creative bent of each experimenter. It might be considered, for example, that the first problem of measurement is to establish the fundamental characteristics that will completely account for the behavior under consideration. However, as in other psychological areas, this is being accomplished along with methods of setting up mathematically useful scoring devices.

The earliest form of the sociometric technique attempted to set up a picture of the group and the individuals within it by asking a question intimately tied up with some group activity of importance to the members. Thus, in analyzing classroom groups the question chosen was, "With whom would you like to sit in school?" When rejections were used, they related similarly to the choosing criterion, "With whom would you not want to sit?" Although this type of question is of obvious usefulness, when used by itself it fails to reveal the elements that enter into the choice or rejection. In order to determine the bases of choice, it is necessary either to correlate sociometric data with other measures or to vary the type of question asked of the subject.

Wherry's study of "buddy ratings" (part II A, chapter 5) employs an indirect method of determining the meaning of leadership choices by including them in a factorial study along with a variety of related ratings and grades. Students' nominations of fellow students with "most" or "least" desirable officer traits were found to have, as hypothesized, high loading on the "leadership" factor, and proved in fact to be the purest measure of leadership.

A more direct approach attempts to elicit the chooser's own perception of his choice. The observation that mutual pairs increased with age had early suggested that mental growth involved choosing to an increasing extent on the basis of expectation of reciprocation from others. Tagiuri, by means of his "relational analysis" (part III C, chapter 6), focuses directly on this perception of the attitudes of other group members, since the chooser is required to designate not only those he prefers or rejects, but also those who will choose or reject him. Tagiuri's studies lead into a further problem of measurement by bringing out the role of personal needs in sociometric choice. Although there is a fair probability that a person will see himself as preferred by a person who actually fails to choose him, it is rare for an individual to perceive a preferred person as likely to reject him. His need to be liked by a preferred person enters into his perception. The measurement of need through sociometric questions has been investigated by Gardner and Thompson, and an adaptation of the sociometric method for either individual or group use has been developed by them for several needs from the Murray list, e.g., need for achievement-recognition, playmirth, succorance, etc.[1]

An aspect of measurement which produces different problems of treatment according to the type of question asked is the use of one-way versus two-way choice. One-way choices are those in which no reciprocation can necessarily be expected by the chooser, as when he chooses another as a leader or when he chooses on the basis of some need, such as dependency, that is complementary to another, such as dominance. This distinction, as well as some of the different treatments possible, is discussed by Criswell in connection with some other sociometric concepts used in personnel administration (part II A, chapter 2). The treatment of one-way choice is likely to become more prominent in the future, if more attention is devoted to personal needs as the basis of choice and to followership as well as leadership and other group roles. Important relation-

---

[1] E. F. Gardner, and G. G. Thompson, *Social Relations and Morale in Small Groups* (New York: Appleton-Century-Crofts, Inc., 1956).

ships may spring from complementary activities, and these may be approached by combining interlocking one-way choice criteria.

The combination of individual scores into a pattern measure is attacked by Massarik and others in analyzing organizational effectiveness (part II A, chapter 3). Unusual difficulties lurk in this particular area. One problem lies in the possibility of overlap between different scores. For example, an individual with large choice output or input or both will have a higher probability of attaining reciprocation, and therefore will automatically tend to have a higher reciprocation score. In the Massarik study, as the authors point out, there is systematic overlap between such scores as perception of prescribed job relationships and perception of actual job relationships.

The attempt to make explicit the many-faceted aspects of sociometric choice is a healthy development, since the use of differently derived sociometric scores as if they were equivalent has been a source of confusion. Examples of such usages have been failure to discriminate between one-way and two-way choice, using statements of prescribed relationships as if they were the same as desired relationships, and drawing no distinction between statements of actual and desired relationships. This has led to ambiguities in the interpretation of the reliabilities, validities, and other results based on these essentially different indices.

Northway's paper on a longitudinal program of research (part II A, chapter 4) adds the time dimension to multi-relational scoring. Her procedure represents not only the status of the child but also the constellation of statuses of those who choose him. This type of approach essentially represents the person as the focus of a network of relations in the group by including not only the choosers of the individual but also those who choose the choosers. Such measures retain typical relational quality of sociometric data that has been lost in simpler types of scoring.

Scores representing entire subgroups or groups are discussed in Criswell's consideration of sociometric concepts in personnel administration (part II A, chapter 2), in which the use of scores representing preference for an in-group over an out-group is considered. In connection with these scores, it is important to note that the choosing group's choices of itself and of the out-group must both be taken care of. Another aspect of scoring of the group as a whole is measurement of the social distance between any two members. A simple way of doing this is to average the value of the choices passing between any pair, giving some differential weighting to first, second, and third choices. Campbell's method of weighting scores (part II A, chapter 1) offers a rationale for weighting of choices and also a suggestion for weighting "no mentions."

Reading the papers that have been mentioned in this discussion will reveal how much remains to be done to approach closer to the ideal of true relational scoring. However, important groundwork is being laid, through identification of relevant attributes of choice and accurate representation of the relational material that must be combined later into more complex scores. Some indices based on relational patterns have been developed.

Studies currently underway on sociometric scaling and bases of choice attest to the vigorous development of work in the field of sociometric measurement. The result is that, even as this book is published, new results will be forthcoming for which the present compilation can provide an essential introduction and foundation.

A RATIONALE FOR WEIGHING FIRST, SECOND, AND THIRD SOCIOMETRIC CHOICES

By Donald T. Campbell

A perennial problem is the differential weighting of the first, second, and third choices in a sociometric or nominations setup. Good standard procedure is to disregard the order of choice and use the total of all mentions. This procedure will provide a perfect rank correlation with any differential weighting formula if the first, second, and third choices, when analyzed separately, rank the nominees in the same order. With large numbers of judges this will indeed be the case in many situations, or near enough so that differential weighting is meaningless. However, the research person often feels that one first choice is worth considerably more than one third choice and would like to have this difference reflected in the final composite score.

When differential weighting is resorted to, the usual practice is to give a series of unit weights to the three choices. Thus, the first choice might be given three votes, the second two, and the third one. The basic unrecognized problem here is not so much the arbitrary character of the differential weighting among first, second, and third choices, as it is the unnoticed differential between no mention at all and third mention. In such a scheme it is assumed that the jump from no mention at all to third mention is equivalent to the jump from third to second and from second to first. This is an obviously false assumption and arises from interpreting the nominations data in a voting type context. In any situation where differential weighting is to be considered, the differential weighting of no mention versus third mention is the most important weighting problem.

A more consistent rationale can be developed by assuming that what a nominations ballot or sociometric questionnaire asks for is the first few rankings of a potential ranking of all personnel aboard. *The best guess as to the value assigned a nonmentioned person is the average of the unused ranks.* If in addition, the assumption made of a normal distribution of the trait in question, the rationale takes a form which emphasizes the special worth of a first mention. The procedure may be illustrated by a hypothetical case of a sociometric study asking for three choices in a classroom of ten pupils. A first choice may be regarded as indicating that the person mentioned lies in the area under the normal curve containing the extreme 10% and bounded by $+1.28\sigma$ and infinity. The appropriate weight for a first choice would be a mean value for this area. But since tables providing this are not readily available, a median may be used, with but little distortion if the total number of persons being chosen from is large. The median is the 5‰σ value, 1.65. The sigma value for a second choice is the median of the area from 1.28 to .88, which is 1.04. The sigma value for the third choice is .67. The sigma value for no choice at all is the median of the remaining 70 per cent of the area, which is —.39. If for computational purposes we give no mention a value of 0, and express the other weights as approximate whole values we get the following: no mention = 0, third choice = 5, second choice = 7, and first choice = 10. For an application in which there are potentially 70 persons who could be mentioned, the sigma values would be 2.45 for first choice, 2.03 for second, 1.80 for third and —.11 for no mention. Approximate whole values for this setting are 12, 10, 9, and 0 respectively, showing increased gap between no mention and third mention, with less interval between third and first. As the potential pool of persons who may be named increases, the similarity between the weighting procedure and the pooling of all mentions disregarding order becomes greater, as far as rank order within the pool is concerned. This procedure of treating the data as ratings rather than as votes should increase the comparability of scores between groups of different sizes. For such purposes, expression of reputational score in terms of an average sigma score value would be indicated.

In view of the general psychometric experience that differential weighting makes little difference, the procedure here outlined is not recommended for general use. For those who persist in preferring some scheme which gives more weight to a first choice than a third, a rational weighting system is here offered.

SOCIOMETRIC CONCEPTS IN PERSONNEL ADMINISTRATION*

By Joan H. Criswell

An essential element of personnel administration is suitable assignment, placement of workers not only in appropriate jobs but also in congenial work groups. In both of these functions sociometric choosing procedures are coming to be recognized as of considerable promise. Thus the group status an individual achieves in various situations might be used to indicate the social skills and insights needed in administration, liaison, or public relations work. In every job also, each worker's group position is important as an element in the maintenance of morale.

But before the most efficient use can be made of these techniques in personnel testing and placement there is need for clarification of fundamental statistical concepts particularly those stemming from a psychometric base. Certain semantic confusions have produced both inadequate experimental design and misinterpretation of results. There has been, for example, widespread failure to obtain reliability coefficients for sociometric tests. There has been discussion of validity when validation was irrelevant, as well as omission of validation which was called for. Some lack of imagination in exploring experimental data has arisen from excessive adherence to psychometric procedures which minimize treatment of interpersonal relationships.

The preceding considerations suggested that an attempt to clarify certain key concepts might lead to more cleancut experimental procedure. The discussion of these points will make few references to specific reports, since comments refer either to unpublished research with which the author has been in contact or to reports of the last ten years, a period already well covered by Loomis and Pepinsky (9). The ideas presented are those that occurred to the writer during a recent review of the literature and which seemed to be of possible value in more sharply focussing personnel research. Definitions offered are intended as suggestive rather than final.

Psychometrics versus sociometrics. A sociometrist working with

---

* The opinions and assertions in this paper are those of the writer and are not to be construed as official or reflecting the views of the Navy Department or the Naval service at large.

psychometricians finds necessary some practical definition of his field which will approximately indicate where psychometrics ends and sociometrics begins. Failure to delimit these areas can lead to setting up an essentially sociometric research in a psychometric way or vice versa.

A working definition used by the writer is that sociometric procedures are those which elicit the pattern of distribution of goal-directed energy in a group, i.e., the strength and direction of inter-individual associations as they occur in the group's orientation toward the achievement of a specified end. Part of the determination of this energy pattern is the measurement of the degree to which the system is characterized by smooth functioning or by dissipation of energy through internal cleavage.

Thus group morale becomes definable as adequacy of amount and smoothness of distribution of the group's goal-directed energy. This concept can be thought of as paralleling that of individual social adjustment: the well adjusted person feels mentally "comfortable" with neither too high nor too low an energy output and without crippling energy conflicts.

Psychometric procedures, even when they sample social behavior, do not generate group structure or express the status of the individual as a function of his attractions to others and theirs to him within the framework of a shared activity. There is, in addition, a fundamental difference between the psychometric rating of traits and sociometric rating of strength of preference.

Ratings of degree of interpersonal attraction are not evaluations in the psychometric sense of an external appraisal with the group roles of rater and ratee eliminated from consideration. In any sociometric rating the interpersonal relation and the group activity are integral to the response made. The rating is an expression of the strength of interpersonal attraction, not an evaluation of an abstract characteristic.

The emphasis of sociometrics on pattern needs to be remembered in planning or evaluating research projects. Definition of the experimental goal should make clear whether psychometric personality ratings or structural delineation is desired. The depth of the structural analysis should also be decided upon, since two types are possible: the one-way technique which produces partial structure, and the more typical two-way technique in which reciprocal or non-reciprocal structures are obtained.

As social measurement has developed in personnel administration great emphasis has understandably been placed on determination of leadership or supervisory ability. This interest has resulted in use of a one-way technique in which the criterion of choice defines complementary group roles for chooser and chosen, and asks for selection of persons for one of the designated roles. Usually individuals are asked to operate within the frame of reference of chooser as follower and chosen as leader. They may, for example, indicate those they would want or not want as squad captains. They may rank the group in order of preference or rate their attraction to each member in the specified role.

In this procedure reciprocal attraction would be in the general pattern of "A chooses B as leader and B chooses A as follower," but only attractions for A or B as leader are obtained. The concept of reciprocation is therefore irrelevant to such a set-up and reciprocation appears only insofar as choosers bring a friendship factor into their expressions of preference. Reciprocal attractions could, however, be directly obtained by dovetailing two one-way experiments, as when supervisors might designate the employees each wants from a clerical pool and at the same time the pool employees might select the bosses they would like from the supervisory group.

The sociogram resulting from one-way procedures primarily delineates concentration of attractions and repulsions on certain individuals. Cleavage may be revealed if subgroups prefer leaders from their own membership. Reciprocal relationships appear in spite of their irrelevance to the criterion requirements because even in selection on a competence basis the factor of companionship enters in.

By-product reciprocal patterns can also appear even in connection with psychometric ratings of "traits" such as personal appearance or honesty, when all members of a group rate each other. Friends may tend to group by rating each other relatively favorably. Methods are being developed for measuring the degree to which a trait rating or a one-way pattern is affected by this submerged two-way pattern. These methods will be touched on later in discussing the sociomatrix.

One-way experiments can be important in determining, for example, whether commissioned officers and recruits have the same evaluation of recruit leaders, or in setting up measures with which to correlate leadership aptitude tests. Misuse of the procedure can occur if the two-way material incidentally obtained is taken as fully representative of group mutuality structures. In this case attempts may be made to determine full structure by in some way partialling out the rated competence factors and leaving the liking or companionship factor. The better and more direct way, if both leadership and mutuality structures are desired, is to use a suitable variety of choice criteria at the start.

The more typical sociometric experiment is aimed at two-way reciprocable interpersonal relations; subjects are asked to choose other persons for work cooperation or recreational association in a specifically designated situation ranging all the way from complexly organized and highly skilled work groups to unorganized leisure-time association. This type of experiment is familiar and requires little discussion; its common defect is failure to explore fully the data obtained.

Significant data are sometimes gathered and then largely discarded, individual social status being determined merely by the number of choices received. The group structure is either not plotted or is plotted and then largely ignored, little attention being paid to specific connections existing between overchosen individuals, overchosen and underchosen, between members of different cliques, etc. Opportunities to enlarge the experiment by obtaining group morale indices or production records are frequently passed up. For this reason the accusation has sometimes justly been made that a so-called "sociometric" experiment was actually psychometric. In these cases data which could have given a multidimensional picture of individuals and of the group were flattened out into a one-dimensional score.

Technique, test, or criterion. The method of choice under a criterion has probably suffered considerably by being called indiscriminately a "sociometric test." This designation has brought with it all the standard concepts of reliability and validity, imperfectly defined in relation to psychometric work and even more confusing when automatically applied to preference data.

A better because non-committal designation would be "sociometric technique," since the procedure is applicable variously as basic research method, as test of social aptitudes, and as criterion for social aptitude tests. This usefulness arises from the fact that the choosing process results in an actual sampling of responses which form an integral part of many situations, in particular, job performance and school progress.

As basic research instrument the technique has not of course been a "test" in the usual sense and has required no routine demonstration of its intrinsic validity and the stability of its findings. Such preoccupations not only raise irrelevant issues but can limit experimentation by implying that stable "reliable" elements of status or structure are more interesting and worthy of study than fluctuating elements.

The use of the word "test" also leads to difficulties when the method really does function in this way. When so used, the test's reliability should be high and validity should be demonstrated by (1) showing that intrinsically valid responses are sampled, as when a type of social status is considered a part of job achievement, or by (2) presenting a coefficient of correlation between the test and whatever related behavior it claims to predict.

The manner of use of the "test," however, has suggested that experimenters believe it to be equipped with built-in reliability and validity coefficients good for all occasions. Reliabilities called for by a particular experiment have been unreported. Or they have been stated with little additional data on how they were obtained, apparently on the assumption that a sufficiently high coefficient requires no comment. Correlation with predicted behavior has been assumed without proof. Degree of chosenness has, for example, been identified with emotional stability, or overchosen individuals have without more ado been designated as leaders. Some of this inaccuracy might be avoided if the procedure were called a "technique" until it has proved its efficiency as a test of specified behavior or social status.

As has been noted, some of the relationships sampled by sociometric methods are a part of actual work behavior and have immediate validity, especially in certain areas such as air combat teams in which sound interpersonal relations are of life-and-death importance. Interpersonal relations are in fact of considerable significance throughout any military organization in which group members must not only work together but share each other's lives twenty-four hours a day, frequently in close quarters and under conditions of hardship. The importance of a "happy ship" in avoiding accidents and performing efficiently is proverbial. For this reason the sociometric technique is important not only as test but as criterion for social aptitude tests or as criterion for itself if previous social status or structure is used to predict later social status or structure.

Sociometrists have usually not seen the possibilities of the technique as criterion measure and this development is at present in the hands of the psychometricians who have used it usually in the form of one-way rating methods. The use of the technique as criterion should be carefully distinguished from the other two meanings as a preliminary to much more extended development of this use in sociometric research. Enrichment of the measurement of social status will result in its greater effectiveness as criterion measure.

A minor confusion results from the fact that the word "criterion" is commonly and very differently used by sociometrists and psychometricians. For this reason the reader should be careful to distinguish between the two meanings in the succeeding discussion. "Criterion of choice" will mean the principle of choosing presented to a group, e.g. choosing an individual to sit by, to study with, etc. "Criterion" used alone will usually refer to the measure of the behavior which a test purports to predict and against which it is therefore validated.

Reliability as internal consistency. In social measurement as in other testing studies internal consistency is secondary to test-retest reliability which is the fundamental kind of dependability aimed at. Internal consistency coefficients cannot always be obtained even in psychometric work (speed tests and many biographical inventories are cases in point). But, when available, consistency coefficients can perform the function of establishing the maximum correlation coefficient of which a test is capable, thus indicating whether reliability is so low that some remedial measures should be taken.

Internal consistency can be determined for some types of one-way sociometric measures in which each group member ranks all or rates some or all of his companions according to his preference for them in a certain role such as supervisor. In this case, the reliability coefficient is an estimate of the stability of the mean ratings of the individuals. For high reliability the within-person variance, that is, the variance of each mean rating, should obviously be much less than the between-person variance, the variance of the entire set of means. If mean ratings range from 1 to 10, then the range of ratings of any one individual should certainly not approach this range. The formula for this reliability coefficient as developed by Horst (5) is:

$$r = 1 - \frac{\dfrac{\sum \dfrac{\sigma_i^2}{n_i - 1}}{N}}{\sigma_M^2}.$$

Where N = the number of persons,

n_i = the number of ratings for person i,

σ_i = the standard deviation of the ratings on person i,

σ_M = the standard deviation of the mean ratings for the N persons,

r = an estimate of the reliability of the individual means, M_i.

The Horst formula would not be suitable for two-way choosing procedures in which small variability of ratings is not the goal. In groups containing a great deal of reciprocated choice considerable variability of rating would be normal. Persons A and B might rate each other 1 but be rated 10 by persons C and D who rate each other 1. Individual ratings would probably vary little only for certain heavily overchosen or underchosen persons.

With two-way choice procedures any method of splitting the group into parallel halves for determination of reliability seems likely to be doomed to failure. Correlation of halves based on alternate choices or random halves of the group of individuals would probably reflect only the sampling variation of the division into halves. The choice process expressed in social structure appears to be a unity.

The lack of internal consistency indices is probably a blessing in disguise, since it will prevent sociometrists from remaining content with the more easily obtained internal consistency coefficient and failing to go on to the more fundamental long-term studies of change in test score. Only now are psychometricians beginning to reduce their reliance on the consistency coefficient in favor of studies of test score shifts over periods of months or years.

Test-retest reliability. The basic form of reliability for any test is the stability of its scores during the time interval over which the criterion is predicted. If the criterion measure, for example, final school grades, occurs one year after the test is normally given, then the test's reliability over that interval is of importance.

As Cureton has pointed out (13, p. 39) obtaining the test-retest coefficient is unnecessary if the validity coefficient is sufficiently high. Thus for an accurately predictive test actual calculation of reliability becomes a minor matter. When validity is low, however, the test-retest coefficient must be known, first, in order to establish that the test is dependable and, second, in order to determine whether real validity is obscured by the unreliability of the criterion. For the latter purpose the reliabilities of criterion and test are obtained, making the test-retest interval of the test as nearly as possible equal to the time interval between test and criterion measure. The criterion test-retest interval could of course be short. The intercorrelation of test and criterion corrected for attenuation then indicates whether satisfactory validity is actually present.

If used as test, the sociometric technique might therefore have to demonstrate a high test-retest reliability over a long time interval. If used as criterion the test-retest interval could be brief, since the criterion is not thought of as extending over a period of time. Insofar as high validity coefficients can be obtained, an analysis of reliability of sociometric measures probably will not be required.

A difficulty of sociometric test-retest administration is of course the dependence of the test on the constitution and characteristics of the social group. Any aggregate of individuals is likely to fluctuate in membership, morale, etc., over a period of time. Another possible influence toward change is the reorganization routinely following the choosing procedure. Such change factors will have to be taken account of in reliability measurement and allowed for through careful experimental design.

A word of caution seems called for on the reporting of reliability coefficients. Group structure presents many elements which can be used for predicting criteria and whose reliability may therefore become of moment. Such factors include number of choices received, number of choices given out, degree of reciprocation achieved, degree of in-group preference shown, or various combinations of measures. Since so much variety is possible, it is particularly important to identify reliability coefficients presented by stating not only the time interval and correlation method employed but also the exact responses studied. Coefficients not fully described are meaningless, however high.

For a further discussion of problems of sociometric reliability together with those of validity the reader is referred to Pepinsky's helpful article on these concepts (11).

Validity. Types of test validity can be roughly divided into three categories: (1) face validity, (2) immediate validity, and (3) predictive validity. For categories (2) and (3) the terms used are supplied by the writer for concepts which are variously referred to in the literature.

Face validity, chiefly important for public relations purposes, represents the degree to which a test looks as if it measures what it is supposed to measure. Some tests "look" valid without actually measuring effectively. Others both look valid and are so in a more fundamental sense. The choosing technique with its production of picturesque sociograms has the advantage of "looking like" social measurement. Its considerable face value has perhaps at times obscured the need for otherwise demonstrating its effectiveness.

The term "immediate validity" may be applied to tests which do not derive their value from predicting related or future behavior, as in "predictive validity," but have immediate significance for personnel or academic action. For example, grades on an academic achievement test may indicate whether the student should be dropped from school, assigned to a special class, transferred to another course, promoted, or graduated. In industry, a promotional examination may have similar significance for promotion or transfer. Tests which have such direct meaning can often be used as proficiency tests or as aptitude tests according to whether the orientation of the examiner is toward present or future action, e.g., toward current assignment or training course graduation. The sociometric test has of course direct meaning in terms of indication of desirable group assignments. This is the "intrinsic validity" which has sometimes been ascribed to it.

An important example of the use of sociometric tests in the armed forces has been its employment as "nominating technique," to establish social status of aviators in air combat groups (12). In this case aviators "nominated" or chose those with whom they would or would not want to fly. The immediate validity here is obvious. Tests having this type of validity can be used as criteria for other measures and in this case combat group status was used as criterion for ratings of personality of aviators.

Probably one of the greatest pitfalls in the use of tests having immediate validity is the assumption that predictive validity is also necessarily present. It would be, for example, incorrect to use air combat group status as an index of peacetime administrative ability without considerable follow-up of aviators in administrative assignments.

"Predictive" or remote validity is really immediate validity once removed. Ultimately a test's validation is in terms of its significance for group action such as graduating a student, or promoting or firing an employee. The test having remote validity predicts behavior which is immediately valid. Thus it may predict school grades achieved or production on the job.

Development of the sociometric test as predictive instrument has consisted of more speculation than experiment. As we have noted, this problem has produced some of the loosest identification of group status with related behavior such as leadership or emotional adjustment. When experimental work increases in this field, a fruitful line of development is possibly the validation of one sociometric test by another. In this case social status in one type of group is used as predictor of social status in another type of group. An application of such procedures in the armed forces would be to predict from certain types of status measures in a recruit training center a man's group position at an isolated shore station or in a submarine crew.

In certain organizational units periodic sociometric tests involving several choice criteria related to job competence could possibly be developed to take the place of efficiency ratings. Such a program would, of course, require that the test be carefully "built into" the organization, with employees and supervisors understanding its purpose and knowing that their choices would be carried out in reassignment.

Measurement of social status. The expression of social status, the individual's position in the group as determined by choices given and received, has shown some hesitance to leave the confines of traditional psychometric method. This is somewhat ironic, since at the same time psychometrics is attempting to develop more rounded measures in the form of pattern scores.

So far sociometry has leaned chiefly on percentile ranks, standard scores, and average ratings. One attempt to develop a different type of score has been Zeleny's inclusion in the status score of a measure of variability around the average rating (14). This looks promising, since the variety of one's impact on others may in itself be an attribute of personality.

In general the direction of progress in this area would seem to be not so much an elaboration of single measures as a development of methods of combining measures. One line of advance might be the more fruitful use of multiple criteria of choice. The writer has previously pointed out the waste involved in using multiple criteria and then discarding much of the data so obtained (2). Several criteria are sometimes used without determining intercorrelations or, even if interrelationships are measured, without measuring the distinctive contribution of each criterion. Choices may be thrown together and results treated as if made under one criterion with resulting ambiguity of interpretation, especially when status so determined is compared with that actually obtained under a single criterion.

In the use of multiple criteria of choice a beginning has been made by such workers as Bronfenbrenner (1) and Jennings (6), but much remains to be done particularly in differentiating the factors entering into choice under criteria which vary according to their emphasis upon ability and official position in the work group as against qualities entering into leisure-time companionship. A fruitful exploration of this problem will appear in the forthcoming second edition of Jennings' *Leadership and Isolation.*

Overall structural indices. In personnel administration individual social status has perhaps received more analysis than has the structure of the employee group taken as a unit. However, studies of morale and production will probably call for increased use of overall indices of group integration or cleavage. Various ratio or percentage measures of this type will be discussed in this section, matric analyses in the next section. In the following paragraphs a few index methods will be used to illustrate different types of approach and perhaps stimulate a more flexible conception of such measurement.

A fundamental dichotomy in development of integration measures is that between relative and absolute indices. Choice of one or the other type of measure may rest on theoretical considerations or on how well a specified ratio works out as predictor of behavior. The ratio developed by the writer (2, 3) for measuring cleavage or integration was a relative one based on the assumption that, as in the Weber-Fechner law, an increment to a reference value carries less psychological weight if the reference value is large than if it is small. Equal increments on the psychological scale thus represent proportional increments to the reference value. In this case the preference of a group for itself over an out-group is expressed as 2.00, if the ratio of in-group to out-group choice is twice as great as that occurring when chance alone determines whether a choice is directed into or away from a group. A value of 3.00 would represent an actual ratio three times as great as chance, regardless of the absolute sizes of the obtained and chance ratios.

Thus if a white group gives W choices to whites and C choices to Negroes and is expected to give on a chance basis W′ choices to whites and C′ choices to Negroes, then the obtained ratio is W/C and the chance ratio is W′/C′. Dividing the obtained (W/C) by the chance (W′/C′) ratio, the preference index of whites for whites is then:

$$R = \frac{C'W}{W'C}$$

A white group which should give 80 per cent of its choices to whites (4:1 ratio) and actually gives 90 per cent to whites (9:1 ratio) is considered to have more self-preference (2.25) than a group which should give 50 per cent to whites and actually gives 60 per cent (self-preference of 1.50).

Another relative approach, one which the writer has used in unpublished research, is to use the logarithm of the previously stated ratio ($R = \log C'W/W'C$) as self-preference measure instead of the ratio itself. This is often done in practice by plotting the values on semi-logarithmic paper. The essential advantage of this logarithmic expression is that it makes the distribution of ratios more symmetrical by pulling in extreme values above 1.00 (the point of neutrality) and expanding those below 1.00. Ratio distributions frequently show considerable skewness and it may be desirable for various reasons to reduce this.

In the second type of approach to cleavage or integration measurement the deviation from chance is expressed as an absolute instead of a relative difference. In one such type of measure the chance per cent of in-group or out-group choice is calculated and subtracted from the corresponding ob-tained per cent. The deviation from chance is of course the same for eithei in-group or out-group choice and is negative when preference for the out-group is shown. According to this method, a white group which should by chance give 80 per cent of its choices to whites and actually gives 90 per cent, shows a self-preference of 10 per cent. A white group which should give 50 per cent in-group choices and actually gives 60 per cent shows the same amount of self-preference.

A procedure showing features of both absolute and relative measures would be to express the absolute percentage deviation from chance as a pro-portion of the maximum deviation. This method might be employed in an attempt to allow for the fact that some groups such as large majorities have only a short distance to go before reaching the maximum self-preference possible, while other groups have a large percentage separating them from the maximum. In the preceding example, one group can show a maximum self-preference of only 20 per cent, while the other can reach 50 per cent. In order to allow for these different maxima one might express preference as the proportion of the maximum achieved. For the preceding two groups the self-preference measures would then be respectively $10/20 = 50$ per cent, and $10/50 = 20$ per cent. Preference for the out-group would have to be divided by the complements of the denominators just given, 80 per cent and 50 per cent.

Application of such a maximum preference method to the ratio first described in this section would of course be difficult if not impossible be-cause of the fact that the maximum ratio of this type has a denominator of zero and therefore cannot be determined. Some type of approximation might, however, be possible.

Undoubtedly other methods could be developed, each giving a differ-ent ranking of groups in order of self-preference. In an unpublished paper Paul Lazarsfeld has presented a valuable discussion of the problem of choosing an appropriate index (8). He points out the possible discrepancies between different types of indices and suggests that at the beginning of an experiment several feasible measures be selected and then tried out on various possible distributions of the data to determine how much the indices conflict in their ordering of the preference of the same groups. If possible methods prove to have large "areas of ambiguity" in which they contradict each other, the experimenter will have to try some combination of them or choose one on the basis of theoretical considerations. Choice of one method rather than another must ultimately be a matter of the judgment of the experimenter.

The sociomatrix. Forsyth and Katz have shown that a matrix of interpersonal ratings or choices can be resolved mathematically into groupings of individuals who tend to prefer each other to the rest of the test population (4, 7). Such analysis shows promise of being particularly useful in populations containing no easily identifiable cleavage-producing categories such as race, sex, or age. Under such circumstances seemingly homogeneous employee groups may nevertheless be analyzable into cliques the basis for which can then be investigated. Additional matrix methods have been recently developed by Leon Festinger (reported in a recent issue of *Human Relations*), and by Luce and Perry (10).

A technique for ordering the sociomatrix on a rational basis as opposed to Katz's trial-and-error basis has been devised by C. O. Beum at the Bureau of Naval Personnel and will be presented later in SOCIOMETRY. A new use of this type of analysis has been to determine to what degree a personal liking factor enters into ratings of competence. If, for example, naval recruiters rate their colleagues on general recruiting efficiency, the extent to which associates rate each other relatively highly and thus form groupings can be separated out mathematically. Other possibilities of the matrix are being explored.

Summary. Discussion was devoted to fundamental sociometric concepts important in personnel administration. An attempt was made to differentiate the sociometric from the psychometric approach so that possibilities of typically sociometric projects could be more fully exploited. Reliability, validity, and scoring of social status were discussed. The structure of the employee group was considered from the viewpoint of analyses by ratio methods and by the sociomatrix. Future developments are seen in the direction of the use of more criteria of choice in order to produce a multi-dimensional picture of social status and group structure which would be expressed in various types of pattern measures. A more flexible attack on analysis of structure by indices may lead to new measures in this field. Finer analysis of the sociomatrix is also in progress.

BIBLIOGRAPHY

1. Bronfenbrenner, Urie. A constant frame of reference for sociometric research. SOCIOMETRY, 1944, 7, 40-75.
2. Criswell, Joan H. The measurement of group integration. SOCIOMETRY, 1947, 10, 259-267.
3. Criswell, Joan H. A sociometric study of race cleavage in the classroom. *Archives of Psychology*, 1939, 233, 1-82.
4. Forsyth, E., and Katz, L. A matrix approach to the analysis of sociometric data: preliminary report. SOCIOMETRY, 9, 1946, 340-347.
5. Horst, Paul. A generalized expression of the reliability of measures. *Psychometrika*, 1949, 14, 21-32.
6. Jennings, Helen R. Leadership and Isolation. New York, Longmans, Green, 1943. (second edition, 1950.)
7. Katz, Leo. On the matric analysis of sociometric data. SOCIOMETRY, 1947, 10, 233-241.
8. Lazarsfeld, Paul. Some notes on the use of indices in social research. Unpublished.
9. Loomis, C. P., and Pepinsky, H. B. Sociometry, 1937-1947: contributions to theory and method. SOCIOMETRY, 1948, 11, 262-283.
10. Luce, R. Duncan, and Perry, Albert D. A method of matrix analysis of a group structure. *Psychometrika*, 1949, 14, 95-116.
11. Pepinsky, Pauline Nichols. The meaning of "validity" and "reliability" as applied to sociometric tests. *Journal of Educational and Psychological Measurement*, 1949, 9, 39-49.
12. Vaughn, C. L. The nominating technique. In G. A. Kelly (Ed.) *New methods in applied psychology*. College Park: Univ. of Maryland Bookstore, 1947.
13. Vaughn, K. W., ed. National projects in educational measurement. A report of the 1946 invitational conference on testing problems, New York City, November 2, 1946. Series I, No. 28, Vol. XI, Aug. 1947.
14. Zeleny, L. D. Selection of compatible flying partners. *American Journal of Sociology*, 1947, 52, 424-431.

SOCIOMETRIC CHOICE AND ORGANIZATIONAL EFFECTIVE-NESS: A MULTI-RELATIONAL APPROACH

By Fred Massarik, Robert Tannenbaum, Murray Kahane and Irving Weschler

I

Introduction

The Multi-Relational Sociometric Survey (the M.S.S.) technique[1] here reported resulted from the authors' continuing interest in human variables associated with organizational effectiveness. Specifically, this technique was developed to identify and analyze several types of inter-personal activities and relations, and to provide a method for expressing the degree of congruence between two or more of these activities and rela-tions in indices which might be associated with available criteria of organi-zational effectiveness.[2]

Traditionally, discussions of organization theory have drawn a distinc-tion between the concepts of formal and informal organization. In a survey of the relevant literature undertaken by the Human Relations Research Group, considerable disagreement was found to exist among writers as to the meaning of these two concepts. In defining formal organization, for example, some stressed the rational, prescribed relations between posi-tions—the blueprint or organizational-chart approach—while others stressed

---

[1] This is the fourth report of the Human Relations Research Group, Institute of Industrial Relations, University of California, Los Angeles, completed under a grant from the U. S. Navy, Office of Naval Research. This group is headed by Dr. Robert Tannenbaum. Special appreciation is due Mr. Eugene Talbot, Dr. Paula Brown, and Mrs. Jacqueline Gordon for their invaluable assistance in connection with the develop-ment of both the M.S.S and this article. The M.S.S. was presented in more popular form in I. R. Weschler, R. Tannenbaum, and E. Talbot, "A New Management Tool: The Multi-Relational Sociometric Survey," *Personnel,* 29 (July, 1952), 85-94. The em-pirical data used for illustrative purposes in the first publication as well as in the current paper were obtained in a pilot investigation conducted in two divisions of Southern California naval research and development laboratory. For the original for-mulations of sociometric theory and technique, see J. L. Moreno, *Who Shall Sur-vive?* New York: Beacon House, 1934 and 1953.

[2] One difficulty involved the establishment of appropriate criteria of organiza-tional effectiveness, particularly because our research was conducted in a laboratory, wherein effectiveness often had to be inferred indirctly from supervisors' ratings and from measures of morale, job satisfaction, and productivity *perceptions.* In another

the rational, prescribed relations between specific persons.[3] On the other hand, in defining informal organization, some included *all* relations between persons not formally prescribed; some, only spontaneously developed affective relations; some, only those relations which are extra-organizational in character (i.e., those not clearly directed toward organizational goals).[4]

From these various definitions, the main point emerges that the people who comprise any organization are related to each other in numerous ways. Further, it may be hypothesized that the degree of congruence between specific relations may have some implications for organizational effectiveness. The research problem, then, becomes that of analyzing selected types of relations, and of developing the appropriate indices showing their interrelations. Although this problem will be discussed more fully in Sections IV, V, and VI, consideration of some key concepts must precede.

Interpersonal activities among people who comprise any organization

---

research project, the Human Relations Research Group is addressing itself to the clearer formulation of measures of effectiveness applicable to scientific research groups.

[3] The following illustrate some shades of meaning in the use of the concept "formal organization":

(a) "A formal, rationally organized social structure involves clearly defined patterns of activity in which, ideally, every series of actions is functionally related to the purposes of the organization. In such an organization there is an integrated series of offices, of hierarchized statuses, in which inhere a number of obligations and privileges closely defined by limited and specific rules." Robert K. Merton, "Bureaucratic Structure and Personality," in his *Social Theory and Social Structure* (Glencoe: Fress Press, 1949), p. 151.

(b) ". . . the most useful concept for the analysis of experience of cooperative systems is embodied in the definition of a formal organization as a system of consciously coordinated activities or forces of two or more persons." C. I. Barnard, *The Functions of the Executive* (Cambridge: Harvard University Press, 1947), p. 73.

[4] The following illustrate some shades of meaning, in the use of the concept "informal organization":

(a) "Informal organization is the network of personal and social relations which are not defined or prescribed by formal organization." Delbert C. Miller and William H. Form, *Industrial Sociology* (New York: Harper, 1951), p. 863.

(b) Informal organization "is composed of the animosities and friendships among the people who work together." *Ibid.*, p. 146.

(c) "By informal organization I mean the aggregate of the personal contacts and interactions and the associated groupings of people. . . . Though common or joint purposes are excluded by definition, common or joint results of important character nevertheless come from such organization . . . informal organization is indefinite and rather structureless. . . . " Barnard, *op. cit.*, p. 115.

may be divided into two main types: those clearly directed toward the attainment of organizational goals, and those not so directed. For the sake of brevity, we shall speak of the first type as "goal-directed," and of the second type as "nongoal-directed."

The first type incorporates those activities which specifically are necessary (as seen by persons in authority) to the achievement of the purposes of the organization. Order-giving, efficiency-rating, and the giving of advice and assistance in work are examples of this type. The second type incorporates those activities not directly essential to the achievement of organizational purposes. Lunching and socializing after working hours are illustrative.

Each activity includes a number of *relations*. For each of the goal-directed activities, five relations are postulated. These are the *prescribed,* the *perceived,* the *actual,* the *desired,* and the *rejected.*

1. *The prescribed relations* are defined by the official sanction of the duly-constituted leaders of the organization. (X has been delegated authority by his superior to give orders in work to Y.) These relations are either explicitly specified or implicitly accepted by persons in authority. They are explicit when they are defined by oral or written directive; they are implicit when their existence within the organization is accepted by those in authority although such existence is not based upon directive. By way of example, in all organizations prescribed order-giving is explicit; in many, however, prescribed giving-of-advice-and-assistance is implicit.

2. *The perceived relations* are defined by persons' perceptions of the prescribed relations. (For example, Y perceives Z as having authority to give him orders in work—even though it is, in fact, X who has such authority.)

3. *The actual relations* are defined by the interactions which in fact take place among persons. (For example, Y regularly receives orders in work from X.) Operationally, these relations can be revealed by two methods—by observation of behavior as it occurs, or by asking individuals to indicate the person(s) with whom they interact.[5] When the latter method

---

[5] Thus we might distinguish an "actual actual" to designate a relation for which data were obtained by direct observation, and a "perceived actual" for which data were obtained by asking individuals to indicate the person(s) with whom they interact. In the pilot investigation, the "perceived actual" was used, but for the sake of brevity, we shall frequently speak simply of the "actual" when referring to the "perceived actual."

is used, the replies represent perceptual data which probably correlate positively, although imperfectly, with data that might be obtained by direct observation.

4. *The desired relations* are defined by persons' preferences regarding interactions with other persons (positive affect). (For example, Y *would like to* receive orders in work from W.)

It is possible here to include *all* preferred interactions or only the one (or ones) *most* preferred. For operational purposes, a choice between these alternatives must be made.

The desired relations are equivalent to the "choices" as used in sociometry.

5. *The rejected relations* are defined by persons' adverse reactions regarding interactions with other persons (negative affect). (For example, Y *would not like* to receive orders in work from X.)

It is possible here to include *all* rejected interactions or only the one (or ones) *most* rejected.

The rejected relations are equivalent to "rejections" as used in sociometry.

In comparing the five relations discussed above, we may view the prescribed relations as organizational norms, and the perceived relations as the psychological corollaries of these organizational norms. The desired and rejected relations may either support these norms (if the prescribed is desired) or contravene these norms (if the prescribed is rejected). The actual relations may be resultants, dependent, among other things, upon the norms, awareness of these norms, and desires and rejections.

For each of the nongoal-directed activities, only three relations are postulated. These are the actual, the desired, and the rejected. Clearly, the prescribed and the perceived relations are not relevant to nongoal-directed activities.

II

DEVELOPMENT AND ADMINISTRATION OF THE RESEARCH INSTRUMENT

1. *The Setting*

The pilot investigation was conducted in a Southern California naval research and development laboratory. The subjects were primarily engineers, physicists, chemists, draftsmen, and supporting administrative and clerical specialists. Specifically, they were the members of two divisions, characterized by presumably contrasting styles of leadership. Division A was headed by an apparently restrictive leader, while Division B was more permissively led.

Prior to the M.S.S. study, other human relations research projects had been conducted in the laboratory, and continuing contact had been maintained with its formal leadership. Thus, a degree of rapport already had been established when the current project was initiated.

2. *Specifying the Principal Activities*

In planning the M.S.S., it became necessary to specify for research purposes a sensibly small number of activities. The selection was made on a common-sense basis, buttressed by interviews with key personnel in the laboratory.[6] The following activities were chosen:

A. Goal-directed activities:
  1) being efficiency rated
  2) turning to others for advice in work
  3) being given directions or orders
  4) presenting major grievances
  5) being designated for a promotion
  6) having one's mistakes in work pointed out
  7) spending time with others during working hours[7]
  8) discussing annoyances arising from work

B. Nongoal-directed activities:
  1) socializing after working hours
  2) having lunch with others
  3) discussing personal problems

3. *Obtaining the Data*

A. The prescribed relations:
  Two sources were utilized to secure information about the prescribed relations of the goal-directed activities: (1) organizational charts and manuals, (2) interviews with top administrators and personnel specialists. These data describe what often is referred to as the "formal organization."

---

[6] This is essentially a type of sampling problem. One might imagine a large universe of all possible activities between individuals in a particular setting, from which a representative sample must be drawn.

[7] Some activities such as this one, are difficult to classify, as they may vary in terms of goal-direction and nongoal-direction.

B. The perceived, actual, desired, and rejected relations:

To secure facts about relations other than the prescribed, a questionnaire was constructed and administered to persons at all levels of the hierarchy. This questionnaire is the basic instrument of the M.S.S.

The following may serve as a prototype to indicate the kinds of questions used:

Goal-directed:

> The perceived: "Who is *supposed* to give you directions (or orders) in your work?"
>
> The actual: "Who *actually* gives you directions (or orders) in your work?"
>
> The desired: "If it were up to you to decide, *whom would you* choose to give you directions (or orders) in your work?"
>
> The rejected: *"Whom would you least want* to give you directions (or orders) in your work?"

Nongoal-directed:

> The actual: "With whom *do* you usually have lunch?"
>
> The desired: "With whom would you *like to be able* to have lunch?"
>
> The rejected: "With whom would you *least like* to have lunch?"[8]

No constraints were imposed on the subjects to limit the number or nature of their responses. More than one answer was permitted, organizational units could be used as choices, and qualifying or qualitative comments could be appended to any reply. The questionnaires were completed by the respondents at their homes and mailed unsigned to the university address of the research team.[9] Code numbers were used so that only the members of the research team could identify individuals. Out of a population of 68, 66 completed questionnaires were obtained.

---

[8] In some cases, the rejection relation was not included, even though it did apply. At the time of the field study, this was done for the sake of economy; but it was realized subsequently that the relevant questions should have been included.

[9] This was done as a further safeguard against the operation of direct or subtle interpersonal pressures such as might be generated by face-to-face contact among the respondents during the filling out of the questionnaire.

The need for a virtually complete return of replies in a sociometric investigation is apparent. High nonresponse would leave such gaps in the matrix as to diminish greatly the value of the data. An instrument such as the M.S.S. may represent a threat to the security of some of the respondents. Therefore, straightforward, satisfactory interpretation of the research project's objectives is essential. Feed-back of data must be handled with caution, for it too may represent a threat. In the pilot investigation, it was emphasized that the survey results would *not* be used as a basis for any sort of administrative action. In fact, it was made clear that no management person would see individual replies; all findings would be available only in such form as to protect the individuals concerned by making identification impossible.[10]

4. *Coding and Preparing the Data for Analysis*

A number had been assigned to each of the respondents, and these numbers became part of the code. Most replies did mention specific individuals, but responses such as "no one," anyone," "people near my desk," "my superiors," etc., also appeared with some frequency and were added to the code.[11]

---

[10] There are certain differences between the use of the M.S.S. as a tool of management and a as research device. When used as a managerial tool, action is a logical consequence of the M.S.S. In academic research, on the other hand, considerable stress is laid on the fact that *nothing* will happen within the organization to modify existing regulations directly as a result of the findings. Clearly, this implies a different type of motivation to cooperate than if change, and particularly change-for-the-better, is promised. There is no reason to believe, however, that the sort of motivation elicited by a promise of action necessarily results in more honest or more valid data than the motivation that exists when it is emphasized that the research results will not be used directly as an instrument for change. Change, brought about indirectly by interest aroused in topics raised by the M.S.S., may nevertheless be a by-product of the research.

[11] The following illustrates some of the categories that were developed to deal with choices other than those for specific individuals:
- A. unnamed persons, e.g., (1) anyone, (2) all, (3) many, (4) some, etc.
- B. self-reference e.g., (1) myself, (2) alone, etc.
- C. "formal" organizational units within the laboratory, e.g.,(1) Power Plant Division, etc.
- D. "informal" groups, e.g., (1) by car pool, (2) the bridge group, etc.
- E. Status units, e.g., (1) my superiors, (2) my subordinates, etc.
- F. functional units, e.g., (1) people who can help me, (2) people who are qualified . . . (6) anyone else who can help me, etc.,

In the pilot investigation, IBM procedures were not used, although this might have been done successfully. Rather, the code designations were transferred to large general-purpose tables from which they could be converted into matrix form.

In order to facilitate analysis and interpretation, a method for organizing the raw data was needed. The method that was developed for this purpose is considered in the next section.

III

A METHOD FOR ORGANIZING THE DATA

Let us recapitulate the basic concepts outlined in Section I. We distinguish two major categories of activities: the goal-directed and the nongoal-directed.[12] For each of the former, five relations are postulated: the prescribed, the perceived, the actual, the desired, and the rejected. For each of the latter type, three relations are postulated: the actual, the desired, and the rejected. The following symbols will prove useful for putting the data into matrix form:

' to indicate an instance of a prescribed relation

o to indicate an instance of a perceived relation

x to indicate an instance of an actual relation

+ to indicate an instance of a desired relation

— to indicate an instance of a rejected relation

G. physical arrangement units, e.g., (1) people near my desk, (2) people in my office, etc.

Also, qualifying remarks were coded, using categories such as the following:

H. frequency of interaction, e.g., (1) always, (2) sometimes, (3) usually, etc.

I. feeling tone of interaction, e.g., (1) friendly, (2) unfriendly, etc.

Following is an example of how a particular response may be coded:

Smith, code number 123, might have replied as follows to the question, "To whom do you turn for advice in your work?": ". . . to Jones; but sometimes I go to other people in the Power Plant Division, or to anyone else who can help me." This would be coded as follows:

Jones—code number for specific individual: 123.

"other people in Power Plant Division" (formal organizational unit)—see C above: C-1.

"sometimes" (qualifying remark for Power Plant Division)—see H above: H-2.

"anyone else who can help me" (functional unit): F-6.

The reliability of the coding was checked, and although no coefficients were calculated, it was apparent that only a trivial number of disagreements between coders appeared.

[12] The goal-directed and the nongoal-directed activities studied in the pilot investigation are listed in full in Section II.

In conventional sociometric matrices, each cell contains information about a particular choice or relationship between two individuals in a particular activity.[13] However, in an M.S.S. matrix cell, for any goal-directed activity such as order-giving, it is possible to indicate all, some or none of the five relations shown above. Thus, an M.S.S. matrix cell contains some variant of the following:[14]

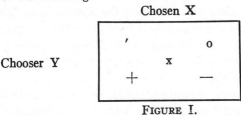

Chosen X

Chooser Y

FIGURE I.

Each symbol is placed in the appropriate position within the cell, as shown in Figure I. Thus, ' always appears in the upper left-hand corner, o in the upper right-hand corner, etc.

For example, the following pattern of relations may be found for the order-giving activity:

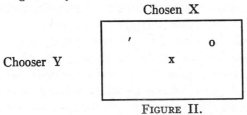

Chosen X

Chooser Y

FIGURE II.

According to Figure II, Y is supposed to take orders from X (prescribed), he believes that X is supposed to give him orders (perceived), and indeed X does give him orders. However, on the affective level, Y neither desires nor rejects X as an order-giver, for we find neither a plus ($+$) in

---

13 Conventional sociometric usage frequently employs the word "criterion" for what we call "activity." For example, see Charles H. Proctor and Charles P. Loomis, "Analysis of Sociometric Data," in Marie Jahoda, Morton Deutsch and Stuart W. Cook, *Research Methods in Social Relations, Part Two: Selected Techniques* (Springfield: Dryden, 1951), p. 562.

14 Actually, it is unlikely that all five of the relations will be found in any one cell. Typically, one person will not be both desired and rejected by the same chooser. This is not to deny the existence of ambivalence as a personality dynamic, although most sociometric methods have not made use of this concept.

the lower left-hand corner of the cell, nor a minus(—) in the lower right-hand corner. (See positions of symbols shown in Figure I.)

A cell that is completely blank indicates that for a particular activity, no relations link the individuals concerned.

For each activity an entire matrix may be formed with the choosers arranged along the ordinate and the chosen along the abscissa.[15] In practice, it may be that more cases will fall along the abscissa than along the ordinate. This is so because a given chooser may select persons outside his own group or organizational unit; he may choose "unnamed persons" (e.g., "my friends"), or entire groups (e.g., "my division"), which of course cannot directly reciprocate the choice.

One can visualize an array of matrices similar to the one just discussed, with each matrix dealing with one particular activity. The following figure shows what this total scheme might look like:

In summary: The M.S.S. scheme indicates the relations (entries in cells) between individuals (x-axis and y-axis) for a number of activities (z-axis).

Among research questions generated by this are the following:

1. For any activity, what relational patterns characterize various organizational units? We shall construct some indices concerned with such patterns. These we shall call *intra-activity indices*. The relevant basic data are the entries in various cells of *any one matrix* defined by the x-y plane in the three-dimensional scheme.

2. What patterns are found in various organizational units as we trace any *one* relation from activity to activity? We shall construct some indices concerned with this. These we shall call *inter-activity indices*. The relevant basic data are the entries for *any one relation,* such as the prescribed, perceived, actual, desired, or rejected, as they appear in a horizontal array of cells along the z-axis, from one matrix to another.

IV

Intra-Activity Indices

Intra-activity indices are constructed on the basis of relation patterns in any one activity. They use as data the cell entries of any one matrix in the x-y plane.

---

[15] Actually the terms "chooser" and "chosen" are not entirely accurate, but will be used in lieu of neologisms, for no adequate terms seem to exist. The inaccuracy

A THREE-DIMENSIONAL SCHEME FOR THE MULTI-RELATIONAL SOCIOMETRIC SURVEY

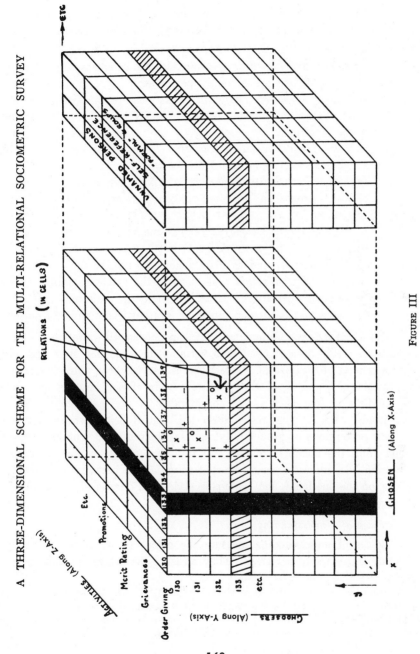

FIGURE III

Intra-activity indices provide information about various aspects of group functioning and about the functioning of the individual in the group. This section will consider the following indices:

1. *Indices of understanding* that measure the extent to which the prescribed relations are correctly perceived.

2. *Indices of normative conformity* that measure the extent to which actual behavior conforms to the prescribed and/or to perceptions of the prescribed.

3. *Indices of affective conformity* that measure the extent to which actual behavior conforms to desires and rejections.

4. *Indices of satisfaction and dissatisfaction* that measure the extent to which prescribed, perceived, or actual relations also are desired or rejected.

5. *Indices of affective atmosphere* that measure the state of balance that exists in an organizational unit between affectively positive choices (desired) and affectively negative choices (rejected).

6. *Indices of centralization* that measure the extent to which choices (prescribed, perceived, actual, desired, or rejected) are concentrated in a particular person or in a particular group of persons.

The hypothesis was formulated that some systematic variations in index magnitudes would be associated with variation in leadership style and with certain criteria of organizational effectiveness. As has been noted before, the two divisions, A and B, of the laboratory were chosen because there was some indication that they varied considerably in the leadership styles of their heads, with A being restrictively led, and B being permissively led. Further, perceptions of productivity, job satisfaction, and morale were obtained from the members of the two divisions. The example, contained in Section VII, indicates some expected co-variations between intra-activity indices, on the one hand, and leadership styles and criteria of organizational effectiveness, on the other.

1. *Indices of Understanding*

Indices of understanding measure the extent to which the prescribed relations are correctly perceived. They measure the degree to which people

---

stems from the fact that when X is prescribed for Y, Y does not necessarily do any choosing—the relevant prescription simply is thrust upon him. Nor is a perception of a prescribed or actual relation really a "choice" in the usual sense of the word. The only genuine choices are the desired and the rejected.

have an accurate idea about the formal organization in which they are involved. By definition, indices of understanding always have the prescribed and the perceived in the numerator.

The following is one possible index of understanding:

$$\Sigma'o / \Sigma' \qquad (1)^{16}$$

In words: "Of the prescribed relations (for a given activity such as order-giving), what percentage also is perceived?"

Each respondent is allowed to make a number of choices in answer to each question. Therefore, it is possible that there could exist perfect congruence between the perceived and the prescribed, yet complete understanding may not prevail since choices in addition to the correct one may be made. Thus, some individuals know with whom they are to interact, yet they may believe that they are also prescribed to interact with persons not so designated. An index can be devised to account for these multiple choices, which should be used to complement index (1). This complementary index is designated in the following manner:

$$\Sigma'o / \Sigma o \qquad (2)$$

Thus, there are two different indices of understanding. Index (1) answers the question, "what percentage of prescriptions is perceived correctly?" and Index (2) answers the question, "What percentage of the perceived is also prescribed?"

An analysis of understanding by organizational units or by individuals may demonstrate gaps in the comprehension of formal structure which may affect the functioning of these units.

---

[16] In computations of all indices, the particular patterns, such as $'o$, are counted whenever the relevant combination of relations appears, whether or not there are any other relations in the cell. Thus $\Sigma'o$ is the sum of all cell entries which contain $'o$, including $'ox$, $'o+$, $'ox+$ $'o-$, $'ox-$, etc., as well as $'o$ alone. Indices, as used in the pilot investigation, are concerned with percentages of relations, rather than with percentages of individuals. Since multiple responses were permitted, this raises some questions of weighting. One individual with numerous choices exerts a relatively greater influence upon an index than an individual with a single choice. What implications this may have empirically would have to be determined by the construction of another set of measures in which the responses of individuals, regardless of number, would be weighted equally. For another possible solution of this problem, see Weschler, Tannenbaum, and Talbot, *op. cit.*, footnote 7, p. 91.

2. *Indices of Normative Conformity*

Indices of normative conformity measure the extent to which reported actual behavior conforms to the prescribed and/or to perceptions of the prescribed. These indices measure the degree to which people report that they do what they are supposed to do, or do what they *think* they are supposed to do. By definition, the actual always appears in the numerator.

As one measure of the degree of normative conformity (with the prescribed as the norm) one may use the proportion of all the prescribed relations which are actual relations as well. This is represented symbolically as:

$$\Sigma'x \,/\, \Sigma' \qquad\qquad (3)$$

A problem concerning multiple responses exists here similar to that encountered with the indices of understanding. This problem can be resolved by using the total number of actual as the base in determining the proportion of actual relations which are prescribed. Symbolically:

$$\Sigma'x \,/\, \Sigma x \qquad\qquad (4)$$

Thus, we have two measures of normative conformity with the prescribed as the norm. Index (3) answers the question, "what percentage of all prescribed relations is also actual?" Index (4) answers the question, "what percentage of all actual relations is also prescribed?"

Further, it is possible to measure normative conformity to relations *perceived* as being prescribed. The relevant indices would be the following:

$$\Sigma ox \,/\, \Sigma o \qquad\qquad (5)$$

$$\Sigma ox \,/\, \Sigma x \qquad\qquad (6)$$

Index (5) answers the question, "what percentage of all perceived relations is also actual?" Index (6) answers the question, "what percentage of all actual relations is also perceived?"

Still another set of measures of normative conformity is concerned with the extent to which an activity that is both prescribed and perceived is also reported as being acted upon:

$$\Sigma'ox \,/\, \Sigma'o \qquad\qquad (7)$$

Index (7) answers the question, "what percentage of all relations that are both prescribed and perceived (understood) is also actual?"

And similarly:

$$\Sigma'ox \,/\, \Sigma x \qquad\qquad (8)$$

Index (8) answers the question, "what percentage of all actual relations is also perceived and prescribed (understood)?"

We might consider some of the psychological meanings of these three sets of measures of normative conformity. The first set, indices (3) and (4), regards conformity as determined by the extent to which behavior corresponds to the organizational blueprint regardless of any other circumstances. In the second set, indices (5) and (6), conformity is concerned with the individual's own view of the organization in which he operates, whether or not this perceptual structuring corresponds to the blueprint. Finally, the third set, indices (7) and (8), is designed to judge conformity against the correctly perceived (or understood) relations only.

If, upon examination of indices (3) and (4), it is found that some persons show relatively little conformity to what is prescribed, then it should be ascertained whether these persons act in accordance with their perceptions of the prescribed—see indices (5) and (6). If they do, then better communication of the prescribed relations becomes the solution, providing it is agreed that organizational goals will be attained most effectively if prescriptions are followed. Another point to note is that when individuals are found to interact with persons neither prescribed for them nor perceived by them, this may be due to the lack of availability of the prescribed or perceived individuals or to hostilities with them.

3. *Indices of Affective Conformity*

Indices of affective conformity measure the extent to which reported actual behavior conforms to desires and rejections. They indicate the degree to which people's behavior is in accord with their preferences for interpersonal contact. By definition, the actual always appears in the numerator. These measures are somewhat similar in purpose to the indices of satisfaction which will be taken up in the next section.

The principal measure of affective conformity is concerned with the following question: "What percentage of all desired (or rejected) relations is also actual?" Symbolically:

$$\Sigma + x \, / \, \Sigma + \qquad (9a)$$

$$\Sigma - x \, / \, \Sigma - \qquad (9b)$$

4. *Indices of Satisfaction and Dissatisfaction*

Indices of satisfaction and dissatisfaction measure the extent to which prescribed, perceived, or actual relations are also desired or rejected. Thus, these indices measure relative satisfaction or dissatisfaction with formal organization and/or with the existing interactions. By definition, indices of satisfaction always have the desired in the numerator; indices of dissatisfaction always have the rejected in the numerator.

One pair of relevant indices may be symbolized as follows:

$$\Sigma'+ \, / \, \Sigma' \qquad (10a)$$

$$\Sigma'- \, / \, \Sigma' \qquad (10b)$$

Indices (10a) and (10b) are concerned with the question, "what percentage of all prescribed relations is also desired (or rejected)?"[17]

A pair of indices focusing on the perceived instead of the prescribed may be represented symbolically as follows:

$$\Sigma o+ \, / \, \Sigma o \qquad (11a)$$

$$\Sigma o- \, / \, \Sigma o \qquad (11b)$$

Indices (11a) and (11b) answer the question, "what percentage of all perceived relations is also desired (or rejected)?"

Variants of these indices, which perhaps are more relevant to management, are the following:

$$\Sigma'o+ \, / \, \Sigma'o \qquad (12a)$$

$$\Sigma'o- \, / \, \Sigma'o \qquad (12b)$$

Indices (12a) and (12b) use the understood relations as the base. They answer the question, "what percentage of all relations that are perceived *and* prescribed (understood) is also desired (or rejected)?"

Still another type of satisfaction and dissatisfaction measure may focus on the actual relations:

$$\Sigma x+ \, / \, \Sigma x \qquad (13a)$$

$$\Sigma x- \, / \, \Sigma x \qquad (13b)$$

In a sense, indices (13a) and (13b) are the converse of the affective conformity measures (9a) and (9b). Indices (13a) and (13b) answer the question, "what percentage of all actual relations is also desired (or re-

---

[17] These indices measure satisfaction and dissatisfaction with reference to relations that are prescribed but *not necessarily* perceived. However, it may be of interest to find out to what extent prescribed relations are desired or rejected, regardless of the extent to which they are also perceived. For example, it may be that superiors designated to fulfill specific functions such as order-giving are well-liked in the roles which they are to fulfill according to the organizational blueprint, but few people are aware that these superiors are indeed assigned these roles. Clearly, the remedy for this kind of situation (which also would be indicated by some of the indices of understanding) would be more effective communication of the organizational prescriptions.

jected)?, while indices (9a) and (9b) answer the question, "what percentage of all desired (or rejected) relations is also actual?"

Indices of satisfaction and dissatisfaction may point to morale problems in various organizational units. When satisfaction indices between activities are compared, the comparisons may indicate those interactions that might be at the root of organizational difficulties.

5. *Indices of Affective Atmosphere*

An index of affective atmosphere measures the state of balance that exists in an organizational unit between affectively positive choices (desired) and affectively negative choices (rejected). If all affective choices are positive, the index figure will be 100; if the number of desired relations is the same as the number of rejected relations, the index figure will be 50; and if all affective choices are negative, the index figure will be 0. Thus, this index may provide some measure of the extent to which a pleasant emotional state characterizes the group.

Symbolically, the index may be stated as follows:

$$\Sigma(+) \, / \, \Sigma(+) + \Sigma(-)^{18} \qquad (14)$$

A variant of this index is concerned not merely with the balance between positive and negative choices, but also considers the extent to which such choices are accompanied by actual relations. It provides information on the ratio of desired-actual relations to the total number of actual relations with positive or negative affect. The following is a symbolic representation of this index:

$$\Sigma(+x) \, / \, \Sigma(+x) + \Sigma(-x) \qquad (15)$$

6. *Indices of Centralization*

An index of centralization measures the extent to which choices are concentrated in a particular person or in a particular group of persons.[19] Let us take an activity such as order-giving. For a hypothetical organizational unit, we note that there are 100 instances of prescription. By simple

---

[18] The plus sign in the denominator indicating addition of $\Sigma(+)$ and $\Sigma(-)$ should not be confused with our symbol for the desired relation which, of course, is also a "+" sign.

[19] Indices discussed so far have focused on relations existing within given organizational units. Here the emphasis shifts to choices received by specific persons. Thus it becomes important to count the total number of times *one particular* type of choice is received by a given person. For example, X may receive the following choice patterns from five people: 'ox, 'ox, '+ '—, 'x—. This would yield the following sum-

count, we find that 80 of these instances involve one person as the order-giver. Only 20 prescriptions are designated for other members of the group. It is clear that here the power inherent in order-giving is concentrated in that one person.

One such index of centralization may be calculated for each relation and the group of indices of centralization can be symbolized as follows:

$$\Sigma(')_x/\Sigma' \qquad (16a)$$
$$\Sigma(o)_x/\Sigma o \qquad (16b)$$
$$\Sigma(x)_x/\Sigma x \qquad (16c)$$
$$\Sigma(x)_x/\Sigma+ \qquad (16d)$$
$$\Sigma(-)_x/\Sigma- \qquad (16e)$$

Each index (16a) through (16e) answers a question of this form: "What percentage of a given relation in a particular organizational unit involves a particular person or group of persons?"

A profile may be drawn, showing indices (16a) through (16e) for a specific superior; such a profile may summarize key aspects of that superior's leadership role. This will be further illustrated in Section VII.

V

OVERLAP BETWEEN INTRA-ACTIVITY INDICES

A consideration of the intra-activity indices suggests that a certain systematic overlap exists between various of the indices.[20]

For the sake of simplicity, we select three of the five relations: the actual, prescribed, and perceived. Representing each as a circle, we note the existence of certain overlapping areas. Each of these areas represents a particular relational pattern. In order to avoid repeating the entire symbolism, we can designate each area by a capital letter. Thus:

---

mary of choices when $\Sigma(')_X$, $\Sigma(o)_X$, $\Sigma(x)_X$, $\Sigma(+)_X$, and $\Sigma(-)_X$ are the respective totals of the prescribed, perceived, actual, desired, and rejected choices given to X:

$$\Sigma(')_X \quad . \quad . \quad . \quad 5$$
$$\Sigma(o)_X \quad . \quad . \quad . \quad 2$$
$$\Sigma(x)_X \quad . \quad . \quad . \quad 3$$
$$\Sigma(+)_X \quad . \quad . \quad . \quad 1$$
$$\Sigma(-)_X \quad . \quad . \quad . \quad 2$$

[20] We are indebted to Dr. Leon Festinger of the University of Minnesota for suggesting this matter.

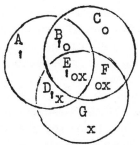

Translating several of the indices into the capital-letter notation, we obtain the following:

Index (1): $\Sigma'o/\Sigma'$ = B+E/A+B+D+E
Index (2): $\Sigma'o/\Sigma o$ = B+E/B+C+E+F
Index (3): $\Sigma'x/\Sigma'$ = D+E/A+B+D+E
Index (4): $\Sigma'x/\Sigma x$ = D+E/D+E+F+G
Index (5): $\Sigma ox/\Sigma o$ = E+F/B+C+E+F
Index (6): $\Sigma ox/\Sigma x$ = E+F/D+E+F+G
Index (7): $\Sigma'ox/\Sigma'o$ = E/B+E
Index (8): $\Sigma'ox/\Sigma x$ = E/D+E+F+G

Rewriting index (6) as (E/D+E+F+G) + (F/D+E+F+G), we note that in fact index (8), which is (E/D+E+F+G), is an important component of index (6). Specifically for Division A, index (8) = 63.64. Obtaining index (6), we find that it yields the figure 78.79. Thus, 15.15 points only (63.64 + 15.15 = 78.79) are accounted for by the component (F/D+E+F+G). It is clear that many of the indices, although of varying psychological meaning, systematically overlap one another.

VI

INTER-ACTIVITY INDICES

In the previous section, we considered a number of measures that used as basic data the entries in the cells of any one matrix in the x-y plane. (See Figure III.) Next, we shall select specific relations, such as the prescribed, perceived, actual, desired, or rejected, and observe them as they appear when we focus on the z-axis, along which the various activities are arrayed.

1. *Indices of Pervasiveness*

An index of pervasiveness measures the extent to which any one relation connects a pair or pairs of specific individuals in a number of activities.

In other words, this index tells us how pervasive ties between two individuals are, as we examine several activities in which the persons may interact. It is possible to construct one index of pervasiveness for each relation. There exists an index of prescribed pervasiveness, perceived pervasiveness, actual pervasiveness, desired pervasiveness, and rejected pervasiveness.

Let us assume that an M.S.S. is designed which covers 20 activities—10 goal-directed and 10 nongoal-directed. The following might be one way of arranging the results showing the relations between individuals X and Y, in which Y is the chooser and X is the chosen. Each "f" represents the number of activities in which a particular relation exists for the individuals concerned.

	Goal-directed activities		Nongoal-directed activities		Total	
	$n_G = 10$		$n_{NG} = 10$		$n = 20$	
Y — X						
	f_G / n_G	(17a)	f_{NG} / n_{NG}	(17b)	f / n	(17c)

In a hypothetical case, $f_G = 7$, and $f_{NG} = 1$. If the relation used happens to be actual, this would mean that Y indicates that in 7 of the 10 goal-directed activities he is in actual contact with X, and that in 1 of the 10 nongoal-directed activities he is in contact with X. Stating these frequencies in percentages for each group of 10, we would say that the pervasiveness index for Y to X in the actual relation is 70 for the goal-directed activities and 10 for the nongoal-directed activities. This would suggest that Y sees himself as actually relating to X primarily in areas of behavior related to work, and considerably less in activities that are oriented toward off-job and personal need satisfactions. For *all* activities, the pervasiveness index would be 55, i.e., Y has actual relations with X in 11 of the 20 activities studied.[21]

2. *A Direct Approach to Inter-Activity Indices*

Instead of constructing measures such as the pervasiveness indices, it is possible to proceed simply by direct observation. We might look at the M.S.S. data, noting the combinations of activities in which a specific relation

---

[21] To justify the calculation of an index for all relations, some assumptions have to be made regarding the exhaustiveness or representativeness of the relations included in the study.

appears for any pair of individuals. For example, it might be that persons who are actual order-givers, frequently also are individuals with whom personal problems are discussed and from whom advice is solicited. Thus, order-giving, advice-seeking, and discussing personal problems may form a cluster, as defined by the appearance of the actual relation.

VII

An Example

Tables I, II, and III contain certain summaries of data, taken from the sociometric matrices, that were obtained in the pilot investigation at the laboratory. These summaries furnish the raw material for the calculation of the *intra*-activity indices. The data were not sufficient to permit calculation of any meaningful *inter*-activity indices.

Table I summarizes the relational patterns for one goal-directed activity, order-giving, and for one nongoal-directed activity, socializing after working hours. As is demonstrated by the formula for the total number of combinations of n different things (the sum of the number of combinations of n things taken 1, 2, . . . n, at a time): $2^n - 1$, there are 31 possible combinations (or relational patterns) for the goal-directed activity (number of relations, n = 5), and 7 different combinations for the nongoal-directed activity (n = 3). However, certain patterns are psychologically inconsistent because they contain both "most desired" (+) and "most rejected" (—). These patterns are marked by asterisks. Excluding these, the number of patterns drops to 23 for the goal-directed activity, and to 5 for the nongoal-directed activity. In fact, for order-giving, only 14 patterns actually were found in Division A, and 19 patterns in Division B. For socializing 4 patterns were found in each of the two divisions.

Table II summarizes relational *totals* for the divisions. The average number of choices per person for each relation is shown in parentheses. Table II may be derived directly from Table I. For example, the total of prescribed relations for Division A in order-giving is found by summing the frequencies of all patterns in which the prescribed (') appears. Specifically, it is the total of patterns 1.1, 2.1, 2.2, 2.3, 2.4, 3.1, 3.2, 3.3, 3.4, 3.5, 3.6, 4.1, 4.2, 4.3, 4.4, and 5.1.

Table III is an extract from the matrices, analogous to Table II, except for the fact that the summary of relational totals is shown for the two division heads only. A similar summary could be prepared for any other person in the organization.

TABLE I
A SUMMARY OF RELATIONAL PATTERNS[1]

			Frequency of Patterns for			
			Order-Giving in		Socializing in	
			Division A	Division B	Division A	Division B
1. One Relation						
Pattern Code	1.1[2]	'	—	3	None	None[a]
	1.2	o	—	1	None	None
	1.3	x	3	9	21	15
	1.4	+	7	9	20	17
	1.5	—	10	9	21	17
2. Two Relations						
Pattern Code	2.1	'o	1	2	None	None
	2.2	˙x	1	1	None	None
	2.3	'+	1	1	None	None
	2.4	'—	—	1	None	None
	2.5	xo	4	8	None	None
	2.6	+o	—	2	None	None
	2.7	o—	—	1	None	None
	2.8	+x	—	7	4	21
	2.9	x—	3	1	—	—
	*2.10	+—	—	—	—	—
3. Three Relations						
Pattern Code	3.1	'xo	9	6	None	None
	3.2	'+o	1	—	None	None
	3.3	'o—	1	—	None	None
	3.4	'+x	—	—	None	None
	3.5	'x—	—	—	None	None
	*3.6	'+—	—	—	None	None
	*3.7	+o—	—	—	None	None
	3.8	xo—	—	1	None	None
	3.9	+xo	1	10	None	None
	*3.10	+x—	—	—	—	—
4. Four Relations						
Pattern Code	4.1	'+xo	11	22	None	None
	4.2	'xo—	1	1	None	None
	*4.3	'+o—	—	—	None	None
	*4.4	'+x—	—	—	None	None
	*4.5	+xo—	—	—	None	None
5. Five Relations						
Pattern Code	*5.1	'+x—o	—	—	None	None

[1]All figures for choices within division.

[2]The patterns are grouped by number of relations in the pattern. The first numeral of each pattern code designates the number of relations in that group of patterns; the second numeral designates the particular pattern within the group. For example: 1.1, one relation, pattern one; or: 3.10, three relations, pattern ten.

TABLE II
A Summary of Relational Totals: Entire Division

	Order-Giving		Socializing	
	A	**B**	**A**	**B**
'	26 (0.93)[1]	37 (0.97)	None	None
o	29 (1.04)	54 (1.42)	None	None
x	33 (1.18)	66 (1.74)	25 (0.88)	36 (0.95)
+	21 (0.75)	51 (1.34)	24 (0.86)	38 (1.00)
—	15 (0.54)	14 (0.37)	21 (0.75)	17 (0.45)

[1]Figures in parentheses indicate "relations per individual." In Division A, 28 persons responded; in Division B, 38 persons responded. Thus, for example: 26/28 = 0.93. There are 0.93 prescriptions per person in Division A.

TABLE III
A Summary of Relational Totals: Received by Division Heads Only

	Order-Giving		Socializing	
	DH:A	*DH:B*	*DH:A*	*DH:B*
'	7	7	None	None
o	9	13	None	None
x	12	16	4	3
+	4	13	2	2
—	11	3	6	4

Table IV is a summary of the intra-activity indices for the two divisions. By way of illustration, let us trace the process by which index (1), an index of understanding ($\Sigma'o/\Sigma'$) was calculated for Division A: To find the numerator, Table I is scanned for all patterns containing the combination 'o. These are patterns 2.1, 3.1, 3.2, 3.3, 4.1, 4.2, 4.3, and 5.1. The figure obtained is 24. To find the denominator it is necessary simply to examine Table II, the line marked '. The figure is 26. Thus index (1) for Division A is 24/26 or 92.31.

A set of criteria against which the indices may be evaluated is provided by a series of responses regarding perceptions by the people in each division of morale, productivity, and job satisfaction. Table V summarizes some of the findings:

³"None" indicates that no such pattern exists for the particular activity. The dash indicates that a pattern exists, but that in the pilot investigation no instances of this were found.

*Denotes inconsistent pattern, which includes both most desired and least desired (rejected).

TABLE IV

INDEX SUMMARY

| | | Order-Giving | | | | Socializing | | |
| | | Division A | | Division B | | Division A | | Division B | |
		Ratio	%	Ratio	%	Ratio	%	Ratio	%
Understanding									
	(1) $\Sigma'o/\Sigma'$	24/26	92.31	31/37	83.78	—			
	(2) $\Sigma'o/\Sigma o$	24/29	82.76	31/54	57.41	—			
Normative Conformity									
	(3) $\Sigma'x/\Sigma'$	22/26	84.61	30/37	81.08	—			
	(4) $\Sigma'x/\Sigma x$	22/33	66.67	30/66	45.45	—			
	(5) $\Sigma ox/\Sigma o$	26/29	89.66	48/54	88.89	—			
	(6) $\Sigma ox/\Sigma x$	26/33	78.79	48/66	72.73	—			
	(7) $\Sigma'ox/\Sigma'o$	21/24	87.50	29/31	93.55	—			
	(8) $\Sigma'ox/\Sigma x$	21/33	63.64	29/66	43.94	—			
Affective Conformity									
	(9a) $\Sigma+x/\Sigma+$	12/21	57.14	39/51	76.47	4/24	16.67	21/38	55.26
	(9b) $\Sigma-x/\Sigma-$	4/15	26.67	3/14	21.43	0/21	0	0/17	0
Satisfaction and Dissatisfaction[1]									
	(10a) $\Sigma'+/\Sigma'$	13/26	50.00	23/37	62.16	—			
D	(10b) $\Sigma'-/\Sigma'$	2/26	7.69	2/37	5.41	—			
	(11a) $\Sigma o+/\Sigma o$	13/29	44.83	34/54	62.96	—			
D	(11b) $\Sigma o-/\Sigma o$	2/29	6.89	3/54	5.56	—			
	(12a) $\Sigma'o+/\Sigma'o$	12/24	50.00	22/31	70.98	—			
D	(12b) $\Sigma'o-/\Sigma'o$	2/24	8.33	1/31	3.23	—			
	(13a) $\Sigma x+/\Sigma x$	12/33	36.36	39/66	59.09	4/25	16.00	21/36	58.33
D	(13b) $\Sigma x-/\Sigma x$	4/33	12.12	3/66	4.55	0/25	0	0/36	0
	(14) $\Sigma+/\Sigma(+)$ $+\Sigma(-)$	21/36	58.33	51/65	78.46	24/45	53.33	38/55	69.09
	(15) $\Sigma(+x)/\Sigma(+x)$ $+\Sigma(-x)$	12/16	75.00	39/42	92.86	4/4	100.00	21/21	100.00
	(16a) $\Sigma(')_x/\Sigma'$	7/26	26.92	7/37	18.92	—			
	(16b) $\Sigma(o)_x/\Sigma o$	9/29	31.03	13/54	24.07	—			
	(16c) $\Sigma(x)_x/\Sigma o$	12/33	36.36	16/66	24.24	4/25	16.00	3/36	8.33
	(16d) $\Sigma(+)_x/\Sigma+$	4/21	19.05	13/51	25.49	2/24	8.33	2/38	7.14
	(16e) $\Sigma(-)_x/\Sigma-$	11/15	73.33	3/14	21.43	6/21	28.57	4/17	23.53

[1]Indices of *dis*satisfaction, for which low values indicate satisfaction, are marked with a D.

Thus it is indicated that Division B consistently exceeds Division A in high or very high ratings in job satisfaction, perceived productivity, and perceived morale. This finding becomes more meaningful when we consider the M.S.S. results. In the sociometric indices of satisfaction, indices (10a), (11a), (12a), and (13a), Division B ranks higher. On all of the indices

TABLE V

A Summary of Perceptual Ratings of Job Satisfaction, Morale, and Productivity

	Job satisfaction of each person in division		Productivity of division		Morale of division	
	% rating high or very high	% rating low or very low	% rating high or very high	% rating low or very low	% rating high or very high	% rating low or very low
Division A	39.3	14.3	28.6	18.6	21.4	53.6
Division B	63.2	7.9	55.2	7.9	81.6	2.6

[1]Adapted from I. R. Weschler, M. Kahane and R. Tannenbaum, "Job Satisfaction, Productivity and Morale: A Case Study," *Occupational Psychology*, XXVI (January, 1952), p. 5.

of dissatisfaction, (10b), (11b), (12b), and (13b), Division A ranks higher. Thus, it would seem that at least as far as order-giving is concerned, the various measures of satisfaction and dissatisfaction vary concomitantly with the measures of job satisfaction, perceived productivity, and perceived morale. The indices of affective conformity, (9a) and (9b), and of affective atmosphere, (14) and (15), show a similar relationship. Here, too, the indices for Division B suggest the more harmonious social situation.

On the other hand, in understanding of prescription, higher indices (1) and (2) are found in Division A. Similarly, for five of the six indices of normative conformity, (3), (4), (5), (6), and (8), measures for Division A are somewhat higher than those for Division B, although the differences generally are slight. Only in index (7), which measures conformity to the understood ($\Sigma'ox/\Sigma'o$) does the index figure for Division B exceed that of Division A.

These findings indicate greater understanding of prescription and a somewhat higher degree of conformity to prescription in Division A than in Division B. But Division B ranks higher than Division A in satisfaction with interpersonal relations, in conformity of behavior (actual) to the desired, and in affective atmosphere. These results make sense in light of the following: (1) Division B provides higher ratings in job satisfaction, perceived morale, and perceived productivity. (2) As indicated by a broad *a priori* analysis of the two divisions, Division A appears to have certain attributes associated with restrictive leadership, while Division B has attributes associated with permissive leadership.

faction, (5) indices of acective atmosphere, and (6) indices of centraliza-

Further evidence is furnished by the indices of centralization. The prescribed, perceived, and actual relations are more centralized in the head of Division A than in the head of Division B—see (16a), (16b), (16c). On the other hand, the head of Division B receives a greater proportion of desired choices than the head of Division A—see (16d), while conversely, and significantly, a much greater proportion of the rejected relations is concentrated in the head of Division A, who heads the division characterized by restrictive leadership.

In examining indices for affective conformity, satisfaction, and affective atmosphere—see (9a), (13a), and (14)—for the activity of socializing after working hours, we observe that again the more harmonious social situation exists in the permissively led Division B. For indices (9b), conformity of actual to rejected, and (13b), dissatisfaction with actual relations, both divisions reveal zero scores. This is not hard to understand in view of the fact that usually, although not necessarily, people will not seek voluntary social intercourse with those they reject. An exception to this may be provided by instances in which socializing is oriented toward an end, such as the influencing of a superior regarding a promotion, even though, in fact, that superior may be rejected. Analogously, the scores for both divisions on index (15), which measures the extent to which socializing interactions with positive affect predominate over those with negative affect, are 100. Again, this is plausible because social contacts outside the job setting will be primarily with those people who are desired as social companions, rather than with those who are rejected in that role.

So far, order-giving has been the only goal-directed activity that we have considered, but we may inquire how the several indices compare when calculated for a number of other activities. Some relevant data are shown in Table VI:

TABLE VI

A COMPARISON OF SELECTED INDICES FOR SEVERAL GOAL-DIRECTED ACTIVITIES
IN DIVISIONS A AND B

	Understanding Index (1) $\Sigma'o/\Sigma'$		Normative Conformity Index (3) $\Sigma'x/\Sigma'$		Satisfaction Index (10a) $\Sigma'-/\Sigma'$	
	Div. A	Div. B	Div. A	Div. B	Div. A	Div. B
Order-Giving	92	84	85	81	50	62
Efficiency Rating	96	76	29	68	54	61
Grievance Handling	86	61	74	58	36	45
Determination of Promotions	59	63	45	50	22	45
Pointing Out Mistakes	79	74	71	80	43	55

For all activities but determination of promotions, understanding of prescription, as measured by index (1), is greater in the restrictively led Division A. Conversely, for all relations, satisfaction, as measured by index (10a), is greater in the permissively led Division B. However, in efficiency rating, determination of promotions, and pointing out mistakes, normative conformity in Division B exceeds corresponding measurements for Division A. At first glance this is puzzling, because, as indeed is the case for order-giving and grievance handling, we would have expected higher conformity in the restrictively led division. This lack of conformity can be explained, however: indices of centralization (not shown here) indicate that the head of Division A assumes much more responsibility for efficiency rating, promoting, and pointing out mistakes than is prescribed for him. Thus, the index of conformity is lowered, because the division head himself has gone beyond the limits set for him by organizational fiat.

Looking at Table VI from a different standpoint, it is apparent that some activities more often rank high on certain indices than others. For example, in understanding and satisfaction, order-giving and efficiency rating typically exceed the other indices in magnitude. Thus, the interpersonal networks for order-giving and efficiency rating are understood more clearly, and accepted somewhat better, than corresponding networks for grievance handling, for the determination of promotions, and for pointing out of mistakes. Normative conformity is highest for order-giving.

In most instances, indices of understanding for the various relations have the greatest magnitudes. They are followed by indices of normative conformity and by indices of satisfaction in that order.

In the pilot investigation, only eleven activities were studied. Thus, the data obtained did not lend themselves to an adequate construction of inter-activity indices.

VIII

Summary

The Multi-Relational Sociometric Survey is an extension of sociometric methodology to a variety of interpersonal activities and relations. Activities may be clearly directed to the attainment of organizational goals (goal-directed, e.g., order-giving) or they may not be so directed (nongoal-directed, e.g., socializing after working hours). Five relations are distinguished: (1) the prescribed, which resembles the organizational blue-print, (2) the perceived, which corresponds to the extent to which persons in the organization are aware of the blueprint, (3) the actual, which indicates the reported interactions among the members of the organization, (4) the desired, which indicates preferences regarding interactions, and (5) the rejected, which indicates aversions to interactions. For goal-directed activities all five of these relations are relevant; for nongoal-directed activities, only the last three are relevant.

A pilot investigation was conducted in a Southern California naval research and development laboratory. Sixty-six subjects, from two contrasting divisions, were studied. The data were organized in the form of a series of matrices, one for each activity. Information on the specific relations was entered in the cells of each matrix. Using the cell entries of any one matrix as raw data, a series of *intra-activity* indices was constructed: (1) indices of understanding, (2) indices of normative conformity, (3) indices of affective conformity, (4) indices of satisfaction and dissatisfaction, (5) indices of affective atmosphere, and (6) indices of centralization. Systematic overlap among intra-activity indices was discussed. Using entries dealing with a given relation as it appears in various activities as raw data, some *inter-activity* indices were also constructed.

An article using the data obtained in the pilot investigation suggests that there are some significant relationships between intra-activity index results, on the one hand, and perceived morale, perceived productivity, job satisfaction, and leadership style, on the other. For example, indices of satisfaction were higher in the more permissively led of the two divisions, which also had higher ratings from its members on morale, productivity, and job satisfaction. Understanding of the organizational blueprint was shown to be higher in the more restrictively led division.

The M.S.S. technique requires considerable further theoretical examination and empirical testing. Indices other than those proposed here may ultimately prove more useful, and various refinements or simplifications are no doubt possible. However, it is suggested that by making the sociometric method multi-relational through the systematic examination of several activities and relations, desirable dimensions of depth and realism are added to the sociometric study of social structure.

A PLAN FOR SOCIOMETRIC STUDIES IN A LONGITUDINAL PROGRAMME OF RESEARCH IN CHILD DEVELOPMENT

By Mary L. Northway

Introduction

The Institute of Child Study is 27 years old (13). In 1953 a federal mental health grant was made for the purpose of studying those factors which influence the development of mental health of children. Coincident with this the Board of Governors of the University of Toronto made available the gracious residence of the late Leighton McCarthy (Canadian Ambassador to the U.S.A.) to the Institute.

Here, in September, 1953, the Institute opened its nursery school for children two and a half to five, and elementary school for children from five to Grade III (to be expanded to grades IV, V, VI in successive years). At present 109 children are enrolled in class groups of 15 to 20. They are at school from 9 to 2.30 lunching with the staff and resting in their classrooms. The appearance of the school is that of a pleasant home and the atmosphere is one which the staff considers salutary for mental health, in which psychologically sound education is expressed through informality and interest. A nominal fee of $150 a year is charged and the children for the most part come from professional and business homes. This selective factor is reflected in the fact that the average I.Q. is about 118 and as high as 160+ in some cases. To be enrolled a child must be in good physical and mental health. Nevertheless, a wide range of disturbances and difficulties that are part of well children's development are encountered.

Although the schools are under the direction of their well-qualified principals and teachers, perhaps a unique feature of the Institute is that all members of the Institute staff and students, whether they be directors, researchers, parent educationists or University teachers (3), have some share in the life of the children (2); thus even the directors are invited to lunch, and a junior research assistant is better known in the kindergarten as an entertaining flautist than as a fledgling statistician. This results in the fact that although research is conducted according to the rigors of scientific method, it reflects continually the influence of association with lively children. Life amongst them saves the researcher from becoming too esoteric or abstract.

181

The Research Programme (9)

The main purpose of the research programme is to study the development of the child in terms of those qualities which influence his mental health. This is defined by the director, W. E. Blatz, as *psychological security* (1, 11).

Social development is an important aspect of mental health and a most useful instrument for probing it is sociometry. The writer's particular problem has therefore been to establish a plan by which a child's sociometric qualities may be appraised from time to time over a period of several years and to record these in such a way that they may be related to other known aspects of the child. As it is hoped that most children will remain in the school over many years, and as age groups are promoted as a whole each year, the groups will remain as constant as possible during the research period.

Our basic data are collected through administering a standard form of a three-criteria three-choice sociometric test to each group of children fall and spring. These are of course given verbally and individually and in most cases included with some other testing or "games". The results are scored, recorded and analyzed in the conventional way and depicted on a sociogram divided into tertiles (4).

As we have stated elsewhere (4) although a great deal of value has come out of the development of a scoring system in sociometry, the interest which has resulted in sociometric status has often obscured the essence of sociometry, namely that its focus is on relationships. "Scores which are statistically identical are rarely sociometrically equivalent" (4, p. 26). Our belief is that the evolution of a child's sociometric pattern may provide a better clue into his mental health than is given by his sociometric status. However in returning our focus to the study of patterns we want to take advantage of the progress which has been made in refining statistical procedures and to incorporate their assets as one important aspect of the patterns. As we are interested not merely in the pattern at one time but in its evolution we hope to compile our data so that we may be able to record and study this.*

Our technical problems therefore have been (1) to devise a means by which patterns may be analyzed, and (2) to devise a means by which

---

* The philosophy implied in this statement is not specific to our sociometric studies but basic to other areas. Thus it is in the item analysis of intelligence test

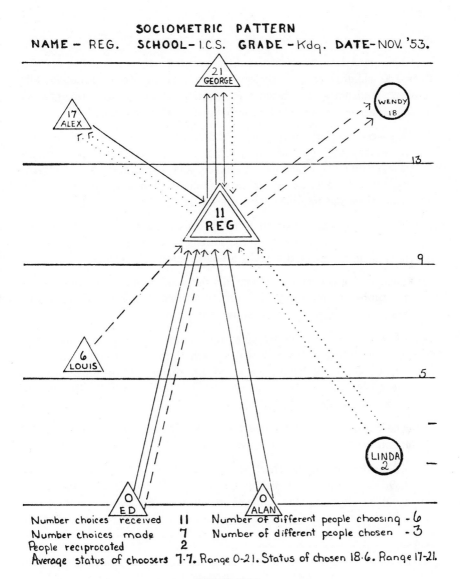

SOCIOMETRIC PATTERN

NAME – REG.   SCHOOL– I.C.S.   GRADE – Kdg.   DATE–NOV. '53.

Number choices received	11	Number of different people choosing – 6
Number choices made	7	Number of different people chosen – 3
People reciprocated	2	

Average status of choosers 7·7. Range 0-21. Status of chosen 18·6. Range 17-21.

DIAGRAM I

183

these may be compared from time to time. The methods so far developed are as follows:

A. *Depicting an Individual's Sociometric Pattern* (Diagrams I and II)

This procedure was reached after working out the patterns of more than 100 children in the Toronto public schools. In consultation with teachers, students and colleagues cooperating in the project we gradually modified various suggested ideas into the following procedure.

(1) A page is divided horizontally into four equal parts. The dividing lines correspond to the points at which scores from a sociometric test are significantly above chance, at chance, and significantly below. Working from the data as set out in a standard sociometric matrix or summary sheet the following steps are taken:

(2) The subject whose pattern is being considered is placed on this diagram at the place where his sociometric score falls. He is represented by a double triangle if a male, a double circle if a female.

(3) Each individual who is chosen by the subject and each who chooses the subject is represented by a circle or triangle and placed on the diagram according to his sociometric status.

(4) Each first choice made by or to the subject is shown by a solid line; each second by a broken line and each third by a dotted line. (It is possible of course by the use of colours to indicate on which criterion the choice was made.) An arrowhead shows in which direction the choice was made.

(5) The choices between the individuals making up the subjects' constellation may be included in a similar fashion.

(6) At the bottom of the sheet space is given for entering relevant data such as: Number of individuals chosen by the subject; number of individuals choosing the subject; number of reciprocals; average and range of status of chosen; average and range of status of the choosers.

---

rather than in the gross score. in the form of the child's ability in reading or numbering rather than the absolute level of achievement that we are interested. The fundamental question changes from one of "how much?" to one of "what kind?" We believe that if the "personality is unique" it deserves to be studied in its uniqueness and not in its similarities to other personalities.

SOCIOMETRIC PATTERN
NAME- JOE   SCHOOL- I.C.S.   GRADE- KDG.   DATE- NOV.'53

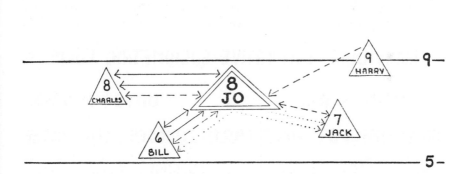

13—

9—

5—

Number choices received 8. Number of different people choosing 4.
Number choices made 9. Number of different people chosen 3.
People reciprocated 3.
Average status of choosers 7.5. Range 6-9.
Average status of chosen 7. Range 6-8.

DIAGRAM II

This gives in one diagram all the sociometric data of a single individual from a single test and sets it forth with fair accuracy and clarity. It is easy to compare the diagram of one child's pattern with that of another and as the two examples used as illustrations show, to see their similarities and differences.

B. *Individual's cumulative sociometric records* (Diagram III)

A practical problem which occurs in all cumulative studies is that of space. Not only do filing cases become cluttered, but unless data are recorded in compact form they become increasingly difficult to work with as the years go by. Therefore consideration has been given carefully to conciseness with relevancy. Presuming that the study is continued for the five years there will be a minimum of ten tests for each child. Records therefore have been devised by which all the data for one child on one test are set forth and can be readily compared with the data from successive tests. To

INDIVIDUAL CUMULATIVE SOCIOMETRIC FORM

NAME - Req.   DATE - NOV. '53.

SCORE	CHOSEN BY	FOR	CHILD	CHOOSES	FOR	SCORE
21	GEORGE	103		GEORGE	111	21
17	ALEX	001		ALEX	033	17
6	LOUIS	200				
2	LINDA	033	1 1			
0	ED	112				
0	ALAN	011				
				WENDY	202	18
7.7.	6.	335	R.2.	3		18.6

DATE - MARCH '54

DIAG.3

186

be able to see what changes and what remains constant about him is of prime consideration.

This type of form originated from a three-year study of nursery school children (10), and has been organized in its present form by my associate, Lindsay Duthie.

Diagram III shows the present form. A sheet is set up to record four test results. Thus the results of these tests can be seen at a glance. In entering the data the following steps are taken:

(1) The child's score is placed in the center column at the level relative to chance: significantly above; significantly below; or around chance.

(2) All those choosing him are placed on the left by name in order of their sociometric test and the criterion and position each chose him *for* is entered. To illustrate: Reg is chosen by George whose status is 21 as first choice on the first criterion and third on the third.

(3) Those whom the child chooses are placed to the right with the criterion and position indicated and the chosens' status. Thus Reg chooses George first on each of the criteria.

(4) At the bottom is given a summary of these data. These are self-explanatory in the diagram. The "R" is the number of reciprocals.

(5) Data from subsequent tests are entered in successive forms. By coding (e.g. encircling in colour) it is simple to see which children's names have appeared on different tests, and to enter by symbols change in the relationship as increasing or decreasing in intensity.

Progress to Date

Since our new school of the Institute was opened in September, a sociometric test has been given in all grades and two tests, four months apart, to the children in nursery school and kindergarten. Data have been recorded into individual patterns and also entered on the cumulative record sheets.

These data have already been made use of in a study (12) relating sociometric status to motor skills and a study (6) relating sociometric status to creativity. They have also been used in preliminary case studies of children of similar sociometric status who differ in sociometric patterns and in preliminary studies of interaction of children with their friends and non-friends (5, 7). They have also been incorporated into routine use for case work with the individual children, and are considered useful as complementary to intelligence, achievement and personality tests in diagnosis and therapy.

FUTURE DIRECTIONS

Although *our* major interest is to trace the change in sociometric patterns of children over a five-year period and to relate these to our total knowledge of each child, there are several other possibilities for using data which have been organized in this way. These, it is envisioned, may be adopted by colleagues and graduate students.

I. *Types:* It is obvious that these patterns may be sorted into types (8). Thus one may attempt to classify "open" and "closed" patterns; or "climbers" (those who choose above themselves) and "pullers" (those who choose below); or "superficial" (receiving a lot of third choices) and "deep" (receiving first choices). Once such classifications are made it is a simple matter using one or more characteristics of the pattern to relate these to other known characteristics of the individual—intelligence, age, economic status, religion, school marks, etc., etc. Such approach lends itself neatly to accepted experimental design and offers researchers at the M.A. and Ph.D. a wealth of hypotheses.

II. *Sociometric structure:* It is obvious that by studying the total sociometric information obtained each year in each grade, it will be possible to ascertain to what extent structures remain constant at different age levels regardless of differing individuals (10). For example, is a degree of sex cleavage typical of kindergarten sociometric structure or does it depend on the individuals making up a kindergarten group of a particular year?

III. *The Whole Child:* Another method falls betwixt the scientific and clinical approach. This is the consideration of the individual's sociometric pattern in relation to all the other known facts about *him*. These other facts include his performance on standardized intelligence, achievement and personality tests including an item analysis of these; his experience as revealed by projectives; descriptive assessment by his teachers and parents, and clinical appraisal by the psychologist. These are considered not only at one time but as he grows and as they change from year to year. Results from such an approach do not immediately lend themselves to neat experimental design. They do, however, enable us to see the child functioning as a whole and how such functioning is reflected in his sociometric pattern.

IV. *Study of the action of individuals of similar sociometric status but different sociometric patterns:* What is the difference in social action between two children such as Reg and Jo whose sociometric patterns are shown in the above diagrams? Both boys have about average sociometric status; both are in kindergarten, differing in age by only two months; both slightly above average in I.Q., differing only by four points; both are considered normal, pleasant children by their teacher.

We have been concerned with how these boys with these different patterns differ in their actual social actions. Observations have been made of the number and content of their contacts, and the content of these in the playroom and on the playground. More specifically, their interaction with their chosen friends has been observed, and tape recorded at a special luncheon party (5). Later their interaction with each other was similarly observed at another party. Too, the teacher has been asked to have them draw a picture of themselves and their friends and to tell her about what they are doing. Also it is planned to watch their interaction with their friends and with their non-friends in the problem situation of putting a new mechanical train together and setting it running around its track. How the decision is reached as to who should "wind it up" offers a natural but superb opportunity for studying the intricacies of social interaction!

V. *Study of "Group Therapy":* It should be quite possible to make objective studies of the effect of planning groups in terms of known sociometric facts. As sociometric results are made known to the teachers and the children discussed with them it is possible to arrange lunch tables, work groups, play activities on the basis of known facts and to ascertain whether through wise use of natural situations the isolated child can be helped to make contacts and the overly social child to become more balanced. Such "group therapy" will however form merely a part in a total mental health programme as one hesitates to interfere unduly with the natural course of what we believe to be a salutary educational achievement.

Conclusion

It is intended from time to time to issue articles in this Journal and elsewhere describing the results of specific studies and giving progress reports. However we believe that the greatest potential value of our programme lies in the fact that we can trace our children's sociometric patterns as they evolve over a period of five years. These, related to the wealth of other information we will have about the children will surely provide answers to some of the besetting problems of social development, social inter-relatedness, and mental health.

Sociometric Studies of Research in Child Development

BIBLIOGRAPHY

1. Blatz, W. E. *Understanding the Young Child,* Clarke, Irwin & Co., Ltd., 1944, pp. 278.
2. Bulletin of the Institute of Child Study, Volume 16, Number 2, June, 1954.
3. Calendar of the Institute of Child Study, 1954-55.
4. Northway, Mary L. *A Primer of Sociometry,* University of Toronto Press, 1952.
5. ———— & Duthie, Lindsay. Children's interaction with their friends at lunch. (In progress.)
6. ———— & McCallum, Margaret. The relationship of sociometric status to children's creativity. (In progress.)
7. ————, Millichamp, Dorothy A., and Duthie, Lindsay. A comparison of two boys of similar sociometric status and differing sociometric pattern. (In progress.)
8. Potashin, Reva. *A sociometric study of children's friendships.* SOCIOMETRY IX: 11.
9. Programme of Research. Institute of Child Study, September 1953, pp. 7 (mimeo) (private report.)
10. Quarrington, Mary O. Developmental Aspects of Sociometric Ratings of Nursery School Children. M.A. thesis, Univ. of Toronto, 1953, p. 48.
11. Salter, Mary D. *An Evaluation of Adjustment Based Upon the Concept of Security.* Univ. of Toronto Studies, Child Development Series, No. 18, Univ. of Toronto Press, 1940, pp. 72.
12. Simonoff, D. Relationship between Motor Development and Sociometric Status in a selected group of Young Children (M.A. thesis in progress.)
13. Staff of the Institute of Child Study. *Twenty-Five Years of Child Study,* Univ. of Toronto Press, 1951, pp. 196.

BUDDY RATINGS: POPULARITY CONTEST OR LEADERSHIP CRITERIA?[*][1]

By Robert J. Wherry
and Douglas H. Fryer

In Brief

The need for criteria against which to test predictors of leadership potential led some of the armed forces personnel research organizations to turn to "buddies," "peers" or coworkers for ratings in preference to evaluation by superiors. Industrial personnel research is also turning to this technique. There has been some criticism that "buddy ratings"[2] are not criteria of leadership, but rather mere popularity contests. This criticism deserves investigation. This study conducted on two Officer Candidate Classes investigates the interrelationship of a dozen different criteria secured from several sources. These included ratings at various times throughout the six-month course by fellow students and by superiors, as well as various course grades. Intensive statistical analysis of the results seem to justify the continued use of buddy ratings as leadership criteria. The buddy nominations (variable 1) measured as early as the first month of training the same factors which they measured three months later. Moreover, what they measured in the first month is the same as that rated by superiors, rating after four months' observation. The ratings by superiors measured something quite different in the first and fourth months. It was not until the fourth month that superiors' ratings reflected the leadership factor which fellow students identified in their first-month ratings.

The Search for Criteria

One problem is common to all groups engaged in personnel research. It is that of developing criteria of performance, efficiency, or behavior against

---

[*] This article is reprinted in full, by permission, from *Personnel Psychology, A Journal of Applied Research* (Vol. 2, No. 2, Summer, 1949, p. 147-159), Erwin K. Taylor, Managing Editor, 1727 Harvard Street, N. Y., Washington 9, D. C.

[1] This study is based upon data collected in connection with Project No. 4071, Personnel Research Section, Adjutant General's Office, Department of the Army. The opinions expressed are those of the authors and do not necessarily express the official views of the Department of the Army.

[2] The term "buddy ratings" is used in some military circles as a popular substitute for sociometric tests. (Editor's Note.)

which to test personnel devices, procedures and methods. This problem is equally present in civilian and military research. In many situations, the only feasible measure consists of a rating of performance. But who can best do the rating—superiors, of whom there are at most one or two who know each worker; or coworker, from whom a number of independent judgments can be secured?

When the war created an urgent need for research in almost every aspect of personnel, the workers in the field were faced with the need for developing criteria for numerous jobs. In many instances selection programs were developed for training courses, and academic success could be used as a criterion for predictors in the aptitude areas. But most of the jobs for which selection was desired encompassed a great deal more than these aptitudes. Leadership, personality and interest factors were at least as important as academic success. To secure criteria against which to test predictors in these areas, research workers were forced to fall back on ratings.

Well aware of the weaknesses of conventional rating methods, the personnel technicians sought to minimize them. To overcome the unreliability of individual ratings they looked for situations in which a number of independent raters could be used. Even though a single rating may be unreliable, the average of a number of such ratings may provide a stable measure relatively free of bias and the idiosyncrasies of every single rater.

They recognize the fact that in any group it was easier to identify and rank the individuals who were extremely good and those who were extremely poor in the job than to rank the middle group. With only one or two raters for each man, this method identifies only extreme groups. However, with a sizable number of raters it was possible to have each rater nominate the best four or five and the poorest four or five members of the group. Subtracting the number of "poor" from the number of "good" mentions and dividing the remainder by the number of possible mentions yielded a continuum usable for criterion purposes.

There was seldom if ever a situation in which the number of supervisors familiar with the efficiency of the worker was adequate to permit multiple nominations. For most jobs, on the other hand, there was a substantial number of coworkers in a position to observe the man's work if only they could, and would, evaluate it properly. The next natural step was to have the nominating of best and poorest workers done by the workers themselves. Many jobs lent themselves very well to this procedure. Groups in which the members worked close together, so that each worker knew the others, seemed so suited.

There were other aspects of peer or coworker ratings that recommended this procedure to the personnel research worker. There are often aspects of a position which the coworker is in a better position to evaluate than is the supervisor: e.g., aspects of personality often carefully concealed from higher-ups.

Under the stimulus of this set of circumstances, evaluation by peers—"buddy ratings," if you will—increased in frequency in armed forces personnel research.

Like all criteria, they suffer from the need to accept them at face value. Standards against which to test them—criteria of criteria—do not usually exist. If there is available a yardstick against which to test a criterion, it would itself become the primary measure and the need for the criterion would at once vanish.

Thus, when the critics of buddy ratings objected and said they were no more than popularity contests, there was little evidence on which to refute the criticism. True, the critics offered no data in support of their contentions. Yet the burden of the proof rests with the advocates rather than with the critics of the procedure.

A Rare Opportunity

Usually the personnel research worker considers himself fortunate to be in a position to secure a single adequate criterion. In developing devices for the selection of enlisted men to attend Army Officer Candidate Schools, the staff of the Personnel Research Section found that it was in a position to collect performance measures from a variety of sources. Further, it was possible to identify the situations in which several different kinds of raters were able to observe trainees. Finally, it was possible to observe a newly formed group that worked at a common task and whose members were in close association with each other.

The Groups We Studied

The studies were conducted at the Signal Corps Officer Candidate School at Fort Monmouth, N. J. The data were gathered in the summer of 1945. Two classes were studied. There were 82 Officer Candidates in the first class and 52 in the second.

The Variables

In addition to scores on a high-level intelligence test (Officer Candidate Test) and academic grades, nine sets of ratings were collected by different methods, from different raters and at different times. The ratings were collected from the first class (82 students) at the end of one, two and four months in the school. In the case of the second class, ratings were collected only at the end of the first month of training. Table 1 describes the several criterion and predictor variables and the pattern of their collection.

In addition to the variables described in Table 1, data were also available on the following:

Retention beyond two months. Officer candidates were discharged at any time during the training period for academic inaptitude, disciplinary reasons, or failure to show promise of having the personality characteristics thought necessary in an officer. For purposes of study each class was divided into two parts, those who were released prior to the end of the second month of work and those who were retained beyond that time.

Graduation. Failure (for any reason) to graduate from OCS and receive a commission represented a waste of time, money and manpower. To determine the relationship between the various other variables and this personnel action, the classes were divided on the basis of whether or not each individual successfully completed the course.

Officer Candidate Test. This is a high level pencil and paper test of general intelligence which had been administered to all applicants for OCS prior to their admission to the school.

Recommendation Blank. This is a standard form sent to civilian acquaintances of the applicant. The names are supplied by the candidate. It is primarily a checklist and rating form which is objectively scored.

OCS Interview. Prior to being selected to attend OCS, each candidate is interviewed by a board of officers. A standardized interview is employed and the members of the board rate the candidate on several traits observable in the interview and thought relevant to officer success. The forms are objectively scored.

Previous Performance. Ratings by non-commissioned officers under whom they had previously served were available for the Officer Candidates studied.

The Analysis

Four separate factorial analyses were computed. Three of the analyses were for the three sets of ratings collected in the first, second and fourth month for class one. The fourth analysis was done for the variables collected on the second class at the end of the first month of training. Four factors were identified by the analyses. The first three of these were common to all four analyses. The fourth was present only for the ratings collected from the first class in its fourth month. (See Tables 5 and 6.)

TABLE 1
The Criterion Variables Studied

No.	Symbol	Nature of Criterion	Obtained from	Reference group	Class one			Class two
					1	2	4	
1	AN-S-S	*Anonymous Nominations by Students by Section:* Each Student nominated 5 men in his section "who possess the personality traits most desirable in an Army officer" and 5 men in his section "who possess the personality traits least desirable in an Army officer." Score in this and other nominating criteria was: "most" mentions minus "least" mentions divided by possible mentions.	Student	Section	x	x	x	x
2	AN-S-C	*Anonymous Nominations by Student by Class:* Same as 1 except nominations were from entire class rather than section.	Student	Entire Class		x		
3	ALR-S-S	*Average Leadership Ratings by Students by Section:* Every student rated each of the other students in his section for 10 leadership qualities on a school form. Each rating form was first averaged for the 10 ratings, and then all forms for a given student were in turn averaged.	Student	Section	x	x	x	x
4	ALR-JTO-C	*Average Leadership Ratings by Junior Tactical Officer by Class:* Same as 3, except that ratings were made by 8 Junior Tactical Officers each rating all men of the class known to him.	Jr. Tactical Officers	Entire Class	x	x	x	x
5	LR-STO-C	*Leadership Ranking by Senior Tactical Officer by Class:* The Senior Tactical Officer ranked the students in each class according to leadership. Position in the ranking was the students score.	Sr. Tactical Officer	Entire Class		x		

195

TABLE 1 (*continued*)

No.	Symbol	Nature of Criterion	Obtained from	Reference group	Class one 1	2	4	Class two
6	AN-JTO-S	*Anonymous Nomination by Junior Tactical Officer by Section:* Same as criterion 1 except that nominations were made by 8 Junior Tactical Officers.	Jr. Tactical Officers	Section			x	
7	AN-TO-C	*Anonymous Nominations by Tactical Officers by Class:* Same as criterion 2 except that nominations were made by the 8 Junior and 1 Senior Tactical Officers by class.	8 Jr. and 1 Sr. Tactical Officer	Entire Class			x	
8	OER-TO	*Officer Efficiency Report by Tactical Officers:* This was a two-section efficiency report consisting of 25 forced-choice items and a 20-point overall scale completed by the most appropriate Junior Tactical Officer, and the same 20-point scale completed by the Senior Tactical Officer.	Jr. Tac. and Sr. Tactical Officers	Individual			x	
9	ALR-AI-C	*Average Leadership Rating by Academic Instructors by Class:* Same as criterion 4 except that forms were completed by Academic Instructors for all students of class known to each.	Academic Instructors	Entire Class	x	x		x
10	AAG-AI	*Average Academic Grades by Academic Instructors:* Based upon an average of daily and monthly objective examinations.	Academic Instructors	Individual	x	x		x

Factor I. *Academic Standing.* Highest loadings for this factor are for academic grades (10), leadership ratings by academic instructors (9), and for the Officer Candidate Test of Intelligence (11). Moderate to small, but always significant, loadings appear also on the Anonymous Nominations by Students (1) and for Average Leadership Ratings by Students (3), indicating that sectional standing among "buddies" was determined in part by the observed performance in the class room. Student nominations by class (2) and all ratings by tactical officers (4, 5, 6, 7, 8) who were unacquainted with classroom performance showed insignificant loadings (with a slightly negative trend) on this factor. The factor is therefore identified as *Academic Standing*.

Factor II. *Leadership*. High loadings on this factor occur for all student nominations and ratings by class or section (1, 2, 3) for all periods for both classes. While loadings are only moderate for early periods for ratings or ranking by tactical officers (4, 5), the loadings become equally high for ratings, rankings, and nominations by the tactical officers (4, 5, 6, 7, 8) after 4 months acquaintanceship. Ratings by academic instructors (9) were low but significant, while those for grades (10) and the OCT (11) were not significant. The fact that both students and officers agree on this factor serves to identify it as *the leadership* factor which both were attempting to rate.

Factor III. *Tactical Standing*. This factor has loadings on all, and only on ratings, rankings, and nominations by tactical officers (4, 5, 6, 7, and 8). Loadings are about equally high for all periods. The lowest significant loading occurs on the officer efficiency report (8), where the nature of the forced-choice items in part controls the ratings. This factor is therefore identified as *standing in tactical performance*.

Factor IV. *Group Difference Correction*. This factor has moderate loadings on only the anonymous nominations *by class* by students (2) and tactical officers (7). The only other loading is a barely significant one for leadership ratings by junior tactical officers by class (4). This factor appears to be a *corrective element* based upon unequal range of leadership ability within the various sections.

Reliability

To be at all useful, a criterion must naturally be reliable, i.e., those who are rated high on the measure at one time should continue to be so rated after an elapse of time. This study permitted the comparison of a number of rating techniques on the first class after the passage of one month and again three months after the original ratings had been made. Table 2 shows these reliabilities. While student nominations and student leadership ratings were about equal in stability after the passage of one month, both were more reliable than ratings assigned by either the Junior or Senior Tactical Officers.

All of the reliability coefficients over a three-month period are smaller than over a one month interval. The reliability of student nominations,

TABLE 2
REPEAT RELIABILITY OF SELECTED CRITERIA

Criterion	After 1 month	After 4 months
1. (Buddy Nominations)	.75	.58
3. (Buddy Ratings)	.76	.17
4. (Superiors' Ratings)	.42	.19
5. (Superiors' Ratings	.58	.28

however, remains at a level that may be considered useful. The reliability of the other three variables is such as to make doubtful their usefulness as criteria. In the case of the student's rating (as distinguished from nomination) and both Junior and Senior Tactical Officer ratings, it is clear that what they measure in the fourth month is something quite different than what they measure in the first month.

Predictability

To the extent that criteria are collected for the purpose of using them as a basis for the testing and weighting of selection instruments, it is essential that they be predictable. The entire philosophy of personnel selection rests on the assumption that, to a degree at least, it is possible to predict in advance of selection which applicants for a job will be more and which less successful. If the measure of success criterion cannot be predicted even by itself, it is neither feasible nor worthwhile to predict it by any battery of personnel instruments.

Table 3 compares the predictability of the nominating technique with that of academic grades for a number of possible selection instruments.

TABLE 3
PREDICTABILITY OF CRITERION 1 (BUDDY RATINGS) AND CRITERION 10 (ACADEMIC GRADES) BY VARIOUS KINDS OF PREDICTORS AFTER ONE MONTH (HIGHER COEFFICIENT IN EACH COMPARISON IS UNDERLINED)

	Buddy ratings (Var. 1)			Academic grades (Var. 10)		
	(1)	Class	(2)	(1)	Class	(2)
Aptitude:						
Officer Candidate Test	.23		.29	.56		.80
Personality:						
Recommendation Blank	.41		.36	.12		.14
Interview	.18		.13	.05		—.04
Previous Performance:						
Ratings by Non-Commissioned Officers	.19		.33	—.15		.15

Comparisons are presented for both class one and class two. The Officer Candidate Test is the only selection instrument for which academic grade is more predictable than buddy nominations. This is gratifying, since the test was included to predict academic success. The other predictors were included to afford measures of the non-academic aspects of leadership.

Relation to Personnel Actions

Personnel who fail the training course for a position (in this case those who do not graduate from Officer Candidate School) represent a waste of time and money. There is obviously no point in hiring employees who will never be put on the job for which they were employed or of sending men who will never become officers to Officer Candidate School. From this point of view, a desirable criterion should be fairly well related to retention in the school and to its successful completion. Table 4 compares buddy nominations and academic grades with respect to their relationship to these personnel actions. Both criteria are equal in their relationship to separation and non-graduation. Thus it would appear that each is measuring an important aspect of success. Since the two criteria have low correlation, it is also clear that each is measuring a different aspect. In this situation, use of only one (and academic success is frequently used alone in such situations) would be doing only half the job. Obviously ultimate

TABLE 4

CORRESPONDENCE OF CRITERION 1 (AN-S-S) AND CRITERION 10 (AAG-AI) TO RETENTION (FOR AT LEAST 2 MONTHS) AND TO GRADUATION

	Buddy Ratings (AN-S-S)	Academic Grades AAG-AI
Retention (at least 2 months)	.70	.71
Graduation	.49	.50

success at Officer Candidate School depends as much on what buddy nominations measure as it does on what academic grades measure.

What Does It All Add Up To?

The analysis of criteria has necessarily been predicated on what amounts to an examination of the internal relationships among the various ratings and other measures of success. The study has looked into the comparative predictability of buddy ratings and such other criteria as academic grades, attrition, and graduation. Moreover, the various available criterion measures have been shown to differ widely in their reliability.

TABLE 5

INTERCORRELATIONS AND RESIDUALS FOR CRITERION MEASURES AND OCT AFTER VARYING NUMBERS OF MONTHS FOR TWO OFFICER CANDIDATE SCHOOL CLASSES AT FORT MONMOUTH IN 1945

(Decimals in Front of Correlation Coefficients Have Been Omitted)

A. Class 1—1 month

	1	3	4	5	9	10	OCT
1		72	30	36	49	38	23
3	01		27	40	44	29	08
4	02	00		60	−13	−10	−05
5	−05	01	03		14	10	−08
9	−02	01	−02	10		71	42
10	−01	02	−02	04	−01		56
OCT	03	−06	06	−06	−01	07	

B. Class 1—2 months

	1	3	4	5	9	10	OCT
1		76	40	45	47	52	39
3	00		27	20	31	40	25
4	01	02		73	26	04	−05
5	06	−02	02		25	10	11
9	−01	−05	04	−05		49	30
10	00	−02	02	−01	01		51
OCT	02	−04	01	08	−09	−03	

C. Class 1—4 months

	1	2	3	4	5	6	7	8	OCT
1		76	59	54	53	48	46	55	19
2	02		60	78	66	62	74	74	−08
3	01	01		44	42	49	29	45	00
4	01	−02	−01		82	76	83	80	−27
5	−07	−03	−03	−03		75	73	70	01
6	02	−02	04	−05	02		65	76	−12
7	02	−01	02	−04	01	02		71	−18
8	03	−01	−04	−06	−02	05	−01		−13
OCT	04	−01	−04	−04	06	−07	05	06	

D. Class 2—1 month

	1	3	4	5	9	10	OCT
1		75	48	48	49	40	29
3	04		32	48	53	30	20
4	04	−07		75	42	25	02
5	−03	03	02		49	29	12
9	−08	01	03	03		60	45
10	05	03	03	−02	02		80
OCT	04	04	−05	−03	00	06	

TABLE 6

FACTOR LOADINGS ON VARIOUS CRITERIA TAKEN AFTER VARYING NUMBER OF MONTHS IN CLASS

(Decimal Points in Front of Factor Loadings Have Been Omitted)

Factor	I. Academic standing				II. Leadership				III. Tactical standing				IV. Group difference correction
Class	1	1	1	2	1	1	1	2	1	1	1	2	1
Months in class	1	2	4	1	1	2	4	1	1	2	4	1	4
Criterion													
1. AN-S-S	41	52	55	30	74	74	64	80	09	10	08	04	17
2. AN-S-C			19				87				09		40
3. ALR-S-S	29	41	28	22	80	72	70	81	00	—10	—10	—04	—11
4. ALR-JTO-C	—16	—09	—11	08	37	50	80	50	65	66	51	67	22
5. LR-STO-C	—01	04	18	19	47	39	69	53	61	79	62	67	04
6. AN-JTO-S			—06				71				43		—09
7. AN-TO-C			—16				60				51		49
8. OER-TO			—08				79				32		09
9. ALR-AI-S	81	56		57	26	21		49	—11	25			15
10 AAG-AJC	90	79		91	02	12		08	09	04			17
11. OCT	55	68	49	80	—03	00	—14	00	—02	00	00	00	02 —09

From the analyses presented above we may make the following tentative conclusions about the use of buddy nominations as criteria:

(1) *From the factor analyses:*

    (a) Buddy ratings appear to be the purest measure of "leadership." Tactical officers are also able to rate this trait but their ratings are quite heavily weighted by tactical standing. Academic instructor's ratings are practically useless for the evaluation of this trait.

    (b) Coworkers are able, at the end of one month, to evaluate leadership to a degree equalled by instructors (tactical not academic) only after four months of observation.

    (c) Nominations (variable 1) which are more reliable than graphic ratings (variable 3) are equally good measures of leadership. They have the added advantage of being easier to secure.

    (d) Nominations by class appear to be better measures of the leadership factor than any other variable. This would appear to indicate the advisability of predicting buddy ratings on the widest base upon which the acquaintanceship of the members of the group permits.

(2) *From the reliability comparisons.* While both nominations and graphic ratings by coworkers show quite satisfactory reliability after one month, the reliability of nominations after four months is outstandingly higher than that of any of the

other variables upon which the test was made. This is probably further evidence of the fact that the nominating technique has the property of early identification of the members of the group who constitute the two extremes of the leadership distribution.

(3) *Predictability.* Except for prediction by the aptitude test, nominations were better predicted by all of the proposed selection devices than was the more commonly used academic grade criterion.

(4) *Agreement with personnel action.* If ability to remain in the school at least two months is considered desirable, it may seem that nominations by buddies are as highly correlated as are academic grades, with this overall measure of success. Similarly, buddy ratings contribute as much as academic grades to the overall criterion of graduation.

The Factor Analysis

Multiple factor analysis was computed on each of four matrices. Three orthogonal factors emerged from each of three of them. The fourth matrix yielded four factors. In each case the final factors were rotated to simple structure. The matrices of correlation and of residuals are presented in Table 5. Table 6 presents the factor loadings. Since three of the four factors found were common to three of the analyses, the loadings are presented together.

B. Statistical Methods and Models

INTRODUCTION

By Leo Katz

Conventionally, a social group is taken to be a well-defined collection of individuals organized for one or more specified activities. It is quickly apparent, to even the most naïve of observers, that the total configuration of the interpersonal relationships is both enormously complicated and subject to continuous change. A process as complicated as this desperately needs a simplified model, at the same time that it limits the applicability of such a model in that it cannot represent the on-going process with any degree of completeness.

Nevertheless, the success enjoyed by the Moreno Sociometric Test in the past two decades indicates quite clearly that, at least for some groups, there is sufficient stability in the configuration that a description of a group at one point in time may be useful for some relatively long period. Furthermore, the description may be quite coarse for individual relationships and still capture a great deal of the flavor of the over-all structure of the group.

Use of the Moreno Sociometric Test as the basic instrument has forced most investigators to employ a model that depicts the group relationship as an aggregate of interpersonal connections. Such a model has definite limitations, although it must be said that, thus far, these limitations have not seriously impeded the progress of the art. Nonetheless, it may be worthwhile to specify these limitations.

First, the Moreno model implies a point-wise atomistic structure which leads quite readily to random models for the group, but does not lead with equal facility to models involving greater interaction in the choices. Practically no attention has been given to the construction of non-null models, and the only statistical distributions obtained so far are those for the purely random case.

Second, there is a traditionally strong tendency to exhibit the quality of the response of one individual to another in the simplest possible way. Even for the simplest kinds of relationships involving people, the response of one individual to another is many-dimensional and, in each dimension, is capable of practically continuous variation in its quality. In conventional application of a sociometric test, most investigators have focused attention on only one aspect of the complex interpersonal relationship. Only rarely has anyone tried to cover, with a number of separate but related sociometric measures, the many facets of this intricate relationship.

Another feature of this tendency toward simple representation, which has the effect of further abstracting the sociometric test from the group situation it is intended to depict, is that most investigators, in order to achieve some manageable simplicity, have agreed to use only two or three categories of the response. Thus, in his early investigations, Moreno used "like," "dislike," and "indifferent" as his three categories. Later investigators have sometimes used "like" and "indifferent" as the two categories of response.

Perhaps the most astonishing aspect of this double, extreme simplification of representation of interpersonal relationships is that the resulting picture of the group is as faithful as it is. The sociometric test, in its most simplified version, has been used as a direct operating tool in the management and manipulation of groups with outstanding success for the past twenty years or more. This suggests that either the many aspects of the interpersonal relationship are highly interrelated or, when only one particular kind of functioning of the group process is under discussion, that it may be possible to select a single sociometric device which will adequately represent the factor or factors in the group that are responsible for the operation in question.

Recognizing that simplicity in the model is a cardinal virtue in scientific explanation, and that a realistic view of the functioning of a group in terms of interpersonal relationships would present an extremely formidable machinery, most investigators have been content to work with models based on one (or possibly two) variables, and have taken values limited in most cases to zero and one. In a few cases, minus one is also included as a possible value. If these limitations are kept firmly in mind the reader should have no real difficulty in assessing the following papers.

Most of the work represented in the papers in this section was done with a view to obtaining probability distributions leading to statistical evaluation of the significance of certain phenomena observed in functioning groups. In some cases the sample space for the investigation has been expressly exhibited. In other cases it is only presented implicitly. In each case the reader should take into account the limitations placed on the quality of the explanation by the statistical methods used. For example, practically all of the early work of Urie Bronfenbrenner is invalidated, due to his almost complete reliance on the binomial probability model and the consequent assumption, for the group, that the choice by one individual of another is made *in vacuo* and independently of his choices of others in the group. It is for this reason that none of his work is represented in the set of papers that follows. These papers have been examined for scientific accuracy; on the whole it would appear that there are no serious errors of omission or commission in the assumptions made. Beyond this, the editors have only two words of advice to the reader: *Caveat emptor!*

FOUNDATIONS OF SOCIOMETRIC MEASUREMENT

By Joan H. Criswell

The tracing of the internal structure of social groups and of the delicate behavioral balances existing between populations demands a mathematical implementation peculiarly its own. Although the temptation may be great, methods of analysis cannot be taken over bodily from such related and more highly developed fields as for example, psychometrics.

One factor making for considerable difference between measurement of group structure and measurement of individual traits is the fact that the former type of investigation involves a variety of asymmetrical frequency distributions widely deviating from the normal. In an investigation, therefore, it cannot be taken for granted that the data are distributed normally, and a problem of first importance is to determine the types of curve involved and the adaptations of method required by such distributions.

Another difference lies in the greater interest of social measurement in the patterns arising from interpersonal relationships. This requires the invention of charts suitable for the visual presentation of such configurations. At present functioning as a means of clarifying the presentation of pattern, these charts might eventually lead to a more extensive development of geometric method than in individual psychology.

A third problem of particular prominence in group measurement arises from the typical use of field investigations in which populations unavoidably vary in such attributes as size and racial or sexual make-up. It is necessary to devise measures which are unaffected by such variations. Several types of measure might conceivably be tested out in the same experimental situation. Already two such indices, to be mentioned in this review, are available.

All the problems mentioned are touched on with different emphases in the two monographs under consideration.* The first question with which the Moreno and Jennings monograph is concerned is the fact that patterns of social interaction might be the product of chance factors rather than of the social preferences of the members of a group. It is thus necessary to know how much the configurations experimentally elicited differ from those which

---

* "Sociometric Measurement of Social Configurations," by J. L. Moreno and Helen H. Jennings, Sociometric Monographs, No. 3, Beacon House, New York, 1945. Pp. 35.

"The Measurement of Sociometric Status, Structure, and Development," by Urie Bronfenbrenner, Sociometric Monographs, No. 6, Beacon House, 1945. Pp. 80.

would be produced if subjects behaved entirely at random under the criterion used.

The social structures under study were obtained by using the sociometric test, the experimenter asking each one of a group of girls living together in a dormitory to choose three fellow members with whom she would like to sit at meals. There were 26 girls in each of seven separate dormitory groups and all made the required three choices. The resulting data showed a heavily skewed distribution of choice, with some persons receiving no choices at all and a quarter of the population attracting to themselves over half of the selections.

To determine what sort of choice configuration would occur in such groups by chance, the authors carried out seven chance drawings. In each drawing the individuals were represented by 26 ballots, three of which were drawn at random for each fictitious chooser. On tabulation, the chance pattern of choice differed markedly from the experimental results, producing a more equitable distribution with fewer unchosen and also fewer heavily chosen individuals. It was found that this chance distribution could be plotted by means of the expansion of a binomial the formula for which was worked out by Paul Lazarsfeld. Chance formulas were also developed for predicting both the number of "mutual pairs" of choices reciprocating each other (A choosing B and B choosing A) and the number of choices which would be unreciprocated. All these formulas have proved important in the evaluation of social structures experimentally determined.

Using the ballot values as points of reference the authors demonstrated large discrepancies between the experimental and chance results. The differences obtained are so great as to appear hardly the result of chance. Nevertheless it would have been interesting to see a more systematic application of some technique for bringing out the statistical significance of these deviations. The chi-square test was applied in only one case, to show that the difference between the number of non-reciprocal relationships predicted by formula was not significantly different from that in the chance distribution of ballots. The test was not applied to any of the differences between actual experimental and chance results, although such an application to all these differences would have considerably strengthened the conclusions reached.

The authors further employed chance values as a base for expressing the extent to which a given structure was present in the organization of the group. Their expression takes the form of a ratio between the number of structures experimentally observed and the number which would occur by chance. For example, the number of isolates (unchosen persons) is expressed as 250 percent greater than the number predicted on a chance basis.

The ratios as stated may be considered incomplete in that they do not include the entire distribution of each structure measured. In expressing the incidence of social isolation, for example, we are interested essentially, not in the number of unchosen persons alone, but in the number of isolates in proportion to the number of non-isolates. This is the complete value experimentally obtained and the corresponding chance ratio of isolates to non-isolates is the value by which the experimental ratio must be divided. Thus the Moreno and Jennings measure which would relate only the experimentally obtained number of isolates to the chance number, can be completed by including the number of non-isolates experimentally obtained and the number expected on a chance basis. This ratio method is useful in sociometric measurement in that it offers a means of expressing the incidence of various structures regardless of the size of the group involved.

Another topic of importance discussed in the monograph is the problem of pattern evidenced in the fact that different groups characterized by the same number of unchosen individuals, mutual pairs, etc., may yet be quite different in social organization. In one population, for example, the pairs may all be unconnected with each other except by unreciprocated choices, while in another they may be connected in chains of varying lengths. The authors point out that in analyzing such differences of pattern the sociogram charting the interrelationship of individuals is of exploratory use, since it aids in preventing the experimenter from overlooking the complexities of configuration involved.

Another approach touched on is the measurement of inter-group attractions and repulsions by means of a ratio method. For example, a group's interest in another group is expressed as that percent of its total choices which it directs toward the other population. Here the authors might well have employed again the chance principles so well discussed earlier in their paper. Since a group's direction of choice toward itself or another group can only be evaluated in terms of the corresponding chance distribution of such selections, the complete ratio of its interest in another social unit in relation to itself would involve the ratio between the choices it actually directed toward the other group and the choices it actually directed toward itself, and the ratio between the corresponding chance values. Dividing the experimentally obtained proportion by the chance ratio would produce a measure of group preference comparable with the previously discussed ratio for expressing the incidence of isolation.

In closing, Moreno and Jennings touch briefly on the elaborate conception of a sociometric scale on which could be arranged the different types of pattern which a group might assume, with complete lack of integration (all choices unreciprocated) at one limit and complete integration (all choices reciprocated) at the other. Some of the statistical complications inherent in such a scale are indicated by the fact, pointed out by the authors, that on each level there are numerous "sociotropic" formations which have the same number of mutual pairs but differ in the positions which the constituent individuals occupy in relation to each other.

The scale is at present chiefly of interest for its suggestion of the types of variation possible in such a framework. The concept of sociotropes is an intriguing one but involves even greater complexity than the authors indicate. Their estimate is that for a group of N individuals the scale would exhibit at each level a number of sociotropes equal to factorial N, the number of permutations of such a group. But they omit to state that except in rare instances there are at each level a variety of configurations in which all individuals occupy the same positions in relation to each other but within this framework show different patterns of choice. Each such configuration is then characterized by its own collection of sociotropic rearrangements. The scale thus acquires three dimensions based on mutuality, choice, and individual position.

For measurement purposes, the number of different permutations of a given configuration is actually less than factorial N, since some permutations of N individuals are sociometrically equivalent in that the subjects may be considered to occupy different positions in relation to each other but the mutual pairs are between the same individuals in both arrangements. That is, a reciprocal pair expressed as A+B is the same as one expressed as B+A.

It cannot be said that the same number of sociotropes would occur at each level of integration, both because there are different numbers of choice configurations at each level and because the number of sociotropes per configuration is not constant. This arises from the fact that the number of possible configurations and sociotropes increases with the number of unreciprocated choices. For this reason the number of different varieties of groups at each level would increase as the scale passed from the highest to the lowest level of integration.

It is suggested in the monograph that the level of maximum integration in the scale may very well not be the best therapeutic level for a group. In fact, excessive mutuality might be suspected to imply a pathological degree of group "introversion". To develop such a scale to an appropriate degree and relate it to measures of group morale would therefore be a valuable research study toward which this paper points the way.

The chance methods presented by Moreno and Jennings are further developed by Bronfenbrenner who takes up the search for a serviceable means of testing for statistical significance the deviations of experimental results from chance values. After various methods were tried out, his final procedure, taken from Carver, was to express any given deviation in terms of the standard deviation of the binomial distribution used in predicting the chance results. The probability of occurrence of such a discrepancy by chance is then obtained by reading from Salvosa's tables the corresponding area under a Pearson Type III curve of skewness comparable with that of the binomial distribution employed.

This method can in many cases be used interchangeably with the chi-square technique, but it may prove of greater value in that it allows for the particular form of the chance distribution used and, further, in that it provides not only a test of significance but also a quantification of the discrepancy in terms of standard units.

The Carver method is of course inapplicable to distributions which do not follow a binomial expansion. This is true, for example, of the chance distribution of mutual pairs for which Bronfenbrenner gives an incorrect binomial formula. In the case of mutual pairs we do not have within the same group a single event repeated *n* times with two possible outcomes, as the binomial theorem requires. Instead we have a collection of interdependent events. When A and B choose each other they inevitably fail to choose numerous other individuals who may or may not choose them, so that their mutual pair enters into the formation of other relationships, either non-reciprocal pairs or pair relationships in which neither of two individuals chooses the other. All three types of pairs must be considered and all are interdependent. Plotting all the theoretically possible arrangements of pairs for any population will show definitely that the chance frequencies do not conform to a binomial expansion. In the case of mutual pairs, therefore, the deviation from chance must be tested by some other method such as chi square. The most probable chance frequency of mutual pairs used in a test of that sort would of course be the mean of the above-mentioned theoretical distribution of pairs and can be arrived at by means of the formula for predicting reciprocal relationships presented in the Moreno and Jennings monograph.

In discussing formulas for predicting the chance frequencies of various types of events Bronfenbrenner includes the mathematical expressions already stated in the Moreno and Jennings article and in Criswell's work on race cleavage. One new formula is reported for determining the probability that a given number of isolates or fewer will occur by chance. This expression is difficult to evaluate, but a question may be raised as to its comparability with other tests of statistical significance. If the chance number of isolates is predicted for a group by means of the binomial expansion, as is done in the Moreno and Jennings study, and the discrepancy of obtained results from chance is tested by chi square, discrepancies judged significant under the latter test frequently appear insignificant under the Bronfenbrenner formula.

A very valuable aspect of Bronfenbrenner's work is perhaps insufficiently emphasized in his presentation, since it is not clearly differentiated from the method of testing for statistical significance. The quantification of discrepancies from chance in terms of standard scores is not only a step in testing for statistical significance but is also an accurate measure of individual social status in the group or of the incidence of some social pattern such as intergroup cleavage. It is independent of group size. Since it takes account of the form of the binomial distribution employed, it may prove superior in certain situations to the ratio method mentioned by Moreno and Jennings and developed by Criswell in the measurement of race cleavage. Unlike the ratio procedure, however, the standard score measure cannot in its present stage of development be applied to the quantification of reciprocation of choice.

The Carver technique has proved uniquely useful as a means of setting objectively the point in the choice distribution above which a group member may be considered to be overchosen and the point below which an individual is underchosen or socially neglected. Previous devices had been to set these points arbitrarily at the first and third quartiles or at one S. D. below and one S. D. above the mean, or to mark off unchosen persons as "isolates" and unusually popular individuals as "stars". Bronfenbrenner supplies a more objective statistical basis for such demarcations of areas, since "neglectees" become those chosen significantly less often than chance would allow and "stars" are those chosen significantly more often.

Carrying his definition of "stars" and "neglectees" into the field of the sociogram, the author refines on Northway's "target diagram", a sociogram which indicates social status by charting the most popular individuals (falling in the highest quarter of the distribution) in the center circle of a series of concentric circles, the least popular individuals (in the lowest quarter) falling in the outermost circle. For Q_1 and Q_3 Bronfenbrenner substitutes the points of statistical significance determined by the Carver method, while the median is transformed to the binomial mean value.

The last chapter of the monograph is devoted to the report of a careful experimental study in which the methods of analysis developed were applied to classes, nursery level through sixth grade, in a small school. The sociometric test was given, every subject making not more than three choices under each of three criteria. There is some suggestion that not all children made the maximum number of choices, thus complicating the problem of prediction and measurement. But whether an adjustment for this situation was devised is not indicated.

The author describes his results as only "suggestive", but this seems overly modest. It is true that for definite conclusions a more extensive geographic sampling would be necessary. However, Bronfenbrenner's data are in line with a considerable body of work already completed. Although a more refined analysis was made than in earlier studies, the results on the whole confirm Moreno's original findings reported in *Who Shall Survive* and Criswell's later study reported in the *Sociometric Review* and *Archives of Psychology*. This confirmation is of considerable interest indicating, as it does, the fundamental importance and remarkable consistency of the tendencies studied. The more recent work is of particular interest in that it involves a quite different geographic area and a higher socio-economic status than did the earlier investigations.

Throughout the studies the same growth of social structure is disclosed the group becoming more strongly knit and more highly differentiated with increase in the age of its members. At higher grade levels there are fewer socially neglected persons, a larger minority commanding more than their share of choices, more mutual pairs, a higher degree of sex cleavage. Thus there is a continuity between earlier and later work in terms of results obtained as well as in terms of statistical method.

The monographs here discussed, both vital elements in the expansion of sociometric method, should be carefully read by experimenters interested in the development of the mathematical techniques so urgently needed to transform social study from a field of speculation into a scientific discipline. The Moreno and Jennings study supplies fundamental formulas for making predictions on a chance basis, while Bronfenbrenner's basic contribution is the standard unit method of expressing social status and structure. These studies and others quoted in their bibliographies constitute a useful starting point for any attack on the considerable problems of social measurement which lie ahead.

DISCUSSION OF PAPERS ON SOCIOMETRY

By E. W. Burgess

If statistics deal with measurement, why is there any necessity for a separate field of sociometry which also is concerned with measurement? The superficial answer might be that statistics is concerned with measurement in general and that sociometry is confined to social phenomena. But there would be no point in creating a new discipline unless there were something in the nature of social phenomena that required the devising of special methods of measurement. If society is conceived as an aggregate of individual organisms, as in population studies, there would be no need of sociometry. But if we take as our subject-matter the person and groups of persons, then the analysis of interpersonal relations and the devising of instruments for their measurement become important. In *Who Shall Survive* Moreno developed an ingenious system of plotting and measuring interpersonal relations.

Sociometry is to be further differentiated from statistics in the fact that the former deals with all types of measurement significant for understanding human behavior and not exclusively with those requiring statistical formulae. Thus the charting of relationships[1] of an adolescent girl to persons in her social world is measurement and permits comparison with similar charts for other girls. True, this charting makes possible simple quantification which is also important. But the charting itself represents measurement which, as in this case, may be more significant than the later quantification.

Most important of all, sociometry places the emphasis upon the social analysis of interpersonal relations which must be made before significant statistical operations are feasible. At present in sociology we unfortunately have a great gap between social analysis and statistics. For the most part analyses of social processes are not oriented toward measurement, and statistical studies deal with aggregates of atomistic items about individuals[2] and not with relationships and processes within groups of interacting persons. The role of sociometry is to bridge this gulf. It must place emphasis

---

[1] See Jessie R. Runner, "Social Distance in Adolescent Relationships," *American Journal of Sociology,* 43, 428-39, November, 1937.

[2] See Ernest R. Mowrer, *Family Disorganization,* University of Chicago Press, 1927. Pp. 130-32 footnotes.

first on the analysis of interpersonal relations and social processes, second, on some mode of representing them in measurable form, and third, upon the using or devising of appropriate techniques statistical or otherwise for the deriving of generalizations susceptible to checking by other investigators.

Finally a word should be said about sociometry in relation to econometry or psychometry (the terms more frequently in use are econometrics and psychometrics). As in sociometry the stress, while on measurement, is upon measurement significant for the creation of a natural science. This means that an analysis must be made of the essential nature of the structure and dynamics of the economic order in econometrics, of the mind in psychometrics and of society in sociometry; that instruments for measurement appropriate in each field must then be devised, and that mathematical or other methods adequate to the problems be worked out. The final objective in all these disciplines is the establishing of significant scientific generalizations which will ultimately constitute a coherent system.

THE CONSTANT FRAME OF REFERENCE PROBLEM IN SOCIOMETRY

By Daisy Starkey Edwards

From the outset of sociometric work, investigators have felt the need of a reference frame which ensures that conclusions may take their place in an integrated scheme of scientific measurement. Moreno[1] had such a standardization in mind when he proposed the introduction of "sociometric indices", derived from ratios. Later, however, Moreno and Jennings[2] suggested that an experimental sociometric situation may be related to a probability measure. This was followed by Bronfenbrenner[3] who elaborated on the general technique foreshadowed by Moreno and Jennings.

Moreno and later investigators are all aware of the fact that "the most acceptable form of statistical treatment would be one which dealt with sociometric situations as a whole, and not with any single series of facts more or less arbitrarily separated from the total picture",[4] but admit that in practice one measurement at a time must be considered, and suggest that a reasonably complete picture is given by:

1. The distribution of the frequencies of the number of choices received by each person, and particularly of those pertaining to large numbers of choices, the recipients of which are denoted by "stars".

2. The number of reciprocated and unreciprocated choices in the group.

3. The number of "isolates".

4. In cases where the group consists of two distinct sub-groups, or more, the number of inter-group choices, or a study of "cleavage".

The problems arising in (1) may be handled mathematically, but the others are not so easy. It is for this reason that one is impressed by the ingenuity of the Moreno and Jennings monograph, as the authors used the experimental results in two ways, firstly, for the situation capable of mathematical treatment; secondly, they took the mechanically obtained experi-

---

[1] Moreno, J. L., *Who shall survive*, Washington, D. C., Nervous and Mental Diseases Publishing Co., 1934.

[2] Moreno, J. L., and Jennings, Helen, *Sociometric Measurement of Social Configurations*, SOCIOMETRY MONOGRAPHS No. 3, Beacon House, New York City.

[3] Bronfenbrenner, Urie, *A Constant Frame of Reference for Sociometric Research*, SOCIOMETRY MONOGRAPHS No. 6, Beacon House, New York City, 1945.

[4] "Foundations of Sociometric Measurement", Joan H. Criswell, SOCIOMETRY, Vol. 9, No. 1.

mental frequencies and compared with the theoretical ones. The statistical χ^2 test confirmed that the two sets of results were in agreement, establishing the machine results were reliable as far as could be ascertained, and it was assumed, secondly, therefore, that the average results of a large number of sortings could be used in the case where the mathematical solution had not been obtained.

It is interesting to find that in the same monograph use is made of "expectation values" in the case of reciprocated choices. The statistician is in the habit of associating the term with a probability distribution, but the authors have evidently taken it here to mean "average value", which for the case under consideration is equivalent, but does not require specific knowledge of the distribution. For instance, in the case of the group of 26 used as an illustration, each choosing three names, the probability of a specific mutual choice is $p^2 = (3/25)^2$, and since there are $^{26}C_2 = 26 \times 25/2$ possible pairs, and because in this case p^2 must be the ratio of the number of cases in which the specific mutual choice occurs to the total number of possible arrangements, evidently $^{26}C_2 p^2$ is the average number of mutual choices occurring in the complete set of arrangements. This result owes its simplicity to the fact that one is not concerned with *how* the mutual choices occur in relation to one another, only in the total number that occurs throughout. It is a very different matter to obtain the frequencies of arrangements containing zero, one, two, etc., mutual choices, because to obtain this data one is forced to consider many different contingencies, for instance, two mutual choices may arise involving three people only, or four, and so on in a more complicated manner for larger numbers of mutual choices.

It would appear that the Bronfenbrenner monograph is open to criticism, on the grounds that he relates the expectation value and obtains probabilities from a binomial distribution of the form $(p^2 + 1-p^2)^{N(N-1)/2}$ for a group of size N. Examining the assumptions which must be made when using a distribution of this type, those relevant to this discussion are

1. Every "success" in the probability sense, here a mutual choice, must have a probability p^2, which is applicable for each independently of the others. In other words, the type of problem in which it would normally be used is, for instance, the case of successive spins of a coin in which the numbers of "heads" are to be counted, and every spin can be counted as a fresh start independent of the others. Moreover

2. The total number of possible "successes" must be the exponent of

the binomial expression, in this case $N(N-1)/2$. Neither of these conditions, are, in fact satisfied. Once a certain mutual choice has been made, both the partners are limited by the fact that they then have to choose one less name from a list of one less, or 2 out of 24 in Moreno's case, and are not, therefore, independent of the first "trial". Furthermore, it is not possible for as many as $N(N-1)/2$ mutual choices to be made, because only Nd choices are made altogether in the general case in which d names are written down, and, therefore, not more than Nd/2 mutual choices are possible. Reference has already been made by Criswell,[4] in general terms, to the breakdown of this type of method, because of the complexity of sociometric situations. It is clear that the use of the Binomial distribution for assessing significance points in the case of mutual choice frequencies is not correct, and the actual distribution is far more complicated. It is not even possible to choose Nd/2 or (Nd-1)/2 pairs at random out of the possible $N(N-1)/2$ when the maximum number of mutual choices is achieved, in fact only those in which everybody's name occurs d times are admissible, as the choices of each person must all be reciprocated.

At the time of writing an acceptable solution in reasonably simple terms is not available, and, while it is not proposed to deny that information on this point would be useful, *it should perhaps be put on record that the number of mutual choices alone can give a very false impression of the degree of integration of a group.* This is probably the reason why Moreno insisted on a structional analysis. For example, consider the case of eight people each making three choices. The maximum possible number of mutual choices is 12, and it could occur in several ways, of which two extreme cases are illustrated.

It is possible that in the extreme case of two cliques shown in (2) some

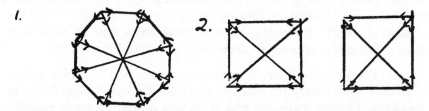

explanation such as race cleavage would be found, and put down in conjunction with the measurement of 12 in the mutual choices category, but, notwithstanding, it is evident that 12 mutual choices alone does not give adequate information. Moreover, on the basis of a significance test it would be considered to be superior to an arrangement such as

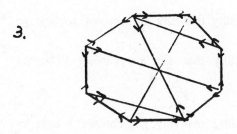

3.

where, although there only 11 reciprocated choices and two unreciprocated choices, there seems little doubt that the group is better integrated than (2). Perhaps it is worth while for potential solvers of the distribution problem to ask themselves the value of their results before embarking on laborious calculations to this end.

The Bronfenbrenner monograph also gives a good deal of attention to the problems of the probabilities of interclass choice and of isolation. We would again express doubts on the validity of the use of the Binomial distribution[5] in connection with the interclass problem. In the first place the formula quoted[6] for the probability of a person in group a choosing one from group b by chance alone appears to assume that the criterion of "choosing" is taken to be the situation in which the name of a certain person from group b appears first on the list of a member of group a. It is for this reason that the formula eventually assumes the simple form $b/(N-1)$, which follows directly from these assumptions. To be consistent with the rest of the publication, in which the *order* of choice has been disregarded, we suggest an amended formula in the form

$$p = \frac{N-1_{c_d} - a-1_{c_d}}{N-1_{c_d}}$$

which is the probability that a certain person in the first group includes somewhere on his list at least one of the second. The further use of the Binomial distribution is vitiated by the fact that subsequent choices of the same person have a different probability from the first. Here, however, we are in a position to indicate how the probabilities of a chance choice of r

---

[5] *Loc. cit.* p. 34.

[6] *Loc. cit.* p. 24.

names, $0 \leqslant r \leqslant ad$, may be ascertained. For simplicity let the first group of a persons be girls, and the second boys.

Let $p_0 =$ probability that any girl chooses no boys $= {}^{a-1}C_d \big/ {}^{N-1}C_d$

Let $p_1 =$ probability that any girl chooses 1 boy $= \dfrac{{}^{b}C_1 \, {}^{a-1}C_{d-1}}{{}^{N-1}C_d}$

Let $p_2 =$ probability that any girl chooses 2 boys $= \dfrac{{}^{b}C_2 \, {}^{a-1}C_{d-2}}{{}^{N-1}C_d}$

and so on.

The total probability of these mutually exclusive events must be one, which may readily be verified, as a check. The probability of all the girls choosing between them no boys, one boy etc., may then be found by making use of the multinomial expansion

$$(p_0 + p_1 x + p_2 x^2 + \ldots \ldots \ldots p_d x^d)^a$$

The coefficient of x^r in this expansion is the probability of the number of choices of boys from the girls' group being exactly equal to r, and the probability of r or less choices is the sum of the relevant coefficients.

In connection with the Bronfenbrenner formula for the probability of i or less isolates[7] stated as

$$1 - \frac{(N-i-2)\,(N-i-3)\,\ldots\ldots\,(N-i-d-1)}{(N-1)\,(N-2)\,\ldots\,(N-d)}$$

we conclude that it is the probability of a given person's including at least one of $i + 1$ specified names, for the subtracted portion is the probability that a person does not include any one of $i + 1$ specified names. It is not clear how the author arrives at the result as a general formula covering the whole sociometric pattern. The following is an outline of a method of arriving at the required probability. In the first place, if k is the maximum possible number of isolates, then $k = N-1-d$. The people who are not isolates name d people not including these, and therefore have no choice, while the isolates choose d from a possible list of $d + 1$. Every different set of k iso-

---

[7] *Loc. cit.* p. 25.

lates corresponds to a distinct sociometric situation, and thus the probability of k isolates is

$$P_k = {}^N C_{N-d-1} \frac{(d+1)^{N-d-1}}{({}^{N-1}C_d)^N}$$

Considering the case of $k-1$ isolates, again, these not named as isolates choose d from a possible list of $d+1$, while the isolates can choose d from a possible list of $d+2$. However, it is obvious that these possibilities include cases where there are k isolates, as any particular set of $k-1$ isolates can have one of $d+2$ more isolates accidentally added in a sociometric diagram containing it, resulting in

$$P_{k-1} = {}^N C_{N-d-2} \left[\frac{(d+1)^{d+2}}{({}^{N-1}C_d)^N} \left[\frac{(d+1)(d+2)}{2} \right]^{N-d-2} - \frac{(d+2)P_k}{{}^N C_k} \right].$$

P_{k-2} follows by successive elimination of additional irrelevant cases in which there are either $k-1$ or k isolates, and so on. The form of these results, ultimately to be added to get probability of i or less isolates, would indicate a complicated algebraical expression for the required probability, involving in the denominator a power of ${}^{N-1}C_d$, and we have been unable to derive Bronfenbrenner's simple result from these premises.

The complexity of the formulae raises the question of whether there is any possibility of modifying the existing technique of sociometric experimentation to meet the requirements of a simple mathematical treatment. It is evident that what is needed is something in which the responses of each individual are independent in the probability sense. An obvious possibility is to ask everyone for a response concerning each member of the group, perhaps, for instance, "like", "neutral", "dislike", which appears to have some support from Moreno insofar as he has at times obtained detailed information from each member of the group about the others. Members of a discussion group in London University who had already applied sociometric technique by the usual method of limited choices, expressed the opinion that this would perhaps not achieve the same object as the normal method. It would force a decision concerning each person from each person, which might not necessarily be forthcoming. However, a summary of the probability results which would follow are included for interest:—

Stardom. The probability that a person writes down "like" about any other person in the group by chance alone is 1/3, and that he makes any other response is 2/3. Hence the probability that any member of the group scores r "likes" by chance alone is $p_r = {}^{N-1}C_r (1/3)^r (2/3)^{N-1-r}$, and the expansion of the binomial $(1/3 + 2/3)^{N-1}$ gives the probabilities of a certain person scoring any number of "likes" from 0 to N–1.

Mutual Choices. The probability of a mutual choice occurring by chance alone is $(1/3)^2$, and any one mutual choice is made independently of any other. Hence the Binomial expansion $(1/9 + 8/9)^{N(N-1)/2}$ gives the probabilities of the occurrence of any number of mutual choices up to the maximum which is obviously $N(N-1)/2$.

Isolates. Define an isolate as one who receives only "neutral" or "dislike" choices. The probability that any one person receives all unfavourable choices is $(2/3)^{N-1}$, and the probability that he receives at least one favourable choice is $(1 - (2/3)^{N-1})$. Hence the probability of exactly i isolates is

$$P_i = {}^N C_i (2/3)^{i(N-1)} (1-(2/3)^{N-1})^{(N-i)}$$

which is the corresponding term in the binomial distribution

$$[(2/3)^{N-1} + 1 - (2/3)^{N-1}]^N.$$

Cleavage. With the previous notation, if the probability of the choice by chance of a certain number of boys names is required, as in the result already found, assuming it immaterial whether the same or different boys are chosen, the problem is the same as that of one girl making a choice from ab boys, and the probability of the choice of r boys (i.e. r "likes") is the term containing $(1/3)^r$ in the expansion of $(1/3 + 2/3)^{ab}$. Bronfenbrenner's very useful remarks on the approximation to the tail area of a Type III curve which applies to the sum of the end terms of the Binomial distribution would, of course, have scope for application in computing the corresponding probabilities.

Thus we have attempted to survey the present work on applications of the theory of chance to the problem of a sociometric frame of reference, and suggested certain modifications to existing published work. The latter have greater claim to accuracy than to utility, and, therefore, we have concluded by suggesting a different method of collecting sociometric data which would lead to less complicated mathematical treatment. It is hoped that the suggested modifications will invoke opinions from field workers regarding the possibility of their practical application.

A METHOD FOR DEPICTING SOCIAL
RELATIONSHIPS OBTAINED BY SOCIOMETRIC TESTING

By Mary L. Northway

The problem of how to show the relationships discovered through the use of a form of Moreno's technique, so that they may be understood most clearly, confronts all those who employ the technique. This article describes a method that we have found particularly valuable for depicting these relationships. The individual's acceptability relative to that of the other members of the group and his own primary choices are shown by this method at one and the same time.

Source of the Data

The method herein described has been used with data from children's classroom groups at the public school, as well as with data from women's fraternity groups at the University of Toronto. These groups were made up of numbers varying from thirty-five to fifty-five individuals, and the social relationships were obtained from choices made on four different questions. Some of these questions restricted choices to individuals actually in the group; others allowed choices to be made either from within or without the group.

The description of the method we have used in these school and fraternity groups is given in this paper. For purposes of demonstrating the method, we here consider a purely fictitious group of only sixteen individuals. The relationships and general pattern follow closely the actual findings we have made in the real groups which we have studied.

Method

A. Obtaining the Data

Each member of the group is asked to give his first three choices for associate on a certain number of bases. In the school groups, we used choices based on items such as companion for one's favorite activity, companion for a classroom project, "best friend" among children actually in the classroom and "best friend" among all children known. In the fraternity questions, questions such as choice for associates on a committee, choice for roommate, etc., were asked. Each individual filled in a mimeographed form giving his choices.

B. Analyzing the Data

Each choice is scored according to the following scale: first choice, five points; second choice, three points; and third choice, two points. A form for

	JANE	BETTY	JO	ROSS	RED	HELEN	KATE	HARRY	JOHN	GEORGE	DICK	MARG	MAUD	MIN	SAM	LILY	.	ACCEPTABILITY SCORE
JANE																		0
BETTY	4																	4
JO				3R	3R													6
ROSS			(10R)															10
RED			3R	6														12
HELEN	2	5																72
KATE	6	5			3													14
HARRY																		53
JOHN			8	2														21
GEORGE																		52
DICK			5	10														42
MARG													(20)					22
MIN		(20)																30
SAM				2	(18)													32
LILY	(15)	10																48
MAUD																		25
Choices in Group	27	40	21	18	34													

FORM 1

Value of choices from each subject to every other subject.
(A few of the choices from this fictitious group are filled in. In actual practice the form is, of course, completed).

analyzing these choices is used (see Form 1). This consists of a series of vertical and horizontal columns; at the head of each column appear the names of all the individuals in the group. The value of the choices each person makes is placed in the column below his name; the value of the choices each person receives is placed in the column opposite his name. Thus, as may be seen in form 1, Jane gave Betty choices to the value of 4 (i.e., third choices on each of two bases). Thus, 4 is placed in the column below Jane's name in the square of the column opposite Betty's name. Jane gives choices of the value of 15 to Lily; 15 is, therefore, placed in the column below Jane's name and opposite Lily's. As this is the highest score Jane gives to any one person the score is encircled.

When the scores of all members of the group have been entered in this way the scores in each column are added. The total obtained from each vertical column shows the value of the choices the individual has given to members of the group. His choices have, of course, been made to outsiders. The total obtained from each horizontal column shows the value of choices each person has received. By glancing across the columns, it may be seen whether this value of choices received (or, as we have termed it, the person's "acceptability score") is made up from several different people, as in the case of Kate, or from merely one or two people as it is in the case of Marg.

Whether or not a person's choice is reciprocated to any extent may be shown in the following way. If one glances down the column under Jo it is seen that Jo chooses Ross with a score of 10 points. Looking at the column under Ross one may see whether or not he gives any of his choices to Jo. It is found he gives Jo a choice with the value of 3. In this case Jo's choice is to some extent reciprocated and so an R is put beside his score.

This form, used as an example of the method, is only partially filled in. In practice the form is, of course, completed for each member of the group.

C. Diagrammatic Representation

From the above form we can immediately read the total acceptability score of each individual and the highest choice each individual gives to any other person. These data may now be organized in the following ways:

1) A distribution curve may be made of the acceptability scores. These, for this present fictitious group, are shown in Figure 1. The distributions we have obtained from both the school groups and the fraternity groups have ap-

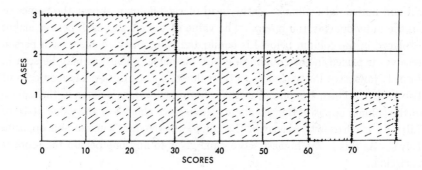

Fig. 1. Distribution of Acceptability Scores

proximated the upper half of a normal distribution curve. The median in every case has been below the average.

2) A "target" diagram may be made. Figure 2 gives an example of this. Four concentric circles whose radii increase are drawn by equal steps. The acceptability scores are divided into quartiles, and each section of the target is marked off in values to correspond with these quartiles. The lowest quartile is on the outside of the target and the highest in the middle. Each subject is placed on the target in the quartile to which his acceptability score belongs. The nearer the center he is the higher his score is.

An arrow is then drawn from each individual to the person to whom he gives his highest composite choice. (This is the encircled number below his name on Form 1.) Thus Jane's highest choice, which went to Lily, is drawn with an arrow from Jane to Lily on the target.

When a subject's highest choice goes to a person outside the actual group an arrow is drawn from him to the outside. See, for example, Ross on Figure 2.

If a subject's highest choice goes to a person who also gives him his highest choice a doubleheaded arrow is used. See Harry and George on the diagram.

In the case of a subject's choosing two persons with equally high choices, arrows are drawn from him to each of them (see Sam, Harry, and George).

These arrows, in each case, indicate the predominating choices found within the group.

In actual practice, especially with large groups, it has been convenient to use counters with each subject's name and score written on them. (White poker chips have served admirably.) These are moved in the circles to which their score belongs and arranged to get the best "fit" among the individuals, i.e.,

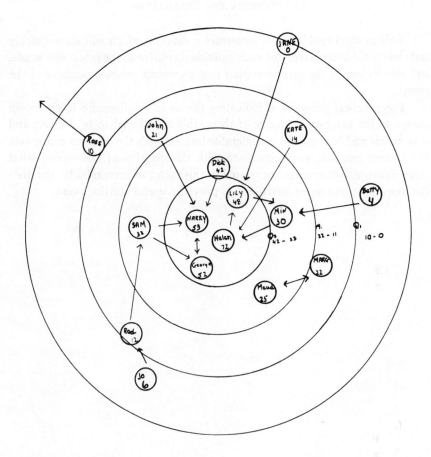

Fig. 2. Target diagram showing scores of acceptability and predominating choices in a Social Group.

to have as few long lines and crossing lines as possible. In plotting the diagram when public school groups are involved, we have found the task simplified by keeping the boys on one side of the diagram and the girls on the other since, at this age, there is very little choosing between the sexes.

The subsidiary choices may also be reached on the diagram but we have found that these confuse the picture, and they are always available from consultation of Form 1.

Conclusions and Evaluation

This method enables us to construct a diagram which will show quickly and clearly the acceptability of each individual relative to the group as a whole, and also to record the predominating choices among various members of the group.

For practical purposes of indicating the social relationships in classroom groups to the teachers in charge of them, this has proved to be a direct and easy means and has aroused considerable interest with the teachers concerned. For further research work concerned with the question of discovering what other individual differences are related to this factor of acceptability, the division into inner and outer quartiles has proved a useful starting point.

A NOTE ON THE USE OF TARGET SOCIOGRAMS*

By Mary L. Northway

During the past eleven years many improvements have been made to my preliminary attempt to devise scoring and graphic methods in sociometry. Scoring on the whole has come to be worked out on a probability basis. However the contribution which has been most widespread is that of the target diagram. It has barged its way into various text books and been highly accepted in lay groups. Undoubtedly it is a picturesque means of symbolizing the sociometric structure of, and relationships in, a group.

The target's very popularity has meant that its limitations and inadequacies have tended to be ignored or excused. Indeed one has had the comment from a group of intelligent, interested, but scientifically naive teachers—"So that's our classroom; wouldn't it be fine if we could help children so that all of them would be in the center circle!"

Safeguards in Using the Target

Two points should be remembered by those using target diagrams:

(1) It is an *abstraction*. Sociometry itself by employing a limited number of criteria and requiring a definite number of choices is an abstraction from the multitudinous permutations of social choice and relationships within a group. The target by depicting only the dominating choices (or else resulting in complete artistic confusion) is a further abstraction from the living situation. Before basing decisions on it one should always consult the original data; the less dominating choices may be as important for both scientific study and therapeutic use as those which are depicted.

(2) It is a *symbol*. To most people the diagram and the word target suggest the archery or rifle range; the assumption is that the purpose is to hit the "bullseye". It is popularly supposed that a higher sociometric score, reflected in position of nearness to the center of the target, is *directly* related to values of good mental health. This is by no means proven.[1] Indeed, while studies have shown personality differences to be related to sociometric level,[2] they have not demonstrated that high status is associated in a one to one

---

* The Target Diagram is a modification of Moreno's Sociogram (*Ed.*).

1 Northway, Mary L. Studies in the Field of Sociometry, Univ. of Toronto Press, (mimeographed) see p. 34f.

2 Northway, Mary L. and Wigdor, Bloosom T. Rorschach Patterns Related to the Socometric Status of School Children. Sociometry 1947, X: 2: 186-199.

relationship with indices of mental health value based on other criteria. It is true that individuals with continually low sociometric scores ("outsiders")[3] frequently show other forms of psychological or social difficulty; but this is not always the case.[4] The need for other criteria than position on the target to evaluate secure development must always be remembered.

Extensions for Improving the Target

1. In depicting the sociograms of a community formed of two or more sub-groups (boys, girls; negro, white; etc.) the target may be segmented scaled to the proportion of the sub-group in the total community; self preference scores indicated and inter-sub-group choices drawn.[5]

2. For depicting number of choices to or from a subject beyond his dominating ones which appear on the sociogram we have found the following device useful. Each subject is placed on the target as usual, with a circle or triangle. Each additional outgoing choice is placed with a small arrow outside his circle; these point to the center of the target if they go to people of higher sociometric status; to the circumference if to individuals of lower sociometric status. Each choice coming to him is recorded inside his circle. Thus his "emotional expansiveness" is depicted.

3. For comparing two sociograms of the same group obtained at different times it has been useful to draw the second on transparent paper which can be superimposed on the original. The changes in each person's status and dominating choices can be readily compared.

4. Obviously the target can be formed according to the statistical division the particular study requires. In studies contrasting cases of high and low sociometric scores we have found division into tertiles useful and based the target sociograms on these.

---

[3] Northway, Mary L. Outsiders, SOCIOMETRY 1944, VII: 1: 10-26.

[4] Potashin, Reva. An Examination of "Withdrawing" as a Personality Characteristic of some Pre-Adolescent Children, Ph.D. Thesis, 1951.

[5] Northway, Mary L. and Quarrington, B. Depicting Intercultural Relations, SOCIOMETRY 1946, IX: 4: 334-339.

A MATRIX APPROACH TO THE ANALYSIS OF SOCIOMETRIC DATA:
PRELIMINARY REPORT

By Elaine Forsyth and Leo Katz

As a general rule, the results of sociometric testing are presented by means of a diagram or graph called a *sociogram* which has for its purpose the illustration of the structure of the group, with its subgroups, cliques, leaders, isolates, and rejectees. The *sociogram*[1] has obvious advantages over verbal descriptions, but it is apt to be confusing to the reader, especially if the number of subjects is large. At present the sociogram must be built by a process of trial and error, which produces the unhappy result that different investigators using the same data build as many different sociograms as there are investigators. Northway (5) has developed a "target-area"[2] device which obviates this difficulty to a certain extent. Even with the gain in systematic placement of individuals afforded by use of this device, the resulting sociograms tend to become rather chaotic if all the data is preserved. The present paper has grown out of an attempt to preserve all the data and present it in an orderly, meaningful manner.

The Matrix Approach

To present sociometric data more objectively, and to make possible a more detailed analysis of group structure, an approach is proposed in which a complete matrix of positive and negative choices is utilized. In starting with the matrix of choices, it is assumed that an individual may choose, reject or ignore each other person in the group, and that his choices and rejections are not limited in number. There is some question as to whether it should also be assumed that each individual chooses himself. It is proposed, in order to keep the matrix general, to use a special mark to designate the individual self choice. We start, then, with a matrix of dimension N x N corresponding to the group of N individuals. The entry in the fourth row and eighth column, e.g., represents the fourth person's feeling toward the eighth. The matrix is comprised of x's along the main diagonal for the self-choices, +'s for positive choices, —'s for negative

---

[1] For the illustration of a sociogram see Moreno, J. L., *Who Shall Survive?*
[2] For the illustration of a target diagram see Northway, Mary L., *A Method for Depicting Social Relationships Obtained by Sociometric Testing.*

choices or rejections, and blanks for indifference or no mention. Figure 1 shows the form in which raw data are recorded:

In essence the method of manipulating the matrix consists of re-arranging the rows and columns in a systematic manner to produce a new matrix which exhibits the group structure graphically in a standard form. From the standpoints of construction and of interpretation this form of presen-

	Joe	Mary	Bill	John	Jane
Joe	×	+	+		
Mary	+	×		−	
Bill	−		×	−	
John		+		×	
Jane	+				×

FIGURE 1.

Read Figure 1 horizontally thus, Joe chooses Mary and Bill and is indifferent to John and Jane. Read column 1 thus, Joe is chosen by Mary and Jane, and rejected by Bill.

tation of sociometric data is superior to the sociogram. We shall first present in some detail the procedure for manipulating the matrix and then discuss some of the consequences, illustrating with an example taken from Moreno's work.

MANIPULATING THE MATRIX

1. *Building the Subgroups.* First select any pair of individuals between whom there exists a mutual positive choice. The rows and columns corresponding to this pair are shifted so that the pair appears in the upper lefthand corner of the matrix. Any other individual in the group who is chosen by both of the original pair will appear in the matrix to have a pair of plus signs in the two rows running across the top of the matrix. If there is any such individual, he is added to the others by shifting his row and column to the third positions to make a subgroup of three. If it is impossible to find anyone chosen by both the original members of the group, the two vertical columns corresponding to the original subgroup may be examined for some person who chooses both members. If an individual choosing both is also chosen by one of them, that individual may be added to the subgroup. In either event, we now have three individuals, each of whom has been chosen by at least one of the remaining two. Adopting the principle that another person may be added to an established subgroup if he is chosen by half or more of the members of the subgroup, we now look for someone who has been chosen by at least two of the three. This process

230

continues, individuals being added and previous members of the subgroup being rechecked at each stage to make sure that at least half of the enlarged subgroup has chosen each member. When no additional person can be added, it is assumed that the subgroup is complete. We now proceed with the matrix reduced by the deletion of N_1 rows and columns corresponding to the N_1 members of the first group. Select again any two individuals making a mutual positive choice and proceed to build up a second subgroup of N_2 members. The process continues as long as subgroups can be formed in this way. The result of this part of the manipulation is a series of subgroups appearing as principal minors of the matrix, in each of which half or more of all choices are positive choices, followed by a number of individuals belonging to no particular subgroup.

2. *Arrangement of subgroups.* For every pair of subgroups formed as above, there are two minors of the matrix, at the intersections of blocks of rows and columns, corresponding to the subgroups. The proportion of rejects or minus signs measures the extent of rejection between the two groups. Rearrange the order of the groups so that the two groups having greatest mutual rejection, as measured by proportion of minus signs, are at the extreme ends of the principal diagonal and the others appear inside in order of diminishing amounts of rejection. This procedure has the effect of moving blocks of minus signs to the upper righthand and lower lefthand corners of the matrix.

3. *Arrangement of non-grouped individuals.* An individual who is not a member may be a satellite of a subgroup in either of two ways. He may choose half or more of the members of the subgroup and be rejected or ignored, or he may be chosen not quite enough to be considered a member of the subgroup. We may indicate this orbital relation by placing the first type at the upper lefthand boundary of the subgroup and the second type at the lower righthand. If an individual is a satellite in both senses the second should take precedence. Those individuals remaining after this operation who are neither in a subgroup nor satellites may be considered to be the genuine isolates in the group.

4. *Cores of subgroups.* One final refinement is indicated by the orbital relationship outlined above. The various members of a single subgroup may be rearranged so that the tighter-knit portion of the group appears at the center as a core. In this way, the subgroups emerge as a tight core surrounded by subsidiary members, in turn surrounded by satellites who are not properly an integral part of the subgroup. Those appearing at the ex-

treme corners of the matrix are the subgroups having the greatest intergroup rejection. Isolates will appear at or near the center of the matrix. Thus, there is no order relationship between the groups at the upper left and lower right. Both are extreme but neither is "better" in any sense.

Once the basic pattern has been produced as a result of these four steps, it may prove desirable to shift some of the matrix around in order to emphasize or illustrate a particular point. However, the basic pattern should be much the same regardless of who has performed the manipulation.

Figure 2 has been reproduced from Moreno (4) and represents the sociometric data collected from Cottage 4 of the New York State Training School for Girls at Hudson, New York. In figure 3, the same data is shown in matrix configuration. In this form, all the information has equal weight, no relations being obscured by reason of unfortunate placing of individuals. Also, some of the secondary relationships are brought to the surface. The subgroup structure has been indicated by dotted lines.

Looking at the matrix, we see that the second subgroup is the largest and contains the major star of the entire group (WR). The first subgroup is connected to the second through their choice of WR, but are not chosen at all by the members of that subgroup. One individual (TA) who is not attached to any subgroup chooses three of the five in the second subgroup but is rejected. It is probable that she would like to join the group but has not been successful in getting herself accepted. She is a satellite of what we have called the first type. The unusual overlapping of the third subgroup on the second and fourth indicates that it is in a state of flux; either it is in process of dissolution with BU and SO drifting one way and SV the other, or it is in process of formation, recruiting members from the other two subgroups. A subsequent check would indicate which is the case.

Considering the positions of the isolates, ET seems to have antagonized some of the members of the second subgroup; but for this, she might have been included in that group. RA, WT, GU and HM seem to be true isolates without any particular pattern of rejections. HM, however, rejects three of the four members of the last subgroup, indicating a concentrated rejection directed against this group. WN and LU, who are otherwise isolates, have formed a mutual bond.

The last subgroup has a curious connection with the second. RG apparently would like to be a member of the second group but is rejected by the leader WR. This rejection is the more significant since it is the only choice, positive or negative, that WR makes. RG, then, forms her own

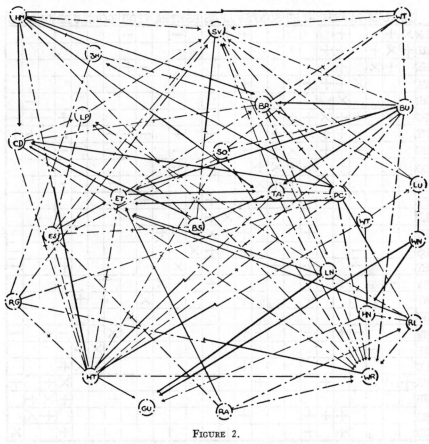

FIGURE 2.

STRUCTURE OF A COTTAGE FAMILY-C4

25 individuals; isolated 0; pairs 28; mutual rejections 1; incompatible pairs 8; chains 2; triangles 4, squares 5, circles 2, stars 7. Distribution 77% Attractions, 23% Rejections. Type of organization, balanced.

Black lines = repulsions. Dot dash lines = attractions. Onesided repulsion or attraction indicated by a line with an arrow. Mutual attraction or repulsion (pairs) indicated by dash across middle of line.

group, none of whom rejects members of WR's group but each of whom is rejected by someone in the WR subgroup. This is the only evidence in the entire group of inter-subgroup potential conflict.

We have departed from the basic matrix pattern in placing the first subgroup in that position. This was done in order to make clear the re-

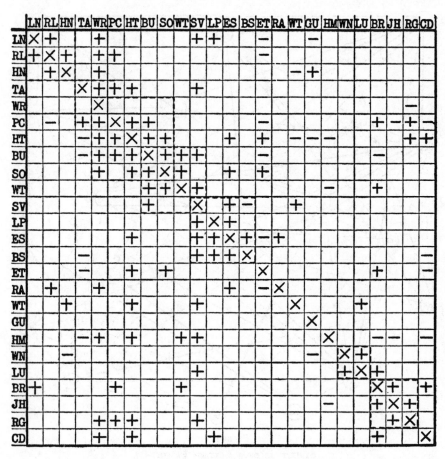

FIGURE 3.

lationship of this group to the second through the leader of the second.

The process has the obvious advantage that different investigators will tend to produce the same or very similar matrices (possibly reversed in order) from the same data. Interpretation of the final matrix pattern is fairly simple. Ganging together is indicated by the principal minors of the matrix; extent of potential conflict between subgroups is indicated by the proportions of rejections in the two non-principal minors at the intersections. Also, the direction of conflict between two subgroups is made apparent as, in the example above, where there is rejection of one group by a

234

second while the second does not reject the first. The relative permanence of the group structure is indicated in terms of the extent to which the sub-groups are well-knit and have absorbed satellites. Stars in the group are indicated by large numbers of positive choices appearing in vertical columns of the matrix. Individuals rejected by the group are indicated by negative signs in a vertical column. There is further indication of the pattern of rejection, which is not obvious from the sociogram, in that the matrix will indicate whether a person is rejected particularly by members of one sub-group or is rejected indiscriminately by the group as a whole.

It also seems possible that numerical standards might be developed as to the "well-knittedness" of a group. There is the further possibility that with development of numerical standards the group as a whole can be characterized in terms of the number, size and relationship of the subgroups, the cohesiveness of the various subgroups, and the number of isolates left in the group.

At present, manipulation of rows and columns in the matrix is a somewhat cumbersome process. Various mechanical methods have been devised but are not wholly satisfactory. It is hoped that a mechanical means will be devised which will materially reduce the labor involved and permit application of these principles to mass data by any investigator. The present approach was developed in attempting to handle more effectively data collected by the Detroit Citizenship Education Study Staff.

BIBLIOGRAPHY

1. Bronfenbrenner, Urie. *The Measurement of Sociometric Status, Structure, and Development*. (Sociometric Monographs, No. 6.) New York: Beacon House, 1945.
2. Cook, Lloyd Allen. *American Sociological Review*, X (April, 1945), 259–61).
3. Jennings, Helen Hall. *Leadership and Isolation: A Study of Personality in Inter-Personal Relations*. New York: Longmans, Green and Co., 1943 and 1950.
4. Moreno, J. L. *Who Shall Survive? A New Approach to the Problem of Human Inter-relations*. New York: Beacon House, 1934.
5. Northway, Mary L. "A Method for Depicting Social Relationships Obtained by Socio-metric Testing, *Sociometry*, Vol. III (April, 1940).

235

SOCIOGRAM AND SOCIOMATRIX
A Note to the Paper by Forsyth and Katz

By J. L. Moreno

Efforts of improving the sociogram and the sociomatrix have been made by various authors (Northway, Dodd, Jennings, Bronfenbrenner, etc.). The attempt of Forsyth and Katz is a valuable contribution in this direction. However, a careful comparison of the sociogram and the sociomatrix contained in their article, both presenting the same sociometric data, does not seem to meet their claim that the sociomatrix is superior and more objective in its presentation than the sociogram. Except for onesided choices or rejections, the matrix offers difficulties. Already pair relations are hard to find, but when it comes to more complex structures as triangles, chain relations, and stars, the sociogram offers many advantages, direct visibility and better opportunities for precise observation. Take for instance a triangle like HT-PC-BU. It is fairly easy to detect in the sociogram, but unless you know from the sociogram or otherwise, that these three individuals form a triangle, one finds it difficult to trace it in the matrix. Or take for instance, the chain relation HT-CD-SV-BU-PC-HT. This chain is easy to follow up in the sociogram but practically impossible to detect in the matrix. Another illustration is the star WR. On matrix and sociogram one can easily see all the individuals choosing WR, but the fact that WR rejects RG and consequently enters into conflict with a key individual (RG) of an important structure consisting of RG-DN-BR-WT-BU, is not noticeable to the examiner of the matrix.

I agree with the authors, however, that the sociogram is badly in need of improvement. The most important task ahead of us it seems to me is to establish *a set of rules* according to which sociograms are to be built.

Up to now sociogram and sociomatrix each offered certain advantages. They supplement each other. In teaching sociometry the sociogram is more plastic and offers an interrelated whole of the group structure to the eye of the student. He has it all before him instead of having to look for the bits in a matrix and piecing them together in his mind. In research work they should be used jointly. However, I believe that a synthesis between sociogram and sociomatrix is possible. Technicians of the matrix should try more and more to put into it what is missing but available in the socio-

236

gram (Forsyth and Katz by arranging the subgroups move into this direction). The technicians of the sociogram should learn from matrix construction and introduce into sociogram building the elements of advantage there.

THE ANALYSIS OF SOCIOGRAMS USING MATRIX ALGEBRA

By Leon Festinger

There is, at present, no adequate analytical device for handling data from one of the most popular measurement techniques in the field of social psychology. Sociometric questions such as "Who are your best friends?" or "What people do you like most to be with?" are increasingly being used whenever an interest in the "structure" or "patterning" of relationships among a number of persons is present. The exact wordings of the questions used represent an almost infinite series of variations, depending upon the context of the study in which the question is asked. The character of the data, however, is always the same. The data obtained are the specific persons mentioned by each one in response to the question.

In the study of groups by means of sociometric data, much attention has been given to the exact pattern of interconnections among individuals. Of importance have been such questions as who are a particular person's friends, what are his relations with the friends of his friends, and what tendencies to subgroup or clique formation exist in the group; how many paths of influence exist among members of a group, over how much of a group does a person's influence extend, what is the nature of the two or three step influence chains that may exist; if an item of information enters a group, how many people will eventually hear about it; who will hear it and from whom, and how far removed from the original source will it be by the time a specific person hears about it?

Without any adequate representational techniques for handling such data, the analysis of the exact patterns of interconnections among members of a group is virtually impossible, unless the group is very small. As the size of the group increases, the complexity of the pattern generally makes it extremely difficult to comprehend by mere inspection. The result has been the relative neglect of this kind of analysis. Investigators have, by and large, contented themselves with analyzing sociometric patterns in such terms as how many choices people receive, what kinds of people get most choices, what proportion of the choices are inside the group, and other such summary measures which serve to relate the sociometric choices to other variables.

Initial attempts at the analysis and description of the exact patterning of interconnections in a group took the form of drawing complicated diagrams where the relations between persons were represented by lines, with arrows on them. These diagrams could then be examined. It is readily understandable that such a diagram would be completely unwieldy if the number of members in the group was large or if the number of choices made by each member was appreciable. There are no rules for operating on such diagrams. One merely arranges them by trial and error so as to make the diagram look as simple as possible, and then one further inspects and examines with the hope that one will be alert enough to see what is to be seen.

It was the recognition of these difficulties that led people like Northway (4) and Cook (2) to attempt to formulate a system which would order the sociometric diagram so as to make it more easily understandable. These attempts, however, still left the analysis of sociometric patterns in a vague and relatively unsystematic state. A large step forward was taken by Forsyth and Katz (3) in suggesting the use of a matrix and some of the manipulations of matrix algebra for the analysis of sociometric patterns. Their idea was to represent the sociometric pattern in a matrix form and then to rearrange this matrix, according to certain principles, in order to have it reveal the subgroupings that were present. The matrix presentation is simply performed by listing the individuals in the group along the rows and along the columns in the same order. The choices that any individual makes are then indicated by the number 1 in one of the squares, such that the row corresponds to the person making the choice, and the column corresponds to the person receiving the choice. The squares along the main diagonal of the matrix are, of course, left blank, since the person is not considered as having chosen himself. Looking across any row reveals who was chosen by that person, and looking down any column reveals from whom that person received choices.

The presentation in this form offers little or no advantage over the more complicated sociometric diagram for direct inspection. Some manipulations of the matrix, however, tend to simplify it. The suggestion of Forsyth and Katz is to rearrange the order of the members of the group so that the numbers in the matrix cluster as closely as possible along the diagonal. More technically, they suggest rearranging the order of the rows and columns so as to minimize the square of the perpendicular deviations of the numbers from the diagonal of the matrix. This rearrangement, once accomplished, will show, clustered together, those people who choose each other frequently, and, relatively separated, those who do not choose each other. It does thus enable us to separate out subgroups which exist, and would seem to be a plausible means of analyzing changes in the pattern of connections in a group from one time to another. Such changes would show themselves in different ordering of the members of the group in the final matrix arrangement from one time to another. It does not seem to be too helpful a method for comparing two different groups, and the labor involved in obtaining the ordering of the matrix which will cluster the choices most closely along the diagonal is quite tedious.

There are other manipulations of matrix algebra which would seem to be of use for the analysis of such patterns of connections among members of a group. When the sociometric pattern is presented in a matrix form, an analysis of some aspects of the structure of the group can be performed by the relatively simple means of squaring and cubing this matrix.[1] The squared matrix is obtained rather readily in the following way: to obtain the number which goes into the cell corresponding to column c and row r of the squared matrix, we multiply each cell in column c of the original matrix by the corresponding cell of row r and then add these products up. The general equation for this multiplication might be written as follows:

$$A^2{}_{rc} = A_{1c}A_{r1} + A_{2c}A_{r2} + A_{3c}A_{r3} + \cdots + A_{nc}A_{rn}.$$

In this equation $A^2{}_{rc}$ refers to the number in the cell of the squared matrix in the r row of the c column; $A_{1c}A_{r1}$ refers to the product of the number in the cell in the first row of the c column and the number in the r row of the first column of the unsquared matrix; $A_{2c}A_{r2}$ refers to the product of the number in the cell in the second row of the c column and the number in the r row of the second column of the unsquared matrix, and so on.

This procedure is actually a rather simple one to carry out. The products of the corresponding cells of a row and a column will yield numbers other than zero only if a *one* appears in both cells which are being considered. Thus, if in a matrix, individual 2 chooses individual 11, and 11 chooses individual 6, this will contribute a number in the row 2, column 6 cell of the squared matrix.

It may be seen from the way in which the squared matrix was obtained that each figure in this matrix represents the number of two-step connections that exist between the specified two members of the group. It is clear, of course, that this relationship need not be symmetrical, just as the one-step connections need not be symmetrical.

The numbers that appear in the diagonal of this squared matrix have a special meaning. They indicate the number of two-step connections that exist from a person to himself, or, in other words, they indicate the number of mutual sociometric choices in which this person was involved.

The meaning of these two-step connections between different people can be important. For example, if the original sociometric choice indicates influence from one person to another, the squared matrix would indicate the extent

---

[1] The application of matrix multiplication to the analysis of sociometric patterns was developed together with Mr. Albert Perry and Mr. Duncan Luce of the Massachusetts Institute of Technology.

of indirect influence that this person has and exactly which other people he influences indirectly. If the original sociometric data indicated channels of communication for information, the squared matrix would tell us who would hear things from whom with the information going through one intermediary.

The cube of the matrix, which gives further information of this sort, is obtained by multiplying the original matrix by the squared matrix in the same manner as the original matrix was multiplied by itself. The formula for obtaining the values of the cells of the cubed matrix would be written similarly as:

$$A^3_{rc} = A_{1c}A^2_{r1} + A_{2c}A^2_{r2} + A_{3c}A^2_{r3} + \cdots + A_{nc}A^2_{rn}.$$

The actual calculation can be performed rather simply.

The meaning of the figures in this cubed matrix is similar to their meaning in the squared matrix. They indicate the number of three-step connections that exist between any two people. The numbers in the diagonal of the matrix now indicate the number of three-step connections from a person back to himself. The implications of these numbers in the diagonal of the cubed matrix will be elaborated on shortly.

It is apparent that these matrices may also be raised to higher powers to obtain the four-step or five-step of even more indirect connections among the members of a group. If we are concerned with a question such as how many people will hear a given item of information in three or fewer steps if it is started with any particular person, the answer may be obtained by adding together the original, the squared, and the cubed matrices. We can obtain such information as who influences the greatest number of people in less than a specified number of steps, which people are influenced by the greatest number of people, and which people are only subject to the influence of a few; which people in the group are most indirectly connected to each other, and how indirect is this connection; and what proportion of the possible connections among the various people actually exist. Being able to handle conveniently and efficiently these aspects of group structure and patterning of connections should make it feasible to study their effects on such processes as communication, influence, social pressures, and many others.

THE DETERMINATION OF CLIQUES

The manipulation of matrices by means of raising them to the third power can, with complete accuracy, determine the existence of cliques of various sizes and with various degrees of "cliquishness." Let us begin by defining an extreme instance of clique formation within a group and then see how we may determine whether or not such cliques exist in any given structure. We will define this extreme type of clique as more than two individuals, all of whom choose each other mutually. In other words, direct one-step symmetrical connections exist between every possible pair of members of such a clique. Clearly, in order to determine the existence of such a clique we would only concern ourselves with the symmetrical submatrix consisting only of mutual choices and not with the complete matrix of connections. If we raise such a symmetrical submatrix to the third power we will obtain all the three-step connections that exist between any two people which involve only mutual choices. What would then be the meaning of a three-step connection from a member back to himself which involves only symmetrical choices, that is, what will be the meaning of the numbers which appear in the main diagonal of this cubed symmetrical submatrix? Numbers will appear in the main diagonal of this cubed matrix if, and only if, there exists a clique, as defined above, within the group. If there does exist such a clique, then numbers will appear in those positions on the diagonal which correspond to those persons who are members of the clique. If only one clique exists in the group, or if more than one clique exists but they contain different members, then the number which appears in the diagonal for a particular individual will bear a given relationship to the number of people in the clique. If the clique is composed of n members, the number appearing in the diagonal for each of the members will be equal to $(n-1)(n-2)$. We may thus immediately determine from this cubed matrix whether or not there exist cliques, who belongs to these cliques if they exist, and how many members each clique has.

It is also possible to distinguish subgroups that are not extreme cliques. These subgroups may be defined on the basis of mutual choices or on the basis of the complete matrix. The best criteria for distinguishing subgroups of less than the extreme degree must still be determined, but it is likely that once defined, they may be relatively easily found by means of matrix multiplication.

This, of course, represents only the beginning of the development of the application of matrix algebra to sociometric data. There are still a number of problems that exist and many indicated areas for extension of the development. I shall mention a few of those which we consider important.

1) Matrices which are cubed or raised to even higher powers will contain in them two kinds of chains or indirect connections among persons. One of these types of chains, which for certain purposes we should like to eliminate, we have called redundant chains. These are chains where one person appears more than once. An example would be: a-b-a-c. For coordinations of these matrices to such things as, say, influence patterns in a group, these redundant

chains do not seem to have much meaning. These redundant chains can be eliminated very easily in the cubed matrix, but we have as yet found no way to eliminate them in matrices of higher power.

2) Thus far we have concerned ourselves with matrices in which only zero or one can appear in a cell. Sociometric data are frequently gathered in two forms such as "Whom do you like most?" and "Whom do you dislike most?" Such rejections are also an important aspect of social structure in a group. It would appear desirable to investigate the potentialities of matrix multiplication using matrices in which any cell can contain either a+1, 0 or — 1.

3) The use of such a technique as matrix multiplication for analysis of a special kind of data immediately suggests extensions of its use. This method of analysis can clearly be applied to any data which consist essentially of relationships among a number of discrete points. In sociometric data the discrete points are people in a group, and the relationships are things like "liking" or "being together with." There are other areas in which the data have a similar form. Bavelas (1), for example, has recently published a mathematical model for dealing with topological structures such as those used by Professor Kurt Lewin. These structures consist of discrete regions having or not having a connectedness relationship. Bavelas deals with such concepts as diameter of such a structure and distance from one part of the structure to another. The technique of matrix multiplication can also clearly be used to operate on such problems.

It also becomes apparent, from a consideration to what kinds of data this analytical device might be applicable, that the relationships among the discrete parts need not be *either/or* relationships. Indeed, most sociometric data are in terms of *either/or* relationships only because the measurement technique is very imprecise. Certainly there are degrees of *friendship* and degrees of *liking* and degrees of *susceptibility to influence*. As yet we are completely unable to handle such data where the relationships among persons can assume continuous values. It would be useful to consider the possibilities for application of matrix algebra to such data.

It is to be hoped that empirical use of these techniques will clarify some of the problems concerning co-ordination to data, and that it will stimulate sufficient interest to push forward further development rapidly.

REFERENCES

1. Bavelas, A. "A Mathematical Model for Group Structures," *Applied Anthropology,* VII (1948), 16–30.

2. Cook, L. A. "An Experimental Sociographic Study of a Stratified 10th Grade Class," *American Sociological Review*, X (1945), 250–61.
3. Forsyth, E., and Katz, L. "A Matrix Approach to the Analysis of Sociometric Data: Preliminary Report," *Sociometry*, IX (1946), 340–47.
4. Northway, M. L. "A Method for Depicting Social Relationships Obtained by Sociometric Testing," *Sociometry*, III (1940), 144–50.

THE DISTRIBUTION OF THE NUMBER OF ISOLATES IN
A SOCIAL GROUP*

By Leo Katz

Summary

The exact chance distribution of the number of isolates in a social group is found in this paper, using methods due to Fréchet. The binomial distribution fitted to the first two moments of the exact distribution is shown to give reasonably good approximation and a slightly coarser binomial approximation is indicated.

INTRODUCTION

Consider a group consisting of N individuals. Each designates d of the others with whom he would prefer to be associated in some specified activity, that is, each chooses d from $N - 1$ possible associates. In the context of the group and the specified activity, an individual is said to be an *isolate* if he is chosen by none of his fellow group members. It is immediately obvious that the number of isolates depends upon the size of the group, the number of choices permitted, and the extent to which the group, as a social organism, provides acceptance for joint activities for the individuals who compose the group. Thus, when N and d are fixed, the number of isolates becomes an important characteristic of the group structure. When it is important to state whether the number of isolates is unusually large or small, it is necessary that the chance distribution of this number be known.

The history of attacks on the distribution problem is brief. Lazarsfeld, in a contribution to a paper by Moreno and Jennings [8], gave the expected (mean) number of isolates as

$$N[(N - d - 1)/(N - 1)]^{N-1},$$

but made no attempt to obtain the distribution. Bronfenbrenner [1] gave (without proof) an incorrect version of the distribution function. He gave the expression, which he claimed was "developed deductively and checked by empirical methods,"

---

* Work done under the sponsorship of the Office of Naval Research at Chapel Hill, North Carolina, and presented at the Chicago meeting of the Institute of Mathematical Statistics, December 27, 1950.

245

$$P(i) = \Pr \{i \text{ or fewer isolates}\} = 1 - \frac{(N - i - 2)^{(d)}}{(N - 1)^{(d)}}, \qquad (1)$$

were $a^{(b)} = a(a - 1)(a - 2) \cdots (a - b + 1)$. This form gives completely nonsensical results in application. Edwards [2] conjectured that the Bronfenbrenner formula gives the probability of a given person's including in his list of d at least one of $i + 1$ specified names. Edwards then gave correctly the probability of the maximum possible number of isolates,

$$P[N-1-d] = \Pr\{N-1-d \text{ isolates}\} = \binom{N}{N-1-d} \frac{(d+1)^{(N-1-d)}}{\binom{N-1}{d}^N}, \qquad (2)$$

where $\binom{a}{b}$, $b \leq a$, is the binomial coefficient $a!/[b!(a - b)!]$. Note that there cannot be $N - d$ isolates, since d persons can be chosen only for a maximum total of $(N - 1)d$ times, less than the Nd choices actually made.

In the last paper cited above, Edwards went on to set up the probability of $N - 2 - d$ isolates by eliminating irrelevant cases from those in which the isolates name d from a list of $d + 2$ while the non-isolates choose d from a list of $d + 1$ names, and indicated that the process might be continued to obtain the probabilities of $N - 3 - d$ isolates, etc. The form of these results, it is stated, would indicate a complicated algebraic expression for the required probability distribution, and the question is then raised whether the existing technique of experimentation should not be modified to meet the practical requirement of simple mathematical treatment.

In this paper, we shall first obtain the exact distribution of the number of isolates on the assumption of random choice, and second, we shall obtain an approximation that *does* satisfy the requirement of simple mathematical treatment. An example will be given to indicate the accuracy of the approximation for a typical application.

EXACT DISTRIBUTION OF THE NUMBER OF ISOLATES

It should first be remarked that any division of the group, into those who are isolates and those who may not be, produces two distinct patterns of choices. Each isolate selects d from among all those in the second group, but each member of the second group must select d from among those members of the second group not including himself. Let

$$p_{i_1, i_2, \cdots, i_k} = \Pr\{\text{individuals } i_1, i_2, \ldots, i_k \text{ are isolates}\}.$$

As an immediate consequence of the remark made above and the symmetry of the situation,

$$p_{i_1, i_2, \cdots, i_k} = \frac{\left(\dfrac{N-k}{d}\right)^k}{\left(\dfrac{N-1}{d}\right)} \cdot \frac{\left(\dfrac{N-k-1}{d}\right)^{N-k}}{\left(\dfrac{N-1}{d}\right)}, \tag{3}$$

for every $(i_1, i_2, \cdots, i_k)$. Setting

$$S_k = \binom{N}{k} p_{i_1, i_2, \cdots, i_k} = \binom{N}{k}\left(\dfrac{N-k}{d}\right)^k \left(\dfrac{N-k-1}{d}\right)^{N-k} \left(\dfrac{N-1}{d}\right)^{-N} \tag{4}$$

the principle of inclusion and exclusion ([3], ch. 4) gives immediately

$$P_{[k]} = \Pr\{\text{exactly } k \text{ isolates in the group}\} = \sum_{j=k}^{N-1-d} (-1)^{k+j} \binom{j}{k} S_j. \tag{5}$$

Equation (5) gives the exact probability of k isolates, in a group of N where each individual makes d choices, as a linear combination of the S_k.

The values of S_k may be computed directly from (4) or recursively, noting that $S_0 = 1$ and

$$\frac{S_{k+1}}{S_k} = \frac{N-k-d}{k+1}\left[\frac{N-k-d}{N-k}\right]^{k-1}\left[\frac{N-k-1-d}{N-k-1}\right]^{N-k-1}. \tag{6}$$

The form of the last term in (6) suggests interesting asymptotic behavior. We are, however, less interested in asymptotic characteristics of the distribution than in its properties for moderate values of N. We may take the asymptotic behavior to give an indication of what may be a reasonable approximation, but the quality of the approximation must be judged by results for typical cases; here, N is usually between 10 and 100. We shall later consider one such typical example in which $N = 26$, $d = 3$.

If we do not require the values of the individual $P_{[i]}$ but are only interested in the moments of the distribution of isolates, it turns out that the S_k quantities are of central importance. Fréchet [4] has shown that

$$\alpha_{(k)} = k!\, S_k, \tag{7}$$

where $\alpha_{(k)}$ is the kth factorial moment of the distribution, given by $\alpha_{(k)} = \sum_{i=1}^{N-1-d} i^{(k)} P_{[i]}$. We shall have occasion to use these factorial moments in the following section.

Approximate Distribution of Number of Isolates

Since we know the exact distribution, an approximate distribution is useful only if it is more easily computed. It is easily shown (see Feller [3]) that, for d fixed, the limiting distribution is Poisson with $\Pr(k) = e^{-\lambda}\lambda^k/k!$, where $\lambda = N(1 - d/(N - 1))^{N-1}$. However, for moderate values of N, the approximation is not good; an example is given later.

Following the procedure of Kaplansky [7] produces a modified Poisson approximation which is quite good. The drawback to this procedure is that computations are almost as difficult as for the exact distribution. Therefore, we seek another approximation to satisfy the dual requirements of accuracy and simplicity.

From (4) and (7), the mean and the variance of the number of isolates are respectively,

$$\text{mean} = a_{(1)} = N\left(1 - \frac{d}{N-1}\right)^{N-1}, \tag{8}$$

$$\text{variance} = a_{(2)} + a_{(1)} - a_{(1)}^2$$

$$= N\left(1 - \frac{d}{N-1}\right)^{N-1}\left[1 + (N - 1 - d)\left(1 - \frac{d}{N-2}\right)^{N-2}\right.$$

$$\left. - N\left(1 - \frac{d}{N-1}\right)^{N-1}\right]. \tag{9}$$

From (9), we see var $(k) = $ mean (k) $[1 - (d + 1)(1 - d/(N - 2))^{N-2} + O(N^{-2})] \approx$ mean (k) $[1 - (d + 1)e^{-d}]$. Since the variance is less than the mean, the binomial distribution, $b(x; n, p)$, is strongly suggested (choice being restricted to simple distributions). We shall not insist that n be an integer; thus, we have essentially a beta distribution. For this distribution, $a_{(r)} = n^{(r)}p^r$ and, fitting the first two moments, we have

$$np = a_{(1)} = N\left(1 - \frac{d}{N-1}\right)^{N-1}, \tag{10}$$

$$\frac{1}{n} = 1 - \frac{a_{(2)}}{a_{(1)}^2} = 1 - \left(1 - \frac{1}{N}\right)\left[1 - \frac{d}{(N-2)(N-1-d)}\right]^{N-2}. \tag{11}$$

Also, since $a_{(r+1)}/a_{(r)} = (n - r)p$, we form the functions,

$$D_r = \frac{a_{(r+1)}}{a_{(r)}} - r\frac{a_{(2)}}{a_{(1)}} + (r - 1)a_{(1)}, \qquad r = 2, 3, 4, \cdots, \tag{12}$$

248

which vanish identically for the binomial distribution. These functions are equivalent to the "total criteria" proposed by Guldberg [6] and Frisch [5] for judging whether an observed series may be approximated by a binomial frequency function. In their work, the approximation is considered to be good when the criterion functions of the moments of the observed series are close to zero. We shall extend the notion to cover the case of approximation of a more complicated probability law by the binomial law.

Setting $r = 2$ and $r = 3$ in (12) gives two functions which are exactly equivalent to the two criteria given by Guldberg (allowing for an omitted term in his second result). Also, the complete set (12) is equivalent to Frisch's total criteria for $g = 1$, $h = 1, 2, 3, \cdots$ in his notation. Since his criteria for all other values of g may be expressed in terms of those for $g = 1$, (12) is equivalent to the complete set of conditions given by Frisch.

Substituting from equation (7) into (12), we have

$$D_r = (r + 1) \frac{S_{r+1}}{S_r} - 2r \frac{S_2}{S_1} + (r - 1)S_1 ,$$

or, using (4) and (6),

$$D_r = (N - r - d) \left(\frac{N - r - d}{N - 1}\right)^{r-1} \left(\frac{N - r - 1 - d}{N - r - 1}\right)^{N-r-1}$$

$$- r(N - 1 - d) \left(\frac{N - 2 - d}{N - 2}\right)^{N-2} + N(r - 1) \left(\frac{N - 1 - d}{N - 1}\right)^{N-1} . \qquad (13)$$

For large N, each power of a fraction in (13) of the form $((a - d)/a)^a$ is approximately equal to e^{-d} and $D_r = 0$, approximately. In the limit, every $D_r = 0$, the asymptotic form of the distribution in this sense is, therefore, binomial. Further, the approximation should remain good even for moderate values of N (particularly when r is small) since the errors made by the exponential approximation are not only small but tend to compensate for each other.

We may, then, use a binomial probability law approximation with p and n given by (10) and (11). (If $1/n$ in (11) is evaluated to terms of $O(N^{-2})$, we find $1/n = (d + 1)/(N - 1 - d)$ or $n = N/(d + 1) - 1$, approximately. This seems consistently to understate the value of n from (11); accordingly, it is suggested that n be approximated by

$$n = \frac{N}{d + 1} - \frac{1}{2} . \qquad (11a)$$

In the next section, we shall compare this approximation with the exact distribution for a typical pair of values of N and d. We also give, for comparison, the Poisson approximation.

TABLE 1

Comparison of the exact and approximate distributions of the number of isolates for $N = 26$, $d = 3$

i	S_i	$P_{[i]}$(exact)	p_i(approx.)	$p_i - P_{[i]}$	$p'_i = \dfrac{e^{-\lambda}\lambda^i}{i!}$	$p'_i = P_{[i]}$
0	1.000 0000	.309 794	.311 098	+.0013	.344 989	+.0352
1	1.064 2429	.402 574	.399 727	−.0028	.367 152	−.0354
2	.474 9281	.214 316	.215 365+	+.0010	.195 370	−.0189
3	.116 8650+	.061 532	.062 473	+.0009	.069 306	+.0078
4	.017 5606	.010 564	.010 354	−.0002	.018 440	+.0079
5	.001 6882	.001 138	.000 943	−.0002	.003 925⁻	+.0028
6	.000 10596	.000 079	.000 039	−.00004	.000 696	+.00062
7	.000 0043 61	.000 003	.000 0002	−.000003	.000 106	+.000103
8	.000 0001 17				.000 014	
9	.000 0000 02				.000 002	

An Example

Moreno and Jennings [8] considered in some detail the case $N = 26$, $d = 3$. Since, also, a number of later writers have treated the same case as a reasonably typical one, we will test the accuracy of the approximation in this situation. The computation of the exact probability distribution seems to be best performed in two stages. In the first, the logarithms of the ratios S_{j+1}/S_j of equation (6) are obtained using 7-place tables, and the S_i themselves obtained from the partial sums of the logarithms. These values appear in the second column of Table 1. In the second stage of the computation, the exact probabilities are found by setting the S_i into (5). The exact probabilities are given to six decimals in the third column of the table.

In the computation of the approximate probabilities, we take advantage of the already computed values of S_1 and S_2 and equation (7) to obtain directly the factorial moments of (8) and (9). From (10) and (11), we have $p = .1717247$ and $n = 6.197378$. We then compute the binomial probabilities, $p_i = b(i; n, p), i = 0, 1, 2, \ldots, ([n] + 1)$, where $[n]$ is the largest integer in n, in the case, 6, using $p_0 = (1 - p)^n$ and $p_i{}^+{}_1/p_i = (n - i)p/(i +)(1 - p)$ as suggested by Guldberg [6] and others. The approximate probabilities, p_i, appear in the fourth column of the table to six decimals. It will be seen that the fit to three decimals is almost exact and certainly good enough for tests of significance. The discrepancies, $p_i - P_{[i]}$, are given in the fifth column. The Poisson probabilities and errors appear in the sixth and seventh columns.

The discrepancies for the "binomial" approximation are not particularly systematic except in the upper tail of the distribution, where the binomial gives zero probability for all numbers of isolates above seven. Although numbers through 22 are possible, they are so unlikely to occur by chance that this possibility may be practically disregarded. For example, the exact probability of eight isolates by chance is about one in ten million. The Poisson distribution appears to be "flatter" than the exact, understating probabilities for the central values and overstating for both tails.

As a further check on the accuracy of the approximation, the values of $\gamma_1 = \mu_2^{3/2}$ and $\gamma_2 = \mu_4/\mu_2^2$ were computed for the exact distribution and for the "binomial" approximation. These computations give $\lambda_1 = .7193$ for the exact, .6993 for the approximate distribution; $\lambda_2 = 3.2620$ and 3.1663, respectively.

REFERENCES

1. Bronfenbrenner, U. "The Measurement of Sociometric Status, Structure and Development," *Sociometry*, VI (1943), 363–97. Reprinted, "Sociometry Monograph," No. 6. New York: Beacon House, 1945.
2. Edwards, D. S. "The Constant Frame of Reference Problem in Sociometry," *Sociometry*, XI (1948), 372–79.
3. Feller, W. *An Introduction to Probability Theory and Its Applications.* New York: John Wiley and Sons, 1950.
4. Fréchet, M. *Les probabilités Associées à un systèm d'événements compatibles et dépendants, actualités scientifiques et industrielles,* Nos. 859 and 942. Paris: Hermann et Cie, 1940 and 1943.
5. Frisch, R. "On the Use of Difference Equations in the Study of Frequency Distributions," *Metron*, X (1932), 35–59.
6. Guldberg, A. "On Discontinuous Frequency Functions and Statistical Series," *Skandinavisk Aktuarietidskrift*, XIV (1931), 161–87.
7. Kaplansky, I. "The Asymptotic Distribution of Runs of Consecutive Elements," *Annals of Mathematical Statistics*, XVI (1945), 200–3.
8. Moreno, J. L., and Jennings, H. H. "Statistics of Social Configurations," *Sociometry*, I (1938), 342–74. Reprinted in this volume.

THE MEASUREMENT OF GROUP INTEGRATION†

By Joan H. Criswell

In the analysis of group structure the sociometric test has so far been most fruitfully employed as an instrument for the treatment of choice volume, that is, the gross number of choices given out or received by an individual or group without regard to the patterns which can be differentiated within these choice totals. This seems to be a necessary starting point for structural analysis, since such volume is more easily handled statistically in view of the fact that single choices represent simpler probability functions than do any patterns of choices. Patterns can be made up of different combinations of choices and therefore introduce statistical problems which become more complex with increase in the number of elements in the patterns. Nevertheless the use of such compound data is a typically sociometric procedure. It does not require that the responses of two or more persons be measured separately and then combined in some way. Instead, their interpersonal relationship is directly measured.

This suggests that experimental findings should be increasingly analyzed into units larger than the single choice. A typical structural investigation might be to determine the curve describing the relationship between degree of reciprocation existing in a work group and the group's morale or efficiency. Reciprocation could also be used as one measure of cleavage between subgroups in a population, cleavage being indicated by low intergroup as compared with high intragroup reciprocation. Reciprocation might also be a function of time, with a curve expressing the relationship between mutuality and the length of a group's life together.[1] Another type of experiment concerns leadership: employees might choose supervisors to work under on certain projects and supervisors choose employees for the same projects, with a subsequent determination of the amount of reciprocation existing between supervisory and subordinate personnel.

---

†The opinions and assertions in this paper are those of the writer and are not to be construed as official or reflecting the views of the Navy Department or the Naval service at large.

[1]For an interesting consideration of time in relation to choice phenomena, see J. L. Moreno, Helen H. Jennings, and Joseph Sargent, *Time as a measure of inter-personal relations*. Sociometry Monograph No. 13, 1946; or see SOCIOMETRY, Vol. III, No. 1, pp. 62-80, January, 1940.

In order to obtain a rounded picture of structure, such experiments could be carried out under a variety of choice requirements. The arrangement of the group may be conceived of as satisfying certain specific needs, a given arrangement depending on which need is uppermost during a certain period. In a section of clerical employees, for example, individuals may be observed to arrange themselves differently according to whether they are proofreading, eating lunch, or having a rest period. Similarity but not perfect correlation may be expected between arrangements under differing conditions. From such considerations has sprung the practise of using the sociometric test with more than one criterion of choice.[2]

In these experiments probably the order of analytic procedure would be to determine first the measures of such masses as the group's distribution of choices within itself, or to itself and to another group, next attempting further to differentiate these areas in terms of reciprocal pairs, finally identifying larger patterns such as cliques or networks. Such progressive differentiation holds interesting possibilities which can only be touched on in the present article. In this paper current methodology will be described and a few additional techniques proposed.

The measurement of reciprocation of choice began in Moreno's work (7) as a determination of the percent of reciprocated choices in school classes and a tracing of age increase in such structures. Similar results were obtained later by Criswell (3). In these early studies age increase showed up in spite of the fact that no adjustment was made for size or race-sex composition of the school class. However, for finer measurement especially in cleavage situations allowances for group differences in size and composition should be made by comparison of results with those which would occur by chance.

For such comparisons the number of reciprocations which a group might be expected to make by chance must be calculated. The formulas which will be given are stated in terms of numbers of reciprocated and unreciprocated choices when it is more convenient to do so. However, reciprocation of choice is essentially a matter of pair formation, since under this experimental condition a selection never exists alone but assumes the existence of another selection which complements it. Obviously a reciprocated choice implies the existence of another choice responding to it, but nonreciprocal choices also occur in two's because the non-occurrence of a reciprocal pair

---

[2]This is considered essential by Moreno for analyzing the social atom (see reference 7) and was found by Jennings to reveal patterning as Moreno predicted (see reference 6).

automatically produces two unreciprocated choices. This fact that the distribution is actually in two's does not affect the chance ratios to be stated. They are therefore given in terms of choices for the sake of simplicity. But the use of pairs becomes important in the tests of significance which will be discussed.

The first formula for predicting the number of reciprocated choices which a group might be expected to make by chance, was developed by Lazarsfeld for distributions presented by Moreno and Jennings (8). It is intended for cases in which each individual makes a designated number of choices under a single criterion, e.g., each member makes three choices of a person beside whom he would like to sit in school class. The formula can be stated as (1):

$$R = N(N-1)p^2$$

in which $R =$ the expected number of reciprocated choices,

$N =$ the number of individuals in the group,

$p =$ the probability that a given individual will be chosen by another individual.

If each individual makes d choices, $p = \dfrac{d}{N-1}$ and $q = 1 - p$.

The corresponding formula for U, the expected number of unreciprocated choices, is (2):

$$U = N(N-1)pq$$

R plus U of course equals T, the total number of choices.

The next step is to extend this formula to experiments in which the subjects choose under more than one criterion, the number of specified choices remaining constant from subject to subject and from criterion to criterion. Each subject may be asked to make two choices of a person to study with, two choices of a luncheon companion, finally two of a baseball teammate.

One method of dealing with results from a variety of criteria has been to list for each subject all his choices made under all criteria, omitting duplication, and to then treat them as if they had been made under a single criterion. The variety of criteria is thus made to function merely as a device for increasing the number of choices and loses the full picture of pair relationships. With a multicriterial setup, however, two treatments using all the choices are possible.

Under the simpler treatment formulas (1) and (2) are used for each criterion separately and the expected amount of reciprocated choice is then the simple sum of the numbers expected under the single criteria. The chance number of reciprocated choices, taking c as the number of criteria used, would then be (3):

$$R_c = cN(N-1)p^2$$

Formula (2) would also be multiplied by c to obtain U_c. T would equal Ncd.

The second and more complicated treatment makes a maximum use of the amount of reciprocation present by employing what might be designated as interstitial or cross-criterial relationships between persons choosing under different criteria. In this case the experimenter takes advantage of the fact that, although A's choice of B may be unreciprocated under criterion 1, B may have chosen A under criterion 2 or 3. Such reciprocation, although not as strong or direct as within-criterion reciprocation, is a type of mutual relationship and may have merit in any measure which attempts to cover every shade of reciprocation present.

A formula for predicting reciprocatal relationships including interstitial ones has been offered by Bronfenbrenner (1), but it is less rather than more sensitive than the usual reciprocation formulas, since it predicts only the number of relationships in which the two participants form one or more reciprocal pairs of either a within-criterion or cross-criterion type. Thus no exact number of choices is predicted. A more precise formula was devised and previously discussed briefly by the writer (5).

In making cross-criterial analyses it is important to remember that all choice relationships are equally eligible for inclusion. There is a temptation to ignore all interstitial mutuals except those between persons otherwise not choosing each other, since in using interstitials the experimenter hopes to salvage subterranean connections between individuals appearing not to be mutually related.[3] Nevertheless it is logically necessary to count all interstitial pairs including those occurring between individuals already choosing each other under a single criterion.

This means that A's choices under criterion 1 are also considered in their relationship to all choices made by the rest of his group under criterion 2, under 3, etc. A in his character under criterion 1 is transplanted temporarily to the group as organized under criterion 2 and his reciprocations counted; then he is similarly transplanted to the group as struc-

---

[3]For differentiating factors tending to draw certain individuals together in some groupings and apart in other groupings, see J. L. Moreno (reference 7) and H. H. Jennings, *Sociometry of Leadership,* Sociometry Monograph No. 14, 1947, or SOCIOMETRY Vol. X, No. 1, 1947.

tured under criterion 3. In his character as chooser under 2 he is also placed in the group structure under 1 and under 3; and so on. The result is that for c criteria each of a subject's choices must be counted c times. Thus if he makes d choices per criterion, his total number of choices under one criterion increases to dc and the total for all his choices is dc multiplied by c, or dc^2. The total, T, for all subjects would then be Ndc^2. If d is constant for all subjects and all criteria, p is the same for whatever criterion the subject's choices are considered under. We therefore have for the expected number of choices the same p, q, and N for c^2 instead of c criteria. The formula for the expected number of reciprocated choices then becomes (4):

$$R_{cc} = c^2 N(N-1)p^2$$

The expression for U_{cc} is similarly formula (2) multiplied by c^2.

In certain investigations the experimenter considers it desirable to permit the subjects to make as many choices as they wish and therefore specifies no special number. In other investigations a number of individuals may make d variable by refusing to give the specified number of choices. In such cases the p and q values must be obtained by the use of averages.

If individuals make different numbers of choices, $d_1, d_2 \ldots d_n$, then each person has a different probability, $\dfrac{d_1}{N-1}$, of choosing any other individual. The chance of a pair between A and B would then be $p_1 p_2 = \dfrac{d_1}{N-1} \dfrac{d_2}{N-1}$. The value of p^2 for the group under one criterion would be the average of these individual probabilities for all possible combinations of N individuals taken two at a time, that is, $\dfrac{N(N-1)}{2}$.

This result can easily be arrived at by obtaining the average value of d and using it as usual in the formula for p. Thus 10 subjects making an average of 2.7 choices apiece under criterion 1 would yield a p^2 of .09 and make 8.1 reciprocated choices by chance under that criterion.

With variable d, p and q of course vary from criterion to criterion and the formulas for T, R, and U, must be modified accordingly. For cases in which c criteria are used, d is the average number of choices per criterion, and cross-criterial relationships are not considered, T equals $N(d_1 + d_2 + \ldots + d_c)$, and the expected number of reciprocated choices is (5):

$$R_c = N(N-1)(p_1{}^2 + p_2{}^2 + \ldots + p_c{}^2)$$

With cross-criterial mutuals used, T equals $Nc(d_1 + d_2 + \ldots + d_c)$, and the expected number of reciprocated choices becomes (6):

$$R_{cc} = N(N-1)[(p_1{}^2 + p_1 p_2 + \ldots + p_1 p_c) + \ldots + (p_c p_1 + p_c p_2 + \ldots + p_c{}^2)]$$

Corresponding U formulas are (7) and (8):

$$U_c = N(N-1)(p_1 q_1 + p_2 q_2 + \ldots + p_c q_c)$$
$$U_{cc} = N(N-1)[(p_1 q_1 + p_1 q_2 + \ldots + p_1 q_c) + \ldots + (p_c q_1 + p_c q_2 + \ldots + p_c q_c)]$$

After chance formulas have been devised the problem arises of expressing the amount of group integration present by relating the experimentally obtained distribution of reciprocated-unreciprocated choices to the chance distribution. A feasible method of accomplishing this is to divide the obtained ratio of reciprocated to unreciprocated choice by the chance ratio calculated from the revelant equations. In all cases $N(N-1)$ and c will cancel out in the chance ratio. Where d is constant throughout, the chance ratio simply reduces to $\dfrac{p}{q}$, regardless of number of criteria or use of interstitial choice. All of the formulas apply to the experimental data whether T is odd or even.

If R_o is the obtained number of reciprocated choices and U_o is the number of unreciprocated, the index of group coherence or integration, I, can for constant d be expressed as (9):

$$I = \frac{R_o q}{U_o p}$$

The other more complicated expressions of I can be obtained by use of formulas (5) through (8). If average d values for different criteria are closely similar, a simpler procedure would be to use one average d based on all choices under all criteria, obtain the p and q values from it and use formula (9).

In the determination of obtained R with inclusion of interstitial relationships care must be taken to count all cross-criterial reciprocations including those between persons who also chose each other within criteria. When obtained R has been counted U can be arrived at easily by subtraction of R_o from T.

For illustrative purposes suppose that 10 children make unlimited choices under two criteria. For criterion 1, the average number of choices made is 2.7; for criterion 2, average d is 3.6. Then, $p_1 = 2.7/9 = .3$, $q = .7$, $p_2 = 3.6/9 = .4$, $q_2 = .6$, $T = Nc(d_1 + d_2) = 126$. The numerator of the chance ratio is, from equation (6): $.09 + .12 + .12 + .16 = .49$. The denominator is, from equation (8): $.21 + .18 + .18 + .24 = .81$. The obtained numbers of choices are: under criterion 1, 12 reciprocated and 15 un-reciprocated; under criterion 2, 20 reciprocated and 16 unreciprocated; under crossed criteria, 40 reciprocated and 28 unreciprocated. Dividing the obtained ratio of 72/54 by the chance ratio of .49/.81 gives 2.20 as the integration index.

Besides determining the degree of integration, it is interesting to measure the amount of intergroup preference exhibited at a given level of integration. One might wish to find out whether a group of Italian and American girls forming 20 mutual pairs had done so without showing any nationality pref-erence. For this determination the total number of possible pairs for the group of N members $\frac{N(N-1)}{2}$, is divided into the number of pairs which would by chance be American-American, Italian-Italian, or Italian-American. The obtained number of pairs is then divided according to these chance pro-portions and compared with the distribution as derived from the experiment. The ratio is calculated between the number of pairs formed within na-tionality groups and the number formed between nationality groups. This is divided by the corresponding chance ratio to give an expression of na-tionality preference as expressed in reciprocation.

In the above procedure the chance distribution of the obtained number of pairs is estimated by determining for each nationality group of n indi-viduals the number of combinations of two which they can form, $\frac{n(n-1)}{2}$, and determining for each possible combination of different nationality groups the number of pairs they can form, $n_1 n_2$. The total of all these pairs is $\frac{N(N-1)}{2}$.

Reciprocation ratios should be a useful supplement to other measures of cleavage based on unreciprocated choice or choice volume in general. A variety of types of indices could no doubt be developed.

A further problem in this type of measurement is the test for signifi-cance of the deviation of the structural index from chance. For this purpose Bronfenbrenner has suggested using tables of the binomial distribution (1). He takes the expected number of reciprocated choices as the mean of a bi-nomial series, expresses the obtained number of reciprocations as a deviation from this mean, and determines from suitable tables how many times the given deviation would be obtained by chance. Although this method applies well to individual choices which are binomially distributed, it is inapplicable to patterns of choice, as the writer has pointed out (4).

In pattern measurement our concern is with the number of patterns of a specified type which a group will produce if arranged by chance alone. The expected value will be the mean number of patterns produced in all possible arrangements of the group by chance. In these arrangements of the total membership the basic element is not the individual, A, or his choice, B, but the individual-making-a-choice, A:B. In a group of three persons making one choice each the elements are then A:B, A:C, B:A, B:C, C:A, C:B. Not all can enter into any one chance arrangement. This suggests the complexity of the chance distribution, since all the elements are involved in prediction.

Whereas the binomial expansion yields the distribution of n unitary independent events, the reciprocal pair or any other pattern is a compound event formable in various ways according to how other events of the same type are made up and therefore hardly independent of them.

A method which seems suitable for any of the experimental findings discussed is to determine the deviation of the obtained from the expected distribution and apply the chi-square test, remembering that pairs, not single choices, are being dealt with. Thus for $T = 80$, $R = 24$, $U = 56$, $R_o = 40$ $U_o = 40$, the test would take the form:

$$X^2 = \frac{(20-12)^2}{12} + \frac{(20-28)^2}{28} = 8.62$$

If a fair number of group indices are available, mean differences between two types of group, e.g., boys and girls, could be evaluated in the usual manner by use of the standard error of the difference between means of indices. Probably in most cases only small numbers of groups would have been used and Student's t-test would have to be applied. Examples of the use of chi square and the t-test on sociometric data can be found in reference. (2).

Although the formulas and methods which have been discussed may appear complicated at first sight they reduce to relatively easily handled numbers. The greatest labor is not in the prediction of chance values but in the counting of reciprocated choices and this work can be greatly reduced if a tabulating machine installation is available. Methods such as those which have been proposed are worth using, since they produce a characteristic sociometric measure and may help to salvage structural material which is at present likely to be discarded.

BIBLIOGRAPHY

1. Bronfenbrenner, Urie. *A constant frame of reference for sociometric research*. Sociometry Monograph No. 6, 1945; or see SOCIOMETRY, Vol. VI, 1943.
2. Criswell, J. H. A sociometric study of race cleavage in the classroom. *Archives of Psychology*, No. 235, 1939.
3. Criswell, J. H. Sociometric analysis of Negro-white groups. *Sociometric Review*, pp. 50-53, New York State Training School for Girls, Hudson, N. Y., 1936.
4. Criswell, J. H. Foundations of sociometric measurement. SOCIOMETRY, Vol. IX, No. 1, pp. 7-13, February, 1946.
5. Criswell, J. H. Measurement of reciprocation under multiple criteria of choice. SOCIOMETRY, Vol. IX, No. 2-3, pp. 126-127, May-August, 1946.
6. Jennings, H. H. *Leadership and Isolation*. Longmans, New York, 1943.
7. Moreno, J. L. *Who shall survive? A new approach to the problem of human inter-relations*. Beacon House, New York, 1934.
8. Moreno, J. L. and Jennings, H. H. *Sociometric measurement of social configurations*, Sociometry Monograph No. 3, 1945; or see Statistics of social configurations, SOCIOMETRY, Vol. I, Nos. 3 and 4, pp. 342-374, January-April, 1938.

STATUS: ITS MEASUREMENT AND CONTROL IN EDUCATION

By Leslie Day Zeleny

Measurement of Status

For some time the writer has set forth the hypothesis that social status, defined as the average intensity of the attitudes expressed toward a person by his associates in a group, can be measured. This article recapitulates previous statements, develops further the hypothesis, and presents additional experimental results from the classroom. (The section on control is omitted in this printing.)

Direction and Intensity of Interpersonal Attitudes

Obviously, the first problem in the measurement of status is the determination of the degrees of positive and negative intensity of interpersonal attitudes in a group. There are at least three ways to do this. One is by patient participation in group activities accompanied by careful observation and reporting of actions and attitudes.[1] Another is by the technique of the personal interview,[2] and a third is by means of a written record.[3] In education, the written record has been found very practical. On the *Group Membership Record*,[4] the members of a group or community of groups, who have had the opportunity to react to one another as values in a particular type of group activity, indicate how they feel about working with each of the members in a new group of which they might be a member. An opportunity is provided for recording one's first few choices for membership in this group, the acceptable members, those toward whom one is indifferent, unacceptable members, and one's last choices.

---

[1] See William Foote White, "Corner Boys: A Study of Clique Behavior," *American Journal of Sociology,* XLVI (March, 1941), 647–64; Frederick C. Thrasher, *The Gang* (Chicago: University of Chicago Press, 1939); and Eliot Chapple and Conrad Arensberg, *Measuring Human Relations: An Introduction to the Study of the Interaction of Individuals* (Provincetown: Massachusetts Journal Press, 1940).

[2] See George Lundberg and Mary Steele, "Some Attraction Patterns in a Village," *Sociometry,* January–April, 1938, pp. 375–419.

[3] See Leslie Day Zeleny, "Measurement of Sociation," *American Sociological Review,* Vol. VI (April, 1941); W. J. Newstetter, J. J. Feldstein, and T. M. Newcomb, *Group Adjustment, A Study in Experimental Sociology* (Cleveland: Western Reserve University Press, 1938): and J. L. Moreno, *Who Shall Survive?* (Washington: Nervous and Mental Diseases Publishing Co., 1934).

[4] Zeleny, *op. cit.*

In this manner, every person may indicate one to five different degrees of intensity of an attitude toward every other member of the group, as follows:

A first choice[5] +1.00 unit
Acceptance +0.50 unit
Indifference 0.00 unit
Unacceptance −0.50 unit
A last choice[5] −1.00 unit

In this manner, the direction and intensity of all interpersonal attitudes may be recorded.[6] (The units of intensity assigned are, of course, arbitrary, but experience has shown them to be very satisfactory.[7])

Social Status Index

To determine any person's status in the group, one may compute the average intensity of the attitudes expressed toward that person, plus or minus the average (or standard) deviation of the individual attitudes from the average attitude. Expressed in a formula, the status of a person, or his social status index, SS, may be given as follows:

$$SS = \bar{I} \pm D \qquad (1)$$

when $\bar{I}$ represents the average of the intensities of the attitudes and D represents the deviation. (For clarity and convenience, the average deviation will be used here; for more refined statistical analysis the standard deviation is better.) When I equals the intensity of an interpersonal attitude, n equals the total possible attitudes that may be expressed toward a person in the group, an N equals the number of persons in the group, then

$$SS = \bar{I} \pm D = \frac{\Sigma I}{n} \pm D = \frac{\Sigma I}{N-1} \pm D. \qquad (2)$$

The *social status index* (*SS*) of a person in a group can then be easily calculated. For example, in the following case,

---

[5] This means a first, second, or third choice depending upon the number in the group (or a last, next to last choice, etc.), see "Measurement of Sociation," *American Sociological Review.*

[6] *Ibid.*

[7] See R. Likert, S. Roslow and G. Murphy, "A Simple and Reliable Method of Scoring the Thurstone Attitude Scales," *Journal Social Psychology,* V (1934), 228–38. It is shown here that arbitrary units are more satisfactory than more complex units used by Thurstone.

Attitudes Expressed Toward A

	I	*D*
From B	+1.0	0.0
From C	+1.0	0.0
From D	+1.0	0.0
From E	+1.0	0.0
From F	+1.0	0.0
	$\overline{I} = +1.0$	± 0.0

$$SS = \frac{\Sigma I}{N-1} \pm D = \frac{1+1+1+1+1}{6-1} \pm D = \frac{5}{5} = +1.00 + 0.00 \text{ units} \quad (3)$$

where +1.00 represents the average intensity of the attitudes expressed toward A and ±0.00 represents the average deviation of the individual attitude intensities from $\overline{I}$.

To compute D, let d represent the development of any one attitude from the mean attitude, then

$$D = \overline{d} = \frac{\Sigma d}{n} = \frac{\Sigma (\overline{I} \frown I)}{N-1} \text{ units} \quad (4)$$

In the above illustration D was computed, as follows:

$$D = \frac{\Sigma(\overline{I} \frown I)}{N-1} = \frac{0+0+0+0+0}{5} = \frac{0}{5} = \pm 0.00 \text{ units} \quad (5)$$

where the sign of the intensities is considered only in relation to the distance of I from $\overline{I}$.

Since, in actual life situations, the interpersonal attitudes differ in magnitude, another SS may be computed illustrating the use of the formula with the inclusion of positive and negative attitudes of differing degrees of intensity. Take the case of B in a group:

Attitudes Expressed Toward B

	I	*D*
From A	+1.0	0.8
From C	+0.5	0.3
From D	0.0	0.2
From E	−1.0	1.2
Form F	+0.5	0.3
	$5\,\lfloor\!+1.00$	$5\,\lfloor 2.8$
	$\overline{I} = +0.20$	$D = \pm 0.56$

263

In this case

$$SS = \frac{\Sigma I}{N-1} \pm \frac{\Sigma(\overline{I} \sim I)}{N-1} = \frac{1.0 + 0.5 + 0.0 + (-1.0) \pm 0.5}{5}$$

$$\pm \frac{0.8 + 0.3 + 0.2 + 1.2 + 0.3}{5} = \frac{1.00}{5} \pm \frac{2.8}{5} = 0.20 \pm 0.56 \text{ units} \tag{6}$$

Thus, the status of B is positive; but it is not high, and there is considerable variability in the attitudes expressed toward B. Perhaps one could say that B's status was not very secure.

Reliability of the Social Status Index

All available evidence indicates that the *social status index* is a reliable measure. The *Group Membership Record,* the measure of the direction, and intensity of interpersonal attitudes, has been shown to be reliable. For example, the product moment correlations between acceptances received on successive administrations of the Record were $r = .910 \pm .029$, $r = .916 \pm .029$, $r = .947 \pm .011$, in three trials ($N = 15, 34, 35$); and similar correlations between choices received were $r = .950 \pm .033$; $r = .938 \pm .024$, $r = .940 \pm .024$, on three trials ($N = 15, 35, 34$). Adding, acceptances and choices together in three additional instances ($N = 29, 29, 28$) $r = .948 \pm .0143$, .961 $\pm .0097$, .956 $\pm .0143$. Furthermore, the *SS* itself, computed in two additional instances, with the use of all five degrees of intensity of interpersonal attitudes, was shown in two experiments to have a reliability correlation of $r = .985 \pm .005$ when $N = 25$ and $r = .852 \pm .036$ when $N = 32$. When used with adults, the *Record* is a reliable instrument.

With children the reliability is not so high, but still high enough to allow the use of the Record with children as young as those in the upper primary and intermediate grades. For example, the coefficient of reliability on two administrations of the Record (five days apart) to a class of twenty fourth-grade children was $r = .79 \pm .0591$.

Validity of the Social Status Index

There is evidence that the social status index is a valid measure of status. First, the conditions under which the *Record* are given impel truthful answers, for if a person does not record his true feeling he will be assigned to a group to which he does not care to belong. Then, a correlation between acceptances "received" by 35 persons and a five man-to-man leadership score determined with the use of the Partridge[8] test was $r = .538 \pm .082$; and a correlation between choices received and the five man-to-man rating was $r = .874 \pm .027$ ($N = 35$).

Of interest, too, is the relationship between symptoms of abnormality as measured by the *Personality Adjustment Inventory*[9] and *social status indices*. Those with the lowest abnormality scores might be expected to show the best social status indices; consequently a negative correlation between the *indices* and the *scores* would imply validity. The correlations in one group of 24 students was $r = .225 \pm .128$. This shows that the *SS* and lack of symptoms of personal maladjustment (neurotic, psychoneurotic and social maladjustment) tend to go together to a small extent. The low negative correlation also indicates, however, that there are other factors than *individual* symptoms of maladjustment that influence status. For example, in another study, correlations between five man-to-man scores (a sociometric rating) and certain characteristics of leaders were: leadership and participation, $r = .59 \pm .074$; leadership and intelligence, $r = .44 \pm .023$; leadership and general knowledge $rho = .763$. Thus, many persons who have an ability to participate in a group, intelligence and knowledge may attain a high status despite certain maladjustments.

All data collected thus far imply that the *social status index* is both a reliable and valid measure of social status.

---

[8] De Alton Partridge, *Leadership Among Adolescent Boys* (New York: Bureau of Publications, Teachers College, Columbia University, 1934).

[9] *The Personality Adjustment Inventory*, arranged by William Hales, Minnesota State Reformatory For Men, St. Cloud, is, in the opinion of the writer, the best of its kind. It gives a total score and diagnostic scores. This test is highly reliable, and will soon be published.

A NEW STATUS INDEX DERIVED FROM SOCIOMETRIC ANALYSIS*

By Leo Katz

Summary

For the purpose of evaluating status in a manner free from the deficiencies of popularity contest procedures, this paper presents a new method of computation which takes into account who chooses as well as how many choose. It is necessary to introduce, in this connection, the concept of attenuation in influence transmitted through intermediaries.

INTRODUCTION

For a considerable time, most serious investigators of inter-personal and inter-group relations have been dissatisfied with the ordinary indices of "status," of the popularity contest type. In the sociometric field, for example, Jennings (1) says, ". . . it cannot be premised from the present research that greater desirability per se attaches to a high [conventional computation] choice-status as contrasted with a low choice-status in any sociogroup without reference to its milieu and functioning." However, in the absence of better methods for determining status, only two alternatives have been open to the investigator. He has been forced either to accept the popularity index as valid, at least to first approximation, or to make near-anthropological study of a social group in order to pick out the *real* leaders, i.e., the individuals of genuinely high status.

The purpose of this paper is to suggest a new method of computing status, taking into account not only the number of direct "votes" received by each individual but, also, the status of each individual who chooses the first, the status of each who chooses these in turn, etc. Thus, the proposed new index allows for *who* chooses as well as how many choose.

For the present discussion, an operational definition of status is assumed, status being defined by the question asked of the members of the group. The same device, then, may be used to study influence, transmission of information, etc.

---

* This work was done under the sponsorship of the Office of Naval Research.

The New Status Index

To exhibit the results of the "balloting," we shall use the matrix representation for sociometric data as given by Forsyth and Katz (2). An example for a group of six persons appears below. In this example, A chooses only F, B chooses C and F, C chooses B, D, and F, and so on. The principal diagonal elements, by convention, are zeroes. The question asked could be, "Which people in this group really know what is going on?"

Chooser	Chosen					
	A	B	C	D	E	F
A	0	0	0	0	0	1
B	0	0	1	0	0	1
C	0	1	0	1	0	1
D	1	0	0	0	1	0
E	0	0	0	1	0	1
F	1	0	0	1	0	0
Totals	2	1	1	3	1	4

In the Forsyth and Katz formulation, the 6×6 array above is referred to as the choice matrix, C, with element $c_{ij} = $ response of individual i to individual j. Further, as pointed out by Festinger (3) for matrices whose elements are 0 or 1, powers of C have as elements the numbers of chains of corresponding lengths going from i through intermediaries to j. Thus, $C^2 = (c_{ij}{}^{(2)})$, where $c_{ij}{}^{(2)} = \Sigma_k c_{ik} c_{kj}$; each component, c_{ik}, of $c_{ij}{}^{(2)}$ is equal to one if and only if i chooses k and k chooses j, i.e., there is a chain of length two from i to j. Higher powers of C have similar interpretations.

The column sums of C give the numbers of direct choices[1] made by members of the group to the individual corresponding to each column. Also, the column sums of C^2 give the numbers of two-step choices from the group to individuals; column sums of C^3, numbers of three-step choices, etc. An index of the type we seek, then, may be constructed by adding to the direct choices all of the two-step, three-step, etc., choices, using appropriate weights to allow for the lower effectiveness of longer chains. In order to construct appropriate weights, we introduce the concept of "attenuation" in a link of a chain.

---

[1] In the sequel, it is assumed that C is a matrix of 0's and 1's.

It is necessary to make some assumptions regarding the effective functioning of an existing link. The first assumption we make is common to all sociometric work, namely, that our information is accurate and that, hence, certain links between individuals exist; and where our information indicates no link, there is no communication, influence, or whatever else we measure. Secondly, we assume that each link independently has the same probability of being effective. This assumption, obviously, is no more true than is the previous one; however, it seems to be at least a reasonable first approximation to the true situation. Thus, we conceive a constant a, depending on the group and the context of the particular investigation, which has the force of a probability of effectiveness of a single link. A k-step chain, then, has probability a^k of being effective. In this sense, a actually measures the non-attenuation in a link, $a = 0$ corresponding to complete attenuation, and $a = 1$ to absence of any attenuation. With this model, appropriate weights for the column sums of C, C^2, etc., are a, a^2, etc., respectively.

We have noted previously that the quantity a depends upon both the group and the context; we now examine this notion in greater detail. Suppose that our interest is in the communication problem of transmission of information or rumor through a group. It is quite evident that different groups will respond in different ways to the same information, and also, that a single group will exhibit different responses to various pieces of information. For example, the information that the new high-school principal is unmarried and handsome might occasion a violent reaction in a ladies' garden club and hardly a ripple of interest in a luncheon group of the local chamber of commerce. On the other hand, the luncheon group might be anything but apathetic in its response to information concerning a fractional change in credit-buying restrictions announced by the federal government.

Some psychological investigations have been directed at exactly this point. It is possible that these, or subsequent studies, may reveal that a is or is not relatively constant among all existing links in a group with respect to a particular context. If it should appear that a is not relatively constant, it will be necessary to consider more complicated models. For present purposes, we shall assume a is relatively constant and that, either by investigation or omniscience, its value is known.

Let s_j be the sum of the jth column of the matrix C, and s a column vector with elements s_j. In the example above, e.g., the row vector $s' = (2, 1, 1, 3, 1, 4)$. We wish to find the column sums of the matrix

$$T = aC + a^2C^2 + \cdots + a^kC^k + \cdots = (I - aC)^{-1} - I.$$

T has elements t_{ij} and column sums $t_j = \sum_i t_{ij}$. Let t be a column vector with elements t_j and u be a column vector with unit elements. Then $t' = u'[(I - aC)^{-1} - I]$.

Multiplying on the right by $(I - aC)$ we have

$$t'(I - aC) = u' - u'(I - aC) = au'C,$$

and by transposition,

$$(I - aC')t = aC'u.$$

But, $C'u$ is a column vector whose elements are the row sums of C', i.e., the column sums of C; *therefore* $C'u = s$. Finally, dividing through by a, we have

$$\left(\frac{1}{a} I - C'\right)t = s.$$

Thus, given a, C, and s, we have only to solve the system of linear equations above to obtain t. Actually, we compute no powers of C although our original summation was over all powers. The process breaks down in case $1/a$ is not greater than the largest characteristic root of C. (See 5, p. 168.) Some experience with computations indicates that reasonable, general-purpose values of $1/a$ are those between the largest root and about twice that root. It is evident that the effect of longer chains on the index will be greater for smaller values of $1/a$. Finally, it is a real advantage in computations to choose $1/a$ equal to an integer. In the numerical example of the following section, the largest root is less than 1.7 and $1/a$ is taken equal to 2.0. There is an extensive literature on bounds for such roots; in this connection, see the series of papers by A. Brauer (6). For matrices of non-negative elements, a simple upper bound for the largest root is the greatest row (column) sum; this bound is attained when all row (column) sums are equal. For the solution, several abbreviated methods of computation are available. See, e.g., Dwyer (4).

The usual index of status is obtained by dividing the column sum s_j by $n - 1$, the number of possible choices. Using the same notion, we obtain as divisor of the t_j, with $(n - 1)^{(k)} = (n - 1)(n - 2) \cdots (n - k)$,

$$m = a(n - 1) + a^2(n - 1)^{(2)} + a^3(n - 1)^{(3)} + \cdots$$

$$= (n - 1)! a^{n-1} e^{1/a}, \text{ approximately.*}$$

Finally, then, the new status index vector is given by $(1/m)t$, where t is the vector solution to the system of equations above.

---

* The approximation improves with increasing n. The relative error $< 1/[a^{n-2}(n - 2)! e^{1/a}]$. For example, when $n = 25$, $a = \frac{1}{2}$, the relative error $< 4 \times 10^{-17}$.

A NUMERICAL EXAMPLE

We shall consider the example of the group of six persons whose choice matrix is given at the beginning of the paper. For this group, conventional technique of dividing column sums by $n - 1 = 5$ produces the

Conventional Status Vector $= (.4, .2, .2, .6, .2, .8)$.

Going beyond the surface question of "How many choose X?" to the deeper question of "Who chooses X?" reveals certain important features of this artificially constructed group. F and D are, apparently, of highest status. A, however, is chosen by both of these though he is not chosen by any of the "small fry" in the group. Is not A's status higher than is indicated by the conventional computation?

Secondly, the positions of the three low-status persons are not identical. B and C choose each other and are chosen by no one else in the group. E, on the other hand, has contact with the rest of the group through D and is in a somewhat different position than B and C.

Other features might be pointed out, such as that F's choice of D is not reciprocated, etc. But this is enough to illustrate the well-known deficiencies in the conventional computations. We pass now to actual computation of the vector t.

We first write out the required equations, using $a = 1/2$ for simplicity. The coefficients of $t_1, t_2, \cdots, t^6$ are the negative of the transpose of C plus $1/a = 2$ added to each principal diagonal term. The equations are

$$
\begin{aligned}
2t_1 \qquad\qquad\quad - \ t_4 \qquad\quad - \ t_6 &= 2 \\
2t_2 - \ t_3 \qquad\qquad\qquad\qquad &= 1 \\
- \ t_2 + 2t_3 \qquad\qquad\qquad &= 1 \\
- \ t_3 + 2t_4 - \ t_5 - \ t_6 &= 3 \\
- \ t_4 + 2t_5 \qquad\quad &= 1 \\
-t_1 - \ t_2 - \ t_3 \qquad\quad - \ t_5 + 2t_6 &= 4,
\end{aligned}
$$

and the resulting values of $t_1, \cdots, t^6$ are 13, 1, 1, 11.4, 6.2, and 12.6, respectively. The approximate computation of $m = 27.71$ agrees fairly well, even here with $n = 6$ only, with the exact value of 26.25. Dividing the t_j by 27.71 gives the

New Status Vector $= (.47, .04, .04, .41, .22, .45)$.

Comparison of the new with the conventional computation above indicates that every change is in the appropriate direction to overcome the shortcomings in the index pointed out previously and the new status indices are in much more nearly correct relative position.

REFERENCES

1. Jennings, H. H. *Leadership and Isolation.* New York: Longmans, Green, 1943 and 1950.
2. Forsyth, E., and Katz, L. "A Matrix Approach to the Analysis of Sociometric Data: Preliminary Report," *Sociometry,* IX (1946), 340–47.
3. Festinger, L. "The Analysis of Sociograms Using Matrix Algebra," *Human Relations,* II (1949), 153–58.
4. Dwyer, P. S. *Linear Computations.* New York: Wiley and Sons, 1951.
5. Ferrar, W. L. *Finite Matrices.* London: Oxford University Press, 1951.
6. Brauer, A. "Limits for the Characteristic Roots of a Matrix," series of four papers in *Duke Mathematical Journal,* I (1946), 387–95; II (1947), 21–26; III (1948), 871–77; IV (1952), 75–91.

ANALYSIS OF SOCIAL INTERACTION AND SOCIOMETRIC PERCEPTION[1]

By Edgar F. Borgatta

Part I. A Review of Literature in the Problem Area

It is characteristic of persons that they constantly assess each other as desirable or undesirable according to some frame of reference (or set). This choice behavior has been, in large part, the central focus of sociometric investigation during the past two decades, stemming directly from Moreno's work (23). This approach, however, has been primarily through the soliciting of response to a sociometric or near-sociometric question. The equally important suggestion that the actual choice performance in interaction be observed, and that the response to the sociometric question (as perception of own response or aspiration) be considered in relation to this actual performance, although central to Moreno's own work, has been neglected by most sociometric investigators. More attention to these forms of observation jointly applied, however, is being given in recent small group research in the laboratory which makes use of both direct observation and pre, during, and/or post meeting questionnaires. The actual performance in interaction has more frequently become the point of reference for asking questions about the discrepancy of perception or aspiration and performance in social situations; today, inferences concerning interaction are being set on firmer empirical grounds.

It was noted early in the sociometric literature, however, that it would be naive to expect a simple relation between the perception of own response (choice reflected in the sociometric questions) and the actual performance in interaction. The immediate complication, of course, is that persons choosing may be rebuffed or accepted, and they themselves are not the sole determiners of the outcome of an encounter. Experience might limit per-

[1] This research, carried out at the Harvard Laboratory of Social Relations, was supported in part by the United States Air Force under Contract AF33(038)-12782 monitored by the Human Resources Research Institute. Permission is granted for reproduction, translation, publication and disposal in whole and in part by or for the United States Government. I am grateful to Samuel A. Stouffer, J. L. Moreno, and Robert F. Bales for encouragement and material contribution through many discussions; to Jonathan Robbin for technical assistance.

formance, for example, but not aspiration. Thus, if we now classify the *summary* observations mentioned, we have at least eight actions possible:

Initiated

1. Actual choice performance of person in interaction
2. Actual rejection performance of person in interaction
3. Choice report by person
4. Rejection report by person

Perceived

5. Actual choice received from other in interaction
6. Actual rejection received from other in interaction
7. Choice report received (object of aspiration of other)
8. Rejection report received from other

The picture, from this point, becomes considerably more complex. Not only is it possible to choose and reject, both at the level of aspiration and of performance, but equally important modes of response are *indifference* and *neutrality*. Moreno's discussion of this area is still the most complete and detailed (23).

Analysis in this area, which is only beginning to mature, soon implicates analysis of other types of extremely relevant aspects of social interaction. The description of the person, we note, is not complete by any means when we have the above observations. The first two, along with 5 and 6, are external and presumably completely objective arbitrary reports of performance. Similarly, once made, the choice or rejection report, as in 7 and 8 above, are objective data. Items 3 and 4, of course, involve in the ordinary formulation the subject's report of his perception of the social situation. The perception, however, is of *his* response to others.

Again, quite early in the sociometric literature Moreno directed attention to another phase (25). In social interaction the response of the individual is dependent not only on his perception of *his* response to others, but also to his perception of the response *of others*. The perception of the response of others may refer to the actual performance or may be anticipatory. This *sociometric self-rating, or sociometric perception,* usually refers to perception of *anticipated* performance of others, although, such anticipated performance may be well rooted in experience. We have again complicated the situation by introducing other orders of data which appear necessary in the frame of reference of social interaction investigation: (a) The perception of the actual performance of others, and (b) the perception of the intended performance of others.

In the analysis of social interaction, however, the perception of the actual performance of others may be considered as part of the experience, or as one of the events upon which the future action is based. That is, since reaction time is involved, response that is other than reflexive or completely conditioned is based on past experience of the organism, or on prediction of the next performance in the situation, the *perception of anticipated action* of other. Our interest in sociometric perception, thus focuses only on perception of anticipated action. The diadic relationships of affective sociometric choice and expected choice (sociometric perception) have been schematized by Tagiuri (27).

Attention to sociometric perception in the literature is yet sparse. We have already mentioned Moreno's original interest (25), and the next instance of use is Maucorps (21) who made the limited application of asking the subjects to predict who, from those they themselves chose, would choose them. This same type of application was recently made by Lundberg and Dickson (20).

Tagiuri (27) generalized the approach to asking that the subjects "guess" from the entire range of persons rather than the narrower field of the already chosen, and Yablonsky (31) has made the same application in a laboratory context.

In a sense, however, serious attention to the area we have identified as sociometric perception began at the turn of the century with the development of the concept of empathy by Theodore Lipps. Implementation of theory in research, however, did not become possible until the development of the Freudian emphasis on insight and transference, the concept of role taking (22), but particularly role playing (24) and the concomitant impetus of the then new "sociometric tests" (23). Moreno's concept of *tele* synthesized this development and is singularly important to this area of conceptualization (23). It is interesting that tele has had at least three major kinds of definition. The first has referred to the minimum transfer of meaning *between* two persons, pointing to an awareness of each other. The reference, thus, is to the minimum condition for the existence of interpersonal relations, and the focus is on process and mutuality. The second type of definition refers to the increased rate of interaction between members of a group. The third definition has been more explicit and essentially is best identified as "two-way empathy." This emphasis of mutuality in the concept in a sense characterizes Moreno's approach of the social through the psychological, or more accurately, the analysis of the psychological in the situational context. Attention to empathy was given by Cottrell (10), and Dymond (11, 12), developed a schema for empirical observation of empathy. Dymond proposed that each subject be asked to *rate* on each of six traits: (a) himself, (b) the other person; *guess:* (c) the self rating the other person will make, and (d) the rating the other person will give him. This development, however, was with ratings rather than with sociometric questions *per se,* but in the direction that interest in sociometric perception has gone (1, 2, 3, 4, 16, 28), the schema was already provided. Asking whether a person "likes" another is not infinitely distant from asking whether a person is "friendly." Both these questions are somewhat different from the purely sociometric question which involves a criterion (activity). The essential difference between the interest in sociometric perception, and empathy as developed on the lines proposed by Dymond, is largely that those emphasizing empathy take as their datum the discrepancy between the "actual situation" and the perception of it, while workers in social perception have been interested in the interrelationships of perception and actual situation as well.

A unique study of tele as two-way empathy in actual situations was made by Toeman (29, 30). A double is an auxiliary ego who attempts to co-experience with the subject in situ. Toeman proposed a scheme for observation and tried to measure the accuracy of double empathy and tele ability.

Most of the empathy studies have dealt with the accuracy of perception of ratings (of personality characteristics) rather than with accuracy of perception of sociometric relationships. However, much experience has been reported which is directly of interest to the student of sociometric perception. Probably the prime reason for inclusion of the empathy approach here is the twofold criticism which has developed: On the one hand, it has been demonstrated that empathic ability corresponds closely to having "conventional" or normal patterns of response, and that having a high empathy score may be directly the function of the fact that ". . . conventional people get good scores on empathy tests because most of their partners (or referents) in the test are also conventional" (19, p. 175). *Projection,* apparently, accounts for the relationship (18, 19). This immediately throws a question on approaches that deal with the identification of (stereotype) response patterns as measures of empathy rather than conventionality (26). There remains, of course, the question of whether there is such a thing as empathy involved in the approach. The more recent writers cautiously agree that there is (14, 19). A second type of criticism is implicit in Gage's (14) suggestion for the use of "standard persons" in the measure of empathy, analogous to the use of the "auxiliary ego" in psychodramatic research, (24) and his raising the question of whether or not accuracy of perception of

275

strangers can be carried over in interpretation to nonstrangers. This questions the comparability and meaning of ratings when certain factors of interaction are or are not held constant. This same type of problem has been raised generally by Moreno and others in relation to sociometric choice scores and other types of indices.

This second problem raised above is a complex one, which ordinarily must be answered by the needs of the researcher. That is, the commonly accepted approach of both sociometric studies and the empathy studies is useful and necessary in the description of structure, but if the intention is to generalize the results for persons into indices of "tendency to," then certain situational factors must be controlled for the indices to have the intended meaning. For example, it has often been noted that in the use of sociometric tests, some account should be taken of the range of acquaintances (23) from which a person chooses or is chosen, rejects or is rejected. Range of acquaintances is not necessarily the same for all persons in a group, especially if the group is of any size. This is the frequently raised question of sociological research: What is the "independent variable," and what are the common factors with which it is heavily loaded? For this simple example, it may be that the important variable is acquaintance, or to make the situation more remote, some general factor common to acquaintance and sociometric popularity which might be named "sociability." But to the point, if there is a focus on the *description of structure* of the community in terms of the reported choices, then the acquaintance information may give more understanding, but it is not necessary in the frame of reference. However, if the focus is on *understanding relationships*, then it would be necessary to control these variables. This is done in the laboratory for acquaintance, as an example, by using unacquainted subjects and allowing them equal opportunity to get acquainted. At one level, this puts a caution to extension of interpretation of certain types of study. For example, if it should be found that sociometric choice and sociometric perception are both a function of acquaintance range (23), there would be questionable meaning to a statement such as that of Goodnow and Tagiuri (16) that where "cleavage" in choice behavior reported exists, if sociometric perception corresponds to it, there is recognition of the bias in choice.

In this connection, we point out that acquaintance and acquaintance span might well be considered more seriously the subject matter of additional investigation. Moreno (23) has indicated that acquaintance may be considered in one sense as the ecological aspect of sociometric investigation. However, like the concept tele, acquaintance appears to have a flexibility in usage which indicates a sensitivity to the importance of the concept for sociological analysis. At one end, acquaintance span may serve to identify the effective range within which choices are made according to various criteria, and in this sense acquaintance is related to the concept of tele as the minimum condition for the existence of interpersonal relations. On the other side, acquaintance may be considered in terms of *degree* of acquaintance. Criteria choice may be associated with high degree of acquaintance, as well as being restricted within acquaintance span, but acquaintance itself may be considered as the non-criterion sociometric question on the lowest level of contact. Essentially, this point of view blends acquaintance in a continuous sequence to such non criteria questions as: "Who do you like?" "Who do you dislike?"

Recently, Ausubel and associates (1, 2, 3, 4) have concerned themselves with an area they name "sociempathy," which focuses on the use of questions concerning sociometric perception and sociometric choice report. Their approach has been with adolescents, and with the use of extensive forms of rating of acceptability of each other member, the prediction of rating of self by other, and the prediction or ratings of other by others. Using "natural" groups, however, their approach differs considerably from that indicated here. Some of their results will be indicated in the report of the present research.

Tagiuri, Blake and Bruner (28) recently reported a study of sociometric perception in therapy groups of ten persons each. The conditions of observation are in this study the sort which would tend to minimize the effect of acquaintance span. Data from their study are not considered here since their method of data treatment is not comparable to this research.

Since this problem area has not yet been schematized succinctly, the following arrangement (23) is offered to indicate the kinds of observation which are necessary to achieve any degree of completeness in the (descriptive) analysis of interaction from a sociometric frame of reference. In addition, acquaintance span of the individual is of importance. All these areas are important to the analysis of social interaction, and 1,3 with 2,2 have been the focal points of study of sociometric perception. The study of empathy would take as the datum the discrepancy of choice relationships found and those perceived.

It is interesting that an important area of study has been essentially by-passed in the study of empathy and perception. The research in accuracy of *teacher* judgments reported first by Moreno (23) and in detail by Bonney (5) and again later receiving attention (6, 15, 17) has in some ways been

SCHEMA

Initiated behavior of the person	*Received behavior of the person*
1, 1. Actual choice performance of person in interaction a. Choice b. Indifference c. Neutrality d. Rejection	2, 1. Actual choice received from others in interaction a. Choice b. Indifference c. Neutrality d. Rejection
1, 2. Choice reported by person a. Choice b. Indifference c. Neutrality d. Rejection e. Don't know	2, 2. Choice report received from others a. Choice b. Indifference c. Neutrality d. Rejection e. Don't know
1, 3. Choice anticipated from others a. Choice b. Indifference c. Neutrality d. Rejection e. Don't know	2, 3. Choice anticipated to be made by person a. Choice b. Indifference c. Neutrality d. Rejection e. Don't know
1, 4. Choice relationship among others perceived by the person a. Choice b. Indifference c. Neutrality d. Rejection e. Don't know	2, 4. Choice relationship among others that others expect the person to perceive a. Choice b. Indifference c. Neutrality d. Rejection e. Don't know

a stepchild of investigators because of the special relationship involved. This type of interest in sociometric perception is located in the schema with 1,4 and 2,2, and legitimately belongs in the area of interest encompassed by the concept of empathy and sociometric perception.

For some aspects of study of interaction, particularly in terms of *general perception* of the situation by the individual, it may not be necessary to ask questions in detail. That is, for example, to answer certain problems defined, the question, "How many persons will want to . . . with you?" may be a satisfactory substitute for the summation of responses to the question, "Who will want to . . . with you?" As we have noted, the procedure the investigator takes should be determined by his objectives, but he should be aware of the limitations and delineations in any given application.

This short review briefly surveys sociometric perception, and not the more generalized area of perception. We have introduced perception of ratings into this discussion only in very limited terms. A conceptual review of the related concepts of empathy and tele, with reference to interaction analysis is projected by this author.

PART II. INTERACTION PERFORMANCE, CHOICE REPORT AND SOCIOMETRIC PERCEPTION—A CROSS VALIDATION REPORT

Sample and design. The research reported below is part of a larger study, sections of which are reported elsewhere (7, 8, 9). In this research, a sample of 126 subjects (Air Force enlisted personnel) was divided into fourteen batches of nine persons each. Within each batch of nine persons grade was held constant, and there were eighteen persons in each of the enlisted grades. Thus, so far as status is reflected in grade, this was held constant in the interaction participation for the study. The batches of nine persons were arranged into groups of three men for experimental purposes, and interaction participation was in *three man groups*. The nine persons in each batch were rotated in the three man groups in such a way that each person participated with different persons each time, and each person participated four times. There were twelve sessions of three man groups in all for a batch of nine persons.

Acquaintance of subjects. Subjects were to be unacquainted when the experiment began for them, and each subject in a batch of nine persons was recruited from a different organization to satisfy this objective. In spite of the fact that two alternates were provided for each batch of nine, it was not possible to satisfy the condition of non-acquaintance entirely. At the general orientation meeting of the experiment, the subjects of a batch were given an acquaintance form in which they were asked to indicate persons with whom they were acquainted, and the degree of acquaintance: Long-time or close friend, long-time acquaintance, and casual acquaintance.

In six of the fourteen batches of nine persons acquaintance was indicated, and in one of these, long-time or close friendship was also indicated. The total number of acquaintance mentions in five of the six groups of nine was twelve, and ten of these were accounted for in five mutual pairs. In the sixth group there were fifteen mentions of acquaintance and five mentions of close friendship. Here, twelve of the acquaintance mentions were accounted for in six mutual pairs, and the remaining three were mixed with friendship mentions as pairs, and one last pair was of mutual friends. Thus, in fourteen groups of nine, eight were completely unacquainted, five were relatively unacquainted and one had about a quarter of the possible mentions. This last group was of Basic Airmen, eight of whom had recently been incarcerated in the same stockade.

Choice report, choice perception, and leadership rating. After each session the three participants were given a short form to complete (in privacy). The instructions were that the first four questions (on enjoying the participation) should be answered only if the statement applied. If there was doubt about a person, the question should not be answered for the person. Instructions were written and verbal to make sure they were understood. The questions referred to the meeting just completed and were: (a) I enjoyed participation in this session with: (*Two blank spaces*). (b) I did *not* enjoy participation in this session with: (*Two blank spaces*). (c) (*Two blank spaces*) will say he (they) enjoyed participation in this session with me. (d) (*Two blank spaces*) will say he (they) did *not* enjoy participation in this session with me. (e) Of the three persons participating in this session, the one who did the most to guide the way it went was: (*Blank*). (f) Of the three persons participating in this session, the one who did the least to guide the way it went was: (*Blank*).

These questions, again, deviate somewhat from a purely sociometric procedure in so much as they refer to past behavior. It would have been possible to have used a question such as: "With whom would you like to participate in one of these sessions again." However, there was little prior experience on such small groups, and there could be no promise of actual sociometric rearrangement of groups. The meaning of these questions was judged to be in context with the purpose of the sociometric test.

From the data collected four indices of *affective* relationship and two of *leadership* relationship were devised. Assuming continuity of meaning between choice and rejection, the indices combine the data from the two affective type questions:

1. *Positive expansiveness,* or the propensity to be a chooser. The score is the sum of the choices made in the four sessions minus the rejections made.

2. *Confidence,* or the propensity to expect to be chosen. The score is the sum of the choices expected minus the rejections expected.

3. *Popularity* (Sociometric choice status). This score is the sum of the choices received minus the rejections received.

4. *Rated expansiveness,* or the expectancy of others that one will be a chooser.

5. *Leadership rating.* This index weights the ratings of highest and lowest, and accounts for the intermediate rating which is not explicit. This score is the number of times a person is said to do *most,* plus eight, minus the number of times the person is mentioned as *least.* The index ranges from 0 to 16.

6. *Leadership self-rating.* This score, parallel to the above, is the number of times a person mentions self as *most,* plus 4, minus the number of times he mentions self as *least.* The index ranges from 0 to 8.

The mean number of choices made was 7.3 (with a maximum of 8) which indicates a high level of acceptability among the respondents in spite of the cautions that were given to choose and reject only where there was no doubt. The question used is not one that is inherently "easy," and the high level of acceptability is probably related to the forced close contact in working together. Since the mean response is high, relationship of external variables to choice behavior is probably depressed; that is, the high mean value for persons indicates that persons who are highly acceptable and very highly acceptable are indistinguishable. Only those who are not acceptable, presumably, are delineated. If other characteristics are related to position in the choice structure, then the strength of relationship will not be indicated since the range of choice positions is limited at the upper end. No special difficulties accrue for these data with any of the other indices.

Ausubel (1), in a sample of 100 high school students found a correlation of .85 for boys and .81 for females between popularity and one's confidence (tendency to expect to be chosen). Popularity correlated .05 and .08 to positive expansiveness (tendency to rate others), and positive expansiveness correlated .59 and .79 to confidence.

In the present study it is seen (Table 1) that the correlation between

TABLE 1.

INTERRELATIONSHIP OF AFFECTIVE AND LEADERSHIP SOCIOMETRIC MEASURES.*

	1	2	3	4	5	6
1. Positive Expansiveness	—	.324	.071	.082	—.088	—.124
2. Confidence		—	.187	.176	.204	.209
3. Popularity			—	.472	.271	.193
4. Rated Expansiveness				—	—.022	.242
5. Leadership Rating					—	.501
6. Leadership Self Rating						—

* Correlations are product moment with level of significance with $a = .05$ is .174.

popularity and confidence is .187, between popularity and positive expansiveness, .071, and between positive expansiveness and confidence, .324. Generally, these results substantiate in direction of relationship the materials presented by Ausubel which involve quite different conditions of group structure and composition of population. It should be noted, however, that the hierarchy of relationship is not the same. This may be accounted for by the high level of choosing in the present sample which might differentially depress the relationship between pairs of variables. It is more likely, however, that in Ausubel's sample the relationships are more crystallized, while here, choice is on the basis of limited experience, and relationships are not so well defined. This would raise the hypothesis that where relationships are not crystallized (as well as non-mutual as suggested by others (1, 27, 28)), sociometric perception will be less accurate. This is consonant with some of Moreno's observations on the operation of the psychological concomitants of interaction discussed in connection with the concept of tele (23). Of some interest is the recurrence of a small positive relation between popularity and positive expansiveness. Since we expect that the correlations have been depressed, we do not discount the plausibility of the relationship as does Ausubel. It may be that a small relationship exists (involving perhaps only five percent of the variance), and this is a legitimate hypothesis to hold for further test. Tagiuri finds this to be a significant relationship.[1a]

In our data we find that positive expansiveness is associated with confidence, but of equal interest is the fact that persons rated as positively expansive are the most popular, and that this is the strongest relationship indicated in the set of correlations. The close connection between the expectation of being chosen and choosing lends weight to the more general hypothesis of the importance of projection (in the non-Freudian sense) in the determination of patterns of choice.

Turning to the leadership rating and leadership self rating, it is seen that a small but significant relationship exists between these ratings and sociometric popularity. Confidence is similarly related to the ratings of leadership. Of particular interest here is the fact that no relationship is indicated between rated expansiveness and the leadership rating, which might well be the expectation. Such a lack of relationship might well point

---

[1a] Tagiuri reports a correlation of .26 with N = 316. Tagiuri also corroborates other relationships reported here. In his sample, positive expansiveness correlated to confidence .53, and being rated expansive with popularity correlated at .68. Personal communication 1954, based on work done in 1951.

to recognition of a dichotomy of supportive behavior (which is expected in the rated expansiveness) and leadership function. This type of hypothesis has been well treated elsewhere, particularly with the concepts of popular and powerful leaders (23). According to this hypothesis, thus, the significant relationship between leadership self rating and rated expansiveness would indicate that an individual who is responded to as a supportive person will tend to mistake this response to mean he has been in a leadership role. Actually, it is seen that positive expansiveness is not related, or possibly, may be negatively related both to leadership rating and self rating.

Performance choice in Interaction.[2] In interaction, subjects participated under two types of experimental conditions designated as (a) *actual behavior* (includes getting acquainted, planning role playing sessions, and free or open discussion—subjects are unaware of being observed during this period, the purpose of the session being identified as role playing participation—24 minutes per session), and (b) *role playing behavior* (includes two periods of role playing in the three man group, each period planned by the three man group itself in the actual behavior—24 minutes per session). Since each subject participated in four sessions with different people each time, the rates of participation represent an average in a sample of small groups, and within limits, a general tendency to perform in the given way. Here we take eight sets of observations of performance for investigation. We identify four of these as measures of expansiveness, and four as measures of popularity. The interrelatedness of the measures across the two types of behavior (actual and role playing) may be viewed in Table 2, variables 7 through 14, particularly the four values bracketed in the main diagonal.

Our measures of expansiveness in interaction are the rates of interaction, and positive expansiveness refers to the rate of acts which are more or less supportive or friendly. While acts which are easily identifiable as unfriendly (showing disagreement, tension, and antagonism) are recorded in the system, the frequently used index of friendly minus unfriendly acts is not used here. Prior experience indicates that in interaction unfriendly acts, if the interaction is to be maintained, are carried out only in the tolerating social situation; that is, if the social system is to maintain itself, hostility can occur only in the circumstances where more permanent underlying ties have already formed or exist, as in the affective climate of the family, the

---

[2] The Bales categories of interaction are used in this study. The detail of the method of observation is in: Bales, R. F., *Interaction Process Analysis*. Addison-Wesley Press, Cambridge, Mass., 1950. Related materials of this study are reported elsewhere (7, 8, 9).

TABLE 2a.

General interaction expansiveness:	7. Rate of total initiation, actual behavior.
	8. Rate of total initiation, role playing behavior.

Positive interaction
expansiveness:

9. Rate of showing solidarity, tension release, and agreement, actual behavior.

10. Rate of showing solidarity, tension release, and agreement, role playing behavior.

General interaction
popularity:

11. Rate of total received, actual behavior.

12. Rate of total received, role playing behavior.

Affective interaction
popularity:

13. Rate of showing solidarity, tension release, and agreement received, actual behavior.

14. Rate of showing solidarity, tension release, and agreement received, role playing behavior.

TABLE 2b.

MEASURES OF EXPANSIVENESS AND POPULARITY IN INTERACTION, ACTUAL BEHAVIOR
AND ROLE PLAYING BEHAVIOR, AND TWO PROJECTIVE MEASURES

	7	8	9	10	11	12	13	14	15	16
7. General interaction expansiveness, actual	—	[.757]	.218	.134	.838	.579	.686	.623	.339	.202
8. General interaction expansiveness, role playing		—	.099	.163	.658	.731	.481	.718	.265	.309
9. Positive interaction expansiveness, actual			—	[.578]	.241	.266	.269	.115	.300	.163
10. Positive interaction expansiveness, role playing				—	.143	.326	.021	.184	.176	.194
11. General interaction popularity, actual					—	[.664]	.722	.649	.341	.217
12. General interaction popularity, role playing						—	.431	.547	.339	.271
13. Affective interaction popularity, actual							—	[.582]	.358	.242
14. Affective interaction popularity, role playing								—	.209	.208
15. Projected expansiveness									—	.686
16. Projected positive expansiveness										—

clique, etc. For this reason we avoided contaminating the measures with known sources of variation. Actually, if this contamination hypothesis is true, using an index of friendly minus unfriendly acts should tend to reduce the size of correlations to external variables while maintaining the hierarchy. Preliminary investigation of the data indicates that this is the case. Our measures of popularity are the rates of acts received, and affective popularity refers to the rate of more or less supportive or friendlly acts received.

It should be noted that the measures of general interaction expansiveness (general activity level) are strongly related to the receiving of responses, both generally and in the positive affective categories. Positive expansiveness in interaction, on the other hand, is not so strongly related to receiving responses.[3]

In addition to the measures of interaction, we here include two measures of expansiveness measured by a "parallel" type projective test, the *Conversation Study*.[4] The *Conversation Study*, consisting of ten pictures of three man groups, requires the writing of protocols of the conversation which is going on. The protocols are gotten in conversation form, and they are scored directly by the Interaction Process Analysis categories. Thematic interpretation is not given here, and we deal only with the data which is in fact parallel to the interaction data. We call the number of acts scored in the ten pictures the *projected expansiveness,* and the number of supportive or friendly acts scored the *positive projected expansiveness* (variables 15 and 16).

Since we have already observed the strong association of general interaction expansiveness and interaction popularity, we are not surprised to see that the two projected measures correlate at a fairly uniform level through *all* the interaction measures. We are, however, considerably interested in the fact that the projected measures correlate with interaction expansiveness and popularity at all. Presumably, this forecasts the possibility of predicting interaction behavior from written materials.

Actual behavior interaction expansiveness, both generally and positively, appears to be more strongly related to projected expansiveness than to positive projected expansiveness. Interaction popularity appears to have this same differential in strength of relationship.

---

[3] A factor analysis of the matrix of interaction across three classes of behavior is in process. When this analysis is completed, data will be available concerning the interrelationship of interaction categories as well as information concerning prediction of behavior as observed under one set of conditions and another.

[4] Qualified person may obtain sample copies of the *Conversation Study* from the author.

TABLE 3.

INTERRELATIONSHIP OF AFFECTIVE AND LEADERSHIP SOCIOMETRIC MEASURES, AND MEASURES OF EXPANSIVENESS AND POPULARITY IN INTERACTION, ACTUAL BEHAVIOR AND ROLE PLAYING BEHAVIOR, AND TWO PROJECTIVE MEASURES.

	7	8	9	10	11	12	13	14	15	16
1. Positive expansiveness	.154	.047	.052	.029	.105	.008	.090	.081	.045	—.018
2. Confidence	.283	.257	—.011	—.001	.256	.177	.123	.200	.256	.278
3. Popularity	.212	.254	.198	.106	.246	.237	.177	.171	.231	.158
4. Rated expansiveness	.117	.117	.060	.034	.183	.138	.033	.107	.259	.197
5. Leadership rating	.549	.707	.116	—.017	.470	.547	.447	.522	.185	.132
6. Leadership self rating	.349	.481	—.016	.004	.405	.359	.256	.483	.301	.237

Relationship between Measures of Choice Report and Interaction Performance. Positive expansiveness does not appear to be significantly related to any of the interaction measures (Table 3). Confidence, or the tendency to expect to be chosen, is significantly associated with expansiveness in interaction, and with popularity in interaction, both generally and affectively. Popularity, which is only slightly correlated to confidence (.187), shows a significant correlation to these measures, but in addition, also to the positive expansiveness in interaction. It is interesting that the only significant relationship in which positive expansivenesss in interaction is involved is that of popularity. Rated expansiveness is apparently significantly related only with general popularity in interaction.

Leadership rating is significantly correlated with general expansiveness, and with popularity in interaction, both generally and affectively. The strength of relationship is quite evident. It is again notable that leadership rating *does not correlate with positive expansiveness in interaction*. These findings not only corroborate the analysis by Moreno of leadership (23), but are exactly those which Bales has observed in his task oriented groups.[5] Because of the high relationship of leadership rating to leadership self rating (.501) we expect these two measures to replicate each other, and we note that the interrelationships to the interaction variables are similarly ordered. The leadership rating, however, appears consistently more strongly related to the interaction variables than does the leadership self rating.

We will remind the reader that the relationships involving variables 1 and 3 (positive expansiveness and popularity) may be depressed because of the distribution of responses (as though the question were an extremely "easy" one). The row vector of positive expansiveness is all positive, and it may be that, in fact, some of the relationships to interaction variables are reliable.

It should be noted that the two types of behavior, actual and role playing, tend to replicate each other consistently. Since it has been indicated elsewhere that the character of the two types of behavior is quite different, both in more molar characteristics and in terms of interaction profile (7, 8, 9), this is at least a partial justification for the use of role playing to examine leadership. In fact, if the leadership rating and the leadership self rating are taken as valid criteria, *it is evident that the measures taken from the role playing consistently correlate higher than those taken from the*

---

[5] Personal communication 1953. For parallel data see: The equilibrium problem in small groups, by R. F. Bales, in: Parsons, T., Bales, R. F., and E. A. Shils. *Working papers in the theory of action.* The Free Press, 1953.

actual behavior. A plausible explanation for this particular finding is that the role playing is not a familiar task for most persons and probably needs to be "kept going." This is not dissimilar to Bales' task-oriented groups where there is a discussion which essentially needs to be discussed. In these circumstances the leader must contribute proportionately more activity to guide the discussion and keep it going than when all persons are in more familiar roles. Essentially, thus, the lower the leadership potential, the more a person is depressed in his activity rate under duress. This is a hypothesis well worth further attention.

Relationship between Measures of Choice Report and Projected Expansiveness. It is again noted that the two "parallel" projective measures, projected expansiveness and projected positive expansiveness, are significantly related to the positively interrelated cluster of measures of choice report and sociometric leadership. Positive expansiveness does not correlate with the projective measures, however. Projected expansiveness appears to be more strongly related to these measures than is positive projected expansiveness. The notable exception is that confidence is just slightly more related to positive projected expansiveness. A somewhat literal but meaningfull interpretation of this is that persons who visualize much supportive behavior (showing solidarity, tension release, agreement) in conversations expect to be chosen more frequently than those who do not. It is of some interest that the projected measures appear to be more strongly related to popularity (which, recall, may be a depressed relationship) than to leadership rating. It is equally interesting that leadership self rating is more strongly related to the projected measures than is leadership rating. These relationships do not satisfy significance requirements, but are at minimum plausible.

Ratings by Superiors, Mental Ability, Age, Rank and Education. The sociometric and interaction measures we have utilized thus far are often taken as valid criteria. It is of particular interest to examine these measures in terms of each other, but it is equally important to examine these in terms of other external systems of gathering data. Here we also examine ratings made by superiors, mental ability, and age, rank and education.

Forms were constructed for the rating of the subjects by their superiors. As in most cases of ratings which are subjective, it is difficult to equate the raters. In order to have some standardization of raters the following procedure for administration was used:

A Major "walked" the forms to the headquarters of the squadrons from which men were drawn for the research. At the headquarters he talked with the squadron commander and explained the forms and their purpose. He then requested that the forms be completed by the officer *"highest up in the squadron organization* who could give a fair appraisal of the airman in question." Ratings were, of course, treated confidentially.

The four items included in the rating form were selected with the assistance of the suggestions made by a large number of staff and tactical Air Force officers. The items were: 17. Ability to understand the requirements of the situation and take necessary initiative; 18. ability to handle men and make himself understood by his men; 19. knowledge of the technical aspects of his job; 20. personal conduct and bearing, and 21. an overall rating was requested as well.

Five alternatives for rating were presented, the center category *intentionally* being that of *average*. Since there is some inclination for extreme ratings to be used routinely in the Armed Services, specificity was added to each alternative, and the middle category read: "Average, as high in this quality as half the enlisted men you have known."

The test of mental ability used was the *SRA Primary Mental Abilities,* intermediate-ages 11-17-Form AH. This factored test is in five parts, 22. verbal meaning, 23. space, 24. reasoning, 25. number and 26. word fluency. Here we have also provided the 27. composite score.

In addition, we provide the data of 28. age, 29. education and 30. rank.

Relationship of Ratings by Superiors, Mental Ability, Age, Rank and Education to Affective and Leadership Sociometric Measures, Interaction Measures, and Two Projective Measures. The choice report measures, expansiveness and popularity, apparently do not correlate with the ratings of superiors (Table 4). There is a suggestion that the ratings by superiors may be negatively correlated to rated expansiveness, and in the case of personal conduct and bearing, a significant correlation to rated expansiveness occurs. The two sociometric leadership ratings are significantly related to ratings of the superior on the ability to understand the requirements of the situation and take necessary initiative, and the overall rating.

Knowledge of the technical aspects of the job, as well as the overall rating and the ability to understand and take necessary initiative are significantly correlated to expansiveness in interaction. Positive expansiveness in interaction, on the other hand, shows no significant relationship to the superior ratings. Popularity in interaction is significantly related to the ability to understand and take initiative, and to the overall rating by superiors. These same relationships hold for the affective interaction popularity in the case of the actual behavior, but not the role playing behavior. It is

TABLE 4.

The Interrelationship of Ratings by Superiors, Mental Ability, Age, Rank and Education with Affective and Leadership Sociometric Measures, Measures of Expansiveness and Popularity in Interaction, and Two Projective Measures.

	1	2	3	4	5	6	7	8	9	10	11	12	13	14	15	16
17. Ability to Understand and Take Initiative	—014	.032	.035	—069	.179	.214	.223	.162	.137	—044	.267	.240	.234	.110	—018	.114
18. Ability to Handle Men	.010	—110	.007	—110	.084	.007	.093	.035	.039	.004	.131	.128	.067	0.60	—134	.013
19. Technical Knowledge	—017	—033	.001	—128	.169	.064	.229	.137	.123	—066	.160	.168	.133	—012	—100	.073
20. Personal Conduct	—122	—068	—020	—178	.116	—037	.059	.003	.064	—138	.043	.095	.112	—093	—199	—083
21. Overall Rating	.006	.087	.063	—064	.211	.202	.192	.069	.107	—104	.220	.213	.194	.050	—081	.092
22. Verbal Ability	—095	.178	.201	.035	.263	.223	.166	.050	.155	—036	.152	.101	.138	.167	2.60	.350
23. Space	.002	.044	.102	—038	.264	.214	.037	.214	—034	.011	.050	.133	.043	.181	.327	.273
24. Reasoning	.006	.187	.099	—115	.111	.201	.053	.120	.136	.075	.014	.067	.047	.196	.440	.484
25. Number	.034	.148	.115	—061	.167	.117	.035	.108	.081	—024	.097	.123	.102	.112	.331	.286
26. Word Fluency	—076	.155	.096	.155	.218	.297	.083	.140	.002	—118	.084	.070	.073	.105	.207	.237
27. Composite rating	—020	.198	.135	—033	.287	.253	.086	.164	.080	—032	.082	.118	.094	.183	.379	.416
28. Age	.027	—114	.009	—116	.087	—105	.024	—089	.018	—174	.017	—043	.135	—054	—334	—270
29. Education	—101	.099	.098	—069	.254	.226	.139	.182	.161	—031	.181	.150	.126	.148	.108	.193
30. Rank	.015	—074	.033	—148	.081	—086	.051	—067	.244	—094	.085	.039	.263	—114	—152	—064

of some interest that the affective measures of interaction in role playing appear to be less related to the ratings by superiors. Similarly, the expansiveness in interaction appears to be more strongly related to the ratings by superiors in the case of the actual behavior. Several types of interpretation are possible here. It may be that superiors confuse activity of personnel while not under pressure with desirable qualities, or it may be that in role playing there is greater variation in the roles of the actual leader, among which is the directive role which may not require high activity. Concomitantly, if the role of the leader is directive, then it may be that affective response will not be forthcoming, *i.e.*, by the very nature of being a leader and directing attention to the task he will be less popular in interaction. In this case, a greater proportion of affective behavior would be anticipated among the non-leaders. In terms of positive expansiveness in interaction we see that this is most probably the case (by restrictions implicit in the correlations).

The ratings by superiors appear to be negatively correlated with projected expansiveness, but unrelated to positive projected expansiveness. Personal conduct and bearing as rated by superiors is significantly related to projected expansiveness.

As with the ratings by superior dealt with above, we shall tend to interpret the materials on the mental abilities by the cluster. Confidence appears to be positively related to the mental ability scores, and verbal-meaning and reasoning show significant correlations. Popularity again presents a positive column of correlations, but only verbal-meaning appears significantly correlated to popularity. Both the sociometric measures of leadership are positively correlated to the mental abilities.

There are significant relationships to the mental abilities among the interaction measures, but here we are more interested in the general relationship than the specific mental abilities. The general expansiveness in interaction is positively related to the mental abilities, and the popularity indices in interaction are also. The positive expansiveness in interaction is not significantly related to the mental abilities, nor are the column vectors all positive. Again, it appears that positive affective activity in interaction is not related to mental ability.

Mental ability appears to be consistently and significantly correlated to projected expansiveness and positive projected expansiveness. Because of the verbal nature of the measure (*Conversation Study*) this would have been anticipated.

Age appears to be significantly negatively correlated to positive interaction expansiveness in role playing. However, this appears to be more a trend item than a sporadic relationship. Age is negatively correlated to all the role playing indices, indicating a greater rigidity in the task. However, this might be a function of greater caution (as distinguished from rigidity) since age shows a negative (but not significant) relationship to confidence. Age is significantly negatively correlated to the two projective measures, but again, this may be a function of the type of tests. However, plausible explanations that fit these data are plentiful. Age is ordinarily expected to correlate to rigidity of outlook for example, and to a more serious and business like attitude. It also happens that age is negatively correlated to the mental abilities, but is positively correlated to the leadership ratings, and this again may serve to indicate the source of the negative relationship found here.

Education is significantly correlated to the two sociometric leadership ratings. It is also apparently related to expansiveness in interaction and in popularity in interaction, both generally and affectively. It is again interesting that there is a zero order relationship in positive interaction expansiveness in role playing, while a plausible relationship of positive interaction expansiveness to education exists. The projective measures correlate with education, and this would be expected because of the close relationship of education to the mental abilities with which we have already dealt.

The factor of rank is a peculiar measure in this matrix, and it serves as a control on the comparability of the batches of nine persons used in the experiment since rank was held constant within each batch of nine persons. The zero order correlations in expansiveness and popularity indicate that the groups were choosing at the same level according to rank. Similarly there was apparently no difference in the groups in level of confidence or in rated expansiveness. Since sociometric leadership was a closed (forced) question, leadership rating and leadership self rating will be at zero correlation if there is no differential choosing of self as leader in the groups. This is evidently the case. On these scores, thus, the batches of nine are seen to be quite homogeneous. The interaction variables appear to be homogeneous over the groups also, except in the case of positive interaction expansiveness and popularity. It is evident that in the actual behavior the persons of higher rank contribute and receive more supportive behavior than do persons of lower rank. There is a suggestion that the projected measures may be negatively correlated to rank. This may be a function of the fact that age is strongly correlated to rank.

SUMMARY

This report deals with the observation of interaction, affective choices reported by persons and expected by persons, leadership ratings of self and by "buddies," leadership ratings given by superiors, intelligence measures, two projective measures, and three items of identification, age, education, and rank. In our presentation we have been interested in the interrelationships within and among the classes of measures.

The measures of sociometric choice and sociometric leadership corroborated results reported in the literature. A strong relationship was found between the tendency to choose and the tendency to expect to be chosen. No appreciable relationship was found between popularity and the tendency to choose. A significant relationship was found between popularity and the expectancy that one will be chosen. The general conclusion to be drawn from these data is that at least two factors are operating in choice behavior persons at this level: (a) There is accurate perception of what the social situation is. And (b), there is projection (in the non-analytic sense).

The measures thus far mentioned deal primarily with acceptability in a social sense. In terms of a leadership criterion we find that there is a small but significant relationship between leadership rating, both by self and by others, and sociometric popularity. Similarly the expectancy that one will be chosen is associated with leadership. Of particular interest, however, is the fact that making many choices, or being a person who would be expected to make many choices at the social level, is not associated with leadership rating. If anything, a large amount of choosing in the social area is associated negatively with being chosen as a leader or choosing self as a leader. This leads to the conclusion that the leadership function and the social leader function are two well differentiated and recognizable roles.

Among our measures of interaction we find that high activity in initiating interaction is associated with receiving many responses, both generally and also in the positive affective area. However, high activity in the positive affective area is not as strongly associated to receiving responses either generally or in the positive affective area. This indicates that persons who are highly active generally attract a great proportion of the positive affective behavior of the co-participants. Persons with low interaction rates tend to attract a small amount of positive affective behavior.

The tendency to choose persons is not significantly related to the interaction measures reported here. The tendency to expect to be chosen at a social level is associated with high activity in interaction and also with receiving many responses in interaction, both generally and in the affective area. Social popularity, as indicated by high number of choices received on the social criterion, is positively correlated to high interaction activity both generally and in the positive area, and also to receiving many responses in both these classes of behavior. An interesting point is that high activity in the positive affective area in interaction is significantly related in the choice behavior of the individual *only in terms of popularity. It is a striking finding that leadership rating does not correlate with activity in the affective area.* An extremely important finding is that the *leadership is found to be highly correlated to high interaction activity,* and also to receiving responses both generally and in the affective area. Again these relationships point to differentiation of roles into at least two categories, that of task leadership and that of support in terms of social and other approval.

It is similarly an interesting finding that the leadership self rating, which may be easy to elicit, and leadership rating show approximately the same pattern of relationship to these criteria.

The interaction behavior reported was of two classes; one called actual behavior and the second called role playing behavior. These two types of behavior tend to replicate each other consistently. The measures external to the interaction observation tend to replicate the findings reported earlier of the consistency of behavior under the two task conditions. It is an important finding that role playing may be used to examine leadership as the observation of actual behavior is. In fact, there is some indication in the data that the role playing may be a better criterion of leadership than the actual behavior itself, if the judgment of contemporaries is taken as a criterion. This may be because the role playing is not a familiar task to the persons and essentially the differential in leadership quality may make itself more evident in the unfamiliar role.

Two projective measures designed specifically to be parallel to the interaction observation measures are reported in this study. It is found that these measures are significantly related to some of the sociometric choice and leadership criteria. General activity level in the projective materials appears to be more strongly related to the sociometric measures than activity only in the positive affective area. The only exception is that expecting to be chosen at a social level is somewhat more related to high activity in the projective measure in the positive affective area. This may point to the fact that persons who visualize much supportive behavior in conversations expect to be chosen more frequently than those who do not. That is, persons who see a rosy world on paper may see a rosy world among their associates. The projective measures appear to be more strongly related to the social criterion than to the leadership criterion. Further, it appears that the leadership self rating is more strongly related to the projective measures than is the sociometric leadership rating received. Some of these relationships do not satisfy significance requirements but are at least plausible.

We have dealt here with two categories of data, interaction and sociometric ratings. A third type, rating by superiors, was also utilized in this study. The ratings by superiors tend to correlate with the sociometric leadership ratings, indicating external validation. High activity in interaction is also positively related to high superior ratings. *Positive affective activity initiated*, however, *shows no significant relationship to the superior rating.* High acceptability at a social level, popularity, is significantly related to high rating by superiors. It is of some interest that in these data the amount of activity in interaction appears to be more strongly related to the ratings by superiors in the case of the actual behavior. It is possible that the superiors confuse activity of personnel while *not under pressure* with desirable qualities, or equally possible, it may be that in role playing there is a greater variation in the roles of the actual leader, among which is the directive role which may not require high activity. This last item, of course, would tend to mask the relationship. If the role of the leader *is* directive, that is, if he has a role which exerts pressure on the others, it may be that affective response on the part of the others in the positive area will not be forthcoming. This is plausible; in our data high affective activity in role playing appears to be less related to superior ratings than this activity in actual behavior.

It is found that intelligence measures are correlated to the expectation that one will be chosen at a social level, and also with being chosen at a social level. The leadership ratings are positively related to high mental ability.

Among the interaction measures it is notable that high activity in interaction and receiving much response, both generally and in the positive affective area, is associated with high mental ability. High activity in the positive affective area, however, is not related to having high mental ability.

REFERENCES

1. Ausubel, D. P. Reicprocity and assumed reciprocity of acceptance among adolescents, a sociometric study SOCIOMETRY, 1953, *16,*
2. ————. Sociempathy as a function of sociometric status in an adolescent group. *Hum. Rel.* (In press)
3. Ausubel, D. P., & Schiff, H. M. Some intrapersonal and interpersonal determinants of individual differences in sociempathic ability among adolescents. *J. soc. Psychol.* (In press)

4. Ausubel, D. P., Schiff, H. M., & Gasser, E. B. A preliminary study of developmental trends in sociempathy: Accuracy of perception of own and others' sociometric status. *Child Development,* 1952, *23,* 111-128.

5. Bonney, M. M. The constancy of sociometric scores and their relationship to teacher judgments of social success and to personality self-ratings. SOCIOMETRY, 1943, *6,* 409-424.

6. ————. Sociometric study of agreement between teachers' judgments and student choices. SOCIOMETRY, 1947, *10,* 133-146.

7. Borgatta, E. F., & Bales, R. F. The consistency of subject behavior and the reliability of scoring in Interaction Process Analysis. *Amer. Soc. Rev.,* 1953, *18,* 566-569.

8. ————. Task and accumulation of experience as factors in the interaction of small groups. SOCIOMETRY, 1953, *16,* 239-252.

9. ————. Interaction of individuals in reconstituted groups. SOCIOMETRY, 1953, *16,*

10. Cottrell, L. S. The analysis of situational fields in social psychology. *Amer. sociol. Rev.,* 1942, *7,* 370-382.

11. Dymond, Rosalind. A preliminary investigation of the relation of insight and empathy. *J. consult. Psychol.,* 1948, *4,* 228-233.

12. ————. A scale for the measurement of empathic ability. *J. consult. Psychol.,* 1949, *13,* 127-133.

13. ————. Personality and empathy. *J. consult. Psychol.,* 1950, *14,* 343-350.

14. Gage, N. L. Accuracy of social perception and effectiveness in interpersonal relations. *J. Pers.,* 1953, *22,* 128-141.

15. Gage, N. L., & Suci, G. Social perception and teacher-pupil relationships. *J. Educ. Psychol.,* 1951, *42,* 144-153.

16. Goodnow, R. E., & Tagiuri, R. Religious ethnocentrism and its recognition among adolescent boys. *J. abnorm. soc. Psychol.,* 1952, *47,* 316-320.

17. Gronlund, N. M. The accuracy of teachers' judgments concerning the sociometric status of sixth-grade pupils. SOCIOMETRY, 1950, *13,* 197-225.

18. Hastorf, A. H., & Bender, I. M. A caution respecting the measurement of empathic ability. *J. abnorm. soc. Psychol.,* 1952, *47,* 574-576.

19. Lindgren, H. L., & Robinson, J. An evaluation of Dymond's test of insight and empathy. *J. consult. Psychol.,* 1953, *17,* 172-176.

20. Lundberg, G. A., & Dickson, Leonore. Inter-ethnic relations in a high school population. *Amer. J. Sociol.,* 1952, *58,* 1-10.

21. Maucorps, P. H. A sociometric inquiry in the French Army. SOCIOMETRY, 1949, *12,* 46-80.

22. Mead, G. H. *Mind, self and society.* Chicago: Univer. Chicago Press, 1934.

23. Moreno, J. L. *Who shall survive?* Beacon, New York: Beacon House, Inc. 1934 (Rev. Ed. 1953).

24. ————. *Psychodrama.* Beacon, New York: Beacon House, Inc. 1945.

25. ————. Sociometry in action. SOCIOMETRY, 1942, *3,* 298-315.

26. Speroff, B. J. A measure of mass empathy. *The status of empathy as a hypothetical construct in psychology today.* A symposium of the American Psychological Association. Mimeograph, Psychol. Dept. of Louisiana State University, 1953.

27. Tagiuri, R. Relational analysis: An extension of sociometric method with emphasis upon social perception. SOCIOMETRY, 1952, *15*, 91-104.
28. Tagiuri, R., Blake, R. R., & Bruner, J. S. Some determinants of the perception of positive and negative feeling in others. *J. abnorm. soc. Psychol.,* 1953, *48*, 585-592.
29. Toeman, Z. The double situation in psychodrama. *Sociatry,* 1951, *1*, 436-446.
30. ————. Clinical psychodrama: auxiliary ego double and mirror techniques. SOCIOMETRY, 1946, *9*.
31. Yablonsky, L. A sociometric investigation into the development of an experimental model for small group analysis. SOCIOMETRY, 1952, *15*, 175-205.

A PROPOSED INDEX OF THE CONFORMITY OF ONE SOCIOMETRIC MEASUREMENT TO ANOTHER*

By Leo Katz and James H. Powell

Summary

An index is proposed to measure the extent of agreement of the data of a sociometric test with another test made at an earlier time or on another test criterion. The index is used to define an index of concordance *between* the two tests. It is shown how the index may be used for either individuals or groups. Tests of the hypothesis that agreement is random are given for all cases and applied to an example.

Introduction

Whenever two or more (sociometric) measurements are made of the inter-personal relationships among one group of individuals, questions immediately arise concerning the extent to which one set of measurements conforms to another. Examples of this kind abound in the literature; we will note only a few.

A second measurement on the same group invariably raises the intriguing question of how much the pattern of relationships observed in the earlier measurement has persisted in the later. Further (and in a more fundamental sense), what is the nature of this persistence? An example of this kind of data was presented to the others by Dr. Hilda Taba of San Francisco State College. In the course of an extensive study of a class of 25 children, she asked each of them, at intervals of about two months, to name the three others they preferred to be seated with, in small groups. The resulting series of measurements provide information on the persistence of choice patterns and, in particular, data to test the hypothesis that the persistence phenomenon is stationary, i.e., dependent only on the time interval between a pair of measurements.

In the study discussed above, the subjects were also asked at one point to name those others with whom they would like to work on a specific activity, namely, mathematics assignments. Noting some conformity of the special choice patterns to the general, we ask whether this is a random effect, and, if not, what is the order of the excess over chance conformity? Similar questions might be raised for other special situations; in this case, the relative

---

* Work done under the sponsorship of the Office of Naval Research.

excesses could be used to determine (inversely) how "special" each situation is, in comparison with the others.

As a final example, and the one to which we shall return for illustration because of the smaller numbers involved, we consider the technique in which each individual is asked to give, first, his choices among the others, and, second, his guesses as to which of the others will choose him. Here, we are usually concerned with whether, and to what extent, the perceived choice configuration conforms to the actual. Also, in this case, to a greater measure than in the preceding, we are interested in the variable accuracy of perception among the individuals in the group.

In each of the last two examples, we encounter the usual confusion of "independent" and "dependent" variables, with neither bearing a causal relationship to the other. In the first example, with measurements in a natural time sequence, there is no possibility of confusion of priority. We shall return to this question in the last section.

THE INDEX

For a group of n individuals there are $n(n-1)$ ordered pairs. Our basic information specifies, for each ordered pair, whether (a) neither relation exists, (b) relation X exists but not Y, (c) Y exists but not X, or (d) both X and Y exist. Following custom, we take relation X to be the prior or "independent" relation; Y the posterior or "dependent" relation. The generic question we ask is: To what extent does the occurrence of relation Y in the ordered pairs conform to the occurrence of relation X? In any specific instance, our data may be summarized as in the fourfold distribution of Table 1.

In Table 1, n_{xy} (for example) represents the number of ordered pairs in

TABLE 1

Joint Distribution of Occurrence of X and Y for a Group of n Persons

	Y	$\bar{Y}$	Total
X	n_{xy}	$n_{x\bar{y}}$	n_x
$\bar{X}$	$n_{\bar{x}y}$	$n_{\bar{x}\bar{y}}$	$n_{\bar{x}}$
Total	n_y	$n_{\bar{y}}$	$n(n-1)$

which relation X occurs and relation Y does not occur, from the first individual to the second of the pair; n_y, equal to the sum of n_{xy} and $n_{\bar{x}y}$, is the number of pairs having relation Y without regard to occurrence or nonoccurrence of X. In this form, it is well known that questions of dependence or concomitant variation depend on the four numbers in the body of the table, and that the marginal totals provide only a frame of freedom for the body of the table when the marginal totals are considered to be known *a priori*. Hence we may take any one of the numbers in the body of the table, say n_{xy}, as the essential variable. Lastly, n_{xy} is known to possess the hypergeometric probability distribution under the hypothesis that X and Y are independent, or, in our terms, that occurrence of Y does not particularly conform to occurrence of X.

We now proceed to construction of an index of conformity (Γ) having the following three properties:

1) $\Gamma = 0$ when X and Y are independent,
2) $\Gamma = 1$ when occurrence of Y conforms exactly to occurrence of X (note that we say nothing about non-occurrences of Y),
3) Γ is estimated by a linear function of n_{xy}.

We first note that, when X and Y are independent, $E(n_{xy}) = n_x n_y/n - 1)$. Since we know that n_{xy} cannot be less than zero nor greater than n_x, we define Γ by the following expression for the conditional expected (mean) value of n_{xy}:

$$E(n_{xy} \mid \Gamma) = \frac{n_x}{n(n-1)} (n_y + \Gamma n_{\bar{y}}). \tag{1}$$

We observe that $E(n_{xy} \mid \Gamma = 0) = n_x n_y/n(n-1)$, which is precisely the condition for statistical independence of X and Y. Secondly $E(n_{xy} \mid \Gamma = 1) = n_x$, i.e., every ordered pair which has relation X also has relation Y and the conformity is complete. Γ is a linear function of $E(n_{xy})$; therefore, we take for our estimate of Γ the solution of (1) with $E(n_{xy})$ replaced by the observed n_{xy}. This gives

$$\hat{\Gamma} = \frac{1}{n_x n_{\bar{y}}} [n(n-1)n_{xy} - n_x n_y]. \tag{2}$$

Equation (1) expresses that the expected value of n_{xy} depends upon the underlying parameter Γ, which may take any value in the interval $[-(n_y/n_{\bar{y}}), 1]$. In most applications, n_y is smaller than $n_{\bar{y}}$. Since the estimate of equation (2) has the appropriate conventional expected values of zero when Y does not conform to X and unity when conformity is perfect, we may (and shall) take the estimate to be our index of conformity.

One advantage of this choice of index is that we have immediately an unbiased estimate of the conceptual underlying parameter. Another advantage, we shall see, is that $\hat{\Gamma}$ lends itself to simple standard tests of the hypothesis that $\Gamma = 0$. Still another advantage, not insignificant from the standpoint of the practitioner is the ease of computation of this index.

Test of the Hypothesis of Absence of Conformity

In most cases in practice, we will believe on intuitive grounds that there actually is some degree of conformity present and shall desire only to estimate that degree. Nevertheless, it is logically necessary that we establish that our belief is well founded. Accordingly, we give in this section a test of the hypothesis that $\Gamma = 0$. It was shown by Katz (2) in 1941 that a "best" test for $\Gamma \neq 0$ against alternatives $\Gamma > 0$ (in the likelihood-ratio sense) is given by the upper tail of the hypergeometric distribution, and that a "best unbiased" test against $\Gamma = 0$ is given by two tails of the same distribution so chosen that the mean value of the tails is equal to the mean of the entire distribution. (Note that, aside from choice of critical regions, this is the well-known Fisher "exact" test for the four-fold table.)

Thus, whenever $n(n - 1)$ is small, we may test the hypothesis exactly, using the recent tables given by Finney (1). When, as is more likely, $n(n - 1)$ is large and each of n_{xy}, $n_{x\bar{y}}$ $n_{\bar{x}y}$ and $n_{\bar{x}\bar{y}}$ is large enough (say, ≥ 2), the χ^2 approximation is adequate. A simple computation gives

$$\chi^2 = \frac{n(n - 1)n_x n_{\bar{y}}}{n_{\bar{x}} n_y} \hat{\Gamma}^2,$$ (3)

with one d.f. Even simpler is

$$z = \sqrt{\frac{n(n - 1)n_x n_{\bar{y}}}{n_{\bar{x}} n_y}} \hat{\Gamma},$$ (3a)

which is approximately normally distributed about zero with unit variance. In case $n_x = n_y$, (3a) reduces approximately to $z = n\hat{\Gamma}$ and the hypothesis is rejected at the 5 per cent level whenever $|\hat{\Gamma}| > 2/n$, approximately.

As always when the χ^2, or the equivalent z, approximation to the exact test is made, one should make the Yates correction, consisting of either adding or subtracting one-half unit from n_{xy} so as to decrease the absolute value of $\hat{\Gamma}$.

THE INDEX FOR AN INDIVIDUAL

One is often in the position of wishing to make tests and estimates, similar to those described above, for the individual members of the group. In these instances, one asks, "To what extent does an individual's pattern of (outgoing) choices persist to a later time or to another criterion of choice?" or "To what extent is the set of an individual's incoming choices unchanged?" In either

TABLE 2

Joint Distribution of Occurrence of X and Y for a Single Individual

	Y	$\bar{Y}$	Total
X	$n_{xy}(i)$	$n_{x\bar{y}}(i)$	$n_x(i)$
$\bar{X}$	$n_{\bar{x}y}(i)$	$n_{\bar{x}\bar{y}}(i)$	$n_{\bar{x}}(i)$
Total	$n_y(i)$	$n_{\bar{y}}(i)$	$n - 1$

case, our data are the observations on $(n - 1)$ ordered pairs and may be exhibited as in Table 2.

In this table, entries are interpreted as in Table 1, except that it is necessary to note that the entries in the body of the table and the marginal totals are those for the ith individual. Everything goes through exactly as in §2 and we obtain the index of conformity for the ith individual,

$$\gamma(i) = \frac{1}{n_x(i)n_{\bar{y}}(i)} \left[(n - 1)n_{xy}(i) - n_x(i)n_y(i) \right]. \tag{4}$$

The tests of §3 hold as before with $\hat{\Gamma}$ replaced by $\gamma(i)$, $n(n - 1)$ by $(n - 1)$, and the marginal totals by the corresponding totals for the ith individual. Here we shall usually require the exact test and, for very small groups, the test may break down in the sense that we are unable to reject the hypothesis of lack of conformity whatever be the value of $n_{xy}(i)$. We shall observe this in the example of §6, in which we deal with a group of ten persons.

THE AMBIGUOUS CASE

In many situations, it is not possible to identify one relation as antecedent or "independent" with respect to the other. In this case, we have exactly the same problem which arises in any regression analysis when we are uncertain as to which regression coefficient is meaningful. Accordingly, we shall use exactly the same device for resolving the difficulty. We define a *coefficient of concordance* as the geometric mean of the two indices of conformity of X with Y and of Y with X. Thus, we obtain

$$C^2 = \hat{\Gamma}_1 \hat{\Gamma}_2 = \frac{[n(n-1)n_{xy} - n_x n_y]^2}{n_x n_{\bar{x}} n_y n_{\bar{y}}}, \tag{5}$$

where C is the coefficient of concordance. We should attach to C the algebraic sign of the factor in square brackets since this is the sign of both indices of conformity.

We observe that $C^2 = \chi^2/n(n-1)$, the mean square contingency of Table 1. (See, for example, Kendall [3], pp. 318–19.) Finally, we note that the test of significance for C is exactly the same as for either index of conformity.

An Example

We shall consider data collected and kindly made available to us by Dr. Renato Tagiuri, of the Harvard University Laboratory of Social Relations. Dr. Tagiuri asked each of a group of ten graduate students first, "Which members of the group do you like most?" and second, "Which members of the group do you feel like you most?" In this situation, armchair philosophizing can construct a case for either argument (a) that these people are fairly sophisticated and, hence, perceive relationships accurately or argument (b) that these people are fairly sophisticated and, hence, conceal their feelings so that relationships cannot be perceived accurately. Obviously, there is a need for objective measurement of agreement. Equally obvious is the ambiguity of the situation, for it is difficult to decide whether we are primarily interested in how well *perceived* relationships conform to the *actual* ones or in the obverse conformity. Since, fortunately, resolution of this dilemma is not the purpose of this paper, we shall assume that the second question is our primary concern although we will make both computations. The data appear in Tables 3 and 3a.

In both tables, the individual's responses appear in rows. Thus, the first individual chooses (in Table 3) the second, third, and fifth and feels he will be chosen by (in Table 3a) the second, fifth, and tenth. For the ith individual, we are concerned with how well the choices he actually receives, the ith column of Table 3, agree with the choices he thinks he will receive, the ith row of Table

TABLE 3
Positive Choices Expressed by Ten Individuals

1	x	x		x					
x	2	x		x					x
x	x	3							
			4				x	x	x
x				5			x	x	
			x	x	6	x			
	x		x	x		7		x	
			x				8	x	
x	x			x		x		9	
x	x		x						10

TABLE 3a
Positive Choices Perceived by Ten Individuals

1	x			x					x
x	2	x		x					x
	x	3			x				
			4				x		x
x				5	x			x	
			x	x	6	x			
			x	x		7		x	
			x				8		
				x		x	x	9	
	x		x				x		10

3a. We first consider individual conformity; the results of these computations are summarized in Table 4.

TABLE 4

Conformity of Actual to Perceived Choices of Individuals

Individual (i)	$n_{xy}(i)$	Pr $\{n_{xy}(i)$ or more$\}$	$\gamma(i)$
1	3	.12	1.00
2	3	.36	.56
3	1	.42	.43
4	2	.17	1.00
5	3	.12	1.00
6	0	1.00	.00
7	1	.58	.24
8	1	.22	1.00
9	3	.048*	1.00
10	2	.083	.57

*Significant at 5% level.

In the case of a small group, such as this, it is difficult to obtain sharp tests of significance for individuals. Thus, while there is perfect agreement with the choices of five individuals, in only one instance (9) can we reject at the 5 per cent level the hypothesis that agreement is by chance alone. We recommend, therefore, whenever it is necessary to examine individual conformity in small groups, that each individual be asked to name approximately *half* the group as those most likely to choose him in order to make the tests as sharp as possible.

The story is quite different when we measure group agreement; here our observations are adequate to construct reasonable tests. Our data and computations are summarized in Table 5.

For a group of ten, the approximate test of §3 indicates significant (5 per cent level) departure from random agreement when $| C | > .20$; the degree of association is measured by $| C |$, where C has the force of a correlation coefficient. In fact, if X and Y are interpreted as variables taking values 0 and 1 only, C *is* the correlation coefficient.

It may be worth while (from the psychologist's point of view) to note that the individuals who took part in this experiment were asked the same two questions with respect to rejections, or negative choices. For these data, the concordance index, C, was .14, not significantly different from zero. We might

TABLE 5

Conformity of Actual to Perceived Choices of Entire Group

Perceived Choices (X)	Actual Choices (Y)		Total
	Y	$\bar{Y}$	
X	19	8	27
$\bar{X}$	12	51	63
Total	31	59	90

$\hat{\Gamma}_1$ (conformity of actual to perceived) = .55,
$\hat{\Gamma}_2$ (conformity of perceived to actual) = .45,
C (concordance between actual and perceived) = .50.

conclude, therefore, that this group is able, to a limited extent, to perceive positive feelings but seems practically unable to discern existing negative feelings.

REFERENCES

1. Finney, D. J. "The Fisher-Yates Test of Significance in 2×2 Contingency Tables," *Biometrika,* XXXV (1948), 145–56.
2. Katz, Leo. *The Test of the Hypothesis of No Association in the Four-fold Table in the Light of the Neyman-Pearson Theory.* Statistical Research Laboratory, Michigan State College, RM-9, 1952.
3. Kendall, M. G. *The Advanced Theory of Statistics,* Vol. I. London: C. Griffin and Co., 1947.

MEASUREMENT OF RECIPROCATION UNDER MULTIPLE CRITERIA OF CHOICE

By Joan H. Criswell

In the use of the sociometric test, the subject is usually asked to select associates under one criterion of choice, for example, to choose persons with whom he would like to eat. Another problem of measurement occurs when he is asked to choose on several criteria, for instance, also those with whom he would like to study, and those with whom he would like to share recreation. The degree of group integration or reciprocation of choice developed by the experimental group must be measured by relating the results obtained to those which would occur by chance.

In the prediction of the number of selections of a given type which would occur by chance in a multi-criterial situation, the problem arises as to whether relationships passing from one criterion to another should be used. Such a relationship occurs when A makes an unreciprocated choice of B under criterion 1 and B makes an unreciprocated choice of A under criterion 2. This produces a sort of interstitial mutual pair, indicating a closer relationship between A and B than would appear from the fact that neither reciprocated the other's choice under any one criterion. The experimenter may therefore wish to include such relationships in his measurements.

It must be emphasized, however, that if one type of cross-relationship is taken into account all such relationships must be counted. This means, for example, that if A and B choose each other under each of two criteria they also form two cross-mutual pairs, A choosing B under criterion 1 and being reciprocated under 2, B choosing A under criterion 1 and being reciprocated under 2. The general rule is that under c criteria with cross-relationships employed, a choice is counted not once but c times. If each of N subjects makes d selections under each of c criteria, an individual makes cd choices per criterion and c^2d choices altogether. The total number of choices counted is thus c times the number actually listed by the subjects and is c^2 times the number made under one criterion only.

The probability of being chosen or not chosen is based on the values of d and N. Therefore, when these values remain constant from criterion to criterion, the basic probabilities are the same for both inter-criterial and intra-criterial relationships. When the experimenter requests that each subject make d choices only under each criterion, it is just as probable that A choosing B under criterion 1 will be reciprocated under 2 as it is that he will be reciprocated under 1. Thus to obtain the chance numbers of reciprocated and unreciprocated choices the fundamental probability formulas[1] for use under one criterion need only be multiplied by c^2 in order to take care of the greater number of choices employed.

With the definitions of N, c, and d, given above and with p equalling $\dfrac{d}{n-1}$ and q equalling $1-p$, the expression for the number of reciprocated choices to be expected on a chance basis (R_{cc}) becomes (1);

$$R_{cc} = c^2 N (N-1) p^2$$

The formula for the chance number of unreciprocated choices (U_{cc}) becomes (2):

$$U_{cc} = c^2 N (N-1) pq$$

Dividing equation 1 by equation 2 gives $\dfrac{p}{q}$ which is the chance ratio of reciprocated to unreciprocated choice. If R reciprocated and U unreciprocated choices are experimentally obtained (counting all cross-criterial relationships), then the extent of group coherence (I_{cc}) can be expressed by the ratio (3):

$$I_{cc} = \frac{Rq}{Up}$$

This formula relates the experimentally derived reciprocation-non-reciprocation ratio to the chance ratio of choice.

The preceding three formulas apply to cases in which Nc^2d (total number of choices) is either odd or even but do not apply where d is not constant from subject to subject and from criterion to criterion. Adjustment for variation in d, methods of testing results on reciprocity for statistical significance, and a fuller derivation of the formulas which have been given will be taken up in a later paper.

---

[1]Moreno, J. L. and Jennings, H. H. Sociometric Measurement of Social Configurations, Sociometry Monographs, No. 3, Beacon House, 1945, pp. 11-12.

PROBABILITY DISTRIBUTIONS OF RANDOM VARIABLES ASSOCIATED WITH A STRUCTURE OF THE SAMPLE SPACE OF SOCIOMETRIC INVESTIGATIONS*

By Leo Katz and James H. Powell

Summary

In this paper, we consider a disjoint decomposition, at three levels, of the total sample space for n-person, one-dimensional sociometric investigations. This results in a structure particularly suited to determination of the probability distributions of a large class of sociometric variables. Systematic methods for obtaining these distributions are presented and illustrated by two examples; while the first is trivial, the second produces a previously unknown result.

It should be remarked that the methods developed here have application in the theory of communication networks and, indeed, in the study of any network situations which may be represented by either of the two models employed in the paper.

Introduction

The simplest model for the organization of a group of individuals is one-dimensional, in the sense that organization for only one activity of the group is considered. Connections between *ordered* pairs of individuals are represented by non-reflexive binary relations. Although a binary model appears superficially to be too barren to show adequately the richness of variability of the response of one individual to another, it is by no means trivial and is precisely the model used in most sociometric investigations, where the relations are lines of communication, authority, liking, etc.

In this model, a particular organization of n individuals has two isomorphic representations, both of which have been used extensively in the literature for descriptive purposes. The older of the two is the linear directed graph on n points, $P_1, P_2, \cdots, P_n$. A connection from man i to man j is represented by a directed line from P_i to P_j, $P_i \rightarrow P_j$; the absence of such a connection, by no line from P_i to P_j. The equivalent matrix representation is an $n \times n$ matrix,

---

* This work was supported by the Office of Naval Research under contract NR 170–115.

$C = (c_{ij})$, where $c_{ij} = 1$ if a connection exists from man i to man j, and $c_{ij} = 0$, otherwise. By convention, $c_{ii} = 0$. Obviously, $c_{ij} = 1$ (or 0) if and only if a directed line exists (or doesn't) from P_i to P_j. Hence, the two representations are isomorphic.

To fix the notation, let $r_i = \Sigma_j c_{ij}$ be the ith row total of C and $s_j = \Sigma_i c_{ij}$ be the jth column total. In the graph, r_i is the number of lines issuing from the point P_i, and s_j is the number of lines terminating on the point P_j. Moreover, $\Sigma_i = \Sigma_j s_j = t$, the total number of directed lines. Finally, let the vectors r and s, with elements r_i and s_j, respectively, be the two n-part, non-negative, ordered partitions of t which represent respectively, the marginal row and column totals of C.

Unless otherwise noted in the sequel, all graphs will be on n points and linearly directed (n-graphs), and all matrices will be $n \times n$ hollow matrices of 1's and 0's. (A matrix is *hollow* if all principal diagonal elements vanish.)

DECOMPOSITION OF THE SAMPLE SPACE

The sample space of the possible organizations of an n-member group is the space of all possible n-graphs or $n \times n$ hollow matrices of 1's and 0's. In this section, we consider a decomposition of the total sample space, Ω, following lines which hold promise of utility for certain investigations. We define first-order disjoint subspaces, Ω_t, $t = 0, 1, \cdots, [n(n-1)]$, as the collections of n-graphs containing exactly t lines. Obviously,

$$\Omega = \bigcup_{t=0}^{n(n-1)} \Omega_t, \tag{1}$$

since the Ω_t are mutually exclusive and exhaustive.

Continuing in the same vein, we define second-order subspaces, $\omega(\rho)$, $\rho = (r_1, r_2, \cdots, r_n)$, as the collections of graphs with r_i lines emanating from P_i, $i = 1, 2, \cdots, n$. Since $\Sigma_i r_i = t$, we have

$$\Omega_t = \bigcup_{(\rho)_t} \omega(\rho), \tag{2a}$$

where $(\rho)_t$ is a generic symbol for non-negative, integral, ordered, n-part partitions of t with all $r_i < n$. In a completely dual manner, we might define alternative second-order subspaces, $\omega(\sigma)$ in terms of n-graphs with s_j lines converging on P_j. In this case, we would have

$$\Omega_t = \bigcup_{(\sigma)_t} \omega(\sigma), \tag{2b}$$

Third-order subspaces are defined by $\omega(\rho, \sigma) \equiv \omega(\rho) \cup \omega(\sigma)$, and are identified with spaces of n-graphs with r_i lines emanating from, *and* s_i lines converging on, P_i. Once again, these sets are exclusive and exhaustive in the sense that

$$\omega(\rho) = \bigcup_{(\sigma)_t} \omega(\rho, \sigma),$$ (3a)

and

$$\omega(\sigma) = \bigcup_{(\rho)_t} \omega(\rho, \sigma).$$ (3b)

We remark that double and triple disjoint decompositions of the larger spaces may also be indicated.

It will be obvious to the reader that there exist isomorphisms among certain of these second and third-order subspaces. It will be less obvious, but important for computations, that these isomorphisms involve *simultaneous* permutations on the elements of the two vectors ρ and σ. We shall not elaborate on this point since it contributes little to the notions with which we are here concerned.

Random Variables Associated with the Structure of the Sample Space

The decomposition described in the previous section imposes a structure on the sample space. In most sociometric investigations, involving randomness in the existence of connections between ordered pairs of individuals, it has been deemed appropriate to assign uniform probability to each of the points in a third-order subspace, at least. In more extreme cases (the vast majority) it is customary to assume that every possible sample point is equally likely. Sometimes this has been done without even specifying which sample points are possible under the conditions of the experiment.

In the context of the particular experiment, it is usually possible for the experimenter to determine that his universe of discourse consists of Ω or one of the smaller subsets we have described. If, *also*, it happens that the random variable under discussion assumes the same value over all the points of each of certain smaller subspaces, the assumption of uniformity of probability within these subspaces will produce the complete probability distribution of the variable. In this section, we investigate these circumstances.

We say that a random variable defined over n-graphs or $n \times n$ hollow matrices is *associated* with the sample space structure of the previous section, if the value of the variable is constant over all points in every $\omega(\rho, \sigma)$ contained

311

in the domain of definition of the variable. Every such variable has a probability distribution which is completely specified as soon as we are able to count the numbers of points in the appropriate subspaces, assuming uniformity of probability on each point. In the next section, we shall present methods for carrying out this enumeration. A variable associated with the structure in the sense of the present definition is necessarily one whose value is somehow determined by, i.e., is a function of, the r_i and s_j, i, $j = 1, 2, \cdots, n$, alone. Indeed, this may be taken as an alternative definition.

To establish that the class of variables associated with the structure has some real substance, we examine a few variables which have been the subjects of sociometric investigations. Gross expansiveness, or average level of expansiveness, has been defined in terms of t alone in the context of the space Ω. Variability in expansiveness is defined as a function (usually a sum of squares) of the r_i $i = 1, 2, \cdots, n$, sometimes in the context of Ω and sometimes in Ω_t. A number of variables have been defined as functions of the s_j, $j = 1, 2, \cdots, n$, in various contexts ranging down to $\omega(\rho)$. Examples are (1) the number of isolates, i.e., the number of $s_j = 0$ and (2) the choice status of the most highly chosen, i.e., $\max_j s_j$. Both of these are usually studied in the context of some $\omega(\rho)$.

Enumeration of the Points in Various Subspaces

In considering the problems of enumeration, it will be more convenient to use the matrix representation because of its more flexible notation. Thus, the total number of matrices (graphs) in Ω is the number of ways in which the $n(n-1)$ elements of C may be specified as either zero or one. By elementary considerations, the number of distinct ways this can be done is

$$\eta = 2^{n(n-1)}. \tag{4}$$

The matrices in Ω_t have t ones distributed over $n(n-1)$ positions; the number of ways this can be accomplished is the number of ways of specifying a particular t of the $n(n-1)$ positions. Therefore, the number of matrices (graphs) in Ω_t is given by

$$\eta_t = \binom{n(n-1)}{t}. \tag{5}$$

where $\binom{a}{b}$, $b \leqq a$, is the binomial coefficient $a!/[b!(a-b)!]$. As is well-known,

$$\sum_i \eta_i = \sum_t \binom{n(n-1)}{t} = 2^{n(n-1)} = \eta.$$

The enumeration of matrices in $\omega(\rho)$ is accomplished by considering, for each i, r_i ones distributed over $(n-1)$ positions. This can be done, independently, for each i, in $\binom{n-1}{r_i}$ ways and thus the total number of matrices (graphs) in $\omega(\rho)$ is given by

$$\eta(\rho) = \prod_1^n \binom{n-1}{r_i}. \tag{6a}$$

By a similar argument, the number of matrices in $\omega(\sigma)$ is given by

$$\eta(\sigma) = \prod_1^n \binom{n-1}{s_j}. \tag{6b}$$

It is easily seen that

$$\sum_{(\rho)_t} \eta(\rho) = \sum_{(\sigma)_t} \eta(\sigma) = \eta_t.$$

The only difficult counting problem arises when we attempt to compute the number of points in $\omega(\rho, \sigma)$. This problem was solved by the authors [3] who showed that this number is given by

THEOREM.
$$\eta(\rho, \sigma) = A\left\{\left[\prod_{i=1}^n (1 + \delta_i)^{-1}\right](\rho, \sigma)\right\}.$$

Where the δ_i are operators on the pair of vectors defined by $\delta_i(r_1, \ldots, r_i, \ldots, r_n; s_1, \ldots, s_i, \ldots, s_n) = (r_1, \ldots, r_i - 1, \ldots, r_n; s_1, \ldots, s_i - 1, \ldots, s_n)$, the symbol $A\{\Sigma a_a (\rho_a, \sigma_a)\}$ stands for $\Sigma a_a A(\rho_a, \sigma_a)$ and $A(\rho_a, \sigma_a)$ is the coefficient of the monomial symmetric function of order corresponding to σ_a in the expansion of the unitary (elementary) symmetric function of order corresponding to ρ_a.

We note that the coefficients $A(\rho_a, \sigma_a)$ are given in tables of David and Kendall [1] for ρ_a and σ_a partitions of t up to $t = 12$. P. V. Sukhatme [5] gave an algorithm for computing $A(\rho_a, \sigma_a)$ for any weight and showed that $A(\rho, \sigma)$ is the number of matrices of element $c_{ij} = 0$ or 1 with fixed row totals r_i and column totals s_j but *without* restrictions on the diagonal elements. We present a very much abbreviated alternative to the proof previously given by the authors in the paper cited above.[1]

---

[1] This alternative proof follows lines of a suggestion by J. S. Frame.

PROOF. $G_n \equiv \prod_{i,j=1}^{n} (1 + x_i y_j)$ generates the $A(\rho_\alpha, \sigma_\alpha)$ as coefficients of terms $\prod_{i=1}^{n} x_i^{r_{i\alpha}} \prod_{j=1}^{n} y_j^{s_{j\alpha}}$, and we may write

$$G_n = \sum_{(\alpha)} A(\rho_\alpha, \sigma_\alpha) \prod_i x_i^{r_{i\alpha}} \prod_j y_j^{s_{j\alpha}},$$

where the sum extends over all a such that

$$0 \leq r_{i\alpha} \leq n - 1, \qquad 0 \leq s_{j\alpha} \leq n - 1, \qquad \sum_i r_{i\alpha} = \sum_j s_{j\alpha}.$$

This is most easily seen if each c_{ij} in a matrix C of 0's and 1's is represented as $(x_i y_j)^{c_{ij}}$. Then, each term in the formal expansion of G_n represents one complete configuration of all the c_{ij}, simultaneously. Finally, in each individual term, the total exponent of $x_i(y_j)$ is the sum $\sum_j c_{ij} = r_i (\sum_i c_{ij} = s_j)$, and the coefficient $A(\rho_a, \sigma_a)$ is the number of distinct configurations of the c_{ij} with the indicated row and column totals.

Minor modification of the same reasoning serves to establish that

$$H_n \equiv \prod_{\substack{i,j=1 \\ i \neq j}}^{n} (1 + x_i y_j)$$

is a generating function for the $\eta(\rho_a, \sigma_a)$.

Next, we observe that

$$H_n = \left[\prod_{i=1}^{n} (1 + x_i y_i)^{-1} \right] G_n.$$

In this equation, the coefficient of $\prod_i x'_i{}^i \prod_j y^s{}_j{}^j)$ in the left-hand member is $\eta(\rho, \sigma)$ and, in the right-hand member, is $\sum_{a1} \sum_{a2} \cdots \sum_{an} (-) \sum_i{}^{a_i} A(\rho - a, \sigma - a)$, where the a_i range over all non-negative integers. Equating these coefficients gives the expanded form of the statement of the theorem.

We note that the last sum in the proof above may be written in finite terms, since, as soon as any $a_i > \min(r_i, s_i)$, the corresponding $A(\rho - a, \sigma - a) \equiv 0$, by the definition of Sukhatme as a number of certain matrices of 0's and 1's.

PROBABILITY DISTRIBUTIONS OF ASSOCIATED RANDOM VARIABLES

It is now clear that we have laid down a program for computing, exactly, the probability distributions for any and all random variables associated with this structure of the sample space. In particular instances, it may be possible to effect certain economies in the computations by exploiting the isomorphisms among subsets so as to avoid duplication.

When the variable in question has constant values on sub-spaces no larger than an $\omega(\rho, \sigma)$, the computations are always formidable, though never impossible. In such circumstances, it would seem desirable to develop approximate distributions for these variables, treating the exact methods as procedures for testing the validity of the approximations over the ranges of group size, etc., to be covered. For *very* small groups, it will usually be feasible to carry out the exact computations.

EXAMPLES

We shall give two examples of random variables associated with the sample space structure. In each, we consider the null case in which each graph in the appropriate sample space is equally likely, i.e., a uniform probability distribution over the sample space.

EXAMPLE 1. One measure of gross expansiveness, equal to the total number of choices made by group divided by size of group, is given by Loomis and Proctor [4] in a contribution to *Research Methods in Social Relations*. In our notation, this index is $E = t/n$.

The distribution problem, in the null case, is easily solved. Clearly, the appropriate sample space is Ω and our random variable, the number of distinct n-graphs with t lines, is constant over the first-order subspaces, Ω_t, in the disjoint and exhaustive decomposition of Ω. Thus, our random variable is associated with the sample space structure and according to Section 4 and the enumeration formulas of Section 5, the required probabilities are given by

$$P(t = k) = \frac{\eta_k}{\eta} = \frac{\binom{n(n-1)}{k}}{2^{n(n-1)}}. \tag{7}$$

EXAMPLE 2. An *isolate* is an individual represented in the graph by a point, P_1, with no terminating lines and in the matrix by a column of zeros, i.e., $s_i \Vert 0$ in the vector σ. The exact probability distribution of the number of isolates for the case $r_i = d(i = 1, 2, \cdots, n)$ was obtained from first principles by Katz [2], in 1950.

Using the methods already developed, we can now easily extend this result to the general case where the ith individual has r_i outgoing connections, the r_i being not necessarily equal.

The most common setting for this problem is in the sample space $\omega(\rho)$. In

315

the null case, we desire the number of n-graphs having a specified number of points with no terminating lines, i.e., a specified number of zeros in the vector σ. Our random variable, X, the number of zero s_j's, is constant over the third order subspaces $\omega(\rho, \sigma)$ in the decomposition of $\omega(\rho)$; thus, it is associated with the sample space structure. Hence, according to Section 4 and the enumeration formulas of Section 5, the probability of exactly k isolates is given by

$$
P(X = k \mid \rho) = \frac{\sum\limits_{(\sigma)_t} I_{A_k}(\sigma)\eta(\rho, \sigma)}{\eta(r)}
$$

$$
= \frac{\sum\limits_{(\sigma)_t} I_{A_k}(\sigma) A \left\{ \prod\limits_{1}^{n} (1 + \delta_i)^{-1}(\rho, \sigma) \right\}}{\prod\limits_{1}^{n} \binom{n-1}{r_i}}, \tag{8}
$$

where A_k is the union of $\omega(\rho, \sigma)$ such that the vectors σ have exactly k vanishing components, and I_A is the indicator function for the set A.

We remark that in some contexts the appropriate sample space might be the larger space Ω_t. However, our enumeration methods will still give us the required probabilities necessary to construct the distribution. In this case, the probability of exactly k isolates is given by

$$
P(X = k \mid t) = \frac{\sum\limits_{(\rho)_t} \sum\limits_{(\sigma)_t} I_{A_k}(\sigma)\eta(\rho, \sigma)}{\eta_t}
$$

$$
= \frac{\sum\limits_{(\rho)_t} \sum\limits_{(\sigma)_t} I_{A_k}(\sigma) A \left\{ \prod\limits_{1}^{n} (1 + \delta_i)^{-1}(\rho, \sigma) \right\}}{\binom{n(n-1)}{t}}, \tag{9}
$$

where the notations are the same as before.

Thus, the probability distribution can be constructed for any index (proposed for the study of group structure) which depends only on the number of isolates in the group. Another such index, equal to the reciprocal of the number of isolates, is given by Loomis and Proctor [4] as a measure of "group integration."

Finally, we note that neither of the distributions (8) and (9) have been given correctly in the literature.

REFERENCES

1. David, F., and Kendall, M. G. "Tables of Symmetric Functions. Parts II and III," *Biometrika,* XXXVIII (1951), 435–62.
2. Katz, L. "The Distribution of the Number of Isolates in a Social Group," *Annals of Mathematical Statistics,* XXIII (1951), 271–76.
3. Katz, L., and Powell, J. "The Number of Locally Restricted Directed Graphs," *Proceedings of the American Mathematical Society,* V (1954), 621–26.
4. Loomis, C., and Proctor, C. *Research Methods in Social Relations.* Part II, Chapter 17, "Analysis of Sociometric Data." New York: The Dryden Press, 1951.
5. Sukhatme, P. V. "On Bipartitional Functions," *Philosophical Transactions of the Royal Society of London,* Series A, CCXXXVII (1938), 375–409.

C. The Reliability and Validity of Sociometric Measures

.

INTRODUCTION

By Robert R. Blake and Jane Srygley Mouton

Basic in the development of social science are questions dealing with the consistency of psychological measures and with the accuracy of predictions made from them. With techniques of measurement that meet the requirements of reliability and validity, the social scientist can contribute to the systematic understanding of the principles governing social conduct. Among the measuring procedures currently available for quantifying social relations are the sociometric methods originally given pre-eminence by Moreno (2). These techniques have been used widely for the last quarter of a century, and by now sufficient technical information about them is available to permit a systematic evaluation of them with respect to both reliability and validity.

Sociometric methods of assessing social relations are shown to possess ample reliability and validity for extended use in systematic research and in social engineering, in the first two sections that follow. Both are organized in a similar way, with the critical features of various experiments summarized so that direct comparisons between comparable investigations can be made. Tables presented show the characteristics of the test populations that have been investigated, the testing conditions that were employed, sociometric method and criteria that were used, the statistical techniques employed for assessing reliability or validity and the conclusions that were drawn.

The summaries demonstrate that sociometric scores constitute a satisfactorily stable basis for measuring individual differences for a wide range of testing conditions, various forms of administration, different test formats, differences in population and a variety of criteria for judgments. Equally important is the conclusion regarding validity. Predictions of performance from sociometric scores have yielded significant results for a variety of work, social, and play situations; in industrial, academic, military, and professional situations. The general conclusion, therefore, is that sociometric methods constitute fundamental techniques that can be expected to have increased significance in the emergence of a science of human relations.[1]

Problems of unusual complexity arise in designing experiments intended

---

[1] Valuable supplemental reading relevant to the issue examined in the following sections also can be found in articles by Witryol and Thompson (4), Lindzey and Borgatta (1), and Pepinsky (3).

to provide a systematic evaluation of the reliability of sociometric measures under precisely defined conditions. Further evidence for the reliability and validity of sociometric measures is provided in the final section, where an experiment is reported in which sociometric indices were employed to predict skill in role-taking. Here it is shown that role-taking skill is predictable from sociometric evidence, and that, at least with children, the skill is general for a variety of roles, rather than specific to the particular role being enacted.

REFERENCES

1. Lindzey, G., and Borgatta, E. F. "Sociometric Measurement," in G. Lindzey (ed.). *Handbook of Social Psychology.* Cambridge, Mass.: Addison-Wesley, 1954, 405–48.
2. Moreno, J. L. *Who shall survive?* ("Nervous and Mental Disease Monograph," No. 58). Washington, D.C.: Nervous and Mental Disease Publishing Co., 1934.
3. Pepinsky, Pauline N. "The Meaning of 'Validity' and 'Reliability' as Applied to Sociometric Tests," *Educational and Psychological Measurement,* IX (1949), 39–49.
4. Witryol, S. L., and Thompson, G. G. "A Critical Review of the Stability of Social Acceptability Scores Obtained with the Partial-rank-order and the Paired Comparison Scales," *Genetic Psychology Monographs,* II (1953), 221–60.

THE RELIABILITY OF SOCIOMETRIC MEASURES [1]

By Jane Srygley Mouton, Robert R. Blake and Benjamin Fruchter

Daily social relations are based on the assessments people make of one another as a product of interaction. Such assessments are direct judgments made without the benefit of formalized scales or any of the standardized techniques of quantification that have become routine in psychological measurement. Many times they are carried through at an implicit and intuitive level, and the judges themselves have difficulty in identifying the clues on which their responses are based. The processes that underlie such judgments may come to recognition or overt expression only under particular conditions, and rarely are they recorded in such a way as to make them accessible for systematic examination. Since these reactions are one of the essential ingredients of interaction, an understanding of the judgmental process on which they are based is important to the developing science of human relations.

The closest formal means of quantifying the assessments people make of one another are the various direct choice techniques. These procedures require members of a specified group to give overt expressions concerning their reactions to one another in terms of an explicit criterion which is standard for the group as a whole. The explicit expression of choice seems to be based on psychological processes similar to those involved in the intuitive or implicit social judgment. It brings them to a level of formal expression, however, thereby permitting the investigator to study certain aspects of this choice process.

In the systematic analysis of direct social judgment, the sociometric techniques of Moreno (34) stand out as the original methods of investigation. These methods and their modifications constitute the closest approximation to the measurement of the judgments people make concerning one another in real life situations. The recording of these judgments provides data permitting systematic study of the cognitive and affective reactions that obtain in human relations.

[1] This research was supported in part by the United States Air Force under Contract Number AF 18(600)-602, monitored by the 3305th Research and Development Group, (Combat Crew Training Research Laboratory) Human Resources Research Center, Randolph Air Force Base, Randolph Field, Texas. Permission is granted for reproduction, translation, publication, use, and disposal in whole or in part by or for the United States Government.

A variety of problems requiring detailed investigation arises from the use of any of the direct assessment techniques. These range from the evaluation of the reliability of choice data, through the use of such data to describe group structure, to the construction of a verifiable theory of social relations. The problem dealt with in this paper is limited to an evaluation of the consistency of choice data and indices derived from them. Do such data satisfy the consistency requirements that they must meet in order to be useful for the systematic measurement and prediction of human relations?

DESCRIPTION OF DIRECT CHOICE DATA

Because sociometric data are sufficiently different from the types of scores with which psychologists are accustomed to deal, it is desirable to examine their characteristics in some detail. A description of a sociometric-type choosing situation is presented below.

DESCRIPTION OF A CHOOSING SITUATION

A typical situation in which sociometric procedures have commonly been used is the classroom. The teacher might introduce the procedure by announcing that the seating was to be rearranged in terms of the preferences that children have for sitting near one another. He might then ask the children to list the classmates with whom they would like to sit by placing the one with whom they would most prefer to sit first in the list, the next most preferred second in the list and so on, including as many names as they wish. Using their responses he would determine which seating arrangement would best satisfy the desires of all the children. Then the seating plan could be changed accordingly. This procedure represents the basic model, but many variations such as the use of a fixed number of choices, the use of a general question about reactions to others, the use of a preference ranking and so on have been introduced.

CONSIDERATION OF THE CHOICE DATA

For a particular respondent the preferences expressed in a choice situation like that previously presented have the effect of separating the total group into two parts, those whom he chooses and those whom he fails to choose. Under certain conditions the respondent is asked not only to name his choices but also to identify those whom he rejects—in the situation just described he would be asked to name those near whom he would prefer not to sit. If rejections are requested and if the group is sufficiently large, so that some members remain unidentified under the list of those who were chosen and those who were rejected, each member's list provides a rough separation of the group into three parts including one made up of those whom he chooses, another of those whom he rejects, and an intermediate part composed of those whom he neither chooses nor rejects. Depending on the form of the assessment questionnaire the group as a whole is ordered so that two or three groupings of other members are made by each individual. It should be noted that the division point by which the subject determines the members he will include in each of the several categories is often an individual decision. The investigator may or may not place restrictions as to how many a respondent should place in this or that category.

PROBLEMS IN INTERPRETING THE MEANING OF RESPONSES

The problems that arise in interpreting the meaning of choice (or rejection) data are numerous with the particular issue depending on the uses to be made of them. The data can be employed for planning or rearranging a social situation or for installing some other administrative change. Criteria for choice that have been used in this way are "With whom would you like to sit?," "Whom would you like for a roommate?," and "With whom would you like to work?" Few technical problems appear beyond eliciting the group's cooperation in supplying the data when the uses are limited to a direct practical application.

Sociometric responses also may serve as one basis for the systematic study of social-psychological processes. This is the case where the choices given are used to derive an index of cohesiveness, to grade individuals in terms of their social acceptability, or to study the leadership phenomena. If they are used for systematic purposes of these kinds problems of a technical sort often arise. One of these problems is concerned with the consistency of sociometric responses.

The problem of consistency has specific application in sociometric measurement. When individuals in a group are asked to evaluate one another in terms of some criterion of choice the responses serve to differentiate the members from one another. While the choices may identify only those members who possess a significant amount of the property defined by the criterion, it is nonetheless a comparative judgment. Those not identified are presumed to possess the characteristics to a lesser degree than those who are identified. One way of assessing consistency would be to determine the extent to which choices from a second administration of the technique characterize the subjects in the same way as choices expressed on the first administration. If they do agree this would mean that two administrations of the same scale produce essentially the same results. If the responses from the second administration fail to correspond with those from the first this would suggest that the use of sociometric procedures in situations which demand a consistency in the data over different periods of time would be unwarranted.

OPPOSING VIEWS WITH RESPECT TO THIS QUESTION

There are opposing views as to whether or not sociometric data should possess the kind of consistency described above. It is maintained that behavior is flexible and adaptive and undergoing such a continuous process of change that reliability coefficients expressing a relationship between two occasions should not be expected to be high. Then a high coefficient would suggest that the sociometric test is not sufficiently sensitive as a measure of changing interpersonal relations to warrant its use for studying the dynamics of social interaction. An alternative view maintains that the behavior of persons is sufficiently invariant from one occasion to the next so that it should be possible to demonstrate consistency of this type. From the standpoint of the latter consideration a high coefficient would constitute the minimum indication of stability necessary for coordinated interpersonal relationships. The studies to be presented later will permit a more detailed examination of these alternative views.

FRAMES OF REFERENCE FOR ANALYZING SOCIOMETRIC RESPONSES

The consistency of sociometric responses can be evaluated from either of two frames of reference. The first involves determining the consistency of choices given, while the second is concerned with evaluating the stability of choices received.

Choices given. In administering a sociometric test each person is asked to nominate from among the remaining group those having the characteristics defined by the criterion used as the basis for response. In order to collect data that are useful for the analysis of consistency subjects are asked to make nominations in the same terms on a second occasion. With data from two different test administrations available the consistency from the first to the second occasions of the choices given can be determined on a person-by-person basis. If a person nominated the same people on the second occasion as he had on the first and this was also true for all the other group members there would be no change in responses on the two occasions, and it could be concluded that for those conditions the choice process was completely stable. With no stability in the choice process the nominations made on the first occasion would bear no consistent relationship to those made on the second. This procedure of determining the per cent change in the responses gives from one occasion to another has been a method for assessing the reliability of sociometric data.

Choices received. The same data can also be examined from the point of view of the distribution of responses received. The reliability of the distribution of choices received is concerned with the degree of consistency in the positions in the distribution of the various individuals on two test administrations, so that the reliability can be very high in terms of choices received while the sources of the choices might change between any two occasions. In this analysis it is unimportant whether or not the person receiving an unchanged number of choices receives them from the same people. What is necessary is obtaining high reliability is that the number of choices received remains essentially the same. The consistency of sociometric data will be evaluated in terms of both choices given and choices received.

Independence of administrations. Assessing the reliability of a measuring instrument requires that the two occasions of its administration be independent of one another. This requirement is based on the following considerations. If the act of assessing performance on one occasion can influence the act of assessing performance on the second then the consistency between the two assessments might be attributed in part to the relationship between the two acts rather than to stability in the performance assessed. If the situation on the second administration is such that the subject can recall the responses given on the first then it is possible for the consistency in response between the two administrations to be high due to the recall and reproduction on the second occasion of the same response as had been given on the first. While this difficulty is a consideration in the method of test-retest reliability analysis the routine conditions of social interaction make it particularly difficult to control in the evaluation of the reliability of sociometric data. In the typical sociometric-type measuring situation the same subjects are present on both occasions, but in this situation the possibility of spuriously high coefficients stemming from recall or other factors is increased.

Time and interaction. In the typical formulation of the reliability issue the critical test has been concerned with determining the degree of agreement between choice data collected on two occasions separated by varying time intervals. The time interval separating two test administrations has been treated as the dimension in terms of which changes in choice data would be expected if such differences were found. In studying consistency in this way, the assumption is made that time is a dimension through which changes in sociometric data can be assessed rather than that time *per se,* is the causative factor responsible for any observed changes. Although differences in time are presumed to be associated with differences in the volume of interactions occurring among group members, the important factor is interaction. In the absence of more valid measures of differences in the amount of interaction, time differences between testing occasions have been used as one basis for assessing the extent to which changes in choice data are likely to be associated with different amounts of interaction. Precise determination would require a more adequate measure of interaction than the dimension of time provides, but the use of time differences in this way allows an approximate evaluation of the reliability of choice data.

Action consequences. In order for conventional conceptions of consistency to hold it is necessary that no significant changes in the situation occur between the first and second test administrations. If a significant change occurs any lack of correlation between the two sets of data could reasonably be attributed to situational variation rather than to response instability.

This is an important consideration in view of Moreno's stipulation that one of the necessary conditions for collecting valid data is that the participants recognize and accept the fact that changes will be introduced into the social situation as a function of the choices that are expressed (34). If this is done then the conditions for a later administration are different to the extent that changes have been introduced. In terms of the previous example, the children would be located close to their preferred seatmates and separated from those they do not prefer as contrasted with the situation that prevailed before the introduction of the sociometrically based changes. If the investigator follows the premise that changes in the situation should be made in order to secure valid data, he has introduced factors that may have a disturbing effect on measured reliability.

Effect of technique of measurement on reliability. A number of different methods of collecting choice data have been employed. Some of them are limited choice (choose 2, choose 3, etc.), unlimited choice, rank order (rank 2, rank 3, to rank the entire group), paired comparisons, and ratings. The method used in the collection of data is a factor to be considered in evaluating the reliability of choice data.

Methods used in computing reliability. A number of studies use the conventional statistical procedures of obtaining the correlation between responses on the first occasion and the responses on the second occasion. Product-moment and rank-difference correlations are the methods which have been employed most frequently to compute reliability coefficients.

Since the distribution of choices is highly skewed it is doubtful that the conditions for applying these methods are sufficiently satisfied in sociometric-type data. As most of the studies have used correlational analysis as the basis for establishing consistency, they will be used in the discussion to follow as one basis for estimating the consistency of sociometric data.

Katz and Powell (28) have devised a technique for computing an index of the extent of agreement between two sets of sociometric choices that have been recorded in matrix form. This index should be a more appropriate statistical technique for estimating reliability than those mentioned above since it is an expression of the extent of agreement of the entries in the two matrices. No assumptions concerning the form of the distributions are involved, but it does assume independence of the two sets of observations (see independence of administrations above) and applies the appropriate probability distributions for testing the significance of the relationship.

THE DATA

The problem of the consistency of sociometric data can be examined by evaluating and contrasting a number of published studies that bear on this topic.

The literature has been difficult to assess for a variety of reasons. Since very little systematic effort has been made to cross-reference sociometric articles appearing in the journals of a half-dozen disciplines it has proved impossible to insure the inclusion of all studies relevant to this particular problem in the present report. A second difficulty is due to the fact that many of the studies report data that have been gathered in connection with some other purpose than the one for which the investigation was undertaken and reported. The consequence is that information significant for interpretation of the reliability issue has often been omitted from the final report. Still other difficulties stem from the inferior quality of theoretical formulation, inadequate research design, and incorrect statistical treatment that characterize a number of studies. Despite these shortcomings, it seems possible to interpret the relevant studies in a meaningful way and to formulate significant issues that can serve to orient future research.

CONSISTENCY OF CHOICES GIVEN

The question of the consistency of choices *given* is concerned with determining the extent to which an individual's choice pattern remains unchanged after an additional period of interaction. A few investigators have supplied data which permit analysis of this problem. These are presented in Table 1.

326

The usual testing procedure has involved asking subjects from the same group to make choices on two occasions. The responses are then examined to determine how many of the choices on the second administration are changed from those that were given on the first. If all choices on the second occasion were identical with those given on the first this would be described as 100 per cent *No Change*. If one-half the responses on the second occasion were different from those of the first this would be expressed as 50 per cent *No Change*, and if two-thirds of the choices were different this would yield approximately 33 per cent *No Change*. If none of the responses on the second occasion agreed with those given on the first this would represent 100 per cent *Change*, meaning that subjects consistently chose different people on the second occasion.

The summaries in the table have been organized to show several features of each study. These include the investigator, the criteria of choice, the technique of choosing, a description of the subjects who were involved in the study, the time interval between test and retest, the extent of acquaintance of group members at the time of first testing, and the per cent change in the choices over the time interval involved. The information available for each of the categories was taken from the original reports. The studies that have been grouped together are alike in that they are all based on a limited number of choices, 7 of the 8 requiring the respondents to give three choices. The subjects range from nursery school children to college students, and the time intervals between the tests extend from two weeks to one and one-half years.

The investigations reported in Table 1 are consistent in showing that a stable relationship exists between two test occasions when the basis for analysis is per cent of *No Change*. This conclusion applies irrespective of the sociometric criterion employed, the age and sex of subjects, the number of group members, the time interval between test administrations, and differences in degree of acquaintance at the time of first testing.

While there is a definite consistency between the two test occasions with choices given on one occasion being repeated on a second occasion, it is also apparent that the consistency is not perfect with different amounts of change being reported in each of the several studies. The specific values range from 27 per cent of *No Change* in the Scandrette (39) investigation to 78 per cent *No Change* in the study by Northway (35).

In view of the difficulties in interpreting raw per cents as presented in Table 1, it is desirable to determine statistical significance by contrasting the observed results with chance expectancy. The index of conformity

TABLE 1
Consistency of Choices Given

Investigator	Criteria	Technique of Choosing	Subjects	Time Interval	Extent of Acquaintance at First Test	Per Cent of Change
Criswell (13)	Seating	Two limit choice	238 children (1st-6th grades)	6 weeks	Unstated	38% No change 42% 1 change 20% 2 changes 69% No change in first choice 49% No change in second choice
Barker (3)	Seatmate	Three limit choice	12 college students	3 months 36 meetings	Strangers	55% No change
Northway (35)	Companions	Three limit choice	36 nursery children	4 months	Unstated	78% No change 83% No change in first choice 78% No change in second choice 74% No change in third choice
Horrocks (25)	Best friends	Three limit choice	905 students (6th-12th grades,10-17 years)	2 weeks	Unstated	% of No change

% of No change

Age	Boys	Girls
10	50%	70%
11	48%	55%
12	63%	63%
13	60%	55%
14	55%	63%
15	60%	70%
16	65%	60%
17	55%	80%

328

(TABLE 1 continued)

Investigator	Criteria	Technique of Choosing	Subjects	Time Interval	Extent of Acquaintance at First Test	Per Cent of Change
Austin & Thompson (1)	Best friends	Three limit choice	404 children (6th grade in 7 schools)	2 weeks	Unstated	40% No change 38% 1 change 16% 2 changes 5% 3 changes
Danielsson (15)	Friends, enemies	Three limit choice	69 adult male Jibero Indians	2 weeks	Unstated	94% No change
Scandrette (39)	Best friends	Three limit choice	78 7th grade students	4½ months	One semester	27.0% No change 32.0% 1 change 34.6% 2 changes 6.4% 3 changes
Singer (41)	Best friends and variations (8 times)	Three limit choice	28 students (7th & 8th grades)	1½ years	Group from 3 schools, previous grade	72% No changes in first choice

developed by Katz and Powell (28) is appropriate for this purpose. It was applied to the data from Criswell (13), Austin and Thompson (1), and Scandrette (39) studies for which there was fairly complete information on the changes between administrations. Since the size of the school classes was not reported an average size of thirty was adopted as a reasonable estimate for this purpose. The index of conformity for choices given on the two occasions in the Scandrette study yielded a coefficient of .55, and for the Criswell study a coefficient of .55 was obtained. These values are significant beyond the one per cent level. The index computed for the data in the Austin and Thompson study is .68, which is also significant beyond the one per cent level.

Additional assumptions concerning the data must be made in order to permit a statistical assessment of the significance of other studies in Table 1. The lowest percentage of *No Change* reported for these investigations is found in the Horrocks study (25). In evaluating these data it was assumed that all the remaining choices in the group of 30 were disagreements, an assumption which would produce the most conservative estimate of the degree of relationship. Based on these assumptions the computed index of conformity is .42, a value that is significant beyond the one per cent level. Similar assumptions were made for Barker's study (3) of 12 college students and a coefficient was obtained of .36. This value is also significant beyond the one per cent level.

The several statistical evaluations shown in Table 2 yield reasonably high coefficients and are significant for each of the studies involved. The relationship between the choices made on two test occasions is greater than chance factors could be expected to produce.

The significance of the reliability might also be interpreted as due to spurious factors such as the dependence between occasions and observers. Because of the inadequacy of the design of investigations from this standpoint there is no way to determine which of these two alternatives constitutes the more correct interpretation of these data.

THE CONSISTENCY OF CHOICE STATUS ON A TEST-RETEST BASIS

The question of consistency of choice status is concerned with evaluating the extent to which an individual's rank remains at the same position in the choice status continuum from one testing occasion to another. Choice status is defined as the position of an individual within a group. The index is derived from choices, ratings, or rankings received from other members on the basis of a specific criterion or a combination of sociometric criteria.

Rather than being concerned with reliability in terms of choices given as in Tables 1 and 2, this section is concerned with consistency of indices based on the number of choices received by each person from the group. The

TABLE 2

EXTENT OF AGREEMENT OF THE CHOICES GIVEN ON TWO ADMINISTRATIONS OF THE SOCIOMETRIC SCALES IN THE STUDIES REPORTED IN TABLE 1

Investigator	Assumptions Made in Computing Index of Conformity	Index of Conformity	Level of Significance
Criswell (13)	Size of class = 30	.55	.01
Austin & Thompson (1)	Size of class = 30	.68	.01
Scandrette (39)	Size of class = 30	.55	.01
Barker (3)	All choices other than *No change* are completely changed	.36	.01
Horrocks (25) Northway (35) Singer (41)	Size of class = 30 Per cent of *No change* is at least 48% and all other choices are completely changed	.42 or greater	.01

volume of choices received by an individual could be relatively stable while the sources of the choices change. The changing source of choices would not affect the size of the reliability coefficient.

A number of studies that assess the consistency of choice status over different periods of time have been published. The procedure usually followed in conducting these studies has been to administer a sociometric test during an early period in the history of a group and then repeat the same test on a later occasion. If choice status is unchanged at the time of the second test the correlation between the two sets of status scores should be high, but if it changes on retest the correlation should reflect this inconsistency between the two occasions.

Certain general characteristics of these studies can be summarized. The groups have generally been composed of from 20 to 50 members, and they have most often been drawn from school classes or from military units. In addition the number of choices permitted the respondent has usually been limited to from three to five though occasionally an unlimited number of choices has been allowed. Most frequently the sociometric criterion has called for choices involving positive expressions only. Finally, the time interval between test and retest has ranged from one day to one and one-half years with the typical study based on a retest after a three month period with both test and retest occurring early in the history of the group. The pertinent features of these studies are abstracted in Table 3.

The studies summarized in Table 3 are grouped in terms of the number of choices allowed. All studies based on a single choice are presented first, and those based on three, five, and an unlimited number of choices follow. Studies involving ratings of the intensity of choices and the method of paired comparisons are given in the last portion of the table. In cases where the PE's were not presented in the original report they have been computed for the purpose of permitting comparisons with other studies. Difficulties encountered in computing the probable errors were due to the fact that the kind of correlation used was not stated. In such cases the correlations were assumed to be either rank-order or Pearson product-moment. The probable errors were computed on the assumption that the correlations were rank-order because it gives the more conservative estimate of significance of the obtained value.

The results indicate that choice status obtained by an individual in a group remains essentially consistent over considerable periods of time. This statement seem to be true for the different techniques of choosing, the criteria used, and the kinds of subjects employed. These variables are discussed below.

Extent of acquaintance. The extent of acquaintance among members at first testing occasion shows some relationship to the consistency of choice status within a group. At one extreme there appears to be some minimum basis for determining the choice status position even at first contact. This is demonstrated in a study by Barker (3) in which twelve college students made ratings at the first meeting of the class with reference to the desirability of one another as seatmates. Three months later ratings were made on the same criterion and a rank-order correlation obtained between the two distributions of choices received. Under these conditions Barker obtained a correlation of .58 $\pm$ .08, suggesting that there is some consistency in response between an initial and a later rating even when there is little familiarity on which to base the first rating.

TABLE 3

TEST-RETEST CONSISTENCY OF CHOICE STATUS

Investigator	Criteria	Technique of Choosing	Subjects	Time Interval	Measurement of Status and Type of Correlation Used	r	PE	Extent of Acquaintance at First Test
Hunt & Solomon (26)	Like best	One limit choice	23 boys, 5 – 8 years	1 – 2 weeks	Total choices received, rank-order correlation	.70	.08	Some previous campers, some new, first week test given six hours after arrival at camp
				2 – 3 weeks		.75	.07	
				3 – 4 weeks		.91	.02	
				4 – 5 weeks		.94	.02	
				5 – 6 weeks		.88	.03	
				6 – 7 weeks		.77	.06	
				7 – 8 weeks		.95	.02	
				1 – 3 weeks		.42	.12	
				2 – 4 weeks		.61	.09	
				3 – 5 weeks		.84	.04	
				4 – 6 weeks		.74	.07	
				5 – 7 weeks		.82	.05	
				6 – 8 weeks		.82	.05	
Hemphill & Sechrest (22)	B-29 crew position	Nominations	94 B-29 crews	Unstated	Unstated	.91 "estimated"		Unstated
Bronfenbrenner (10)	Work, play, seating	Three limit choice for each criterion	14 Nursery	7 months	Composite raw scores rank-order correlation[1]	.27	.17	First test given third week in October
			20 Kndgtn.	7 months		.67	.08	
			21 1st Gr.	5 months		.48	.11	
			14 2nd Gr.	5 months		.28	.18	
			29 3rd – 4th Gr.	5 months		.52	.09	
			29 5th – 6th Gr.	5 months		.59	.08	

[1] The choices received on each criterion were correlated with the total choices received on all four criteria. These correlations are spuriously high due to the fact that the total choices received included the choices for the individual criterion with which it was correlated.

(TABLE 3 *continued*)

Investigator	Criteria	Technique of Choosing	Subjects	Time Interval	Measurement of Status and Type of Correlation Used	r	PE	Extent of Acquaintance at First Test
Damrin (14)	Plan dance, vacation, seating, living by, picture taken with	Three limit choice for each criterion (choices weighted 3, 2, 1)	156 girls	8 weeks	Averaged weighted choices	.86	.01	Unstated
Northway (35)	Companions for play activities	Three limit choice (choices weighted 5, 3, 2)	36 Nursery	1 month 2 – 3 months 3 – 4 months	Total weighted choices	.63 .57 .56	.07 .08 .08	Unstated
Northway, Frankel, Potashin (36)	Unstated	Unstated	Classroom groups, 20% membership change	1 year 1 week 1 week		.60 .80 .90		Unstated

(TABLE 3 continued)

Investigator	Criteria	Technique of Choosing	Subjects	Time Interval	Measurement of Status and Type of Correlation Used	r	PE	Extent of Acquaintance at First Test
Witryol & Thompson (49)	Take to another class, play with, activity in school and out of school[2]	Three limit choice	6th grade, four different classes		Total choices on all 4 criteria, Pearson correlation			Unstated
			I 22	1 week		.94	.02	
			II 14			.71	.05	
			III 18			.69	.09	
			IV 18			.96	.01	
			I 22	4 weeks		.66	.08	
			II 15			.83	.06	
			III 18			.69	.09	
			IV 17			.94	.02	
			I 21	5 weeks		.60	.10	
			II 18			.64	.10	
			III 17			.80	.06	
			IV 17			.90	.03	
Wherry & Fryer (47)	Personality traits desirable for officer	Five limit choice	134 Army OCS	1 month 4 months	(Most)— (Least) possible	.75 .58	.03 .04	1 month
Williams & Leavitt (48)	Roommate, fairness, humor, best officer, leadership	Five limit choice for best, one choice for worst	100 OCS Marines, average age 21 years[3]	3 weeks	Sum of (all) choices minus rejections	.78	.04	2 weeks in platoon

[2] Tetrachorics were computed in the study with standard errors supplied by the authors.
[3] See Table 1, footnote 4.

(TABLE 3 *continued*)

Investigator	Criteria	Technique of Choosing	Subjects	Time Interval	Measurement of Status and Type of Correlation Used	r	PE	Extent of Acquaintance at First Test
Zeleny (52)	To work in groups	Five limit choice	15 college students 35 college students 34 college students	1 day	Choices	.95 .94 .94	.03 .02 .02	Unstated
McIntyre (30)	Roommate, sharing of recreation	Five limit choice	One floor of men's college dormitory, (approx. 70)	6 months	Pearson	.65	.05	2 months in dormitory
Bonney (9)	6–8 choosing situations (i.e., send Valentine to, vote for class officers, vote for librarian)	Choice mostly unlimited (choices weighted 5, 4, 3, 2, 1)	48 children, in 2nd grade, two 3rd grades 42 – 57 children (30% turnover)	1 year	Total weighted choices as a per cent of class total	.84 .77 .67	.02 .04 .05	Unstated
Byrd (11)	Actors for play	Unlimited choice	27 4th grade	2 months	Rank-order of total choices	.89	.04	2 months
Jennings (27)	Working, living	Unlimited choice and unlimited rejection	133 girls 12 – 16 yrs. N.Y. Training School	8 months	Total choices minus total rejections	.65 .66	.04 .04	Various

(TABLE 3 continued)

Investigator	Criteria	Technique of Choosing	Subjects	Time Interval	Measurement of Status and Type of Correlation Used	r	PE	Extent of Acquaintance at First Test
French (17)	Go on liberty with, volunteer for tough assignment with, for Acting Chief Petty Officer	Unlimited choice	16 companies (42 – 54 men per company) Naval recruits 17 – 20 years	9 weeks 8 weeks 5 weeks	Number of choices	(see sub-table below)		1 week

Correlation With Final Test (10th Week) by Companies

Week of Initial Test	Company	Liberty		Mission		Leader		Total	
		r	PE	r	PE	r	PE	r	PE
First week	102	.38	.08	.53	.07	.63	.06	.54	.07
	103	.49	.09	.72	.05	.69	.05	.43	.08
	104	.63	.06	.79	.04	.83	.03	.83	.03
	105	.28	.09	.40	.08	.35	.09	.27	.09
	Mean	.46	.08	.64	.06	.66	.06	.56	.07
Second week	98	.43	.08	.48	.08	.60	.06	.56	.07
	99	.40	.08	.36	.08	.54	.07	.41	.08
	100	.62	.06	.57	.07	.83	.03	.71	.05
	101	.56	.07	.65	.06	.90	.02	.75	.04
	Mean	.51	.07	.53	.07	.76	.04	.63	.06
Fifth week	94	.76	.04	.89	.02	.88	.02	.86	.03
	95	.82	.03	.81	.04	.87	.03	.86	.03
	96	.82	.03	.82	.03	.82	.03	.84	.03
	97	.78	.04	.92	.02	.96	.01	.93	.01
	Mean	.80	.03	.87	.03	.90	.02	.88	.02

337

(TABLE 3 continued)

Investigator	Criteria	Technique of Choosing	Subjects	Time Interval	Measurement of Status and Type of Correlation Used	r	PE	Extent of Acquaintance at First Test
Gibb (18)	I Group members (socio-telic) II Personal friends (psycho-telic) III Influence	Unlimited choice	10 groups college men (10 each) 20 groups officer candidates (10 each)	3 sessions 3 hrs. each —unstated interval	Tetra-choric coefficients, standard error	(See sub-table below)		Unstated
Murray (33)	Best friends	Unlimited choice	43 retarded children	12 weeks 12 weeks	Choices received	.33 .50		Average of 14 months
Zeleny (51)	Work in groups	Rating of yes, no, indifferent; three limit choice	3 college classes (29 in each)	1 day 6 days	Weighted sum of rankings received	.95 .96 .96 .94 .97 .96	.01 .01 .01 .01 .00 .00	Unstated

Sub-table (Gibb):

Sessions	Officer Candidates		Students			
	1 & 2	2 & 3	1 & 2		2 & 3	
			r	PE	r	PE
I	.45	.50	.66	.07	.78	.09
II			.80	.06	.78	.09
III	.77	.64	.83	—	.78	—

(TABLE 3 *continued*)

Investigator	Criteria	Technique of Choosing	Subjects	Time Interval	Measurement of Status and Type of Correlation Used	r	PE	Extent of Acquaintance at First Test
Zeleny (52)	Like	Rating of yes, no, indifferent	15 college students 35 college students 34 college students	1 day	Likes or acceptances received	.91 .91 .95	.03 .02 .01	Unstated
Zeleny (53)	Like	Rating of yes, no, indifferent; first three choices and last three choices	20 4th grade students	5 days	Weighted sum of rankings received	.79	.06	Unstated
Barker (3)	Desirability as a seatmate	Rating of pleased, indifferent, sorry	12 college students	3 months 36 class meetings	Rank-order, composite group rating	.58	.08	Strangers
McKinney (31)	Members of discussion group	Rating of yes, no, indifferent; check positive negative reasons	29 9th grade	2 weeks	Rank-order, $\dfrac{Yes - No}{N - 1}$ positive minus negative reasons	.94 .97	.02 .01	Unstated

(TABLE 3 continued)

Investigator	Criteria	Technique of Choosing	Subjects	Time Interval	Measurement of Status and Type of Correlation Used	r	PE	Extent of Acquaintance at First Test
Seeman (40)	OSAS (friendship)[4]	Rating on 1–6 point scale	5th grade approx. 40	Re-test	Pearson, mean scores	.90	.02	Unstated
Taylor, E. (43)	OSAS friendship	Rating on 6 point scale ratings (weighted 15, 10, 5, 2, 1)	8th grade; 31 traditional students, 32 unclassified students, 27 progressive students	4 months 3 months 3 months	Weighted scores	.90 .89 .66	.02 .03 .08	Unstated
Wherry & Fryer (47)	10 leadership qualities	Rating	134 Army OCS's in two classes of 82 and 52 members each	1 – 2 months 1 – 5 months	Averaged ratings	.76 .17	.03 .06	1 month
Lippitt (29)	Like best	Paired comparison	13 nursery children selected from 5 others; 10 nursery children	1 – ½ months	Rank-order of choices	.64 .50	.20 .17	Unstated

[4] The Ohio Reputation Scale is composed of short descriptive items concerning reputation. Choices were made as to individuals within the group that fitted the descriptions given on the scale.

(TABLE 3 *continued*)

Investigator	Criteria	Technique of Choosing	Subjects	Time Interval	Measurement of Status and Type of Correlation Used	r	PE	Extent of Acquaintance At First Test
Witryol & Thompson (49)	Like best	Paired com- parison	6th grade, four differ- ent classes		Pearson			Unstated
			I 25	1 week		.98	.01	
			II 20	1 week		.99	.00	
			III 19	1 week		.96	.01	
			IV 21	1 week		.97	.01	
			I 25	4 weeks		.93	.02	
			II 20	4 weeks		.98	.01	
			III 19	4 weeks		.92	.02	
			IV 21	4 weeks		.97	.01	
			I 25	5 weeks		.94	.02	
			II 20	5 weeks		.96	.01	
			III 19	5 weeks		.90	.03	
			IV 21	5 weeks		.95	.01	

341

The relationship between the amount of acquaintance and the degree of consistency between choices received is reported in a study by Hunt and Soloman (26). Sociometric choices of boys in a summer camp were correlated on a week-by-week basis from the first and second week to the seventh and eighth week. The correlations between successive weeks increased in magnitude with time. They were lowest at the beginning of the camping session and higher between successive weeks later in the session. As the degree of acquaintance between group members increased the size of the correlations between choice distributions increased.

This generalization is given further support in a study by French (17) in which choices were made by sixteen companies of Naval recruits at the end of the first, second, fifth, and tenth weeks of training. Several different sociometric criteria were used as the basis for measuring choice status. With an increase in the amount of acquaintance prior to the first test there was a consistent increase in correlations of choices received on the first and final occasions. In general, the lowest correlations were obtained between the tests taken at the end of the first and tenth weeks, with higher correlations being obtained between the second and tenth weeks, and the highest correlations found between choices received at the end of the fifth and tenth weeks of training.

Relevance of criteria and consistency of status. There is some evidence that the more relevant the criterion of choice is to the purpose for which the group meets the more consistent the measured status positions between testing occasions. This set of relationships is suggested in the study by French (17) cited above. Choices received on the criterion of "going on liberty with" yielded lower retest correlations than the choices received on "volunteering for a tough assignment," and choices received on the criterion of "Acting Chief Petty Officer" yielded higher correlations than either of the other two criteria. This conclusion is only tentative since there was no independent means by which to assess the relevance of the criteria to the purpose for which the groups were organized.

Age of subjects. The stability of choice status may be determined in part by the age of the subjects making the choices. The statement that relates these variables to one another is that the closer the subjects are to adult age the more stable their choices and the higher the resulting correlation between tests. The studies using older children as subjects report higher retest correlations than studies using nursery and kindergarten age children as subjects. This possibility can be evaluated by contrasting studies reported by Bronfenbrenner (10), Lippitt (29), and Northway, Frankel, and Potashin

(36) all of which deal with nursery and kindergarten children with those by Bonney (9), McKinney (31), Seeman (40), Taylor (43), Byrd (11), and Zeleny (51), a series of studies using older children as subjects. By comparison with these investigations, studies based on the sociometric responses of college students and adults such as those by Zeleny (51) (53) and Hemphill and Sechrest (22) yielded the highest test-retest correlations. The interpretation here is complicated by the fact that the time interval was also much shorter. Although there are studies in the table which appear to produce results which are inconsistent with this interpretation, the generalization seems valid that the choice status received by older children and young adults is more stable. The studies relevant for making this interpretation are not equated with respect to other factors such as time interval between test and retest, relevance of criteria, and technique of choosing which also appear to be significantly related to the test-retest correlation.

Technique of choosing. The consistency of choice status over a period of time appears to vary with the technique of choosing. This was investigated directly in a study by Witryol and Thompson (49). Both the paired comparison technique and various sociometric choosing situations were used with four classes of sixth grade children. The tests were given at one, four, and five week intervals, and the sociometric choices for the various choosing situations were combined into a total score. The results show that the paired comparison technique gave the higher and more consistent correlations over the various time intervals covered by the study.

Time interval between test and retest. A general statement with respect to time interval is that the longer the period elapsing between test and retest the lower the resulting correlation. With the exception of the study reported by Taylor (43), the general validity of this statement is shown in investigations by Northway (35), Northway, Frankel, and Potashin (36), Wherry and Fryer (47), French (17), Lippitt (29), Hunt and Soloman (26), and Witryol and Thompson (49). In these studies the longer the time interval between two testing occasions the greater the possibility that changes in interpersonal attitudes will occur. Such changes would be reflected by differences in sociometric choices which might have the effect of lowering the correlation for status positions between test and retest.

Summary. Granting the general consistency reflected by the test-retest correlations, there appear to be several contributing factors that are related to their magnitude. These include the extent of acquaintance, the relevance of the choice criterion to the activity of the group, the age of subjects, the technique of choosing, and the time interval between test and retest.

TABLE 4

CONSISTENCY OF CHOICE STATUS WITHIN A SINGLE TEST OCCASION

Investigator	Criteria	Technique of Choosing	Subjects	Type of Correlation Used	Correlation	Extent of Acquaintance
Grossman & Wrighter (19)	Seating, Walking home, playing, class officer, best friend	Three limit choice	4 classes of 6th grade N = 117	Spearman-Brown split-half	.93 .96 .96 .97	Unstated
Bass & White (4)	7 sociometric items	Rating	75 frat. members	Correlated split-half for 7 items	.90 or above	Unstated
Ricciuti & French (38)	Leadership potential or aptitude for service	Rating	633 Naval Academy Midshipmen	Split-half method (composite ratings)	.90	Cruise
Taylor, F. (44)	Friend, like	Rating	3 therapy groups 7 females, 9 males 4 males and 4 females	W	.72 .54 .52	3 months acquaintance
Heinicke & Bales (21)	Leadership	Ranking	College students high consensus groups 6 gr. N = 5 4 gr. N = 6	W	.500 or higher	Not acquainted at beginning of 6 week interaction

Consistency of Choice Status within a Single Test Occasion

The problem of the consistency of choice status has been approached in still a different way by analysis of data within a single test occasion. When this procedure is used the number of choices received by each person from one half the group is contrasted with the number of choices received from the other half. This method of analysis resolves many of the technical problems of evaluating consistency such as the independence between administrations and so on. The studies using this method that have been reported are summarized in Table 4.

The studies in Table 4 are consistent with those described in Table 3. Regardless of the technique of computing the index of agreement for choice status received, whether from data representing choices received on two different occasions or from data obtained on a single testing occasion, the studies agree in demonstrating that sociometric assessments have a significant degree of reliability.

Intercorrelations among Techniques

The consistency of sociometric data can also be evaluated by contrasting results obtained with different sociometric measurement techniques administered in succession. One could employ two different techniques of gathering sociometric choices on the same criterion and then study the extent of agreement between them; for example, the results by the method of paired comparisons can be contrasted with those from a limited direct choice technique. If the status positions given by both techniques are roughly comparable the intercorrelation between these two ways of measuring status would yield a value which should be at least as high as the reliability coefficient of the least reliable of either of the two techniques. If status position as assessed by one technique is distinctly different from that obtained through use of a second, then the intercorrelation between the measures would be lower. In the latter case it would have to be assumed that the resulting index of status for an individual is contingent upon the technique used in measuring it; whereas in the former the status could be treated as essentially independent of the procedure employed in assessment.

Four different studies which are concerned with intercorrelating different techniques of measuring status position are summarized in Table 5. The same categories have been used in Table 5 as were used in previous tables. Twelve different pairs of combinations of techniques of choosing are represented. Frequently the technique for computing the correlations reported in Table 5 was not indicated. In these cases the same procedure as was used to evaluate the reliability coefficients in Table 3 was employed in computing the PE's. The rank-order correlation was assumed because it gives the more conservative estimate of the significance of the reliability coefficient.

The correlations in Table 5 are statistically significant, but some pairs of techniques seem to produce much higher intercorrelations than others. The technique that produces the lowest intercorrelations with other measures is apparently the two or three limit fixed choice. It seems that the larger the number of choices allowed including unlimited choices the higher the correlation between the measures and the greater the consistency of the derived index of status position. In order to make these generalizations, however, the results of several studies must be combined and reference made to Table 3 as well as Table 5.

The study by Witryol and Thompson (49) referred to in Table 3 shows that for four classes of 6th graders the paired comparison technique yielded higher retest correlations and showed less fluctuation as the basis for measuring status position than did the three choice technique. This finding suggests the the test-retest consistency of paired comparison data is greater than that for three limit choice data. On the other hand, in view of the correlations between these two measures shown in Table 5, it can be inferred that the variations in the correlation coefficients appearing there seem to be associated with the three choice technique and its lower reliability. These two considerations taken together lead to the tentative statement that the paired comparisons technique may be the more stable of the two procedures for the measurement of choice status. This possibility is given further support by results reported by Eng and French (16). They found that the paired comparison technique yielded consistently high correlations with unlimited choice and mean rank, and lower correlations with the two and five limit choice technique.

The results of the Taylor (44) (45), Eng and French (16), and Ausabel, Schiff, and Gasser (2) studies can also be contrasted with one another from the point of view of this possibility. The correlations between ratings and rankings are high (Taylor), between rankings and limited choices (Eng and French) and between choices and ratings (Ausabel, Schiff, and Gasser) are comparatively low. From these results it can be inferred that the limited choice technique is the common factor responsible for the lower intercorrelations. This interpretation is given further support by the Eng and French study where the limited choice technique showed the lowest correlations of any technique with the several other measures. This finding is not unexpected, as each member makes judgments on only a portion of

TABLE 5
INTERCORRELATIONS AMONG TECHNIQUES

Investigator	Criteria	Technique of Choosing	Subjects	Time Interval	r	PE	Extent of acquaintance at first test
Eng & French (16)	Desirability as a room-mate	Unlimited choice[1] vs. paired comparison vs. rank-order	32 sorority members	3 sessions at 1 week intervals	(See sub-table below)		Unstated
Taylor, F. (44) (45)	Like as a friend	Rating ($+1, -1, 0$) vs. preference ranking	3 psychotherapy groups 7 females; 4 males and 4 females; 9 males.	Administered in succession	.91 / .95	.02 / .02	3 months / 5 months
Ausubel, Schiff & Gasser (2)	Friendship	Three limit choice vs. ratings (1 – 5 points)	2 classes – 3rd grade 2 classes – 5th grade 2 classes – 7th grade all classes – 11th grade all classes – 12th grade	Administered in succession	.73 .29 .42 .42 .49	.05 .10 .07 .08 .07	Unstated

(The r / PE values for Taylor and Ausubel fall under the "Five limit choice" heading.)

Sub-table (Eng & French):

	Mean rank		Unlimited choice		Five limit choice		Two limit choice	
	r	PE	r	PE	r	PE	r	PE
Paired comparison	.97	.01	.90	.02	.73	.06	.54	.09
Mean Rank			.89	.03	.74	.06	.55	.09
Unlimited choice					.78	.05	.65	.07
Five limit choice							.75	.06

[1] The unlimited choosing situation was presented as the first technique with the choices ranked in order of preference. The first and second choices of each were used as the data for computing the status on the two choice category. The rank-order of preference was the third technique used and the first five choices were used for computing the status in the five choice category.

347

(TABLE 5 continued)

Investigator	Criteria	Technique of Choosing	Subjects	Time Interval	r	PE	Extent of acquaintance at first test
Witryol & Thompson (49)	Like least, take to another class, play with friends, activities in school and out of school	Paired comparison, vs. three limit choice	I 23 6th grade classes	1 day	.82	.05	Unstated
			II 15	1 day	.41	.15	
			III 19	1 day	.67	.09	
			IV 18	1 day	.89	.03	
			I 23	1 week	.80	.05	
			II 19	1 week	.77	.07	
			III 18	1 week	.36	.14	
			IV 18	1 week	.90	.03	
			I 23	5 weeks	.64	.08	
			II 19	5 weeks	.62	.09	
			III 18	5 weeks	.54	.11	
			IV 20	5 weeks	.86	.04	

the scale with the limited choice technique, and the part of the scale not covered by his choices is assumed to be compatible with the judgments of others.

INTERCORRELATIONS AMONG CRITERIA

Another way to evaluate the consistency of choice data on a single occasion involves examining the intercorrelations of criteria. Given the same technique of choosing, to what extent is status position as measured on one criterion related to status position as measured on a second criterion?

Assuming that the choice process is differentiated for various criteria, a justification for this kind of analysis can be seen in terms of the functional equivalence of the items which serve as the basis for choice. If essentially the same basis for choice characterized two criteria which are stated in different verbal terms then it would be expected that if the choice process for the two criteria is the same or similar the correlation between them should be high. Furthermore, correlations should be low for the items which are not functionally equivalent. The difficulty in making this kind of analysis is that there is no independent means by which functional equivalence of sociometric criteria can be established. Under these conditions more functional equivalence is likely to be assumed for those items that produce high intercorrelations and less functional equivalence assumed for those that do not. In the absence of a measure in terms of which equivalence can be independently determined, it will be possible only to point out where the intercorrelations appear to be consistent with *a priori* assumptions of the degree of functional equivalence of items.

The data presented in Table 6 are difficult to interpret for additional reasons. Studies showing substantial intercorrelations among choice criteria are not equated in terms of other variables. In some cases a complication stems from the fact that different techniques of choosing were used for the different criteria thereby making it difficult to determine whether the obtained results are to be attributed to differences in the functional equivalence of criteria or to differences in the technique of choosing. As in Table 5, where the type of correlation coefficient was not indicated PE's were computed for the rank-order method.

There is some degree of positive intercorrelation among all choice criteria. This finding suggests that the choice process is rather general with the same persons receiving a higher number of choices even when the criteria for choosing are different. In addition to consistently significant intercorrelations between positive choices, Table 6 can also be interpreted as showing that the more psychologically similar the two criteria the higher the result-

TABLE 6

INTERCORRELATIONS AMONG CRITERIA

Investigator	Criteria	Technique of Choosing	Subjects
Young (50)	OSAS[1], ORS,[2] composite socio-metric score based on criteria of sit with, help with school work, president of class, play on team, go on picnic, stay all night (at home), best friend	Rating, Nomination, Two limit choice	41 7th grade students
Williams & Leavitt (48)	Roommate, sense of humor, leadership, fairness, best officer	Five limit choice for best and five limit choice for worst	100 OCS Marines (18 – 26 years average age 21)

Young (50):

	r	PE	ORS		Sociometric Composite	
OSAS			.83	.03	.90	.02
ORS					.88	.03

Williams & Leavitt (48):

	H		L		F		O	
	r	PE	r	PE	r	PE	r	PE
R	.56	.05	.78	.03	.95	.01	.69	.04
H			.11	.06	.58	.04	.39	.05
L					.94	.01	.95	.01
F							.85	.02

[1] See Table 3, footnote 4.

[2] The Ohio Reputation Scale is composed of short descriptive items concerning reputation. Choices were made as to individual's within the group that fitted the descriptions given on the scale.

(TABLE 6 continued)

Investigator	Criteria	Technique of Choosing	Subjects	r	PE		II		III		IV	
McKinney (31)	Membership in discussion group, personal appraisal	Ratings (+1, 0, −1) Choice of positive and negative reasons	27 9th grade students	.96	.01							
				.98 (retest two weeks later)	.01							
Maucorps (32)	I Toward which members feel most drawn	Unlimited choice (+1) 3 highest indicated (+3); eight limit choice;	35 French officers at special training school			I	.81	.04	.74	.05	.84	.03
	II Work in groups	Choice, 3 highest, 3 next highest, 3 lowest indicated (weighted +3, +1, −3);				II			.90	.02	.89	.03
	III Team for final exam	Unlimited choice (+1) 4 highest (+3)				III					.89	.03
	IV Posted with at head-quarters											
Smucker (42)	Best friends and rejec-tions, repre-sent college	Unlimited choice and rejection, four limit choice	Girl's dormi-tory (approxi-mately 75)	.64								

(TABLE 6 continued)

Investigator	Criteria	Technique of Choosing	Subjects	r	PE
Gibb (18)	Sociotelic group members, psychetelic – personal friends, influence leaders	Unlimited choice	10 groups college men (10 in each) / 20 groups officer candidates (10 in each)		
Hackman & Moon (20)	Leader of a committee, committee members	Two limit choice	2 laboratory sections of college students	.86	.85
Holzberg (23)	I Debating / II Planning party / III Student council representative / IV Make a decision for you	Five limit choice and rejections with weighting	47 student nurses (20 – 22 years)		

Officer Candidates

Sociotelic

Sessions	1		2		3	
Influence	.38	.10³	.46	.09	.65	.08
Leader	—		—		.59	.11

Psychetelic

	1		2		3	
Influence	—		.54	.09	.64	.08
Leader	—		—		.65	.10

College Students

Sociotelic

Influence	.53	.13	.25	.16

Psychetelic

Influence	.30	.15	.36	.15

Holzberg (23)

	II	III	IV
I	.86	.85	.79
II		.83	.81
III			.67

³ Tetrachorics were computed in the study with standard errors supplied by the authors.

(TABLE 6 continued)

Investigator	Criteria	Technique of Choosing	Subjects	r	PE
Taylor (45)	I Liking	Rank-order Ratings (+1, −1, 0)	Combined three psychotherapy groups; 7 females; 4 males and 4 females; 9 males		
	II Public popularity				
	III Influence of group	Ratings (+1, −1, 0)		III	
				I .92	.02
				II .57	.16
Bates (5)	Contributing most to group task, effective leaders	Rank-order, three limit choice	18 college	.83	.05

Chowdhry & Newcomb (12)	Criteria	Technique of Choosing	Subjects		I		II		III		IV	
	I Most capable as president	Three limit choice[4]	4 groups:									
			34 in Religious Group	R	.95	.01	.89	.03	.81	.04	.67	.07
	II Most influential		30 in Political Group	P	.96	.01	.97	.01	.84	.04	.95	.01
	III Represent group at convention		36 in Medical Fraternity	F	.87	.03	.70	.06	.53	.09	.86	.03
	IV Like as friends		46 in Medical Sorority	S	.96	.01	.93	.01	.61	.10	.68	.06

4 The choices received on each criterion were correlated with the total choices received on all four criteria. These correlations are spuriously high due to the fact that the total choices received included the choices for the individual criterion with which it was correlated.

353

(TABLE 6 continued)

Investigator	Criteria	Technique of Choosing	Subjects	r PE									
					M r	M PE	P r	P PE	S r	S PE	ORS r	ORS PE	OSAS r	OSAS PE
Wardlow & Green (46)	I Review for a quiz (mental)	Three limit choice (weighted 3, 2, 1 points)	37 adolescent girls in 1st year home-making	M			.32	.10	.61	.07	.52	.08	.61	.07
	II Weiner roast (social)			P					.57	.08	.52	.08	.60	.07
	III Play basketball (physical)			S							.39	.10	.51	.08
				ORS									.50	.08
	IV OSAS (friendship)	Rating (1–6 points)		Mean Correlation	.52	.08	.51	.08	.52	.08	.49	.09	.56	.08
	V ORS (reputation)	Choice												

ing correlations between them. This is borne out in the study by Williams and Leavitt (48) where the intercorrelations of "roommate," "leaders," "fairness," and "best officer," are consistently high. With criteria that appear to be less closely related the intercorrelations of status position is lower. This is shown in the same study where the criteria when correlated with "sense of humor" criterion yielded the lowest intercorrelations. In the case of the study by Smucker (42) where the two criteria are "best friends" and "representatives of the college," the resulting intercorrelations of status position are somewhat low.

The same finding appears in the study by Wardlow and Greene (46) where criteria based on social relations are more highly intercorrelated than are judgments based on physical abilities. Examples of studies in which intercorrelations are high and in which the criteria are functionally closely related to one another are those published by Bates (5), Maucorps (32), McKinney (31), and Young (50).

CONSISTENCY OF SOCIOMETRIC JUDGMENTS UNDER CONDITIONS OF EXPERIMENTAL VARIATION

Two investigations deal with the problem of consistency of sociometric judgments of personal and social characteristics when factors that might produce a spuriously high correlation between the two testing occasions have been systematically excluded. Both investigations report evidence supporting the view that individual characteristics can be judged consistently under these conditions.

The first study reported by Bell and French (6) used twenty-five previously unacquainted student volunteers from an introductory course in psychology. Over a six week period each subject participated in six five-man discussion groups with each group composed of five men who had not met previously. This procedure required a total of 30 thirty-five minute group discussions with a different topic for discussion at each meeting. At the end of each session, the participants were asked to rank the group members for the position of discussion leader in a hypothetical second meeting of the group. Bell and French show that the rankings an individual received in any one group in which the member participated are significantly related to his average ranking in the other five groups, with the average correlation being .75. They conclude that leadership status would seem to be a stable individual characteristic with seventy-three per cent of its variance measured reliably, and that .75 is probably a minimum estimate due to sources of unreliability in the measurements themselves. In other words, if the measures themselves were completely reliable the consistency of judgments in the individual situation with the average of the judgments in the other five groups might have been as high as .91.

A second study dealing with the consistency problem in the same general way is that by Blake, Mouton, and Fruchter (7). In this investigation, thirty-three college students who were unacquainted with one another at the beginning of the experiment were organized into eleven three-man discussion groups for a fifteen minute discussion period. They were then reorganized into new groups so that no person worked in the second test situation with another person whom he had previously known in the first situation. In addition to changes in group membership the discussion topic also was changed in the second session. Finally the trained observers who watched each group during the first period observed the discussion of three different people during the second session. Both subjects and observers were asked to rank the performance of the members on a twelve item scale of personal and social characteristics that was filled in after each session. These data permit determination of the extent to which personal and social charac-teristics are reliably judged from one discussion situation to another when the discussion topic, group membership, and the observers are changed. The results support the proposition that judgments of behavior under conditions of short-term interaction can be reliably made even when factors that might produce spurious consistency between judgments have been systematically eliminated. Items that were most reliably judged were leadership, contribu-tion to group decision, and dominance position within the group.

Both the Bell and French and the Blake, Mouton, and Fruchter studies agree in demonstrating that it is possible to make judgments of individual personal and social characteristics that are consistent from one occasion to the next even where the group membership and discussion topic are different in each of the sessions.

DISCUSSION AND SUMMARY

This paper has dealt with the problem of assessing the reliability of sociometric judgments. By way of introducing the issues involved in this question a typical social situation within which such judgments might be made was described, and the alternative arguments as to whether or not such judgments should be consistent over time was discussed. This was followed by an analysis of the use of a time measure between testing occa-sions as the basis for assessing the degree of consistency in such judgments. Other problems which arise in assessing the reliability of sociometric data include the problems involved in assuming independence between the administrations of the same sociometric technique, the introduction of administrative changes based on the sociometric judgments given at the first administration as these changes might affect the responses given on the second occasion, the differences in the techniques of measurement or the number and ordering of the choices given, and finally the methods used in computing the index of reliability were discussed.

A total of 53 studies bearing on the reliability of sociometric judgments were then summarized under six different headings. The basis for classification was the way in which consistency was investigated whether from the standpoint of the consistency of choices given between two testing occasions, the consistency of choice status received from a single test administration or from two test occasions spaced by a time interval, the degree of intercorrelation between different techniques of measuring choice status, or the intercorrelations of the different sociometric criteria used as the basis of choice. In the final section the studies were concerned with experimental manipulation of the conditions under which the sociometric judgments were made.

Two important generalizations can be stated on the basis of the studies of the consistency of sociometric judgments that have been reported. The first is that it is possible for group members to make consistent judgments. The second is that there are factors that seem to be associated with the magnitude of the reliability of these judgments.

That reliable judgments can be made over a wide range of conditions has been demonstrated in a number of different ways. One series of investigations has shown that choices, when evaluated in terms of their source, are consistently made. This means that the choices a person gives on one occasion are likely to be duplicated on a second administration of the same criterion. Another way in which consistency has been demonstrated involves stability in terms of the number of choices received. This has been investigated both in terms of the consistency of choices received, with a choice status index based on a single test occasion, and the consistency between indices based on the number of choices received on two different occasions. The findings lead to the conclusion that the choice status characteristic of a person is rather constant over time.

The consistency issue has also been examined from the standpoint of the technique used in collecting the choice data. The technique may involve unlimited or fixed choice, the paired comparison procedures, or ranking and rating methods. Each of these has produced reliable data, but there is some evidence that when other factors that might influence the results are rendered inoperative the paired comparison method produces the most reliable choices.

Various criteria have also been intercorrelated to determine the extent of agreement between them as the basis for judging the consistency of choice responses with the finding that as long as the basis for choice is positive or involves a positive attribute consistency of judgments seems to be the rule.

Finally, two experimental studies that manipulated the conditions under which choices were given have been reported. These studies, which present the most rigorous analysis of reliability that has yet been made, agree in showing that when factors that could produce spurious agreement between the two sets of sociometric judgments are systematically excluded a significant relationship between independent assessments of the same person's performance on different occasions remains.

The second general conclusion is that certain factors seem to be associated with the magnitude of the consistency of sociometric judgments that is obtained. While not all these factors have been subjected to critical experimental analysis, enough evidence concerning these relationships is available to justify their presentation in a series of testable hypotheses. These are listed below.

HYPOTHESES

1. The longer the time interval between test and retest the less the consistency of sociometric judgments.

2. The closer the age of the subjects to adulthood the more the test-retest consistency of sociometric judgments.

3. The longer the subjects have known one another prior to the first test the greater the consistency in sociometric judgments between test and retest.

4. The more relevant the criterion of choice by which judgments are made to the activity of the group the greater the consistency of sociometric responses between test occasions.

5. The larger the number of discriminations required by the techniques of choosing the greater the consistency of sociometric judgments between test and retest.

6. The larger the group from which choices are made the greater the consistency in sociometric judgments between test occasions.

7. The larger the number of discriminations elicited by the measurement technique the greater the correlation between the measures derived from those techniques on a single occasion.

8. Where strength of choice preference is indicated by the ordering of choices the stronger the choice the less the change in choices given between test occasions.

9. The greater the similarity of criteria of choosing in terms of social-psychological considerations the larger the correlations between them.

These hypotheses need to be subjected to further empirical investigation in order to establish more clearly the conditions under which they are valid. In addition, experiments are needed to identify other factors that may be critical with regard to reliability of sociometric data even though studies reported to date have not identified them.

REFERENCES

1. Austin, Mary C., & Thompson, G. G. Children's friendships: A study of the bases on which children select and reject their best friends. *J. educ. Psychol.,* 1948, 39, 101-116.

2. Ausubel, D. P., Schiff, H. M., & Gasser, E. B. A preliminary study of developmental trends in sociempathy; Accuracy of perception of own and others' sociometric status. *Child. Develpm.,* 1952, 23, 111-128.

3. Barker, R. G. The social interrelations of strangers and acquaintances. SOCIOMETRY, 1942, 5, 169-179.

4. Bass, B. M., & White, O. L., Jr. Validity of leaderless group discussion observer's descriptive and evaluative ratings for the assessment of personality and leadership status. *Amer. Psychologist,* 1950, 5, 311-312.

5. Bates, A. P. Some sociometric aspects of social ranking in a small face-to-face group. SOCIOMETRY, 1952, 15, 330-341.

6. Bell, G. B., & French, R. L. Consistency of individual leadership position on small groups of varying membership. *J. abnorm. soc. Psychol.,* 1950, 45, 764-767.

7. Blake, R., Mouton, Jane, & Fruchter, B. The reliability of interpersonal judgments made on the basis of short-term interaction in three-man groups. *J. abnorm. soc. Psychol.,* 1954, 49, 573-578

8. Bonney, M. E. The constancy of sociometric scores and their relationship to teacher judgments of social success and to personality self ratings. SOCIOMETRY, 1943, 6, 409-424.

9. Bonney, M. E. The relative stability of social, intellectual, and academic status in grades II to IV, and the interrelationships between these various forms of growth. *J. educ. Psychol.,* 1943, 34, 88-102.

10. Bronfenbrenner, U. A constant frame of reference for sociometric research: Part II. Experiment and inference. SOCIOMETRY, 1944, 7, 40-75.

11. Byrd, E. A study of validity and constancy of choices in a sociometric test. SOCIOMETRY, 1951, 14, 175-181.

12. Chowdhry, Kamla, & Newcomb, T. M. The relative abilities of leaders and non-leaders to estimate opinions of their own groups. *J. abnorm. soc. Psychol.,* 1952, 47, 51-57.

13. Criswell, Jean H. Social structure revealed in a sociometric test. SOCIOMETRY, 1939, 2, 69-75.

14. Damrin, Dora E. Family size and sibling age, sex, and position as related to certain aspects of adjustment. *J. soc. Psychol.,* 1949, 29, 93-102.

15. Danielsson, B. Some friendship and repulsion patterns among Jibaro Indians. SOCIOMETRY, 1949, 12, 83-105.

16. Eng, Erling, & French, R. L. The determination of sociometric status. SOCIOMETRY, 1948, 11, 368-371.

17. French, R. L. Sociometric status and individual adjustment among naval recruits. *J. abnorm. soc. Psychol.,* 1951, 46, 64-72.

18. Gibb, C. A. The sociometry of leadership in temporary groups. SOCIOMETRY, 1950, 13, 226-243.

19. Grossman, Beverly, & Wrighter, Joyce. The relationship between selection-rejection and intelligence, social status, and personality amongst sixth grade children. SOCIOMETRY, 1948, 11, 346-355.

20. Hackman, R. C., & Moon, R. G., Jr. Are leaders and followers identified by similar criteria? *Amer. Psychologist,* 1951, 5, 312.

21. Heinicke, C., & Bales, R. F. Developmental trends in the stature of small groups. SOCIOMETRY, 1953, 16, 7-38.

22. Hemphill, J. K., & Sechrest, L. A. A comparison of three criteria of air crew effectiveness in combat over Korea. *Amer. Psychologist,* 1952, 7, 391.

23. Holzberg, J. D., Posner, Rita. The relationship of extrapunitiveness on the Rosenweig Picture-frustration study to aggression in overt behavior and fantasy. *Amer. J. Orthopsychiat.,* 1951, 21, 767-779.

24. Horowitz, M. W., Lyons, J., & Perlmutter, H. V. Induction of forces in discussion group. *Hum. Relat.,* 1951, 4, 57-76.

25. Horrocks, H. E., & Thompson, G. G. A study of the friendship fluctuations of rural boys and girls. *J. genet. Psychol.,* 1946, 69, 189-198.

26. Hunt, J. McV., & Solomon, R. L. The stability and some correlates of group status in a summer camp group of young boys. *Amer. J. Psychol.,* 1942, 55, 33-45.

27. Jennings, Helen H. *Leadership and Isolation.* (2nd ed.), New York: Longmans, Green, 1950.

28. Katz, L., & Powell, J. H. A proposed index of the conformity of one sociometric measurement to another. *Psychometrika,* 1953, 18, 249-256.

29. Lippitt, Rosemary. Popularity among preschool children. *Child. Develpm.,* 1941, 12, 305-332.

30. McIntyre, C. H. Acceptance by others and its relation to acceptance of self and others. *J. abnorm. soc. Psychol.,* 1952, 47, 624-625.

31. McKinney, J. C. An educational application of a two-dimensional sociometric test. SOCIOMETRY, 1948, 11, 356-367.

32. Maucorps, P. H. A sociometric inquiry in the French army. SOCIOMETRY, 1949, 12, 46-82.

33. Murray, H. The sociometric stability of personal relations among retarded children. SOCIOMETRY, 1953, 16, 113-141.

34. Moreno, J. L. *Who Shall Survive?* (2nd ed.), Beacon, New York: Beacon House, 1953.

35. Northway, Mary L. Social relationships among preschool children: Abstracts and interpretations of three studies. SOCIOMETRY, 1943, 6, 429-433.

36. Northway, Mary L., Frankel, Esther B., & Potashin, Reva. Personality and sociometric status. *Sociometry Monogr.,* 1947, No. 11.

37. Popinsky, Pauline N. The meaning of "validity" and "reliability" as applied to sociometric tests. *Educ. Psychol. Measmt.*, 1949, 9, 39-49.

38. Ricciuti, H. N., & French, J. W. Analysis of ratings of leadership potential at the U. S. Naval Academy. *Amer. Psychologist*, 1951, 6, 392.

39. Scandrette, O. C. Friendship in junior high 7th graders. *Clearing House*, 1951, 25, 364-366.

40. Seeman, M. A situational approach to intra-group Negro attitudes. SOCIOMETRY, 1946, 9, 199-206.

41. Singer, A. Certain aspects of personality and their relation to certain group modes, and constancy of friendship choices. *J. educ. Res.*, 1951, 45, 33-42.

42. Smucker, O. Near-sociometric analysis as a basis for guidance. SOCIOMETRY, 1949, 12, 326-340.

43. Taylor, E. A. Some factors relating to social acceptance in eight-grade classrooms. *J. educ. Psychol.*, 1952, 43, 257-272.

44. Taylor, F. K. The patterns of friendliness and dominance in a therapeutic group. *J. ment. Sci.* 1950, 96, 407-425.

45. Taylor, F. K. Quantitative evaluation of psycho-social phenomena in small groups. *J. ment. Sci.*, 1951, 97, 690-717.

46. Wardlow, Mary E., & Greene, J. E. An exploratory sociometric study of peer status among adolescent girls. SOCIOMETRY, 1952, 15, 311-316.

47. Wherry, R. J., & Fryer, D. H. Buddy ratings: Popularity contest or leadership criteria? SOCIOMETRY, 1949, 12, 179-190.

48. Williams, S. B., & Leavitt, H. J. Group opinion as a prediction of military leadership. *J. consult. Psychol.*, 1947, 11, 283-291.

49. Witryol, S. L., & Thompson, G. G. An experimental comparison of the stability of social acceptability scores obtained with the partial-rank-order and the paired-comparison scales. *J. educ. Psychol.*, 1953, 44, 20-30.

50. Young, L. L. Sociometric and related techniques for appraising social status in an elementary school. SOCIOMETRY, 1947, 10, 168-177.

51. Zeleny, L. D. Sociometry in the classroom. SOCIOMETRY, 1940, 3, 102-104.

52. Zeleny, L. D. Sociometry of morals. *Am. Soc. Rev.*, 1939, 4, 799-808.

53. Zeleny, L. D. Status, its measurement and control in education. SOCIOMETRY, 1941, 4, 193-204.

THE VALIDITY OF SOCIOMETRIC RESPONSES

By Jane Srygley Mouton, Robert R. Blake and Benjamin Fruchter

Sociometric responses have been studied to determine their relationship with variables that are classifiable as performance criteria. Results thus far obtained suggest that the sociometric type score may have considerable value as a basis for predicting a variety of criteria that evaluate performance. Investigations dealing with the validity of sociometric responses, involving studies conducted within the industrial setting, in military organizations, and in educational situations, including summer camps, are summarized in the present paper.

Types of Investigations Summarized

Some of the investigations to be presented were conducted under field conditions with no effort made to control sources of variance that would result in spurious relationships between the variables under examination. Others were designed specifically to evaluate the degree of relationship between sociometric responses and criterion measures under specifiable conditions. Techniques of data analysis range from interpretive judgments unsupported by tests of significance concerning the validity of sociometric responses to the use of detailed statistical tests for determining the relationship between the variables under investigation.

Studies summarized in this report are of two types. They include validation for distributions of sociometric choices received by individuals and distributions of sociometric choices received by groups. Investigations were included if the criterion measure used for validation purposes was based on a behavioral or performance measure or on observers' ratings of behavior where such judgments could be considered as independent of the sociometric test responses. Such criterion variables as personality test data, intelligence test scores, or socio-economic status, age, or sex are excluded. Also excluded are reports analyzing perceptual judgments as contrasted with direct sociometric choices.

Relationships between Sociometric Responses Received by Individuals and Performance Criteria

Studies based on the distribution of choices received by individuals are presented in Table 1. The situations in which the investigations were conducted serve as the basis for subgroupings. The first section reports industrial studies. Military studies are presented in the second. The third includes studies in educational situations and summer camps.

Several aspects of each study are reported in the summaries presented in Table 1. The first column indicates the name of the investigator and the year the study was reported. The next two divisions provide descriptions of subjects used and the conditions of data collection. The fourth column describes the basis for the sociometric choice. The fifth category contains information about the performance measure employed. The final column presents the obtained results. A brief statement of conclusions drawn by the investigator also is presented in the last column.

STUDIES WITHIN INDUSTRY

Prediction of performance within the industrial situation from sociometric responses is presented in the first section of Table 1. The studies are consistent in reporting that positive sociometric criteria choices received by individuals are correlated with effectiveness in performance on external criterion measures.

The number of choices received has been studied from two points of view. One concerns the validity of choices for work partners when the distributions of choices received is directly correlated with the performance criterion. Studies such as those by Springer (35) and Van Zelst (37) are examples of investigations conducted in this way. Both report that ratings by coworkers for desirability as work partners and other job related activities correlate with positive attitudes toward work and with quality and quantity of performance on the job. Consistent with these results is the reported finding that accident proneness is inversely correlated with choices received (34). The latter finding is confirmed in two investigations in nonindustrial situations (12, 42).

Choices received have been employed for combining partners into work units whose performance efficiency is then evaluated. Van Zelst (38, 39) has shown that after regrouping construction workers on the basis of a sociometric criterion, construction costs for work done by these workers decreased as compared with a control group in which the pairings were made on other than sociometric considerations. Studies (31, 36) relating production to sociometric distributions that have been conducted in the industrial situation also are reported in Table 2.

TABLE 1

EVALUATION OF THE RELATION BETWEEN SOCIOMETRIC RESPONSES RECEIVED BY INDIVIDUALS AND A
VARIETY OF INDIVIDUAL PERFORMANCE MEASURES

Section 1: Studies in Industry

Investigator	Subjects	Test Conditions	Sociometric Criteria	Performance Criteria	Results and Conclusions
Van-Zelst (1952) (38)	2 work groups of 38 carpenters & 36 brick-layers.	Checks made for stability & re-grouping of teams. Teams which were mutual 1st choices made no changes; 2nd—1 change; 3rd—4 voluntary changes and 6 to incorporate new workers. Worked together 5 months on the job.	Listing of 3 choices for teammates in the 2-man work-teams which were then joined into 4-man groups.	Cost of house construction index; engineers' estimates; monthly turnover records; all compared with a previous 9-month period.	After voluntary re-grouping, a superior level of out-put. Drop in rate of turnover, 5% savings in total production.
Springer (1953) (35)	100 male candidates for leadman in North American Aviation.	Rated by 3 co-workers who were not candidates for lead-man.	5-point near-sociometric scale on job performance and knowledge co-operation, ability to train others, and suitability for promotion to leadman.	2 supervisors rated each candidate for same variables as used by co-workers.	Relationship between ratings of each candidate by 1 supervisor and 1 co-worker (these ratings chosen at random from those available). job knowledge 15 job performance quality .25* quantity .33* cooperation .33*

TABLE 1 (*continued*)

Investigator	Subjects	Test Conditions	Sociometric Criteria	Performance Criteria	Results and Conclusions
					fitness for pro-motion .39* Supervisors' ratings were more conservative and more reliable than co-workers. Correlations with asterisks are significant.
Van Zelst (1952) (39)	4 work groups. 2 of carpenters (20, 19), 2 of bricklayers (16, 16).	One group with a group of carpenters and brick-layers was a con-trol; experimental group re-grouped by choice. The groups had been previously equated; covered a 3-month period.	Experimental groups chose work partner.	Job satisfaction, turnover rate, index of labor cost, index of materials cost.	Experimental group was su-perior on all 4 criteria. Turn-over rate very low (critical ratio 14.65). Financial savings such that every 29th house was "free," rela-tive to cost of construction by control group.
Van Zelst (1951) (37)	60 carpenters & bricklayers in 4 groups.	5-point paper-pencil scale, filled in anony-mously.	Rating co-workers on desirability as work-partners; like & dislike.	Kerr *Tear Ballot for Industry*.	Popular workers were satis-fied with jobs, more secure, better attitude toward management and co-workers; more confidence in manage-ment and in supervisors.

TABLE 1 (*continued*)
Section 2: Military Studies

Investigator	Subjects	Test Conditions	Sociometric Criteria	Performance Criteria	Results and Conclusions
Halpin (1954) (18)	353 aircrew members in 52 B-29 crews.	Tested at MacDill AFB in 1950, 33 retested in Japan in 1951. "Forming new crew" question given to 27 crews.	Revised form of Hemphill & Coon's Leader Behavior Description Questionnaire. Scores: Consideration and Initiating Structure-interaction. Crews asked with whom they'd like to form a new crew. Satisfaction of each crew with its Commander computed.	Rating of performance by a squadron & wing commander.	Both in training and combat a trend toward negative correlation between superiors' ratings & the Consideration scores, and positive correlation between these ratings and the Initiating-Structure scores. Crew Satisfaction index was the reverse; correlated positively with Consideration and negatively with Initiating Structure.
Hollander (1954) (22)	9 sections of cadets at Naval Pre-Flight School N = 268.	After 3 months of training.	Nominate 3 cadets as *best* & *least* qualified for hypothetical student commander. A leadership score for each was derived.	Officer-like qualities (e.g., military bearing).	Officer-like qualities correlated with leadership scores +.55; with authoritarian r —.06
Hoffman & Rohrer (1954) (21)	Marines being screened at OCS. Group	Each group had 6 platoons.	Group I wrote a descriptive paragraph about 1st 5 and last	Platoon standing given each member by platoon officer.	Rho coefficient between Group II scores & criterion of .84. Scale then used on Groups III

TABLE 1 (*continued*)

Investigator	Subjects	Test Conditions	Sociometric Criteria	Performance Criteria	Results and Conclusions
(19)	I-518 (1951), Group II-172 (1952), Group III-142 (late 1952), Group IV-145 (early 1953) in platoons of about 45.		5 choices for good officers. From these a 4-point scale drawn up, refined & keyed after testing on Group II, then validated on Groups III and IV.		& IV with following results: Platoon N Rho A 47 .88 B 49 .78 C 46 .84 D 49 .84 E 49 .90 F 47 .85
Rigby, Hoffman, Rohrer, Wilkins (1953) (29)	145 Marine Corps enlisted men going through a screening course.	Two criteria given at end of week for each of 3 weeks. Third given only once.	Peer rankings of potential affectiveness as officers. Nomination of peers for 17 social and military tasks. Peer Evaluation Scale.	Rank order of members representing pooled judgments of Marine Corps assessment staff.	The three sociometric measures highly related to each other and to the criterion.
Goodacre (1951) (14)	12 6-man squads in the Army.	6-man groups given tests before going into field to do a military problem.	Choice of buddies in social, garrison and tactical situations.	Success in 12 field problems.	Rho Field score & Garrison .62 Field score & Social .78 Field score & Tactical .75 Field score & Group Cohesion .77
Hemphill & Sechrest	94 B-29 aircrews in com-	Testing done in the Pacific com-	Make up air crew from the squadrons by se-	Average circular error bombing	Correlations between sociometric nominations and

TABLE 1 (*continued*)

Investigator	Subjects	Test Conditions	Sociometric Criteria	Performance Criteria	Results and Conclusions
(1952) (20)	bat.	bat area.	lecting crew members for each position. "On-crew," vs. "off-crew" index computed for each man.	data from combat missions were obtained from official records.	bombing accuracy, .36
Zeleny (1947) (42)	48 cadet observers in AF flying school.	5 choices, 5 rejections	Would you like to fly in a team with the other cadets?	Success as cadets avoiding of accidents.	High status cadets usually chosen as flight leaders. High status cadets showed high flying ability. Low status cadets had more crashes.
Williams & Leavitt (1947) (41)	1,193 Marine Corps Officer Candidates. 240 OCS student and 100 combat platoon leaders in experiment.	Judgments by platoons made, at end of 2 and 5 weeks of OCS. Nominate 5 best & 1 worst in platoon.	All-round ability as a combat officer. Personal traits, desirability as a roommate, sense of humor, fairness in making military court decisions, leadership in an emergency.	OCS pass-fail. Ratings of combat proficiency by superiors immediately following military campaign.	Sociometric judgments after 2 weeks of OCS correlated .33 with pass-fail (N = 240), .47 with combat ratings (N = 100). Sociometric judgments after 5 weeks of OCS correlated .40 with pass-fail (N = 1193, .43 with combat rating (N = 100).
Wherry & Fryer (1949) (40)	2 groups of 82 & 52 officer candidates.	Nomination at end of 1 month of OCS.	Nominations for most and least desirable as officers.	Retention in OCS for 2 months. Academic grades, graduation.	Correlation of nominations with retention in OCS at the end of the 2nd month, .70; with graduation, .49.
Dugan (1953)	167 crew-members of	1 peer rating in training, 1 while	Peer rating.	In training: proficiency tests,	Highest correlations between proficiency scores in training

TABLE 1 (*continued*)

Investigator	Subjects	Test Conditions	Sociometric Criteria	Performance Criteria	Results and Conclusions
(7)	29 B-29 air-crews.	in combat.		ratings of in-structors and flight checks. In combat; ratings from superiors.	and peer ratings of proficiency in combat.
French (1951) (11)	16 companies of Naval Re-cruits. 42-45 men in each. N = 860.	Data collected from 4 companies at the end of 1st and 10th weeks; 4 others at end of 2nd and 10th weeks; 4 others at end of 5th and 10th weeks; 4 others at end of 10th week only. Length of course, ten weeks.	Nominations for man to go on liberty with; to volunteer with for a tough and danger-ous assignment; nominations for job of acting chief petty officer.	Sick bay attendance of men and number of disciplinary offenses.	Status in company negatively and significantly related to sick bay attendance and dis-ciplinary offenses. Sick bay attenders less acceptable as liberty companions, but equally acceptable as leaders. Disciplinary offenders less acceptable in all situations, but not consistently as mis-sion companions and leaders. Correlations with sick bay attendance appear during 1st week of training; with disci-plinary offenses after 2nd week.
Izard & Rosenberg (1954) (24)	168 Naval Cadets in 1 group, 332 in another.	Test 1 to Group I, 2 to Group II.	Long form, 420-item forced-choice personality test scored for leader-ship. Short form, 106 items.	Aptitude-for-Serv-ice ratings.	Correlation between test and criterion: Group I .26 Group II .28

TABLE 1 (continued)

Section 3: Studies in Educational Situations

Investigator	Subjects	Test Conditions	Sociometric Criteria	Performance Criteria	Results and Conclusions

Carter & Nixon (1949) (6)	100 boys from 2 high schools.	Questionnaire sent to each boy after he had worked at 3 tasks with a boy he didn't know. He was to answer anonymously & return his nominations.	Which 5 of the 50 boys from your school would you pick as a leader in an intellectual, a clerical, and a mechanical situation?	Work score on tasks done in pairs as rated by 2 observers; rating by school supervisors. Score on activities done in high school, i.e., clubs, etc.	Generally low correlation between criteria. Leadership in intellectual and clerical tasks tend to be associated with each other more than leadership in mechanical tasks. Correlation of leadership scores & other criteria:
					
					Supervisor's ratings:
					
					       1 School 2
					Intellectual .53 .43
					Clerical .66 .56
					Mechanical .51 .68
					
					    Activity score
					       1 School 2
					Intellectual .50 .29
					Clerical .60 .44
					Mechanical .51 .65

Bass & White (1950) (1)	87 members of a college fraternity.	Rating done on ballots—high middle, and low.	7 items. Selecting who runs things in the fraternity. Whom would you select to address an audience, etc.?	47 members who participated in "leaderless group discussions," 2 observers rated each of 8 in a group as	Sociometric test and observers' choices correlated between .25 and .60 (rho).

TABLE 1 (*continued*)

Investigator	Subjects	Test Conditions	Sociometric Criteria	Performance Criteria	Results and Conclusions
Gibb (1950) (13)	10 groups of college students, 20 groups from OCS at Lackland AFB.	Each group met for 3 3-hour sessions. Questions given during and at end of sessions.	Sociotelic & psychotelic types of sociometric ratings of co-members. Each group chose a leader, then re-chose if they wished. Sociometric questions as to member preferred for a friend, etc.	to who led the discussion. Rated for leadership by 2 non-participant observers.	Correlation between psychotelic & sociotelic .70; between leadership ratings and sociometric .45; between leadership ratings & psychotelic .42. Sociotelic group more inclusive than psychotelic. Leadership, i.e, influencing behavior, cannot be measured by sociometric tests, only sociotelic or psychotelic criteria.
Lippitt, Polansky & Rosen (1952) (25)	64 boys, 40 girls—1948. Lower socio-economic background. Disturbed children, 63 boys & 65 girls —1950 Middle class, not disturbed. All in summer camps.	1st and last weeks of 4-week camp session. Data collected by picture-ranking technique.	1st study a composite study of attributed power. 2nd study "Who has influence?" Ranking technique by cabins of 8 members.	Frequency of successful influence attempts and the frequency of contagion initiation observed & coded by adults.	Real consensus in each group on who ranks where. 1948 study average Population N rho M-camp 64 .52 8 groups Boys w-camp 40 .71 8 groups Girls

TABLE 1 (*continued*)

Investigator	Subjects	Test Conditions	Sociometric Criteria	Performance Criteria	Results and Conclusions
Polansky, Lippitt & Redl (1950) (27)	8 boys & 8 girl groups in 2 camps for low socio-economic disturbed children 11-15 years in age.	Test by personal interview with each.	Sociometric ratings by each of degrees of liking, prestige of the others.	Observers watched groups to determine influencing behavior, status indicators, & incidents of contagion. The camp counsellors rated children as to: Adult relatedness group relatedness impulsiveness group belonging-ness need feeling of accept-ance by group	Relationship of Prestige to Observed influence: Contagion Influence Frequency of Successful Influences Influence Attempts Aver-age Rho .61 .55 .49
Rosen (1953) (32)	16 cabin groups of pre- and young adoles-cent boys in 2 4-week camps. 1 group of 63 assumed mal-adjusted due to agency refer-rals, other 65 adjusted.	Individual inter-views.	Rank cabin members, including selves, on "who is best at get-ting the others to do what he wants them to do."	2 research teams observe influence behavior daily.	Better adjusted boys more perceptive than the others about their own and others behavior have greater power attributed to them. Are actu-ally observed to be rela-tively more successful in in-fluencing others.

TABLE 1 (*continued*)

Investigator	Subjects	Test Conditions	Sociometric Criteria	Performance Criteria	Results and Conclusions
Hunt & Solomon (1942) (23)	2 groups of boys, age 5-8, 23 in one group, 22 in the other. High middle class back-grounds. 8 weeks at camp.	Sleeping & seating arrangements made 1st day, in-terviews repeated each week.	Sleeping & seating choices; interviews on whom each liked best.	Ratings by camp counsellors on personal traits; generosity, physical attrac-tiveness, ordered activity, obedience to counsellors, lack of egocentricity.	Frequency of altering choices of best liked declines like a trial & error curve. All personal traits rated except obedience to counsellors were significant. Prestige slightly correlated with group status.
Lippitt (1941) (26)	45 children in 3 groups. Pre-school age.	Testing done in school after children were acquainted with investigator, 5 retested after 6 weeks	Each child asked to cite preference for one of two names in a pair. Every name paired with every other.	Teacher ratings of child's popularity. A battery of other tests.	Correlation of pupil prefer-ence & teacher rating for the 3 groups: $.23\pm.17$, $.54\pm.17$, and $-.07\pm.14$. Child ranking of popularity with coöperation: $.44\pm.15$; $.65\pm.14$; $.24\pm.14$. Popularity with peers unre-lated to constructive-de-structive situation, gross mo-tor items, amount of direc-tion and compliance, amount of interaction. Low posi-tive correlation with paper cutting.
Bonney & Powell	10 sociometri-cally ranked	As many choices as desired.	Choices for work and play.	Observation of be-havior and classifi-	Only 5 of the 25 behavior categories showed signifi-

TABLE 1 (*continued*)

Investigator	Subjects	Test Conditions	Sociometric Criteria	Performance Criteria	Results and Conclusions
(1953) (4)	high & 10 socio-metrically ranked low children from a group of 42, first grade.			cation into behavior categories in 7 10-min-ute and 11-min-ute periods over 4 months.	cant difference between the 2 groups. Highly acceptable more likely to be conforming in class, smile more often, coöperate in voluntary group participation, make more voluntary contributions to the group, play alone less frequently. They also exhibit unfavorable behavior categories, too.
Fuller & Baune (1951) (12)	11 boys & 11 girls in 2nd and then 3rd grades. Mean I.Q. 133, 7-8 years. Has 5 times as many accidents as average child.	Oral by individual.	Choose 2 to have lunch with, go to movies with, work in class with.	First aid referrals. H.O.W. Behavior rating scales. Fuller Affectivity Interview Blank.	Less popular children receive more injuries than more popular & larger proportion of social injuries, i.e., those involving other children. Less popular score lower on the Fuller Affectivity and higher on the H-O-W Behavior scale. More popular have fewer problem tendencies than social isolates.
Polansky, Lippitt & Redl	104 children in summer camps, 1 of	Interview, sorting of subjects' pic-tures into classi-	Near sociometric choices, prestige choices. Near or	Direct observation of amount of time spent together, of	Popularity not an index of group status. Little correspondence found between

TABLE 1 (*continued*)

Investigator	Subjects	Test Conditions	Sociometric Criteria	Performance Criteria	Results and Conclusions
(1950) (28)	boys, 1 of girls, 10-14 years.	fied boxes. Test given twice, end of 1st and 3rd weeks.	liking choices made for own group & the whole camp.	influence. Rankings by counsellors— every 4 days.	whom a child says he likes to be with and whom he is with.
Byrd (1951) (5)	2 7th grade pupils.	Children free to choose as many others for play as they wished. Choices made privately.	Situation I—children to choose persons they wished for a play. Situation III—1 week after play was given, repeat as in 1.	Situation II—4 days after I, children did actually choose persons for plays and presented them.	Rho's on degree of constancy from one situation to another Situation I & II .76±.09 Situation II & II .80±.08 Situation I & III .89±.04
Greenblatt (1953-54) (15)	27th grade classes.	Test given 1949 and 1950.	Sociometric test unspecified.	Mental health tests; participation at 3 school dances. 2 observers.	Girls with high mental health and high sociometric scores are found less often in rôle of non-participant at dances than girls of low mental health and sociometric scores. Findings for boys inconclusive.
Bock (1952) (3)	16 in 9th grade physical science class, 6 girls 10 boys.	Students worked on a problem in pairs. Observer noted the amount of interaction. Class could group freely.	Choose 3 in the class with whom you prefer to work.	Amount of interaction, timed by an observer each minute.	Much interaction between mutual choices but not all. Also secondary interaction. Primary or extensive interaction between unreciprocated choices, to some extent.

375

TABLE 1 (*continued*)

Investigator	Subjects	Test Conditions	Sociometric Criteria	Performance Criteria	Results and Conclusions
Bates (1952) (2)	6 groups of 8 members, college students in a Social Disorganization class. Largely unacquainted. 2 sessions a week for 8 weeks.	Test given at end of 3rd, 10th & 15th sessions & at end of experiment.	List the S's in order as to who contributes most to carrying out task. Pick 3 who most lived up to each of 9 norms selected from group questionnaires & tape recordings, also 3 who least lived up to norms.	Observers recorded amount and content of interaction.	Correlation between 3rd sociometric ranking: and communications sent .85 and communications received .91 and total communication .92 Correlations of sociometric rankings & those named as leaders .83
Schachter (1951) (33)	4 types of clubs, 8 of each type, 5-7 members. 3 Ss in each group acted as deviate, model, and slider. Clubs organized by experimenter.	After session of the clubs in which instructed Ss acted their part, ranking and nominating to committees took place.	Assignment of group members to committees which were in order of desirability. Executive, Steering, and Correspondence. Also members ranked each other as to desirability as a club member.	Number and time of communications addressed to instructed Ss during club sessions. Committees elected by the members.	Deviate strongly rejected in sociometric choices. With cohesiveness constant, rejection greater in relevant than irrelevant groups. With relevance constant, rejection greater in cohesive groups. Communications to deviate increase, except by strong rejectors; to model are few and constant, to slider decrease during the meeting.

TABLE 1 (*continued*)

Investigator	Subjects	Test Conditions	Sociometric Criteria	Performance Criteria	Results and Conclusions
Speroff & Kerr (1952) (34)	44 Negro & 46 Spanish-speaking manual workers in a steel mill. In work groups of 6 each.	Men knew each other well. Choices made within racial groups.	With whom would you like to work most? Least?	Number of accidents during 3 years previous.	Index of desirability (Likes squared minus number of dislikes squared) was correlated with the number of accidents. Correlation of —.54 between interpersonal desirability index and number of accidents. Least desirable workers have more accidents.
Gullahorn (1952) (17)	12 clerical workers in an office of 37.	No limit to number; 3 usually chosen as maximum. One hour interview with each worker.	Choice for best friend.	Amount of direct interaction as recorded by an observer over a 2-week period.	Interaction most related to spatial distance & next most to friendship choices.

MILITARY STUDIES

Military studies are summarized in three ways in the second section of Table 1. The first group is concerned with the degree of correspondence between sociometric response distributions and superiors' ratings on variables such as leader behavior (18), military bearing (22), and officer potential (19, 29). Significant relationships between sociometric choices by peers and performance ratings given by platoon (19), squadron and wing officers (18) and other staff raters (29) are reported.

The second set relates sociometric responses to criterion performance measures used in evaluating Officer Candidate School students. Significant and positive relationships are reported between peer nominations given in training and the Officer Candidate School (40), in-training proficiency tests (7, 14), and flight checks (7). Other criteria such as flight accidents (42) and frequency of sick bay attendance and number of disciplinary offenses (11) have been found to be negatively related with number of choices received when the sociometric criterion measures a positive aspect of behavior. The relationship reported here is consistent with the finding relating sociometric choices to accident proneness in industry, as reported earlier in this paper (34).

A third set of military studies relates sociometric response distributions to a variety of performance measures other than those described above. Significant relationships between peer nominations during training, including Officer Candidate School training programs, and later performance, as determined by measures of combat effectiveness as reported (7, 20, 41). These studies suggest that measurements involving sociometric choices constitute useful indicators of future military proficiency. Number of choices received is associated positively with effectiveness in military activities. Choices are inversely associated with criterion variables that measure negative factors in military performance.

Studies in the Educational Situation

The final section in Table 1 summarizes investigations relating sociometric choices to performance in the educational situation. Training situations include the formal school system and other programs like summer camps and nursery schools.

The first studies in Section 3 are concerned with leadership behavior. Sociometric choices received on leadership items are related to observers' ratings of leadership behavior in group discussion and in other types of group tasks. Correlations between observers' evaluations and peer nominations of leaders, for example, range from .25 to .60 for group discussion activities (1, 13). On intellectual, clerical and mechanical work tasks, correlations between leadership ratings and both superior's ratings and an index of school activities range from .12 to .66, with intellectual and clerical tasks yielding higher correlations than are reported for leadership and performance in mechanical tasks (6).

Attributed influence, measured by near-sociometric scales, has been correlated with observers' ratings of successful influence attempts (26, 27, 32). Studies of children in camp situations report correlations ranging from .49 to .71 between status as determined by sociometric choice and observed success in influencing others. Popular children are more frequently imitated than are children who are less popular (26, 27).

The volume of sociometric responses received has been studied in connection with observers' ratings of behavioral characteristics exhibited under informal conditions involving play. Positive correlations between friendship choice and characteristics such as coöperation, obedience, generosity, and conformity have been demonstrated (4, 23, 27). As in other settings, a positive sociometric choice also has been found to be inversely related with accident proneness in the school situation (12).

Volume of interaction also has been investigated as a criterion variable on the assumption that the frequency of contact between people constitute a positive dimension of social conduct. Four different studies report positive correlations between sociometric choices received and frequency of interaction (2, 3, 5, 15). Office girls have also been found to spend more time in interaction with those who receive a high number of friendship nominations (17). One study has failed to confirm this relationship (28), and another study, using communication as the index of interaction, has shown that under certain conditions frequency of interaction may be inversely correlated with choices for association (33).

RELATIONSHIP BETWEEN GROUP SOCIOMETRIC SCORES AND GROUP PERFORMANCE

The validity of sociometric responses can be assessed from a second point of view. Rather than validating the distribution of choices received by individuals against a criterion measure, the distribution of choices, received can be evaluated on a group or "team basis." The performance measures used for this purpose are criteria that discriminate between groups rather than individuals. Studies based on differences between groups rather than individuals are summarized in Table 2.

TABLE 2

EVALUATION OF THE RELATIONSHIP BETWEEN GROUP SOCIOMETRIC SCORES AND A VARIETY OF GROUP PERFORMANCE MEASURES

Investigator	Subjects	Test Conditions	Sociometric Criteria	Performance Criteria	Results and Conclusions
Strupp & Hausman (1953) (36)	99 aircraft maintenance mechanics, 9 crews & supervisors.	Part of a larger testing program.	Nomination or rejection of fellows on 12 choice criteria.	Supervisors rated job performance. 3 management supervisors ranked crews on productivity.	Sociometric measures indicating attractiveness of crew and crew chief to members of crew correlated highly with productivity criterion.
Rock & Hay (1953) (31)	7 men selected from 40 applying for positions, on a job evaluation committee.	Two leaders chosen from others as being qualified to be good leaders.	Choose partner for various social & work purposes.	How committee works under leadership of each.	Committee working under predicted leaders evaluated twice as many jobs. Members participated more when acting as leaders. When a member was leader, his leadership was non-directive & group took over.
Roby (1952) (30)	90 11-man bomber crews.	Bomber crews in training at Randolph.	Sociometric rating.	Various performance measures to indicate effectiveness of sub-group performance.	High degree of personal liking is associated with superior performance of the crew as a whole.
Ziller (1953) (43)	94 10- & 11-man bomber crews in training.	Test given before problem solving; confidence ques-	Sociometric questionnaire on 3 measures of cohesiveness & crew integration;	Success in problem solving involving 5 possible approaches & 5	Crew attraction positively related to group problem-solving flexibility.

TABLE 2 (*continued*)

Investigator	Subjects	Test Conditions	Sociometric Criteria	Performance Criteria	Results and Conclusions
		tionnaire given after introduction to problem but before solving it.	questionnaire on group confidence.	degrees of flexibility. California F-Scale & "Social Rigidity or Conformity Scale" after problem solving.	
Fiedler (1954) (8)	53 B-29 crews.	Sociometric rating. Assumed Similarity Score by comparing predictions command or makes for his most & his least preferred coworker on sample personality test item.		Radar Bomb Scores.	Significant relation between AC's Assumed Similarity Score & Radar Bomb Scores only in crews having a certain sociometric structure, i.e., where AC and keymen mutually chose each other.
Greer, Galanter & Nordlie (1954) (16)	63 infantry squads of 9 men. Had worked together from 1 month to 2 years	Top and bottom 13 squads interviewed. During the interview, neither the interviewer nor the inter-	List squad according to how well you like them. Make a list of order in which everyone, including self, is liked by the group as a whole. Thus a de-	Effectiveness in solving a field problem set up & observed by superiors. 4 missions in the problem.	Effective squads significantly better at perceiving preference hierarchy than less effective ones.

TABLE 2 (*continued*)

Investigator	Subjects	Test Conditions	Sociometric Criteria	Performance Criteria	Results and Conclusions
		viewee knew from what category squad the member came.	rived preference hierarchy was made up from sociometric rating and each man's perception of it derived as a discrepency score.		
Fiedler (1954) (10)	25 Army tank crews, 5 men in crews.		Sociometric ratings Assumed Similarity Score of commander. (See Fiedler (8)).	Unspecified objective criteria.	Where commander and key-men mutually chose each other the commanders ASo correlated significantly with objective criteria as in the bomber crews.
Haythorn (1953) (19)	16 NROTC sophomores. Working in groups of 4, rotating so each worked with another only once.	At end of each of 5 sessions each ranked the group & members in it as to leadership desirability. Afterwards Cattell 16 Personality Factor Questionnaire given.	Select best & poorest leaders in the group.	Rating of workers & observers on group's success, morale, cooperation, productivity, cohesion, talkativeness, competitiveness, job-completion, motivation, friendliness, social interaction. While	Significant relationship between degree subjects were chosen by co-workers & extent group was rated high in morale, coöperation, cohesiveness, motivation, & interest in job-completion by co-workers.

TABLE 2 (*continued*)

Investigator	Subjects	Test Conditions	Sociometric Criteria	Performance Criteria	Results and Conclusions
				working on reasoning, mechanical assembly, discussion tasks.	
Fiedler (1954) (9)	22 3- and 4-man surveying teams.		60-statement questionnaire, 7-point scale, predicted how most & least cooperative worker would fill in questionnaire & other measures.	Ratings of survey teams by instructors.	Evidence suggests that the more effective surveying teams tend to be less congenial than relatively ineffective teams.
Fiedler, Hartmann & Rudin (1952) (10)	Members of 14 high school basketball teams.	Tested at beginning of season & a 2nd group of 7 good & 5 poor teams were tested at end of season.	With whom can you play best & least well? And other measures.	Proportion of games won used as criterion of team's effectiveness.	More effective basketball teams confer status on task-centered persons; less effective teams confer status on warm, relationship oriented individuals.

The attractiveness of a group to its members has been related to measures of the effectiveness of group performance. In industrial studies, productivity has been employed as a measure of group efficiency. Crew effectiveness is one basis for judging the adequacy of military performance. The studies reported show that the more attractive a group to its members the greater its efficiency. Personal liking within the crew (30, 43) and group attractiveness in the industrial situation (36) are associated with superior performance by the work team. Mutuality of choice within a crew also is related to its effectiveness (8). Results not consistent with this generalization have been presented in an investigation showing that less effective basketball and surveying teams are more congenial and have warmer interpersonal relations than do more effective ones.

The relationship between the rôle structure of a group and its efficiency is dealt with in one study in Table 2. When leaders chosen by sociometric procedures act as leaders, their groups are more efficient than when members, not seen as leaders, are assigned that rôle (31). This finding is similar to one reported earlier showing a positive relationship between sociometric choice for leaders and observers' ratings of effectiveness in leadership behavior (1, 13).

Measures of morale, coöperation, and cohesiveness have been employed to describe group characteristics. A relationship between ratings of co-workers for leadership desirability within the group and positive ratings on group variables such as morale has been reported (19). The conclusion is consistent with the findings reported above showing that work groups in which the teams are paired on a sociometric basis are more productive than are groups in which workers are paired by other than sociometric procedure (38, 39).

SUMMARY

Studies relating sociometric response distributions to variables classifiable as performance measures have been summarized in the present paper. While the reports included are of uneven quality, the consistency in the findings that have been reported by different investigators can be taken as evidence that the sociometric choice provides a valuable method of measuring personal and group characteristics. The sociometric distribution being validated and the criterion employed to assess performance have been based on either individual or group measures.

The validity of sociometric choices has been determined for both immediate and distant criteria. Number of choices received on positive sociometric criteria has been found to predict such performance criteria as productivity, combat effectiveness, training ability, and leadership. An inverse relation also has been confirmed in a number of studies that show number of choices received to be negatively correlated with aspects of behavior considered to be undesirable, including such variables as accident-proneness, sick bay attendance and frequency of disciplinary offenses. The finding for accident-proneness has been observed in industrial, military, and educational settings and for both children and adults. The results thus far reported indicate that sociometric choices merit more intensive analysis as a basis for predicting a variety of performance criteria than they have yet received.

REFERENCES

1. Bass, B. M. and O. L. White, Jr. Validity of leaderless group discussion observers' descriptive and evaluative ratings for the assessment of peronality and leadership status. *Amer. Psychol.,* 1950, 5, 311-312.

2. Bates, A. P. Some sociometric aspects of social ranking in a small face-to-face group. SOCIOMETRY, 1952, 15, 330-341.

3. Bock, R. D. A synthesis of time sampling and sociometric testing. *Ibid.,* 263-271.

4. Bonney, M. E. and J. Powell. Differences in social behavior between sociometrically high and sociometrically low children. *J. ed. Res.,* 1953, 46, 481-496.

5. Byrd, E. A study of validity and constancy of choices in a sociometric test. SOCIOMETRY, 1951, 14, 175-181.

6. Carter, L. F., and Mary Nixon. An investigation of the relationships between four criteria of leadership ability for three different tasks. *J. Psychol.,* 1949, 27, 245-261.

7. Dugan, R. D. Comparison of evaluation of B-29 crews in training and in combat. *Amer. Psychol.,* 1953, 8, 343-344.

8. Fiedler, F. E. Interpersonal perception and sociometric structure in prediction of small team effectiveness. *Ibid.,* 1954, 9, 365.

9. ————. Assumed similarity measures as predictors of team effectiveness. *J. abnorm. soc. Psychol.,* 1954, 49, 381-388.

10. ————, W. Hartmann, and S. A. Rudin. Social perception measures as predictors of effectiveness in basketball teams. *Amer. Psychol.,* 1952, 7, 313.

11. French, R. L. Sociometric status and individual adjustment among Naval recruits. *J. abnorm. soc. Psychol.,* 1951, 46, 64-72.

12. Fuller, E. M., and H. A. Baune. Injury-proneness and adjustment in a second grade. SOCIOMETRY, 1951, 14, 210-225.

13. Gibb, C. A. The sociometry of leadership in temporary groups. *Ibid.,* 1950, 13, 266-343.

14. Goodacre, D. M., III. The use of a sociometric test as a predictor of combat unit effectiveness. *Ibid.,* 1951, 14, 148-152.

15. Greenblatt, E. L. Two adidtional studies in the dynamics of school structure of class room seating and school dances. *J. ed. Res.,* 1953-54, 47, 261-270.

16. Greer, F. L., E. H. Galanter, and P. G. Nordlie. Interpersonal knowledge and individual and group effectiveness. *J. abnorm. soc. Psychol.,* 1954, 49, 411-414.

17. Gullahorn, J. T. Distance and friendship as factors in the gross interaction matrix. SOCIOMETRY, 1952, 15, 123-234.
18. Halpin, A. W. The leadership behavior and combat performance of airplane commanders. *J. abnorm. soc. Psychol.*, 1954, 49, 19-22.
19. Haythorn, W. The influence of individual members on the characteristics of small groups. *Ibid.*, 1953, 48, 276-284.
20. Hemphill, J. K. and L. Sechrest. A comparison of three criteria of air crew effectiveness in combat over Korea. *Amer. Psychol.*, 1952, 7, 391.
21. Hoffman, E. L. and J. H. Rohrer. An objective peer evaluation scale. *Ed. Psychol. Meas.*, 1954, 14, 332-341.
22. Hollander, E. P. Authoritarianism and leadership choice in a military setting. *J. abnorm. soc. Psychol.*, 1954, 49, 365-370.
23. Hunt, J. M., and R. L. Solomon. The stability and some correlates of group status in a summer-camp group of young boys. *Amer. J. Psychol.*, 1942, 55, 33-45.
24. Izard, C. E. and N. Rosenberg. Prediction of peer leadership ratings by forced choice test under varied conditions. *Amer. Psychol.*, 1954, 49, 397.
25. Lippitt, R., N. Polansky, and S. Rosen. The dynamics of power. *Human Relat.*, 1952, 5, 37-64.
26. Lippitt, Rosemary. Popularity among preschool children. *Child Develop.*, 12, 1941, 305-332.
27. Polansky, N., R. Lippitt, and F. Redl. An investigation of behavioral contagion in groups. *Ibid.*, 1950, 3, 319-348.
28. Polansky, N., R. Lippitt, and F. Redl. The use of near-sociometric data in research on group treatment process. SOCIOMETRY, 1950, 13, 39-62.
29. Rigby, M. K., E. L. Hoffman, J. H. Rohrer, and W. Wilkins. Three approaches to peer evaluation. *Amer. Psychol.*, 1953, 8, 421.
30. Roby, T. B. The influence of subgroup relationships on the performance of group and subgroup tasks. *Ibid.*, 1952, 7, 313-314.
31. Rock, M. L., and E. N. Hay. Investigation of the use of tests as a predictor of leadership and group effectiveness in a job evaluation situation. *J. soc. Psychol.*, 1953, 38, 109-119.
32. Rosen, S. Some perceptual and behavior components of social influence in small groups, as predicted by interpersonal adjustment in previous social environments. *Amer. Psychol.*, 1953, 8, 424.
33. Schachter, S. Deviation, rejection and communication. *J. abnorm. soc. Psychol.*, 1951, 46, 190-207.
34. Speroff, B., and W. Kerr. Steel mill "hot strip" accidents and interpersonal desirability values. *J. clin. Psychol.*, 1952, 8, 89-91.
35. Springer, Doris. Ratings of candidates for promotion by co-workers and supervisors. *J. app. Psychol.*, 1953, 37, 347-351.
36. Strupp, H. H. and H. J. Hausman. Some correlates of group productivity. *Amer. Psychol.*, 1953, 8, 443-444.
37. Van Zelst, R. H. Worker popularity and job satisfaction. *Personnel Psychol.*, 1951, 4, 405-412.
38. ———. Sociometrically selected work teams increase production. *Ibid.*, 1952, 5, 175-186.

39. ————. Validation of a sociometric regrouping procedure. *J. abnorm. soc. Psychol.*, 1952, 47, 299-301.
40. Wherry, R. J. and D. H. Fryer. Buddy ratings. popularity contest or leadership criteria? SOCIOMETRY, 1949, 12, 179-190.
41. Williams, S. B., and H. J. Leavitt. Group opinion as a predictor of military leadership. *J. consult. Psychol.*, 1947, 11, 283-291.
42. Zeleny, L. D. Selection of compatible flying partners. *Amer. J. Sociol.*, 1947, 52, 424-431.
43. Ziller, R. C. Leader-group rigidity and group cohesiveness; determinants of group problem-solving processes and concomitant affective group behavior. *Amer. Psychol.*, 1953, 8, 459-460.

ROLE PLAYING SKILL AND SOCIOMETRIC PEER STATUS

By Jane Srygley Mouton, Robert L. Bell, Jr. and Robert R. Blake*

In this experiment the hypothesis tested is that children of high peer status differ from those of low peer status in role playing ability, with the former having greater skill than the latter in enacting assigned roles in standardized role playing situations. Although peer status often has been regarded as directly and positively associated with role taking ability, there has been little previous experimental work on this problem (5, 6, 8, 9, 10). Validation of the hypothesis under systematic conditions would demonstrate that one of the correlates of sociometric position is the ability to portray social roles effectively in "as if" situations.

Experimental Design

The general plan was for three observers to evaluate the behavior of each of twenty-six negro preadolescent subjects who enacted three different role situations opposite the same adult collaborator. Since subjects, of whom 15 were boys and 11 girls, were all the students in the high sixth grade at the Blackshear Elementary School, Austin, Texas, the range of talent is inclusive of a class group and is only subject to whatever restrictions limit participation in school.

The Three Role Playing Situations

All subjects enacted three different scenes with the adult collaborator, a 21 year old male negro graduate student, who had no previous acquaintanceship with any of the children. For one role playing situation (mischievous student) a table and some chairs were in the room, but in the other two scenes both the subject and the collaborator took standing positions. Each subject entered the room alone. None had the opportunity of seeing any of the others enacting the situation. The subject was told the particular role to be enacted during that session, with each scene introduced by the adult collaborator through a standard statement designed to prompt the subject to begin his enactment of the situation. Throughout the enactment the collaborator made only such remarks as were necessary in order to re-

* Appreciation is expressed to Dr. Edgar F. Borgatta of the Russell Sage Foundation for suggestions given with respect to the interpretation of the findings of this study.

spond appropriately to the subject's role behavior. Five minutes were allowed for enacting a role. The child then returned to class, and the next child was brought to the role playing room and so on until all 26 children had been in the role playing situation once. The sequence was then repeated for each of the other two roles.

To minimize order effects the experimental design employed provided for the systematic counter-balancing of the three situations as shown in Table 1. For one third of the children the first enactment portrayed an

TABLE 1

ORDER OF ROLE PRESENTATION

Subject	First 1, 2, 3,	Second Observers 4, 5, 6	Third 7, 8, 9
1	Sad Friend	Angry Playmate	Mischievous Student
2	Sad Friend	Mischievous Student	Angry Playmate
3	Angry Playmate	Sad Friend	Mischievous Student
4	Angry Playmate	Mischievous Student	Sad Friend
5	Mischievous Student	Sad Friend	Angry Playmate
6	Mischievous Student	Angry Playmate	Sad Friend
.	.	.	.
.	.	.	.
.	.	.	.
26	Sad Friend	Mischievous Student	Angry Playmate

unhappy friend who is sad. For another third of the total group the second scene involved the sadness role, and for the remaining one third the last enactment concerned sadness. The two other role enactments were ordered in the same way so that each role preceded and followed the other roles an equivalent number of times.

Sad Friend. The first role, referred to as A, is that of a young elementary school student who is sad because he (she) has not been invited to a party given by his (her) best friend. The following instructions introduced role A:

"I would like for you to act out a little scene with me, like in a play or in the movies. Instead of giving you a lot of words to memorize, I want you to make up the words as we go along. Here is the way we will do it: You are to play the role of a person who is very sad because he (she) was not invited to a party given by his (her) best friend. I am an adult friend and I will start the scene by asking you why you are so sad. Then you will start playing your part. You may tell me all about how you feel about your friend for leaving you out. You may play the part in any way that you feel like. Do you understand?"

Angry Playmate. The second role, referred to as B, is that of a student who is extremely angry with a fellow playmate. The following instructions were given:

"I would like for you to act out a little scene with me, like in a play or in the movies. Instead of giving you a lot of words to memorize, I want you to make up the words to the play as we go along. Here is the way we will do it: You are to play the role of a person who is very angry with me. Think of me as a fellow playmate. I want you to come up to me and start arguing about why you are mad at me. You may argue with me about anything you feel like. Please forget that I am older than you and say anything to me that you would to anyone else your own age. I want you to be *so angry* that I will hardly be able to get a word in edgewise. Do you understand?"

If the subject hesitated instead of beginning an argument, the collaborator said:

"Hello, John. I saw Jack the other day and he said that you were very angry with me. Why? I can't remember having ever done anything to you."

Mischievous Student. The third role, role C, is that of a student who is called into the principal's office for being mischievous. The following instructions were used:

"I would like for you to act out a little scene with me, like in a play or in the movies. Instead of giving you a lot of words to memorize, I want you to make up the words to the play as we go along. Here is the way we will do it: You are to play the role of a person who has been sent to the principal's office for 'cutting up' in class. I will play the part of the principal. I will start by asking you what you were doing in class to cause the teacher to send you to the office. You may be sorry for what you did, you may be a smart alec, or you may act in any other way that you want. Do you understand?"

390

Rating Scales

The behavior elicited in each role playing enactment was evaluated on 10 seven-category rating scales comparable with those employed successfully in an earlier study (1). Each item assessed a significant personal, social, or situational characteristic to be observed in the role playing enactment. Emphasis in the selection of items was placed on evaluating characteristics of the performance as contrasted with assessing personality characteristics as such. The categories on each scale ranged from an extremely positive aspect of the behavior through neutral or moderate categories to an extremely negative aspect of the behavior. Scales with abbreviations are shown in Table 2.

TABLE 2

RATING SCALES USED IN EVALUATING THE ROLE PLAYING ENACTMENTS

Item	Abbreviation Used in Text
1. Rate the subject in terms of the extent to which he showed signs of being frustrated.	Frustration
2. Rate the subject in terms of the extent to which he seemed shy about playing the scene.	Shyness
3. Rate the subject in terms of the difficulty he had in expressing himself.	Difficulty
4. Rate the subject in terms of the clarity with which he expressed himself.	Clarity
5. Rate the subject in terms of the extent to which he showed interest in the task.	Interest
6. Rate the subject in terms of the extent to which he seemed anxious for the scene to end.	Anxiousness
7. Rate the subject in terms of how satisfied he seemed with the way he played the scene.	Satisfaction
8. Rate the subject to the extent to which he seemed hesitant (paused) in making up his mind to speak.	Hesitancy
9. Rate the subject in terms of the extent to which he wanted to give a good performance.	Good Performance
10. Rate the subject in terms of the extent to which he seemed effective in playing the role (in terms of how "real" he seemed in the role).	Effectiveness

Observers

Nine members of a Social Research Class at Huston-Tillotson College acted as observers. Prior to the experiment they were familiarized with the rating scales to be used but they had had no prior experience with role playing situations and were unacquainted with the children. To insure unbiased ratings they judged in complete independence of one another and were informed neither of the technical problems being investigated nor of the specific contents of the roles being enacted. As shown in Table 1, each observer rated the behavior of the same child in one role only. This arrangement resulted in each child being evaluated in three different roles and by three different observers for each role. Through employing this design, it is possible to eliminate systematically any bias that might arise if the same observer were to evaluate the performance of any child in two or more different roles.

Determination of Peer Status

Peer status was determined before the role playing situations were enacted. Students were told that the sociometric information was confidential and that it would in no way affect grades or class standings. The following positive and negative sociometric items were administered by the class instructor: (1) name the three persons in the class whom you like the most; (2) name the three persons in the class whom you like the least. The "liking" cirterion was selected for use on the assumption that the popular child is more adaptable in his peer relations and, therefore, more capable of flexibility in playing roles in a range of interpersonal situations. Two different indices of peer status were employed in conducting the analyses, one involving a simple frequency distribution of number of choices received and the other based on McGuire's formula for determining peer status (7).

RESULTS

Reliability of Scales

Inter-observer product-moment reliability coefficients were computed for each scale, for each role, and for each of the three pairs of observers. Average correlations also were computed by *z* transformation for the three observer pairs combined for each role as well as for the three roles taken together.

Eight of the ten rating scales yielded significant reliability coefficients for each of the combinations of raters and roles. The three scales with reliability coefficients above .80 are "showed signs of frustration," (1); "difficulty in expression," (3); and "effectiveness in playing the role," (10). Five additional significant scales, all with average coefficients above .60 are "seemed shy in playing the scene," (2); "degree of clarity in expressing himself," (4); "interest in the task," (5); "anxious for scene to end," (6); and "hesitancy in deciding to speak," (8). Two of the scales, "satisfaction with the scene," (7) and "desire to give a good performance," (9), are not significant at the 1 per cent level, though the latter scale is significant beyond the 5 per cent level of confidence.

Comparable results are obtained when reliability coefficients for each role are considered separately. Only the latter two items (7 and 9) failed to yield significant consistency between observers for each role evaluation. Similar results also are obtained in the comparison of raters. For the eight scales which have significant reliability on a combined rater and combined role basis, 70 of the 72 possible comparisons of ratings between observer pairs are significantly reliable beyond the 1 per cent level.

Conspicuous is the fact that the eight scales that yield a significant degree of reliability for any one role yield significant reliability coefficients on the two other roles as well and that the two which fail to approach significance are unsatisfactory for all three roles. Since no observer rated the same child in more than one role and since the order in which children played the various roles was systematically varied, so that no one role appeared more frequently at the beginning, in the middle or as the final role in the sequence than any other, the findings take on added significance. They indicate that when the sample represents an essentially unrestricted range of talent reliable judgments of role playing performance can be made even by observers with a minimum of psychological training.

Taken with the investigation by Stanton and Litwak (11), in which the reliability of judgments was determined in a different way than used here, both studies agree by demonstrating that role playing behavior is subject to reliable assessment under a range of conditions, with different types of judgments and with judges with different degrees of training. Borgatta and Bale's (3) evaluation of the reliability of role playing behavior also is consistent with the findings reported above.

Intercorrelation of Scales

With the exception of items 7 and 9, intercorrelations between rating scales are sufficiently high to suggest that the different scales did not differentiate between specific characteristics of role playing behavior. Since individuals rated low on one performance characteristic of role playing behavior also were rated low on others, effectiveness in the role playing situation employed is apparently more or less global in nature. The intercorrelations indicate further that scale 10, "effectiveness in playing the role," is probably as satisfactory as any of the scales as a single basis for assessing overall aspects of role playing behavior. Additional research is needed, however, in order to determine which particular scales are most useful in discriminating specific aspects of performance for designated types of role playing situations and with different types of subjects.

Intercorrelation of Roles

Even though no observer evaluated the performance of any child in two different role situations, the consistency of the same subject's behavior, as judged by different observers, is unusually high. With the exception of items 7 and 9 inter-role correlations all are significant and range from .70 to .97. That is to say, children who were judged to be effective in the enactment of role A, for example, also were seen to be effective in their enactments of roles B and C. The finding that role playing ability is individually consistent throughout the three different role playing situations that were employed suggests that role playing skill may be relatively independent of the specific role requirements of concrete situations, particularly when subjects represent an essentially unrestricted talent range as they did in this study. This finding has important theoretical implications. If borne out in further research it would indicate that role playing effectiveness within a single role constitutes a basis for evaluating general adaptability to the requirements of different role playing situations. Also consistent with this point of view are findings by Borgatta (2) who has reported relatively high consistency in behavior for individuals from role playing to actual situations, with somewhat less consistency to projective situations. Taken together, both sets of results indicate that social behavior with interpersonal components is sufficiently stable and self-consistent that differences among individuals are preserved through changes in roles and from role playing to actual and projective types of situations.

Peer Status and Role Playing Skill

Findings already presented demonstrate that individual differences in role playing performance can reliably be judged and that differences between individuals seem to be general rather than specific to the role playing situation. Therefore, since skill in role playing can be regarded as general and since it distinguishes one individual from another, the significant next step is that of identifying other characteristics of the person which are associated with role playing skill. The analysis which follows tests the hypothesis that sociometric position is a critical factor associated with role playing skill.

Since the sociometric distribution was somewhat skewed, with fewer subjects at the high end of the distribution, the most appropriate test of the hypothesis is through the use of X^2. The X^2's shown in Table 3 were computed from 3 x 3 tables. The sociometric distribution was divided into approximately equal groups of high, middle, and low peer status. Rating scales also were collapsed into three categories to avoid low theoretical frequencies in any of the cells.

Inspection of Table 3 shows a clear, definite and consistent relationship between sociometrically measured peer status, computed by McGuire's formula, and ratings of role playing effectiveness. Children with high sociometric status positions received the largest number of positive scale ratings on their role playing enactments, those of low sociometric status

TABLE 3

RELATIONSHIP BETWEEN PEER STATUS AND ROLE TAKING ABILITY

	Role A		Role B		Role C			
Item	X^2	P	X^2	P	X^2	P	r	P
1. Frustration	42.19	.01	68.99	.01	55.92	.01	—.78	.01
2. Shyness-Assurance	49.20	.01	47.36	.01	33.16	.01	—.70	.01
3. Difficulty	52.80	.01	38.04	.01	56.29	.01	—.71	.01
4. Clarity	30.13	.01	33.97	.01	40.26	.01	—.73	.01
5. Interest	10.09	—	15.83	.01	31.46	.01	.55	.01
6. Anxiousness	58.18	.01	35.09	.01	47.50	.01	—.63	.01
7. Satisfaction	2.53	—	6.45	—	2.53	—	—.34	—
8. Hesitancy	34.19	.01	25.60	.01	54.43	.01	—.73	.01
9. Good Performance	3.36	—	2.26	—	5.66	—	.19	—
10. Effectiveness	46.40	.01	29.29	.01	64.61	.01	.70	.01

positions received the least favorable ratings, while middle status children received ratings of intermediate values. The relationship between peer status and role taking effectiveness is significant for the eight scales with significantly high reliabilities and for the three role situations employed to evaluate it. Furthermore, since the three roles were highly intercorrelated, they were combined into a single role playing score based on the average of the nine judgments in order to obtain a single estimate of role playing skill. The role playing score was then correlated with the McGuire peer status index to determine the strength of association between sociometric position and role playing skill. Correlations by items are —.78 (frustration), —.70 (shyness), —.71 (difficulty), .73 (clarity), .55 (interest), —.63 (anxiousness), —.34 (satisfaction), —.73 (hesitancy), .19

(good performance), and .70 (effectiveness). All of the reliable scales are, therefore, significantly associated with sociometric position with the relationship between the two variables being in the predicted direction. Similar results were obtained when the raw frequency of positive choices received constituted the sociometric variable.

Children of high peer status were judged in the role playing situations as showing less frustration, acting with more assurance, having less difficulty and showing greater clarity in expression than were children of low status. Furthermore they were seen as neither anxious nor hesitant and finally as manifesting interest and as being more effective in enacting the requirements of the role situations. These are types of characteristics which commonly are employed in describing socially effective children. One interpretation based on the summary report by Carter (4) is that peer status appears to covary with a cluster of factors that can be designated as individual prominence and achievement. This cluster includes the idea of noticeability and competence of the individual in social affairs. If peer status is regarded as representative of this cluster of social characteristics, the strong association between peer status and role taking skill in the situations described should not be surprising since observations of the role playing situation were in terms of characteristics commonly related to social competence, *i.e.*, frustration, assurance, clarity of expression, hesitancy, and overall effectiveness. The suggested interpretation of the relatively close association between peer status and role taking ability, therefore, is that the social skills underlying peer status are ones which are accentuated in the enactment of social roles of the kind employed in this study. Additional research to provide a definitive basis to account for the association between sociometric peer status is needed now that the presence of such a fundamental relation has been established.

Summary

The hypothesis tested in the present investigation is that children of high peer status differ from those of low peer status in role playing ability, with the former having greater skill than the latter in enacting assigned roles in standard role playing situations. Nine observers evaluated the behavior of each of 26 negro preadolescent children who enacted three different roles opposite the same adult collaborator. Experimental arrangements were such that no child was observed enacting two different roles by the same observer. The order in which the roles were enacted also was varied so that each role occurred in each position in the sequence equally often.

Ten seven-category rating scales were employed by observers who independently judged the role playing performance. Three-choice limit sociometric responses on the criteria "like most" and "like least" were used as the basis for determining peer status position for each child. McGuire's formula was employed as the index of peer status.

The several analyses reported are internally consistent and lead to four general conclusions. The first is that independent observers achieve substantial agreement with one another in rating the same role playing enactment. The second is that rating scales are highly intercorrelated, indicating that at least for the scales and testing conditions employed, it is difficult to distinguish specific individual differences in the effectiveness with which a role is portrayed. The third conclusion is that role playing behavior is judged consistently, independently of the particular content of the role being enacted. The final conclusion is that the sociometric status position of a child among his peers is significantly associated with ability to enact a role effectively, with high status children receiving significantly more favorable observer ratings of their performance than those that are received by low status children. The interpretation of the association offered is that since the significant components involved in peer status appear to be individual prominence and achievement as described by Carter (4) in such terms as confidence, striving for recognition, bold, forceful, and not timid, the same or similar factors are present in the behavior of those who are able to enact roles effectively. Children who were effective in role playing were described as low in frustration, clear in expression, assured, and unhesitant. Having established a fundamental link between sociometric peer status and role playing skill, further research now is required to determine the causative basis of the association.

REFERENCES

1. Blake, R. R., Mouton, J., & Fruchter, B. The reliability of interpersonal judgments made on the basis of short-term interactions in three-man groups. *J. abnorm. soc. Psychol.,* 1954, 49, 573-78.
2. Borgatta, E. F. Analysis of social interaction: actual, role playing, and projective. *J. abnorm. soc. Psychol.,* 1955, 51, 394-405.
3. Borgatta, E. F., & Bales, R. F. The consistency of subject behavior and the reliability of scoring in interaction analysis. *Amer. Sociol. Rev.,* 1953, 18, 566-569.
4. Carter, L. F. Recording and evaluating the performance of individuals as members of small groups. In A. P. Hare, E. F. Borgatta, & R. F. Bales (Eds.), *Small groups.* New York: Alfred A. Knopf, 1955, 492-497.
5. Coleman, W. Role playing as an instructional aid. *J. educ. Psychol.,* 1948, 39, 429-435.

6. Hartley, E. L., & Hartley, R. E. *Fundamentals of social Psychology.* New York: A. A. Knopf, 1952.
7. McGuire, C., & Clark, R. A. Sociographic analysis of sociometric valuations, *Child Develpm.* 1952, 23, 129-140.
8. Moreno, J. L. *Who shall survive?* Beacon, New York: Beacon House, Inc., 1953.
9. Sarbin, T. R. The concept of role taking. *Sociometry,* 1943, 6, 273-285.
10. Sarbin, T. R. Contributions of role taking theory. *J. abnorm. soc. Psychol.,* 1952, 41, 117-124.
11. Stanton, H. R., & Litwak, E. A short form test of interpersonal competence. *Amer. sociol. Rev.,* 1955, 20, 668-673.

PART III
Major Areas of Exploration

A. Childhood and Early Adolescent, High School and College Level

INTRODUCTION

BY MERL E. BONNEY AND MARY L. NORTHWAY

Sociometric studies in the areas of childhood and adolescence include a wide range of topics. Since many of these topics are dealt with in other divisions of this volume, attention will be centered in this section on some general relationships between personality traits and sociometric choice-status. Various aspects of personality adjustments as they are related to sociometric data are presented in the five articles included in this section. However, these introductory remarks will not be confined to these five studies.

In the first place it is clear that different populations yield different results, in regard to relationships between measurements of choice-status and other forms of personality assessments such as self-ratings and ratings by observers. Apparently much depends on the kind of measurement techniques used, the content of these instruments, and the nature of the group studied.

In Kuhlen and Bretschs' study of high school students who responded to the Mooney Problem Check List, those students classified as "unacceptable" on the sociometric test were found to be much more characterized than were well-accepted students by such problems as lacking necessary social skills, not having close friends, having serious family conflicts, and being unhappy in school.

When Feinberg[1] asked two thousand high school age boys to check items on his Personal History Questionnaire, he found his highly accepted subjects to be characterized by very favorable parental relationships, by unusually good school adjustments, by active participation in sports and social events, by the feeling that they got along exceptionally well with their classmates, and by the belief that they had many close friends. The reverse conditions were found to be characteristic of the rejected boys, although there were a few variations from the above relationships according to socio-economic levels.

In the college level studies reported by French and Mensh and by Powell,[2] very little relationship was found between high or low choice-status among peers in a sorority house and in a girls' dormitory, on the one hand, and self-ratings on personality traits, on the other. These findings are obviously contrary to the results reported in the two preceding studies.

---

[1] M. R. Feinberg, "Relation of Background Experience to Social Acceptance," *Journal of Abnormal and Social Psychology*, XLVIII (1953), 206–14.

[2] M. G. Powell, "Comparisons of Self-Ratings, Peer Rating, and Expert's Rating of Personality Adjustment," *Educational and Psychological Measurement*, VIII (1948), 225–34.

It will be noted that in the two high school studies the content of the personality-assessment instruments dealt with particular problems and with personal history items, whereas in the two college studies the content of the personality measurements dealt with *personality traits* such as sociability, confidence, and neurotic tendency. It is quite possible that the different results obtained by these several studies is at least partly due to these differences in the content of the measuring instruments. It seems likely that specific problems such as those included in the Mooney Problems Check List and the kind of items included in the Personal History Questionnaire can be responded to with much less ambiguity of meaning than is possible when rating oneself on a trait like *confidence,* or when answering a series of questions which are then scored and designated *neurotic tendency,* as on the Bernreuter scales. It seems plausible that the more a measuring instrument deals with definite and overt behavior adjustments the more the results are likely to be related to sociometric test results, since the latter are based largely on personal evaluations of overt behavior.

Before leaving these studies, mention should be made of the fact that, from the standpoint of ratings by their sorority peers, the girls of highest sociometric status in French's and Mensh's study were reliably superior to those of lesser rank on the traits of sociability, fairmindedness, and sense of humor.

One point upon which we can be sure is that anyone who wants to arrive at an adequate personality assessment of any person or group must not be content with any one method of appraisal. This point is made especially clear in Powell's study in which self-ratings, ratings by observers, and sociometric choice-status are shown to be in considerable disagreement with each other.

We should not expect self-adjustment as measured by personality questionnaires to correlate closely with findings from sociometric testings: the one is measuring responses of individuals to a prepared list of questions; the other is measuring how well these same individuals are perceived by others in their respective groups as being sources of satisfaction for their personal or their group-activity needs, and often with respect to only one kind of criterion. In a broad sense, we can say that the first kind of measuring instrument is an assessment of an individual's worth or value as *he perceives himself,* while the second is an assessment of his social worth or value *as perceived* by others in the group tested. The first is based on self-stimulus value, the second on social-stimulus value.

Another point about which we can be sure is that even though in most studies those who are highly chosen can, as a group, be shown to be reliably superior to those who are poorly chosen, in *some* personality characteristics there is no one combination of traits that is invariably found to be true of particular individuals in either of these extreme categories. As a matter of fact, there is such a wide range of traits, and of combinations of traits, found at all levels in a sociometric hierarchy, that it is impossible to designate any one personality type that is likely to be found at any sociometric position, whether high or low.

This wide variability in terms of particular individuals who are either desired or undesired by others in their respective groups is readily understood when it is realized that a person's sociometric position is determined not simply by what he *is* but also by how he utilizes his personal-social assets to meet the needs and desires of others. Since this inter-action process is bound to be affected by many variables, it is not surprising that no one combination of traits has anything like universal value in arousing favorable responses from one's associates.

Faith in the importance of having the "right traits" can be over-done if one does not realize that no matter how many good traits a person has, they will not materially help him unless he is in a social situation in which he is freely evaluated for what he is. Some of the more evident barriers standing in the way of these free evaluations are racial, national, religious, and social class differences. In other words, individual personality traits are seldom given a fair chance to operate in determining inter-personal preferences except between people who are fairly similar in ethnic and socio-economic levels.

That traits are always perceived, not as isolated psychological variables, but as "figures on a ground," is well illustrated in Cook's [3] study of a tenth-grade class. His upper and middle class students were seen as possessing to a marked degree nearly all favorable traits listed on the form used, while the lower class students were viewed, especially by higher class students, as possessing to a marked degree a long list of undesirable traits. While it is within the realm of possibility that these reputations were closely in accord with objective facts, it is much more likely that they were heavily affected by the "social grounds" of the raters and the rated, so that when they were asked to list names of each other under the various trait-descriptions on the *Guess Who* measurement, their listings must have been much affected by their looking at each other through the distorted lenses of social-class stereotypes.

That the "right traits" alone cannot account for either high or low sociometric status is further emphasized by data from numerous studies which have placed major importance on an individual's capacity to adapt and to *integrate*

---

[3] L. A. Cook, "An Experimental Sociographic Study of a Stratified Tenth Grade Class," *American Sociological Review*, X (1945), 250–61.

his traits with on-going social processes around him. Some people have good intentions, are honest, sincere, and cheerful, and even have generous impulses toward others, and yet cannot establish satisfying relationships with others because of over-responding, or because of responding inappropriately or "out of tune" with the feelings or needs of others. They cannot *fit* themselves smoothly into emerging and ever-changing social processes. Their responses lack rapport and wholeness.

It is doubtful that the chief trouble with socially maladjusted individuals is ever that they have too much of certain virtues, i.e., that they are too honest, too humble, or too generous. Instead, it seems that the chief difficulty is always one of *quality-level* and of integration, rather than simply one of quantity or of frequency.

The importance of social behavior being intimately tied in with the responses of others is emphasized in Kidd's analysis of reasons for rejection of men in a college dormitory, when he concludes that among the chief reasons for being rejected were ego-centricity and obnoxious aggressiveness against others. These kinds of behavior are the direct opposite of adaptability to differences in others, of trying to think as others think, and of trying to *relate* oneself to others rather than to dominate them.

The above statements also find support on the positive side in Jennings' descriptions of highly chosen girls in the New York State Training School for Girls, when she says that these girls were characterized by "ability to establish rapport quickly and effectively with a wide range of other personalities and to win their confidence under varying circumstances."

Lest anyone think, however, that individuals who are high in sociometric choice-status are simply people who are nice and tolerant, and who are hyper-conformists, attention must also be called to some other statements from Jennings' descriptions of highly desired girls, such as, that these girls were characterized by taking a stand for what they considered to be right, by taking the initiative in efforts to enlarge the social space for interchange of ideas and activities, and by calling to account those girls who tried to exclude other girls from participation in various activities.

Other studies, too, have shown that those who stand high in desirability and in prestige with their peers are not rubber-stamps but, instead, are much more likely to be forthright in their personal relationships and to be outstanding in socially constructive aggressiveness. They are often characterized by a good integrated balance of *both* friendly and aggressive traits.

It is worth noting, too, that the *quality-level* of a sociometrically high individual is a mirror of the *quality-level* of the group members involved in the testing. The kind of person who is highly chosen depends very much upon the kind of choosers.

Those who are psychologically adequate and secure direct a large proportion of their choices to others who are likewise adequate and secure. Their inter-personal attractions are based primarily on ego satisfactions and self-realization. They desire to affiliate with another person chiefly because of such factors as pride in this person's abilities and achievements, shared interests and values, cooperative efforts carrying mutual benefits for both, mental stimulation, and persistent concern for the other person's happiness and self-enhancement. Likewise, in selecting leaders, the adequate and the secure direct nearly all their choices to those whom they believe will represent their group to the best advantage to all.

On the other hand, it is well known that there are many people whose inter-personal attachments and selections of leaders are heavily determined by immature and neurotic conditions within themselves. They tend to seek from others only the lower-level or more basic satisfactions, such as sex, security from physical or social harm, comfort and reassurance, and personal prestige values; or, in more extreme cases, even punishment, domination, and abuse, in order to assuage feelings of guilt and worthlessness.

To the extent that lower-level motivations are operating in sociometric choosing, we would expect to find some individuals receiving more choices than an objective appraisal of their personal and social worth would warrant. The degree to which such lower-level motivations are operating in any particular testing situation can be known only through a rather intensive knowledge of the personality needs of the choosers. This calls for more study of the peculiar satisfactions arising from the inter-personal attachments within a group than is generally available. Such studies would seem to be a most fruitful area for psychological investigation.

Finally, in regard to personality change, we can see from Cook's study the need of centering our efforts on both the individual *and* the social situation, in order to improve the *quality-level* of the personal-social behavior of all the members of a group; with the end in view, not of developing particular traits, but of improving total effectiveness in the art of social living.

SOCIOMETRIC STATUS AND PERSONAL PROBLEMS OF ADOLESCENTS

By Raymond G. Kuhlen and Howard S. Bretsch

The kinds of personal problems which characterize adolescents who are socially unacceptable as contrasted with the problems of those who are acceptable to their age mates should provide some clues as to how sociometric status might be promoted in school or out-of-school situations. "Personal problems," of course, have several meanings. Since a "personal problem" grows out of the frustration of a motive, evidence of its existence or non-existence should provide insights into what motives are currently most important to an individual, and into the kinds of situations that are hampering his development and adjustment. Or a person's "problem" may reflect the mechanisms by which he is adjusting to social failure, particularly if his mode of adjusting is unacceptable to himself or others and results in further frustration. Further, the personal problems that are characteristic of the socially unacceptable may reveal the extent to which such individuals are sensitive to their actual social status. In total, such analysis should be a source of possible hypotheses as to the reasons for, or the results of, lack of social acceptability, and thus would have certain implications for adults who have responsibility for the supervision and direction of adolescents, for counselors and guidance workers, curriculum planners, and school psychologists. Presumably, too, data bearing on this issue would be of interest to psychologists interested in development, especially those who teach teachers or prospective teachers.

PROCEDURE

The data reported in this paper were obtained from 692 ninth graders (326 boys and 366 girls) representing practically all of the beginning ninth graders in a city of approximately 87,000 population in central New York State. Mean age of the subjects was 14.6 years, with a standard deviation of 8 months. Though evidence (3) suggests no difference between the proportions of the two sexes who at the ninth grade are having dates, it should be noted that girls at this age are, in the main, post-pubescent; boys as a group are just reaching pubescence. Girls thus might be expected to have more the usual high-school advantage in social orientation and interest.

Sociometric status was determined for each of these youngsters by asking each to record on a specially prepared questionnaire the names of others in his own classroom whom he would choose as first or second choices for various activities that 9th graders might be expected to engage in. Six activities (including attendance at movies, going for a walk, making things (as model airplanes, dresses, etc.), playing outdoor and indoor games, and studying school work) were listed, and thus each child could make up to 12 choices. The number of times each child was mentioned by his classmates was tabulated and reduced to a score comparable to scores from other classrooms by dividing by the number of children in the room at the time of testing. The major portion of the data reported in this paper relates to the top and bottom 25 per cent of the distribution of scores so obtained. By focusing attention upon these extreme groups it was expected that some insights might be obtained into the nature of the relationships between social acceptability and personal problems.

Personal problems were identified by means of a modified version of the Mooney Problems Check List, Junior High Form (4). This check list included 235 problems of all sorts and was originally based on the written statements of some 4,000 students who were asked to describe briefly the problems that worried them most. The original blank directs the subject to indicate only those items that represent problems to him. Inasmuch as it is not possible under this plan to be sure that an item not checked has not been simply overlooked, the directions were changed to require some kind of a response to each item. Subjects were thus asked to respond by encircling an "N," an "S," or an "O" (for never, sometimes, and often), depending upon the extent to which an item represented a problem for him. The problems have been grouped by Mooney into the following areas: (1) Health and physical development, (2) psychological reactions with others, (3) home and family, (4) psychological relations to self, (5) school problems, (6) social and recreational activities, (7) moral and religious problems, (8) finance and employment, and (9) future vocation and education. These problem categories show the variety of the problems sampled. In the analysis to follow our concern will be with the specific problems and not with these broad classifications.

RESULTS

The general finding is that the unaccepted children have more problems than the more accepted. This is shown in Table 1 which gives the mean number of problems "often" and "sometimes" checked by the two extreme quartiles and by the middle half. The greatest difference between the groups is to be found in problems checked as *often* present rather than in those checked as *sometimes* present. In fact, very little difference existed between the extreme groups on *total* problems "sometimes" encountered. Thus it would seem that the problems characterizing the unacceptable adolescents are (on the whole) of a more serious, or at least more persistent, nature.

Table 2 shows the contrasts between the acceptable and the unacceptable children with respect to problems that *often* bothered them. For purposes of presentation only those showing differences of 10 or more between percentages checking are shown. Most of these differences are significant at the 5 per cent level, but only a few at the 1 per cent level. The problems differentiating these socially acceptable and unacceptable girls were (as the table shows) primarily problems suggesting lack of social skill on the part

TABLE 1.

The mean number of problems checked as "often" or "sometimes" occurring by individuals who were chosen by their classmates with varying frequency.[a]

Group	"Often"		"Sometimes"	
	Boys	Girls	Boys	Girls
Most frequently chosen group	32	24	55	68
Middle half	32	29	67	67
Least frequently chosen group	48	38	58	69
Difference (high-low)	16[b]	14[c]	3[d]	1[d]

[a]Each of the four extreme groups (boys, girls; acceptable, unacceptable) has an "N" of approximately 75.
[b]Significant at the 5% level.
[c]Significant at the 1% level.
[d]Not significant.

of the girls with lesser status, or at least a *desire* for *greater* skill. Of the differences great enough to be included in the table only two ("Getting information about best courses to take in high school," and "Getting information about possible jobs") are checked more frequently by the popular girls, suggesting a greater concern about future status on the part of such individuals.

The picture with respect to the boys is not so clearly one of social concern. While items relating to social graces did differentiate the popular and the unpopular, many such items did not. (Perhaps this is due to the greater immaturity of boys and their generally lesser social interest). There were, however, indications of subjective social insecurity on the part of the unaccepted, as evidenced in their greater checking of such problems as "being unhappy," "feelings too easily hurt," "having no one for a pal." There is also a strong suggestion of greater family difficulty among the unaccepted boys. "Mothers," "fathers," "brothers," and "sisters" are all more often problems! Problems with respect to allowance and lack of freedom at home

TABLE 2.

Problems checked as "often" present which differentiated accepted and unaccepted boys and accepted and unaccepted girls. Negative signs indicate preponderant checking by the unaccepted group. Differences marked by an asterisk are significant at the one per cent level; those in italics, at the five per cent level.

Problem	*Unaccepted*	*Accepted*	*Diff.*
Data For Boys			
Having to wait so long before starting work	22	3	—19*
Wanting to buy my own clothes	29	11	—18*
Going to shows	33	16	—17*
Having to earn my own spending money	23	8	—15*
Teacher too strict	23	8	—15*
Losing temper	18	3	—15*
Disliking school	26	11	—15
Feeling that nobody understands me	15	1	—14*
Boy friend	34	20	—14
Developing better posture	25	11	—14
Wanting more freedom at home	14	1	—13*
Girl friend	29	17	—12
Using correct manners	26	14	—12
Brothers	19	7	—12
Wanting to quit school	15	3	—12*
Father	15	3	—12*
Making a date	22	11	—11
Making a good appearance	18	7	—11
Sisters	18	7	—11
Wanting more time to myself	18	7	—11
Not getting enough exercise	15	4	—11
Mother	15	4	—11
Getting rid of people I don't like	14	3	—11
Data For Girls			
Getting acquainted with people	32	10	—22*
Disliking school	19	1	—18*
Bashfulness	23	7	—16*
Wanting to learn to dance	26	11	—15
Wearing glasses	18	4	—14*
Meeting people	27	13	—14
Selecting suitable clothes and knowing how to wear them	28	14	—14
Knowing how to act at a party	23	10	—13
Girl friend	26	13	—13
Using correct manners	27	16	—11
Being left out of things	11	1	—10*
Getting my parents to like my friends	14	4	—10
Wanting to quit school	10	1	—9
Getting information about possible jobs	9	24	13*
Getting information about best courses to take in high school	12	23	11

suggest that the home is handicapping some of these boys in achieving the social adjustment and acceptance among their peers. Finally, there is evidence of an unfavorable attitude toward school among the least acceptable group. Among boys this is suggested by *dislike for school,* and for both sexes in the wish *to quit school.* This finding is in line with the hypothesis (suggested later in the "discussion" section of this paper) that the school by its very social nature forces awareness of social deficiencies and inequalities upon children. Thus quitting school and dislike of school may in some cases at least be simply an escape by unacceptable children from an intolerable social situation.

The problems checked as occurring "sometimes" which differentiate the unaccepted and the accepted groups by a difference of at least 10 are shown in Tables 3 and 4. It is noteworthy in contrasting these tables with Table 2 that while the differences in problems occurring "often" showed predominate checking by the unaccepted group, in the case of problems occurring "sometimes" about as many differences favored one group as the other. (This would be expected from results presented in Table 1.) Also, certain items that were checked predominately by the unacceptable group as occurring *often* were checked more frequently by the accepted group as occurring *sometimes.* In short, a more acceptable social status (and presumably a more active social life) results in certain problems not characteristic of the unaccepted, and in a more universal occurrence on a *sometimes* level of problems that characterize the unaccepted on an *often* level. Thus "selecting clothes and knowing how to wear them" and "getting acquainted with people" are checked with greater frequency as *often* problems by the unaccepted girls, but more frequently as *sometimes* problems by the accepted girls. These contrasts are reasonable since active social life presumably would be more apt to result in such problems arising at least occasionally. Other items checked by the socially acceptable girls show more problems regarding dating ("having dates," "knowing what to do on a date," "making a date"), and presumably it is this greater heterosexual activity and social life that accounts for more of the popular girls being bothered about "yielding to temptation" and "having a guilty conscience"! (Note that "refusing to do what the crowd wants" was more frequently a problem for the *unaccepted* girl). Greater exuberance ("having too much pep for my own good"), budget problems, and too much social activity (i.e., "wanting more time to myself") also are implied in the responses of the more socially accepted girls.

The problems listed in Table 3 which were more frequently checked by the unaccepted girls contain a remarkably large proportion of items relating to physical factors. Such items as "stomach trouble," "headaches," and "never feeling quite well" suggest the possibility that this concern for physi-

TABLE 3.

Problems checked as "sometimes" present which differentiated accepted and unaccepted girls. Negative signs indicate preponderant checking by the unaccepted group. Differences marked by an asterisk are significant at the one per cent level; those in italics are significant at the five per cent level.

Problem	Unaccepted	Accepted	Diff.
Never feeling quite well	35	13	—22*
Headaches	63	41	—22*
Being lonely	53	33	—20*
Developing better posture	49	33	—16
Stomach trouble	32	17	—15
Getting information about best courses to take in high school	54	41	—13
Textbook hard to understand	54	41	—13
Wanting to buy own clothes	40	27	—13
Slow with numbers	38	25	—13
Being overweight	29	16	—13
Joining clubs	33	20	—13
Refusing to do what the crowd wants	26	13	—13
Having too many colds	26	14	—12
Too few school activities	27	16	—11
Unhappy home life	14	3	—11
Not getting enough exercise	32	22	—10
Learning to see the funny side of things	27	17	—10
Yielding to temptation	36	58	22*
Wanting more time to myself	22	41	19*
Selecting suitable clothes and knowing how to wear them	28	46	18
Disliking certain people	54	71	17
Getting into arguments	40	57	17
Not smart enough	42	58	16
Budgeting my money	30	46	16
Being too self-conscious	44	59	15
Having too much pep for my own good	13	28	15
Having dates	19	34	15
Knowing what to do on a date	33	46	13
Talking back to my parents	32	45	13
Getting acquainted with people	28	41	13
Making a date	28	41	13
Wondering if I'll be successful	50	61	11
Having a guilty conscience	40	51	11
Wondering what becomes of people at death	31	42	11
Getting rid of people I don't like	30	41	11
Hurting people's feelings	24	35	11
Feeling that nobody understands me	31	41	10
Finding where I belong in the world	30	40	10

cal symptoms may be a *result* of the social frustrations these youngsters are encountering rather than a cause or a mere concomitant. Yet problems such as "being overweight" and "developing better posture" suggest (as would be expected) that the physically unattractive are more often among the unaccepted group. In this table, much more than in the table dealing with the "often" responses, there is evidence that the unacceptable girls are aware of (and willing to admit as at least occasionally bothering them) their actual lack of status. Thus they more often check such problems as "being lonely," "joining clubs," and "too few school activities."

Examination of the data in Table 4 for the boys show differences similar to those found among the girls. Physical deficiencies (real or imagined) more often characterize the unacceptable boys, and other items point to their greater recognition of difficulty in getting along with people. More of the accepted boys *occasionally* have problems in connection with dating and social appearance and, curiously, more of them "sometimes" sense the need for a more pleasing personality. There is also the suggestion that the accepted group are more concerned with their futures. This last point (evidenced in the table by such problems as "finding where I belong in the world" and "deciding on an occupation") involved item differences which

TABLE 4.

Problems checked as "sometimes" present which differentiated accepted and unaccepted boys. Negative signs indicate preponderant checking by the unaccepted group. Differences marked by an asterisk are significant at the one per cent level; those in italics are significant at the five per cent level.

Problem	Unaccepted	Accepted	Diff.
Being unhappy	44	24	—20*
Getting tired very easily	30	12	—18*
Feelings too easily hurt	36	18	—18*
Too little money for shows, sports	27	12	—15
Having no one for a pal	18	3	—15*
Seldom find things I like to do	32	18	—14
Trouble in getting along with people	32	18	—14
Not getting enough exercise	27	14	—13
Death in family	27	14	—13
Lack of appetite	26	13	—13
Unhappy home life	18	5	—13
Don't get along with my teacher	38	26	—12
Wanting to quit school	26	14	—12
Being underweight	29	17	—12
Getting proper medical care	18	7	—11
Wanting a more pleasing personality	23	46	23*
Knowing what to do on a date	15	38	23*
Making a date	21	42	21*
Trying to break off a bad habit	30	45	15
Developing a better posture	30	45	15
Using correct manners	33	47	14
Making a good appearance	34	47	13
Headaches	33	45	12
Having dates	18	30	12
Deciding on an occupation	32	43	11
Finding where I belong in the world	26	37	11
Getting information about possible jobs	25	36	11

were not statistically reliable, but some credence can be placed in the trends in view of the occurrence of similar (but lesser) differences in items like them, but which are not reported in the paper. The same trends also occurred in the data for the girls.

DISCUSSION

Before discussing the implication of these results, it should be recalled that the subjects who provided the data were ninth graders. As adolescents, they are at an age when about half of them are having dates (3) and when, for a number of reasons, matters pertaining to social relationships and social adjustment might be expected to be assuming new importance, when diverse problems relating to social acceptability begin to arise. In the first place, as studies of interest changes show, the period of adolescence and early adulthood is the age of greatest social interest, and these youngsters of 15 are just on the threshold with the accentuated interest that newness of experience brings. Second, by the ninth grade there is considerable interest in the opposite sex on the part of both girls and boys (2), and "social status" now implies status in the eyes of the opposite sex, whereas only a few years earlier the opposite sex was largely ignored or avoided. And finally, sheer presence in school (with the increased social activity—clubs, parties, etc.— which characterizes junior and senior high school life) makes it probable that the ignored child will be more aware of the fact that he is not accepted and is not a participant than he would be if not in school.

In view of these conditions, it is surprising to find that the differences in responses to social items were not more extensive and pronounced than they were. In fact the emphasis on *differences* in the foregoing presentation of results should not obscure the fact that, in general, problems most frequently mentioned by the accepted group were also among those most frequently mentioned by the unaccepted group. The general excess of problems checked as "often" existing (noted in Table 1) appeared to result from a more frequent checking of all kinds of problems by the unaccepted group. Thus with respect to the general question of identifying factors related to social acceptability, the findings reported in this paper are much in line with those reported in other studies dealing with personality test results: social status determined by means external to the child do not correlate highly with measures of personality and adjustment which depend upon the child's subjective judgment and personal response. Yet in evaluating adjustment both "external" and personal evaluations must be taken into account. There is, as pointed out above, some indication (when *individual*

413

items are examined) of the nature of the psychological reactions of those lacking in social status. In general, children low in social status among their peers reveal in their "problems" feelings of social insecurity, a sense of isolation, a sensitivity to lack of social skills,—and the existence of home and school problems that appear to be related in significant ways to their lack of status. However, the relative lack of relationships found here emphasizes again the importance of multiple approaches to the study of the problems of individual children. *Feelings* of unacceptability constitute a problem regardless of externally determined status.

From a practical point of view, the findings focus attention upon two aspects of the problem of improving status: (1) the possibility of the school's aiding the adjustment of these young adolescents by programs designed to develop social skills, and (2) the obstacle to progress from school efforts offered in numerous cases by home circumstances. The data distinctly seem to emphasize the possibility that some progress may be made in improving the social status of unaccepted children (or their attitudes toward their status) by the teaching of social skills. The "problems" revealed by the above analysis reveal "felt needs" that might be met by a planned school program. Informal dancing instruction at noon or after school or in gym classes, instruction in making and acknowledging introductions in English classes, instruction in grooming and eating in home economics courses,— these represent only a few of the possibilities. The statements of children themselves regarding the means by which they overcame social obstacles indicate how school instruction has occasionally helped, but also suggest how little effort the schools expend in this direction (1). The teaching of concrete skills to meet anticipated problems is a fundamental method of eliminating these problems. In this connection, it is worth noting that efforts expended in this direction are *academically* important. It is probable that if social adjustment and acceptance is improved, drop-outs will be fewer (the unaccepted children disliked school and wanted to quit), and if stress generated in social situations is decreased, academic efficiency may increase. These hypotheses are worthy of careful investigation.

The vast contributions that the home (or the school) makes to adjustment will not be apparent in a study emphasizing problems, but with this limitation in mind it is well to observe that the home does present a great number of obstacles to social development. Not infrequently the situation is such that once the parents are sensitized to the need they can do much to remove minor handicaps that stand in the way of their offspring, and bring about psychologically important changes in the home environ-

414

ment. In other instances, however, the home situation is so bad that it constitutes an extreme obstacle to what the school, or any other agency, might do to promote a child's development, unless radical changes are made in long established living patterns, or in socio-economic status. Thus in another group which the present writers have studied sociometrically a brother and sister were social isolates. Their teacher commented that they were from a very poor family, had a minimum of clothes (which nonetheless were clean), saw others only at school, and appeared generally introverted. Another isolate comes from a large family housed in a small dirty house (several children sleep in a single bed); her appearance is untidy, hair unkept. Once or twice a year children from this family are sent home "to get the inhabitants cleaned out of their hair." Yet the teacher comments that the girl is a "sweet-looking child and if given half a chance will probably develop well." Another girl is highly intelligent, talented in music, and on the honor roll. However she is "chosen" by no one under conditions similar to those of this study. Her home is "strict" and old-fashioned to an extreme. The girl dresses in old-fashioned, though immaculate clothes, is religious to almost a fanatic degree, has no use for the "worldly desires" of her age mates. It is little wonder that she is an isolate. Examples such as these, of course, only illustrate maladjusted homes whose maladjustments are being passed on to the children. In many such cases the contributions that the school alone will make to improved adjustment are probably minor compared to the extent to which the home will counterbalance such efforts.

SUMMARY

Sociometric status was determined for almost 700 ninth graders, and evidence was obtained as to the personal problems characterizing these individuals. In general it was found that those who were least accepted by their grade mates (roughly the bottom quartile) had reliably more personal problems pressing enough to be checked as "often" present than did the top quartile in acceptability. However, there was little difference between the accepted and unaccepted children with respect to the total number of problems checked as occurring "sometimes." Practically all of the item differences on "often" responses show predominate checking by the unaccepted group, with the items showing greater concern with social skills, unhappiness and lack of status, family problems, and dislike of school. On items checked as "sometimes" problems the accepted group checked more items relating to social activities, moral concerns (for the girls) presumably growing out of broader heterosexual activities, concern over the future education and job. The unaccepted groups checked such items as those involving health factors, and revealing unhappiness and a sense of lack of status.

REFERENCES

1. Hutson, P. W., and Kover, D. R., Some problems of senior-high-school pupils in their social recreation, *Educational Administration and Supervision,* 1942, 28, 503-19.

2. Kuhlen, R. G., and Lee, B. J., Personality characteristics and social acceptability in adolescence, *Journal of Educational Psychology,* 1943, 34, 321-340.

3. Punke, H. H., Dating practices of high-school youth, Bulletin of the *Nat'l Ass'n of Secondary School Principals,* 1944, 28, 47-54.

4. Mooney, R. L., Surveying high-school students' problems by means of a problem check list, *Educational Research Bulletin,* 1942, 21, 57-69.

SOME RELATIONSHIPS BETWEEN INTERPERSONAL JUDGMENTS AND SOCIOMETRIC STATUS IN A COLLEGE GROUP[1]

By Robert L. French and Ivan N. Mensh

Popular analyses of personality commonly take the form of judgments or ratings of an individual with reference to various trait dimensions. Since judgments of this sort evolve from personal interaction within a group framework, it is reasonable to expect that they will bear some relationship to the sociometric features of the group concerned. Sociometric choices or rejections are themselves personal judgments which may rest to some extent upon specific trait evaluations. But more important, perhaps, in a group of known characteristics the sociometric position of an individual furnishes some clues to his opportunities for observing or being observed by others, to the opinions he will hear and value, to his own insecurities and aspirations, to various factors, in brief, which may conceivably influence the ratings he gives and receives. This approach to interpersonal judgments, then, may reveal significant functional aspects of sociometric structures.[2] It may also contribute to an understanding of the conditions under which valid judgments of personality may be obtained.

The work reported here is exploratory in nature, designed to obtain evidence concerning the relation of the sociometric status of an individual to: (1) the group's rating of him with reference to several personality characteristics; (2) ratings of him by individuals of varying sociometric status; (3) his ratings of himself.

PROCEDURE

The subjects comprised the 34 girls living in one of the sorority houses on the Northwestern University campus. All of the girls had lived together for at least two months during the academic quarter in which they were studied. Eleven girls had not lived in the house prior to that quarter, but they as well as the others had been affiliated with the sorority for at least two previous quarters. The ratings and sociometric data reported here

[1] This study was supported by a grant from the Research Committee of the Graduate School of Northwestern University.

[2] Other important correlates of sociometric structure have, of course, been reported by various investigators. See, for example; Moreno, J. L., *Who Shall Survive?* Washington, D. C.: Nervous and Mental Diseases Publishing Co., 1934; Jennings, H. H., *Leadership and Isolation.* New York: Longmans, Green and Co., 1943.

were obtained in one evening at the sorority house after several prior contacts with the girls, both individually and collectively.

Ratings

Each girl was asked to rate herself and every other girl on each of six traits: punctuality, sociability, fairmindedness, intelligence ("intellectual quickness"), self-confidence, and sense of humor. The instructions read:

"On each of the following six pages you are asked to rate every girl in the house on a particular trait. For example, on the first page you will find the following heading:

IS SHE PUNCTUAL OR LATE FOR APPOINTMENTS?

	Always prompt		Occasionally late			Frequently late		Always late
	9	8	7	6	5	4	3	2	1
Jane Doe		√							
Mary Roe							√		

On the left hand side will be listed the names of all girls in the house. Start at the top and rate each girl in turn, including yourself. In rating each girl, ask yourself: "Is she punctual or late for appointments?" Think carefully of as many concrete incidents as possible; then make a check-mark somewhere on the line after the girl's name to indicate how punctual she is (See above illustration for Jane Doe.) The numbers from 1 to 9 at the top of the page show roughly the degrees of punctuality represented by points along each line, "9" signifying the highest degree, and "1" the least. The descriptions above the numbers further define their meanings. Try to locate each check-mark as accurately as possible, using the numbers and descriptions as general guides.

"After completing the punctuality ratings, go on to each of the following pages in turn, and rate each girl on the traits there described."

The scales for the remaining traits were arranged similarly. Questions and descriptive statements with their approximate corresponding scale numbers were as follows:

Is she sociable and friendly, or does she tend to avoid people?
    (9)   Enjoys people; spends most of time with others
    (6-7)   Usually likes to be with people
    (3-4)   Often prefers to keep to herself
    (1)   Aloof; almost always prefers to be alone

Is she fair-minded or prejudiced in her judgments of people and issues

    (9)   Always impartial and fair-minded
    (6-7)   Tries to be fair; usually just
    (3-4)   Judgment often affected by strong feelings
    (1)   Partial and prejudiced; intolerant

Is she intellectually quick or slow as compared with other girls in the group?

    (9)   Always grasps the essentials immediately
    (6-7)   Usually catches on quickly
    (3-4)   Often slow in getting the point
    (1)   Always slow in understanding

Is she self-confident or does she doubt her own ability to handle situations ?

    (9)   Self-assured in all situations
    (6-7)   Usually has confidence in herself
    (3-4)   Often needs reassurance from others
    (1)   Always doubtful of own adequacy.

Does she display a sense of humor?

    (9)   Sees the funny side of everything
    (6-7)   Usually sees the amusing side of things
    (3-4)   Often needs jokes explained to her
    (1)   Takes everything literally

In the analysis of results, each rating was given the numerical value of the column in which it fell. In order to eliminate the effects of rater differences in central tendency and variability of ratings, these "raw ratings" were converted to "standard ratings". This involved determining the mean and standard deviation of the ratings given by each subject on each trait (excluding her self-rating), and the deviation of each rating from the mean in terms of standard deviation units. Each standard score thus derived was converted to a score on an arbitrary scale ("T-scale") with a mean of 50 and standard deviation of 10. Thus, if a rater gave another subject a raw rating of 6, and if all of the ratings which she gave on this trait averaged 7.50 with a standard deviation of 1.50, the rating of 6 would be converted to a standard rating of 40. It could then be compared directly with any standard rating given by any rater on any trait. In order to facilitate comparison of any rating given with the mean rating received by the rater from the group as a whole, a "standard mean rating" was computed for each subject on each trait. Raw ratings received by each subject were averaged, the characteristics of the distribution of means for all subjects on the trait determined, and each mean then converted to a value on a T-scale. A subject receiving a standard mean rating of 50, then, would be considered average by the group, and so on.

Sociometric data

After completing the ratings, the subjects filled out a form on which they were asked the following questions:

> "If you were to choose a room-mate at the present time, what three girls now living in the house would you consider *first?*"
> "Under the same conditions, what three girls now living in the house would you consider *last?*"

Although order of first and last choices was obtained, it was not considered in analyzing the data. The first three choices in each case were treated equally as "choices", and the last three as "rejections".

The sociogram showed that 25 of the girls formed a relatively well-integrated group, or series of sub-groups, while the remaining 9 were relatively isolated. Each of the girls in the "majority group" had at least one mutual choice within the group, and but one girl made a choice (unilateral) outside of it. Of the total of 75 rejections made by the 25 girls, only 12 went to other girls within the group. In the "minority" or "isolate" group, three of the girls were held together in a chain of mutual choices, and three others received one choice apiece, but with these exceptions all appeared to be so isolated from the majority structure and from each other as to warrant considering them an isolate group.

In order to analyze the relationships between ratings and sociometric status, the subjects were divided into three "status groups", as follows: (I) members of the majority group receiving no rejections; (II) members of the majority group receiving rejections; and (III) members of the minority or isolate group.[3] Tables 1 and 2 show the sociometric characteristics of the three groups.

Statistical analyses

The data obtained were subjected to analyses of variance to test the significance of differences between status groups with respect to various

---

[3] A continuous measure such as that developed by Bronfenbrenner did not appear desirable because it weights each choice equally and does not allow a measure based on consideration of choices, mutual choices and rejections in combination. Cf. Bronfenbrenner, U. The measurement of sociometric status, structure and development. *Sociometry Monographs,* 1945, No. 6. Without taking into account all of these factors, it does not seem possible to describe status differences as sensitively as perusal of the sociogram would suggest is necessary. The result may be, of course, that we are dealing here with more than a single status continuum.

TABLE 1
CHOICES, MUTUAL CHOICES AND REJECTIONS RECEIVED BY MEMBERS OF STATUS GROUPS

Subject	Group I (N = 15)														
	A	B	C	D	E	F	G	H	J	K	L	M	N	O	P
Times Chosen	2	2	2	4	4	3	4	6	8	7	6	4	4	6	2
Mutual Choices	1	1	2	2	3	2	1	2	3	1	2	1	2	3	1
Times Rejected	0	0	0	0	0	0	0	0	0	0	0	0	0	0	0

Subject	Group II (N — 10)									
	A	B	C	D	E	F	G	H	J	K
Times Chosen	2	4	1	3	4	3	2	3	3	5
Mutual Choices	2	2	1	2	1	3	1	2	1	2
Times Rejected	2	3	3	1	2	1	6	5	1	1

Subject	Group III (N — 9)								
	A	B	C	D	E	F	G	H	J
Times Chosen	2	2	1	0	1	1	0	0	1
Mutual Choices	2	1	0	0	1	0	0	0	0
Times Rejected	10	13	6	4	11	2	21	5	5

TABLE 2
NUMBERS OF CHOICES AND REJECTIONS WITHIN AND BETWEEN THE STATUS GROUPS

		Group Making Choices			Group Making Rejections		
		I	II	III	I	II	III
Group	I	26	25	13	—	—	—
Receiving Choices	II	19	4	7	6	6	13
and Rejections	III	—	1	7	39	24	14
Total		45	30	27	45	30	27

aspects of the ratings. In each case the analysis involves a single classification, status-group, with one measure for each member of each group,—mean rating given, mean rating received, or whatever the case may be. With a total of 34 measures, there are 33 degrees of freedom, 2 for "between groups" and 31 for "within groups" or error.

RESULTS

Ratings received from all other individuals

To what extent is the group judgment of an individual on particular traits related to sociometric status? Table 3 shows the means of the standard mean ratings received by members of the several status groups on each trait, together with the F's obtained in the analyses of variance. Statistically significant values of F are noted for sociability, fairmindedness and sense of humor. Evaluation of the mean differences between each pair of groups by

TABLE 3

STATUS GROUP MEANS FOR STANDARD MEAN RATINGS RECEIVED BY INDIVIDUAL MEMBERS
OF THE GROUPS

	Punctuality	Sociability	Fair-mindedness	Intelligence	Confidence	Humor
Group I	52.33	55.46	57.00	52.93	51.00	55.80
Group II	52.20	43.70	43.30	50.80	49.20	45.80
Group III	43.33	48.22	45.22	44.00	48.66	45.22
F	2.76	5.13*	11.19**	2.42	0.17	5.47**

*Significant at 5% level
**Significant at 1% level

means of the t test reveals that Group I is significantly superior to Group II in all three traits and to Group III in all but sociability, and that Group II and III do not differ significantly in any. In the three traits showing no significant F's, Group I tends likewise to have the highest standing.

Is the dispersion of ratings received by an individual a function of his sociometric status? In Table 4 it will be observed that mean variability is consistently least for Group I, and greatest for Group III, and that significant values of F are obtained for the same traits noted above, sociability, fairmindedness and humor. Application of the t test to group differences in these traits shows Group I significantly less variable than Group III in all three traits, and less variable than Group II in sociability and fairmindedness. Between Groups II and III there are no significant differences. Apparently, then, individuals having the most favorable positions in the sociometric structure receive the highest ratings in certain characteristics, and the group as a whole shows greatest agreement in its ratings of these individuals.

Ratings of own and other status groups

The question arises next as to whether the different status groups tend to agree in their ratings of their own and other groups. Or, to put it in a different way, is the sociometric status of the rater a factor in ratings which

TABLE 4

STATUS GROUP MEANS FOR STANDARD DEVIATIONS OF STANDARD RATINGS RECEIVED BY INDIVIDUAL MEMBERS OF THE GROUPS

	Punctuality	Sociability	Fair-mindedness	Intelligence	Confidence	Humor
Group I	6.38	6.12	6.71	7.29	7.09	7.17
Group II	6.82	8.36	8.47	8.05	7.73	8.51
Group III	7.59	8.41	8.82	8.58	8.04	9.23
F	1.95	6.87**	9.20**	1.96	1.22	3.42*

*Significant at 5% level
**Significant at 1% level

she assigns to individuals of a given status? To gain some information on this point we computed for each individual the mean of standard ratings which she gave to members of a particular status group on each trait. (Self-ratings were excluded.) The mean ratings assigned to a given group by individual members of the three groups were then subjected to analysis of variance separately for each trait. Table 5 shows the F values found in

TABLE 5

STATUS GROUP MEANS FOR MEAN STANDARD RATINGS GIVEN BY MEMBERS TO EACH STATUS GROUP
(self-ratings excluded)

Ratings Given to	by	P	S	F	I	C	H
Group I	Group I	52.13	53.84	54.55	52.03	51.43	53.63
	Group II	51.23	53.40	54.29	52.45	50.74	53.58
	Group III	51.23	53.61	54.63	51.50	50.96	51.79
	F	1.13	0.39	0.28	1.17	0.38	3.52*
Group II	Group I	52.12	46.25	46.87	51.24	49.47	47.89
	Group II	51.31	45.07	45.95	48.73	49.33	47.79
	Group III	50.78	45.72	44.01	50.31	49.06	46.26
	F	0.86	1.21	4.27*	3.66*	0.06	1.30
Group III	Group I	44.69	48.48	46.45	45.49	48.75	46.29
	Group II	46.16	49.22	46.48	47.43	49.28	46.25
	Group III	46.40	48.57	48.77	46.90	48.89	51.26
	F	1.37	0.27	3.22	2.15	0.12	10.24**

*Significant at 5% level
**Significant at 1% level

these analyses, together with the group means of the mean ratings given by members of each group. To illustrate reading of the table,—the mean of mean standard ratings in sociability given by individuals in Group II to Group I is 53.40. In most cases considerable agreement may be noted among the groups in their ratings of a given group. Statistically significant exceptions are found in several instances, however, notably in the case of humor, where Group III rates itself higher and Groups I and II lower than do these latter groups. In the case of fairmindedness, ratings of Group II differ significantly, and differences in ratings of Group III approach significance, largely because Group III rates itself higher and Group II lower than do Groups I and II. Again, there is a significant difference of opinion concerning the intelligence of Group II, with individuals in Group II rating other members of that group lower than do the other groups. In some cases, then, the status relationships between rater and individual rated appear to have influence on ratings.

Self-ratings

How is sociometric status related to judgments of one's self? In Table 6, showing status group means for standard self-ratings and the *F*'s obtained in the analyses of variance, there appears to be no relationship; members of the various groups seem on the average to think about equally well of themselves, and in some cases this is quite well indeed.

But self-judgment cannot, perhaps, be considered adequately by itself without reference to group judgment of the individual. To evaluate the agreement between the two, the difference between standard self-rating and standard mean rating received in each trait was computed for each individual. The means of these differences for the status groups are given in Table 7, together with values of *F* indicating that the groups differ significantly in degree of conservativeness in self-ratings of all traits but self-confidence. Application of the *t*-test to mean differences in these five traits shows that Group I is significantly more conservative than Group II in self-ratings of all traits but punctuality and intelligence, and more conservative than Group III in all traits but sociability. Between Groups II and III the differences are not significant.

Recalling that members of Group I generally receive the highest ratings from the entire group, one might ask if this finding with respect to self-

TABLE 6
STATUS GROUP MEANS FOR STANDARD SELF-RATINGS BY INDIVIDUAL MEMBERS
OF THE GROUP

	Punctuality	Sociability	Fair-mindedness	Intelligence	Confidence	Humor
Group I	46.93	54.13	52.27	50.73	44.60	54.53
Group II	47.56	51.60	50.70	54.90	48.70	55.90
Group III	46.89	50.44	54.00	52.33	44.33	52.11
F	0.01	0.68	0.48	1.08	0.54	0.61

TABLE 7
STATUS GROUP MEANS FOR DIFFERENCES BETWEEN STANDARD SELF-RATINGS AND STANDARD
MEAN RATINGS RECEIVED BY INDIVIDUAL MEMBERS OF THE GROUP

	Punctuality	Sociability	Fair-mindedness	Intelligence	Confidence	Humor
Group I	—5.40†	—1.33	—4.73	—2.20	—6.40	—1.27
Group II	—4.00	7.90	7.40	4.10	—0.50	10.10
Group III	3.56	2.22	8.78	8.33	—4.33	6.89
F	3.70*	3.75*	6.92**	4.38*	1.35	7.11**

†Negative difference indicates self-rating lower than mean rating received
*Significant at 5% level
**Significant at 1% level

ratings is any more than a reflection of the oft-demonstrated fact that individuals standing high on a trait tend to under-rate themselves, whereas those standing low tend to over-rate themselves.[4] Is sociometric status necessarily involved at all here? In order to obtain some evidence on this point, the self-ratings in each trait were subjected to analysis of covariance, in which the self-ratings in the three groups were adjusted for group differences in mean rating received, the adjustment being based on the average regression of self-rating on mean rating within the groups. Table 8 shows

TABLE 8

STATUS GROUP MEANS FOR STANDARD SELF RATINGS, ADJUSTED FOR GROUP DIFFERENCES IN MEAN RATINGS RECEIVED; AND OTHER DATA OBTAINED IN ANALYSIS OF COVARIANCE

	Punctuality	Sociability	Fair-mindedness	Intelligence	Confidence	Humor
Group I	44.48	51.55	51.38	49.70	43.86	51.57
Group II	45.82	54.67	51.52	54.61	49.21	58.10
Group III	52.74	51.34	54.58	54.37	45.22	54.61
F	2.62	0.68	0.55	2.36	1.31	3.80*
r	0.75	0.56	0.13	0.48	0.67	0.61
b	0.9226	0.4810	0.1246	0.3429	0.6944	0.5162

*Significant at 5% level

the adjusted mean values, the average regression coefficients (b's), average correlations within groups (r's), and the values of F obtained in analysis of variance of the adjusted values. The adjusted mean values can be regarded as what the mean self-ratings would most probably be if there were no group differences in mean ratings received. Comparison of these values with the unadjusted means in Table 6 shows some changes in ranking; on every trait either Group II or Group III is now highest in self-rating. Higher F's are also noted in Table 8, especially for punctuality, intelligence, and humor, the last being significant at the 5% level of confidence. Evidently, then, with respect to at least one of the traits, low sociometric status may involve some factor or factors other than standing on the trait which makes for higher self-ratings.

DISCUSSION

In considering these findings, it should be remembered that they have been obtained under quite specific conditions. One sorority group is probably not representative of all sororities, let alone of groups in general. Moreover, only one sociometric criterion was employed, choice of roommate, and

---

[4] For a summary of this literature, see, for example, Guilford, J. P., *Psychometric Methods*. New York: McGraw-Hill, 1936.

although this seems to be the most important one for this type of group, other criteria might yield somewhat different results. Also, the criterion was "unrealistic" in the sense that no actual changing of roommates was contemplated; there is, however, no evidence to indicate that this fact made any difference.

Common sense would predict that high-status individuals would be rated high on certain traits by the whole group, for the traits in question, sociability, fairmindedness, and sense of humor—undoubtedly have high social value in a group of this sort. However, as with any finding of a relationship between measures of personality characteristics and social effectiveness, the interpretation is far from clear. Do individuals attain high status because they manifest these traits? Or do they develop these traits in consequence of having attained high status? Or are they merely thought by raters to stand high in these respects because they have high status or are admired as individuals? Or does high status permit the conspicuous display of these traits without there necessarily being any fundamental personality differences?

Probably all of these interpretations apply in some degree. The data permit no decision, although with respect to certain traits some evidence pointing toward the last-mentioned possibility appears in the cases of disagreement among status groups. Thus members of Group III rate other members of that group considerably higher in humor, and members of Group I somewhat lower, than do the members of Groups I and II. What accounts for these discrepancies? Do low status individuals have both less humor and lower standards of humor so that they rate each other relatively high? But if so, why do they agree with the other groups as closely as they do in their ratings of Group I and II? One suspects, in accord with everyday observation, that the low-status individual may display a perfectly adequate sense of humor among his peers, but in the presence of high-status individuals feel constrained to banalities. Longitudinal studies of the relation between sociometric position and personal judgments in a group of this sort would throw more light on this and other possible factors. In any case, the present data suggest that the social structure of a group must be considered in evaluating its judgments of particular individuals.

To account for the tendency of individuals rated low by the group to rate themselves higher, it is usually assumed that they are aware of their failings, and attempt to mask these defensively in the case of socially important traits by inflating their self-ratings. We need not inquire here whether these deficiencies involve fixed personal characteristics or just a mat-

426

ter of group opinion; it is enough to note that on most of the traits there is some relationship between group opinion and self-ratings, as indicated by the correlations in Table 8, which would suggest that the individual in rating himself is affected by group opinion (or something related to it). But the question may be raised as to whether this tendency to self-inflation derives fundamentally from the individual's awareness of low standing on a particular trait, or from the more general complex of factors comprising his sociometric status, since in general low status is associated with low standing on important traits. The analysis of covariance of self-ratings is aimed at this question. If when the effects of status group differences in mean ratings received are eliminated, there remain significant group differences in self-ratings, then some factor associated with sociometric status, other than general opinion of the individual on that trait, must be implicated. The results indicated that while apparently this does not hold true of some traits, there is a good possibility that it does in regard to humor, and perhaps also punctuality and intelligence. Although not conclusive, the data warrant the hypothesis that low sociometric status involves generalized feelings of insecurity which predispose to inflation of certain types of self-ratings. It is easily conceivable, futhermore, than even in the case of other traits, where self-inflation may occur regardless of sociometric status, the motivation may come from perceiving low standing as a threat to status, rather than from merely wanting to be as good as possible, or something of that sort, but this is a more difficult matter to test. Finally, it goes without saying that personality differences of various sorts may complicate self-rating tendencies in individual cases.

SUMMARY

An exploratory investigation of the relationships between sociometric status of members of a college sorority and their ratings of themselves and other members on certain personality traits indicates: (1) that individuals of high status are rated high by the group on traits which are presumably most valued socially; (2) that the sociometric status of the rater is in some cases a significant factor in his ratings of other individuals; and (3) that sociometric status, although not directly related to self-ratings, is found to be a factor in some self-ratings when the effects of differences in ratings received from the group are eliminated statistically. The findings suggest that an understanding of the judgments which an individual makes of himself or which others make of him must take into account the social structure of the group concerned. Further research is needed to isolate the factors underlying these relationships.

427

AN ANALYSIS OF SOCIAL REJECTION IN A COLLEGE MEN'S RESIDENCE HALL*

By John W. Kidd

The problem. Taking the cue from Moreno and associates in the statement that, "The most elusive problem up to date has been the measurement of rejection," (11, p. 16) the general problem which this study was designed to answer in part is: What is the nature of social rejection? As limited by the site and design of the study, the problem more specifically is: What are some factors significantly associated with those individuals most highly rejected by their peers among the 639 residents of Abbot Hall, a residence hall for men at Michigan State College, during the winter term of the 1949-50 academic year?

The literature. A review of the literature seems to justify the following hypotheses: 1) rejection is characterized by non-participation in extra-curricular activities (1; 7, p. 493; 8, p. 204); 2) rejection is positively associated with low prestige status (5, p. 260; 14, p. 220); 3) rejection is positively associated with being a lower classman (15, pp. 28-9); 4) rejection is positively related to poor home adjustment (6; 18); 5) personality characteristics are the most important characteristics determining rejection (2; 4); 6) rejection is positively correlated with academic failure (1; 3; 8, p. 204); 7) rejects disrupt group harmony (14, pp. 225-7); 8) rejects are likely to be egocentric (9, p. 134; 10, p. 335; 12; 13; 14, pp. 225-7; 16, p. 37; 17, p. 45); 9) the behavior of rejects is compensatory for inner frustration and is often aggressive (9, p. 134; 10, p. 335; 12; 13; 14, pp. 225-7; 16, p. 37; 17, p. 45); 10) an individual's rejection status is likely to be the same in different but similar groups (9, p. 205; 13, p. 139); 11) behavior leading to or accompanying rejection is positively related to lack of security (9, p. 134); and this study was designed to test in part, among others, all but number 10 of these.

Hypotheses. Based upon the literature, social and psychological theory, and the experiences of the investigator, the following hypotheses, sub-hypotheses and criteria of measurement were structured as bases of the study:

I. Rejection is associated with those individuals who are identified by their

---

*(A summary of a Doctor's dissertation of the same title, Michigan State College, East Lansing, 1951)

peers as strange, different, atypical, or lacking in prestige at the time they become group members.

A. Rejection is associated with those individuals whose past experience has produced values, appearance, or behavior identifiable by the group as different. Measurable evidence of such differences may be revealed by:
1. atypical race;
2. atypical nationality;
3. atypical religion;
4. atypical community background;
5. atypical family relationship.

B. Rejection is associated with those individuals who are characterized by prestige-detracting traits, including:
1. relatively low chronological age;
2. relatively low college classification;
3. relatively low occupational category of the father;
4. relatively low family income.

II. Rejection is associated with those individuals who, through inability or lack of motivation, fail to comply with the group's expectations of acceptable behavior, and which may be attributed to a deficiency in role-taking.

A. Rejection is associated with those individuals whose interaction with other group members is relatively restricted. Measurable evidence of such restricted interaction may be revealed by:
1. low leadership-prestige status in the group;
2. selecting relatively few others as friends;
3. rejecting relatively few others as friends;
4. participating in relatively few spectator and extra-curricular activities;
5. taking on relatively less part-time employment where such employment brings one into proximity with considerable numbers of one's peers;
6. being rated lower by themselves and Resident Assistants on participation in dormitory affairs;
7. being rated lower by themselves and Resident Assistants on over-all social participation.

B. The self-images of the most rejected individuals are likely to be inaccurate in terms of the group judgment, as evidenced by: (self-image)
1. a feeling of being rejected by one's peers;
2. a feeling of being deficient in:
   a. scholastic effort;
   b. over-all social participation;
   c. participation in the affairs of the group;
   d. social and personality adjustment;
   e. citizenship.

429

(group judgment)

1. the extent to which the group rejected the most rejected individuals;
2. the extent to which the group considered those most rejected to be deficient in:
   a. scholastic effort;
   b. over-all social participation;
   c. participation in the affairs of the group;
   d. social and personality adjustment;
   e. citizenship.

C. The most rejected individuals' behavior is often typical of reaction to frustration, that is, it is likely to be aggressive and/or withdrawing, as evidenced by:

1. relatively low academic achievement in relation to ability;
2. relatively frequent changes of residence and/or drop-outs;
3. admitted feelings of insecurity;
4. low rating by selves and Resident Assistants on scholastic effort;
5. low rating by selves and Resident Assistants on citizenship;
6. low rating by selves and Resident Assistants on social and personality adjustment;
7. being characterized by one's peers as being aggressive and/or withdrawing in his interpersonal relations;
8. case studies of some of the most rejected individuals.

Methodology. A Moreno type of sociometric questionnaire was administered to the 639 residents of the hall under an aura of demonstrated sincerity and anonymity of the respondee of which 94% were returned. In the questionnaire the following information was requested: 1) the names of one's best friends with desirability as a roommate being the criterion; 2) the names of those one would be most reluctant to accept as friends; 3) the names of those one would most prefer as Resident Assistant (a student administrative functionary in charge of from 50-75 students in a section of the residence hall); 4) the names of those one would least prefer in that capacity; 5) reasons for rejecting those under 2) above; 5) race; 6) state or country if other than U. S. in which one was reared; 7) college classification; 8) father's occupation; 9) approximate income of family during previous year; 10) size of community in which reared; 11) religious preference; 12) parents, step-parents, etc. lived with before entering college and how long; 13) age; 14) grade-point average; 15) expectation of being selected and rejected by others; 16) degree of security in feeling about the future.

Ratings by selves and Resident Assistants on points used in the study along with information about spectator and extra-curricular activities were obtained from the Annual Men's Residence Reports. Other information needed was obtained from college records.

From the questionnaire returns each resident was assigned a friendship score and a leadership score. In each case the score equalled the number of times chosen minus the number of times rejected. Seeking approximately 100 from each extreme of such a distribution to serve as selects and rejects the nearest feasible numbers were 96 rejects and 102 selects. These groups were then compared on various traits, through the application of the Chi square technique, in order to detect those ways, if any, in which they differed significantly.

The evidence. The evidence of the first or background hypothesis may be observed in Table I. The subhypothesis that atypicality was associated with rejection found support. Rejection, as distinguished from selection, was significantly associated with being from an atypical regional background— particularly foreign nationality—and being from a city of more than 100,000 population as well as ethnic atypicality as represented by a combination of atypical regional and religious background.

The group was so predominantly Caucasoid that race is considered to have been inadequately tested. Atypicality of family relationship as related

TABLE I

SUMMARY OF RELATIONSHIPS BETWEEN REJECTION AND BACKGROUND FACTORS

Factor	Evidence	Rejection apparently related to
College classification	p .05—	Lower classman
Community background	p .05—	City of more than 100,000
Regional background	p .05—	Foreign nationality
Religious preference	p .1+*	Other than Protestant or Catholic
Ethnic type (composite of two above)	p .05—	Foreign ethnic type
Parental relationship	p .2—*	Living with other than two natural parents
Parental relationship	p .2—*	A childhood change of relationship
Age	p .1+*	Less than 21
Occupation of father	no relationship indicated	
Family income	no relationship indicated	
Race	no relationship indicated	

* not significant
p is probability of occurring through chance alone; .05 or lower considered significant.

to rejection failed to stand the usual test of statistical significance though such would have occurred through chance alone approximately one time in five.

Of the four prestige-detracting traits studied, only being a lower classman was significantly associated with rejection as opposed to selection.

The tests of significance of the various criteria used to measure evidence on the second, or behavioral, hypothesis are presented in Table II. The tabulation of reasons for rejection given by the rejectors are in Table III. The subhypothesis that rejection is associated with restricted interaction found support to the extent that rejection was significantly associated with 1) low leadership-prestige status; 2) restricted rejection and selection of others;

TABLE II

SUMMARY OF RELATIONSHIPS BETWEEN REJECTION AND BEHAVIORAL FACTORS

Factor	Evidence	Rejection related to
Leadership-prestige status	p .001—	Low status
Rejection of others	p .01—	Few rejected
Selection of others	p .001—	Few selected
Spectator and extra-curricular activities	p .001—	Few activities
Part-time employment	p .05—	Unemployment
Participation in dormitory affairs[3]	p .001—	Little participation
Participation in dormitory affairs[4]	p .001—	Little participation
Over-all social participation[3]	p .02—	Little participation
Over-all social participation[4]	p .05+*	
(evidence on restricted interaction)		
Expectations of selection	p .001—	Low expectation[1]
Expectations of rejection	p .2—*[2]	
Scholastic effort	p .2—*[1]	
Participation in dormitory affairs	p *[1]	
Over-all social participation	p *[1]	
Citizenship	p *[1]	
Social and personality adjustment	p *[1]	
(evidence on inaccuracy of self-image)		
Grade-point average (ability constant)	p .01—	Low average
Moves and drop-outs	p .001—	Moving and dropping out
Security-insecurity[4]	p .5+*	
Family income unknown	p .01—	Income unknown
Scholastic effort[4]	p .05—	Little effort
Scholastic effort[3]	p .5+*	
Citizenship[4]	p .1—*	
Citizenship[3]	p .1—*	
Social and personality adjustment[4]	p .01—	Poor adjustment
Social and personality adjustment[3]	p .001—	Poor adjustment
(evidence on frustration-insecurity)		

* not significant; [1] accurate self-image; [2] inaccurate self-image; [3] Resident Assistant rating; [4] self-rating; p is probability of occurring through chance alone—.05 or lower considered significant.

TABLE III

ARBITRARY COMBINATIONS OF MOST FREQUENT FREE-RESPONSE REASONS GIVEN FOR
REJECTION IN ORDER OF FREQUENCY

1. Superiority role (Conceited, big-shot ideas, egotistical, overconfident, cocky, know-it-all, selfish, braggart, superiority complex, superior air, intrusive, social climber, extrovert, argumentative, sarcastic, spoiled, unreasonable, domineering, overbearing, must have own way, others always wrong, aggressive, belligerent, temperamental, bully, chip-on-shoulder) 231
2. Loud (Noisy, boisterous, prankster, talkative) 122
3. Inconsiderate (No regard for others, no respect for others, uncooperative) 84
4. Immature (Juvenile, childish) 57
5. Inferiority role (Unfriendly, timid, too quiet, independent, introvert, retiring, inferiority feelings) 48
6. Profane (Vulgar, crude, ill-mannered, low morals, loose morals, foul-minded, cursing) 40
7. Irresponsible, (Untrustworthy, unreliable, two-faced, sly, untruthful) 28
8. Untidy (Insanitary, unclean, slovenly) 22
9. Pessimist, (Griper, complainer, moody) 18
10. Odd (Screwy, silly, simple, sex-crazy, naive, helpless, narrow, straight-laced) 14
11. Effeminate (Affected, girlish) 11

3) restricted spectator and extra-curricular activities; 4) restricted part-time employment which brings one into contact with group members; 5) low rating on group participation by selves and others; 6) low rating on over-all social participation by others.

The second subhypothesis to the effect that rejection is associated with those holding inaccurate self-images was supported by only one of the criteria utilized, i.e., the rejects, as compared with the selects, were rejected significantly more than they stated they expected.

The subhypothesis to the effect that rejects are frustrated and insecure was supported by a significant relationship between rejection and 1) low academic achievement in relation to ability; 2) more frequent moves and drop-outs; 3) being ignorant of the family income. In addition, the tabulation of reasons given for rejecting others, as shown in Table III, points to egocentric, aggressive behavior as that most typical of rejects. An intensive study of the nine most rejected individuals offers further support to this proposition, in that those individuals were, in eight cases, most often described as conceited, loud, inconsiderate, etc., while one was considered to be primarily pessimistic and inferior in feelings.

Conclusions and implications. Of the background factors considered which might produce a rejected status through making an initial impression on the group of being different or lacking in prestige, only being a foreigner in the national or ethnic sense and being from a city of more than 100,000 population were significantly associated with rejection as opposed to selection, as marks of atypicality, and being a lower classman as a mark of low prestige. While race was not adequately tested due to the nature of the population studied, and while unusual parental relationship as well as relatively low age approached statistical significance in apparent relationship, there was no indication that either low family income or low rated occupation of the father were related to rejection.

Among the behavioral characteristics examined, the following were significantly related to rejection as opposed to selection: 1) low leadership-prestige status; 2) restricted rejection and selection of others; 3) restricted spectator and extra-curricular activities; 4) lack of part-time employment; 5) self-rating and rating of observers on being restricted in participation in the affairs of the group; 6) rating by observers as being restricted in over-all social participation; 7) inaccuracy of self-image in expecting less rejection than received; 8) low grade-point average in relation to ability; 9) more frequent moves and drop-outs; 10) not knowing the family income; 11) rating selves low on scholastic effort; 12) being rated by selves and observers as poor in social and personality adjustment. In addition, a tabulation of the reasons given for rejection placed emphasis on ego-centric, inconsiderate, aggressive behavior most frequently, and withdrawing, odd, juvenile behavior generally second most important. A study of the nine most rejected individuals indicated that eight of them were primarily egocentric, inconsiderate, boisterous, etc., and one pessimistic and withdrawing.

Generally, then, it appears that rejection accompanies marked atypicality as to origin and belief systems and classification in a low local prestige rank—specifically, lower classman, and that many commonly held criteria of acceptability such as family income, occupation of father, were not applied in the group studied.

Personality traits which are typical of reaction to frustration and/or insecurity, i.e., aggression and withdrawal, were significantly associated with rejection. The reject appears to interact with group members less than does the select.

It may be concluded that marked atypicality results in an initial rejection by the group accompanied by barriers to interaction established both by the group in its ostracism and the individual in his different values and communicative handicaps which renders the gaining of acceptability more difficult than for the average group member.

Further, the reject appears to be maladroit in role-taking, failing to become completely aware of the group definitions and expectations, or, in the event this conclusion is unwarranted, he then must be either inept in his attempt to comply with group expectations or lack the motivation to do so.

For a counseling or advisory program in residence halls which seeks social acceptability for the individual as part of the educational product, the following implications seem to be justifiable:

1. In the case of foreigners and others from markedly different ethnic backgrounds:

    a. attempt to bring them to a realization of the many differences likely to exist between their previous cultural values and the values of the culture in which they now find themselves;

    b. suggest that the mark of an educated man is spontaneity and adaptability—that they may make certain adjustments to these different values without forever forsaking their earlier values to which they may return;

    c. attempt to get over the idea that to really understand another individual and anticipate his actions and reactions, one must think as he thinks; therefore adjustment to the values of a group and the individuals therein necessitates taking on the roles of various individuals within such a group;

    d. show that effective role-taking is essentially a communicative process, a matter of interpersonal relations of a sympathetic sort; that to effectively put oneself in another person's place one must at least temporarily abandon bias, prejudice, dogma, and *a priori* answers;

    e. explain that being thwarted in attempting such a goal-response as gaining social acceptance tends to lead to frustration and reduce rationality to rationalization;

    f. arrange situations, programs, activities, and conditions in so far as feasible to increase the sheer quantity of contacts by foreigners with more typical group members.

2. In the case of other rejects:

    a, b, especially c, d, and e above, plus

    f. calling their attention as the situation permits to the kinds of behavior typical of the most rejected persons, and how adjustment to norms of acceptable behavior in such a group constitutes a vital part of the educational process and is real preparation for successful living in American society.

REFERENCES

(Abbreviated from original to only those items referred to in summary)

1. Alexander, Norman, and Ruth J. Woodruff, "Determinants of College Success," *Journal of Higher Education,* 11:479-85, December, 1940.

2. Austin, Mary C., and George C. Thompson, "Children's Friendships: A Study of the Bases on Which Children Select and Reject Their Best Friends," *Journal of Educational Psychology,* 39:101-16, January, 1948.

3. Bonney, Merl E., "A Study of the Relationship of Intelligence, Family Size, and Sex Differences with Mutual Friendships in the Primary Grades," *Child Delvelopment,* 13:79-100, March, 1942.

4. ————, "Personality Traits of Socially Successful and Socially Unsuccessful Children," *Journal of Educational Psychology,* 34:449-72, November, 1943.

5. Cook, Lloyd Allen, "An Experimental Sociographic Study of a Stratified 10th Grade Class," *American Sociological Review,* 10:250-61, April, 1945.

6. Flotow, Ernest A., "Charting Social Relationships of School Children," *Elementary School Journal,* 46:498-504, May, 1946.

7. Hill, Reuben, "An Experimental Study of Social Adjustment," *American Sociological Review,* 9:481-94, October, 1944.

8. Janney, J. E., "A Technique for the Measurement of Social Adjustment," *Journal of Experimental Education,* 7:203-5, March, 1939.

9. Kuhlen, Raymond G., and Beatrice J. Lee, "Personality Characteristics and Social Acceptability in Adolescence," *Journal of Educational Psychology,* 34:321-40, September, 1943.

10. Moreno, J. L., Helen Hall Jennings and Joseph H. Sargent, *Time As a Quantitative Index of Inter-personal Relations.* Sociometry Monographs, Number 13, New York: Beacon House, 1943. 344 pp.

11. Northway, Mary L, "Outsiders," SOCIOMETRY, 7:10-25, February, 1944.

12. ————, "Sociometry and Some Challenging Problems of Social Relationships," SOCIOMETRY, 9:187-98, May-August, 1946.

13. Smucker, Orden Curtiss, "A Sociographic Study of the Friendship Patterns on a College Campus." Unpublished Doctor's dissertation, Ohio State University, Columbus, 1945.

14. Steele, Samuel C., "Friendship Patterns on a College Campus." Unpublished Master's thesis, University of Rochester, New York, 1938.

15. Thomas, "Attitudes of Liking and Disliking Persons and Their Determining Conditions." Unpublished Master's thesis, University of Illinois, Urbana, 1936.

16. Winslow, Charles N., and Muriel N. Frankel, "A Questionnaire Study of the Traits that Adults Consider To Be Important in the Formation of Friendship with Members of Their Own Sex," *Journal of Social Psychology,* 13:37-49, February, 1941.

17. Woolf, Maurice D., A Study of Some Relationships Between Home Adjustment and the Behavior of Junior College Students," *Journal of Social Psychology,* 17:275-86, February-May, 1943.

LEADERSHIP AND SOCIOMETRIC CHOICE*

By Helen H. Jennings

Leadership phenomena "happen"; in the human setting of some spot where people get into interaction on a *tele*,[1] or feeling, basis, behaviors of a "leadership" sort occur. The study of leadership phenomena, however, is complicated by the questions: leadership in what respect? for whom? in what sort of group? and what kind of psychological position in respect to the given population did the individual showing leadership have *at the time* he displayed it?

The choice process in a community structures it psychologically in a particularlized fashion along the lines of association for work and living together important to its population. Such work groups and living (housing) groups may be called *sociogroups* since association is founded on a socio- (collective) -criterion. The tele (or choices) expressed for members in these sociogroups, may be called *sociotele*. Then there are other "groups" which have no sociocriteria, in this sense, where association, equally real and important, is strictly a "private" matter; this tele is similarly "personal" and may be called *psychetele*.[2] Psychetele has a pri-

---

* Prepared by the author from data more fully reported in *Leadership and Isolation*, Longmans, Green, 1943 and 1950.

[1] As Moreno demonstrates, the tele process of attraction and repulsion must be considered dependent upon both individuals in a relationship, even though the flow of feeling on the part of one individual towards the second may be unknown by the second, as the direction this takes is not random but depends upon the second person. The tele factor is therefore not viewed as the subjective, independent product of each person. J. L. Moreno, *Who Shall Survive?* Beacon House, 1934. J. L. Moreno and H. H. Jennings, "Statistics of Social Configurations," *Sociometry*, I: 342-374, January-April, 1938, p. 363 ff.

[2] The writer finds these distinctions upon comparing the choice process in sociogroups and psychegroups in the same population—this analysis reveals that "psychegroup choice prominence" differs greatly in its meaning from "sociogroup choice prominence." (*Op. cit.*, 2nd edition.) The definitions are given to reflect the finding that an unrestricting criterion (leisure-time) shows a structural picture of interrelationships based almost exclusively on personality-to-personality compatibility, whereas "restricting" criteria (*working*, and/or *living* in same group) show other bases. The results also suggest that sociogroups can function together sometimes as one *multisociogroup* for given purposes but that psychegroups (as thus defined) are not so constructed that their combining could be usually an enlarging and desirable function; in fact, such endeavor might defeat their very objectives.

vate, personalized base. (I, as Mary Jones, feel towards you, Sally Smith, thus and so . . .). Sociotele has a collective, impersonalized base freer of the uniqueness of private personality aspects of response. (I, an employed woman holding membership in this union, feel towards you, as an employed woman also holding membership in this union, thus and so . . .). The membership of a given psychegroup may also overlap and be part of a sociogroup, but *while functioning as* sociogroup members, the individuals apparently "expect to" relinquish roles appropriate in psychegroup membership.[3]

By psychegroup is not meant, in sociological terms, any face-to-face group, often called "primary groups." There are such groups which never become either in part or totally what is here meant by the term psychegroup. The psychegroup as here used is an inter-personal structure *where* the uniqueness of the individual as a personality is appreciated and "allowed for" with varying degrees of spontaneous indulgence and affection, of the kind he seeks. It is where one counts "altogether" as a person, not merely as an individual or as a member of sociogroup. In industry it springs up in the informal grouping that comes to exist as men work side by side. In the filing room of a telephone company, it is the similar informal grouping that "happens." But in such psychegroup formations, as these develop inside socio-groups, it appears, the individual must consider his participation "separately" from his participation as a sociogroup member. Obviously, even in the most inviting psychegroup, no millenium exists psychologically, but relative to other inter-individual groupings, it exists to a greater extent. Similarly, it appears that in a particular sociogroup, only certain aspects of personality are appreciated by other members, as only certain aspects are appropriate to the tasks important in the specific sociogroup life. The differences in structure apparently result from such mores, inherited, cherished or worked towards. Within the sociogroup, there may be many members chosen by others as sociogroup members who *at the same*

---

[3]This reminds the writer of the situation of a psychologist, a social case worker, a sociologist, or a physician. Each carries a "role" respectively appropriate and demanded in his sociogroup. But when any one of them enters his psychegroups (informal friendship or family groups), he must drop this role and base his interrelations in total person-to-person terms. Only physicians who have the advantage of having been at the game of shifting roles longer seem to recognize this. And perhaps it is true that even they have over-played by shifting too completely, letting members of their psychegroups have such privacy as to die at their own convenience without any "unasked for" advice. See, J. L. Moreno, *Sociodrama,* Psychodrama Mon. No. 1. Beacon House, 1944, N. Y.

time are rejected or unchosen by these same individuals in the latter's several psychegroups.

It is the confusion between a sociogroup and a psychegroup or rather the lack of a clear-cut delineation between them that has complicated study of leadership phenomena.

The problem of this report is to review what relation is found between sociometric choice-status in sociogroups and the behavior individuals show at the time they display a given choice-status. In this report, a sociogroup is defined as a group which has psychological structure *in relation to* a sociocriterion important enough to cause inter-personal choice to arise distinctly in relation to it.

PART II

THE EXPERIMENT

The Problem

This study[4] explores the choice process as it operates in a community and the individual's social-contact range in relation to it; it further, analyzes general behavior dynamics in this setting. The present report will discuss only the data important to a minimum consideration of sociometric choice and leadership.

The Subjects

The laboratory of the research was the New York State Training School for Girls: a closed community comprising over 400 individuals. The population consists of girls committed by the Children's Courts of the state and represents a cross-section of the socially and economically underprivileged of the state's population as a whole. To be admitted, the girl must be over 12 and under 16 years of age and of normal intelligence.

The Sociometric Test

The sociometric test, devised by Moreno,[5] discloses the feelings which individuals have in regard to one another in respect to membership in the groups in which they are at a given moment (ideally all groups in which they are or could be). It is an *action* test. The criterion for choice must have explicit meaning for the subject and offer him the specific opportunity to give information for reconstruction (or retention) of the situations in which he is.

---

[4]*Op. cit.*
[5]*Op. cit.* p.

The results are put into operation to the optimal satisfaction of *all* subjects.[6] Thus, in respect to the criterion of the group's formation, the psychological position of every member in the composition of the group's structure is brought to light. By periodic testing, in like manner, changes in this structure can be traced, followed, and evaluated.

Validity and Consistency

Choice behavior, as one kind of behavior, is valid just as any behavior is valid, providing choices are made on criteria holding significance for the subjects. The research examines how individuals behave in choice and rejection, under the same conditions of testing, at intervals 8 months apart. The question is rather one of examining *how stable* is such behavior, for the same individual, at two time points 8 months distant.

Data on the individual's behavior in general, however, are examined to throw light on the meaning of the choice behavior shown by the individual or towards him by others. (In the present reporting, data particularly of interest to an understanding of leadership phenomena in this setting only are summarized).

As previously employed, the sociometric test was found to have an average reliability of .95 based on data given on four successive weeks with a five-choice allowance on one criterion (tent-mates in summer camps).[7] Zeleny found, at the college level using also five choices and one criterion (membership in a discussion group), reliability coefficients ranging from .93 to .95 on re-administering such a sociometric test on successive days.[8] These coefficients are based on the extent to which the subject is chosen by others on two or more occasions; they thus relate to the *choice-position* the individual *receives from others*. The more stringent comparison which the present study makes, by use of unlimited choice and a much longer re-test interval, also reveals that even under these conditions, there is a fairly high correlation.[9]

A comparison of the individual's *consistency with himself* on separate occasions (his extent of expenditure of choice) could not be made in pre-

---

[6]J. L. Moreno, *op. cit.*, p. 269 ff. Also, J. L. Moreno and H. H. Jennings, *Sociometric Control Studies of Grouping and Regrouping.* Sociometry Monographs No. 7, Beacon House, 1947.

[7]Wilber I. Newstetter, Marc J. Feldstein, and Theodore M. Newcomb, *Group Adjustment*, Western Reserve University, 1938, p. 35.

[8]Leslie Day Zeleny, "Sociometry of Morale," *Amer. Sociol. Review*, IV: 799-808, Dec., 1939, p. 804.

[9]Jennings, *op. cit.*, pp. 27-31, 57.

vious research as the extent to which the subject could choose others was allotted in advance. This reveals that the individual shows *a characteristic repertoire* in choice expression for others.[10] In a study of boys in several open communities Deutschberger[11] results confirm this finding for the individual living in a "stable" community. However, when the community undergoes rapid population changes, the individual's full emotional repertoire is not maintained and he tends to "drop" others who are "unlike" himself (in religion and race). Hence, "need and occasion" appear involved, as Deutschberger points out.

The Test Instructions

The following protocol material[12] illustrates the simplicity and direcness of the approach used:

> "You will notice that your paper is divided into 8 squares or boxes. In the first 'Yes' box, marked 'live with,' write the name of whatever girls there are anywhere on the campus or in your own house whom you would prefer to live with. In the 'No' box of 'live with,' write the names of whatever girls there are anywhere on the campus or in your own house whom you would prefer not to live with. Do the same for the 'work with' boxes. Then those you would prefer not to work with, place in the 'No' box for work. Next, do your 'recreation or leisure' and then, your 'study or school' boxes, having in mind the same instructions. . . . The 'No' boxes should contain only the names of those, *if any,* whom you definitely *don't* want in your group for the particular functions or function, which it happens to be. The 'Yes' boxes should contain only the names of those, *if any,* whom you definitely *do* want in your group for the particular functions or function, which it happens to be. . . . Do the boxes in any other order than that suggested if you prefer."

The second technique used was a social contact listing or "test."[13]

Dates and Spacing of Tests

The first tests were given during the last week of December, 1937. The test-population included all individuals (443) comprising the popu-

---

[10]*Op. cit.,* p. 58, 215, 219.

[11]Paul Deutschberger, "Interaction Patterns of Changing Neighborhoods," Sociometry, IX: 296-315, November 1946.

[12]The complete protocol appears in H. H. Jennings, "A Sociometric Study of Emotional and Social Expansiveness" in Roger G. Barker, Jacob S. Kounin, and Herbert F. Wright (edrs.), *Child Behavior and Development.* 1943.

[13]For these results, see *op. cit.,* pp. 62-65 ff.

lation as of January 1, 1938. Re-tests were given during the first week of September, 1938, to all individuals (457) comprising the population as of September 3, 1938.

The Method of Choice Analysis

The method of analysis is a comparison of the number of *different* individuals reacted to positively (chosen) or negatively (rejected) by the subjects, with the number of different individuals reacting positively or negatively to the subjects. The data used in the analysis include all choices and rejections either on the criterion of living or on the criterion of working given to or received by 133 subjects present for both tests and occupying the same housing units on both occasions.

Problem of this report

Is there any relation between behavior shown in interaction with others and the sociometric choice-status of the individual? In order to examine behavior at different "points" in choice-status, "under-chosen" is defined as placing 1 S. D. below the mean of the test-population; "over-chosen" as placing 1 S. D. above the mean; and "average-chosen" as placing approximately at the mean, in number of individuals choosing the subject. The number of under-chosen positions are 41 (19 on Test I and 22 on Test II); the number of over-chosen positions are 43 (22 on Test I and 21 on Test II); for a basis of comparison, 41 other positions placing nearest the mean on either test were selected.

PART III
FINDINGS

In the community, elections of a House Council were held in the fall of 1937.[14] The individual receiving the highest number of votes automatically became a member of the Community Council. The election was held under the supervision of the Club Director and the ballots were closed. Four members were elected to the Council in each house. For the purpose of comparing membership in the Councils with rank in positive choice received from others, only data for the two members in each living unit receiving the highest (and second highest) number of votes are used. The reason for this is twofold. In the voting for Council membership in the respective living units, the voting is limited to the individuals

---

[14]The election data, given to the writer by the Club Director of the community, by oversight were not included in the 1st edition of *Leadership and Isolation*.

living in the respective units; in the present research the subjects were free to choose other subjects residing anywhere in the community. Secondly, the majority of votes might be cast for only one or two individuals, and those attaining membership in the respective Council because of receiving the third or fourth highest number might not be receiving a very large number.

This comparison reveals that of the twenty such Council members (two from each of the ten housing units of this study), eighteen or 90 per cent place among the over-chosen (as defined in this study: 1 S. D. above the mean). The two Council members who do not so rank, place just below this point. When allowance is made for the difference between being chosen from a community wide base and being elected from the limited house population, it is evident that there is practically a one-to-one relationship between being elected to represent the house body in matters concerning the group and being chosen by community members on the sociometric criteria of living and/or working with them.

Approximately three months intervened between this election and the time of Test I. During this period, it would have been possible for elected Council members to lose their standing with their respective house population, had members been elected who were found incapable of representing and acting in behalf of the group to the satisfaction of their "electorate."

Observation of the personalities of over-chosen and study of the motivations given for choice provide the following clues to their choice-status. These appear, to a greater or less extent, to hold for each over-chosen subject.

enlarges the social space[15] for interchange of ideas and activities

secures more and more responsibilities to be held by members in their work groups, in their housing units, and in the community as a whole

takes definite stands on what he considers "right" and will ."fight" for it

aids the average (average-chosen) individuals to broaden their conceptions of their potential capacities; shows faith in their abilities by "taking it for granted" that they *can* and want to contribute to their own development and to the life of the community

shows ability to establish rapport quickly and effectively with a wide

---

[15]*Op. cit.*, pp. 3, 215, 219.

443

range of other personalities and to win their confidence under varying circumstances

insists on an "impersonal" fairness and succeeds in gaining respect for this level of interaction between members

raises the level of conduct of average members by "demanding" considerate behavior towards the less able (in the sense of less contributing members)

calls "to account" individuals who attempt to exclude participating by the relatively non-contributing or "destructively" contributing members; shows towards them "protective" behavior

exhibits anger and censuring almost exclusively towards only those members whom they consider "should know better" rather than towards all alike

"controls" and "destiny" of "non-adjusting" members (*i.e.*, non-adjusting to the kind of regime instituted by such behaviors as listed above) by influencing other members to aid them, by "blocking" their possible satisfactions in "non-adjusting" behaviors, and by "obliging" other members to show respect for them in the community as a whole (*e.g.*, not to carry unfavorable reports about them into the "networks" by telling "out-group" members of occurrences which would "prejudice" their standing in the community)

causes others to feel he aids them to meet their "problems"

These behavior tendencies are confirmed and further expanded when housemother reports commending or "complaining" of the individual's behavior are examined in relation to the individual's choice-status. To the over-chosen are attributed three times as many incidences of initiatory behavior in making innovations without permission, twice as many incidences showing planning and organization, four times as many occasions showing initiative in starting new projects, and over four times as often behavior exhibiting ingenuity in changing conduct of "problem" members or fostering understanding between new members and others, and about twice as often rebellious behaviors, as recorded for average-chosen members. In these reports, the incidences for under-chosen are none or but half as frequent as for average-chosen.

To the under-chosen are attributed twelve times as many incidences of behavior actively or passively interfering with the group's activities, as to the over-chosen, while such incidences are practically missing for the average-chosen. For the over-chosen are reported seven times as great an incidence of retaliatory behavior (among other over-chosen) than for average-chosen and this behavior is rare for under-chosen. (Could this reflect less earnest competition to give occasion for such behavior among the latter members?)

On the other hand, the most often spontaneously given "praise" of the housemother by the over-chosen is her listening to and considering the members' opinions in planning; such comment is made only a third as often by the average-chosen and not at all by the under-chosen.

Thus, it appears the under-chosen show in common many varieties of behaviors the effect of which may tend to separate and draw individuals apart rather than to bring them together. The average-chosen show somewhat less than half as great an incidence of such behaviors, and about twice as great an incidence of behaviors the effect of which may tend to bring individuals into constructive relationship with one another. Further, in the very behaviors in which the average-chosen outrank the under-chosen, the over-chosen in turn are found to exceed the average citizen by approximately twice as great an incidence. And in those behaviors which "make new events happen" or "enlarge the kind and extent of activity" the over-chosen surpass the average citizen by over four times as great an incidence.

Just as isolated-from-choice positions and over-chosen positions are but two ends of one continuum, so behaviors when analyzed in relation to such choice-status of the individual (at the time he has the particular choice-status) appear as forming extremes on one continuum—at the one end showing expressions disruptive (or "clogging") to the life of the group and at the other, expressions conducive to an expanding life for the group. Sociometric choice for the individual thus appears to depend directly upon the nature of the group *in which he is to be functioned with*.

In the sociogroup for living in the same housing unit, this living together apparently becomes both an "art and a business." Individuals whose behaviors in interaction with other individuals lead the membership as a whole or some section of it to a more rewarding and fulfilling experience appear to earn sociometric choice proportionately. Similarly, the sociogroup for working in the same unit shows like trends.[16]

Thus for the citizen who would earn choice, it appears as much a matter of what behaviors he rarely exhibits as it does a matter of what behaviors he may frequently show which will determine what choice-status

---

[16]For an analysis of *working* and *living*, differentiated according to these criteria, see *op. cit.*, pp. 226-232. The individual's program consisted of one-half day of academic school and one-half day of "work" (practice of the elected vocation); the latter was "work" in which the individual was to earn a livelihood.

he will hold in a sociogroup for work or living.[17] The average citizens of this study are not in any sense average in all constructive behaviors; it is rather that the sum-total of their behaviors taken as a whole redounds to their remaining average contributors to the community life: the incidence of behaviors having a negative import for inter-personal exchange (in common work and living) appears to offset those having a positive import sufficiently in the case of such individuals to "hold them down" to an average-status.

Leadership and isolation appear, from this study, as phenomena which arise out of individual differences in inter-personal capacity for sociogroup participation and as phenomena which are *indigenous to the specific milieu of the sociogroup* or sociogroups *in which they are produced.*

Individuals who emerge as leaders in one sociogroup may or may not emerge in a similar role in another community or even in another sociogroup in the same community. Likewise, individuals who classify as isolates in terms of choice from their associates in one sociogroup in a given community may or may not change in choice-status in another sociogroup in the same or another community.

Nevertheless, it may be hypothesized that when certain qualities have become pronounced and integrated in the personality expression of the individual (such a quality as relatively great freedom from self-concern sufficient to enable him to be concerned with matters affecting many others than himself), these are likely to persist, for they reflect a high level of emotional growth and maturity, and thus may be expected to act favorably upon his future relationships with persons in other sociogroups.

It would also appear, similarly, that certain qualities (such a quality as relative inability to observe and orient one's actions to the elements of a situation and the persons comprising it) may, unless outgrown, continue to act unfavorably upon the individual's future relationships.

The "why" of leadership appears, however, not explainable by any personality quality or constellation of traits. Some individuals are found who are as emotionally mature and as resourceful in ideas as the leader-individuals of this study, yet they were not "allowed" a role of leadership nor chosen more than the average citizen of the community. The why of leadership appears to reside in the inter-personal contribution of which

---

[17]Living, in the sense of common housing unit for many persons, is not to be understood as the same as living in one's family; the latter group is ideally a psychegroup formed with the fullest possible spontaneity. Also, in this study, it did not involve room-mate choice; each individual has a single room.

the individual becomes capable in a specific setting eliciting such contribution from him. Similarly, isolation appears as but the opposite extreme on this continuum of inter-personal sensitivity between the membership and the individual in the sociogroup.

The over-chosen "personalities" showing certain behaviors in common differ markedly from one another in the "style" of these behaviors and the "style" they show *in contact with* specific other individuals. As persons, they are very "unlike." (Similarly, isolates and near-isolates differ greatly from each other.)[18] An analysis of their ways of behaving (depending upon toward whom) shows the leadership they exert to be definable as a *manner of interacting with others*—a manner which moves others in directions the latter apparently want to happen even though they may be doing little themselves towards attaining such directions. It is as if these individuals recognize and think more of the needs of others than others think of their own needs. The leader-individuals often take actions in behalf of others whom they do not choose and who do not know of the effort made for them.[19] Such actions by the average individuals almost invariably involve others whom they choose and thus may be inferred to be of more personalized interest to them.

While the varieties of styles of leadership (and of isolation) are many, nevertheless a number of characteristics of leader individuals stand out as common attributes. The social milieu is "improved" from the point of view of the membership through the efforts of each leader. Each widens the area of social participation for others (and indirectly his own social space) by his unique contribution to this milieu. Each leader seems to sense spontaneously when to censure and when to praise and apparently is intellectually and emotionally "uncomfortable" when others are "left-out," and acts to foster tolerance on the part of one member towards another.[20] (At the same time they give little quarter

---

[18]*Op. cit.* p. 166 ff.

[19]For example, three times as frequently the over-chosen individual, as compared with the average-chosen subject, made "unasked-for-suggestions to the psychologist for the welfare of others." Further, "visits to the psychology office in behalf of another individual (instead of self)" were made approximately seven times as often by over-chosen individuals as by average-chosen, and not at all by under-chosen.

[20]It should be understood that "leadership" can take precisely the opposite trends than those taken by the leadership found in this test-community; it obviously can take the direction of securing objectives wanted by some section of a population at the expense of some other section of the population—such "group-

to each other—other leaders.) (By contrast, the isolates and the near-isolates appear relatively "self-bound," behaving in ways which tend to show little capacity to identify with others or to bridge the gap between their own personalities and others as members of the sociogroup.)

The leadership thus exhibited in the community by various members appears, in each instance, to reflect a "style" of leadership—a particularized way of behaving derived from the personality attributes of the individual-in-an-over-chosen position. Actually, however, the "success" of several "types" of personality in achieving leadership-status through their ways of behaving while a member of the population appears to depend, in turn, upon the fact that the population itself is comprised of so great a variety of personalities that no one personality has a constellation of attributes necessary to win an exclusive position in esteem and influence necessary to a role of exclusive leadership. Each leader makes a contribtuion *to some "parts"* of the membership which all members do not equally want or need. There may be very little overlap between the individuals who "support" one leader and those who support another.

Leadership appears as a process in which not one individual has a major role but in which relatively many share. The superior capacity which one individual may have to recognize *and respond* to the needs of others does not show itself as a generalized capacity which may relate him to *any other individuals*. It appears in the special sensitivity between the individual and *specific* other persons, resulting in interaction between them.

The psychological structure resulting from choice behavior on the part of members of the test-community, this research finds,[21] may be most accurately envisioned as *an equilibrium in flux*. The movements which take place continually within it are compensatory movements which do not disturb the total structure viewed as a totality. The total structure tends to retain its characteristics from one time to another *even though the respective positions of its carriers* (the members of the population) alter from time to time. The shifts "upward" and "downward" that are shown

cleavage" points are frequent in our public schools, along socio-economic, racial, and religious lines and result in secret sororities, fraternities and "unlisted societies," and behaviors related thereto. Intergroup Education, American Council on Education, Hilda Taba *et al., Sociometric Work Guide for Teachers,* 1947. The writer is Specialist in Group Relations on this project.

[21] *Op. cit.,* pp. 210, 226.

in the choice-status of the individuals in the population are, so to speak, bound to occur since interaction cannot be static. The reasons for this stability and this slowness of flux within the structure appear in the behaviors distinguishing choice-status. A social process of interaction *by and towards* the individuals respectively "isolated" or "lifted" to leadership is found to form the very basis of the isolation and of the leadership. Personality *per se in so far as it is reflected in social structure* is the capacity for interplay with other personalities, for responding to and being responded to, in a reciprocal situation, in which the individual is in common with other individuals.

PART IV

BROADER IMPLICATIONS

In view of the interlocking dependence of one sociometric situation upon another in the structure of a sociogroup, *no* leader-position is "better" or "worse" than another—each is simply different—and none should be assessed certainly in a quantitative hierarchy. This would similarly hold for intermediary and network positions and for unchosen positions alike. It is obvious that intermediary positions are indispensable in the functioning of the sociogroup structure as a whole; it is also obvious that every link in a network is a phenomenon which if it had not developed would cut off into dead-ends the communication possibilities at a given point in question.[22] But even if we assume that this given link were severed towards the end of the network, it is as yet impossible to assess whether the loss resulting would correlate with the simple number of individuals left without linkage to the structure. What is thrown into the network below a given point and what receptivity is given to what is thrown into it above a given point may affect the life of the sociogroup all out of proportion to the "technically measured" importance of the part of the structure in which the individuals are who are "severed out" towards the lower end of a network.

It is less obvious what importance unchosen (and sometimes highly rejected) positions can have for a structure. The difference between

---

[22]Theodore M. Newcomb, *Personality and Social Change*, Dryden Press, 1943, Chaps. 3, 9, 14 and 15. Newcomb shows that the kind and direction of relationships developed in a community are closely tied in with attitudes representative of the dominant trends of thought in the community. (*E.g.*, the individual's attitudes would be more affected by "with whom" he had a relationship than even by a course of study he might take.)

the unchosen positions, however, is indicated by the directions of their sociotele relationships to persons in other positions in the structure. The fact that the sociometrically speaking "lesser" people on a sociogram do not tend to conglomerate together is first noted; the fact that they break up into diverse directions in seeking relationships is next to be noted. But the implications of these choice behaviors in the psychology of the choice process is the important fact for understanding the behavior of persons in leadership-positions. Through the fact of the unchosen looking to them, through the "flattery" and "charity" and "understanding" and "getting a hearing" that they optimistically expect to receive from the individuals in leadership-positions, the behaviors of the latter are to a considerable extent affected and determined, and these in turn affect the behaviors of the average-chosen towards the unchosen. (Scapegoating is prevalent or not depending largely upon the behavior of the leadership-position people in their attitudes and stands towards such conduct and their attitudes towards such conduct is determined by the expectations which those "to be scapegoated" hope to get from the "top" persons of influence.)

Thus the ideas which the unchosen have, as well as the ideas of the over-chosen, are important in the sociogroup life. And moreover, the ideas of the unchosen are important for what ideas the over-chosen will consider fitting in interaction, and these in turn are of pre-eminent importance for the behaviors of the average-chosen—the great "sociometric middle-class." If the unchosen did not look "up" (as they almost invariably do in this test-community), the over-chosen might not feel the "tele-pull" of their looking to them.

For the needs of a population to find outlets for fulfillment a widely ramified psychological structure, sociometrically speaking is a necessity. Without a certain minimum publicity being spread to others by those who know and approve the individual's "way of leading," no individual can have a leadership-position beyond his immediate interrelationships. It is here where the power of networks enters. In the test-community, knowledge of fellow members' ways of behaving could be widespread as the psychological inter-individual structure was so well developed. Hence, sociometric choosing did not have to be "in the dark."

In any community where this is not the case, there likely will not be found similar correlation between kinds of behavior displayed by the individual and the choice-status he shows concomitantly. Even if, in our test-community, such a high correlation had not been found, this would not, of necessity, invalidate sociometric choosing as a method under which the leadership-positions may be currently located. It would simply have suggested two lines of investigation: (1) Was the election for sociogroup representation bonafide? (That is, was the elected individual to be allowed to function *as such* representative, or was it an election in name only, where the electorate knew or suspected the elected individual would not actually carry the authority to represent them?) (2) Was knowledge on the part of the population of its own membership sufficient to make the electorate intelligent about its voting on the given criterion?

Even in a population of four to five hundred, there must be sufficient psychological geography for the network communication to function. One individual cannot know 500 others but he can be in authentic communication with the trends of thought of the more influencing members through relationships with immediate persons whose opinions he trusts. Unless the community has a well-developed and actively functioning structure of psyche-group life, any sociogroup life cannot well develop and consequently no authentically based community life can emerge. The "community" then may be likened to the population of a hotel—no basic communication happening among its "membership." For effective sociometric community structure to "grow" and stay in full sense, some aspects of living in the "community" must be carried on by the population in common—*under conditions where the manner of their being carried on* makes a difference. Such structure does not "come forth" regardless of the controls instituted to thwart or distort its development.

The aristo-tele position, so called by Moreno,[23] because the individual in it could exert influence all out of proportion to its sociometric prominence, may be thought of as a "feeder-to-leaders" since he is an individual who receives hardly any choices from the population as a whole but receives a high degree of tele preference from individuals who *do* receive a great number of choices from the population as a whole. Such leader-feeders, however, are not and should not be thought of as in actual positions of leadership, from a sociometric standpoint. They are *given* influence *at the discretion* of those in leadership-positions; it is only through them that their ideas are given practice in actuality and except for them, their ideas would wait for an audition and might never find receptivity.

---

[23] *Op. cit.*

451

(This is quite aside from consideration of how important the feeder-leader may be to the individual in a leadership role. The latter may be almost wholly dependent upon the "sustenance" in ideas, strategies, and even emotional inspiration he gets from the former. But the fact remains that the feeder-leader *does not himself* personally exert leadership.

It may be concluded that the receipt of sociometric choice in a sociogroup means the passing of a reality test implied in the criterion for choice in the sociometric test for such situation. The individual gains such choice as he "passes" such test on the basis of demands related to the needs of specific persons in the defined situation involving him and them.[24] Thus choice expressed by one individual towards another registers, in this definite sense, an active decision in favor of collaboration with him in the life situation involved. For this reason, the writer prefers the term "desirability" rather than "acceptability" to describe sociometric choice-status: "acceptability" can imply a passive or tolerant attitude merely towards the chosen person. Similarly, the term "supporter" would seem more fitting than "follower" to imply the active reciprocity involved in leadership.

Whether leadership, as found in the sociogroups of this study, appears in any similar expressions in the psychegroups of this test-population, is a separate (though related) question.[25] In the sociogroup, it is noted, the newcomer often chooses the over-chosen leader-individuals. For psychegroup affiliation, he seldom does. It is as if the individual could find compatibility in his psychegroup best with individuals *psychologically located*

---

[24] In an earlier report ("Structure of Leadership," Sociometry, I: 99-143, July-October, 1937, p. 133), the writer found wide discrepancy between results on the basis of a "popularity vote" (for "The one I consider is most popular") and results based on sociometric testing. "Popularity" in a void (*i.e.,* minus a definition: popular for what?) shows no correlation with sociometric choice-status and related behaviors.

[25] In group work, a distinction has been made between formed groups and natural groups. In settlements and in informal educational and recreational agencies, "formed groups" may consist of either protected groups where each of the individuals presents a special problem so that they cannot be absorbed into other groups (in the settlement, *e.g.,* these may be mentally retarded or neurotic persons). An interest group is one where an interest is set up and individuals are recruited around the interest (such as art, music, dancing, etc.). The group work emphasis is, in a sense, to transfer the interest group (sociogroup) into a psychegroup so that the kinds of inter-personal relationships are established which will better enable each individual to work out his individual psyche problems. It is significant that the psychegroup, as defined in this report, seems spontaneously to operate on this premise. *Op. cit.,* 2nd edition.

more nearly like himself, but in the sociogroup selects individuals who can importantly create a milieu benefiting many members.

The fact remains that sociogroup members are persons and there will always be a residuum of the psychegroup in the structure that develops in the sociogroup. But it would seem equally certain that individuals can learn (and come to prefer) to function almost wholly in respect to the purpose at hand, outside of the psychegroup position they feel they and others have within the sociogroup—this by adherence in their behaviors *to their role* as sociogroup members who see the other members in the same role, and, in this regard, worthy of such consideration. They will then see slipping into their psychegroup roles (even though experiencing them at the same time) as falling "out of role" appropriate to sociogroup performance.

As a sociogroup member, it appears, the individual must show capacity to subjugate any special interest of his own psychegroup within the sociogroup. Cliques are, upon investigation, often found to be of this formation—lacking motivation or skill for enjoying sociogroup membership.[26] The over-chosen sociogroup members show pronounced spontaneity in shifting roles. Because the size of the psychegroup tends to be small, none of them are important from a network standpoint; it is when the members of psychegroups have relationships in several sociogroups, however, that the community becomes a "community" in inter-individual exchange and leadership phenomena.

BIBLIOGRAPHY

1. Criswell, Joan Henning. "A Sociometric Study of Race Cleavage in the Classroom." *Archives of Psychology,* No. 235, January, 1939.
2. Deutschberger, Paul. "Interaction Patterns in Changing Neighborhoods." SOCIOMETRY, IX: 303-315, November 1946.
3. Jennings, Helen Hall. *Leadership and Isolation.* New York: Longmans, Green, 1st ed., 1943, 2nd ed., in preparation.
4. ————. "A Sociometric Study of Emotional and Social Expansiveness," in R. G. Barker, J. S. Kounin, and H. F. Wright (edrs.), *Child Development.* New York: McGraw-Hill Book Company, 1943.
5. ————. "Sociometric Studies," a supplement in J. L. Moreno, *Who Shall Survive?* (see below)
6. Intergroup Education, American Council on Education, Hilda Taba, *et al.,* "Sociometric Work Guide for Teachers," and others. 1947.

---

[26]*Op. cit.,* 2nd edition.

7. Moreno, J. L. *Who Shall Survive?* New York: Beacon House, 1934.
8. ————. and Jennings, H. H. "Statistics of Social Configurations," SOCIOMETRY, I: 342-374, Jan.Apr. 1938.
9. Newstetter, W. I., Feldstein, M. J., and Newcomb, T. M. *Group Adjustment.* Cleveland: School of Applied Social Science, Western Reserve University, 1938.
10. Sanders, Irwin T. "Sociometric Work with a Bulgarian Woodcutting Group," SOCIOMETRY, II: 58-68, October 1939.

OUTSIDERS

A study of the personality patterns of children least acceptable to their age mates.

By Mary L. Northway

Every school room is a social group and the relationships among the members form patterns similar to those in other groups. There are the leaders, the cliques, the reciprocal companionships and the isolated members. Because of the potential dangers isolated individuals hold for a democratic society and because of the effects isolation has on personality development, we have been concerned with studies of the children who are least acceptable to their age mates. These studies have not consisted merely of scientific observations, but have included co-operative attempts with the school to devise ways and means by which personalities in their still plastic stages may be guided towards better social integration.

The School Setting

One aspect of these studies has been the intensive investigation of children who at the beginning of the study were in a small public school, in grades 5 and 6. In these we have followed the same children for a period of two years; there were eighty children in all. At the time the study began the school was a newly opened institution in a middle class district of a suburb of Toronto. The buildings and equipment were functionally adequate for the needs of the growing child and attained the highest standards advocated by modern education. The principal and staff were enlightened in child development and actively interested in the children's individual development and social relationships.

The Tools We Used

Working closely with the teachers our eyes were focussed on the lively, human unpredictable group the teachers see, rather than on the theoretical statistical child of the text books. Our records were designed to catch the human, whole child as much as possible. Over the two year period these records consisted of:

1. The school's basic records, age, family, health status, school progress, special difficulties, interviews with parents.
2. Intelligence tests, group and individual.
3. Reports on psychologists' interviews with the children.
4. Time sample studies of class room participation.

5. Observational records of the child on the playing field and in special situations, *e.g.*, music groups, public speaking, school entertainments, team games.
6. Lists of the officers and members of clubs within the school.
7. Reports on children's participation in selected discussion groups.
8. Children's compositions on such topics as "the kind of person I like."
9. An analysis of the school year book (written by the children themselves).
10. Sociometric testing within the classrooms.

ANALYSIS OF THE DATA

From the two year study the results are being analyzed in three ways: (1) to show the sociometric pattern of the groups and the changes in it; (2) to discover personality characteristics related to various degrees of social acceptability (these will form the basis of a later paper in this journal); (3) to study the personality patterns of the children who were least acceptable to their companions.

SOCIOMETRIC TESTING AS A SCREENING TEST

Sociometric testing was used as our device for discovering the least acceptable children. The form of test (12) used consisted of questions asking the child for his choice of associates in four actual school situations. For each situation he had to report his first three choices (3). The choices of each child received were scored, 5, 3 and 2 for a first, second and third, respectively. These were then placed on a "target diagram" the children in the highest quartile in the center, those in the lowest in the outer circle (10). Individual choices were drawn with lines connecting one child with another. During the two years the test was given in October and May of each year.

In previous studies (1, 2, 4, 6) it had been determined that all children whom psychiatrists had designated as "recessive" were found in the lowest quartile of acceptability, but that all the children in the lowest quartile were not recessive. The sociometric test can therefore be used as a screening test for selecting recessives. As children of other characteristics are also screened out our study was directed to a thorough study of children who were "outsiders." This finding led us to our investigation of personality patterns of children within this division.

Other studies, such as Loeb's (6), had investigated factors which might be related to degree of social acceptability. She found insignificant relationships between acceptability and age, mental age, and I.Q., and only a slight relationship with success in certain school subjects; the one significant relationship discovered was that between discrepancy of rank in ability and achievement scores. Those children whose rank in achievement in school subjects was above their rank in mental age were found to have significantly higher acceptability scores. Therefore in commencing our study we had two clues about characteristics of children in the lowest quartile: (1) that recessive children were likely to be found (2) that the children's ability was not highly directed to achievement in school work.

THE OUTSIDERS

The children whose scores were in the lowest quartile (in our target diagrams the outer circle) were called "outsiders." In each classroom there were ten such children. From observing and interviewing these children and discussing them with the teachers the most apparent fact was the different personalities and forms of behaviour shown. Some were noisy and difficult to manage in class, others quiet and unassuming; some had high I.Q.'s, others low; some were attractive looking, others wan and thin; some did good school work, others poor or erratic; some were given no choices by their companions, others scored as much as fourteen; some came from economically good homes, others from poor; some participated to the minimum amount in class discussion, others received high class participation scores. The only factor common to all was that they were all among the least acceptable fourth of the group.

In compiling our information, however, it seemed that several children in the group showed similar characteristics. Although these were contradicted by other children the similarities present led us towards sub-classification within the group. The working basis in setting up these sub-categories was in terms of the therapeutic measures the staff and ourselves were suggesting as means of guiding the child to better socialization. In all, three distinct personality patterns were found: (1) Recessive children, (2) Socially uninterested children, and (3) Socially ineffective children.

THE RECESSIVE CHILDREN

There were six children among the eighty children in the two classrooms of the school* of whom two may be considered severe cases and four mild. They are listless, lack vitality, usually under par physically, either below normal in intelligence, or ineffective in their use of the ability they have;

---

*"Studies of Recessive Children" by Griffin, Laycock & Line, 1938, on file Canadian National Committee for Mental Hygiene estimate 5 - 6% of children in the school population will be found to be recessive.

careless in appearance, care of possessions, work habits; lack interest in people, activity or events of the outside world. They seem to exist rather than live, and throughout careful interviews with these children, observation of them or discussion with those familiar with them, no inner drive or outgoing interest could be located.

This recessivism varies from severe to mild. The child whose energy seems to be sufficient merely to keep him alive and carry him through the day without drive or thrill exemplifies the severe form. The child who does not participate actively in events but at least takes a slight interest in what is going on and what happens to him is of a milder form. (See cases I and II).

SOCIALLY UNINTERESTED CHILDREN

These children superficially appear to be similar to the truly recessive children. They are not liked by the others nor do they appear to make any effort in either formal class activities or social affairs of the school. They are often quiet and retiring. However, on closer examination it is found that they are much better developed in their care of person and possessions and that they have interests. Those interests are personal rather than social. A child's energy may be directed towards art, music, science, hobbies, reading or to affairs of the home. Some of these children are merely quiet with and uninterested in other children; some are shy and uncomfortable with them; some are bored and critical of them and some rather objectively and impersonally interested in observing what other children do without in any way attempting to participate with them. These children accept requirements of classroom procedure with passivity and rarely try to rebel or initiate any changes. Nine children in the school group were considered to be of this type. (See cases III and IV).

SOCIALLY INEFFECTIVE CHILDREN

Children of this third group differ completely in their superficial behaviour from the former group; they are often noisy, rebellious, delinquent in classroom affairs, boastful and arrogant. They are a nuisance to the teacher and the life of the classroom. They appear to be diametrically opposite from recessive children. However, this is not true, for they have in common the lack of acceptance by classmates and these manifested forms of behaviour seem to have arisen as rather ineffective, naïve attempts to overcome the basic social insecurity and isolation from group life which they experience. They have vitality and are keenly interested in social affairs, but because of failure in the establishment of social relations, they make effortful, conspicuous, and often foolish and futile attempts to be recognized and accepted by the social group. There were five of these children in the group. (See cases V and VI).

EXTENSION OF THE STUDIES

These three personality patterns which were categorized from the intensive school study were substantiated by analyses in other schools and camps. Twenty-eight teachers from as many schools using their own classrooms as subjects wrote case histories of the children who were in the outer quartile of acceptability. Most of these cases, it was found, could be categorized into the three types. However, the teachers' descriptions added and re-emphasized certain points; the recessive children they mentioned over and over again as "dirty", "untidy", "no care of his books", "sloppy work book", "uncombed hair", "nice clothes but always untidy." These children may be said to be lacking in basic personal organization. They also stated these children had always been peculiar children as long as the school had known them.

Reviewing the cases of lowest acceptability from our earlier camp studies (11) similar patterns were found to be present. (See cases IV and VI.)

The characteristics vary of course from case to case, but the real types seem clear cut in their basic symptomology. However, the real value of the differentiation lies in terms of the treatment which may be used with each group.

TREATMENT

In these studies we have attempted to discover in what ways the facilities and the personnel of the school itself may be used constructively to help the child in the establishment of better social relationships and personal integration.

With the truly *recessive* child, at least as he is found in the upper grades, the school has made little progress. Superficially the child has been helped to take better care of himself and his possessions and mere guidance on his school work has been given. Attempts to use small groups or individual children as socializing agents have not been very successful, nor have attempts to develop interests had more than temporary influence. These children seem to present serious pre-psychotic conditions and perhaps the school's best contribution is to be able to locate them and to refer them to qualified specialists. They show many of the schizoid tendencies and in many cases should not be called recessive at all, for they have never developed a personality from which to recede. As no energy or interests can be found directed to outward activities or social relations it must be that such energy as they have becomes increasingly ingrown and is therefore symptomatic of schizoid development.

The other groups, however, respond favorably to treatment within the school itself. We have found that the *socially uninterested* child may fairly readily be helped towards the establishment of social relationships. His very interest regardless of what it may be forms the basis for re-direction. The child who is interested in music and can be given opportunity to use inconspicuously this interest in some form of social participation for the benefit of the group soon begins to discover satisfaction arising from it. The factor of *inconspicuous* participation is important. We have found it most unwise to "put the child, as it were, socially on the spot," on the basis of his talent. To have the musical child play for the whole school or the artistic child give a talk to the Home and School Club is unwise. If the child fails he becomes the laughing stock of the group, and because of his lack of social security, failure in performance will be unduly tragic to him. If he succeeds he becomes established in the role of a musician, "the guy who's always playing the violin" rather than as a person. Therefore to bring the interest inconspicuously into social participation (see case **IV**) avoids these dangers and gives the child the means of finding himself acting with the group rather than for the group. Insightful teachers, given a little understanding of these general principles, handle such children well and develop ingenious methods for dealing with the particular case. With older children the technique of using one or two of the youngsters to whom the child is favourably inclined (as shown by his choices) as intermediary to help this youngster into group participation can be effective. Explaining the child and the situation to those already accepted children gives them an opportunity to advance their socialization towards concern for and help of others.

These socially uninterested children present a hopeful prognostic picture if treatment of the kind suggested is provided. However, they present so many characteristics of the recessive child that if care is not given them they may become recessive in the true sense. Their very interests may lead them further from social contacts or, if it should break down through force of circumstances, or become stagnate through no freshening by social impetus, psychotic symptoms may quickly increase.

The *socially ineffective children* also need help in the establishment of social relations and legitimate forms of social responsibility in the school offers a way to increase their sense of status. Confidence of the teacher and participation in school sports and games are valuable. It seems wise to give as little attention as possible to the child's undesirable form of behaviour either through reprimand or punishment or obvious concern. This social attention is exactly what the child is seeking and any activities which receive it will continue. However, in cases where certain superficial forms of behaviour such as boasting of his family's position and possessions is one of the objectionable factors, a teacher who has won his confidence may point out to him the effect this is having on other children and suggest forms of behaviour which they would find more pleasant. Insight into himself is sometimes gained by group discussion about what characteristics we like and dislike in people, but such treatment is secondary to establishing in the child a sense of acceptance and status.

If nothing is done for these children beyond traditional punishment for the more severe misdemeanors it is doubtful that they will become schizoid, but they may become delinquents, rebels, misanthropes or paranoids or at best unhappy people who are usually a social nuisance.

ETIOLOGY

In all these children, failure in the establishment of adequate social relationships is the common-factor. The causes of this can be understood only in terms of our knowledge of personality development in the family, play group, school and gang. With both the socially uninterested and the inefficient child, at some point social learning has been inadequate to meet social situations and the child has taken refuge in withdrawing to non-social interests or by hitting blindly at the problem without finding a satisfactory solution. In order to understand any one case it is necessary to know the particular factors in the background of that child's social development.

The recessive child, however, seems to show more than a failure in social development. Preliminary studies with babies and young infants* leads us to suppose there may be innate temperamental differences in children in terms of their vitality and readiness for contact with the world and their adaptability to change. Some infants are enclosed within themselves, resistant to changes in routine, unresponsive to people. If this temperamental factor does exist it may be the predisposing factor in later recessivism. However, added to this, the picture the teachers give of lack of basic personality organization suggests that lack of family consistency and affection,

---

*Investigations now being conducted by Dr. Eleanor Long with children under two years at the Infants' Home, Toronto.

and failure to guide the child in the establishment of both adequate habit patterns and self organization in the pre-school years may be important factors.

MENTAL HYGIENE POINT OF VIEW ADOPTED IN OUR SCHOOL STUDIES

In using the social acceptability scale we have frequently found the assumption being made by teachers and others, that the attainment of a high social acceptability score was considered the desirable position for a child to hold. From our observations of children the assumption that increased social acceptability and optimal personality development are directly related seems unwarranted. It is true that those children with zero or very low scores present problems, but beyond that we have no evidence for believing high acceptance is better than acceptance by a few friends and acquaintances. As long as our society is such that it requires its artists, its thinkers, its quietly effective people as well as its leaders, its salesmen, its flamboyant figures it would seem necessary we help a child form the kind of adjustment which is most adequate for him. The youngster with his few loyal friends, a socialized point of view, and ability to play his part in a group may be as adequate and happy a person as the very highly acceptable child who is the center of the group. Because we live in a culture evaluating business and therefore the arts of salesmanship and influence, we have set extraordinary values on extravert qualities; with children perhaps the most unfortunate thing we do is to insist that to be successful they must drive towards winning friends and influencing people. The teachers who can use the qualities of the reserved artistic child, the quietly effective thinker, for the increased benefit of the group as a whole is thereby establishing a truly democratic society within which each person contributes according to his unique qualities and profits in terms of his unique experience.

INTERPRETATION

The sciences of man are becoming increasingly aware that man cannot be understood except in his society, and that society cannot be understood except in terms of man. Personality patterns reflect the social development of a child but they also are important in determining what his place in society shall be. The outsiders are dangerous to themselves in terms of their future development as potential psychotics or misfits, and to society in terms of their drive for social domination to compensate for their lack of social assimilation. Diagnosis through use of sociometric testing at the school level is useful, but guidance cannot be carried out solely by trained clinicians but must come through the efforts of enlightened parents and teachers who have normal contacts with the child in his everyday world. Because, however, at the upper public school levels personality patterns are already fairly stabilized, it is important that increasing attention be given to the emergence of these characteristics in the pre-school child and that effective means of guiding his social development at that level be ascertained.*

CASES — *Recessive Children*

I. *Doreen*

Doreen is a tall, scrawny girl of 13. Through the two years of our study she has always been among the least acceptable of the children. Last spring a serious lung operation was performed from which she is still convalescing. Her I.Q. rating has gone up from 70 to 79 and her social acceptability from 0 to 2 casual choices.

Teacher's Report

Background. Doreen has been a special case for study for some years. She attended another school for several years and presented the same set of problems to the staff there. However, the situation a few years ago was not as acute as now. Her brilliant sister, Anna, was two or three years behind her in that school but now Anna has caught up to her and is really far ahead in all class activities. Last year our doctor told the parents that Doreen had a chronic lung and bronchial tube infection that could be remedied. The remedy was a serious operation. The parents, especially the father, would not consent. In June 1942 the case was at a standstill. However, during the summer the operation was performed and Doreen returned to school about the middle of September. We also had suggested in June that Doreen attend a private school or our own Central School so that she would not be embarrassed by comparisons with Anna. Our suggestion was not accepted.

As we see Doreen. She is still not well but I believe she is better than last year. We all feel sorry for her and we try to find opportunities to encourage her. She is not interested in School and merely goes through the routine.

Social Relations. None of the girls in the class seems to be genuinely interested in Doreen. The boys think she is dumb and let it go at that. A Roman Catholic girl from another school is Doreen's only friend. This girl frequently comes to our school after 4 o'clock, but she is now becoming interested in other girls and the activities of our school and is paying less attention to Doreen. This is an unfortunate development. Doreen sings in the United Church Choir and goes to Sunday School regularly. She also attends the C.G.I.T. Her leader says that at first she disliked everything the other girls liked; never wanted to be agreeable and would be very critical of others. At election

---

*Recent studies (to be reported in this journal) indicate that social relationships at the upper pre-school level are fairly stabilized in a group of children attending nursery school.

time Doreen was nominated for treasurer but missed out and protested that the voting was unfair. She eventually gave in but did not seem satisfied. The leader thinks that lately Doreen has been more sociable. Her parents *say* that she likes C.G.I.T. and seldom misses. Incidentally, her sister Anna is the president of the group.

Treatment. The most tangible angle of Doreen's problem seems to be that of health. She is still convalescing from her operation and this year all of her activities have been modified accordingly. It is too soon to expect to see evidence of the group's acceptance of Doreen. We are encouraging her by giving her things to do within her ability. Her music test indicates that she has some native ability (more than Anna) and we are coaxing her along in this activity. She *says* she wants to be a musician in later life. We wish we could convince the parents to put Doreen in another school. Another attempt to persuade them is under way now. If Doreen is not set on the road to proper adjustment this year, we hate to think of what will happen.

Psychologist's Report

C.A. — 13 — 11	Social Acceptability (3rd test)	
M.A. — 10 — 8	Score — 5	Rank — 40/40
I.Q. — 79	Classroom participation rank — 8	

Doreen seems very worried and uncertain during the Binet test. She kept asking about the test—why it was being given, to whom it was being given and why she in particular had been chosen to try the test.

She has a very low I.Q. and it is hardly likely that she will attain academic success. It does not seem advisable for her to continue very long in the regular schools.

One of her major difficulties is her sister. Anna is more than a year her junior, quite attractive, bright and most popular individual in her class. Doreen is very sensitive about this situation and tried to steer away from any questions about Anna.

Doreen asks a great many questions about her own work in class and very often gives wrong answers. Her hand seems to be raised all the time. Doreen seems quite disinterested and unexcited about school. She did, however, brighten up a little when she talked about a girl friend who does not go to this school, and when she talked about a party she had gone to a few days before.

Doreen has a few interests—she sings in a choir and likes to go to a show. But she is completely overshadowed by her sister. Doreen is not pretty and her face is covered with sores and blemishes. She was ill in the hospital last summer which may account for the lethargic way she seems to drag herself around.

Child's Own Report

The kind of person I like best is one who is polite and very nice, and who is interesting, the person who has a great sense of humour and is lots of fun and who is a good sport and who has a sense of modesty and quick understanding and even temper.

II. *Teddy*

Teddy is eleven and is in grade 7. He is a big fat boy with glasses. He has an I.Q. of 128 but his interests in school or the children are nil. His work is erratic, sometimes showing considerable brilliance, at others being sloppy, unfinished, stupid and untidy. The school has tried to spot interests and get Teddy into things. But efforts seem to be futile and he is becoming more withdrawn and vague.

Socially Uninterested Children

III. *Cedric*

Cedric is a boy with few social contacts but a real interest in art.

Psychologist's Report

		Grade 6. School.	
C.A.	11.1	Social Acceptability score	5
M.A.	15.4	Social Acceptability rank	35/38
I.Q.	138	Class Participation score	12
		Class Participation rank	15/38

Data obtained through an Intelligence testing interview.

General Impression. Cedric is a rather shy and quiet boy who talked very little either about the test or himself. Although he is low in social confidence, he is very certain about his work and gave his responses to the test in a very confident and dogmatic way. He has a slight stammer which was not apparent till after about 15 minutes of conversation. He rarely looked directly at me, preferring to look beyond me even when answering questions.

Family. Ced (He prefers this to Cedric) is the only child of rather old parents (according to Miss S.). He is asked to help out in his dad's men's store on occasion but doesn't like selling very much. His parents take him to the show every Friday night and he rarely goes with any other boys. His parents, however, are not trying to keep him entirely to themselves as he belongs to the Boy Scouts.

Social Relationships and Interests. Although he has some pals at the Cubs, Cedric doesn't seem to care much for them and sees them only at meetings, etc. There is only one boy from his class in the same pack; they aren't friends really. Cedric is not a member of any gang at school or in the neighborhood but says he likes Jack F. best and goes around with him the most. Since Jack is the most popular boy in the class it does not seem likely that this is a real friendship.

Cedric is not at all fond of reading and rarely goes to the library. He spends some time at home with his mechano set but his real interest is in drawing and most of his time is thus taken up. At school also, art is his favorite subject, and he also likes social studies and gym, although he does not seem to be a very sturdy lad.

Test Performance. Cedric made hardly any comments about the test and seemed to want to concentrate on getting the answers right rather than talk about himself. He likes the test whenever he thought he had answered correctly, which occurred quite often, but when we reached the more difficult items, his stammer became worse. Cedric was always very definite about his answers and he always felt they were right. When he guessed for the meaning of some of the vocabulary words he was disappointed that they were not right, even though he was not sure of their meaning. When I said "that's. fine" or commented on how well he was doing, he perked up noticeably and smiled but if I forgot to do this, or if he thought his answer was not correct he looked ashamed. Cedric gave his responses very quickly and since it was difficult to get him to talk much, the test was very short.

Summary and Suggestions. Cedric is an only child with but one real interest and apparently no real friends. He is not a friendly sort of lad, and although his participation score is rather high, it seems likely that he speaks out in order to show others that he is not so dull as perhaps they think. He is a bright boy but it may be that his parents are trying to push him ahead faster than he can take it, and the pressure seems to be too great emotionally. His interest in art could be extended so as to include other children perhaps, but if he constantly expects recognition from them and from the teacher something else must also be done to help him.

Boy's Own Report

The kind of person I like is one who is always agreeable, who is loyal and can be trusted. He should have consideration, a good loser and some humour.

IV. *Gwen*

Gwen was sixteen when she was first sent to camp. She did not want to come. Although she spoke little she told us that as soon as camp was over she was going into a convent. She cabined with a group of four interested campers who enjoyed all activities thoroughly and worried because they could not get Gwen to take part. She went off sketching by herself at every opportunity. Sports she said bored her and the table conversation she found "dumb". No pressure was put on her to join in camp activities. However, her counselor with subtle insight into the situation one day asked her if she would be good enough to help the girls who were putting on a play by using her talent for drawing to make the backdrops. For several days Gwen worked in a room just off the stage making her designs. When the play was produced its success was increased by the original backdrops Gwen had made. She gained her sense of achievement through the group's success and experienced for the first time the satisfaction that arises out of being part of a common enterprise.

This episode marked a turning point in Gwen's camp life. From then on she took part in all activities involving creative and artistic activity and gradually assumed real responsibility for organizing these. The camp staff never could decide just how successful the summer had been for when Gwen left her ambition to go into a convent had changed into an ambition to go on the stage!

At the beginning of the season her acceptability score was zero, by the end she was accepted by her own group of cabin mates and received good status among the campers as a whole.

Socially Ineffective Children

V.   Ken

Ken is a bright looking little boy of 12. His acceptability has dropped during the last two years. Although he was liked eighteen months ago, very few children choose him at present. He is always talking and making a noise and emphasizing how superior he is to the other children.

Teacher's Report—Ken

Background. Ken has a brother and sister both older than he is. His mother is French Canadian. His father is in business and is away from home a great deal of the time. There have been several occasions in the past two years when I needed the help of the parents but I have not succeeded in getting active support. Ken's academic position was not good enough last June to promote him into Grade 7. We promised him the opportunity of trying another set of examinations at the beginning of September. He worked diligently during September and we promoted him into Grade 7. He immediately slipped back into last year's careless habits and we have had to prod him continually to keep him up with Grade 7.

Ken as we see him. Almost everyone—pupils and teachers—agree that Ken talks too much. However, he is a likable sort of lad, with a ready smile but is inclined to be bold and saucy. He gets into a number of scraps but faces the consequences and pays the price. At the present time he, with two other boys, is in wrong with the police for climbing up on a roof of a factory and jumping off into a snowdrift. He ran away when he first saw the police but decided that they "wouldn't do much to him for just a little thing like that", and went back to the officer. The school interceded for him and he promised to play fair with us and try to stay out of trouble. However, before this situation cleared away, he was caught stealing bags of candies in the stores. He admits that he stole the candies and says it is not the first time. He seemed to be sorry that he didn't play fairly with us and shed a few tears about it. We're inclined to think that he is so plastic that he takes the form of whatever group he happens to be with. So far we are making very little progress with Ken.

Social Relations. Ken had been in Grade 7 only a week or so when the acceptability test was taken so that I believe it did not show his true position. I think it will rank higher in the next test with this group. (It did not.) His name was recently mentioned by members

467

of the Hi-Y Club as a nominee for membership. This group, which is made up of boys of Grade 8, turned him down unanimously. They said he was silly and not reliable.

Treatment. On numerous occasions we have talked to Ken about being a nuisance in class and on the field. He is always ready to discuss the question. He talks easily and freely admits that he is in the wrong. He says he forgets and the first thing he knows he has done something "stupid."

Psychologist's Report

Kenneth Eric — Grade 7.

C.A. 12.5   M.A. 12.2   I.Q. 98   Social acceptability

Father in business.

Ken announced his name was Kenneth E. —. His father works in the —— business. On being asked if he ever went down to the factory he said, very firmly, "My father doesn't work in a factory — he works in an office."

He asked for reassurance continually and at one point very politely requested to know "Why am I being asked these questions?"

He likes going skating but has had a recent appendix operation (which he referred to frequently) which keeps him from sports at present.

There are no special events Ken is looking forward to, although, "we might have a Valentine party, but we have so many parties here."

Ken has a bicycle which he used to ride with the boys to the airports—"a club of us went but the club is broken up now. There were rules and discipline and the boy whose house it was at was president. They played games and ate. It broke up because we broke things at my house. We broke the chandelier and it cost $10.00."

Ken doesn't like art but likes the rest of school all right. (We had noticed Ken being very objectionable in an art class).

Child's Own Report

The type of person I like is: Clean in appearance, pleasant to talk to and has a good sense of humour, but there are many other important details. When you are gone away from him he will be loyal to you. Then when other boys have done something good compliment them— not to be a bad sport about it. Say you are playing at something—a fort for instance—will work pleasantly to build a fort of his own. If he has the quality of minding his own business he will not interfere. But if you are a good sport tell him to build a fort nearby and we could have great fun. If a person has all those things he's a good enough fellow for anybody.

VI.   *Matilda*

Matilda was twelve when she came to camp. She lived with a "Victorian" mother and grandmother while father was off on business.

In acceptability she scored zero. She was dirty, careless and physically awkward. She had no sense of her own or other people's property. She borrowed her cabin mates' clothes indiscriminately and when they were dirty rolled them up in the corner.

Matilda made a great effort to attain attention. She talked incessantly and every few days picked out a new favorite whom she would follow around for as long as possible.

The camp at that time followed the policy of playing up individual talent as a means of developing group recognition. Matilda soon announced her talent was elocution. So she was allowed to perform at the camp concert. The result was unfortunate. The more pathetic Matilda's recitation was the louder became the laughter. Later she took an interest in nature study and was encouraged by the nature study leader to prepare five minute talks on the life of the chipmunk and give these to the camp assembly. This not only harmed Matilda still more, but damaged the entire nature programme.

Matilda used a technique common to children desiring social approval. She gave gifts. If her gifts had been of the kind twelve year olds like she might have had some success. Unfortunately her father was in a business that carried old fashioned embroideries. Samples of these were bestowed on all of Matilda's admired campers. The effect was disastrous.

We recommended a programme planned to teach Matilda the basic routines of washing and dressing and care of possessions. Also the public appearances were to be abolished. However, these suggestions were not put into effect and the child left camp completely as ineffective socially as she had been before this opportunity.

BIBLIOGRAPHY

1. Bonney, Merl E. "A Study of Social Status on the Second-grade Level." *The Journal of Genetic Psychology,* Vol. LX, June 1942, pp. 271-305.
2. Criswell, Joan H. "A Sociometric Study of Race Cleavage in the Classroom." *Archives of Psychology,* No. 235, January 1939.
3. Griffin, Laycock and Line. "A Study of Recessive Children." (Unpublished report, Canadian National Committee for Mental Hygiene, 1940).
4. Hill, F. M. "A Comparative Study of the Psychometric Performance, School Achievement, Family Background, Interests and Activities of Shy and Normal Children." (Unpublished M.A. Thesis, University of Toronto Library, 1941).
5. Jennings, Helen H. "Structure of Leadership—Development and Sphere of Influence." *Sociometry,* Vol. 1, Nos. 1 and 2, 1937.
6. Loeb, N. "The Educational and Psychological Significance of Social Acceptability and Its Appraisal in an Elementary School Setting." (Unpublished Ph.D. Thesis, University of Toronto Library, 1941).

7. Kephart, Newell C. "A Method of Heightening Social Adjustment in an Institutional Group." *American Journal of Orthopsychiatry*, Vol. 8, No. 4, pp. 710-717, 1938.

8. Kerstetter, Leona M. "Reassignment Therapy in the Classroom," in collaboration with Joseph Sargent. *Sociometry*, Vol. 3, No. 3, 1940.

9. Moreno, J. L. "Who Shall Survive? A New Approach to the Problem of Human Relations." 1934. Obtainable at Beacon House, Inc., New York City.

10. Northway, M. L. "A Method of Depicting Social Relations Obtained by Sociometric Testing." *Sociometry*, Vol. 3.

11. ————. "Appraisal of the Social Development of Chi'dren at a Summer Camp." University of Toronto Studies, Vol. 5, No. 1, 1940.

12. ————. "Social Acceptability Test." *Sociometry*, Vol. 5, No. 2, May 1942.

B. Community, Industry, and the Armed Forces

INTRODUCTION

By Charles P. Loomis and Charles H. Proctor

Among the important concepts to emerge in modern social science are the following: social system, reference group, social clique or informal group, status-role, stratification, and social power. Although sociometry, with its sociogram and the various sociometric indices and procedures, has no monopoly among the various influences contributing to the development and validation of these concepts, its importance cannot be denied. Sociometry has provided a sort of bridge, imaginary or real, between the social system and the personality system, a bridge that is perhaps too often taken for granted.

When attempts are made to explain and analyze the social interaction among people in a small group situation, this bridge is more clearly recognized, and the efficacy of sociometric theory and methodology is apparent. However, as interest focuses on explaining social interaction in an institutional framework, or within formal organizations, or wherever it appears appropriate to characterize social interaction as action in conformity to social or cultural norms— here sociometry has been less frequently admitted. Increasingly, as research interest is geared to problems of social change within institutions and formal organizations, the "informal" portion of interaction patterns assumes greater importance. Among social scientists in general, it is now believed that the formal or bureaucratic structure of large-scale organizations, if they are to function effectively, must be articulated to ubiquitous informal structure involving cliques and similar systems. So goes the theory, but concrete studies specifying the nature of these relationships are often lacking. The most concrete demonstrations of these relationships are sociometric in nature.

FINDINGS: THE COMMUNITY

The first selection to be presented in this chapter, a summary of a pioneering study by George Lundberg, is among the first sociometric treatments of social status. It illustrates the importance of the sociogram, as originally conceived by Moreno, in describing the interaction of persons in various status-roles and power positions within the social system of the community.

The second selection presents a sociogram designed to describe the interaction pattern of a village community of family-sized farms, and stresses important aspects of social structures. Two types of leader roles, the family-

471

friendship or clique-leader role, and the community-wide prestige-leader role are depicted. Also, the cliques as ascertained by factor analysis, and the status structure as determined by local community residents used as judges, are presented. To our knowledge, this sociogram and another[1] that describes the same components of a large *hacienda* are the only sociometric descriptions in existence that describe clique structure, social status, and leader roles, in one sociogram. The selection illustrates the advantages of combining information of this type in the sociogram. Another article using these sociograms illustrates how sociometry is contributing to the improvement of the typological analysis of social systems.[2]

The third selection presents an analysis of the informal social systems appearing in the sociograms mentioned in the preceding paragraph. This selection represents one of the few attempts at the application of factor analysis in the differentiation of various criteria used in sociometric groupings. These criteria range from the family-friendship type embodied in the question "In case of a death in the family, whom would you notify first?" to the community-as-a-whole type represented in "What persons would you pick to represent you and the people of this place on a commission in the case of a great catastrophe?" The function of informal groupings in social change is also discussed.

The fourth selection summarizes the earliest attempt to apply sociometric procedures to a rural non-English speaking community—the village of El Cerrito, New Mexico. This article attempts to designate various roles, frequency of interaction and family-clique groupings.

The fifth selection ranks with Moreno's early studies as published in *Who Shall Survive?* as one of the early demonstrations of reference group behavior. It is perhaps still the most clear-cut demonstration of this type of behavior on a community basis. Settler groups on a large resettlement colony (Dyess, Arkansas) left the colony or remained, in accordance with their clique groupings as formed for the most part after arrival.

---

[1] Charles P. Loomis, *et al, Turrialba—Social Systems and the Introduction of Change* (Glencoe, Ill.: The Free Press, 1953), Chapter 3. The principal sociogram presented in the second selection, "Southtown," which follows, is really of San Juan Sur, a family-sized farming community in the Turrialba area of Costa Rica. One of the contributions of this sociogram and the one of a nearby large estate, Atirro, is to highlight the differences in social structure of communities of family-sized farms and large estates. With the ideological struggle over the advantages and the disadvantages of these two types of system raging throughout the world, especially in the underdeveloped areas, this comparison is important.

[2] Charles P. Loomis and John C. McKinney, "Systemic Differences Between Latin American Communities of Family Farms and Large Estates," *American Journal of Sociology*, March, 1956.

The sixth article, "A Summary of Findings from Community Studies Reported in *Sociometry*," is just that.

FINDINGS: INDUSTRY AND THE ARMED FORCES

Sociometry is distinguished by its provision of the kind of information used in decision making, in the practical-affairs as well as the scientific-research worlds. This dual outlook was evident in the selections discussed in the preceding subsection of this introduction. Now, as we turn to the articles chosen under the Industry and Armed Forces categories, the same duality is present. In these four selections an association can be found between Industry and a theoretical emphasis (selections seven to nine), versus the Armed Forces and a practical emphasis (selections ten to thirteen). Certainly, this association is not to be taken too seriously; nevertheless, it is to some extent representative of published work.

One of the major questions in this field has continued to be: Under what conditions do informal groups arise and persist? In the seventh selection some of these conditioning factors of the informal group within in a bureaucracy are examined. The conclusions to which Gullahorn is drawn are similar to those which have arisen when the same problem is studied in other settings.[3] Such variables as nearness (in a time-space sense) and community of interests, have appeared frequently in sociometric studies, and exhibit an interrelation with the form of the informal groupings.

Speroff's approach to the empirical relationship between interpersonal preferences and job satisfaction is direct, and the inconclusive results are perhaps familiar.

In the ninth selection by Weiss and Jacobson, an attack upon the problem of the meshing of informal and formal structures has been commenced. This selection is weighted in the direction of methodology, but has been included so as to indicate the fruitfulness of handling problems of social structure under a combined informal-group and formal-organization viewpoint. The common ground is an organization-wide, work-contact network which is represented faithfully and compactly in matrix form. This article illustrates a tendency, common to many studies of formal organization, in which the role of sociometric methodology is that of providing a convenient device for summarizing interpersonal structure at the contact-no-contact level.

---

[3] Leon Festinger, Stanley Schachter, and Kurt Back, *Social Pressures in Informal Groups: A Study of Human Factors in Housing* (New York: Harper and Bros., 1950).

473

The tenth selection represents an approach to one of the major practical questions in this field. Administrators frequently have some measure of control over the allocation of people into work- or learning-groups. And in many instances, sociometric data have been collected in the hope that through their use such allocations can be improved. Zeleny has elaborated a series of techniques by which allocation can be objectified and they appear to give "satisfactory" results.

The use of sociometric data to make predictions of the efficiency of individual and group performance appears to be widespread and almost always accurate. Goodacre's study contains the elements common to these studies: a measure of the informal group structure and climate; a measure of effectiveness; and finally, a demonstration of their intimate relationship.

Halpin's study employs methods of eliciting interpersonal attitudes which, although close relatives of the conventional sociometric test, may depart too far from it to be admitted as such, but the resulting demonstration of relationship between style of leadership and the superiors' versus subordinates' rankings is a recurring theme of many sociometric investigations.

The last selection is a classic example of the use of a sociogram to diagnose a network of interpersonal relations.

THE SOCIOGRAPHY OF SOME COMMUNITY RELATIONS

By George A. Lundberg and Margaret Lawsing

Can the informal and private affinities and nucleations of an ordinary community be discovered and charted with any degree of accuracy, and if so, what does this elementary and basic societary structure reveal?

As a first attempt to answer this question, we undertook a complete house-to-house canvass of a small Vermont village.[1] Ninety-four per cent of the families gave the desired information, the wife being most frequently the source of the information secured.[2] The bulk of the interview consisted of (1) scoring the living room according to the Chapin scale, designed to measure socio-economic status, (2) securing certain additional information regarding occupation, family size, general housing conditions, and kinds of reading matter. This information is not relevant to the present report and will therefore not be analyzed at this time. (3) In the course of the interview, or at its conclusion, the person interviewed was asked to name her most intimate friends in the community,[3] after having been assured that this, in common with other information secured, would be kept strictly confidential.

It is recognized, of course, that the results secured and partially analyzed below are merely verbal testimony of friendship groupings voluntarily contributed by the persons interviewed.[4] Under these conditions we would be likely to miss (1) illicit friendships, love affairs, and other attachments not approved by the community or otherwise embarrassing to the reporting individual. This would include all so-called subconscious attachments, if any. (2) The friendship patterns reported would not be complete for the whole community, because other members of the family than the housewife would be members of

---

[1] Population about 1000; area, about one square mile. Businesses and services: two furniture factories, two dry goods stores, two general stores, three confectionery stores, four grocery stores, three barber shops, one bank, real estate office, two garages, one grist mill, two filling stations (plus five pumps in connection with other stores), one plumbing shop, one heating shop, four churches, one school, one doctor, one fire station.

[2] Since a village of this type merges gradually with the surrounding country, a number of families outside of the village limits are included in our data. Two hundred fifty-six families were successfully interviewed out of a possible 272 in the area canvassed.

[3] Information as to friends, visiting, and social correspondence with persons outside the community was also gathered, but is not here analyzed.

[4] Corroboration of the verbal testimony was attempted through interviews with certain local people after the main field work had been completed, and also through a study of the social columns of the local newspaper. While the groupings thus revealed are less complete than those secured through the interviews, they corroborate, as far as they go, the interview results.

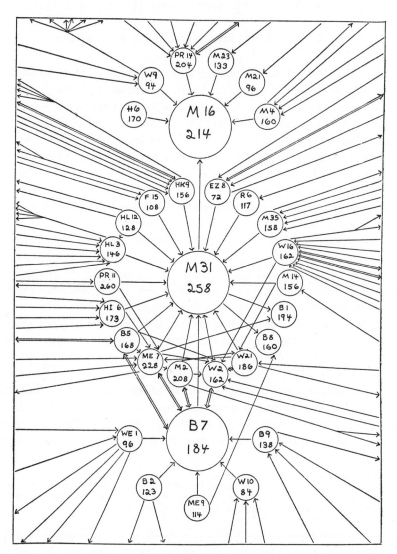

CHART I.—"Friendship Constellation in a Village." Each person is represented by a circle. The letter and the first number in the circle is the code symbol of the person. The second number is that person's score of socio-economic
status on the Chapin scale. Each arrow represents a choice made or received
according to the direction of the arrow. Mutual choices are represented by
doubleheaded arrows.

476

other groups that we did not attempt to chart. This is perhaps more true of the children than of the father in a community of this kind, and less true of either than it would be in a large urban community. (3) We did not attempt to secure the negative or repulsion patterns for fear of compromising the success of the whole study. The results secured, however, may be said to represent a highly reliable account of the friendship nuclei of the housewives of this village *as they were willing to have the investigator know these relationships* in the fall of 1936. As such, the purely verbal nature of the behavior studied is significant from some points of view, even if we make no assumption whatever as to its correlation with other friendship behavior. (4) Finally, it is recognized that the results secured represent only the general friendship patterns, as regards, perhaps, primarily recreational or prestige association, i.e., "social" in the limited sense of the "visiting" type of association. One's friends are usually chosen with reference to special types of association. Thus, Moreno, for example, found that girls would sometimes choose different companions for work associates than for housemates. We secured in this study perhaps primarily the "social" type of patterns.[5] These are, however, very spontaneous and basic forms of social nucleation. They represent, perhaps, the individual's own estimate of his social status.

Of 256 persons successfully interviewed, only 3 cases of completely isolated persons were found. (Twenty-nine others admitted no friends in the village, but mentioned friends in the adjoining areas. Thirteen of these 29 were also mentioned as friends by others in the village.) All of these three isolated cases were older people without relatives, some of them with organic defects such as deafness. They were very eager for contacts and urged the interviewers to come back for further visiting.

Forty-six persons gave only one other person as their friend, and in 13 of these cases the choice was mutual. Only one of these pairs (men) was exclusive in the sense that neither member made any other choices, though both were chosen by several others. All of the other 12 pairs were women. More complicated forms of triangles and other patterns of the various types classified

---

[5] The term "friendship," like most other sociological terms, is too general and vague a category to allow conclusions as to just what relationships it covers in a given case. In the present study, the person interviewed was asked to name confidentially her best friends in the community. The aim was to secure the names spontaneously volunteered in response to what appeared to be a casual inquiry at the end of an interview dealing entirely with other matters. If further interpretation was requested, the interviewer explained that what was desired was the names of people with whom "social" visiting for other than business or professional reasons most frequently took place. The problem of the interpretation of this verbal behavior in terms of other behavior remains, of course. But this is true of all behavior. It takes on meaning in proportion as it is related to some larger pattern, and verbal behavior is not in this respect unique.

above wait upon further analysis. These groupings are not commonly themselves isolated but have one or more ties with other similar groups.

At the opposite extreme from the isolated persons stands the "star" or the person who is the object of a large concentration of choices. The most conspicuous of these cases, with her satellites, is depicted in Chart I (M31). She is the "lady bountiful" of the village—a widow of about 60 years, of old and reputable family, wealthy, and generous in her donations to all village undertakings, from uniforms for the fire department to the major charities. Her donations are apparently the chief basis for her prestige. This person was mentioned as a friend by 17 people, most of them with heavy social ramifications of their own. Yet the "star" herself mentioned only one person (a physician and politician, not among the 17 satellites) as her friend. The intricacy of the interrelationships among the satellites as shown in the lower part of the constellation indicates a very definite clique of high social potential (i.e., number and mutuality of choices). Two mutual triangles converge upon B7 (a banker's wife) who has, in addition, a group of five satellites whose choices she does not reciprocate. These satellites are recipients of a total of 21 choices by persons outside of the constellation here depicted. The satellites of the main star, M31, receive from the outside a total of 46 designations as friends. The magnetic power of M31 in the community as well as the high interaction among her satellites depicted in the lower part of Chart I indicates a societal structure which would have to be considered in the description and explanation of a great many aspects of this community's behavior.

TAPPING HUMAN POWER LINES

By Charles P. Loomis

If power is a fact in social and community life, action groups can increase their effectiveness by understanding its distribution and operation. Many factors combine to sustain persons and groups in power positions. Here we shall try to understand the influence of two of these factors—*prestige,* or social status, and *position in the communication system.* Our focus will be on the *informal* groups in the community, the family and friendship groups which have neither officers, formal procedures, nor similar characteristics of organizations.

A person with prestige, or social status, is one who has characteristics which his society or his community values. All societies have standards by which individuals and groups are rated in importance. Many communities have their own special standards in addition to those of the larger society, and sometimes community standards assume even greater importance in the minds of people than the standards of the larger society. In our society, typical prestige-laden traits are wealth, position in organizations, culture, reputation for such things as civic mindedness, intelligence, congeniality, and many others.

Communication is the process by which information passes through a group and by which opinions and attitudes about the information are formed and modified. Intimate friendship and family groups are particularly important in the communication process, because for most people the network of communication is incomplete without these groups. Almost everyone is a member of a friendship or kinship group. But probably less than half the people in the communities, particularly where there are many low income people, can be reached directly through the communications issued by formal organizations.

Few people are on an intimate face-to-face basis with more than two or three dozen others. Thus, those who are key members of informal groups and are frequently contacted by other members, or those who have access to more than one informal group, are in positions of power. They can influence others by giving information or by editing, distorting, or withholding it. Sometimes these key persons also have high prestige, but not always. In fact, their power may be rooted in the intimacy and influence they have with low-status groups whom the prestige persons cannot reach without their help. This is why it is important for people to know *both* the prestige and communication systems in order to work effectively as an action group in a community.

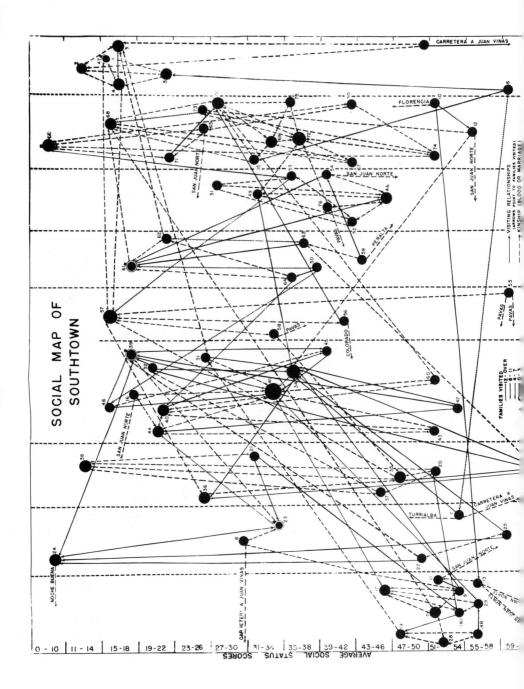

SOCIAL MAP OF SOUTHTOWN

An Example of Prestige and Communication Systems

The social map shows both the prestige and the communication systems of a rural neighborhood which we shall call Southtown. On the map families are represented by circles. Circles representing high-prestige families are near the top, low-prestige families at the bottom, with others in between as indicated by the scale of average status scores. Communication, as illustrated by informal visiting, is represented by connecting lines between the families. Broken lines show which visiting families are bound by kinship relationships. Dotted lines show which are bound by god-parent or god-child ties, called church relationships. Solid lines show informal visiting among other friends. Arrows indicate the direction of the communication, and whether it is one-way or mutual. The larger circles represent the more frequently visited families. Circles with a ring around them are families designated as prestige leaders in the community (not just in their own set), because they were chosen by 10 or more people as those from which they would want someone to represent them on a commission before the president or governor. Such leaders are all in the upper part of the chart. What we have been calling friendship groupings are represented by the families between the vertical lines. In Southtown, as in most rural areas where there is little opportunity to move up and down the social ladder, most groups are family-friendship groups.

Why Prestige and Communication Systems Should be Mapped

An experience may demonstrate the importance of having data concerning communities, comparable to those in the illustration. When we began to work in Southtown we found the people suspicious and unwilling to give information. We learned later that the head of the family represented by circle No. 66, Mr. Bull, had gone to the county-seat and talked with officials responsible for relief, taxes, and law enforcement in the neighborhood. Fortunately we had explained our mission to these officials, and Mr. Bull returned from the county-seat with the changed opinion that our mission was for the good of the village. In a matter of hours through the network of relations described on the social map, he communicated his findings and his own judgment without leaving his farm. As the map shows, Mr. Bull (No. 66) has high prestige and commands a key position in the network of communication. The attitude of the community toward our workers changed from one of suspicion to one of active cooperation in only a few hours. The people who at first were "not at home" to us suddenly became friendly, almost as if by magic, and often sent their children to ask us to visit them next.

Using the data revealed on the map, the Agricultural Extension Service invited a select group to attend a demonstration of improved farm practices. The heads of families who combined prestige leadership with friendship-family leadership (Nos. 23, 39, 61, and 66), the prestige leader who didn't hold leadership in friendship-family groups (No. 47) and the friendship-family leaders (Nos. 24, 34, 38, 41, and 57), were the people selected to view the demonstration. The next day I visited a sample of all the families just to chat and see which families would know about the demonstration that only the leaders saw. Everyone without exception knew of it.

MEANING OF THE MAP FOR ACTION GROUPS

Most of the family-friendship groups extend from the top of the chart to the bottom. Southtown is not a highly stratified community. In many communities the size of Southtown, rigid systems of social stratification would divide the people into classes or even into castes (groups in which the members can never hope to change their status by acquiring the symbols of prestige). Such stratification restricts social movement and communication between the various levels. If class or caste restrictions on communication were strong in Southtown the groupings between the vertical lines would tend to center in class groups, rather than extending from the top of the map to the bottom. The group at the lower left of the chart—a lower class group—is the one example of isolation on a class basis in Southtown.

Where neighborhoods and communities are highly stratified, a social action group must be able to relate its goals to the desires and needs of each of the social segments it is trying to reach. And it must communicate its goals in terms that are meaningful and appealing to each particular segment. In communities where the class lines are not rigidly drawn, a proposal for action can often be communicated through the entire community by getting prestige leaders to accept it. The proposed idea then becomes a prestige item for the whole community. Prestige items may appeal across caste or class lines in stratified communities, but it is less likely. In Southtown, where there is little stratification, a practice adopted by a prestige leader will spread much more rapidly than if a low-prestige person adopts it, other things being equal. This does not mean that the friendship-family leaders and others of lower status do not have a part to play in changing community practices or attitudes. In fact, the more stratified the community or the less "open" the lines of communication between classes, the less a group initiating change may rely on ordinary downward spread, and the more it must seek the co-operation of the key people in each of the class groups involved in the action plan.

To understand the change process, one must know both the prestige and the communication systems of the community. In all stable communities a more or less informal power structure exists that must be reckoned with before major changes can be made. When the change involves a program such as reorganizing a school district or building a hospital, the prestige leaders may do no more than grant or withhold permission. Or they may campaign actively for or against the change. Sometimes leaders such as 47, 61, and 66 in the illustration will merely tell others who ask them that they think the change is good or bad for such and such reasons. In such instances, they usually tailor their reasons to fit the sentiments of the one who asks. But whether the prestige leaders employ active or passive methods, they use the communication system mapped in the illustration to spread their point of view.

INFORMAL SOCIAL SYSTEMS*

By Charles H. Proctor

In conjunction with the sociological study of Turrialba communities made in 1948, questionnaires were administered to heads of households in San Juan Sur and Atirro.[1] In San Juan Sur we find a cluster of seventy-five small family-operated farms. Their proximity and their participation in community-wide activities (organized largely around the school) mark the community as a unit. Atirro is a large coffee and sugar cane *hacienda*. There are 77 families living in two geographic clusters (Atirro proper and Pueblo Nuevo). Work activities are directed through a pyramid of authority and are oriented toward profit-making. These two communities are representatives of the two broad categories (small-farm and *hacienda*) of communities found in much of Latin American rural sociology.

As a part of the questionnaire used in these two communities, nine sociometric questions were included. These were:

1) "Among the people that you know, whom do you consider as most capable, honorable, active, and who are concerned with the problems of you and the people of this place?"
2) "If you were to leave for a few days, whom would you leave in charge of your affairs?"
3) "Whom do you invite to parties at your house?"
4) "In case of a death in the family, whom would you notify first?"
5) "Would you name those families from whom you would borrow money if it were necessary?"
6) "Which families do you visit most frequently?"
7) "If you are sick who are the first friends or relatives who come to see you?"
8) "Who are the persons in whom you have confidence and with whom you discuss your personal problems?"
9) "What persons would you pick to represent you and the people of this place on a commission in the case of a great catastrophe?"

---

* Adapted from Charles P. Loomis, *et al, Turrialba,* Chapter IV.

[1] For a more complete background and analysis, see Charles P. Loomis, and John C. McKinney, *op. cit.;* and Reed M. Powell, "A Comparative Sociological Analysis of San Juan Sur, a Peasant Community, and Atirro, an Hacienda Community Located in Costa Rica, Central America" (Ph.D. dissertation Michigan State University, 1951); C. P. Loomis, and R. M. Powell, "Sociometric Analysis of Class Status in Rural Costa Rica— a Peasant Community Compared with an Hacienda Community," *Sociometry,* XII (Feb.–Aug., 1949), 144.

Each person was asked (1) to give three names in response to each question, (2) to state the relationship of the three persons to the respondent's family, and (3) to tell where the three persons lived.

METHODOLOGICAL PROBLEMS

As in many other sociometric studies,[2] it seemed apparent that the nine questions were tapping two basic types of interpersonal structure. In order to demonstrate this, a coefficient of association between choice patterns was computed for all pairs of sociometric questions. This coefficient is essentially a correlation between a_{ij}'s which are equal to 1, when i chooses j on the ath question and zero otherwise; and b_{ij}'s which are equal to 1, when i chooses j on the bth question and zero otherwise; over all $n(n-1)$ pairs ij (where n is the number of choosers, and i and j identify particular individuals).

Regardless of the roughness of the coefficient, it was obvious that the choice patterns generated by questions 1 and 9 were distinct from the choice patterns generated by questions 2 through 8. The choice patterns found by questions 1 and 9 are quite similar, while there is considerable similarity among the choice patterns found by questions 2 through 8.

Comparing San Juan Sur with Atirro, we find that the relationships among choice patterns for the differing criteria stay essentially the same. This finding reinforces our belief in the basic differences between these criteria, at least in Costa Rican rural culture.

As to the differences between these two types, there is much room for speculation. In our analysis they were named community-leadership (questions 1 and 9) and family-friendship (questions 2 through 8). These terms reflect some of the content of the criteria. There are other differences. The questions 1 and 9 are less indicative of social relationships; they (particularly question 1) are sort of "guess who" sociometric questions. Many of the questions 2 through 8 reflect family obligations.

When we looked more closely at the patterning of the choices it was found that the distribution of choices received was J-shaped for the community-leadership questions, and almost normal for the family-friendship questions. Thus, most members of the communities were agreed upon a few persons as their leaders or prestige figures or both, while almost everyone is included in the family-friendship network.

---

[2] H. H. Jennings, *Leadership and Isolation* (New York: Longmans, Green and Company, 1950), p. 274 ff., has a discussion of sociogroup and psychegroup.

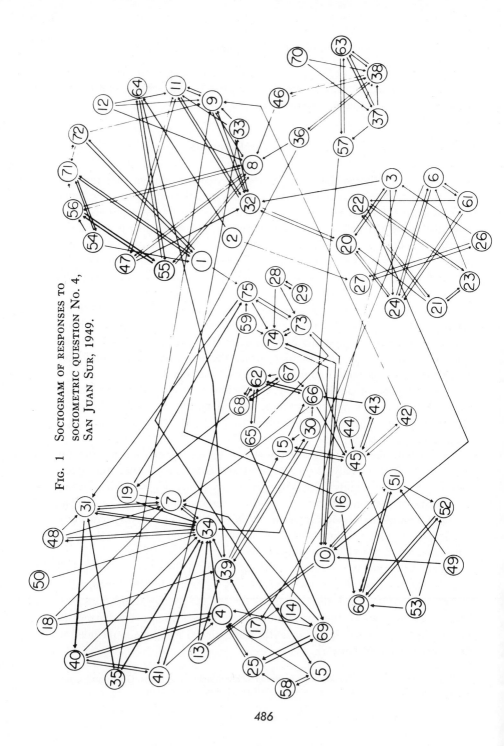

Fig. 1 Sociogram of responses to sociometric question No. 4, San Juan Sur, 1949.

It was when we began to look at the family-friendship choice patterns as revealed by a sociogram analysis that differences between San Juan Sur and Atirro appeared. Question 4 was selected as typical of the family-friendship cluster of questions. To initiate drawing of the sociogram, a coefficient of agreement between the outgoing choice patterns of every pair of family heads was computed. When one of them chose another, this was also called an agreement. These coefficients also were in the form of correlation coefficients so that a factor analysis was performed on the resulting $n \times n$ matrix.

The clusters of individuals, indicated by this factor analysis, were then arranged and rearranged in a sociogram. In San Juan Sur, nine such clusters were delimited, but only too frequently there arose a question as to whether a cluster was sufficiently "identified." It was not possible to set up objective criteria for identifying clusters. The sociogram of San Juan Sur (Figure 1) shows the originally delimited clusters (arranged in circular pattern), and also the lack of clear-cut boundaries between clusters.

In Atirro, our procedure of using this coefficient of agreement produced an interesting problem. In the first place the boundaries of particular small clusters seemed to be clear-cut. The geographically-isolated Pueblo Nuevo could be split away as well as some other "cliques" (A, B, and F in Figure 2). The remainder of the family heads appeared to divide into three large clusters (C, D, and E). However, one of these clusters was united less by in-cluster choices than by out-cluster choices. This shows that attention to out-going choices can cause the identification of clusters which have no internal ties. This also happened in the case of cluster F, in which there was strong agreement among out-going choices, i.e., choices directed outside of Atirro.

Looking at the two sociograms, it would be difficult to sustain any conclusion that family-friendship structures differed from family-sized farm to *hacienda*-type community. Nevertheless certain differences are suggestive as well as in accord with our general knowledge of possible differences.

1) The number of mutual choices in San Juan Sur is greater (52) than the number in Atirro (36). An explanation of this appears to involve the following: Average length of residence in Atirro is less than in San Juan Sur; the Atirro population is a more transient group, being less tied to the land. Many choices were made to relatives living outside of Atirro, and thus "wasted" for purposes of reciprocation. (2) Mentions seem to concentrate more on certain individuals in Atirro than in San Juan Sur. (Compare Nos. 52, 74, 70, and 23 in Atirro, with their counterparts, Nos. 34 and 7 or 45 in San Juan Sur.) Explanation: Due to the absence of the appropriate kin, people in Atirro observe

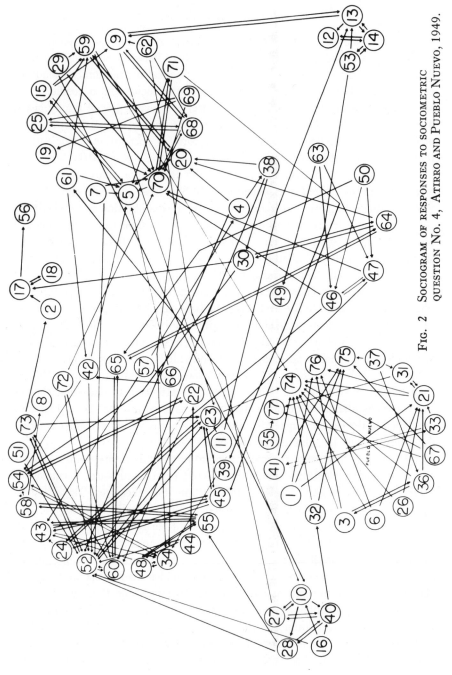

FIG. 2   SOCIOGRAM OF RESPONSES TO SOCIOMETRIC
QUESTION NO. 4, ATIRRO AND PUEBLO NUEVO, 1949.

more universalistic criteria in making their selections, and agreement among them brings about the "concentrating" which in turn reduces the degree of reciprocation.

Other differences between San Juan Sur and Atirro are revealed when we investigate the relationships between aspects of family-friendship structure and certain characteristics of the family heads, such as age, land tenure, length of residence, and social status rank position. In general, the clusters in San Juan Sur evince an internal heterogeneity, while those in Atirro an internal homogeneity with respect to the economic positions and social status rank of the members of the clusters. The *hacienda*-type community is stratified in a broader sense than that of just economic role.

How may analyses of this type be of value to action programs? In starting to answer this question, we may assume that in so far as conflicts between goals of the program and the goals of persons with whom the program is working are eliminated, the program will enjoy greater acceptance. With respect to existing consensus on goals, some observed differences between San Juan Sur and Atirro can be emphasized. Division of a community into family-friendship groups may be interrelated with differences in attitudes or normative structures. Since differences in normative structures are frequently associated with such outward characteristics as occupation, income, age, etc., we compared family-friendship groups with respect to these characteristics. In San Juan Sur the over-all picture was one of within-clique heterogeneity and cross-clique homogeneity of outward characteristics. The inference was that since clique divisions followed family divisions, normative structures did not differ from one clique or family to another. On the other hand, in Atirro we found some cross-clique differences in the outward characteristics of residence or ecological position and "more or less proletarian" position in the economic system of large *haciendas*. The latter difference is probably associated with differences in normative structures along clique lines. This distinction can be further emphasized by remembering that in San Juan Sur one individual was by far the most important community leader, while in Atirro there were several persons named as community leaders.

Consequently, in San Juan Sur a greater degree of consensus on normative structures permeates informal interaction, while in Atirro there appears to be less universal acceptance of norms. This has obvious implications for action programs. Whereas in San Juan Sur the support of an action program by the community leader could in itself signify general acceptance, in Atirro it is necessary to explore the reactions of several leaders.

INFORMAL GROUPINGS IN A SPANISH-AMERICAN VILLAGE*

By Charles P. Loomis

El Cerrito, New Mexico, like many Spanish-speaking villages, is characterized by an interaction pattern which is family-centered. The visiting relations of this family-sized farming community in San Miguel county are described in the sociograms presented, Figures 1 and 2. As indicated by these two sociograms, most of the visiting is carried on among relatives. Only two out of 108 visiting relationships were not among relatives. Figure 1, which describes the visiting relations with the respective geographic location of the houses retained, is so complicated that the reader will find it difficult to determine the clique or family-friendship groupings. In Figure 2 the circles representing the families have been rearranged so that those who visit others most frequently are placed close to one another, thus permitting the clique or family-friendship groups to manifest themselves. An attempt is made in this sociogram to indicate the frequency of visiting and to specify the kinship relationships involved. Few communities manifest clique groupings, the interaction patterns of which are so completely dominated by kinship. Frequency of visiting is directly proportional to the degree of blood relationship. In the Latin-American cultures, the age of the head of the family is an important determinant of his status and authority. Age is respected in this culture. From the sociogram, it is obvious that most clique or family-friendship groups in the village include a family designated as having grandchildren. These family-friendship groupings with their central families with grandchildren constitute the so-called "larger family," common in Latin America and in other familistic cultures. Family 9 is the key family of the village and the "larger family" of which it is a part has members who maintain frequent visiting relationships with most of the other "larger family groupings." There are several families which are unrelated in the village; nevertheless, the village is notably lacking in antagonistic relationships. Many rural villages in Latin America and elsewhere have bitter feuds carried on by family members of opposing factions. In El Cerrito such a feud did exist until toward the end of the last century when one group got the upper hand and drove the other group out. Sociometry more than any other influ-

* Summarized from the article appearing in *Sociometry,* February, 1941, and the report by Olen Leonard and Charles P. Loomis, *Culture of a Contemporary Rural Community—El Cerrito, New Mexico,* Rural Life Studies, Nov., 1941 (Washington, D.C.: U.S. Dept. of Agriculture). Can be found in compilation, Charles P. Loomis, *Studies of Rural Social Organization in the United States, Latin America, and Germany* (East Lansing: State College Book Store, 1945), Chapter 16.

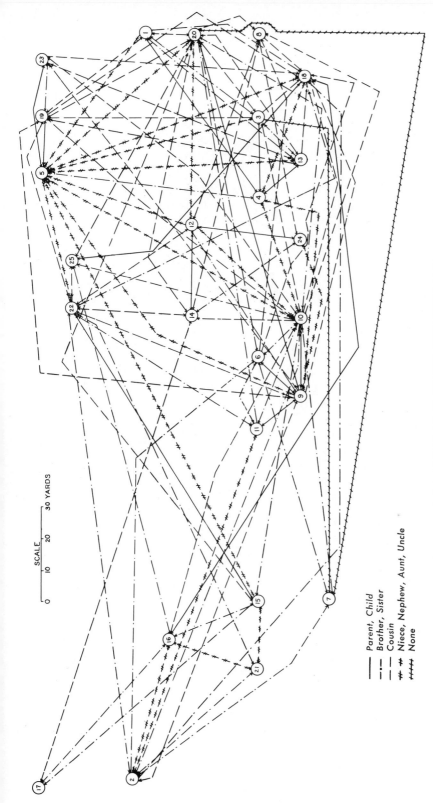

——— Parent, Child
—·!— Brother, Sister
—·|— Cousin
╫ ╫ Niece, Nephew, Aunt, Uncle
╫╫╫ None

FIG. I   VISITING OF FAMILIES, EL CERRITO, NEW MEXICO, 1940

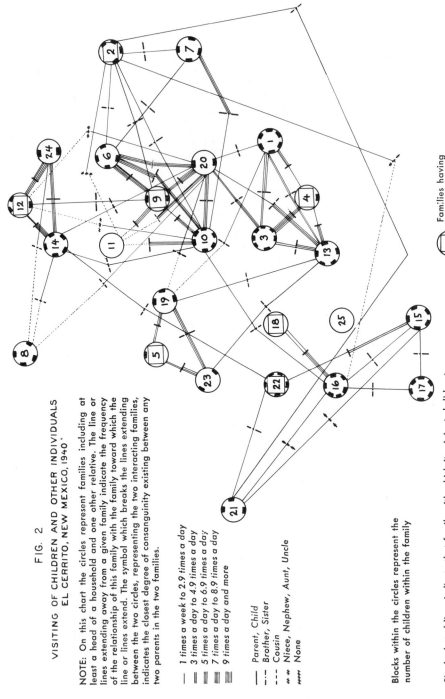

FIG. 2

VISITING OF CHILDREN AND OTHER INDIVIDUALS
EL CERRITO, NEW MEXICO, 1940¹

NOTE: On this chart the circles represent families including at
least a head of a household and one other relative. The line or
lines extending away from a given family indicate the frequency
of the relationship of this family with the family toward which the
line or lines extend. The symbol which breaks the lines extending
between the two circles, representing the two interacting families,
indicates the closest degree of consanguinity existing between any
two parents in the two families.

—— 1 times a week to 2.9 times a day
=== 3 times a day to 4.9 times a day
≣≣≣ 5 times a day to 6.9 times a day
▦▦▦ 7 times a day to 8.9 times a day
▨▨▨ 9 times a day and more

—— Parent, Child
–—– Brother, Sister
––– Cousin
++ Niece, Nephew, Aunt, Uncle
ⱳⱳⱳ None

Blocks within the circles represent the
number of children within the family

Single dotted lines indicate that family with which it originated did not
reciprocate; i.e., the relationship is not mutual because the family closest
                did not have children that entered the other home

⬜ Families having
grandchildren
in El Cerrito

492

ence has made students of rural life aware of the many impórtant sub-systems of rural neighborhoods and communities.[1]

----

[1] Until the advent of sociometry, many rural sociologists believed that the neighborhood was "the next group beyond the family which had sociological significance." See Charles P. Loomis and J. Allan Beegle, *Rural Social Systems* (New York: Prentice Hall, 1950), Chapter 5, for a description of how rural sociologists used sociometry to overcome the "blind spot" of the neighborhood, and established the importance of clique and other social systems now widely used in studies in the diffusion of improved farming practices and in the function of the community generally.

INFORMAL SOCIAL SYSTEMS AND DECISION-MAKING*

By Charles P. Loomis

Dyess Colony, Arkansas, some 40 miles north of Memphis, a settlement hewn out of the jungle of the Mississippi delta and the largest of the New Deal resettlement projects, offers the best example of informal group influence in administration and local decision-making known to the author.[1] The chief problem in the administration of the colony was the large turn-over of settlers. In view of the fact that the settler families came from low income groups, most of whom were rural families on relief, and in view of the fact that the settlement and the farms to which they were assigned increased their material level of living very substantially, the exodus of colonists was difficult to understand.

Officials of the Federal Emergency Relief Administration (having bought 18,999 acres of rich but jungle-covered land, cleared enough of it to build homes for 484 families, roads, and the various community services for people with only relief payments and goods standing between them and starvation) hoped they would create a peaceful settlement with satisfied farm families. A co-operative grocery store was built and stocked, a co-operative hospital with a two-doctor clinic under a co-operative plan provided the best medical services most of the families had ever had, and a much-used lending library which provided books for both children and adults. In fact, few community services were lacking. But to the surprise of the officials, between May, 1936 and April, 1938, 40 per cent of the families left the project. The sociologists studying the project during this time saw few families, among those who stayed, who were satisfied or happy with their new homes and community. How can we explain this exodus equalled on none of the dozens of other federal projects built during the period?[2]

The exodus of families is related to various events as indicated by Figure 1 which presents the fluctuations of the exodus of colonists and the reasons given by families for leaving the project. Often, of course, the reasons as given to the administration may not have been the real reasons or they may have

---

* Published for the first time in this volume.

[1] See Charles P. Loomis, *Studies of Rural Social Organization in the United States, Latin America and Germany,* Chapter 2; and "Sociometrics and the Study of New Rural Communities," *Sociometry,* II (1939), 56–76, upon which this article is based.

[2] For descriptions and analyses of these colonies, see Charles P. Loomis, *op. cit.,* and Russell Lord, Paul H. Johnstone, *et al., A Place on Earth, A Critical Appraisal of Subsistence Homesteads* (Washington, D.C.: USDA, 1942).

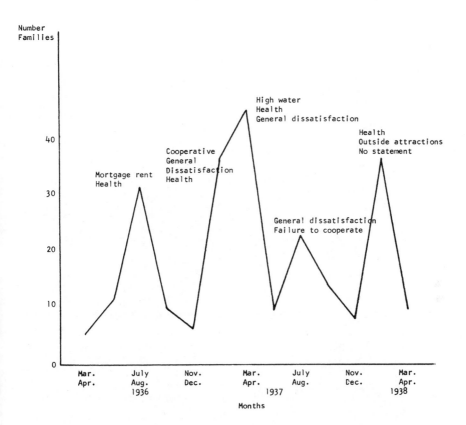

Fig. 1 Number of families moving from Dyess Colony, Arkansas, by months with prevailing reasons for leaving as reported by the heads of the households to Project Officials, March 1936–April 1938. (Includes 252 families.)

been reasons of the "last straw" variety. Also, when families gave no reason, the administrator entered his own interpretation. This may have been recorded as dissatisfaction, failure to co-operate, etc. All of the reasons for leaving, given in Figure 1, are related to events which transpired early in the history of the project.

When the project was conceived by the congressmen from Arkansas, and when arrangements had been made for its development, the local press reports described the possibility of a virtual paradise. Thousands of applications were

FIGURE 2

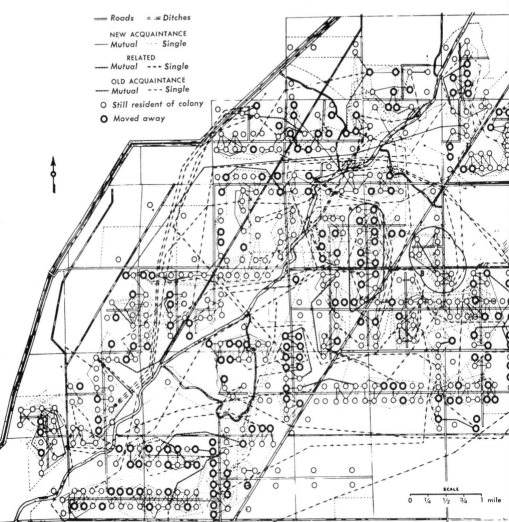

Each ring designates a residence; each line, a visiting relationship. Solid lines indicate that relationshps were mutual, or 2-way; broken lines, that they were single, or 1-way. As differentiated by the legend, these visits took place between families who had known each other before they moved to the project, those who met after arriving on the project, or those who were related by blood. Note that most of the families in the in-group represented by the encircled area "A" left the project, whereas all of the families in the in-group represented by the encircled area "B" remained.

496

filed and only those who, from the brief questionnaire, seemed most likely to succeed were accepted. From our interviews, we learned that only a few settlers thought of the land yet to be cleared, the amortization payments, the difficult farming operations, and, more important, the first experience in living in a community most aspects of which were controlled by the Federal Government. When these and other conditions materialized, the settlers could choose from a wide variety of complaints with which to justify leaving the colony. These complaints, however, provided necessary but not sufficient "causes" of the exodus.

The clue to the chief factor in settler exodus from Dyess Colony was revealed to us when the administrator told us that it appeared to him that people had to leave to see what a good thing they had on the colony. He said that many families who left, voicing all kinds of gripes and dissatisfaction, later begged to be permitted to return. The suggestion was made that there was something involved in decision-making in the colony which was not present when the families were separated from their neighbors outside.

After the investigators had made a sociometric chart describing the visiting relationships of the families as of May, 1936, and indicated on this chart those who had left with a special designation (thick black circle), as on Figure 2, the processes involved in leaving the project and those requests to be permitted to return became more apparent.

The sociometric chart, Figure 2, is a sort of map of relationships. Each family is represented by a circle. The lines between the circles indicate the type of visiting relationships the families carried on. Visiting relationships between kinfolks, old acquaintances made since moving to the colony are designated by special symbols on the lines. The mutual relationships can also be differentiated from one-way relationships. The chart describes the informal communication during the early days of the clique or friendship groups with their near neighbors. More or less closed systems of visiting families such as those designated as A and B on Figure 2 can be noted throughout the project. Most of these groups, as can be noted from the comparison of groups A and B on Figure 2, are either composed predominantly of movers or non-movers. It can be demonstrated that there was little difference in the soil or agricultural or other nonsocial conditions involved in the adjustment of the small, informal "neighbor" groups who were movers like group A and those who were non-movers, like B.

In a community such as Dyess Colony, made up of families which typically believed they had been promised paradise but who were actually confronted with the backbreaking work of clearing the land, and who could only, by dint of hard work and perseverance, eke out an existence, one might expect the evaluation of the total situation would be formed as it was discussed by neighbors from day to day. The tremendous amount of interaction, following each change in government regulations and concerning other problems (those of Figure 1), was in large part carried on in the small friendship groups such as A and B on Figure 2. In some of the groups, the frustration rose to a feverish pitch with families leaving in anger. In other groups, because of the different nature of their leadership or composition, counsel of patience or "it can't get worse, it may get better," prevailed. Some groups had realistic contact with the outside world and took a relativistic attitude: "It's bad and it'll be a long hard battle, but it would be worse if we left." Thus, within the various informal groups, the final evaluation differed greatly. Those who left in rage and haste could not stay together after leaving; and soon they were viewing in a different light those sources of frustration on the project which seemed so much a part of reality when supported by conversations with opponents of the administration. Letters of mover families who wished to return proved that the decision to leave was due more to exaggerated dissatisfaction with the project developed in the atmosphere of separate informal groups than to rational considerations and impartial, calculated deliberation by separate families.

As stated above, 40 per cent of the families on the project in May, 1936, had left by April, 1938. Many others were anxious to take their places. Also, the policy of the colony was to permit the non-movers to apply for and trade their places for those which were left if they so desired. The coming of new colonists, the trading of farms, and improved roads and transportation resulted in a rearrangement of the informal groupings so that they were no longer, after two years, small social systems like A and B on Figure 1. Any one family's friendship group might have within it colonists from all parts of the colony so that the groups formed complicated mosaics with as many as half a dozen groups having members in the area where previously Group A or Group B on Figure 2 prevailed.

As the years passed and the federal government finally withdrew selling its equity, arrangements which prevail in rural America generally replaced the original bureaucratic structure of the colony. The development of the community facilities, the clearing of the land, the settlement to permanent families was finished. Whether the same mistakes will be made again when similar operations are set in motion remains to be seen.

A SUMMARY OF FINDINGS FROM COMMUNITY STUDIES REPORTED IN *SOCIOMETRY**

By Charles H. Proctor

A considerable number of sociometric studies of communities have been carried out and a large number of them are reported in the pages of *Sociometry*. To summarize the findings of these studies is the purpose of the following discussion. The studies reported in *Sociometry* represent varied selections by investigators from among the possibilities inherent in the design of sociometric research. Many types of communities provided the settings. Choice or naming criteria differ. Experimental units include individuals, families, subgroups, or entire communities. A fairly wide collection of sociometric indices or structural properties of the choice matrix has been employed. The auxiliary variables characterizing the experimental units are numerous. Finally, many theoretical schemas are represented among the inquiries.

A rough empirical typology could be constructed to distinguish: (1) those studies done in small towns or rural areas, using a diffuse friendship criterion (e.g., visiting), examining a variety of experimental units and sociometric measures, and primarily concerned with exhibiting and analyzing the dependence of the sociometric structure upon those features of the experimental units usually included as control or independent variables in community surveys; from (2) the studies done in metropolitan areas, using the criteria of "communication" or "influence," focusing on the individual person, on two- and three-person connections or "chains," and analyzing the dependence of opinion change and decision-making processes upon the sociometric structure. In short, friendship studies can be distinguished from influence studies.

The story of the influence studies is currently being enacted by the "adoption of practices" and mass communications specialists. It would be premature to attempt a summarization of this area. The investigations summarized below are largely of the first type.

Shepard Wolman (*July–October, 1937*)

In order to assign 35 families to houses in a newly constructed Resettlement Administration village, each family was asked to indicate three others they would like as neighbors. The houses were then assigned on the basis of the

---

* Published for the first time in this volume.

sociometric data. Six months later a retest, using a hypothetical reassignment as criterion, was carried out. The position of each family in terms of both incoming and outgoing choices was discussed with reference to occupational, geographic, and personality characteristics of the choosers and the chosen.

One of the significant findings was that "the leader individuals [the highly chosen] of the first test were active, participating figures in project affairs during the pre-settlement period and early days of project occupancy; whereas the newly developed centers of attraction among the first settlers are families in whom sociability, good neighborliness and mildness predominate." The dependence of sociometric structure on "task" emphasis was apparent.

George A. Lundberg (July–October, 1937)
George A. Lundberg and Mary Steele (January–April, 1938)

In a rural Vermont village, 199 housewives named their best friends. An average of 2.3 choices were made. By a combination of making assumptions and examining choice patterns, the sociometric structure was depicted in a series of eight "charts." About thirty housewives were included in each chart. Numbers of mentions received were used to identify the "stars" who were then proposed as centers or "nuclei" of "inner groups" of persons naming the star, plus others who named those of the inner group. The delineation of two such subgroupings required identification of multiple nuclei as inner groups. Seven charts were found in this manner. The eighth chart consisted of isolates and semi-isolates, a residual subgrouping.

The meaning of these seven subdivisions was further amplified by the computation of indices of amount of internal interaction and of cohesion. About 20 to 30 per cent of the possible within subgroup relationships were reported. The ratios of ingroup choices per person to outgroup mentions per person were in the neighborhood of three, reflecting the predominance of ingroup naming.

Mean socio-economic score and mean "cultural" score varied systematically across the eight charts. Three identifiable clusters of charts showed significantly different mean socio-economic scores. For the collection of persons with scores around the median socio-economic score, 60 per cent of their choices went to others of higher socio-economic status. Occupational differences, when socio-economic status was removed, did not appear to exist. Kinship ties were not prominent in the mentions, nor was geographic location a determinant of the subgroupings. Church membership did appear to be "one of the clearest factors associated with these groupings."

Passing to the aspects of sociometric structure found within the charts, the authors examined such patterns as: mutuals, non-mutual chains, stars chosen by the ingroup, stars chosen by the outgroup, strategically placed positions, isolates and semi-isolates. As these patterns were identified in the charts, the authors explored their implications for the influence and popularity of the persons involved, combining this with a discussion of the background characteristics of the individuals. Some evidence of the existence of a saturation point of amount of interstimulation was found. As ingroups increase in size, the interaction index drops.

Irwin T. Sanders (October, 1939)

In a village near Sofia, Bulgaria, woodcutting groups were named and assigned to sections of the forest by the local government unit, and leaders were also appointed officially. The thirty heads of households of one of these groups were asked to name five others in the group with whom they would prefer to cut wood, and the five they would eliminate from their work groups. Answers were requested "out of kindness and because of your desire to help," and the response was complete. The first three choices were utilized in the analysis.

Attention to choices-received, allowed the identification of eight (actually there were nine) highly chosen individuals, none of whom were the officially appointed leaders. Among four of the leaders, all possible relationships, except one, were reciprocal bonds. Mentioning of kin appeared to be in accord with group-wide assessments of ability rather than family loyalty. However, all under-chosen individuals chose at least one relative, while only half of the others chose at least one relative. That is, individuals rejected as workers, would prefer to include persons with kinship ties in their work groups. Examination of the choices between the seven family groupings yielded similar distinctions of over- and under-chosen as when choices among individuals were studied. "Family clusters can be said to have a status in the same sense that individuals do."

The existence of a clear distinction between over- and under-chosen persons and family clusters (a bimodal frequency distribution of choices-received) probably arose from the criterion of "cut wood with."

Rose Cologne (February, 1943)

The Self-Help Center was located in a poverty-stricken district of a large city. The 27 members were asked to select work companions (usually three were named) for six categories of work-groups. Each individual's connectedness into the group choice pattern was represented by an index number based upon the order of choices and reciprocation. Individuals were ranked on the basis of their scores on this index for each of the six activities. Differences in rankings from activity to activity were immediately apparent.

Through further information on respondents' reasons for making choices, the nature of the dependence of the sociometric structure upon the type of task and the individual's competence for the task was uncovered. Where technological skills were less universally distributed among the members, the factor of differential skill explained the choices made. In other cases "personality" factors or social skills became important.

Paul Deutschberger (November, 1946)

The investigator administered and, six months later, readministered sociometric questionnaires covering friendships to 480, nine- to sixteen-year-old, white males in one "stable" and two "unstable" neighborhoods in both New York and Pittsburgh. Stability here referred to the amount of shift in population composition (e.g., ethnic and racial) going on at the time of the study. Five indices were calculated for each individual:

1) Friendship range: number of friends weighted by time spent with friends.
2) Group participation per cent: portion of friendship range allotted to members of more-than-two-person groups.
3) Diversity per cent: portion of friendship range allotted to friends of races or religions other than those of the respondent.
4) Location per cent: portion of friendship range allotted to friends living more than a quarter mile from respondent.
5) Diversity-location per cent: portion of that amount of friendship range allotted to friends living more than a quarter mile from respondent which went to friends of other races or religions.

The data summarized by examination of four means, for each of the indices. The four basic populations being compared were: stable neighborhood-first test, stable-second test, unstable-first test, and unstable-second test. In this way the nature of the dependence of the level and direction of change through time of the indices on stability was revealed. The use of an analysis of variance model, plus recognition of the correlations between the first and second tests would have avoided some of the cumbersomeness of the examination of mean values and would have provided more sensitive tests of the changes through time. Even so, many differences were obviously statistically significant.

A decrease in stability was associated with:

1) Decrease in friendship range,
2) Increase in group participation among thirteen- to sixteen-year-olds, although not among nine- to twelve-year-olds,
3) Decrease in diversity per cent,
4) Decrease in location per cent, and
5) Decrease in diversity-location per cent.
6) While group participation for the thirteen- to sixteen-year-olds increased through time in the unstable neighborhoods, it decreased in the stable ones. No such tendency to decrease through time was found among the nine- to twelve-year-olds.
7) While diversity per cent decreased through time in the unstable neighborhoods, it increased in the stable ones. This was still true for the diversity-location per cent.
8) While location per cent decreased through time in the unstable neighborhoods, it increased in the stable neighborhoods.

Although the report notes a decrease through time in friendship range in unstable neighborhoods against a maintenance of friendship range in stable neighborhoods, this difference does not approach the magnitude of the results 6, 7, and 8.

Charles P. Loomis (November, 1946)

The visiting patterns of 61 heads of households in a rural small town in Hanover, Germany, were found to depend upon party affiliations and occupational differences. Visiting connections were more frequent within party subgroups than across the party classifications. The Nazis and Communists exhibited this tendency more so than did the Social Democrats. Both full-time farmers and the craftsman-salaried workers categories manifested ingroup preferences, while the small farmers and wage workers maintained a considerable number of visiting relationships across this occupational difference.

Henrik F. Infield (February, 1947)

Fifteen veterans who were working to establish a co-operative farm in Saskatchewan were requested to name four others with whom they would prefer to: work, eat, hunt or fish, go to town, visit sporting and social affairs, talk over problems of the farm, talk over personal affairs; and near whom they would prefer to bunk. Only numbers of choices-received (showing a familiar skew distribution) and the numbers of first-choice and other-choice mutuals (41 and 51) were tabulated. However, the raw data were presented in matrix form. That taking the test "stirred the group up" and a prognosis of healthy development of the farm were the findings emphasized in the report.

T. Wilson Longmore (August, 1948)

In a village near Huanuco, Peru, 161 families were requested to "Name up to three families whom you visit most frequently." It was found that 26 per cent of the families reported no visiting. Of the visiting relationships reported, 56 per cent were with kin, 8 per cent with god-parents, and 36 per cent with friends. Sixty per cent of visits were from persons of relatively lower income to others of relatively higher income. But a strong within-income-class pattern of visiting was not uncovered.

Alexander P. Hare and Rachel T. Hare (November, 1948)

From interviews with seventy student-veteran families in a university housing community of 1,000 families, lists of each family's friends and acquaintances were obtained. Twenty-two per cent mentioned no friends; the median number of friends mentioned was two. Median number of acquaintances was nine.

Increases in numbers of friends were associated with:

1) Greater length of residence, which association was in part attributed to the positive relationship between length of residence and length of marriage which also is related to numbers of friends,
2) Presence of children,
3) Greater amount of social activity,
4) Less money spent on recreation outside of home.

In 48 per cent of the friendships, "the husband is the leader in initiating family friendships."

Irwin T. Sanders (November, 1949)

Housewives living on two dissimilar blocks (a "block" was defined as "the houses on both sides of a street between intersections") in Lexington, Kentucky, were asked to name "three women along this street to discuss how you could help toward winning the war." In the lower-middle class block of 37 houses, 39 per cent of the choices crossed the street, while ten of the 21 mutuals were between women on different sides of the street. In the substandard block of 17 houses, 53 per cent of the choices and four of the seven mutuals crossed the street. This evidence was used to question the organizational practice of defining a block as bounded by four different streets.

REFERENCES

1. Wolman, Shepard. "Sociometric Planning of a New Community," *Sociometry*, I (July–October, 1937), 220–54.
2. Lundberg, George A. "Social Attraction-Patterns in a Rural Village: A Preliminary Report," *Sociometry*, I (July–October, 1937), 77–80.
3. Lundberg, George A., and Mary Steele. "Social Attraction-Patterns in a Village," *Sociometry*, I (January–April, 1938), 375–419.
4. Sanders, Irwin T. "Sociometric Work with a Bulgarian Woodcutting Group," *Sociometry*, II (October, 1939), 58–68.
5. Cologne, Rose. "Experimentation with Sociometric Procedure in a Self-Help Community Center," *Sociometry*, VI (February, 1943), 27–67.
6. Deutschberger, Paul. "Interaction Patterns in Changing Neighborhoods: New York and Pittsburgh," *Sociometry*, IX (November, 1946), 303–15.
7. Loomis, Charles P. "Political and Occupational Cleavages in a Hanoverian Village, Germany," *Sociometry*, IX (November, 1946), 316–33.
8. Infield, Henrik F. "A Veterans Cooperative Land Settlement and Its Sociometric Structure," *Sociometry*, X (February, 1947), 50–70.
9. Longmore, T. Wilson. "A Matrix Approach to the Analysis of Rank and Status in a Community in Peru," *Sociometry*, XI (August, 1948), 192–206.
10. Hare, Alexander P., and Rachel T. "Family Friendship within the Community," *Sociometry*, XI (November, 1948), 329–34.
11. Sanders, Irwin T. "The Use of Block Leaders in Effective Community Mobilization," *Sociometry*, XII (November, 1949), 265–75.

DISTANCE AND FRIENDSHIP AS FACTORS IN THE GROSS INTERACTION MATRIX*

By John T. Gullahorn

It is not safe to ignore the sheer fact of contiguity as a factor in inter-action, despite the fact that many investigators might consider it an un-interesting variable in comparison with personality, friendship, and other such factors. During the course of a study of the social organization of clerical workers, it was discovered that even where the conditions of work do not require cooperative effort the gross interaction rate among the employees was largely determined by distance. Friendship and business necessity were additional factors.

The study was conducted in an office of 29 women and 8 men in a large eastern corporation. Two months were spent observing the group and learning the work of the office. In addition, two and a half months were devoted to interviewing the workers and in continued observation. The last two weeks were spent recording gross interactions.

The investigator sat in one corner of the office where all but four of the workers could be observed. Every 15 minutes he looked about the entire office and recorded in code which persons were engaged in conversation. Because it was sometimes impossible to tell who was talking to whom, each person was marked as interacting with every other person in the conversa-tion group. It was necessary for the investigator to leave his desk to make the observation unless he was already walking about the office. There was no apparent objection to his wandering around a little more often than customary. In fact, only one person mentioned it. Whenever he was engaged in conversation with one of the employees when an observation fell due, the investigator waited until the discussion had ended before making his observation. This meant that the observations were not uniformly spaced at 15 minutes; however, any variation was at random. It was possible to keep observations roughly at four per hour, with no two closer than five minutes apart. Only in a few cases were observations less than ten minutes apart.

It would have been desirable to set up a more sophisticated observation

* The research on which this paper is based was conducted for and under the direction of Professor George C. Homans and was financed by the Laboratory of Social Relations at Harvard. The writer wishes to express appreciation to Professor Homans and Professor Samuel A. Stouffer for permission to publish this portion of the study.

program whereby detailed data on each interaction could have been obtained. This was not possible, however, under the conditions in which the study was conducted. The system of observation which was adopted was apparently not disturbing to the workers, so that it may be assumed they continued talking with each other in a normal fashion, neither increasing nor decreasing the frequency of their conversations to make an impression on the observer.

The situation was ideal for observing the effects of distance on interaction, especially among a group of twelve girls who worked in one section of the office. Conversation between the girls did not necessarily occur on business matters. Each performed a self-contained clerical task, and the jobs of all the girls were similar. The work did not require cooperation, but occasionally one girl would help another with her task. Many of the conversations among the girls were overheard by the investigator, and a large majority of them concerned personal rather than business matters. The girls in this group formerly worked in two separate offices. They were brought together as a single work group about a year and a half before the study began. This meant, of course, that some firm friendships had formed among girls in each of the two separate offices before the merger. The influence of interaction as a factor in friendship will be suggested if friendships form between the girls formerly in different offices who now interact most frequently with each other. The age and length of service of each of these girls is given below, with those formerly in Office "A" on the left and those formerly in Office "B" on the right. Those who joined the group after the merger are centered beneath the other two.

TABLE I

OFFICE "A"				OFFICE "B"			
	Age	Company Service			Age	Company Service	
		Years	Mos.			Years	Mos.
Baldwin	22	4	— 7	Casey	30	10	
Carey	22	1	— 9	Hall	27	3	— 2
Doherty	21	2	— 6	O'Malley	21	4	— 4
Donovan	19	2	— 8	Rafferty	25	8	— 3
Lenihan	26	7	— 3	Rioux	23	1	— 10

ENTERED OFFICE AFTER MERGER

	Age	Company Service	
		Years	Mos.
Fahey	34	3	— 5
Murray	19	1	— 6

507

The group was seated in one corner of the room in three rows of four girls each, with each row separated from the others by file cabinets. The girls could look over the files to speak with those on the other side, but not with as great ease as they could talk to those within their own rows. It is in connection with the seating arrangement that the gross interaction matrix makes most sense. It is given at this point so the two can be readily compared. If the matrix is arranged by rows the relationships stand out most clearly.

TABLE II

INTERACTION MATRIX*

		Row I				*Row II*				*Row III*			
		Baldwin	Fahey	Rioux	Murray	Doherty	Rafferty	Hall	Donovan	Casey	Carey	O'Malley	Lenihan
Row I	Baldwin	—	53	23	8	0	5	2	2	0	1	1	16
	Fahey	53	—	26	9	0	2	3	0	2	1	0	1
	Rioux	23	26	—	75	1	4	1	2	2	1	0	0
	Murray	8	9	75	—	0	2	1	3	1	1	1	1
Row II	Doherty	0	0	1	0	—	24	26	18	4	8	7	2
	Rafferty	5	2	4	2	24	—	6	30	20	19	21	3
	Hall	2	3	1	1	26	6·	—	51	7	5	3	2
	Donovan	2	0	2	3	18	30	51	—	3	7	1	1
Row III	Casey	0	2	2	1	4	20	7	3	—	46	42	20
	Carey	1	1	1	1	8	19	5	7	46	—	69	30
	O'Malley	1	0	0	1	7	21	3	1	42	69	—	53
	Lenihan	16	1	0	1	2	3	2	1	20	30	53	—
	Total	111	97	135	102	90	136	107	118	147	188	198	129

Grand Total: 1558

Row Totals:	Frequency	Percentage of Grand Total in Each Row	Within-Row Total	Percentage of Within-Row Interaction in Each Row Total
Row I	445	28.56	388	75.95
Row II	451	28.95	310	68.74
Row III	662	42.49	520	78.55

* All names used in this matrix and throughout the paper are fictitious.

It will be noted that with five exceptions, all numbers within the blocked-off sections, which indicate within-row interactions, are larger than

508

those outside these sections. These five scores occur between Lenihan and Baldwin, Hall and Casey, Rafferty and Casey, Rafferty and Carey, and Rafferty and O'Malley. But before going into the individual scores more thoroughly, the interaction between rows deserves attention. If chance alone operated in determining the frequency of interaction between girls, each one should interact approximately the same number of times with each of the others. As is evident from the matrix, this is not the case. Considering the interactions of each girl with only those in her own row as opposed to interactions outside the row, and then the total figures for each row, the following results are obtained:

TABLE III

INTERACTION BY ROWS

	Inside Row	Outside Row			Total
		1-Row Distant	2 Rows Distant	Total	
Row I	388	28	29	57	445
Row II	310	28(I)	113(III)	141	451
Row III	520	113	29	142	662
Total	1218	141	58	340	1558

In the totals above, of 1558 interactions, 78.18 per cent took place within the row in which the girl sat. The girls interacted with those outside their rows 21.82 per cent of the time. Distance is obviously the gross determinant of rate of interaction as shown in these figures.

One other condition should hold if proximity is the main factor influencing rate of interaction in this situation: Interaction should occur more often between the adjacent rows than between the two end rows. The data are found in the Outside-Row interactions in Table III. Row I's interactions (28 with the adjacent row and 29 with that two rows distant) are contrary to expectations. In Row III and in the total outside-row interactions, it is clear that interaction is much greater between girls in adjacent rows than between those two rows distant from each other.

The total data and those for Row III confirm the anticipated results. Those for Row I reflect the influence of a close friendship between a girl in Row I and one in Row III (Lenihan and Baldwin). Their total interactions of 16 show up in the outside interactions of 57 for that row and load the results. In the larger outside interaction of 142 by Row III this one relationship does not hide the effect of distance even though the same 16 interactions enter into its total. If only the total figures or those for

509

Row III had been available, they would have masked friendship as a factor in the Row I results.

How much distance influences the rate of interaction is even more striking when the contacts of individual with individual are considered, ranking those for each person with all the others by frequency. For Row III, as an example, the following results are found, with F indicating frequency of interaction and R the row in which the interactant sits.

TABLE IV
INDIVIDUAL INTERACTION RATES FOR ROW III GIRLS

Casey:			Carey:			O'Malley:			Lenihan:		
F	Person	Row	F	Person	Row	F	Person	Row	F	Person	Row
46	Carey	III	69	O'Malley	III	69	Carey	III	53	O'Malley	III
42	O'Malley	III	46	Casey	III	53	Lenihan	III	30	Carey	III
20	Lenihan	III	30	Lenihan	III	42	Casey	III	20	Casey	III
20	Rafferty	II	19	Rafferty	II	21	Rafferty	II	16	Baldwin	I
7	Hall	II	8	Doherty	II	7	Doherty	II	3	Rafferty	II
4	Doherty	II	7	Donovan	II	3	Hall	II	2	Hall	II
3	Donovan	II	5	Hall	II	1	Donovan	II	2	Doherty	II
2	Rioux	I	1	Rioux	I	1	Murray	I	1	Donovan	II
2	Fahey	I	1	Murray	I	1	Baldwin	I	1	Murray	I
1	Murray	I	1	Baldwin	I	0	Rioux	I	1	Fahey	I
0	Baldwin	I	1	Fahey	I	0	Fahey	I	0	Rioux	I

It will be noted that not one of the persons had more interactions with anyone outside her row than with the least frequent of the row members. In one case there was a tie, that of Rafferty receiving as many contacts with Casey (20) as Lenihan did. Casey sat at the outside end of her row, Lenihan at the other end. In this case friendship also entered in. Casey and Rafferty were key members of the nucleus of one clique of girls; Lenihan was not a member of this clique. Casey had also mentioned in her interview that Rafferty was her best friend in the office, and Rafferty mentioned Casey as her best friend. In every case except one, that of Lenihan's 16 contacts with Baldwin, there is a constant decrease of frequency of interaction as distance increases by rows. Most frequent interaction occurs within the row; second most frequent, between adjacent rows; least frequent, between the two end rows.

If each of the 12 girls' interactions with all the others is arranged as in the preceding table by frequency of interaction, there are 12 sets of 11 diadic interaction frequencies, or a total of 132 relationships. It may be assumed that if distance is the determinant, then in each case interactions with each girl within the row will be highest; those with the adjacent row, second highest; and those with girls two rows distant, lowest. There were only nine relationships which did not conform to this expectation.

In addition it is found that if relationships within each row are considered alone, then in only one case does any girl interact more with a girl two or three desks away than with those sitting next to her. If the distances are considered for the entire row, with the end girls talking most with those adjacent to them, next most with the girl two desks away, and least frequently with the girl three desks away, only one additional exception results.

Summary

(1) Interaction within the row is far greater than is interaction of each row with the other two.

(2) Interaction is more frequent between adjacent rows than between those separated by another row.

(3) Within each row, the girls interact more frequently with those seated nearest them than with any others.

(4) With few exceptions, the frequency of interaction diminishes as the distance within the row increases and also as the distance by row increases.

Discrepancies in the distance data are understandable in terms of friendship choices. A discussion of friendship preference data will aid in clarification of these aberrations.

Analysis of Friendship Choices

The friendship choices were secured during the interviews which were held with each worker. The interviews were intensive and lasted a minimum of one hour. They were for the most part nondirective, but one question that was always asked was, "Who are your best friends around here?" In almost every case the question was introduced when the employee was discussing the friendliness of the office staff in general. No limit was set on the number of friends who could be mentioned, but most of the women in the office did not name more than three. Two of the 12 girls in the group that has been discussed chose none of the girls in their work group; one chose five within the group. A matrix of friendship choices for the office gives the following, with those for the girls being discussed blocked off by double lines.

There is a cluster of mutual choices involving O'Malley, Casey, Rafferty, and Hall (Table V). Carey chose each of these and was chosen by one of them. Rioux was selected by two, but chose no girl in the group. Murray,

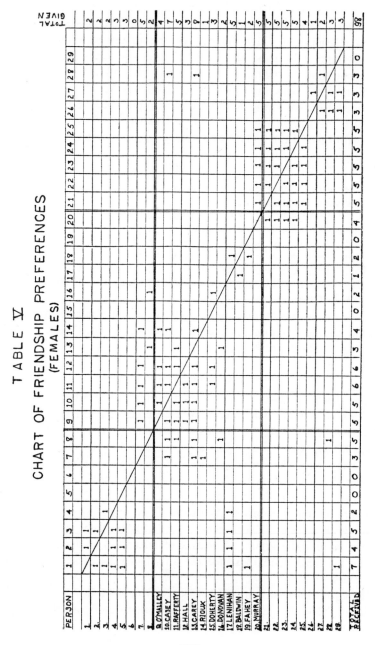

TABLE V

CHART OF FRIENDSHIP PREFERENCES
(FEMALES)

who appears to be unchosen if viewed only within this work group, becomes a well integrated member of a clique when her mutual preference choices with the younger girls are revealed, as in the lower right corner of the chart above. The relationships within the group stand out most clearly if shown in diagrammatic form (after a sociogram).

FRIENDSHIP PREFERENCE DIAGRAM

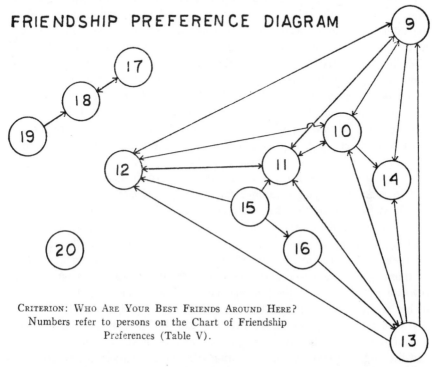

CRITERION: WHO ARE YOUR BEST FRIENDS AROUND HERE?
Numbers refer to persons on the Chart of Friendship
Preferences (Table V).

On the basis of the friendship choices it would be predicted that when proximity was not the main determinant of interaction rate, the mutual choices indicated in the diagram would exert the strongest pressure for frequency of interaction. Considering the data already presented, it is found that in Table IV Baldwin, who should have come at the end of the group listed under Lenihan, actually had a higher frequency of interaction with her than did anyone else outside her own row. They were mutual friendship choices, and neither chose any other girl within the work group. Reference to the Interaction Matrix (Table II) will show that five cases were found in which interaction outside the row was larger than the lowest within-row frequency. All of these cases—Lenihan and Baldwin, Hall and Casey,

Rafferty and Casey, Rafferty and Carey, and Rafferty and O'Malley—were also mutual friendship choices. Friendship here suggests an explanation for the discrepancies when distance is considered as the gross factor in the interaction rate.

One surprising discovery is the low interaction rate between Rafferty and Hall, who sat next to each other and who were mutual friendship choices. To explain this it is necessary to look at information secured in the interview with Rafferty. She remarked of her neighbors, "I'll still just sit at my desk some days and not say a word to either [Alice Hall] or [Elizabeth Doherty]. Actually neither one of them has anything to talk about. They're both nice, but . . ." And again, "But some of the girls will make dirty cracks intended to hurt you. Most of the time their remarks are humorous, but sometimes they aim to hurt. I guess I do the same thing myself. I called [Alice Hall] 'fatso' the other day, and I've made other digs at her. But they usually start when she makes me mad by insulting someone else." Several others complained of Hall's barbed tongue, so this may help explain her low interaction rate within her friendship circle. It also suggests varying meanings for the word *friendship*.

It is to be expected that interactions outside a girl's own row will be highest with those who represent mutual friendship choices, as shown in the diagram. There are twelve such relationships outside the girl's own row. Of these, ten represent the highest outside interactions, two do not. Both of those which are lower than the rate with other individuals outside the row are with Hall, and the personal peculiarities influencing the frequency of her friends' interaction with her have already been mentioned.

One interesting pair is Murray and Rioux. Neither chose as a friend any of the girls in this work group. The two sat next to each other. They had the highest frequency of interaction (75) of any pair in the group. It is possible that this high frequency is partly explained by the fact that neither left her seat frequently to talk with friends outside her row.

Friendship has been shown to be of some importance in determining the frequency of interaction, but distance appears to be the most important factor among the girls being discussed. Further evidence is found in the fact that in every case the two persons with whom each girl interacted most frequently were in her row. For only one girl was one of these two a mutual friendship choice; and she was second, not first, in frequency of interaction with the girl concerned. No person who ranked top in frequency of interaction with any girl was a mutual friendship choice. However, if one-way friendship preferences are considered, the picture is more encouraging to a belief that friendship counts highly. If the two persons who interacted most frequently with each girl are considered, it gives a total of 24. Of these, 11 were also friends by at least a one-way choice.

There is some support in the data for the hypothesis that persons who interact frequently will tend to develop sentiments of friendship, other things being equal. Three clear-cut cases tend to substantiate this hypothesis. One of the eleven one-way friendship choices which were among the top pair in frequency of interaction was that of Fahey for Baldwin. Fahey sits next to Baldwin, and the two were observed to interact 53 times. Fahey was new to the office and did not have close friends, so Baldwin was one of her two choices. Her other choice was a woman who had sat within speaking distance until two months before the observation period, and with whom Fahey had her third highest interaction rate of 23 even while she sat some distance away. During the earlier period, the rate would doubtless have been much higher.

The second case is Doherty. She was shy, and she had no close friends in the office group. She selected as her best office friends those in her work row, with whom she interacted more frequently than with anyone else in the office. It was suggested previously that friendships which formed between girls who were in different offices before the merger would be between those who interacted most frequently. The case of Doherty conforms with this expectation. Two of her three friendship choices were with girls formerly in office "B," while she was in office "A." These were the two girls with whom she had her most frequent interaction.

Carey was previously in office "A." She chose both O'Malley and Casey from the office "B" group as friends, and her highest interaction rate was with these two girls. She had a high rate of interaction with Rafferty, who sat outside her row, and she and Rafferty were mutual friendship choices. Rafferty was formerly in office "B."

THE OFFICE CONTEXT IN WHICH THE GROUP OF TWELVE WORKED

The other women in the office were divided into two groups: (1) the younger girls, all nineteen years of age or younger and, with one exception, having six months service or less; and (2) the senior women, who were from 33 to 54 years of age and who had from 14 to 26 years of service.

The younger group supports the hypothesis that those who interact frequently tend to develop sentiments of friendship. They came into the office without previous acquaintance with the girls with whom they worked. They interacted most frequently with each other. They soon formed their own clique and occasionally went out as a group after business hours. With one exception, each one of these girls chose all of the others as friends.

Among the senior women business and proximity result in the greatest frequency of interaction. In no case does one of this group interact as frequently with those who represent mutual friendship choices as she does with her neighbors or with those with whom she has to discuss business matters. With one exception, they all interact more frequently with both of the two latter groups than with mutual friendship choices. One of the women, Boyle, had her highest number of interactions (23) with Fahey, who chose her as friend. Most of these interactions were initiated by Fahey's leaving her desk and going to Boyle's. As Fahey mentioned that she frequently consulted Boyle on business, it cannot be assumed that all of these interactions came about solely because of her liking Boyle. It does appear, however, that the frequent interaction led to her choosing Boyle as a friend.

The men in the office have not been discussed, but it was found that among them business matters were the most important influence on the rate of interaction, except for one man who talked excessively because of what was assumed to be a feeling of personal insecurity.

Interaction rates differed among the various groups of women as shown in the following table. The young girls had the least service. The intermediate group, which has been discussed at length, was between the other two in both average age and seniority. The senior women had the highest average age and the longest service in the company.

TABLE VI

INTERACTION BY SENIORITY GROUPS

	Inside			Outside			Range for Inside Interaction		
	Mean	High	Low	Mean	High	Low	Mean	High	Low
Young girls	112.17	144	93	2.00	3	1	16.17	21	11
Intermediate	148.12	240	71	4.69	18	0	21.94	27	16
Senior women	93.00	121	61	4.43	7	1	19.14	24	14

The high rate of inside interaction, that is, interaction with other persons working in the office, for the intermediate workers probably indicates that they do not feel particularly insecure in their positions. There are many suggested explanations, such as the belief by many of these girls that they will soon be married; or the possibility that they have passed the stage experienced by a new worker when she doubts her abilities, and they have not yet reached the stage when they feel their entire career is tied up with the one company which employs them. Range in the table above refers to the number of persons interacted with during the observation period. In this too the intermediate group was highest. It will be noted that the senior women were lowest in frequency of interaction, while the younger girls were lowest in the range of interaction.

In a lengthier friendship analysis not reported in this paper, clear-cut distinctions turned up between the three major work groups of women which have been indicated above. The younger group formed the most tightly knit clique in the office. The intermediate girls had a clique of some strength with a nucleus of four girls and several who were marginal members. The senior women had no clique under the rigorous definition which was used, requiring that a clique be composed of three or more persons each of whom chose all of the others. By liberalizing this slightly they did have a clique of four with a few others tied in to some degree. It appears that the younger workers are the most friendly and the least selective in their friendships. The women who have worked longer for the company are likely to be more discriminating in choosing their friends.

SUMMARY AND CONCLUSIONS

It is evident in the above analysis that distance was the most important factor in determining the rate of interaction between any two employees in the group studied. This influence held up consistently throughout all of the relationships explored. When distance alone did not serve as an index of interaction it was found that friendship was likely to be the controlling influence. Other factors included the necessity for discussing business matters and such personality factors as feelings of insecurity.

BIBLIOGRAPHY

Bales, R. F., *Interaction Process Analysis.* Cambridge: Addison-Wesley Press, Inc., 1950.

Chapple, E. D., "Measuring Human Relations: An Introduction to the Study of Interaction of Individuals," *Genetic Psychology Monographs,* February, 1940.

Festinger, Leon, Stanley Schachter, and Kurt Back, *Social Pressures in Informal Groups.* New York: Harper and Brothers, 1950.

Homans, George C., *The Human Group.* New York: Harcourt, Brace and Company, 1950.

Moreno, J. L., *Who Shall Survive?* New York: Beacon House Inc., revised and enlarged edition, 1952.

Moreno, J. L., "Sociometry, Experimental Method and the Science of Society," *Sociometry Monographs,* No. 22.

Moreno, J. L., and Helen H. Jennings, "Sociometric Control Studies of Grouping and Regrouping," *Sociometry Monographs,* No. 7.

JOB SATISFACTION AND INTERPERSONAL
DESIRABILITY VALUES

By B. J. Speroff

Background

Both management and labor have been keenly interested in and aware of the salient role that job satisfaction and employee morale play in the industrial climate. Measuring employee job satisfaction thus has received considerable attention within recent years, and morale or job attitudinal surveys have been eagerly employed by large and small industrial concerns alike. From these surveys and studies a plethora of interrelationships and interpretations about the various factors found, and of their effects, have been reported on in ascertaining employee satisfaction (3).

Out of this mass of facts, figures, and interpretations one can readily perceive the dynamic relationship of employee morale and job satisfaction to interpersonal relations. Both morale and job satisfaction have been defined in terms of the attitudes one holds towards the job, co-workers, confidence in management, and so on, so that in the end one's dealings with others influences his job satisfaction outlook (2). Thus, the effects of group identification and group acceptance help to determine one's status within the organization and thereby the extent to which satisfaction is derived from the job. Bellows (1), in this vein, points out that the manner and degree to which one is accepted by the group and adjusts to his fellow co-workers play a vital part in the employee's attitudes toward a host of job-related factors all of which go to make up for job satisfaction (or the lack of it).

A great deal of attention also has been drawn to the study of group interaction, leadership, and the relationship of these factors to morale and productivity. Sociometry (9) was developed as a new psychological technique and has been adapted to measure morale through a systematic analysis of group and subgroup formations and in this way determining to what extent group and subgroup formations affect the organization's structure and functions. Outstanding among these studies have been those of Lewin (7), Lippitt (8), and Jenkins (4), which have dealt with the climate of the work group under differing leadership approaches with respect to productivity of the work groups and morale level of work groups. Most of these studies, however, have not had their roots in, and application to, the industrial scene as such. Outside of a study by Van Zelst (13) little has been done or reported on in the literature in an attempt to explore the relationship between interpersonal acceptance or desirability of workers and job satisfaction. This study was undertaken in order to explore the relationship between job satisfaction and worker interpersonal acceptance; specifically, to determine whether job satisfied and happy workers are also popular or desired workers.

SUBJECTS

The subjects in this study were the combined personnel from two small independently owned unorganized plants located in a small midwestern town. One plant manufactured lawn and porch furniture ($N = 22$) and the other handwoven machine belts ($N = 14$). In a previously reported study (10), using these same subjects, a correlation of —.76 was found between job satisfaction scores and the number of job related interview sessions that took place between the plant manager and workers over a one year period. This finding indicated that high employee morale is inversely related to the frequency of such job-related sessions.

PROCEDURE

In the present study the same personnel's job satisfaction scores were already available. Job satisfaction was determined by means of the *Kerr Tear Ballot for Industry, General Opinions* (6), a standardized and validated instrument utilizing the tear method of response which assures complete anonymity. The test itself consists of 10 items relating to job security, company welfare, supervisory ability, working conditions, interpersonal relationships, income, communications, confidence in the "intentions" of management, confidence in the "good sense" of management, and personal happiness. Each worker was also asked to write down the name of the worker he would "most like" to work with and the worker he would "least like" to work with if he had his choice. In both plants each of these work groups was small enough and every man knew every other man for a period of at least five years so that a wide sociometric choice was possible.

RESULTS AND DISCUSSION

The mean age of these male, manual, non-supervisory workers was 47.0 years, which is considerably higher than the mean age of other reported worker groups who have been tested on the Tear Ballot. The mean job satisfaction score for these combined groups was 44.6 which, also, is considerably higher than any other previously reported for any worker group (norm is

38.1). Each worker's sociometric standing was calculated by means of the empirical formula:

Likes — Dislikes = Interpersonal Desirability Value (12).

Some workers received as high as five "like" nominations, others received as low as three "dislike" nominations while many workers received neither "like" nor "dislike" nominations. The mean Interpersonal Desirability Values score for the combined groups was .66.

Intercorrelations between these variables—job satisfaction, age of worker, and interpersonal desirability values—were calculated. Significant correlations were found between one's job satisfaction score and one's age (.64) as well as between one's interpersonal desirability values score and one's age (.50), but no statistically significant correlation was found between one's job satisfaction score and one's interpersonal desirability value score (.31).

In a previously reported study (11) the author found that age and worker popularity correlated significantly which relationship was similarly borne out in this study, but this finding is at variance with the findings of Van Zelst (13), who found no relationship between age of worker and job satisfaction score. In his report Van Zelst stated that a lack of relationship between age and the other variables could be due to the fact that his group was "slightly higher than the norm for similar groups in job satisfaction and to be relatively homogeneous in regards to age," which, however, was also the case in the present study. It is interesting to note another point of variance between these studies, also. In the present study no significant relationship was found between one's job satisfaction score and his interpersonal desirability values score, yet Van Zelst found a significant correlation, albeit he stated that "the high correlation . . . may be somewhat overestimated. . . . This possibility is corroborated by the high intercorrelation of these variables with total job satisfaction score." However, in view of these contradictory results it would seem that a retest of the hypothesis would be in order using a larger sample and perhaps a more refined sociometric technique.

SUMMARY

A group of 36 workers from two small unorganized plants were administered a standardized job satisfaction questionnaire and were also asked to name the individual they would "most like" to work with and "least like" to work with, in order to derive a measure of interpersonal acceptance or popularity for each worker. This study was undertaken in order to determine the nature of the relationship between the interpersonal desirability of workers and their job satisfaction as measured by the *Kerr Tear Ballot for*

Industry, General Opinions. It was found that no significant relationship exists between worker popularity and job satisfaction, but that age is significantly related both to job satisfaction and to interpersonal acceptance.

REFERENCES

1. Bellows, R. *Psychology of Personnel in Business and Industry.* New York: Prentice Hall, 1949.
2. Blum, M. *Industrial Psychology and Its Social Foundations.* New York: Harper, 1949.
3. Hoppock, R. *Job Satisfaction.* New York: Harper, 1935.
4. Jenkins, J. G. *The Nominating Technique: Its Uses and Limitations.* EPA, Atlantic City, April, 1947.
5. Kerr, W. A. Summary of Validity Studies of the Tear Ballot. *Personnel Psychology,* 1952, 5, 105-113.
6. Kerr, W. A. *Tear Ballot for Industry, General Opinions.* Chicago: Psychometric Affiliates, 1948.
7. Lewin, K., Lippitt, R., and White, R. K. Patterns of Aggressive Behavior in Experimentally Created Social Climates. *J. soc. Psychol.,* 1939, 10, 275-301.
8. Lippitt, R. Field Theory and Experiment in Social Psychology: Autocratic and Democratic Group Atmospheres. *Am. J. Sociol.,* 1939, 45, 26-49.
9. Moreno, J. L. Foundations of Sociometry. *Socio. Monog.,* 1943, No. 4.
10. Speroff, B. J. Job Satisfaction Study of Two Small Unorganized Plants. To Appear in *Occupational Psychol.*
11. Speroff, B. J. *Addendum Findings on Interpersonal Desirability Values, Accidents, Age, and Reported Worries of Steel Mill Personnel.* Paper Presented in Section on Clinical Psychology, A.A.A.S., St. Louis, Dec., 1952.
12. Speroff, B. J., and Kerr, W. A. Steel Mill 'Hot Strip' Accidents and Interpersonal Desirability Values. *J. clin. Psychol.,* 1952, 8, 89-91.
13. Van Zelst, R. H. Worker Popularity and Job Satisfaction. *Personnel Psychol.,* 1951, 4, 405-412.

THE STRUCTURE OF COMPLEX ORGANIZATIONS*

By Robert S. Weiss and Eugene Jacobson

Sociometric techniques have been used most frequently in the study of small group structure.[1] The utilization of sociometry in the study of large and complex social systems, such as the bureaucratic organization, has generally been limited to the construction of indices, e.g., frequency of communication, or amount of out-group as compared with in-group contact. These indices are then treated as characteristics of individual members of the organization, and the structural context in which they were developed is generally lost.

The use of sociometry to determine the over-all structure of a complex organization probably owes its rarity to an absence both of basic structural concepts and of efficient methods for the manipulation of large masses of sociometric data. This paper proposes both a set of structural concepts and a methodology, which together state a practical approach to the sociometric analysis of complex structures.

The approach is based on certain assumptions about the nature of large organizations. To begin with, a complex unit, such as the government agency, the labor union, the church, the military unit, the school, and the industrial plant, can be seen as having a fabric of roles that constitutes the "structure" of the organization. Individual members contribute in accordance with the prescriptions of the roles they perform and co-ordinate their activities with each other in accordance with the relationships of their roles to other roles in the structure. This structure can be assumed, in most cases, to remain relatively constant despite changes in personnel through promotion, transfer, retirement, or recruitment. If a member of a relatively stable organization is replaced, the new member will ordinarily be expected to re-establish the work relationships that the previous incumbent had maintained, with changes only in the more peripheral contacts.

---

* The research reported here was supported by a grant from the Office of Naval Research Contract N6-onr-232, task order II. It is part of a more inclusive study directed by Eugene Jacobson. The authors acknowledge the assistance of Stanley Seashore in the design and analysis of the study; John R. P. French, Jr. and Joan Criswell, who aided in the design of the sociometric instrument; Theodore Newcomb, Ronald Lippitt, and Ronald Freedman, who supervised dissertations during which much of the analysis was developed; Daniel Katz, for guidance in the initial design of the study; Orabelle Poll, who conducted the first phases of the analysis; and Drs. Katz, Newcomb, and Dorwin Cartwright, for helpful comments on this paper.

[1] See, for example, Gardner Lindzey and Edgar F. Borgatta, "Sociometric Measurement," in Gardner Lindzey (ed.), *Handbook of Social Psychology* (Cambridge: Addison Wesley Press, 1954).

The Structure of Complex Organizations

An organization's structure reflects the co-ordination patterns within it, and its analysis and description is essential to the understanding of the division of labor, the communication processes, and the adjustment and growth mechanisms of the complex unit. As a first approximation, the organization chart, when it exists, provides an introduction to this analysis and description. But even the best chart is an over-simplified description of the organization. Rather than being designed to reproduce the structure, it is usually intended primarily to establish lines of authority and to define the limits of administrative units. It is useful as a description of the actual structure only to the extent that working contacts are confined to charted authority relationships or relationships within administrative units.[2]

Intensive study of a complex organization will generally require a more complete description of structure than that provided by the standard organization chart. It is the purpose of this paper to present an objective and reproduceable method for arriving at this description. The method consists of an analysis of the role relationships reported by members of the organization at a given point in time.

How the Method was Developed

The Human Relations Program of the Survey Research Center has been conducting studies of the determinants of effectiveness of complex organizations since 1947.[3] In the winter of 1949, a study in a government agency was designed to investigate relationships among variations in patterns of communication and variations in employee attitudes. Methods for measuring the relevant attitudes in the areas of job performance, relationships with superiors and subordinates, organization goals, communication, power, and individual career mobility were available. But the corresponding task of measuring variations in patterns of communication and interaction demanded the development of descriptive and analytic methods not previously used. The structural analysis that follows is the product of an attempt to develop a systematic description of interaction patterns.

_____

[2] A set of research monographs, *Studies in Naval Leadership,* published 1949–54 by the Personnel Research Board of the Ohio State University, under the direction of Carroll Shartle, presents extensive empirical analyses relating some aspects of organization chart representations of structure and sociometric choice. The work directed by Ralph Stogdill and reported by Ellis Scott is particularly relevant.

[3] Studies completed by 1952 are summarized in Daniel Katz and Robert Kahn, "Some Recent Findings in Human Relations Research in Industry," in E. G. Swanson, T. M. Newcomb, and E. L. Hartley (eds.), *Readings in Social Psychology* (New York: Henry Holt and Company, 1952).

THE BASIC DATA

The structure of the complex government agency was found through what was basically a sociometric analysis. The procedures differed from those used to find choice patterns in a small group primarily in that more people were involved and the choice criterion was different. The number of persons, in this case about 200, made it necessary to replace the ordinary cut-and-dry analysis with more systematic procedures.[4] The criterion used was one calculated to produce data which would be co-ordinate to the elements of structure. We assumed that the elements of structure were role relationships; reports of work contacts were used as a criterion.

To obtain the basic information about attitudes and patterns of interaction, each of the 196 members of the professional and administrative staff of the agency was interviewed privately in sessions that lasted from one to three hours. When the interview was about two-thirds completed, each respondent was asked to fill out a "Personal Contact Checklist" form.[5] Instructions were:

> Now go back over the past two or three months and think of the people (in the organization) with whom you have worked most closely. We would like to get the names of the people with whom you work most closely. Write their names in here. You will notice that we want some who are higher than you in the organization, some lower than you, and some at the same level.

After the respondent had listed his co-workers, he was asked to indicate the frequency of his contacts with them, reason for the contact, subject matter discussed, and the relative importance of the contact, each on a four- or five-point scale.

About 2,400 work relationships were reported by the 196 respondents. Of these, 44 per cent were reciprocated. That is, if individual A reported that he worked with B, B also reported that he worked with A. Reciprocation was

---

[4] Some systematic analysis methods have been proposed, notably by Duncan Luce and Albert D. Perry, "A Method of Matrix Analysis of Group Structure," *Psychometrika,* No. 14, 1949; and by Luce, "Connectivity and Generalized Cliques in Sociometric Group Structure," *Psychometrika,* No. 15, 1950. In these studies a group was defined as consisting of a set of individuals who were of a certain degree of closeness to each other. This definition proved inappropriate for the problem discussed in this paper. It seemed, on theoretical, intuitive, and practical grounds that "groups" of individuals should be defined in terms of their separateness from each other rather than in terms of their degree of inner connectedness, if the ultimate objective is the description of a complex organization consisting of a set of groups.

[5] This sociometric form is reproduced in Eugene Jacobson and Stanley Seashore, "Communication Practices in Complex Organizations," *Journal of Social Issues,* VII, No. 3 (1951), 28–40.

strongly related to reported frequency and importance of contact. Eighty per cent of the 409 contacts reported as "several times daily" and of "utmost" or "great" importance were reciprocated. Only 19 per cent of the 565 contacts reported as "several times monthly" or "several times yearly," and of "some," "little," or "no" importance were reciprocated. Reciprocated reports of work relationships were primary data for the bulk of the analysis, although some use of unreciprocated choices was made to clarify ambiguous contact patterns.

DEVELOPMENT OF A MATRIX

To reduce this mass of reported contacts to a graphic representation of the organization structure, the matrix analysis suggested by Festinger[6] and by Forsyth and Katz[7] was used as a guide. An IBM punching and listing procedure was used for the construction of the 196 x 196 matrix.[8]

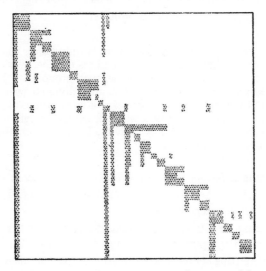

FIG. 1   SCHEMATIC IMPRESSION OF ORIGINAL MATRIX

[6] Leon Festinger, "The Analysis of Sociograms Using Matrix Algebra," *Human Relations,* II (April, 1949), 153–58.

[7] Elaine Forsyth and Leo Katz, "A Matrix Approach to the Analysis of Sociometric Data," *Sociometry,* IX (November, 1946), 340–47.

[8] The listing technique developed by Orabelle Poll, working with Ian Ross, is described in O. Poll, H. Ruderman, and D. Zipperstein, "Methodological Report of a Sociometric Study of Personnel in a Government Agency" (Survey Research Center, 1950, hectographed).

A schematic diagram of this matrix is shown in Figure 1. Individuals who report a contact appear in the left margin. Those reported as contacts appear along the top margin. Respondents were listed sequentially in organization chart order, and, as a result, most persons were located in the matrix near most of the others with whom they worked. The dark blocks along the diagonal from the upper left to the lower right indicate clusters of reports. The long vertical lines indicate individuals who were reported as contacts by a large number of respondents.

ANALYSIS OF THE MATRIX:
SEPARATING THE WORK GROUPS

In breaking down the initial matrix into the structural components, a set of structural concepts that identified the elements and suggested operations to be used in the analysis was proposed as follows:

> a. *Work group* was defined as a set of individuals whose relationships were with each other and not with members of other work groups (except for contacts with liaison persons or between groups).
> b. *Liaison person* was defined as an individual who worked with at least two individuals who were members of work groups other than his own.
> c. *Contact between groups* was defined as a single working relationship between members of sets of individuals who would otherwise be classified as separate work groups.

The concepts of *liaison pair* and *double contact between groups* were also used in the analysis. Their definition is analogous to the definitions of liaison person and contact between groups.[9]

The basic approach to the determination of the structure of the organization was to isolate the separate *work groups by* removing *liaison persons* from the matrix and omitting *contacts between groups*. When this was done, and the separate groups had been identified, it could be shown how the organization co-

---

[9] These concepts correspond in many respects to the concepts of articulation point, bridge, articulation pair, and double bridge in the mathematics of graph theory. The concept of separate work group corresponds to the graph theory concept of component. These correspondences are described in Robert S. Weiss, "An Application of Graph Theoretical Concepts to the Analysis of Sociometric Information" (Survey Research Center, 1953, hectographed). An elementary introduction to the concepts of mathematical graph theory appears in Frank Harary and Robert Z. Norman, *Graph Theory as a Mathematical Model in Social Science* (Ann Arbor: Institute for Social Research, 1953).

ordination structure was established through the activities of the liaison persons and the existence of the contacts between groups.

The technique used in isolating work groups required that the matrix be symmetric across the main diagonal. In other words, it was necessary that there be an entry in the cell corresponding to B's report of contact with A whenever there was an entry in the cell corresponding to A's report of contact with B. The original unreciprocated matrix could be made into a symmetric form either by adding entries in the proper cells when a report was not reciprocated, or by deleting unreciprocated entries. The second method was chosen because the close relationship between reciprocation and importance and frequency of contact suggested that the simplification would not be at the cost of essential information. A general impression of the matrix of reciprocated contacts is presented in Figure 2.[10]

From this symmetric matrix, the work groups were isolated through the following procedures:

1) The large matrix was separated, more or less arbitrarily, along the diagonal from upper left to lower right corner into smaller matrices called *segments* that retained as many of the total contacts as possible. These arbitrary separations are indicated in Figure 2 by dashed lines. There is good reason to believe that the structure finally developed is one that will be arrived at in all details no matter what original arbitrary segment division is made, but the labor required will vary somewhat depending on segment inclusiveness.[11]

2) The individual who had the greatest number of contacts outside of his segment was tentatively considered to be a liaison person and was removed from the matrix, together with his contacts. Then the individual with the next greatest number of contacts outside his segment was removed, and so on, until no person remained in the matrix who had more than one contact outside his segment.

3) Within each segment, persons who had no contacts with others in the segment were removed from the matrix and tentatively considered to be isolates.

4) Rows and columns within the segments were reordered to bring persons who reported contacts with each other into adjacent positions. When the reordering was accomplished, the separate groups were, in most cases, identified by inspection.

---

[10] IBM procedures for developing matrices of reciprocated contacts are reported in the Poll, Ruderman, Zipperstein memorandum and in Ian Ross, "Matrix Multiplication by Means of Punched Cards" (Research Center for Group Dynamics, 1950, mimeo).

[11] The analysis reported here has been replicated from written instructions with essentially identical results. The directions are included as an appendix to Robert Weiss, *Processes of Organization* (to be published by the Institute for Social Research).

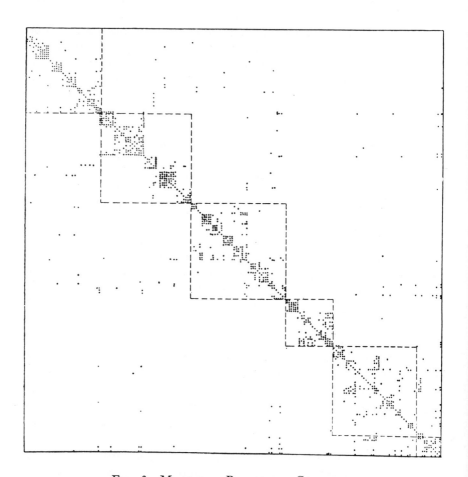

FIG. 2   MATRIX OF RECIPROCAL CONTACTS

5) More than 80 per cent of the structure could be, unambiguously and economically, identified by the procedures outlined above.   The remaining blocks of interaction within segments, however, demanded a more detailed and rigorous analysis to determine whether they were ultimate separate units or whether they were still capable of being separated.   If they were separable, that meant that they contained liaison persons.   All persons who had the contact pattern that would allow them to contact all other persons in the unit with a

minimum number of steps were considered to be potential liaison persons.[12]   If their removal from the group caused it to break into separated units, they were classified as liaison persons.

6) Upon completion of step 5 above, there were three lists of persons:

    a. members of separated work groups
    b. tentatively identified liaison persons
    c. tentatively identified isolates

7) Only reciprocated reports had been used up to step 6. The unreciprocated data were then used to make more certain assignment of liaison persons and isolates. Tentative isolates who reported frequent contact with one of the separated groups, or who were reported as frequent contacts by one of the separated groups, were assigned as members of groups. Tentative liaison persons, whose frequent contacts were all with one of the separated groups, even though some were not reciprocated, were considered to have membership in that group.

8) The end product of this set of operations was two lists of persons:

    a. About 82 per cent of the respondents could be classed as members of the twenty-two primary separate work groups that formed the basic framework of the organization. These people had the bulk of their contacts within their respective groups.

    b. The twenty-two work groups were held together by a network of liaison persons who were the remaining 18 per cent of the respondents. One-third of these liaison persons had many contacts with each other and few with any single work group. They were characterized as a *liaison set.* The rest of the liaison persons were assigned to the primary work groups in which they had frequent contacts as *liaison group members,* or remained as *liaison individuals.*[13]

---

[12] These potential liaison persons are, in the language of graph theory, *central* to the unit. The assumption is that the set of central individuals includes the set of liaison persons, but exceptional cases can be constructed. A method for locating liaison members of a set has been developed by Frank Harary and Ian Ross, "Identification of the Liaison Persons of an Organization Using the Structure Matrix" *Management Science,* I (April–July, 1955), 251–58. The less rigorous technique used in the original analysis is described in Weiss, *Processes of Organization.* Contacts between groups may also be found by these techniques. The two participants in a contact between groups appear as liaison individuals under most conditions. Certain problems in this area have not, however, been solved as yet.

[13] Only one person could be classed as an isolate. This individual was an observer on leave from another organization.

For a matrix of 200 persons, after the data have been punched, tabulated, and reproduced in reciprocated matrix form, the analysis described here can probably be compiled by one person in something under forty hours. Some parts of the analysis can be completed by an electronic digital computer, such as MIDAC. Ian Ross, University of Michigan, has developed a program for the analysis of interaction data from groups of up to forty individuals.

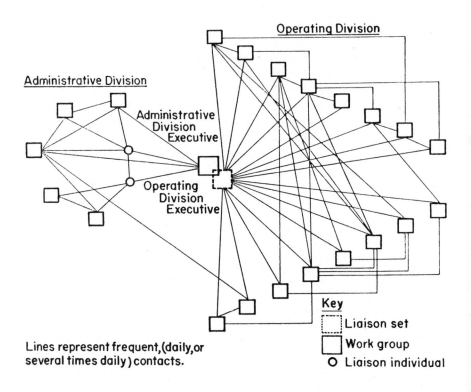

SCHEMATIC REPRESENTATION OF THE
STRUCTURE OF THE ORGANIZATION

Fig. 3.

Description of the Structure

The first result of the analysis was a representation of the structure of the
organization as it existed in fact. In Figure 3 the squares represent work
groups (separate groups plus *liaison group members*), the two circles in the
Administrative Division represent *liaison individuals* without group assignment, and the dashed square in the center of the diagram is the *liaison set* of
persons, none of whom have group assignment but who work closely with each

530

other. The lines connecting these elements indicate the existence of one or more working relationships among the elements.

The individuals who work in the Administrative Division of the organization have few contacts with persons in the Operating Division. There is only one frequent working relationship reported; this is between a minor executive in the Administrative bureau and one of the Operating Division work group members, and probably results from an unusual task that required temporary collaboration. Co-ordination between the Divisions is achieved partly by the dual membership of one person who is a member of high status both in the Administrative executive group and in the liaison set that includes the Operating Division executives. Weekly and semi-weekly meetings, usually formal, bring the two executive groups together. The overlapping membership of the executive groups is indicated in the diagram by the overlapping corners of the square.

STRUCTURAL ANALYSIS

In addition to this purely descriptive treatment of the organization as a unique structure, the analysis allows us to look for relationships that might be found in any organization. Two examples are:

> a. The relationship between the position of an individual in the organization and his attitudes toward his job, co-workers, and the organization's goals.
> b. The relationship between the goals and methods of operation of a work group or larger segment of the organization, on the one hand, and the structure of that work group or segment.

Position and Attitudes

The position of each member can be described in a number of ways: his assignment to one work group rather than another; the relative centrality or peripherality of his position in the structure; whether his position was that of a liaison person, ordinary work group member, or relative isolate; his relationship to others in his work group; and a large number of other relevant indices. We have related several of these measures to identification with the organization, attitudes toward supervision and communication, and other relevant attitudes. Results obtained do not lend themselves readily to generalization. There are systematic relationships, particularly between internal structure of the working groups and attitudes toward supervision and communication, but few of the attitudes seem to be dependent primarily upon structure. Most of them are conditioned by the respondent's past experience and aspirations, and the nature of the roles he is required to perform. These findings appear in other reports.[14]

Goals, Methods of Operation, and Structure

The structures of the two major units, the Administrative Division and the Operating Division, differed in a number of respects, including size of work group, extent of contact among work groups, methods of co-ordinating work groups, and structure of the executive group. It was possible to relate these structural differences to the nature of the different goals of the Divisions. The major goal of the Administrative group was the administration of internal policy in a consistent fashion and with sufficient attention to detail to make errors unlikely. The structure of this Division is hierarchic, with little direct contact between executive and work group member. The work groups tend to correspond to formally prescribed units and to be relatively isolated from one another.

The structure of the Operating Division which has a very different major goal, contrasts sharply with the structure of the Administrative Division. The major goal of the Operating Division is to respond flexibly and effectively to a changing environment. Since accountability is less important than effective co-ordination in this Division, work groups tend to be small and there is a great deal of contact among them irrespective of formal requirements. The executive group has direct contact with the work groups and there is much less evidence of adherence to hierarchic "channels" of interaction than appears in the Administrative Division. The structure is less like that formally prescribed, less hierarchic, and probably more fluid.

The effect on structure of particular forms of division of labor was investigated by comparing work groups where each member was responsible for a specific job with groups where each member was responsible for certain operations involved in performing the group task but not for any finished unit of work. Clear differences in co-ordinative relationships within these two kinds of groups emerged. In groups whose members were each responsible for all

---

[14] One analysis that used some of these data has been published in Dwaine Marvick, *Career Perspectives in a Bureaucratic Setting* (Ann Arbor: University of Michigan Press, 1954). A formal method for using the sociometric data as a basis for establishing a status ranking is reported by Orabelle Poll as *The Application of Scaling Techniques to Partially Ordered Stratification Systems* (M.A. Thesis, Department of Sociology, University of Michigan, 1951). Other material is presented in Weiss, *Processes of Organization*.

operations on a portion of the total task, the formally prescribed co-ordinative relationships, those between supervisor and supervised, predominated. In groups whose members each specialized in a few operations, on the other hand, informal co-ordinative relationships, between individuals not hierarchically related, were more common.

A number of other areas for investigation have been proposed. Once the basic structural data about a complex organization are available, variations in pattern can be related to indices of over-all unit effectiveness. In this study, another analysis is under way relating distribution of contact patterns within sub-groups to organization morale.

Summary

We have described a methodology for the determination of the structure of a complex organization, including techniques for gathering, classifying, and analyzing data. This methodology has proved useful in furnishing an accurate description of the structure of a complex organization, and in allowing us to investigate the effects on individuals of their position in the structure and the relationship between the goals of parts of the organization and their structure.

SELECTION OF COMPATIBLE FLYING PARTNERS*

By Leslie D. Zeleny†

Summary

Though mutual confidence is essential in flying, pairs of cadet pilot-observers, flying partners in an Army Air Forces flying school, were picked alphabetically, without regard to human relations. Sociometric tests, in which each man stated his most and least preferred choices of partner, were set up; and the degrees of interrelationship among members of "elements" of five to seven men were mathematically expressed. On the basis of the tests, it was possible to place nearly all cadets with compatible partners. A man's status in the whole group was also computed by comparing his fellows' acceptances and rejections of him.

To explore the possible usefulness of sociometry for the selection of compatible flying partners among cadet pilot-observers and for the study of other aspects of group life among flyers, a "flight" of forty-eight cadet-observers in an advanced Army Air Forces flying school was studied. In their training it was necessary for two cadet pilot-observers to fly a single-engine two-seated aircraft, taking turns in flying and in "aerial observing." The degree of compatibility of flying teams was, obviously, a factor conditioning the training experience.

Compatibility was, however, ordinarily given little consideration. Rather, it was customary for members of a flight to be listed in alphabetical order, divided into "elements" of five to seven cadets each, and assigned to a flight instructor. Thus each element consisted of alphabetically listed cadets; and it was the easiest way to make a team by taking them in pairs from the list. This often created flying teams of a relatively low degree of compatibility.

An improvement was the selection of flying teams with the aid of sociometry. Since a cadet actually placed his life in the hands of his partner when the latter flew the aircraft, there was ample motive to make positive and negative

---

* The basic data in this article are taken from the *History of Brooks Field, Texas, 1917–1943*, an official publication of the Army Air Forces, with permission of the Public Relations Officer, Brooks Field, Texas, granted February 7, 1946. The author of the history which is declassified and of the study, is the author of this article.

† Formerly Captain, Army Air Corps. Served with the Army Air Forces Central Flying Command and the North African Division, Air Transport Command. Experiments conducted in the summer of 1943; detailed interpretation, 1946.

choices of members in one's element and flight, especially when it was understood that new partners would be selected, as far as possible, upon the basis of mutual compatibility.

The sociometric test contained the following written directions:

To help make the best flying teams, will you kindly indicate how you feel about flying with each of the cadets in your flight? Below is a list of the names of the cadets in your flight.

1) If you would like to fly with a particular cadet in a flying team, encircle "Yes" after his name. If you would not like to fly with a particular cadet in a flying team, encircle "No" after his name. If you do not know how you feel about flying with a cadet, encircle "I" for "indifferent." Remember, your choices may determine with whom you will fly the next few weeks. (Follow the foregoing directions now. Then read on.)

2) Examine the name of each cadet after which "Yes" has been encircled; place a "1" to the upper right of the "Yes" following the names of the five cadets who are your FIRST FIVE CHOICES as persons with whom to fly. (Do this now. Then read on.)

3) Examine the name of each cadet after which a "No" or "I" has been encircled; place an "L" to the upper right of the "No" or "I" following the names of the five cadets who are your LAST FIVE CHOICES in your flight as persons with whom to fly.

Each flying cadet chose or rejected as many persons as he wished in his relatively closed community. Since these cadets had been in the advanced school only a short time, the degree of acquaintance with cadets outside of their elements was limited, except in cases where they had been known before in lower flying schools. There was only one criterion for the choice, i.e., "flying with" another cadet in a flying team.

The pattern of choices and rejections in the flight is shown graphically in Chart I, "Choice of Flying Partners." In the columns are shown the reactions[1] of each cadet to every other cadet.

Not only does Chart I show the reaction of each cadet to every other cadet; but, what is important, the reaction of every cadet to every other in each *instructional element* is shown also.

Consider the compatibility of a flying team composed of the first two members of Element I; that is, selected at random, as was the practice. No. 1's

---

[1] The verbal responses were translated into mathematical symbols, as follows: $\text{Yes}^1 = +1.0$; $\text{Yes} = +0.5$; $I = 0.0$; $\text{No} = -0.5$; $\text{No}^L = -1.0$. (And and I^L was converted into a -0.5).

CHOICE OF FLYING PARTNERS FLYING CADETS CHART I

CHOICES EXPRESSED BY CADET NO................

FLYING CADETS	1	2	3	4	5	6	7	8	9	10	11	12	13	14	15	16	17	18	19	20	21	22	23	24	25
						ELEMENT I																			
1		0	0	.5	.5	0	1*	.5	1	0	0	0	0	.5	0	0	0	0	0	.5	-.5	1	.5	.5	0
2	-1		0	.5	0	1	0	0	.5	-.5	0	0	0	-.5	0	0	0	-.5	1	-1	0	-1	-1	1	0
3	-1	-1		-.5	0	-1	0	0	.5	-.5	-.5	0	-.5	0	0	-.5	0	0	-1	0	-.5	.5	-.5	-1	0
4	0	0	1		.5	1	0	.5	0	0	0	0	0	-.5	0	-.5	0	0	-.5	0	-.5	0	-.5	-.5	0
5	1	1	1	.5		0	.5	0	1*	0	-.5	1	0	0	0	-.5	0	0	0	-1	-.5	.5	-1	-.5	.5
6	1	1*	1	.5	.5		.5	0	.5	0	0	0	-1	0	0	0	0	0	-.5	0	.5	-.5	.5	1	0
7	1	0	0	-.5	0	0		0	.5	0	0	0	0	0	0	0	0	0	0	0	0	.5	-.5	-.5	0
		MORALE INDEX +.25							ELEMENT II															
8	-1	0	0	.5	0	0	-1		.5	.5	0	1	0	0	0	0	0	0	0	0	0	-.5	1	1	0
9	0	0	1	0	1	.5	.5	1		1	0	1	0	1	1	0	0	0	0	.5	0	1	.5	-.5	1
10	0	1	0	0	.5	0		1	.5		0	-1	1	0	0	0	0	0	0	0	0	.5	.5	1	0
11	0	0	0	0	0	0	0	0	1	.5		1	0	0	0	0	0	0	-.5	-.5	-.5	.5	-.5	-.5	0
12	0	0	0	0	0	0	0	0	1	-.5	1*		1*	0	.5	0	0	0	0	0	-.5	.5	-.5	-.5	0
13	0	0	0	0	0	0	0	1*	.5	1	0	1		0	0	.1*	0	0	0	0	1	1	1	1	0
		MORALE INDEX +.50									ELEMENT III													
14	.5	0	1	0	0	0	0	0	.5	0	0	0	0		1	0	.5	1	1	0	-.5	1	.5	-.5	0
15	0	0	0	0	0	0	0	0	.5	0	0	0	0	-1		0	.5	0	0	0	-.5	.5	-.5	-.5	.5
16	0	0	0	0	0	0	0	1	0	1	0	0	1	1	.5		1	0	-.5	.5	1	.5	1	.5	0
17	0	0	0	0	0	0	0	0	.5	0	0	0	0	.5	1	1		1*	1	.5	-.5	1	-.5	-.5	1
18	0	0	0	0	0	0	0	0	.5	0	0	0	0	1	.5	1	1*		1	0	0	1	-.5	-.5	1
19	0	0	0	0	0	0	0	0	.5	0	0	0	0	0	1	0	1	1		0	-.5	.5	.5	-.5	1*
												MORALE INDEX +.60							ELEMENT IV					
20	0	0	0	0	0	0	0	0	.5	0	-1	0	0	0	0	0	1	0	1		-1	1	0	-.5	1
21	0	1	0	0	0	0	0	1	0	0	0	0	1	0	0	1*	0	0	0	0		1	1*	1*	1
22	0	-.5	0	0	0	0	0	0	.5	0	0	0	0	.5	0	0	1	1	0	1*	-.5		.5	-.5	.5
23	-.5	0	0	0	0	0	0	0	.5	0	0	0	0	0	0	0	0	0	0	0	1*	.5		1	.5
24	-1	1	0	-.5	0	.5	0	0	0	1	0	0	0	0	0	1	0	-1	-.5	1	1*	0	.5		.5
25	0	0	0	0	0	0	0	0	1	0	0	0	0	0	1	0	1	0	1*	0	0	1	.5	1	
																		MORALE INDEX +.40						
26	0	0	0	0	0	0	0	0	-.5	0	0	0	.5	.5	0	0	0	0	0	-1	-.5	.5	-.5	-.5	1
27	0	0	0	-.5	0	0	-1	0	0	-.5	0	0	0	.5	0	0	0	0	0	0	1	.5	-.5	.5	.5
28	0	0	0	-.5	0	0	-1	-1	-.5	-.5	0	-.5	-1	-.5	0	-1	0	0	0	0	1	-1	-.5	-.5	0
29	.5	0	0	0	0	0	-.5	0	.5	0	0	0	1	0	0	0	0	0	0	1	0	1	-.5	-.5	0
30	0	0	0	0	0	0	0	0	.5	0	0	0	0	0	0	0	0	0	0	0	0	1	-.5	-.5	0
31	0	0	0	-.5	0	0	0	0	-.5	0	0	1	-1	-.5	0	-.5	0	0	0	0	-.5	.5	-1	-.5	0
32	0	-.5	0	-.5	0	0	0	0	.5	0	0	0	0	1	0	-.5	0	0	0	0	-.5	.5	-.5	-1	0
33	0	0	0	0	0	0	0	0	.5	0	0	0	0	0	0	-.5	0	0	0	-1	-1	.5	-.5	-1	0
34	0	-.5	0	0	0	0	0	0	.5	0	0	-.5	0	0	0	-.5	0	0	0	0	-1	.5	-.5	-.5	0
35	0	0	0	0	0	0	0	0	0	0	0	0	0	0	0	-.5	0	0	0	0	-.5	.5	-.5	-1	0
36	0	0	0	0	0	0	0	0	-.5	-.5	0	0	-.5	0	0	-.5	0	-1	-1	0	-.5	.5	-.5	-.5	0
37	0	0	0	-.5	0	0	0	0	0	1	0	0	.5	-.5	0	0	.5	0	0	1	-.5	.5	-.5	-.5	0
38	0	0	0	-.5	0	0	0	0	0	0	0	0	0	0	0	0	0	0	0	1*	0	.5	-1	-.5	0
39	0	0	0	0	0	0	0	0	.5	0	-1	0	0	0	0	0	0	0	0	0	-.5	.5	-.5	-.5	0
40	0	-.5	0	0	0	0	0	0	.5	0	0	0	0	0	0	0	0	-1	0	0	-1	.5	0	-.5	0
41	0	0	0	-.5	0	0	0	0	0	-.5	0	0	0	0	0	0	0	0	0	1	.5	.5	0	-.5	0
42	0	0	0	0	0	0	0	.5	-.5	-.5	0	0	0	0	0	0	0	0	0	0	1	.5	0	-.5	0
43	.5	0	0	0	0	0	.5	0	.5	0	0	0	.5	0	0	0	0	0	0	.5	1	.5	1	1	0
44	0	0	0	0	0	0	0	0	0	0	0	0	0	0	0	-.5	0	0	0	0	0	0	-.5	-.5	0
45	0	0	0	0	0	0	0	0	.5	0	0	-.5	0	0	0	0	0	-1	0	0	1	.5	.5	-1	0
46	0	0	0	-.5	0	0	0	0	.5	-.5	0	0	0	0	0	0	0	0	0	0	.5	.5	0	0	0
47	0	0	0	0	0	0	0	0	0	0	0	0	0	0	0	-.5	0	0	0	0	-.5	.5	-.5	-.5	0
48	0	-.5	0	0	0	0	0	0	.5	0	0	0	0	0	0	0	0	0	0	0	-.5	.5	-.5	-.5	0

CHOICES "RECEIVED" BY

FLYING TEAMS	ELEMENT I	ELEMENT II	ELEMENT III	ELEMENT IV
	1–7	8–9	14–15	20–22
	2–6	10–13	16–17	21–23
	4–5	11–12	18–19	24–25
	3–			

CHOICES EXPRESSED BY CADET NO................

Left-side labels: CHOICES "RECEIVED" BY (rows 8–37) and CHOICES "RECEIVED" BY (rows 38–48).

FLYING CADETS	26	27	28	29	30	31	32	33	34	35	36	37	38	39	40	41	42	43	44	45	46	47	48	IR	IE
1	.5	0	0	0	.5	.5	0	0	0	0	.5	0	0	.5	0	0	.5	1	0	0	0	0	0	+.21	.00
2	0	0	0	-1	-1	-.5	-1	0	-1	0	0	0	0	-.5	0	0	-1	.5	-1	0	0	-.5	0	-.21	+.03
3	0	0	0	0	-.5	0	0	0	0	0	0	0	0	-1	0	0	0	0	0	-.5	0	-.5	0	-.21	+.11
4	0	0	0	0	-.5	0	0	0	0	0	0	0	0	0	0	-.5	-.5	0	0	-.5	0	-.5	0	-.07	-.06
5	0	0	0	0	-.5	-.5	0	0	0	0	-.5	0	0	0	0	-.5	-.5	0	0	-.5	0	-.5	0	-.01	+.05
6	0	0	1	0	0	-.5	0	0	0	0	0	0	0	0	1	-.5	0	0	0	-.5	0	-.5	0	+.10	+.05
7	0	-.5	0	-.5	-.5	0	-.5	0	0	0	0	0	0	0	0	0	0	1	0	-.5	0	0	0	-.02	-.01
8	0	0	0	0	-.5	-.5	0	0	-1	0	-.5	0	-1	0	0	-1	.5	-.5	0	0	0	-.5	-1	-.08	+.12
9	-1	0	0	0	-.5	0	0	0	0	0	0	0	0	.5	1	-.5	0	1	0	0	0	0	0	+.19	+.33
10	0	0	0	0	-.5	0	0	0	0	0	0	0	0	0	0	-.5	.5	1	0	-.5	0	-.5	0	+.10	+.03
11	0	0	0	0	.5	.5	.5	0	0	0	0	0	0	0	0	-.5	0	1	0	0	0	-.5	0	+.04	-.04
12	0	0	0	0	-.5	.5	.5	0	0	0	0	0	0	.5	0	0	.5	1	0	0	0	-.5	0	+.07	+.03
13	.5	0	0	1	-.5	.5	0	0	0	0	1	1	0	1*	0	-.5	1	1*	0	0	0	-.5	0	+.30	+.05
14	1	1	0	0	0	.5	1	0	0	0	0	0	0	-.5	0	0	0	0	0	-.5	0	-.5	-1	+.15	+.10
15	.5	0	0	0	0	0	0	0	0	0	0	0	0	0	0	-.5	0	0	0	-.5	0	-.5	0	+.01	+.14
16	0	0	0	0	0	.5	0	0	0	0	0	0	0	1	0	-.5	.5	.5	0	-.5	0	-.5	0	+.23	-.03
17	.5	0	0	0	0	.5	0	0	0	0	0	0	0	0	0	0	-1	0	0	-.5	0	-.5	0	+.11	+.16
18	0	1	0	0	0	.5	0	0	0	0	0	1	0	0	0	0	-.5	0	0	-.5	0	-.5	0	+.15	-.01
19	1	0	0	0	0	.5	0	0	0	0	0	0	0	0	0	-.5	0	0	0	-.5	0	-.5	0	+.08	-.01
20	1	1	0	-1	0	1	-.5	0	0	0	0	0	1	0	0	0	0	0	0	-.5	0	0	0	+.08	+.06
21	-1	0	0	0	0	.5	0	0	0	0	0	0	0	-.5	0	0	.5	1	0	.5	0	-.5	*0	+.19	-.24
22	.5	1	0	0	1*	.5	0	0	0	0	0	0	0	0	0	0	0	0	0	-.5	0	0	0	+.13	+.47
23	-1	0	0	0	-.5	0	0	0	0	0	0	0	0	.5	0	-.5	1	.5	0	.5	0	-.5	0	+.02	-.12
24	-1	0	0	-.5	-1	.5	0	0	-1	0	0	0	0	.5	0	-.5	1	1	0	-.5	0	-.5	0	-.03	-.23
25	1	0	0	0	0	.5	0	0	0	0	0	0	0	0	0	-.5	0	0	.5	-.5	0	-.5	0	+.15	+.21
ELEMENT V																									
26		1	0	-1	0	.5	0	0	-1	0	0	0	-1	-.5	0	-.5	0	0	0	-.5	0	-.5	0	-.09	+.09
27	.5		0	0	0	.5	0	0	0	-1	1	-1	0	1	-1	1	1	-1	.5	-.5	0	-.5	0	-.22	+.12
28	.5	0		-1	-1	.5	-1	0	.5	0	-1	0	0	-1	-1	-1	0	-.5	-1	-.5	-1	-1	0	-.39	+.09
29	0	1	1		1	.5	.5	0	0	0	0	0	0	.5	0	0	1	.5	0	.5	0	0	1	+.15	+.07
30	.5	0	0	1*		1	.5	0	0	0	0	0	0	-.5	0	0	0	.5	.5	.5	0	0	0	+.07	-.14
31	-1	0	0	-1	1		-1	0	0	0	0	0	-1	-1	0	0	0	-1	-1	-.5	-1	-.5	-1	-.32	+.34
MORALE INDEX +.18 / ELEMENT VI																									
32	.5	0	0	0	.5	1		0	1	1	1	0	1	-.5	0	-.5	0	0	0	-.5	0	-.5	1	+.08	+.03
33	0	0	0	-.5	-.5	.5	-1		-1	1*	-1	-1	0	0	0	-.5	0	0	0	-.5	0	-.5	0	-.17	+.04
34	.5	0	1	0	-.5	.5	1*	0		1	0	0	0	-1	0	.5	0	0	-1	0	0	-.5	0	-.04	+.01
35	0	0	0	0	0	.5	1	1	1		0	1	1	-.5	0	-.5	0	0	0	-.5	0	0	0	+.04	+.10
36	0	0	0	0	0	.5	1	0	0	.5		1*	-1	-.5	0	-1	0	-1	0	0	0	-.5	0	-.13	+.05
37	0	0	0	0	-.5	.5	.5	0	0	1	1*		0	0	0	-.5	0	.5	0	.5	0	-.5	0	+.08	+.04
MORALE INDEX +.37 / ELEMENT VII																									
38	-.5	0	0	0	-.5	.5	1	0	1	0	1	0		0	-1	1*	0	.5	1	-.5	1	-.5	1	+.10	.00
39	-.5	0	0	-.5	-1	0	-1	0	0	0	1	0	0		1	-1	1*	1	0	1	0	-.5	0	-.02	-.01
40	0	0	0	-1	-.5	0	-.5	0	0	0	0	0	-1	.5		0	5	1	0	1	0	-.5	0	-.04	.00
41	.5	0	0	1	1	1	0	0	0	0	0	0	1	0	0		0	.5	1	.5	1*	.5	1	+.24	-.20
42	0	0	0	1	-.5	-.5	0	0	0	0	0	0	0	1	-1	-.5		-1	-.5	1	0	-.5	1	-.08	+.04
MORALE INDEX +.08 / ELEMENT VIII																									
43	.5	0	0	1	.5	.5	0	0	0	0	0	1	0	1	1*	.5	1		0	1	0	-.5	0	+.30	+.23
44	0	0	0	0	0	.5	0	0	1	0	0	0	0	0	0	1	0	-1		-.5	1	.5	0	.00	+.02
45	-.5	0	0	-.5	-1	0	-.5	0	0	0	1	-1	0	1	0	.5	1	.5	-1		-1	-1	0	-.08	-.10
46	.5	0	1	0	.5	.5	0	.5	0	0	0	0	0	0	0	1	0	.5	1	.5		.5	1	+.17	+.04
47	-.5	0	0	0	1	.5	0	.5	0	1	0	0	0	0	0	1	0	0	1	.5	1		1	+.12	-.34
48	.5	0	0	0	0	1	1	0	1	0	0	0	1	0	0	1	0	0	1	-.5	1	1*		+.03	.00
MORALE INDEX +.25																									

	ELEMENT V	ELEMENT VI	ELEMENT VII	ELEMENT VIII
FLYING TEAMS	26–27	32–34	38–41	43–45
	29–30	33–35	39–40	44–46
	31– ?	36–37	42–	47–48

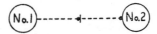

Fɪɢ. 1.—The degree of compatibility of the first two cadets in Element I.*

response to No. 2 was one of rejection (-1), and the response of No. 2 to No. 1 was one of indifference (0). The degree of compatibility is shown graphically in Figure 1. The degree of compatibility may be expressed mathematically. When compatibility is defined as the average of the units of intensity of the interpersonal choices and rejections in a group $(\bar{I})$ plus or minus the average deviation of the intensities from $\bar{I}(D)$.

$$C \text{ (compatibility index} = \bar{I} \pm D . \quad (1)$$

When I equals the intensity of a choice or rejection, n equals the total possible interpersonal reactions, and N equals the number of persons in the group, then

$$C = \bar{I} \pm D = \frac{\Sigma I}{n} \pm \frac{\Sigma d}{n} = \frac{\Sigma I}{N(N-1)} \pm \frac{\Sigma(\bar{I} \sim I)}{N(N-1)} \text{ units}, \quad (2)$$

$$\bar{I} = \frac{\Sigma I}{N(N-1)} = \frac{-1+0}{2(2-1)} = \frac{-1}{2} = -.5 \text{ unit}, \quad (3)$$

$$D = \frac{\Sigma(\bar{I} \sim I)}{N(N-1)} = \frac{.5+.5}{2(2-1)} = \frac{1}{2} = .5 \text{ unit}, \quad (4)$$

$$C = -.5 \pm .5 \text{ unit}, \quad (5)$$

where the $-.5$ represents the average intensity of the interpersonal reactions and the D represents the average deviation.[2] Thus, the social relations in the

---

* The graphic representation of units of positive and negative choice is as follows:

(1)———◀ +1.0 UNITS   (3)┠--------┤ ±0.0 UNITS

(2)——•—┤ +0.5 UNITS   (4)┠---•---┤ −0.5 UNITS

(5)┠-------┤ −1.0 UNITS

[2] Leslie Day Zeleny, "Measurement of Sociation," *American Sociological Review*, VI (April, 1941), 173–88. The sociation index is the same as the compatability index used here.

FIG. 2.—The degree of compatibility of two sociometrically selected cadets in Element I.

first team, chosen by rule-of-thumb methods, were incompatible to a measurable degree, i.e., $-.5 \pm .5$ unit. A simple inspection of Chart I showed that cadets Nos. 1 and 7 would have made a more compatible team. The interpersonal response may be expressed graphically, as in Figure 2. Cadet No. 1 chose Cadet No. 7, and the choice was mutual. In mathematical symbols the relationship may be expressed as follows:[3]

$$C = \bar{I} \pm D , \tag{6}$$

$$\bar{I} = \frac{\Sigma I}{N(N-1)} = \frac{1+1}{2(2-1)} = \frac{2}{2} = 1 \text{ unit}, \tag{7}$$

$$D = \frac{\Sigma(\bar{I} \sim I)}{N(N-1)} = \frac{0+0}{2(2-1)} = \frac{0}{2} = 0 \text{ unit}, \tag{8}$$

$$C = 1 \pm 0 \text{ unit}. \tag{9}$$

The social relations in a sociometrically selected flying team were compatible to the degree of 1 ± 0 unit.

Thus, by inspection, by graphic representation, and by mathematical

TABLE 1

COMPATIBILITY INDICES FOR
EIGHT INSTRUCTIONAL ELE-
MENTS IN THE FLIGHT*

Element	C
I	$+.25$
II	$+.50$
III	$+.60$
IV	$+.40$
V	$+.18$
VI	$+.37$
VII	$+.08$
VIII	$+.25$

* D not computed.

---

[3] *Ibid.*

symbols, the degree of compatibility of flying teams could be shown and the most compatible teams selected. In the instance of the flight of flying cadets shown in Chart I, it was possible to place nearly all the members in compatible flying teams. The notation at the bottom of Chart I shows possible compatible flying teams within each element. Sociometry made this recommendation possible. In actual practice a number of these recommended teams were used by flying instructors with satisfactory results.

The degree of compatibility among the cadets in an instructional element could also be measured; and a *compatibility index* computed for each element, as follows. Thus Table 1 shows the compatibility or morale indices for each element in the flight. The range of compatibility indices was relatively great, spreading from a high of .60 in Element III to a low of .08 in Element VII. Thus chance, as a method for selecting elements, was hardly productive of a uniform degree of compatibility in instructional elements. Adjustments in the composition of instructional elements could have been made.

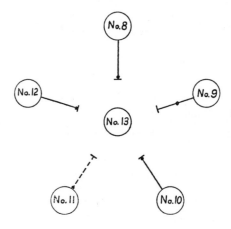

Fig. 3.—The status of Cadet No. 13 in Element II. ($SS = +.7 \pm .36$ unit.)

The search for a scientific method of determining flying partners also provided additional data. Of importance was the social status given to each flying cadet by his flying associates, called "choice-status" by Jennings.[4] The status of each cadet was measured in terms of the average intensity of the

---

[4] Helen Hall Jennings, *Leadership and Isolation* (New York: Longmans, Green and Co., 1943), p. 219.

choices and rejections expressed toward him by his flying associates. Diagrams of the status of two cadets in Element I serve to make clear the meaning of status in this instance (Fig. 3). Cadet No. 13 was accepted as a flying partner by every member of the unit except No. 11, who remained indifferent. Mathematically, the position of No. 13 may be expressed as follows:

$$SS = \bar{I} \pm D = \frac{\Sigma I}{n} \pm \frac{\Sigma d}{n} = \frac{\Sigma I}{N-1} \pm \frac{\Sigma (\bar{I} \sim I)}{N-1} \text{ unit,} \tag{10}$$

$$\bar{I} = \frac{\Sigma I}{N-1} = \frac{1+.5+1+0+1}{6-1} = \frac{3.5}{5} = +.7 \text{ unit,} \tag{11}$$

$$D = \frac{\Sigma (\bar{I} \sim I)}{N-1} = \frac{.3+.2+.3+.7+.3}{6-1} = \frac{1.8}{5} = .36 \text{ unit,} \tag{12}$$

$$SS = +.7 \pm .36 \text{ unit.} \tag{13}$$

Thus Cadet No. 13 came only .3 unit short of obtaining a "perfect" status among his associates with respect to membership in a flying team.

Much different was the social status of Cadet No. 33, as shown in Figure 4. No. 33 was rejected for flying by all except one of his associates, who accepted him with 1 unit of positive intensity. Mathematically, his position may be expressed as follows:

$$SS = I \pm D, \tag{14}$$

$$\bar{I} = \frac{\Sigma I}{N-1} = \frac{-1+(-1)+1+(-1)+(-1)}{6-1} = \frac{-3}{5} = -.6 \text{ unit,} \tag{15}$$

$$D = \frac{\Sigma (\bar{I} \sim I)}{N-1} = \frac{.4+.4+1.6+.4+.4}{6-1} = \frac{3.2}{5} = .64 \text{ unit,} \tag{16}$$

$$SS = -.6 \pm .64 \text{ unit.} \tag{17}$$

Thus Cadet No. 33 came only .4 unit from attaining complete rejection.

In a similar manner it was possible to compute the status of each cadet in his flight. These are given in Chart I. The $\bar{I}R$'s in the right-hand column of Chart I are the same as the SS, without D. These scores, not running so high or so low as scores in the elements because of lack of acquaintance, ranged from a high of $+.30$ in the case of Cadet No. 13 to a low of $-.39$ in the case of Cadet No. 28.

Those enjoying high status usually possessed two qualities: exceptional ability in flying and personal qualities of leadership. On the other hand, those

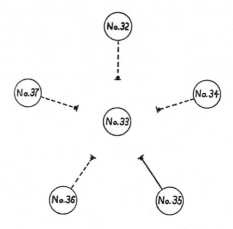

Fig. 4.—The status of Cadet No. 33 in Element VI. $(SS = -.6 \pm .64$ unit.)

with low status generally possessed exceptionally low ability in flying and un-attractive personal qualities. Obviously, however, flying ability or reputation for flying ability was the primary basis of choice. There were two checks on the validity of the social-status index of cadets as computed, outside the urgency of the situation in which the choices were made. The first was a tendency for those with exceptionally high status, in this and other instances, to be selected, without previous knowledge of the director of flying, as flight instruc-tors. In the second place, it was found during a certain period that cadets (other flights included) with low status were more often involved in crashes than others. To be more specific, the average SS or $\bar{I}R$ of six cadets involved in aircraft accidents officially classified as "serious" was $-.06 \pm D$. During the same period seven cadets were in officially classified "minor" accidents. Their average status score was $+.11$. Of the thirteen cadets who had been in accidents, only one had a high status score. Probably, he was flying with a cadet with a low status score, and it was an incompatible team.

Cadets varied in the number and intensity of their choices and rejections for others, called by Jennings "emotional expansiveness."[5] Take, for example, the emotional expansiveness of Cadet No. 13 within his assigned element (Fig. 5). Among the cadets in Element II, Cadet No. 13 was indifferent to three of his immediate associates and desirous of flying with only two of them. His expansivenesss may be expressed mathematically, as follows:

---

[5] *Op. cit.*, p. 219.

$$EE \text{ (emotional expansiveness index)} = \bar{I} \pm D = \frac{\Sigma I}{n} + \frac{\Sigma d}{n} \left. \right\} \quad (18)$$

$$= \frac{\Sigma I}{N-1} \pm \frac{\Sigma (\bar{I} \sim I)}{N-1} \text{ units},$$

$$\bar{I} = \frac{\Sigma I}{N-1} = \frac{0+0+1+0+1}{6-1} = \frac{2}{5} = .40 \text{ unit}, \quad (19)$$

$$D = \frac{\Sigma (\bar{I} \sim I)}{N-1} = \frac{.4+.4+.6+.4+.6}{6-1} = \frac{2.4}{5} = .48 \text{ unit}, \quad (20)$$

$$EE = +.40 \pm .48 \text{ unit}. \quad (21)$$

Thus, Cadet No. 13, while receiving .7 ± .36 unit of intensity of choice for flying partner, responded only to the extent of .40 ± .48 unit of intensity, slightly more than half of the intensity "received." When the whole flight was considered, Cadet No. 13's *EE* index was only .05 (see *ĪE*, average intensity of choices expressed, on Chart I).

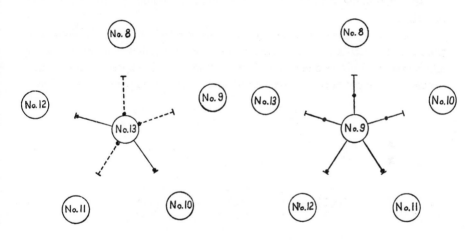

FIG. 5.—The emotional expansiveness of Cadet No. 13 in Element II. (*EE* = +.40 ± .48 unit.)

FIG. 6.—The emotional expansiveness of Cadet No. 9 in Element II. (*EE* = +.7 ± .24 unit.)

Much different was the emotional expansiveness of Cadet No. 9, as is shown in Figure 6. Thus, No. 9 responded positively emotionally to every member in his element. The degree of his emotional response may be expressed mathematically as follows:

$$EE = \bar{I} \pm D \tag{22}$$

$$\bar{I} = \frac{\Sigma I}{N-1} = \frac{.5 + .5 + 1 + 1 + .5}{6-1} = \frac{3.5}{5} = .7 \text{ unit}, \tag{23}$$

$$D = \frac{\Sigma(\bar{I} \sim I)}{N-1} = \frac{.2 + .2 + .3 + .3 + .2}{6-1} = \frac{1.2}{5} = .24 \text{ unit}, \tag{24}$$

$$EE = .7 \pm .24 \text{ unit} . \tag{25}$$

Also, No. 9's *EE* (*ĪE* on Chart I) index for the whole flight community was +.33. It was clear that No. 9 was markedly more emotionally expansive in his element and in his unit than was No. 13.

Examination of the array of *EE* indices (*ĪE*'s on Chart I) shows that they vary from a + .47 for No. 22 to a − .34 for No. 47. Thus cadets varied immensely in the acceptance of their associates as flying partners. It was immensely more difficult to find satisfactory flying partners for some cadets than for others.

Social adjustment, defined as the average intensity of mutual choices and rejections between a cadet and each of his associates, plus or minus the average deviation, could be diagrammed and mathematically expressed in the same manner as compatibility, social status, and emotional expansiveness. Take,

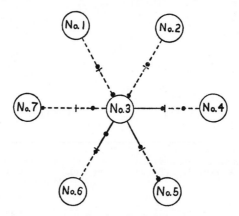

Fig.7.—The social adjustment of Cadet No. 3 in Element I. ($SA = -.13 \pm .56$ unit.)

for example, the case of Cadet No. 3 (Fig. 7). Cadet No. 3 was rejected by four of his six associates in the element, while choosing two of those who rejected him. Such a constellation of choices and rejections revolving about one person as a nucleus is called by Moreno[6] and Jennings[7] a "social atom." However, they would not limit the mutual responses to a "closed" community—the element—as is done in this instance. They would add the responses in the flight, as we shall do presently. Mathematically, social adjustment may be expressed as follows:

$$\left. \begin{array}{l} SA \text{ (social} \\ \text{adjustment index)} \end{array} = \bar{I} \pm D = \frac{\Sigma I}{n} \pm \frac{\Sigma d}{n} = \frac{\Sigma I}{2\,(N-1)} \right\} \quad (26)$$

$$\left. \pm \frac{\Sigma\,(\bar{I} \sim I)}{(2N-1)} \text{ units}, \right.$$

The adjustment of No. 3 in his "social atom" is negative. In this manner it is possible to show the degrees of social adjustment of each cadet in his element or flight.

$$\bar{I} = \frac{\Sigma I}{2\,(N-1)}$$

$$\left. = \frac{-1+0+(-1)+0+(-.5)+1+0+1+(-1)+.5+0+(-.5)}{2\,(7-1)} \right\} \quad (27)$$

$$= \frac{-1.5}{12} = -.13 \text{ unit},$$

$$D = \frac{\Sigma\,(\bar{I} \sim I)}{2\,(N-1)}$$

$$\left. = \frac{.87+.13+.87+.13+.37+1.13+.13+1.13+.87+.63+.13+.37}{2\,(7-1)} \right\} \quad (28)$$

$$= \frac{6.76}{12} = \pm .56 \text{ unit},$$

$$SA = -.13 \pm .56 \text{ unit}.$$

Inspection of the status indices ($\bar{I}R$) on Chart I and emotional expansiveness indices ($\bar{I}E$) on the same chart show numerous types of relationships be-

---

[6] J. L. Moreno, *Who Shall Survive?* (Washington, D.C.: Nervous and Mental Disease Pub. Co., 1934), pp. 141–46.

[7] *Op cit.*, p. 219, and chap. v. "The Patterning of Interrelations."

TABLE 2

RELATIONSHIPS BETWEEN SOCIAL STATUS
AND EMOTIONAL EXPANSIVENESS

Type	Description	Specific Illustration (Cadet No.)	$SS(\bar{I}R)$	$EE(\bar{I}E)$
I..	A *high-status* cadet, who *accepts* his associates	43	+.30	+.23
II..	A *high-status* cadet, who *rejects* his associates	41	+.24	−.20
III..	A *low-status* cadet, who *accepts* his associates	31	−.32	+.34
IV..	A *low-status* cadet, who *rejects* his associates	45	−.08	−.10

tween status and emotional expansiveness. The types given in Table 2 may be easily recognized.

Each of the four types of cadets lived in a different type of "social world" and probably needed to be handled differently. Type I may be considered well adjusted to his associates in the flight, for his human relations in the flying community are, for him, relatively happy. The situation is the opposite in Type IV, for whom the situation is relatively unhappy. Type II is a potential leader, who rejects his potential fellows, thus finding the situation none too pleasant; and Type III experiences frustrations, for, though he desires to fly with his associates, he is rejected.

The classification of cadets according to the foregoing types should give flight instructors and flight surgeons valuable clues to the diagnosis of both stable and unstable emotional conditions among flying cadets, and perhaps other flyers, too. In this connection it is to be observed that psychoneurosis was the most frequent cause of the elimination of both pilot-observers and nonpilot-observers from flying status. Though accurate data are not available, it can be stated that low-status cadets were much more likely to be eliminated from the training program than others.

This study, though incomplete because of the limitations to research imposed by more urgent military duties and the unavailability of records, demonstrates how opportunities for cadets to express spontaneous choices and rejections with respect to flying partners provided a better basis for the selection of compatible flying teams than the random method in use. It showed, also, the limitations of the older method of forming flying teams and instructional elements upon the basis of random selection.

The study demonstrates, too, methods for identifying leaders and isolates among flying cadets and shows how to represent graphically and symbolically the status, emotional expansiveness, and social adjustment of cadet flyers within a community of flyers.

It is believed that the general methods outlined in this study are suggestive of further studies that could be made with respect to the determination of leaders and followers in flight crews and, perhaps, small groups of many kinds.

THE USE OF A SOCIOMETRIC TEST AS A PREDICTOR OF COMBAT UNIT EFFECTIVENESS[1]

By Daniel M. Goodacre, III

The Institute for Research in Human Relations, under contract with the Personnel Research Section of the Adjutant General's Office, was assigned to "develop measures of effectiveness for small combat units." A Moreno technique, the Sociometric Test was one of the predictors developed. A field problem for scout squads of reconnaissance platoons was developed as a criterion of the effectiveness of that squad's field performance. The scout squad is made up of six armed men with full field equipment and two jeeps; one jeep contains a radio and the other has a light machine gun mounted upon it. Under "normal" combat conditions the squad leader and two of his men ride in one jeep while the assistant squad leader rides in the other jeep with the remaining two men. The field problem consisted of twelve tactical situations, such as an air attack, the outposting of a road junction, a withdrawal, etc., which were constructed to represent battlefield conditions, as nearly as possible. These twelve situations had been agreed upon by a group of military experts to be representative of the normal combat functioning of this type of unit. The field problem required about six hours to complete and was run over a circular course covering a wide variety of terrain features. All of the twelve squads used in the problem were from the same regiment, had had about the same amount of training, and were tested at the same military reservation. The rating of combat behavior was done by personnel from the Institute and the military on a standardized rating form while closely following the squads in the field. The squads to be tested were first given the various predictors, including the Sociometric Test, and were then taken to the problem area and conducted through the field problem.

The purpose of constructing the Sociometric Test was to develop a paper and pencil measure of group cohesion; the assumption being that group cohesion and group performance are related. It was further hypothesized that Army social interactions may be categorized into three areas of interaction. These areas are:

First, a *Non-Military Area* that is thought to consist of social interactions that take place outside of the military structure while on a leave

---

[1] This paper was in part presented at the 1951 meeting of the American Psychological Association.

or pass status off the reservation. This area is represented in the Sociometric Test by the following questions:

> If you were going on pass what man (or men) would you *want* to go on pass with and what man (or men) would you *not want* to go with?
> If you were going to a party or dance tomorrow what man (or men) would you *want* to have there and what man (or men) would you *not want* to have there?
> If you had a leave to go home what man (or men) would you *want* to invite to your home and what man (or men) would you *not want* to invite to your home?

Second, a *Garrison Area* consisting of on the reservation social interactions that occur within the military structure but which are of a non-tactical nature. This is represented by the following questions:

> If you were going to chow what man (or men) would you *want* to sit with and what man (or men) would you *not want* to sit with?
>
> If your outfit was having a good movie tonight what man (or men) would you *want* to go with and what man (or men) would you *not want* to go with?
>
> If you were told to pick the men whom you wanted to live in a tent or barracks with what man (or men) would you *choose* and what man (or men) would you *not choose*?

Third, a *Tactical or Field Area* of social interactions occuring "in the field" which are structured by a tactical military situation. This area is represented by the following questions in the test:

> During an attack what man (or men) would you *choose* to share a foxhole with and what man (or men) would you *not choose* to share a foxhole with?
>
> If you were to lead an advance through an enemy town what man (or men) would you *choose* to cover you and what man (or men) would you *not choose* to cover you?
>
> If you were wounded what man (or men) would you choose to help you back to an aid station and what man (or men) would you *not choose* to help you back to an aid station?

The nine questions above were selected from a collection of suggested items gathered by interviewing combat veterans of World War II. The criteria for the selection of the items were that they:

1. Tap situations that occur with a high degree of frequency in all Army combat units.
2. Overlap as little as possible.

3. Be worded so that it would be both possible and logical for the respondent to make a positive, negative or no response choice.

Three different scores can be arrived at by assigning a unit weight to each of the positive and negative responses and summing different combinations of these responses. The three different scores and the methods of obtaining them are:

1. A score indicating the expressed attitude of one member of the group towards the rest of the group may be obtained by summing all of that individual's responses.
2. A score indicating the expressed attitude of the group towards any member of the group may be found by adding all of the responses made by others about that particular individual. This score may be thought of as an index of leadership or leadership potential.
3. A score indicating the extent of group cohesion may be derived by adding all of the response the group made. This score is the one which is to be considered here.

The present format was developed in an attempt to minimize three factors which often have been found to be quite bothersome in the construction of sociometric tests. These three factors or difficulties are the halo effect produced in subsequent items by the patterning of previous responses, the tendency for a respondent to change a choice already made after discovering that the question has another aspect to it (either positive or negative), and the paucity of responses when written responses are required of a non verbally oriented population such as we are dealing with here. These three difficulties have been somewhat minimized in this format by:

1. Putting each item on a separate page to reduce the "halo effect" of previous responses.
2. Presenting the entire question, both the positive and negative side of it, first as a unit, and then asking for the positive or negative choice *after* both aspects have been considered, to reduce the tendency of some respondents to change responses after they have once been made.
3. Having the respondent write each man's name only once to reduce the possibility of limiting the number of responses as a result of the respondent's resistance to a writing situation.

A rank order coefficient of correlation was run between the total score (the index of group cohesion) received on the Sociometric Test by each squad and the total score received on the field problem by each squad. This correlation produced a rho of .77 which is significant for a N of 12 (squads) above the 1% level of a confidence. Other rho coefficients found were:

Criterion and Garrison area   .62
Criterion and Social area   .78
Criterion and Tactical area   .79

As would be expected from the above statistics these three areas of social interactions are highly intercorrelated, with the Tactical and Social Areas correlating highest (rho of .84) and the Garrison Area correlating somewhat lower with the other two areas (rho's of .68 and .76). The lower correlations of the Garrison Area with the other two areas may be partiallly understood when the rho's between each question and the criterion of field performance are examined. It was found that two of the garrison questions (going to chow and going to a movie) had rho's of only .46 and .44 while the other seven of the questions all correlated with the criterion with rank order coefficients of correlation ranging from .63 to .75. It is felt that the two "weak sisters" in the Garrison Area are weak because they involve social interactions of a less intimate degree of association than the other items. This is manifested in the observation (at the military reservation where the testing was conducted) that inter-personal choices in these two situations (going to chow and going to the movies) are made relatively casually and indiscriminately as compared to, say, those made when going on a pass.

It is regrettable that reliability coefficients cannot be reported for the Sociometric Test but a rapid turnover of personnel in the units used in the study occurred shortly after the testing as a consequence of the outbreak of hostilities in Korea. This prevented re-testing of the original sample.

INDEX OF GROUP COHESION AND TOTAL FIELD PROBLEM SCORE
FOR EACH SQUAD

Squad	Index of Group Cohesion	Total Field Problem Score
A	210	85
B	193	82
C	256	77
D	160	74
E	178	68
F	185	66
G	185	65
H	171	64
I	186	63
J	119	58.3
K	38	57.8
L	108	57

The correlation of .77 indicates that the group cohesion score received on the Sociometric Test is related in a positive manner to performance on the Scout Squad Field Problem. It is felt that this Sociometric Test could be applied with equal facility to any other Army combat unit and with changes of terminology in a few questions it could be applied to almost any small organized unit in the armed forces or industry as a predictor of group performance. Further research, however, would have to determine the effectiveness of that prediction of other groups.

THE LEADERSHIP BEHAVIOR AND COMBAT
PERFORMANCE OF AIRPLANE COMMANDERS*

By Andrew W. Halpin

The fresh attention which social psychology has focused upon small group behavior (4, 12) is reflected in current research on military leadership. Stouffer (13) and others (3, 6, 8, 10) have discussed the military significance of primary groups, and have indicated the need for research on leadership within such face-to-face groups. The 11 members of the B-29 crew constitute a group of this kind. The crew, however, is part of a larger hierarchical organization in which the airplane commander is responsible to squadron and wing superiors who evaluate his combat performance and that of his crew. The present study is an analysis of the relationship between the crew's perception of the leadership behavior of the airplane commander and (a) ratings of his combat performance made by his superiors, and (b) an index of his crew's satisfaction with him as a commander. Thus, the analysis involves a comparison between the crew's description of the commander's behavior and two independent evaluations of the effectiveness of that behavior: one by his superiors and the other by his crew.

In ordinary parlance, the concept of leadership is used in an evaluative sense. To say that a man displays leadership implies that this is "good" or "effective" leadership. The evaluation of leadership, however, is only one aspect of the problem. A more primary task is to describe the behavior of the leader in terms of psychologically meaningful dimensions. If a description of the leader with respect to specific dimensions of behavior and an evaluation of the effectiveness of that behavior can be obtained independently, then it becomes possible to ascertain how much each dimension contributes to favorable evaluation. Furthermore, one also may determine whether this contribution changes when the source of evaluation is changed.

Evaluations of leadership may be obtained readily enough by means of various rating schedules. On the other hand, the measurement of a group's description of its leader's behavior is a less commonly used procedure. Hemphill and Coons (7) have devised a technique for this purpose, a Leader Behavior Description Questionnaire. This instrument was used originally with

* This study was sponsored jointly by the Human Resources Research Laboratories, Department of the Air Force, and The Ohio State Leadership Studies. It is one of a series of Studies in Aircrew Composition supervised by Dr. John K. Hemphill. The author is indebted to Dr. Hemphill for his many valuable suggestions, and to Mrs. Janet W. Bieri for her assistance in analyzing the data. The full data upon which this partial report is based are reported elsewhere (5). The opinions expressed are those of the author and should not be regarded as having the endorsement of the Department of the Air Force.

nonmilitary groups. Later, two forms of the questionnaire (130 and 80 items respectively) were designed specifically for the aircrew situation (5). Both questionnaires are in multiple-choice format, and the frequency with which the leader engages in the behavior described is indicated by marking, for each item, a statement containing one of five adverbs: always, often, occasionally, seldom, or never. The following items are illustrative:

1) He tries out his new ideas on the crew.
2) He rules with an iron hand.
3) He gets crew approval on important matters before going ahead.
4) He does personal favors for crew members.

PROCEDURE

In order to develop empirical keys for the Leader Behavior Description Questionnaire, a factor analysis[1] was made of the responses obtained from a sample of 30 questionnaires. The procedure was based upon an extension of an iterative factor analysis technique (14, 15). Although seven factors were extracted, after the completion of rotation it was found that the last three accounted for only approximately 6 per cent of the variance common to the seven. Because no meaningful interpretation could be made of these relatively unrepresented factors, nothing more was done with them. The four remaining factors have been designated as: Consideration, Initiating Structure-in-Interaction, Production Emphasis,[2] and Social Awareness. The first two of these account for approximately 50 and 34 per cent respectively of the common variance. These factors, Consideration and the Initiating Structure-in-Interaction, are the only two pertinent to the present study. Other investigators have noted the relevance of these two aspects of leadership. Freud (2), for example, has discussed the importance of consideration and libidinal ties in the relationship between the leader and the group. Similarly, Homans' concept of the leader "originating interaction" (9, ch. 16) corresponds essentially to what is referred

---

[1] Dr. B. James Winer, University of North Carolina, made this factor analysis and constructed the dimension keys.

[2] Production Emphasis refers to a manner of motivating the crew to greater activity by emphasizing the mission or job to be done. Social Awareness (Sensitivity) appears to measure the airplane commander's sensitivity to and awareness of social interrelationships and pressures existing both inside and outside the crew. It may represent activities on the part of the airplane commander which often have been referred to as "sizing up the situation." This factor does not indicate the extent to which the airplane commander acts in accord with these insights, but merely indicates his awareness of social pressures originating from either within or outside the crew. There appears to be a distinction between being aware of these social pressures and taking appropriate action with respect to them.

to here as Initiating Structure-in-Interaction. Furthermore, these two dimensions of leader behavior are analogous to constructs which have been developed in the field of personality theory: for example, to Rank's (11) principles of love and force and to Bronfenbrenner's (1) dimensions of support and structure.

High positive loadings on the Consideration factor are associated with behavior indicative of friendship, mutual trust, respect, and a certain warmth in the relationship between the airplane commander and his crew. High negative loadings appear on items which suggest that the commander is authoritarian and impersonal in his relations with members of the crew. Consideration thus refers to the extent to which the airplane commander, while carrying out his leadership functions, is considerate of the men in his crew.

High positive loadings on the Initiating Structure factor occur on items which imply that the airplane commander organizes and defines the relationship between himself and the members of his crew. He tends to define the role which he expects each member of the crew to assume, and endeavors to establish well-defined patterns of organization, channels of communication, and ways of getting jobs done. This factor probably represents a basic and unique function of leadership. It is possible that other factors, including Consideration, primarily represent facilitating means for accomplishing this end.

On the basis of the factor analysis, keys were constructed for these two dimensions of leadership behavior. The Consideration key of 28 items[3] has an estimated reliability (corrected by the Spearman-Brown formula) of .94. The corresponding estimate for the 29-item Initiating Structure key is .76.

The 130-item form of the Leader Behavior Description Questionnaire was administered to 353 members of 52 B-29 crews who attended the Combat Crew Training School at MacDill Air Force Base during the autumn of 1950. In order to determine whether the crew members agreed on how they described their leaders on the Consideration and the Initiating Structure dimensions, an analysis was made of the dimension score variance associated with the airplane commander who was described. Specifically, the between-crew and within-crew variances were compared for each dimension separately. The F ratio, in the case of both dimensions, was significant at the .01 level. The corresponding unbiased correlation ratios are .54 and .36, thus indicating a tendency for the crew members to agree in their perception of their commander's leadership behavior. Accordingly, crew mean Consideration and crew mean Initiating Structure scores were used as indices for describing the leader's behavior on

---

[3] In the 80-item form of the questionnaire, there are only 15 items on each of the keys. The estimated reliabilities are .93 and .86 respectively.

TABLE 1

CORRELATIONS BETWEEN THE AIRPLANE COMMANDER'S CONSIDERATION AND INITIATING STRUCTURE SCORES AND (A) SUPERIORS' RATINGS OF HIS COMBAT PERFORMANCE, AND (B) CREW'S SATISFACTION INDEX

SUPERIORS' RATINGS OF COMBAT PERFORMANCE	IN TRAINING ($N = 33$†)				IN COMBAT ($N = 29$‡)			
	CONSIDERATION	INITIATING STRUCTURE	$r_{12.3}$	$r_{13.2}$	CONSIDERATION	INITIATING STRUCTURE	$r_{14.5}$	$r_{15.4}$
(1)	(2)	(3)			(4)	(5)		
A. Technical competence on arrival overseas	−.24	.11	−.31	.23	−.02	.24	−.18	.29
B. Technical competence at present time	−.21	.10	−.27	.20	−.22	.19	−.38*	.36
C. Effectiveness of working with crew members	−.14	.14	−.21	.21	−.13	.27	−.33	.40*
D. Conformity to SOP	.03	.37*	−.13	.39*	−.25	.32	−.52**	.54**
E. Performance under stress	−.22	.15	−.31	.26	−.12	.16	−.24	.26
F. Attitude and motivation to be effective	−.15	.20	−.25	.28	−.34	.16	−.50**	.42*
G. Over-all effectiveness as a combat crew member	−.20	.22	−.32	.33	−.23	.28	−.46*	.48**
Crew's Satisfaction Index	.48*	−.17	.63**	−.48*	.64**	.35	.57**	−.03

* Significant at the .05 level.
** Significant at the .01 level.
† For Ratings B and E, $N = 32$; for Satisfaction Index, 27.
‡ For Rating E, $N = 28$; for Satisfaction Index, 27.

these dimensions. For 52 crews, the correlation between these ascribed Consideration and Initiating Structure scores is .45, which is significant at the .01 level.

During the summer of 1951, data from three sources were collected in Japan on 33 of the 52 airplane commanders who had been described by their crews at MacDill Air Force Base. First, 29 of the 33 commanders were described again on the Leader Behavior Description Questionnaire (80-item form). Second, the squadron and wing superiors rated all 33 commanders with respect to seven criteria of combat performance. The rating for each criterion was made on a nine-point scale. The commanders were evaluated by from one to four raters, with 73 per cent of the ratings secured from more than a single rater. Third, the members of 27 crews answered the question, "If you could make up a crew from among the crew members in your squadron, whom would you choose for each crew position?" The ratio between the number of votes the incumbent commander received and the number of votes cast was used as an index of the crew's satisfaction with his leadership. Accordingly, the data consist of two descriptions of the leader's behavior—one in training and one in combat—and two evaluations of his combat performance, one by his superiors and the other by his crew. The superiors' ratings and the Satisfaction Index then were correlated with the Consideration and the Initiating Structure scores ascribed to these commanders by their crews, both in this country and in the Far Eastern Air Force. In each case, partial as well as zero-order correlations were computed, that is, for the Consideration scores with the Initiating Structure scores partialled out, and for the Initiating Structure scores with the Consideration scores partialled out (see Table 1).

RESULTS

In both the training and the combat situation, there is a trend toward negative correlations between the superiors' ratings, and the Consideration scores, and positive correlations between these ratings and the Initiating Structure scores. The partial correlations accentuate this trend, which is more marked in the combat situation than in the training situation. One notes particularly that in the case of the rating on "over-all effectiveness as a combat crew member," which perhaps best represents the way the superiors, in day-to-day operation, evaluate the airplane commander, both partial correlations based upon the crews' perception of the commander's behavior in combat are statistically significant.

On the other hand, the correlations between the leadership dimensions and the Satisfaction Index show a trend in the opposite direction. The zero- and first-order correlations between this index and the Consideration scores, whether in training or combat, are positive and statistically significant. Conversely, the correlations with the Initiating Structure scores, although not consistently significant, tend to be negative.

The four entries in the lower right-hand corner of Table 1 succinctly illustrate the two trends. It will be recalled, however, that the correlation between the leadership dimensions, as described, is .45. Thus, although the relationship between the dimensions is described as one of relative independence, the contribution of these dimensions to the effectiveness of the leader is evaluated both by superiors and subordinates as antithetical. Furthermore, the superiors and the subordinates each view this antithesis in an opposite way.

Summary

1) In developing a Leader Behavior Description Questionnaire on which the members of 52 B-29 crews described the behavior of their airplane commander, two major dimensions of leadership were identified: Consideration and Initiating Structure-in-Interaction. The correlation between these dimension scores is .45.

2) While in training in this country, 33 airplane commanders were described by their crews on this questionnaire. Later, 29 of these commanders on combat assignment in the Far Eastern Air Force were again described by their crews. Ratings on seven aspects of the combat performance of these commanders were secured from their administrative superiors. An index of each crew's satisfaction with its commander was also computed.

3) A trend toward negative correlations was found between the superiors' ratings and the Consideration scores, and positive correlations between these ratings and the Initiating Structure scores. Conversely, the correlations between the Satisfaction Index and the dimension scores showed a trend in the opposite direction. Thus, the superiors and subordinates were inclined to evaluate oppositely the contribution of these dimensions to the effectiveness of leadership. This difference in evaluation confronts the leader with conflicting role expectations. It is suggested that the role conflict so induced constitutes the core of "the dilemma of leadership." Further research is needed to determine the precise techniques which different leaders use in their attempt to resolve this conflict, and to analyze the consequences of these techniques for both the personal adjustment of the leader and the effectiveness of the group.

REFERENCES

1. Bronfenbrenner, U., "Toward an Integrated Theory of Personality," in R. R. Blake and G. V. Ramsey (eds.), *Perception: An Approach to Personality*. New York: Ronald, 1951. Pp. 206–57.
2. Freud, S. *Group Psychology and the Analysis of the Ego*. London: Hogarth, 1948.
3. Grinker, R. R., and Spiegel, J. P. *Men under Stress*. Philadelphia: Blakiston, 1945.
4. Halpin, A. W. "Current Conceptual Trends in Small Group Study: Social Psychology," *Autonomous Groups Bulletin,* VII (1952), 4–17.
5. Halpin, A. W., and Winer, B. J. *The Leadership Behavior of the Airplane Commander*. Washington, D.C.: Human Resources Research Laboratories, Department of the Air Force, 1952.
6. Havron, M. D., Fay, R. J., and Goodacre, D. M, III. *The Effectiveness of Small Military Units* (Personnel Research Section, AGO, Report No. 885). Washington, D.C.: Department of the Army, 1951.
7. Hemphill, J. K., and Coons, A E. *Leader Behavior Description*. Columbus, Ohio: Personnel Research Board, Ohio State University, 1950.
8. Homans, G. C. "The Small Warship," *American Sociological Review,* XI (1946), 294–300.
9. ———. *The Human Group*. New York: Harcourt, Brace, 1950.
10. Mandelbaum, D. G. *Group Dynamics of Military Units*. (Prepared for the Working Group on Human Behavior under Conditions of Military Service.) Washington, D.C.: Department of Defense, Research and Development Board, 1951.
11. Rank, O. *Will Therapy and Truth and Reality*. New York: Alfred Knopf, 1950.
12. Smith, M. B. "Social Psychology and Group Processes," *Annual Review of Psychology,* III (1952), 175–204.
13. Stouffer, S. A. *et al. The American Soldier (Adjustment during Army Life,* Vol. I). Princeton, N.J.: Princeton University Press, 1949.
14. Wherry, R. J., and Gaylord, R. H. "The Concept of Test and Item Reliability in Relation to Factor Pattern," *Psychometrika,* VIII (1943), 247–64.
15. Wherry, R. J., Campbell, J. T., and Perloff, R. "An Empirical Verification of the Wherry-Gaylord Iterative Factor Analysis Procedure," *Psychometrika,* XVI (1951), 67–74.

THE NOMINATING TECHNIQUE AS A METHOD OF EVALUATING AIR GROUP MORALE

By John G. Jenkins

It was my good fortune to be associated, during World War II, with some particularly fine Navy flight surgeons. At the outset, I had very little idea what they did, and, certainly, they had rather less than half that amount of knowledge of what I did. Nor was the clarification of the issue aided by the fact that I wore three stripes and the insignia of a pharmacist.

The luck of the draw threw me into very close contact with these flight surgeons, however, and it gave me a deep appreciation of what their military function was. In a good many cases, it also gave the flight surgeon some idea of what an aviation psychologist did with his time, and often it led to a lasting professional friendship. Flight surgeons who had suspected that Ph.D.'s in psychology were essentially amateur psychiatrists were much molified to learn that we were essentially finger-counters. And they began to like us better when they learned that our type of finger counting could often be used to fill out gaps in their own best efforts. In a surprisingly large number of cases, the paranoid atmosphere of our early contacts gave way to a feeling of mutual appreciation and to a realization that the research techniques of the psychologist could be used effectively to supplement the natural contributions of the flight surgeon.

Since the last six years have, I trust, clearly established my own friendly relationship with aviation medicine, let me address my main topic by suggesting that a sympathetic outsider like myself ultimately learns to distinguish three types of flight surgeons. The lowest type (and he does, unfortunately, occur) is the Minimal Duty Flight Surgeon. I am tempted to call him the Flight-Pay Flight Surgeon. He is a physician who has qualified for flight surgeons' wings, but he does not like flying, he does not like pilots, and his only apparent interest in aviation lies in the slight increase it means in his pay. The pilots soon spot such a man and take delight in offering him rides and generally trying to make him unhappy. They have no respect for him, and they regard his contribution to an air group as rather less than nothing. Fortunately, he appears to be a rather rare type, for he is not a credit to the medical profession and he is not a help to an active and functioning air group.

The second type I would call the good Sick Bay Flight Surgeon. His identification is primarily with basic medical activities and only very secondarily with the air group. The men like him; they respect him; but his influence is almost entirely through somatic medicine. When the men are sick or injured, they will choose this man over all other medical help; but they do not expect to see him on the flight deck. The pilots will readily turn to him with a pilonidal cyst or with an aerotitis media; they will track him down when something hurts somewhere; but they are unlikely to go to him when they find—suddenly perhaps—that they have had a bellyful of flying. These men, as I see them, are a real credit to the medical profession; but they are, for me at least, something less than full-scale flight surgeons.

The third type, I believe, should be designated as Flight Deck Flight Surgeons. (Naturally I do not mean to limit such men to carrier-based aviation; they are just as readily to be found among shore-based units or among those who fly the big boats). The thing that marks these men is their emphasis—through the way they live—on the first word in their title. Whatever else anyone may say, these men are identified with *flight* and with the pilots who produce *flight*. Their job, as they live it, is not to take care of sick pilots so much as to keep well ones in the air. Anything, mental or physical, that hampers the pilot or the air group in actual flying is meat for this sort of flight surgeon. Men of this sort, as I have seen them, can be the most important influence in the whole air group for keeping pilots flying and, if necessary, fighting in the air.

It is the Flight Deck Flight Surgeon, of course, who is deeply concerned with the morale of air groups. The Flight-Pay Flight Surgeon does not care about this matter, since his basic concern is to put in his minimum flying hours per month—preferably in a trainer and within a few miles of the home airport. The Sick Bay Flight Surgeon cannot be deeply concerned about all air group morale, since his primary orientation is always toward somatic pathology and its skillful remedy. But the Flight Deck Flight Surgeon finds morale his primary criterion of the welfare of the group, and toward the maintenance of morale he bends his best efforts.

Believe me, I am not talking in terms of vague and hypothetical types. I have known all three. With the first type, I can find nothing in common; and I suspect that his own medical confreres can find but little more. For the Sick Bay Flight Surgeon, I have keen respect. He is a medical practitioner of a high order but, since his interests do not outrun the orbit of somatic medicine, I share but little common ground with him. Whatever our group of one hundred psychologists in Naval Aviation Psychology may have been able to learn about air group morale was always in company with the third type—the Flight Deck Flight Surgeon.

At the risk of appearing to offer only conventional compliments, let me say that I have the highest admiration for the real Flight Deck Flight Surgeon. Our records show man after man of this type identified by the pilots themselves, working against heavy odds for the welfare of his air group. He had gained the confidence of the men by flying whenever he could and by showing that he liked to fly. His normal station was on the flight deck, and he was always the first man on hand if there was a deck crash or barrier crash of any sort. Because he actually likes to fly, the men talked to him about flying, and this led them to talk to him about themselves and their fears and hopes. He was always an invited member of informal—and sometimes illicit—social celebrations staged by the air group. He it was who talked straight to the skipper—or, if necessary, to the admiral—when a key man had had enough and had to be grounded for a while. Such men often complained to me that they practiced very little medicine, but for my book the medical profession had no better representatives.

I hope that this long introduction will be pardoned. In preparing this paper, I tried to get along without the introduction, but always found myself going back to it. The reason is simply that any objective aid in determining air group morale will be of interest chiefly, if not altogether, to the Flight Deck type of flight surgeon. Realizing that, I had to identify him before I could show how methods developed by a group of nonmedical psychologists could be of possible use in appraising the morale of those who pilot airplanes.

It is necessary to add a further word of explanation. Psychologists were initially brought into Naval Aviation for a single purpose. They were asked to set up batteries of tests to help pick the better risks among those who applied. Our group in the Navy had a two-year head start on the program, having already begun the long process of test-validation on Navy pilots in 1939. Like any other battery of tests, our battery could be used only at the expense of rejecting a considerable number of false positives. The air training command accepted this, however, and used our tests in screening more than a quarter of a million applicants during the war. The best key to their appraisal of the practical usefulness of the tests is to be found in the fact that the Command itself three times raised the basic cutting score of the test-battery, while the war was going on.

Now, for reasons of obvious necessity, our test-battery was standardized to predict only outcome of training. We could say that men scoring high would show few washouts in training and that men scoring low would exhibit high rates of failure. That was all. We could not even hazard a guess as to how these men would perform in combat. For all we knew, by selecting those who did not wash out, we might be selecting docile well-behaved conformers, who would do well on a training station tour of duty but fold up when facing lethal combat. As of 1944, we did not know, but we everlastingly thought we should know.

As early as 1942, we had discussed this point with the line officers of the training command. We had sought to convince them that some of us must go out into the combat area, if we wished to find out how the tests were doing in so far as picking good combat pilots was concerned. Initially, this suggestion evoked only tolerant amusement. Somewhat later, it met only with the resistance of any novel—and presumably impractical—idea. Ultimately, it brought forth, in early 1944, the startled question, "Well, why the hell shouldn't some of them go out there and see!"

That is how five of us come to receive orders to go out and live with combatant air groups in the combat zones. One of the five—the writer—spent only six months in all aboard ship, in intensive study of a single air group. The other four were out for more than a year in the combat zone. We carried no ready-made solution out with us. In fact, we tried a number of techniques which proved completely abortive. Ultimately we came to use what we have called the "nominating technique," first applying it in long individual interviews and ultimately using it as a group-response technique. In that way, it was possible, while the war was still going on, to obtain responses from more than 2,500 combatant pilots, all given in the war zone and while the air group was engaged in active combat. This mass of data, as I shall try to show you, gave us not only combat data for the further validation of our tests, but it provided as well a significant key to the morale of various air groups.

Let me describe the technique itself. Basically it runs this way: Our observer lives with an air group long enough to gain the acceptance of the group and to establish rapport with them. If he is a good listener, shows a moderate capacity for distilled spirits, has a restrained interest in certain games of chance, and, above all, likes flying and those who fly, the process need not take too long.

At this point he asks to have the air group assembled, at a time convenient to the members, and he explains his mission. He shows that the facts he gains will have practical significance in developing other air groups, and he guarantees anonymity for each response. Beginning with individual interviews, he then asks each pilot two questions—and it will be noted that these questions are realistic (not speculative), that they are functional (not evaluative), and that they ask for determinants (and not mere lists of names).

The questions are:

1) Assume that you are being shifted to a new air group tomorrow, and that you may select your own combat teammates. On what two men—living

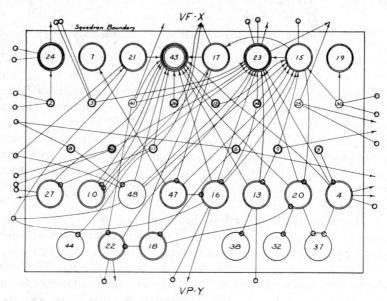

VF-X

FIG. 1

Legend — A Lt. (jg) nominates an Ens. for "low" and a Lt. Cdr. for "high."

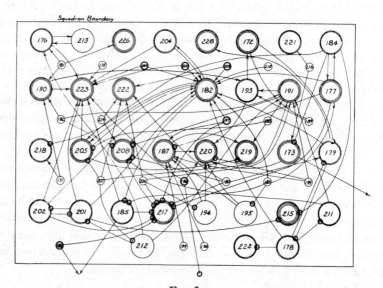

FIG. 2

Legend — A Lt. (jg) nominates an Ens. for "low" and a Lt. Cdr. for "high."

or dead—would you most like to fly wing in combat? Why would you select those two men?

2) What two men would you least like to have flying wing on you in combat? Why?

It should be noted again that we are talking about transfers such as did actually occur; that we are asking the respondents to *name* pilots at the two extremes, not to rate them; and that we also asked them to give *specific reasons* for their choice. We believe these three characteristics to be most important in determining the outcomes we obtained.

Now, what did we get? Well, we got the names of somewhere around 10,000 men designated at the one extreme or the other. The list of *different* names is actually much shorter than that, for many men were named more than once. With those named only once, it is difficult to say how much credence should be put in the nomination. When, however, four independent pilots pick a certain man as their best or worst choice for a combat-teammate, it is difficult to think in terms of chance determinants. In this way, we could and did build up our own file of those chosen for top and those chosen for bottom; and we could establish our level of assurance where we wanted by using only specified multiple nominations.

Once this file was available, we began to find that we had materials that bear directly on the social structure of air groups. It comes about in this way. One of my colleagues suggested borrowing a technique from sociology and using it to see what would happen to our nominations in a series of groups. So we took the idea of the sociometric diagram, developed originally by the sociologist, Moreno, and plotted our available air groups according to his techniques.

What we did was simply this. When a pilot named a man as H, that is, as one of the men he wanted with him in combat, we drew a line from the nominator to the man nominated, ending it in an arrow. For the man nominated as L, not wanted, we ended the line in a circle. Now let us apply that to Figure 1.

It is seen that the skipper (No. 43) is picked as H more often than anyone else in the squadron, and that he gets no L nominations. The executive officer (No. 23) shows a similar pattern. It is interesting to note that the third highest group of nominations goes to a lieutenant (jg) (No. 15) who was perhaps twenty-fifth in official rank in the squadron. I lived with this group at some length, and I am sure that the diagram correctly represents the facts of their daily relationships.

It will be noted also that no man gets any grouping of L nominations. Only one man gets as many as two circles, and most of the L nominations are given outside the structure of the present squadron. There is no evidence of cliques. The diagram should be that of a squadron with high morale, good combat effectiveness, and high resistance to combat-fatigue. The history of the squadron shows that to be the case.

The diagram means little until we contrast it with the diagram for another squadron (Fig. 2). Here, the skipper (No. 215) has only two nominations, and both of them are L. There is leadership in this squadron, but it is not in the officers officially designated to lead. Looking at the diagram closely, it will be seen also that the men can find enough L nominations within the squadron, so that they do not have to go outside for them. From the way the arrows and circles run, there may be seen evidence of internal breakdown and of cliques. This should not have been a squadron of high morale, and the record assures us that it was not.

Now, two cases do not establish a principle. We are still working over data to check out other squadrons and other groups to see how well the sociometric diagrams correspond to their clinical history. In terms of studies made in industry and elsewhere, it is a reasonable bet that the technique will stand up well enough to have practical usefulness. Meanwhile it is available for flight surgeons who wish to try it out professionally.

I may add that I have been delighted with the way practical men react to these diagrams. One veteran air officer told me: "Why that's just the way our air group is. But I'll be damned if I thought it could ever be put down in black and white." An experienced flight surgeon remarked that it put down in rather precise form the basis upon which he, by intuition, had had to base his daily intercourse with his air group. I have shown these diagrams to many line officers, and my most common experience has been to find that Captain X takes it away from me so that he can explain it to Captain Y. Finally, I may state that I reported on the technique last month to a group of business executives gathered for a week-end meeting at Harvard, and that my mail from industrial concerns has been singularly heavy since then.

The technique gains credibility if you review the reasons given by the Navy pilot for their nominations. We started out with a file of about 10,000 statements as to why X was nominated for H while Y was nominated for L. Consistency ran so high that we found we could reduce all of these statements to about twenty-five basic categories. In other words, the combatant pilots showed very high agreement as to what they wanted and did not want in their combat mates. Let me take just a minute to review the highlights of this situation for you.

They wanted the team player who could be counted on, not the lone wolf who was out to make a name for himself.

They wanted the man who helped those in trouble, even at his own risk, not the man overly interested in his own safety.

They wanted the man who genuinely liked to fly, not the man who flew by default.

They wanted the man who was aggressive and forceful in combat, and they had only scorn for the man who could find "good reasons" to avoid combat.

They wanted the good shipmate who fitted well into the group in the ready room and not the temperamental irritable chap who added unnecessarily to the strain of getting ready to fly.

They chose the steady, smooth formation flier and wanted no part of the unpredictable erratic gent who had to be watched in the air.

Interestingly enough, they wanted the man who was adequate in perception and judgment; and they voted strongly against the man who failed to size up total situations, couldn't remember instructions, or committed Dilberts, even if his courage was unquestioned.

Aviation skills were mentioned, but here adequacy rather than virtuousity tended to be stressed.

That is a partial list of the qualities, good and bad, established by reference to actual pilots rather than to abstract traits. I mention the list simply because it seems to me to add to the solidity I believe the nominating technique contains. It is not a panacea. It is still in the research stage. It requires skill and time to use. Properly used, however, I believe it may ultimately afford the flight surgeon a practical and objective tool for getting at the morale of operating air groups and for discussing this morale with the appropriate line officers.

C. Perceptual Sociometry

INTRODUCTION*

By Renato Tagiuri

Much of our life is spent in what appears to be well-co-ordinated inter-action with people. This is no accident, of course, for among the many possible ways in which we may act, only a few are appropriate to a given interpersonal situation. This relative smoothness of operation reflects the fact that a person knows fairly well what the other person does, feels, wants, and is about to do. Perception and evaluation of other persons is an extremely crucial aspect of our existence; but while this is one of the many things we seem to do quite well, it is also true that we know little about the "principles" in terms of which we operate. This is one of the skills we develop very early in life and, as adults, we engage in this process most of the time without paying much attention to how we do it.

The question arises as to whether these processes of perception and cognition should be investigated as a phenomenon *sui generis,* or whether it is better to arrive at an understanding of person-perception on the basis of studies of perception and cognition of simpler, inanimate events. There is no doubt that as a source of physical energy, a person (or animal) is not different from a thing. When dealing with persons, however, we "perceive" not only characteristics analogous to properties of objects, but we also perceive intentions, purposes, motives. We perceive, in short, characteristics of a *psychological* event that has mental representations and strivings of its own. We believe it unlikely, therefore, that we could arrive at an understanding of how we perceive or become aware of this kind of phenomena, by building up from knowledge of perception of events that do not share these specific properties.

It must be clear that we do not perceive an event such as "honesty" in the same direct way in which we perceive, say, a color. Rather, we arrive at such perceptions by evaluating a host of cues, some pertaining to the object person, some inherent in the situation. What is involved, then, is largely a process of inference in which, it must be remembered, the experience of the perceiver plays a major role.

The process of person-perception has many facets. In order to behave appropriately, we may have to assess a person's traits, his intentions, feelings, attitudes, capacities, or his role-related behavior. We may have to "know

---

* This paper was prepared in conjunction with research on interpersonal perception carried out at Harvard University and sponsored by the Office of Naval Research (contracts No. N5–ori–07646 and 07670).

about" what a policeman is likely to do in the role of policeman, or we may have to evaluate a temporary state, like anger, or the intention to help. In forming an impression, there is always a purpose—though at times weak—and the impression may vary with the purpose.

We can distinguish three major elements. There is the *situation* in which the person to be judged is embedded. We do not need to "look" at the person who has lost a loved one to make a good guess about how he feels. Then there is the *person*, apart from the situation. If we did look at him or talk to him, we would probably be able to conclude that he is sad even without knowing about the circumstances mentioned above. Usually, however, the cues from both of these sources point in the same direction, thus increasing the likelihood that our judgment is correct. But there is a third major source of variation in this system; the *perceiver* himself. He is selectively tuned to perceive certain events in preference to certain others, and when the task is ambiguous enough, as complex events can often be, he will select and interpret the evidence accordingly.

Against the background of these general comments on person-perception (11, 60), we can now place the present section, which is concerned with the perception of feelings of like and dislike among members of small groups.

It is important to consider first why, of all the conceivable facets of a person's behavior that are evaluated by others, one should focus on this particular one for study. Essentially, like-dislike between members is one of the aspects of interpersonal behavior that are highly relevant to a very broad range of social situations. Evidence for this claim is abundant and can be found in a great variety of contexts. Developmental and dynamic psychology have placed the issue of being and feeling accepted at the center of their theories of personality development. In sociology, Homans, after analytically whittling down his co-ordinates to three, selected *activity, interaction,* and sentiments of *like* and *dislike* for a systematic description of human interaction. Factor analytic studies of mutual ratings by members of small groups (13, 12, 28, 6, 66) concur on the presence of three basic factors in group behavior—influence and initiative, task-competence, and like-dislike. While the first two factors may not always apply to all groups, the last one must always be considered. Finally, we might regard the liking-disliking attitude of others as the social analogue of those features of the *nonsocial* world that reveal its actual or potential beneficial vs. harmful characteristics.*

The factor of like-dislike between members is, indeed, so basic that where efficient operation depends upon specifically nonaffective relationships, such as

---

* Cf. also, dimensions resulting from Osgood's semantic differential studies (47).

in a military group organized along hierarchical lines, special safeguards have to be built into the system to avoid, as much as possible, the interference of such affective elements as "favoritism." No characteristic of others seems so ego-involving as their positive and negative attitudes toward us. Perhaps this fact is related to the present social climate in which interaction between men especially favors—in the language of Parsons—particularistic as against universalistic bases. Focusing specifically upon this aspect of relationships between people, sociometry has thus dealt with a most important set of events, and its widespread appeal and usefulness are largely based upon this fact. Newstetter and Feldstein (44) go so far in this general direction as to suggest that what is called *social adjustment* may be understood as the level of mutually satisfactory interaction between individual and group, and that this in turn is based primarily upon the group acceptance of the individual, on the one hand, and the individual's acceptance of the group, on the other.

Standard sociometric procedures simultaneously provide two types of data about any member of a group: (a) information about his affective response to the others and (b) information about others' affective response to him. But the investigator's knowledge of the feelings between the members of a group—the data of traditional sociometry—constitutes an incomplete picture of the interpersonal relationship. A more useful description of a relationship between two persons should include their perceptions of each other's feelings. For behavior does not consist of the response to the properties of the stimulus field objectively or consensually specified, but rather, of the reaction to what is perceived by or known to the subject. Therefore, while standard sociometric data constitute very useful information, understanding of behavior in interpersonal settings can be advanced further if one has access also to information regarding the *subject's view* of it.

The importance for psychological studies of having, in addition to "objective" information, the subject's own representation of it can be illustrated rather dramatically by the following example. The *objective* social situation of A, B, and C is very favorable; in each case there are eight or more individuals "who would like to work with" them. The *subjective* evaluations, however, are quite different. A and B both expect to be sought out, but they differ crucially, for A is quite correct in guessing that certain particular persons will choose him, while B, though confident, guesses the wrong people. C seems to assess the situation as very unfavorable and is not willing to guess that anyone wants him as a roommate. In terms of the objective situation C is like A and B, while his subjective picture is more like that of D, who is not chosen by anyone and knows it. D and E have similar objective situations in that they are both completely unchosen, but while D correctly recognizes it, E does not perceive himself as an isolate and makes four guesses, which are, of necessity, wrong. It is easy to see how the action of, and reaction to, these five persons would differ in the group situation, and it must be very clear that it is the combination of objective and subjective pictures that would help in predicting the different courses of their behavior.

One of the advances brought about by the addition of the perceptual component in sociometric work is the gain in the refinement with which the members of a group and the dyadic relationships among them can be described. If, as is most frequently the case, the dimension of like-dislike is simply trichotomized (i.e., like, dislike, omission), then the variables for describing individuals, deducible from the data, are essentially, expansiveness and popularity. With the perceptual component this array is considerably increased to include, among others, measures of "warmth," "transparency," "apparent popularity," as well as many measures of accuracy. By means of the above methods, 45 different types can be usefully differentiated instead of only six (10, 53, 59). By considering the perceptual dimension, Goodnow and Tagiuri (21) were able to refine the analysis of cleavage between subgroups. Newstetter and Feldstein (44) advanced the concepts of spurious and concealed acceptability, and thus distinguished cases that are accepted less than it appears to observers, from those that are accepted more than it may seem.

Let us now consider the essential components of the phenomena in question. First there is the actual feeling network itself. This represents "reality" and is one of the possible definitions of the stimulus. There is, of course, a difference between what the members feel and what they say they feel, but since we have no satisfactory way of distinguishing between these two, we shall not attempt to keep them separate. Then there is the perception of the actual network of feelings. This perceptual aspect can, in turn, be analyzed into various components. There is, for one, the perception of one's own position in the network. Second, the perception *by members* of relationships existing between other members of the group. Finally, there is the perception of the relationships *by observers outside* the group. Each of these perceptions can be looked at in two somewhat interdependent ways. We may ask about *which members* like John or *how many* people like John. The first is a specific question about the particular preferences or dislikes of individuals. The second question requires a judgment of a volumetric or level type. The latter evaluation may be correct even though the specific judgments may be all wrong.

Some of the components listed above were studied, sporadically, during the past three decades. In 1930, Newstetter and Feldstein reported observations on whether camp counselors could place each camper on a scale of acceptability to their peers. They found that the counselors' ratings correlated with acceptance, on the average, better than .75. With T. M. Newcomb, these writers again reported on this problem in 1938. Moreno published some observations on fifth graders in 1931: "The estimates of the teachers as to who were their most desired and least desired pupils from the viewpoint of the children were surprisingly inaccurate" (40, p. 428). In 1934, again Moreno reports on this question. After asking boys and girls in all classes from kindergarten through eighth grade to indicate which children they wished to have in their classroom and sit next to,

> . . . each teacher was asked to write the name of the boy and the girl in her classroom whom she would judge will receive most of the choices from their classmates and the two will receive next most; also the name of the boy and the girl whom she would judge will receive the least choices and the two who will receive next least. In 48% of the instances the teachers' judgments coincided with the findings through the sociometric test in respect to the two most chosen boys and girls; in 38% of the instances in respect to the two least chosen boys and girls in her classroom (41, p. 25).

Here the perceiver is "outside" the group, and here the question is of the volumetric or level type, but limited to the identification of who received most and next most, fewest and next fewest choices.

Strangely enough, these independent initial reports stirred no one to go into this problem further. We find nothing in the literature until 1942, when again Moreno in his paper, "Sociometry in Action," referred to a "self-rating" type of sociometric test in which he would have an individual (a) list all the persons involved in a certain situation, (b) choose and reject them according to preference, and (c) guess how each person felt towards him. However, Moreno's hints were not followed and he himself did not write again on this problem until 1954.

In 1943, Bonney published his systematic study of teachers' perceptions of interpersonal feeling between their pupils. A brief excursion into this area was made in 1949 by Maucorps, who was the first to study recognition of *specific* choices by group members—yet he inquired only about whether a member felt reciprocated *by those he himself chose*. This is the last of the isolated efforts. From 1951 on, a stream of studies on various aspects of the problem began to appear.*

Notice that investigations began with teachers' or counselors' accuracy, then turned to the awareness of the group members themselves. The former

---

* A complete list of references (up to 1956) to these works is given at the end of this introduction.

deals with understanding others in order to help them, the latter with understanding of one's own situation with emphasis upon the relationship of perception to feelings and actions.

Unfortunately, many of the writings on this problem have focused almost exclusively on accuracy of various kinds and its correlates. This is an excessively narrow approach and, as Cronbach has shown (14), one fraught with artifacts and relationships that make interpretation of results extremely difficult. The chaotic results obtained from these studies are due to a small number of major difficulties. First, we really do not have a satisfactory criterion against which to match the judgments. The criteria used—objective behavior, ratings by the object person, ratings by experts, consensual ratings by peers or experts—have very different psychological implications. Second, the disparity of tasks and abilities subsumed under the various operations called measures of "accuracy" have been glossed over. Most accuracy scores contain seven different, and not necessarily correlated, components. Finally, the majority of studies are inconclusive because of the lack of representativeness of the design employed. As a result, investigations yield data that are difficult to interpret and impossible to compare. It is the process rather than its achievement that one must investigate if a broad understanding of the phenomenon is to be reached (60).

On the assumption that behavior is a function of what is thought to be there, rather than of what indeed is there, it becomes important to know just how behavior and perception relate. While a number of simple hypotheses connecting behavior and perception have been popular in the literature, the relationship is probably quite complex and dependent upon a number of parameters. It is often assumed that there is a connection between the accuracy of one's evaluations and characteristics such as personal adjustment and other, more specific traits (36). It is also proposed that such accuracy in some way mediates interactions with others so as to make them more "effective" leaders and clinicians. A recent article by Steiner (52) dispels any such simple notions by indicating a number of complicating and limiting factors. The relationships between perception, personality, overt behavior, and effectiveness are much more complicated than was originally assumed (19). Accuracy, in fact, is a rather awkward concept that seems to have caused more embarrassment than enlightenment. There is no question, however, that understanding of behavior cannot be reached without considering the meaning that a situation has for the person. The methods described in this section have permitted a systematic and quantitative approach to this old problem and perhaps uncovered certain erroneous ways of formulating it.

Some regularities in the relationships under scrutiny have emerged by now. For one thing, it is apparent that—individual differences apart—people in general do better in identifying others' feelings and status than would be expected on the basis of appropriate chance models. This is true of all the accuracy measures referred to above when *positive* feelings are being judged. Negative feelings are more difficult to identify. Attempts at studying correlates of accuracy, of whatever type, where concerned with *judge*-variables, have, with very few exceptions, produced negligible coefficients and have yielded little insight into processes. In fact, the various accuracy measures themselves do not correlate. When, on the other hand, *stimulus* variables were related to the accuracy with which the feelings or status of the stimulus person were perceived, or when perceptions by particular individuals of particular object-persons were examined, striking discoveries were made (1, 2, 58, 26).

The lack of intercorrelations among accuracy measures is often attributed to the different skills and processes involved. This is, probably, one important consideration. What also contributes to this lack of relationships is the extreme dependence of results upon judgmental sets and upon the distributions of the variables that are to be judged. The manifestations of this crucial non-ability component have not yet been clearly analyzed in their implications for perception of feelings and status.

Perhaps the most important and general relationship brought to light is the strong interplay between feelings perceived and feelings held. We tend to feel toward people the way we perceive them to feel toward us, while at the same time we tend to perceive others' feelings for us in accordance with our feelings for them. These two aspects of the process are, of course, fused together. And in so far as both accuracy and mutuality are above chance, these associations reflect good integration between people's feelings as well as between perception and feelings. This strong interplay between perception and choice, plus the regularities in mutuality of feelings, operate selectively to limit the varieties of combinations of feelings and perceptions of feelings that define the dyads of a group.*—A dyad can be thought of as "tending" toward the actualization of these couplings. The intra-individual coupling is much stronger than the inter-individual one, and sometimes leads to certain inter-individual anomalies and imbalances.

Enough work has appeared by now to give some perspective of what is needed before a fairly thorough understanding of the topic in question is reached. More attention must be given to perception of negative feelings; the

---

* Tagiuri and Bruner, in preparation. Cf. also T. M. Newcomb's 1956 Presidential Address: "The Prediction of Interpersonal Attraction," American Psychological Association, Chicago.

majority of studies consider only positive ones. The effect upon judgment of certain non-ability variables, such as judgmental sets, must be analyzed for the various conditions of judgment encountered. The populations on which these studies are conducted need to be diversified; most studies deal with children, teachers, and therapeutic groups. More cross-cultural materials need to be obtained and compared. Terminology needs to be made uniform. There is the broad question, mentioned above, of the approach to the problem: more emphasis must be given to the process, less to perceptual or cognitive achievement. Observations made on the perception of interpersonal feelings must be integrated with the vast and rapidly expanding literature on perception of persons. Finally, there is need for vigorous qualitative studies in which the process of judgment or perception is carefully analyzed as it takes place.

BIBLIOGRAPHY

(Note. This bibliography lists all the works up to mid-1956 bearing directly on the problem of perceiving positive and negative feelings among members of groups. These items are marked with an asterisk.)

1. *Ausubel, D. P. "Reciprocity and Assumed Reciprocity of Acceptance among Adolescents, a Sociometric Study, *Sociometry,* XVI (1953), 339–48.
2. *Ausubel, D. P. "Sociempathy as a Function of Sociometric Status in an Adolescent Group," *Human Relations,* VIII (1955), 75–84.
3. *Ausubel, D. P., and Schiff, H. M. "Some Intrapersonal and Interpersonal Determinants of Individual Differences in Sociempathic Ability among Adolescents," *Journal Social Psychology,* XLI (1955), 39–56.
4. *Ausubel, D. P., Schiff, H. M., and Gasser, E. B. "A Preliminary Study of Developmental Trends in Sociempathy: Accuracy of Perception of Own and Others' Sociometric Status," *Child Development,* XXIII (1952), 111–28.
5. Bales, R. F. *Interaction Process Analysis, A Method for the Study of Small Groups,* Cambridge, Mass.: Addison-Wesley Press, 1950.
6. Bales, R. F. Personal communication (1956).
7. *Bonney, M. E. "The Constancy of Sociometric Scores and Their Relationships to Teacher Judgments of Social Success and to Personality Self-Ratings," *Sociometry,* VI (1943), 409–24.
8. *Bonney, M. E. "Sociometric Study of Agreement between Teachers' Judgments and Student Choices," *Sociometry,* X (1947), 133–46.
9. *Borgatta, E. F. "Analysis of Social Interaction and Sociometric Perception," *Sociometry,* XVII (1954), 7–32.
10. *Bruner, J. S. "On Social Perception." Paper read at the Seminar of the Office of Naval Research, January, 1954.
11. Bruner, J. S., and Tagiuri, R. "The Perception of People," in G. Lindzey (ed.), *Handbook of Social Psychology,* Vol. II Cambridge, Mass.: Addison-Wesley, 1954. Pp. 634–54.
12. Clark, R. A. "Analyzing the Group Structure of Combat Rifle Squads," *American Psychology,* VIII (1953), 333.
13. Couch, A., and Carter, L. F. "A Factorial Study of the Rated Behavior of Group Members." Paper read at meeting of Eastern Psychological Association, March, 1952.

14. Cronbach, L. J. "Processes Affecting 'Understanding of Others' and 'Assumed Similarity,'" *Psychological Bulletin*, LII (1955), 177–93.
15. *Crow, Wayman J. "A Methodological Study of Social Perceptiveness." Unpublished Ph.D. dissertation, University of Colorado, 1954.
16. Eng, E. W. "An Approach to the Prediction of Sociometric Choice," *Sociometry*, XVII (1954), 329–39.
17. *Falorni, M. Luisa, Pera, S., and Vecchioni, V. "Contributo allo studio dell' analisi relazionale a mezzo di tecnica di 'supposizione' intesa come estensione del metodo sociometrico," *Rassegna di Medicina Industriale*, XXIV (1955), 92–100.
18. *Festinger, L., and Hutte, H. "An Experimental Investigation of the Effects of Unstable Interpersonal Relations in a Group," *Journal of Abnormal and Social Psychology*, XLIX (1954), 513–22.
19. *Gage, N. L., Leavitt, G. S., and Stone, G. C. "Teachers' Understanding of Their Pupils and Pupils' Ratings of Their Teachers," *Psychological Monographs*, Vol. LXIX, No. 21 (1955).
20. *Gilliam, Sylvia, and Levenson, B. "Interpersonal Attitudes among School-Children." Center for Field Studies, Graduate School of Education, Harvard University. Mimeographed preliminary report of the Russell Sage Project, 1955.
21. *Goodnow, R. E., and Tagiuri, R. "Religious Ethnocentrism and Its Recognition among Adolescent Boys," *Journal of Abnormal and Social Psychology*, XLVII (1952), 316–20.
22. Gottheil, E. "Changes in Social Perceptions Contingent upon Competing or Cooperating," *Sociometry*, XVIII (1955), 132–37.
23. *Gronlund, N. E. *The Accuracy of Teachers' Judgments Concerning the Sociometric Status of Sixth-grade Pupils*. ("Sociometry Monograph," No. 25.) New York: Beacon House, 1951.
24. *Gronlund, N. E. "Sociometric Status and Sociometric Perception," *Sociometry*, XVIII (1955), 122–27.
25. *Gronlund, N. E. "The Relative Ability of Home-room Teachers and Special-subject Teachers to Judge the Social Acceptability of Pre-adolescent Pupils," *Journal Educational Research*, XLVIII (1955), 381–91.
26. *Gronlund, N. E. "Generality of Teachers' Sociometric Perceptions: Relative Judgment Accuracy on Several Sociometric Criteria," *Journal of Educational Psychology*, XLVII (1956), 25–31.
27. *Gronlund, N. E. "The General Ability to Judge Sociometric Status: Elementary Student Teachers' Sociometric Perceptions of Classmates and Pupils," *Journal of Educational Psychology*, in press.
28. Hemphill, J., and Coons, A. *Leader Behavior Description*. Columbia: Personnel Research Board, Ohio State University (undated).
29. Horowitz, M. W., Lyons, J., and Perlmutter, H. V. "Induction of Forces in Discussion Groups," *Human Relations*, IV (1951), 57–76. (Collected relevant data but did not report results.)
30. *Husquinet, A. *L'adaptation scolaire et familiale des jeunes garçons de 12 à 14 ans*. Paris: Les Belles Lettres, 1954.
31. *Hutte, H. *De invloed van moeilijk te verdragen situaties op groepsverhoudingen*. Leiden: Stenfert Kroese, 1953.
32. *Katz, L., Tagiuri, R., and Wilson, T. R. "A Note on Estimating the Statistical Significance of Mutuality," *Journal of General Psychology*, LVIII (1958), 97–103.
33. Lindzey, G., and Borgatta, F. E. "Sociometric Measurement," in G. Lindzey (ed.), *Handbook of Social Psychology*, Vol. I. Cambridge, Mass.: Addison-Wesley, 1954. Pp. 405–48.
34. Lippitt, R., Polansky, Redl, F., and Rosen, S. "The Dynamics of Power" in D. Cartwright and A. Zander (eds.), *Group Dynamics*. Evanston, Ill.: Roe, Peterson and Co., 1953. Pp. 462–82. (Collected relevant data but did not report results.)
35. *Luce, R. D., Macy, J., and Tagiuri, R. "A Statistical Model for Relational Analysis," *Psychometrika*, XX (1955), 319–27.
36. *Lundberg, G. A., and Dickson, Leonore. "Interethnic Relations in a High School Population," *American Journal of Sociology*, LVIII (1952), 1–10.

37. *Maher, H. "Personality Adjustment and Social Adjustment." Unpublished honors thesis, Harvard University, 1952.
38. *Maucorps, P. H. "A Sociometric Inquiry in the French Army," *Sociometry*, XII (1949), 46–80.
39. *Moreno, J. L. *Plan and Technique of Developing a Prison into a Socialized Community*. New York, 1931. Second edition entitled *Application of the Group Method to Classification*. New York: National Committee on Prisons and Prison Labor, 1932.
40. *Moreno, J. L., with Jennings, H. L., and Stockton, R. "Sociometry in the Classroom," *Sociometry*, VI (1943), 425–28.
41. * Moreno, J. L. *Who Shall Survive?* Washington, D.C.: Nervous and Mental Disorder Publishing Co., 1934.
42. *Moreno, J. L. "Sociometry in Action," *Sociometry*, III (1942), 298–315.
43. *Moreno, J. L. "Current Trends in Sociometry," *Sociometry*, XV (1952), 146–63.
44. *Newstetter, W. I., and Feldstein, M. J. *Wawokiye Camp, a Research Project in Group Work*. Cleveland: School of Applied Social Sciences, Western Reserve University, 1930.
45. * Newstetter, W. I., Feldstein, M J., and Newcomb, T. M. *Group Adjustment: A Study in Experimental Sociology*. Cleveland: School of Applied Social Sciences, Western Reserve University, 1938. Pp. 154.
46. *Och, M. "Estimation of Group Opinion and Its Correlates in Sociometric Status." Unpublished honors thesis, Harvard University, 1953.
47. Osgood, C. E. "The Nature and Measurement of Meaning," *Psychological Bulletin*, XLIX (1952), 197–237.
48. Parsons, T., and Shils, E. A. "Values, Motives, and Systems of Action," in T. Parsons and E. A. Shils (eds.), *Toward a General Theory of Action*, Cambridge, Mass.: Harvard University Press, 1952.
49. *Schiff, H. M. "Personality Correlates of Judgmental Response Sets in the Perception of Sociometric Status." Unpublished doctoral dissertation, University of Illinois, 1953.
50. *Schiff, H. M. "Judgmental Response Sets in the Perception of Sociometric Status," *Sociometry*, XVII (1954), 207–27.
51. *Singer, E. "An Investigation of Some Aspects of Empathic Behavior," *American Psychologist*, VI (1951), 309–10 (abstract).
52. *Steiner, I. "Interpersonal Behavior as Influenced by Accuracy of Social Perception," *Psychological Review*, LXII (1955), 268–74.
53. *Tagiuri, R. "Relational analysis: An Extension of Sociometric Method with Emphasis upon Social Perception," *Sociometry*, XV (1952), 91–104.
54. *Tagiuri, R. "Analisi relazionale: un'estensione del metodo sociometrico con particolare riferimento alla percezione sociale," *Bollettino di Psicologia Applicata*, 1954, No. 6, pp. 3–14.
55. *Tagiuri, R., Blake, R. R., and Bruner, J. S. "Some Determinants of the Perception of Positive and Negative Feelings in Others," *Journal of Abnormal and Social Psychology*, XLVIII (1953), 585–92.
56. *Tagiuri, R., Bruner, J. S., and Kogan, N. "Estimating the Chance Expectancies of Diadic Relationships within a Group," *Psychological Bulletin*, LII (1955), 122–31.
57. *Tagiuri, R., Bruner, J. S., and Kogan, N. "Calcolo delle probabili relazioni diadiche in un gruppo," *Bollettino di Psicologia Applicato*, 1955, No. 7–8, pp. 3–14.
58. *Tagiuri, R., Kogan, N., and Bruner, J. S. "The Transparency of Interpersonal Choice," *Sociometry*, XVIII (1956), 624–35.
59. *Tagiuri, R. "Studies in Perception of Interpersonal Feelings," in *Research Reviews*. Washington, D.C.: Office of Naval Research, April 1956. Pp. 15–21.
60. Tagiuri, R., *et al*. "Person Perception," *SSRC Items*, X (1956), 2–5.
61. *Taylor, F. K. "The Three-dimensional Basis of Emotional Interactions in Small Groups. I," *Human Relations*, VII (1954), 441–71.
62. *Taylor, F. K. "The Three-dimensional Basis of Emotional Interactions in Small Groups. II," *Human Relations*, VIII (1955), 3–28.
63. *Taylor, F. K. "Awareness of One's Social Appeal," *Human Relations*, IX (1956), 47–56.

64. *Weinberg, H. "A Relational Analysis of a Co-ed High School Class." Unpublished term paper, Harvard University, 1952.
65. *Wessman, A. E. "Group and Self Perceptions: A Case Study." Unpublished term paper, Harvard University, 1951.
66. Wherry, R. J. *Factor Analysis of Officer Qualification, Form OCL-2B.* Columbus: Ohio State Univer. Research Foundation, 1950.
67. Yablonsky, L. "A Sociometric Investigation into the Development of an Experimental Model for Small Group Analysis," *Sociometry,* XV (1952), 175–205.

THE ACCURACY OF TEACHERS' JUDGMENTS CONCERNING THE SOCIOMETRIC STATUS OF SIXTH-GRADE PUPILS

By Norman E. Gronlund

Synopsis

This study is an attempt to determine the accuracy of teachers' judgments concerning the degree to which sixth-grade pupils are accepted by their classmates, and the relationship of certain variables to the accuracy of these judgments. The acceptance of sixth-grade pupils by their classmates was determined by a sociometric test and referred to as the pupils' sociometric status.

The method of investigating the problem consisted of the following procedures: A sociometric test administered to the pupils in forty sixth-grade classes requested each pupil to choose the five classmates with whom he would most prefer to work, the five classmates near whom he would most prefer to sit. In addition, each pupil was requested to respond to eight questions concerning the freedom he had in carrying out routine class activities.

Each teacher, in the same forty classes, made judgments concerning the sociometric status of her pupils on the criteria of work companion, play companion, and seating companion. Each teacher also indicated which three boys and three girls she most preferred and which three boys and three girls she least preferred as pupils in her class. Information concerning the teacher's training and experience were obtained for each teacher.

The above data were analyzed with standard statistical procedures and found to be consistent with the following conclusions:

1. There is a difference between teachers in the accuracy of their judgments of the sociometric status of sixth-grade pupils in the classroom. Correlation coefficients representing the average accuracy of each teacher's judgments ranged from .268 to .838, with a mean of .595.
2. There is *no* difference in the accuracy of teachers' judgments of the sociometric status of boys and girls.
3. There is a difference in the accuracy of teachers' judgments of the sociometric status of pupils among the criteria of work companion, play companion, and seating companion.
4. There is *no* relationship between the average accuracy of the teachers' judgments of the sociometric status of pupils and each of the following variables: age of teacher, years of teaching experience, length of time in present position, semester hours of college training, recency of college training, semester hours in education courses, semester hours in psychology courses, size of class, marital status of teacher, and length of time the teacher had been in contact with the class.
5. There is a relationship between taking a course in Child Development and more accurate judgments of the sociometric status of pupils.

6. There is a tendency for teachers to over-judge the sociometric status of pupils they most prefer, and to under-judge the sociometric status of pupils they least prefer.

7. There is a negative relationship between the degree to which a teacher's judgments are biased in the direction of her preferences and the accuracy of her judgments of sociometric status.

8. There is *no* relationship between the freedom pupils have in class and the accuracy of teachers' judgments of sociometric status.

CHAPTER I

INTRODUCTION

Statement of the Problem

One of the objectives of modern education is the social adjustment of pupils. The extent to which pupils are chosen by their classmates as work companions, play companions, and seating companions is one evidence of social adjustment. This acceptance by peers is highly valued and sought after by the pupil and represents an important domain of pre-adolescent behavior. It should be of major concern to the teacher who is largely responsible for the social development of the members of her class. In an attempt to carry out this responsibility teachers are constantly making judgments concerning the relative acceptability of various members of the class. The extent to which these judgments are accurate determines, in part, the effectiveness of her efforts in this area.

This study is an attempt to determine the accuracy of teachers' judgments concerning the degree to which sixth-grade pupils are accepted by their classmates, and the relationship of certain variables to the accuracy of these judgments.

Definition of Terms

In order to clarify the terms used in this study, they are defined as follows:

Sociometric test—an instrument which "requires an individual to choose his associates for any group of which he is or might become a member."[1]

Criterion—basis on which associates are chosen on a sociometric test.

---

[1] Jacob L. Moreno, *Who Shall Survive?* First Ed., Washington, D. C.: Nervous and Mental Disease Publishing Co., 1934. P. 11. Second, Revised Ed., Beacon House Inc., Beacon, N. Y., 1951.

In this study the criteria are work companion, play companion, and seating companion.

Sociometric status—degree to which a pupil is accepted by his classmates, in terms of the number of choices he receives from them on a sociometric test.

Teacher preference—status of pupil in terms of whether the teacher most prefers or least prefers having him in her class.

Teacher judgment—relative position of pupils to his classmates in terms of the teachers' estimate of his sociometric status.

Nature of the Study

The general nature of the study is revealed in the statement of the problem. While this reflects the central theme throughout the study there are a number of specific questions for which answers are sought. These questions are listed below to help clarify the exact nature of this study.

1. To what extent are teachers accurate in judging the sociometric status of all pupils in the classroom?
2. Is there any difference between teachers in the accuracy of their judgments?
3. Is there any difference in the accuracy of teachers' judgments of boys and girls?
4. Is there any difference in the accuracy of teachers' judgments on the criteria of seating, play, and work?
5. What is the relationship between the average accuracy of the teachers' judgments and each of the following variables?
   a. Age of teacher.
   b. Years of teaching experience.
   c. Length of time in present position.
   d. Semester hours of college training.
   e. Recency of training.
   f. Semester hours in education courses.
   g. Semester hours in psychology courses.
   h. Size of class.
   i. Marital status of teacher.
   j. Length of contact with class.
   k. Whether or not the teacher had a course in Child Development.
6. Do teachers over-judge those boys and girls they most prefer, and under-judge those boys and girls they least prefer as pupils in class?
7. If the above phenomenon exists, what is the relationship between the degree to which this bias is present in a teacher's judgments and the accuracy of her judgments?

8. What is the relationship between the amount of freedom the pupils feel they have in class and the accuracy of teachers' judgments?

Delimitations of Study

This study is restricted to forty women teachers at the sixth grade level teaching in the Flint, Willow Run, and Ypsilanti public schools. Only women teachers were included in this study for several reasons. First, the teachers at this grade level are predominantly women. Second, to include the few men teachers that were available at this grade level would only tend to complicate the results.

Several considerations also prompted the decision to confine this study to the sixth grade level. First, it was desired to obtain a situation in which the teachers were with the same group for the major part of the day. Second, the pre-adolescent period is one of the most important stages in the pupil's social development. Finally, the reliability of the sociometric test has been shown to increase with age, at the elementary level, thereby providing the most reliable bases against which to compare the teachers' judgments.

The selection of the Flint, Willow Run, and Ypsilanti public schools was prompted by the deep interest of the administrators and teachers in problems of social adjustment. The fine coöperation of these administrators and teachers in carrying out this research in their classrooms is gratefully acknowledged.

Method of Investigation

A sociometric test was administered to forty sixth-grade classes. On this test each pupil was asked to choose five classmates with whom he would prefer to work, five classmates with whom he would prefer to play, and five classmates near whom he would prefer to sit. In addition, each pupil was requested to respond to eight questions concerning the freedom he had in carrying out routine class activities.

In the same forty classes the teacher was asked to make judgments concerning the sociometric status of each pupil on the criteria of seating companion, play companion, and work companion. Further, the teacher was asked to indicate which three boys and three girls she most preferred as pupils in her class, and which three boys and three girls she least preferred as pupils in her class. Personal data information regarding the teachers was obtained from school records where possible. Where the school records were not available the teacher was requested to provide the desired information on a personal data sheet.

Organization

The next chapter will review the literature related to this problem. Chapter III will describe the method of investigating the problem, including the procedures and instruments used, description of the subjects, and method of collecting data. Chapter IV will present an analysis of the data and the results of that analysis. Chapter V will contain a summary, conclusions, and implications for further research in this area.

CHAPTER II

Related Literature

The literature pertinent to this study falls into three categories: (1) that concerning the use of sociometric tests; (2) that concerning the accuracy of adults' judgments of sociometric status, in childhood and adolescent groups; and (3) that concerning factors which may possibly be related to the accuracy of adults' judgments of sociometric status, in childhood and adolescent groups.

The literature on sociometric testing is voluminous and much of it has no direct bearing on the present problem. Since this is a study of teachers' judgments of pupil sociometric status, only that literature on sociometric testing will be reviewed which is pertinent to this problem.

Sociometric Tests

Moreno,[1] who devised the sociometric technique, defines it as follows:

> An instrument to measure the amount of organization shown by social groups is called a sociometric test. The sociometric test requires an individual to choose his associates for any group of which he is or might become a member.

He cautions that the accurate giving of the test is important if it is to be correctly called sociometric. The two specifications that he sets up to meet this requirement are that the test must "determine the *feelings* of individuals towards each other and, second, to determine these in respect to the *same criterion*."[2]

The sociometric test devised by Moreno was first used in a public school by him in Brooklyn, New York. The boys and girls of all classes

---

[1] Jacob L. Moreno, *Who Shall Survive?* Washington, D. C.: Nervous and Mental Disease Publishing Co., 1934. P. 11.

[2] *Ibid.*, p. 15.

from the kindergarten through the eighth grade were requested to choose among their classmates those whom they would most prefer to have sit near them. The results of this first attempt to use a sociometric technique in a classroom were described by Moreno[3] as follows:

> As a consequence of the test given to these pupils a complex structure of the class organization was uncovered, widely differing from the prevalent one. A number of pupils remained unchosen or isolated; a number chose each other, forming mutual pairs, triangles, or chains; others attracted so many choices that they captured the center of the stage like others.

The most extensive research done with the sociometric test in the classroom, and a logical extension of Moreno's original work, was that by Bronfenbrenner.[4] He conducted a sociometric study of 151 elementary school children from the nursery school through the sixth grade. Although his primary purpose was to set up and evaluate a scoring method for sociometric testing, his contributions were many. In the fall and spring term the children at all grade levels were asked to name the classmates they would like best to work with, play with, and have sit near them. These three criteria were selected on the basis of observation of the classes. They were considered to be the ones common to all grade levels; familiar to all members of the group; equally available for all members to participate; and least influenced by extraneous environmental factors.

In deciding whether to use the number of choices received by each child or the number of different persons by whom he was chosen, as the best unit for fine discrimination, Bronfenbrenner[5] states:

> A comparison of indices based on both types of unit revealed that while negative deviations from the expected value were equally marked in one or the other distribution, extreme deviations *in excess* of chance expectancy were obtained only when the number of *choices* rather than the number of *different persons* choosing was utilized for computing indices.

Using the number of choices as an index of sociometric status he made no distinction between a first, second, third, etc., choice. This was prompted by the difficulty of determining the social significance of different choice levels; the dubiousness of assigning a priori values; and the complication of the scoring procedure wth weighted choices.

---

[3] Ibid., p. 24.

[4] Urie Bronfenbrenner, "A Constant Frame of Reference for Sociometric Research: Part II, Experiment and Inference," SOCIOMETRY, 7 (February, 1944), 40-75.

[5] *Ibid.,* p. 44.

Through the development and application of a formula based on the Pearson Type III Curve Bronfenbrenner[6] found that the number of choices a pupil receives on a sociometric test is a reliable index of sociometric status, within certain restrictions. In this regard Bronfenbrenner[7] states:

> In summary, for sociometric situations involving as many as three criteria with five choices allotted per person, the total number of choices received by each child may be used with reasonable confidence as a reliable index of sociometric status provided the number of criteria and choices allotted remains constant for all groups tested.

He contends that this holds true if the groups include no less than ten and no more than fifty persons.

Comparing the fall and spring sociometric results, using a total number of choices each child receives as an index of sociometric status, Bronfenbrenner[8] found that sociometric status remained fairly stable. In regard to his findings in this respect, he concludes:

> In classroom situations, marked shifts in sociometric status are comparatively rare. On the whole, children tend to retain the same general social position and this tendency becomes more pronounced in older age groups.

This finding is in general accord with that of Bonney[9] who found sociometric status as stable as that of intelligence and academic attainment. He administered a sociometric test, intelligence test, and general achievement test to the same class of students for three consecutive years when they were in the second, third, and fourth grades. Correlations between the scores of successive grade levels in these measurements were quite high with sociometric status approximately as stable over the three years as intellectual and academic status.

While general ability of sociometric status has been shown, to obtain a true index of the reliability of the sociometric test is a difficult problem. Newstetter, Feldstein, and Newcomb allotted thirty fourteen-year-old boys in a summer camp five choices each for tentmate at two-day intervals,

---

6 *Ibid.*, p. 68.

7 *Ibid.*, p. 69.

8 *Ibid.*, p. 73.

9 Merl E. Bonney, "The Relative Stability of Social, Intellectual, and Academic Status in Grades II to IV and the Inter-Relationships between these Various Forms of Growth," *Journal of Educational Psychology,* 34 (January, 1943), 88-102.

the results of which correlated $.92\pm.02$.[10] Jennings[11] found similar results in a training school for girls using an unlimited number of choices. A four-day re-test of approximately twenty-eight girls on the criterion of *work with, live with, spend leisure time with,* and *study with* yielded a reliability coefficient of .96. Zeleny[12] allotted five choices for membership in a discussion group at two-day intervals, the results of which correlated between .93 and .95. Although these reliability coefficients are high there can be little doubt that the memory factor played a large part in the repetition of the choosing situation. On the other hand, a low correlation between sociometric tests several months apart would not necessarily mean the instrument is unreliable, but may be merely indicating the real changes that have taken place in the social development of the group. In addition to the findings of Bronfenbrenner and Bonney, Jennings[13] also found that sociometric status was fairly stable over several months. A re-test of 131 girls after an eight-month period correlated .65. Despite the fact that "reliability" in its usual meaning cannot be directly applied to the sociometric test, a fair degree of stability of sociometric status is indicated.

Although the sociometric test is said to be valid by definition, in that it purports to measure choice behavior, it is desirable for the purposes of this study to determine if sociometric status is related to other evidences of social adustment.

Jennings[14] has presented data to show that the behavior descriptions of those who receive few choices on the sociometric test are quite different from those who are highly chosen. The personality descriptions were obtained from an analysis of the "complaints" and "commendations" of house mothers concerning each of 124 girls living in a training school for girls. The under-chosen members of the group were characterized most frequently as exhibiting behavior disagreeable to the house mother such as quarrelsome, complaining, nervous, aggressive, and dominant behavior. In addition they were most frequently described as interfering with the group's activities, and exhibiting attention-seeking behavior. On the other

---

[10] Wilber J. Newstetter, Mark J. Feldstein, and Theodore M. Newcomb, *Group Adjustment: A Study in Experimental Sociology.* Cleveland: School of Applied Sciences, Western Reserve University, 1948. Pp. 35.

[11] Helen H. Jennings, *Leadership and Isolation.* New York: Longmans, Green and Co., 1943. P. 31.

[12] Leslie D. Zeleny, "Sociometry of Morale," *American Sociological Review,* 4 (December, 1939), 804.

[13] Jennings, *op. cit.,* p. 57.   [14] Jennings, *op. cit.,* pp. 144-163.

hand, the over-chosen members were characterized most frequently by behavior regarded as "Commendatory" by the house mother, such as co-operative even disposition, initiative, non-attention-seeking, etc., behaviors.

A similar relationship between behavior descriptions and number of choices received on a sociometric test in a classroom situation was found by Olson.[15] He asked teachers in ten elementary school classes to make comments about each child concerning factors that may affect the number of choices received on a sociometric test. The social and emotional factors were categorized and compared to the number of choices the children received. Those children classified as ill, sulky, conduct problems, bossy, new in class, and shy tended to be below the mean in number of choices received; whereas those classified as good natured, quiet, friendly, well adjusted, and dependable tended to be above the mean in the number of choices received.

Bonney[16] also found significant differences in the personality traits of those highly chosen by their classmates and those chosen by few. He administered a sociometric test to three fourth-grade classes and compared the results with teacher and pupil ratings of members of the class, on twenty personality traits. In describing the personality traits which distinguished the high chosen from those receiving few choices, Bonney[17] concludes:

> . . . the traits which proved most significant in differentiating between the popular and unpopular children may be organized into two syndromes. The first syndrome is composed of strong, aggressive personality traits such as leadership, enthusiasm, daring, and active participation in recitations. The second syndrome is not so definite but is composed of traits which count the most in direct inter-personal contacts, such as a pleasing appearance, a cheerful disposition, and friendly attitudes.

Kuhlon and Lee[18] conducted a similar study on sixth, ninth, and twelfth grade students with similar findings. Those receiving the largest number of choices were judged most frequently as being popular, cheerful

---

[15] Willard C. Olson, *Child Development.* Boston: D. C. Heath and Company, 1949. Pp. 200-201.

[16] Merl E. Bonney, "Personality Traits of Socially Successful and Socially Unsuccessful Chidren," *Journal of Educational Psychology,* 34 (November, 1943),449-472.

[17] *Ibid.,* p. 458.

[18] Raymond G. Kuhlon and Beatrice J. Lee, "Personality Characteristics and Social Acceptability in Adolescence," *Journal of Educational Psychology,* 34 (November, 1943), 321-340.

and happy, enthusiastic, friendly, able to enjoy jokes, and to initiate games and activities.

In a study concerning the relationship of personal problems to sociometric status Kuhlen and Bretsch[19] administered a sociometric test and the Mooney Problem Check List to about 700 ninth-graders. On the problem check list the students were asked to check each item in the category of never, sometimes, or often. They found that those with lowest sociometric status (bottom quartile) checked more personal problems "often" than the top quartile in sociometric status. Those personal problems that were checked "often" by the low sociometric status group revealed greater concern with social skills, unhappiness and lack of status, family problems, and dislike of school.

Northway[20] made an intensive study of the personality traits of this low sociometric status group (lower quartile). In a sociometric study of eighty fifth and sixth grade pupils she selected the twenty least chosen members for special clinical study concerning their personality make-up. She found that this low sociometric status group fell into three distinct personality patterns—the listless, recessive children; the quiet and retiring, socially uninterested children; and the noisy, rebellious, socially ineffective children.

The past several studies have shown that sociometric status is related to other evidences of social adjustment. In this respect the sociometric test may be considered valid for the purposes of this study.

Judgment of Sociometric Status

Ever since Moreno devised the sociometric technique there has been some question concerning the extent to which an outside observer could judge the sociometric status of members of a group. In his original administration of the test to all classes of the first eight grades of a Brooklyn public school Moreno[21] asked the teachers to judge which boy and girl would receive most of the choices from their classmates and which two would receive next most. In addition he asked them to judge which two would receive the least choices and which two would receive the next least. Concerning the over-all accuracy of the teachers' judgments he stated:

---

[19] Raymond G. Kuhlen and Howard S. Bretsch, "Sociometric Status and Personal Problems of Adolescents," SOCIOMETRY, 10 (May, 1947), 122-127.

[20] Mary L. Northway, "A Study of the Personality Patterns of Children Least Acceptable to Their Age Mates," SOCIOMETRY, 7 (February, 1944), 10-25.

[21] Moreno, *op. cit.*, p. 25.

In 48 per cent of the instances the teachers' judgments coincided with the findings through the sociometric test in respect to the two most chosen boys and girls; in 38 per cent of the instances in respect to the least chosen boys and girls in her classroom.

He found that the degree of accuracy varied with the grade level, having its highest point in the kindergarten and first grade and declining as the grade level increased. The average degree of accuracy was thirty per cent at the sixth grade level. This declining accuracy he attributes to increasing complexity of groups, and the development of a social cleavage between adults and children. Concerning the lack of insight teachers have into children's groups Moreno[22] comments:

> The teachers' judgments concerned only the extremes in position. The average positions of individuals are, it is evident, far more difficult to estimate accurately. The intricacies of the children's own associations prevent the teacher from having a true insight. This fact appears as one of the great handicaps in the development of teacher-child relationships.

It is regrettable that more research workers did not follow Moreno's cue and explore this important area. Only a few studies are available concerning the adult's ability to judge the sociometric status of members of childhood and adolescent groups. In the majority of these investigations this judgment of sociometric status was incidental to other purposes, and consequently a limited number of subjects were used.

Bonney[23] in a sociometric study of the fifth grade had three teachers, at the end of the year, make judgments concerning the pupil's sociometric status. The teachers were asked to place the pupils in five categories—highest group, above average, about average, below average, and lowest group. They were told they need not place the same number in each group. Comparing this teacher grouping of pupils with the sociometric results Bonney[24] found that "approximately ninety per cent of the children were placed by the teachers, either in the same quintile, or only one removed from that in which they were placed by pupil choices."

In another, more comprehensive study, by Bonney[25] thirteen teachers

---

[22] Moreno, *op. cit.*, p. 54.

[23] Merl E. Bonney, "The Constancy of Sociometric Scores and Their Relationship to Teacher Judgments of Social Success, and to Personality Self-Ratings," SOCIOMETRY, 6 (November, 1943), 409-424.

[24] *Ibid.*, p. 419.

[25] Merl E. Bonney, "Sociometric Study of Agreement Between Teacher Judgments and Student Choices," SOCIOMETRY, 10 (May, 1947), 133-146.

were asked to make judgments concerning the sociometric status of 291 high school students. The students were asked to select their two best friends. The results of this choosing situation were divided into three groups—high, middle and low. The high group consisted of those students who received three or more choices and contained forty-five students; the middle group one or two choices and contained thirty-five students; and the low group no choices and contained thirty students. Each category had approximately an equal number of boys and girls. Three months after the students made their choices the thirteen teachers were asked to rate the students in the high, middle, or low group on the basis of their estimate of how many choices each student received. An "unable to judge" category was used where the teacher did not know the student well enough to judge. The teachers were told how many students were included in each group on the basis of choices and were told to try to place the same number in each group. However, this could not be done due to the large number of "unable to judge" ratings. Approximately forty-four per cent of the ratings fell in this category. Of the remaining ratings twenty-one per cent were in the high group; twenty-three per cent in the middle group; and eleven per cent in the low group. The average accuracy of teachers' judgments was forty-five per cent for the high and middle group, and twenty-eight per cent for the low group. However, the few ratings in the low group plus the large number of ratings in the "unable to judge" category make the results of dubious value, if not altogether uninterpretable.

A much more limited study was carried out in a summer camp. In this setting Newstetter, Feldstein, and Newcomb[26] asked six counselors to make judgments concerning the sociometric status of thirty fourteen-year-old boys, who had been allotted five choices each for tentmate preference. The counselors rated these thirty boys on a seven-point scale for sociometric status. The correlation between the counselors' judgments and the boys' choices revealed a mean coefficient of .756±.20. The reiability of the ratings was determined by correlating the judgments of raters for a one-week interval. These correlations ranged from .830 to .998, with a mean correlation of .945±.01.

While these results are encouraging and reveal that an adult can have considerable insight into the group life of children and adolescents, as measured by a sociometric test, they cannot be transferred *in toto* to the classroom situation. The informality and freedom of camp life is quite differ-

---

[26] Newstetter, Feldstein, and Newcomb, *op. cit.*, pp. 35-53.

ent from the usual classroom routine. In addition, the restriction of the camp population to boys simplifies the judgment situation over that of the classroom where sexes are mixed.

This may provide a good point to sum up the major shortcomings of all of the above studies in judgment of sociometric status. No mention was made of differences between the judges in any of the above studies. The underlying assumption seemed to be that all adults are equally capable of judging sociometric status in childhood and adolescent groups. Certainly one would expect the judges to vary in the amount of insight they have into group structure. This area may have been avoided due to the limited number of judges used, which is a second shortcoming of the above studies. While Moreno's[27] study shows that the accuracy of teachers' judgments declined gradually from the kindergarten to the seventh grade, might that not be explained in part by differences of the ability of teachers to judge sociometric status, rather than solely on the basis of declining insight into older age groups. The fact that the accuracy of teachers' judgments in this study increased from twenty-five per cent in the seventh grade to forty per cent in the eighth grade would tend to indicate such an assumption. Regardless, the lack of information on the differential ability of the teachers to make such judgments plus the limited number of teachers at each grade level causes the results to be questionable.

In Bonney's[28] fifth grade study only three teachers were used, which would limit the value of any statements that could be made about differential ability to make such judgments. In his[29] more extensive study at the high school level thirteen teachers were used, but they were asked to judge the sociometric status of students, approximately half of whom they did not have an opportunity of observing in groups. Another criticism of this latter study might be that he had the teachers make their judgments three months after the administration of the sociometric test. While large shifts in sociometric status are rare, it is to be expected that some shifts in status will take place over a three-month period.

Factors Affecting Judgment of Sociometric Status

Due to the few studies in this area of judgment it should be important to consider what are some of the factors that may possibly influence the

---

27 Moreno, *op. cit.*, p. 28.
28 Bonney, *op. cit.*, p. 419.
29 Bonney, *op. cit.*, pp. 133-146.

judgment of sociometric status. Travers[30] in a study concerning the judgment of the opinions of groups found that "the individual tends to overestimate the percentage of the group being judged who thinks as he does." It would be valuable to know if such a bias exists in the teachers' judgment of a sociometric status. Stated another way, would the teacher tend to overestimate the sociometric status of pupils she most prefers? The possibility of such a bias existing is revealed in a statement by Stokes.[31] He states:

> One common error on the part of teachers is to confuse social adjustment between children with social adjustment between adults and children. The two are not necessarily antithetical but it is perfectly possible for a child to achieve satisfactory relationships between himself and his teachers, and yet fail to make himself acceptable to his peers. The converse is equally true; and all the shades of variation between these extremes also.

If teachers do tend to confuse social adjustment between children with social adjustment between adults and children then Tryon's[32] findings would imply that the teacher's judgment of a sociometric status would be more accurate with girls than with boys. She made a study of the personality characteristics 350 pupils considered desirable in each other, and concludes, in part:

> For the twelve-year-old girl, quiet, sedate, non-aggressive qualities are associated with friendliness, likeableness, good humor, and attractive appearance. Behavior which conforms to the demands and regulations of the adult world is admired.
>
> At the twelve-year level the idealized boy is skillful and a leader in games; his daring and fearlessness extends beyond his social group to defiance of adult demands and regulations. Any characteristic which might be construed as feminine by one's peers such as extreme tidiness or marked conformity in the classroom is regarded as a weakness.

If such sex differences exist in traits pre-adolescent pupils consider de-

---

30 Robert M. W. Travers, *A Study in Judging the Opinions of Groups.* Archives of Psychology, No. 266. New York: Bureau of Publications, Columbia University, 1941. P. 66.

31 Stuart Stokes, *The Sociol Analysis of the Classroom.* Division on Child Development and Teacher Personnel, American Council on Education, January, 1940 P. 2.

32 Caroline M. Tryon, *Evaluations of Adolescent Personality by Adolescents.* Monographs of the Society for Research in Child Development, IV. Washington: National Research Council, 1939. P. 77.

sirable in one another then it is conceivable that the teacher's judgment of the sociometric status of girls would be more accurate than that of boys.

Bonney,[33] who made a similar study concerning the sex differences of personality traits on the fourth-grade level, found that traits admired by adults consistently favored the girls although the sex differences were not large.

Although there are no studies directly concerning the personal data variables which may possibly affect the teachers' judgments of pupil sociometric status in the classroom a study by Kelly and Perkins[34] may shed some light on this area. They determined the relationship between various personal data variables and the teachers' knowledge of child and adolescent behavior, as measured by an objective test, for both grade school and high school. A brief summary of their conclusions follows:

There were significant relationships between mean scores and the following variables:

1. Number of years of training. For both grade school and high school.
2. Number of courses in education. For both grade school and high school.
3. Number of courses in psychology. For grade school.
4. Recency of training. For grade school.
5. Length of time in present position. For grade school.
6. Subject taught. For high school.
7. Age for high school.
8. Sex for high school.
9. Marital states. For high school.
10. Having children. For high school.

Since the first five personal data variables show a significant relationship to the elementary teachers' knowledge of child and adolescent behavior it would be interesting to determine if this relationship exists in the application of that knowledge to a restricted area, as represented in the present study.

Summary

The sociometric test has been described and its use in classroom situa-

---

[33] Merl E. Bonney, "Sex Differences in Social Success and Personality Traits," *Child Development*, 15 (March, 1944), 63-79.

[34] Ida B. Kelley and Keith J. Perkins, *An Investigation of Teachers' Knowledge of and Attitudes toward Child and Adolescent Behavior in Every Day School Situations*. Purdue University Studies in Higher Education, XLII. Lafayette, Indiana: Purdue University, 1941. P. 101.

593

tions illustrated. Studies have revealed that the total number of choices received by an individual on a sociometric test may be used as a reliable index of sociometric status, where no more than three criteria and five choices are used, and where the groups include no less than ten and no more than fifty persons.

It has been shown that sociometric status is fairly stable. It has also been shown that sociometric status is related to other evidences of social adjustment.

Several studies concerning the judgment of sociometric status have been reviewed and their shortcomings pointed out. Their major shortcomings were insufficient number of judges, and lack of information concerning the differential ability of judges to make such judgments.

Several factors which may possibly affect the accuracy of teachers' judgments were revealed in the literature. These were personal bias, sex differences among pre-adolescents, and personal data variables among teachers.

It may be concluded that the literature pertinent to this problem has furnished many valuable leads, but has not satisfactorily answered any of the questions raised in the first chapter.

CHAPTER III

Method of Investigating the Problem

This study has been defined, in the first chapter, as an attempt to determine the accuracy of teachers' judgments concerning the degree to which sixth-grade pupils are accepted by their classmates, and the relationship of certain variables to the accuracy of these judgments.

General Procedure

The general procedure used in this study may be described as follows: A sociometric test was administered to forty sixth-grade classes. On this test each pupil was asked to choose five classmates with whom he would prefer to work, five classmates with whom he would prefer to play, and five classmates near whom he would prefer to sit. The number of choices each pupil receives on each of the above criteria, indicates the degree to which he is accepted by his classmates as work companion, play companion, and seating companion. This acceptance is referred to as the sociometric status of the pupil. In addition to the sociometric test each pupil was requested to respond to a pupil activity form. This form was concerned with the freedom the pupils had in choosing their own companions for routine class activities. It was used to measure the opportunity pupils were given to exhibit choice behavior, observable to the teacher.

In the same forty sixth-grade classes each teacher was requested to make judgments concerning the sociometric status of the pupils in her class. These judgments were made separately for boys and girls in the following manner. The teacher wrote the names of the boys, in her class, in alphabetical order on a previously prepared teacher judgment form. To the right of the boys' names were three columns, one each for work companion, play companion, and seating companion. In the work companion column the teacher ranked the boys in the order in which she judged they would be accepted by their classmates as work companions. This was repeated for each boy's acceptance as play companion and seating companion. Continuous ranks were used in each column with the teacher ranking from the ends of the distribution toward the center. When the teacher had completed her judgments for boys the above procedures were repeated for girls, on a separate judgment form.

This procedure provided six sets of judgments for each teacher: one each for the sociometric status of boys as work companion, play companion, and seating companions; and one each for the sociometric status of girls as work companion, play companion, and seating companion. Thus the teacher's judgments of boys and girls could be compared directly with the sociometric results on each criterion, and the accuracy of her judgments determined.

In addition to these judgments each teacher was requested to indicate which three boys and three girls she most preferred as pupils in her class, and which three boys and three girls she least preferred as pupils in her class. This information was sought in order to determine the relationship between the teacher's preference for certain pupils and the accuracy of her judgments.

Personal data information regarding the teachers was obtained from the school records where possible. When the school records were not available the teacher was requested to provide the desired information on a personal data sheet.

DEVELOPMENT OF INSTRUMENTS USED IN THIS STUDY[1]

A brief discussion of the development and nature of the instruments used in this study follows.

---

[1] Copies of the instruments used in this study are in the appendix, in the order in which they are described here.

Sociometric Test

Several considerations were necessary in the selection of criteria for the sociometric test. First, they had to be familiar to all teachers, as well as all pupils, at the sixth-grade level. Second, they had to be concerned with activities which occurred within the realm of the teacher's daily observation. Third, they had to concern activities where the choice of classmates was a normal procedure. Finally, they had to concern activities which were common from class to class. It was decided that the only criteria which adequately met these requirements were the three used by Bronfenbrenner.[2] These are work companion, play companion, and seating companion.

The criteria were placed in statement form, and the directions indicated the pupils' choices were to be in terms of the children they most preferred for each activity. The three statements of choice appear on the sociometric form as follows:

1. I would choose to *work* with these children:
2. I would choose to *play* with these children:
3. I would choose to have these children *sit near* me:

A space for five names was left under each statement, and the pupils were requested to make five choices for each. The use of five choices was prompted by a desire to obtain the sociometric status of the pupils on each criterion. Five choices were necessary to obtain the proper spread of scores for this purpose. In addition, Newstetter, Feldstein, and Newcomb[3] found that the reliability of sociometric status, on one criterion, increased with the number of choices up to five. Choices beyond that number made no appreciable change.

The choosing, on each criterion, was confined to pupils within their own class. This was necessary since the teacher's judgments were to be based on the classroom situation. This was thought to be a normal choice procedure, in keeping with the pupil's usual class experience. During regular class hours the pupil's choice of work, play, and seating companions is restricted to his own classmates. The mere physical environment confines his choice behavior to this group.

At the top of the sociometric form the pupil's name, school, age, and sex were requested. This information was used to describe the student

---

[2] Bronfenbrenner, *op. cit.*, p. 43.

[3] Newstetter, Feldstein, and Newcomb, *op. cit.*, p. 35.

population, and enabled the sociometric results to be analyzed separately for boys and girls.

Pupil Activity Form

This form was devised in an attempt to obtain information regarding the freedom of activity the pupils had in class. The assumption underlying its construction was as follows: If pupils were allowed freedom in carrying out class activities, and selecting their own companions for these activities, they would be exhibiting overt choice behavior observable to the teacher. Thus the teacher would have a better basis for her judgments of sociometric status than where this freedom was not permitted. Consequently it was expected that her judgments would be more accurate. The above assumption was to be tested by determining the relationship between the responses to the pupil activity form and the accuracy of the teacher's judgments.

This form consisted of eight questions to which the pupils were asked to respond. The first question was concerned with the number of different pupils they studied or worked with in class during the past week. Numbers from one to fifteen followed the question and the pupils were asked to underline the most appropriate number. Questions two, five, and seven were concerned with whether or not the pupils were permitted to choose their own work, play, and seating companions in class. The remaining questions were concerned with the freedom allowed the pupils in their daily associations with classmates. Each of these last seven questions was followed by two alternatives and the pupils were instructed to underline the one which best answered the question.

The pupils were requested not to put their names on this form since the majority of the questions concerned the teacher. It was believed that this would prevent the pupils from fearing exposure of their answers, and would thereby elicit more honest responses.

Teacher Judgment Forms

In the construction of the teacher judgment forms it was decided that several requirements had to be met. First, the teachers' judgments of sociometric status should be separate for boys and girls. This was considered necessary since boys and girls seldom choose members of the opposite sex as comparions at the sixth-grade level. The varying number of boys and girls in each class would tend to complicate the results if they were not considered separately. Second, the teachers' judgment should be in terms of the same criteria used in the sociometric test administered to the pupils. This was considered necessary in order to make the teachers' judgments comparable to the sociometric results. Third, the teachers' judgments should be in the form of continuous ranks. This would force the teacher to judge the relative acceptance of each pupil. In addition, it would provide a type of judgment familiar to the teacher, since she is constantly comparing one pupil with another during the course of her teaching. Fourth, the teachers' judgments should be made from the extremes of the distribution toward the center. It was believed that this procedure would enable the teacher to make her judgments more easily and more efficiently.

In accord with the above considerations, two similar judgment forms were constructed—one for the teacher's judgments of girls, and one for the teacher's judgments of boys. The forms were arranged in such a way that the names of the boys and girls could be written in alphabetical order on their respective sheets. To the right of the names were three columns, one each for seating companion, play companion, and work companion. This arrangement permitted the teacher to rank the pupils in the first column, fold it back underneath the page, and then rank the pupils in the next column, etc., obtaining as independent judgments as possible on each criterion.

Two instruction sheets accompanied the teacher judgment forms. The first sheet explained the nature and purpose of the sociometric test given to the class, and the general nature of the judgments to be made by the teacher. The second sheet outlined in detail the specific procedures to be followed in making her judgments. The teachers were instructed to rank the boys in each column first, and then rank the girls in each column.

Although the instructions requested the teacher to circle the rank numbers of those who they believed would receive no choices on the sociometric test, this aspect of the instructions had to be deleted. The majority of the teachers stated that all pupils would receive some choices, and therefore no isolates could be indicated. The sociometric results later indicated that this was true.

Teacher Preference Form

This form provided a space for the teacher to list the names of the three boys and three girls she most preferred as pupils in her class, and the three boys and three girls she least preferred as pupils in her class. The accompanying instructions requested the teacher to base her preferences on the assumption that her class was to be divided into two sections, and she was to choose the pupils she would most and least prefer in her section. She was further instructed to make her selections solely on the basis of how much she would, or would not, enjoy having them as pupils in her section.

This instrument was used to determine the relationship between the teacher's preference for certain pupils and the accuracy of her judgments. It was believed that the extremes of the teacher's preferences were sufficient for the above purpose.

Teacher Personal-Data Form

The personal-data form was constructed for the obtainment of information on the teacher's age, length of teaching experience, length of time in present position, total number of semester hours of college training, recency of college training, number of semester hours in psychology, whether or not a course in child development had been taken, and whether single or married. The length of time the teacher had been in contact with her class was obtained directly from the teacher.

These personal-data variables were collected in order to determine their relationship to the accuracy of the teacher's judgments.

DESCRIPTION OF SUBJECTS

The subjects consisted of forty teachers and 1,258 pupils in forty sixth-grade classes from the Flint, Willow Run, and Ypsilanti public schools. The distribution by schools of sixth-grade classes included in the study may be seen in Table I. Examination of this table reveals that the majority of classes were located in the Flint public school system. The city of Flint is a typical industrial metropolis which contains a cross-section of most creeds, nationalities, and social classes.

The school system in Flint varies in type of organization at the elementary level. The majority of the elementary schools are organized under the *platoon system*. With this arrangement the pupils spend half of the day with a home-room teacher. The remaining half-day is spent by the pupils in special classes, with a different teacher for each class. All of the Flint elementary schools included in this study, except one, are organized under the *platoon system*. This lone exception is Doyle, which is organized along traditional lines.

All sixth-grade classes from Flint, included in this study, were home-room classes where the teacher spent at least a half-day period with the pupils. The remaining sixth-grade classes, from Willow Run village and Ypsilanti, are organized along traditional lines, with the teacher spending the entire day with the pupils.

TABLE I

DISTRIBUTION BY SCHOOLS OF SIXTH-GRADE CLASSES INCLUDED IN STUDY

Name of School	Number of Sixth-Grade Classes	Number of classes Included in Study
Flint		
Civic Park	3	3
Cody	2	2
Cook	1	1
Dort	3	3
*Doyle	2	1
Durant	2	2
Garfield	3	3
Homedale	1	1
*Jefferson	2	1
Lewis	3	3
Martin	1	1
*McKinley	2	1
Oak	2	2
Stevenson	2	2
Walker	3	3
Washington	2	2
Zimmerman	3	3
Willow Run		
Foster	2	2
Ross	1	1
Spencer	1	1
Ypsilanti		
Central	2	2
Total	43	40

*These three classes were eliminated because the teacher had already administered a sociometric test to her class.

Willow Run village is a war-born government housing project made up largely of industrial workers. Ypsilanti is a small college and industrial city.

Pupil Population

The 1,258 pupils were fairly evenly divided by sex. There were 632 boys and 626 girls. The average age of the boys was 11.8, while the average age of girls was 11.5.

The number of pupils per class ranged from fifteen to forty-three, with an average of thirty-two. The pupil population was almost entirely white. Only five of the 1,258 pupils were colored and they were distributed among four classes.

Teacher Population

The teachers participating in this study consisted of forty women all of whom were white. The personal-data factors describing the teacher population are presented in Tables II through VIII.

TABLE II
AGES OF TEACHER POPULATION (N = 40)

Age	Frequency
21-25 years	4
26-30 years	3
31-35 years	0
36-40 years	1
41-45 years	4
46-50 years	10
51-55 years	9
56-60 years	4
60-65 years	5

Mean age = 47.5 years.

TABLE III
YEARS TEACHING EXPERIENCE AND YEARS IN PRESENT POSITION (N = 40)

Years	Frequency—Teaching Experience	Frequency—Present Position
1- 3	3	7
4- 6	3	7
7- 9	1	4
10-12	1	4
13-15	2	0
16-18	4	1
19-21	3	5
22-24	3	5
25-27	8	5
28-30	12	2

Mean Years Teaching Experience = 20.5.
Mean Years Present Position = 13.6.

TABLE IV

SEMESTER HOURS CREDIT EARNED IN COLLEGE (N = 40)

Semester Hours	Frequency
61- 70	2
71- 80	0
81- 90	4
91-100	2
101-110	2
111-120	16
121-130	10
131-140	0
141-150	4

Mean Semester Hours = 114.0.

TABLE V

RECENCY OF COLLEGE TRAINING BASED ON MIDPOINT BETWEEN FIRST AND LAST DATES OF TRAINING (N = 40)

Years	Frequency
1925-1926	6
1927-1928	3
1929-1930	9
1931-1932	8
1933-1934	5
1935-1936	2
1937-1938	0
1939-1940	1
1941-1942	1
1943-1944	5

Mean Year = 1932.

TABLE VI

SEMESTER HOURS CREDIT EARNED IN EDUCATION COURSES (N = 40)

Semester Hours	Frequency
10-12	4
13-15	4
16-18	2
19-21	8
22-24	12
25-27	3
28-30	2
31-33	1
34-36	1
37-39	2
40-42	1

Mean Semester Hours = 22.2.

TABLE VII

SEMESTER HOURS CREDIT EARNED IN PSYCHOLOGY COURSES (N = 40)

Semester Hours	Frequency
3- 4	8
5- 6	12
7- 8	4
9-10	4
11-12	4
13-14	0
15-16	2
17-18	2
19-20	2
21-22	2

Mean Semester Hours = 8.9.

An examination of the first six tables will reveal that there is a wide spread of all personal-data variables among the forty teachers. The average teacher, representing this group, would be approximately forty-seven years of age with twenty years of teaching experience. Approximately thirteen of these years would have been spent in her present position. She would have 114 hours of college credit, half of which would have been earned before 1932. Twenty-two of these credits would be in education courses, and approximately nine in psychology courses. In general, the teacher population is a rather highly experienced and mature group.

Table VIII reveals that eighteen of the teachers were single, in comparison with twenty-two married. Sixteen of the teachers were with their

TABLE VIII

DIVISION OF TEACHER POPULATION ACCORDING TO MARITAL STATUS; LENGTH OF CONTACT WITH CLASS; AND WHETHER OR NOT TEACHER HAD COURSE IN CHILD DEVELOPMENT (N = 40)

	Frequency
Single	18
Married	22
One Semester with Class	16
Two Semesters with Class	24
Had Course in	
Child Development	15
No Course in	
Child Development	25

classes only one semester. This situation resulted from the fact that some elementary schools in Flint have mid-year promotions. The remaining twenty-four teachers were with their classes the entire year. Of the forty teachers participating in this study, fifteen had taken a course in Child Development and twenty-five had not taken such a course.

COLLECTION OF DATA

The data used in this study were collected during the last three weeks of May, 1949. The administrative and supervisory officials of the Flint, Willow Run, and Ypsilanti public school systems were contacted early in May and arrangements were made to meet with the forty sixth-grade classes. A schedule of meetings with the classes were set up and the investigator contacted each class during its regular school time. The fine coöperation of the principals and teachers enabled this research to be carried out in a natural setting.

The teachers prepared their classes for the arrival of the investigator, but the pupils were not informed of the nature of their participation. The teachers, likewise, were made aware of the fact that the investigation was a study concerning teacher judgment, but the exact nature of the study was not revealed to them until the time of the sociometric testing.

Procedure in Collection of Data

In contacting each of the forty sixth-grade classes the investigator was introduced to the teacher by the principal. After giving the teacher a brief explanation of the nature and purpose of the investigation, out of hearing of the students, the teacher introduced the investigator to the class and then turned the class entirely over to him, returning to her desk. The verbal introduction and directions, of the investigator to the pupils, were standard for all classes. The verbal directions were as follows:

> I am making a study of classroom groups to find out what a classroom would be like if every pupil would choose his own *work companions,* his own *play companions,* and his own *seating companions.*
>
> On this sheet that I shall give you (demonstrating sociometric form) there is a place for the names of *five pupils with whom you would most prefer to work; five pupils with whom you would most prefer to play; and five pupils whom you would most prefer to have sit near you.* Write here (pointing to spaces for names) the names of those whom you would choose. You may choose anyone *in this class* you wish, including those pupils who are absent. Your choices will not be mentioned to anyone else. Give both first and last names. Spell them the best you can.

Please make your choices thoughtfully and carefully, for the value of this whole study depends on how accurately you do this.

When I give you this sheet (demonstrating sociometric form) print *your name, school*, whether you are *boy or girl*, and give your *age*—at the top of the sheet. When you have done this please look up, so I will know you are ready to start. Do not write any choices on your paper yet.

At the conclusion of those verbal directions a copy of the sociometric test was passed to each pupil. After all students had completed filling in the personal data at the top of the form, the investigator said:

Now, place number—in the top right-hand corner of your paper..

This referred to a code number assigned to each class, to prevent mixing up the sociometric tests from different classes. It also enabled the teachers' responses to be anonymous to everyone but the investigator. When the pupils had placed the code number in the top right-hand corner they were told:

Remember!

1. Your choices must be from pupils *in this class,* including those who are absent.
2. You must give both *first* and *last* names, spelling them the best you can.
3. Your choices will *not be seen* by anyone else.
4. You may choose a pupil for more than one thing if you wish.

With the above reminder the pupils were given permission to start. The adequacy of the above directions, and the rapport established with the pupils, was revealed by their response to the test situation. All pupils approached the task seriously and diligently. Every one of the pupils, in all classes, made five choices for each criterion. None of the pupils wrote in a fictitious name, or the name of a person outside of their class.

When the pupils began the sociometric test the investigator gave the teacher a self-addressed envelope which contained the Teacher Judgment Forms and the Teacher Preference Form. These forms, and the envelope, each bore the code number which was assigned to her class. The teacher was requested to read the directions for each form, to make certain they were clearly understood. In addition to its major purpose this procedure kept the teacher occupied at her desk, thus preventing her from observing the pupils' responses to the sociometric test.

When the pupils had completed the sociometric test, they were collected by the investigator. A copy of the Pupil Activity Form was then passed to each pupil, with the following directions:

There are eight questions on this sheet. Please read each question, and *underline* the answer which you think best answers the question. Please do not ask any questions about this sheet, but do it the best you can.

You need not put your name on this sheet, but place number— in the top right-hand corner.

The pupils were then told to begin. When the Pupil Activity Form was completed by the students it also was collected by the investigator. None of the teachers had seen any of the responses, either to the Sociometric Test or the Pupil Activity Form.

Before the investigator departed he checked with the teacher to make sure the procedures for making her judgments and preferences were clearly understood. At this time, the teacher was reminded that in recording her judgments there could be no ties in rank. The teacher was then requested to complete the forms as soon as possible and mail them to the investigator.

The adequacy of the above procedure was revealed by the quick return and the completeness of the responses to the forms. The majority of the teacher-forms were received within a few days after the sociometric testing of the class. The remainder were received within two weeks after the testing. All teachers had filled out the forms according to the directions.

The personal-data factors, concerning the teacher, were gathered from the school personnel records in the Flint school system. In the other two schools a personal-data form was included in the envelope left with the teacher. She was requested to fill it out along with the other forms.

SUMMARY

The general procedure used in this study has been described. In brief, it consisted of measuring the acceptability of pupils to their classmates by means of a sociometric test, and having teachers make judgments concerning that acceptance. In addition, information was gathered on the freedom of activity the pupils had in class, the teachers' preferences for certain pupils, and personal-data factors regarding the teacher. Information on these variables was obtained in order that their relationship to the accuracy of the teachers' judgments might be determined.

The development and nature of the instruments used in this study was discussed. These instruments are the sociometric test, pupil activity form, teacher judgment forms, teacher preference form, and the personal data-form for teachers.

The subjects were described as forty teachers and 1,258 pupils from forty sixth-grade classes in the Flint, Willow Run, and Ypsilanti public schools.

The specific procedures used in collecting the data were described, and the verbal instructions to pupils were illustrated.

It was decided that a description of the analysis of data, collected in this study, would have little meaning without a presentation of the results derived from that analysis. They are therefore presented together in the following chapter. It will suffice here to state that all statistical procedures, used in the analysis, are based on standard formulas.

CHAPTER IV

ANALYSIS OF DATA AND RESULTS

The preceding chapter described the method used in investigating this problem. This chapter presents an analysis of the data obtained.

ACCURACY OF TEACHERS' JUDGMENTS OF SOCIOMETRIC STATUS

To determine the extent to which teachers are accurate in judging the sociometric status of all pupils in the classroom the sociometric results were analyzed separately for boys and girls, on each of the three criteria, and their relationship to the teachers' judgments determined. This procedure was carried out for each class in the following manner.

The number of choices each pupil received on each of the three criteria of the sociometric test were tallied separately for boys and girls. Each choice was given a value of one regardless of whether it was first, second, third, fourth, or fifth choice. This procedure provided six sets of sociometric results for each class. Three sets of sociometric results represented the sociometric status of boys as work companion, play companion, and seating companion, and three sets represented the sociometric status of girls on the same criteria.

The teacher's judgments of sociometric status were separate for boys and girls, in the form of continuous ranks, on each of the three criteria. These ranks were converted into standard scores, with a mean of zero and standard deviation of one, using Fisher's[1] conversion table. Thus the degree of relationship between the six sets of teacher's judgments and the sociomet-

---

[1] Ronald A. Fisher, and Frank Yates, *Statistical Tables for Biological, Agricultural, and Medical Research.* Edinburgh: Oliver and Boyd, Ltd., 1948. P. 66.

TABLE IX
CORRELATION COEFFICIENTS REPRESENTING THE ACCURACY OF TEACHERS' JUDGMENTS
OF THE SOCIOMETRIC STATUS OF BOYS AND GIRLS IN FORTY SIXTH-GRADE CLASSES

Class Number	Boys			Girls			Average Accuracy of All Judgments
	Work Companion	Play Companion	Seating Companion	Work Companion	Play Companion	Seating Companion	
1	.265	.112	.480	.643	.502	.509	.419
2	.418	.610	.457	.299	.530	.368	.447
3	.931	.668	.690	.661	.529	.550	.671
4	.012	.640	.657	.599	.414	.577	.483
5	.727	.321	.662	.509	.446	.348	.502
6	.386	.490	.645	.724	.442	.700	.565
7	.288	.062	.568	.131	.205	.355	.268
8	.780	.546	.414	.394	.216	.065	.403
9	.791	.637	.811	.618	.538	.607	.667
10	.365	.360	.627	.712	.557	.666	.548
11	.458	.750	.688	.811	.357	.348	.569
12	.860	.541	.868	.536	.701	.492	.666
13	.791	.687	.521	.652	.792	.744	.698
14	.376	.572	.468	.530	.415	.609	.495
15	.739	.544	.563	.616	.294	.598	.559
16	.480	.079	.464	.899	.905	.843	.612
17	.487	.506	.679	.681	.844	.798	.666
18	.443	.677	.410	.385	.549	.581	.508
19	.603	.627	.626	.738	.572	.748	.652
20	.221	.443	—.105	.758	.552	.606	.413
21	.590	.585	.721	.686	.585	.636	.634
22	.796	.710	.752	.757	.332	.753	.683
23	.553	.544	.625	.372	.505	.558	.528
24	.693	.772	.618	.688	.434	.720	.654
25	.671	.886	.640	.593	.504	.334	.605
26	.858	.544	.821	.872	.866	.899	.810
27	.643	.473	.591	.846	.795	.827	.696
28	.842	.775	.642	.374	.561	.595	.632
29	.234	.858	.686	.795	.796	.787	.693
30	.621	.633	.540	.672	—.114	.511	.477
31	.867	.816	.856	.778	.827	.885	.838
32	.801	.381	.784	.780	.399	.669	.636
33	.713	.682	.644	.426	.525	.643	.605
34	.655	.536	.662	.750	.737	.713	.675
35	.551	.592	.666	.876	.190	.764	.607
36	.715	.693	.499	.654	.584	.725	.645
37	.308	.400	.337	.645	.670	.658	.503
38	.778	.834	.814	.807	.796	.813	.807
39	.700	.389	.713	.634	.295	.611	.557
40	.698	.774	.759	.683	.604	.736	.709
Mean	.593	.569	.614	.640	.531	.624	.595

ric results, for each class, could be determined by Pearson product-moment coefficients of correlation. Table IX presents these correlation coefficients for all forty classes. *The degree of relationship expressed by these coefficients is henceforth referred to as the accuracy of the teachers' judgments of sociometric status.*

An examination of this table reveals that all except two of the 240 coefficients are greater than zero and positive. The mean accuracy of the teachers' judgments for boys on the criteria of work companion, play companion, and seating companion is .593, .569, and .614, respectively. The mean accuracy of the teachers' judgments for girls on the same three criteria is .640, .531, and .624, respectively. The last column on the right presents the average accuracy of all of the judgments of sociometric status, for each teacher. An examination of these coefficients will reveal that they vary from .268 to .838 with a mean of .595. Apparently teachers differ rather widely in their ability to make such judgments.

The questions raised in Chapter I concerning the sources of variation in the accuracy of these teachers' judgments, and the relationship of certain variables to this accuracy will now be considered. It was decided that the best means of securing answers to these questions would be to place them in the form of null hypotheses. This will be done, as each question is considered in the following pages.

Variations in the Accuracy of Teachers' Judgments of Sociometric Status

There were three questions raised in Chapter I concerning the variation in the accuracy of teachers' judgments. These may be stated in the form of null hypotheses as follows:

There is no difference between teachers in the accuracy of their judgments of the sociometric status of pupils in the classroom.

There is no difference in the accuracy of teachers' judgments of the sociometric status of boys and girls in the classroom.

There is no difference in the accuracy of teachers' judgments of the sociometric status of pupils in the classroom on the criteria of work, play, and seating companion.

The above hypotheses were tested by applying an analysis of variance to the 240 correlation coefficients, in Table IX, representing the accuracy of teachers' judgments of boys and girls on each criterion. The results of this analysis are presented in Table X.

An examination of this table reveals that the variation among teachers in the accuracy of their judgments is significant beyond the one per cent level.

TABLE X

ANALYSIS OF VARIANCE OF THE 240 CORRELATION COEFFICIENTS REPRESENTING ACCURACY OF TEACHERS' JUDGMENTS

		Degrees of Freedom	Sum of Squares	Mean Square
(1)	Teachers	39	3,276,548	84,041
(2)	Pupil	1	2,432	2,432
(3)	Criteria	2	243,482	121,741
	Remainder	197	4,900,879	24,878
	Total	239	8,423,341	

Levels of Significance

$$(1) \quad F = \frac{84,041}{24,878} = 3.3770 \qquad \begin{array}{l} 1\% = 1.69 \\ 5\% = 1.45 \end{array}$$

$$(2) \quad F = \frac{2,432}{24,878} = .0978 \qquad \begin{array}{l} 1\% = 6.76 \\ 5\% = 3.89 \end{array}$$

$$(3) \quad F = \frac{121,741}{24,878} = 4.8935 \qquad \begin{array}{l} 1\% = 4.71 \\ 5\% = 3.04 \end{array}$$

These data are inconsistent with the hypothesis that there is no difference between teachers in the accuracy of their judgments of the sociometric status of pupils in the classroom.

The source of this difference between teachers, in the accuracy of their judgments, will be sought later by determining the relationship between certain selected variables and the average accuracy of the teachers' judgments.

In addition, these data are consistent with the hypothesis that there is no difference in the accuracy of teachers' judgments of the sociometric status of boys and girls in the classroom.

A further examination of Table X reveals that the variation in the accuracy of teachers' judgments among the three different criteria is significant beyond the one per cent level. This finding is inconsistent with the hypothesis that there is no difference in the accuracy of teachers' judgments of the sociometric status of pupils in the classroom on the criteria of work, play, and seating companion.

Since such a difference exists it would be of some value to determine the comparative accuracy of the teachers' judgments on each criterion. An examination of the correlation coefficients in Table IX reveals that the mean accuracy of the teachers' judgments is lowest on the play companion criterion, both for boys and girls.

The question immediately arises as to the significance of these differences. Is the mean accuracy of the teachers' judgments on the play companion criterion significantly different from that on the criterion of seating or work? The answer to this question was determined by applying the Fisher t-test to determine the significance of the difference between means.

The results presented in Table XI, reveal that there is no significant difference between the mean accuracy of the teachers' judgments on the criteria of seating and play, or work and play, for boys. However, the difference between the mean accuracy of the teachers' judgments on these same criteria is significant beyond the five per cent and two per cent levels, respectively, for girls. It appears that the tendency for teachers to be less accurate in their judgments of the sociometric status of pupils on the criterion of play. is more pronounced for girls than boys. The teachers' judgments of girls probably accounts for the major part of the variation among criteria revealed by the analysis of variance.

TABLE XI

SIGNIFICANCE OF DIFFERENCE BETWEEN MEAN ACCURACY OF TEACHERS' JUDGMENTS ON DIFFERENT CRITERIA

Variables	N_1	N_2	M_1	M_2	t	P
Boys						
1. Seating-Play	40	40	.614	.569	1.09	>.10
2. Work-Play	40	40	.593	.569	.51	>.50
Girls						
1. Seating-Play	40	40	.624	.531	2.11	<.05
2. Work-Play	40	40	.640	.531	2.49	<.02

RELATIONSHIP OF SELECTED VARIABLES TO THE AVERAGE ACCURACY OF TEACHERS' JUDGMENTS OF SOCIOMETRIC STATUS

It has been shown that there is a significant variation among teachers in the accuracy of their judgments of the sociometric status of pupils in the classroom. The question immediately arises as to the relationship of certain variables to this difference between teachers in their ability to make such judgments. The variables which were considered important in this respect are the personal-data variables concerned with the training and experience of the teachers, as well as the size of class with which the teachers' judgments were concerned.

Eight of the variables were of a continuous variety and their relationship to the average accuracy of the teachers' judgments may best be tested by placing them in the form of a null hypothesis, as follows:

There is no relationship between the average accuracy of the teachers' judgments of the sociometric status of pupils in the classroom and each of the following variables:

(1)   Age
(2)   Years of teaching experience
(3)   Length of time in present position
(4)   Semester hours of college training
(5)   Recency of college training
(6)   Semester hours in education
(7)   Semester hours in psychology
(8)   Size of class.

The above hypothesis was tested by the following procedure. The correlation coefficients representing the accuracy of the teachers' judgments on each criterion, for boys and girls, were averaged for each teacher. This average accuracy of all the judgments, for each teacher, may be seen in the last column of Table IX. The personal-data variables were collected on a personal-data form and are presented in Tables II through VII in Chapter III. The size of class was obtained from analysis of the data and ranged from fifteen to forty-three pupils per class. The degree of relationship between these variables and the average accuracy of the teachers' judgments

TABLE XII

Correlation Coefficients Representing the Degree of Relationship Between the Average Accuracy of Teachers' Judgments and Certain Selected Variables
(N = 40)

Variables	Average Accuracy of Teachers' Judgments	t	P
1. Age	—.021	—.132	.895
2. Years of Teaching Experience	—.035	—.217	.829
3. Length of Time in Present Position	—.021	—.128	.898
4. Semester Hours of College Training	.014	.087	.931
5. Recency of College Training	.017	.104	.917
6. Semester Hours in Education	.010	.060	.952
7. Semester Hours in Psychology	.040	.249	.805
8. Size of Class	—.007	—.045	.964

was obtained by means of Pearson's product-moment coefficients of correlation. The resulting coefficients are presented in Table XII.

An examination of this table reveals that all correlation coefficients are near zero. To determine if any of the coefficients were significantly different from zero Fisher's t-test was applied and the values of P determined. All of these values are greater than .80, which means that one could expect correlations of this size or greater, eighty, or more, times out of a hundred if the true correlation were zero.

These data are consistent with the hypothesis that there is no relationship between the average accuracy of the teachers' judgments of the sociometric status of pupils in the classroom and each of the eight selected variables.

These results are somewhat surprising, especially since a study[1] discussed in Chapter II showed that variables three through seven were significantly related to elementary teachers' knowledge of child and adolescent behavior, as measured by an objective test. Two possible explanations may be presented to account for the lack of relationship found in this study. First, the accuracy of the teachers' judgments of sociometric status in the classroom is not dependent merely upon general knowledge of a child and adolescent behavior, but upon the application of that knowledge to a restricted area. Second, the judgment of sociometric status is a specific type of judgment dependent upon insight into group life, which apparently is not obtained from general training or experience.

The lack of relationship between the size of class and the average accuracy of the teachers' judgments may be partly explained by the restricted range in class size. The number of pupils per class ranged from fifteen to forty-three. It is possible that the accuracy of the teachers' judgments of sociometric status is not affected by class size within this range.

RELATIONSHIP OF OTHER VARIABLES

In addition to the eight variables treated above, three variables, considered to be important, were of a dichotomous variety and required separate treatment. Stated in null hypothesis form:

There is no difference in the accuracy of teachers' judgments of the sociometric status of pupils in the classroom, between:

(1) Those teachers who are single, and those who are married.
(2) Those teachers who were with the class two semesters,

---

[1] Kelly and Perkins, *op. cit.*, p. 101.

and those who were with the class one semester.
(3) Those teachers who had taken a course in Child Development, and those who had not taken such a course.

To test the above hypothesis the mean accuracy of the teachers' judgments were calculated for the teachers in each category. The significance of the difference between these means was determined through application of the Fisher's t-test. The number of teachers falling in each category, the mean accuracy of the teachers' judgments, and the significance of the difference between means is presented in Table XIII.

TABLE XIII

SIGNIFICANCE OF DIFFERENCE BETWEEN MEAN ACCURACY OF TEACHERS' JUDGMENTS
FOR THREE SELECTED VARIABLES

	Variable	N_1	N_2	M_1	M_2	t	P
1.	Marital Status	18 single	22 married	.611	.582	.79	>.10
2.	Length of time with Class	24 Two Semesters	16 One Semester	.604	.581	.61	>.10
3.	Course in Child Development	15 Yes	25 No.	.678	.545	12.96	<.01

This table reveals that the difference between the mean accuracy of judgment of the eighteen single teachers and the twenty-two married teachers is not significant at the ten per cent level. A difference this large or larger would be expected ten, or more, times out of a hundred, by chance alone, if the true difference were zero.

The difference between the mean accuracy of judgment of the twenty-four teachers who were with their classes two semesters and the sixteen teachers who were with their classes one semester is also not significant. It is possible that teachers know their pupils well enough after one semester to make such judgments, and a longer contact with the pupils does not improve the accuracy of these judgments to any significant degree. Further research would be required to verify such a possibility.

A further inspection of Table XIII will reveal that there is a significant difference between means on the last variable. The difference between the mean accuracy of judgment of the fifteen teachers who had taken a course in Child Development and the twenty-five teachers who had not taken such a course is significant far *beyond* the one per cent level. Less than once out of a thousand would such a difference occur by chance if the true difference were zero. An inspection of the means reveals that this difference is in favor of more accurate judgments by those teachers who had taken a course in Child Development.

This finding must be interpreted in light of the type of Child Development course taken by these fifteen teachers. The majority of these teachers had taken an in-service course, offered in Flint, through the cooperation of the University of Michigan. The content of the course centered around the development of the whole child, with a great deal of emphasis on social adjustment. In this area the class members were made familiar with the theory of the sociometric technique and its application to the classroom.

In regard to the above course description several explanations appear possible for the more accurate judgments made by teachers taking such a course. First, taking the course while in service may have provided an immediate application of the principles of child development learned, thus increasing the practical benefits of the course. Second, the emphasis in the course on social adjustment may have made the teachers more aware of the social adjustment of the pupils in their classes, thus focusing their attention on this important area. Third, familiarity with the sociometric technique and its application in the classroom may have made the teachers more conscious of overt signs of choice behavior in the classroom, thus increasing the accuracy of their observations.

It is, of course, entirely possible that none of the above explanations are valid. It may be that those teachers who are more conscientious, and more concerned about the social adjustment of their pupils, to begin with, elect to take such a course. The data presented here can only reveal that there is a relationship between taking a course in Child Development, as described above, and greater accuracy in teachers' judgments of sociometric status of pupils in the classroom. Further research would be required to identify the cause of this relationship.

These data are consistent with the hypothesis, regarding the first two variables, that there is no difference in the accuracy of teachers' judgments of the sociometric status of pupils in the classroom, between: those teachers who are single, and those who are married; those teachers who were with the class two semesters, and those who were with the class one semester.

These data are inconsistent with the hypothesis, regarding the third variable, that there is no difference in the accuracy of teachers' judgments of the sociometric status of pupils in the classroom, between: those teachers who had taken a course in Child Development and those who had not taken such a course.

RELATIONSHIP BETWEEN TEACHERS' PREFERENCES FOR CERTAIN PUPILS
AND ERRORS IN THEIR JUDGMENTS OF THE SOCIOMETRIC
STATUS OF THOSE PUPILS

It will be recalled that each of the forty teachers in this study was requested to indicate which three boys and three girls she *most* preferred as pupils in her class, and which three boys and three girls she *least* preferred as pupils in her class. These data were gathered to determine if the teacher's preference for certain pupils was related to the errors in her judgments of the sociometric status of those pupils. In view of a study[1] quoted in Chapter II, it seemed probable that a teacher may over-judge the sociometric status of those pupils she most prefers and under-judge the sociometric status of those pupils she least prefers. To determine if such a tendency existed the following null hypotheses were tested.

Teachers do not *over-judge* the sociometric status of the three boys and three girls they *most* prefer as pupils in class.

Teachers do not *under-judge* the sociometric status of the three boys and three girls they *least* prefer as pupils in class.

The procedure used in testing the above hypotheses was to compare the teachers' judgments with the sociometric results, for the pupils in each of the four preference groups, and to determine the amount and direction of the teachers' judgment error. However, before this comparison could be made it was necessary to convert both the teachers' judgments and the sociometric results into total comparable scores. This was done for each class in the following manner.

It will be recalled that the teacher's judgments were separate for boys and girls. These judgments were in the form of continuous ranks on each of the three criteria for boys, and each of the three criteria for girls. These ranks had been converted into standard scores, with a mean of zero and a standard deviation of one, as previously described. Thus each boy had a standard score representing the teacher's judgment of his sociometric status on each of the three criteria. An average of these three standard scores would yield the teacher's judgment of the total sociometric status of each boy in her class. The teacher's judgment of the total sociometric status of each girl in her class could be computed the same way. Since the standard scores were averaged the resulting distributions for boys and girls would still have a mean of zero and a standard deviation of one.

---

[1] Travers, *op. cit.*, p. 66.

To make the sociometric results, for boys and girls, comparable to these teachers' judgments the following procedure was used. The number of choices each boy received on the three criteria of the sociometric test were totaled. These total sociometric scores for boys were converted into standard scores with a mean of zero and a standard deviation of one. The total sociometric scores for girls were computed in the same way, and converted into similar standard scores.

The above procedure provided two sets of comparable standard scores for each boy and girl in class: one set representing the teacher's judgment of the total sociometric status of the pupil, and one set representing the total sociometric status of the pupil as measured by the sociometric test.

The average amount of discrepancy between these two sets of standard scores was computed for each of the following groups: three boys *most* preferred by the teacher; three boys *least* preferred by the teacher; three girls *most* preferred by the teacher; and three girls *least* preferred by the teacher. If this discrepancy indicated the teacher had *over-judged* the sociometric status of those pupils she *most* preferred, or *under-judged* the sociometric status of those pupils she *least* preferred it was designated as a *positive-judgment error*, since it was in the direction of the teacher's preference. If this discrepancy indicated the teacher had *under-judged* the sociometric status of those pupils she *most* preferred, or *over-judged* the sociometric status of those pupils she *least* preferred it was designated as a *negative-judgment error;* since it was away from the teacher's preference.

The above procedure was carried out for each of the forty classes. Table XIV presents the average amount and direction of error in the teachers' judgments of the pupils in each of the four preference groups. An examination of this table will reveal that the majority of judgment errors are positive for each preference group. This indicates a tendency for more teachers to *over-judge* those pupils they *most* prefer and to *under-judge* those pupils they *least* prefer. The last column on the right presents the total judgment error for each teacher. It will be noticed that only five of the values are negative. In other words, thirty-five of the forty teachers made greater judgment errors in the direction of their preferences.

A further examination of Table XIV will reveal that the mean error of the forty teachers' judgments is positive for each preference group. Had no relationship been present between the teachers' judgments and their preferences, for the pupils in these groups, one would expect random errors of judgment with resulting means of zero. Thus the significance of these means can be determined by applying the Fisher t-test to determine if

TABLE XIV

Average Amount[1] and Direction[2] of Error in Teachers' Judgments of the Sociometric Status of Boys and Girls They Most and Least Prefer as Pupils in Class

Teacher Number	Boys		Girls		Total Judgment Error for Each Teacher
	Three Most Preferred	Three Least Preferred	Three Most Preferred	Three Least Preferred	
1	+ .72	+1.04	+ .30	.00	+2.06
2	+ .52	+ .33	− .09	+ .77	+1.53
3	+ .09	− .08	+ .14	+ .15	+ .30
4	+ .51	+1.00	+ .02	+ .10	+1.63
5	− .42	+ .38	+1.00	+ .62	+1.38
6	+ .74	+ .04	.00	+ .37	+1.15
7	+ .75	+ .24	− .02	+ .52	+1.49
8	− .11	+ .67	+1.05	+ .28	+1.89
9	+ .17	+ .23	+ .64	+ .97	+2.01
10	− .57	+ .66	+ .28	+ .66	+1.03
11	− .54	+ .52	+ .40	− .05	+ .33
12	+ .30	− .24	− .52	+ .22	− .24
13	+ .20	+ .23	+ .13	− .15	+ .41
14	− .14	+ .73	+ .31	+ .29	+1.19
15	− .42	− .59	− .16	− .24	−1.41
16	+ .80	− .34	.00	+ .01	+ .47
17	+ .07	+1.39	.00	+ .21	+1.67
18	+ .14	+ .12	+ .24	+ .85	+1.35
19	+ .59	+1.09	− .18	− .16	+1.34
20	+ .98	+ .06	− .19	− .27	+ .58
21	+ .14	+ .86	+ .19	+ .36	+1.55
22	+ .12	− .14	− .07	+1.10	+1.01
23	+ .04	+1.09	+ .59	+ .28	+2.00
24	− .15	+ .09	+ .67	+ .02	+ .63
25	+ .48	+ .18	− .47	+ .23	+ .42
26	− .16	+ .27	− .10	+ .11	+ .12
27	+ .36	+ .41	.00	− .43	+ .34
28	+ .18	+ .26	+ .63	+ .38	+1.45
29	− .53	.00	+ .01	+ .06	− .46
30	− .65	+ .12	+ .01	+ .68	+ .16
31	− .04	+ .14	− .25	− .28	− .43
32	+ .28	+ .72	− .16	+ .93	+1.77
33	+ .58	+ .39	+ .34	+ .71	+2.02

[1] Amount of error is expressed in standard scores with a mean of zero and standard deviation of one.

[2] Direction is expressed by algebraic sign. Plus (+) indicates error in the direction of the teachers' preference. Minus (−) indicates error away from teachers' preference.

TABLE XIV (*continued*)

Teacher Number	Boys Three Most Preferred	Boys Three Least Preferred	Girls Three Most Preferred	Girls Three Least Preferred	Total Judgment Error for Each Teacher
34	+ .02	— .09	+ .30	+ .73	+ .96
35	+ .41	+ .63	+ .07	+ .33	+1.44
36	— .13	+ .39	+ .02	+ .36	+ .64
37	+ .59	+ .93	+ .05	— .09	+1.48
38	+ .42	+ .19	— .04	+ .03	+ .60
39	— .47	+ .13	+ .40	— .20	— .14
40	— .26	+ .51	+ .40	+ .49	+1.14
Mean	+ .14	+ .37	+ .15	+ .27	+ .93

they are significantly different from zero. This was done for the mean error of judgment in each group. The results are presented below in Table XV.

TABLE XV

Significance of the Mean Error of the Forty Teachers' Judgments for the Three Boys and Three Girls Most and Least Preferred by the Teacher

Group	N	M	t	P
Boys				
Most Preferred	40	.14	2.05	$<.05$
Least Preferred	40	.37	5.33	$<.01$
Girls				
Most Preferred	40	.15	2.73	$<.01$
Least Preferred	40	.27	4.52	$<.01$

This table reveals that all four means are significantly different from zero if the five per cent level of significance is accepted. Three of the means are significant beyond the one per cent level. Means this large or larger would be expected less than once out of a hundred by chance if the true means were zero.

These data are inconsistent with the hypothesis that teachers do not *over-judge* the sociometric status of the three boys and three girls they *most* prefer as pupils in class. Likewise, these data are inconsistent with the hypothesis that teachers do not *under-judge* the sociometric status of the three boys and three girls they *least* prefer as pupils in class.

BIAS AND THE ACCURACY OF TEACHERS' JUDGMENTS

It has been shown that teachers' judgments of sociometric status have a tendency to be biased in the direction of their preference for having or not having certain pupils in class. The question immediately arises as to the relationship between the degree to which a teacher's judgments are biased in this way, and the accuracy of her judgments of all pupils in the classroom.

To determine if there is such a relationship the following null hypothesis was tested.

> There is no relationship between the degree to which teachers' judgments of sociometric status are biased in the direction of the three boys and three girls they most and least prefer as pupils in class, and the accuracy of their judgments of the sociometric status of all pupils in the classroom.

To test the above hypothesis it was necessary to calculate the total amount of bias entering into each teacher's judgments of the three most and three least preferred boys and girls. The last column on the right in Table XIV presents this total. When this total amount of bias for each teacher was correlated with the average accuracy of each teacher's judgments of the sociometric status of all pupils in the classroom a coefficient of —.37 was obtained. The negative relationship expressed by this correlation coefficient reveals a tendency for a larger bias in teachers' judgments to be associated with less accurate judgments. Applying a Fisher t-test to this correlation coefficient it was found to be significantly different from zero. A coefficient this large or larger would be expected only twice out of a hundred by chance if the true correlation were zero.

These data are inconsistent with the hypothesis that there is no relationship between the degree to which teachers' judgments of sociometric status are biased in the direction of the three boys and three girls they most and least prefer as pupils in class, and the accuracy of their judgments of the sociometric status of all pupils in the classroom.

RELATIONSHIP BETWEEN THE FREEDOM PUPILS HAVE IN CLASS AND THE ACCURACY OF THE TEACHER'S JUDGMENTS OF SOCIOMETRIC STATUS

As previously discussed, it appeared probable that a teacher who allowed pupils greater freedom in class activities would be more accurate in her judgments of sociometric status. This was based on the assumption that more overt choice behavior would be exposed to the teacher, resulting in a better basis for her judgments. To determine if such an assumption is tenable the following null hypothesis was tested.

There is no relationship between the freedom pupils have in class, as determined by their responses to eight items on a pupil-activity form, and the accuracy of teachers' judgments of sociometric status.

It will be recalled that the pupils in each of the forty classes were requested to respond to a pupil-activity form, indicating the range of activity they had in class and the freedom they had in carrying out this activity. The pupils' responses to the eight questions on this form were scored in the following manner.

The first question requested each pupil to indicate how many classmates he worked or studied with during the past week. The responses to this question were scored, for each class, by taking the median number of pupils indicated.

The remaining seven questions had two alternative answers: one indicating freedom of pupils to choose their own companions, move around in class, and associate with other class members; the other alternative indicating lack of freedom in these areas. The responses to each of these seven questions were scored, for each class, by calculating the difference between the number of pupils selecting each alternative. If this difference was in the direction of more pupils indicating freedom of activity it was assigned a plus (+). If this difference was in the direction of more pupils indicating a lack of such freedom it was assigned a minus (—). To make these scores comparable for all classes they were divided by the number of pupils in class.

The above procedure provided an index of pupil freedom on each question for all forty classes. Since each question was concerned with freedom in a specific activity it was decided to correlate the index of pupil freedom on each question with the accuracy of the teachers' judgments of boys and girls on each criterion.

Table XVI presents the resulting correlation coefficients. An examination of these coefficients will reveal that they are all small and approximately evenly divided between positive and negative. They range from —.373 to .363. The Fisher t-test was applied to each of these coefficients to determine if any of them were significantly different from zero. It was found that only two were significantly different from zero at the five per cent level. These were the extreme negative and positive values just men-

TABLE XVI

CORRELATION COEFFICIENTS REPRESENTING THE DEGREE OF RELATIONSHIP BETWEEN THE ACCURACY OF FORTY TEACHERS' JUDGMENTS OF SOCIOMETRIC STATUS AND PUPILS' RESPONSES TO EIGHT ITEMS ON A PUPIL-ACTIVITY FORM

| Items on Pupil-Activity Form | Accuracy of Teachers' Judgments | | | | | |
| | Boys | | | Girls | | |
	Work Companion	Play Companion	Seating Companion	Work Companion	Play Companion	Seating Companion
1	.135	—.123	—.090	.010	—.050	—.013
2	—0.45	.210	.070	.139	—.091	—.036
3	.149	—.025	.128	.177	.014	.148
4	—.126	—.051	—.292	—.373*	—.082	—.234
5	.152	—.100	—.109	.013	—.019	—.159
6	.363*	.143	.111	.072	.167	.095
7	—.012	.044	.309	.064	.163	.067
8	—.193	—.169	—.034	.208	.183	.040

*Significantly different from zero at the five per cent level.

tioned. It would be expected on the basis of chance alone that two of these correlations would exceed the five per cent level of significance so one can conclude that the data are consistent with the null hypothesis that no relationship exists between the variables under discussion.

Since the relationship between the class response to each item and the teacher's judgments of the boys and girls on each criterion was not significant it was decided to correlate the total score on the pupil-activity form, for each class, with the average accuracy of the teachers' judgments. This yielded a correlation coefficient of .133, which was not significantly different from zero at the ten per cent level.

These data are consistent with the hypothesis that there is no relationship between the freedom pupils have in class, as determined by their responses to eight items on a pupil-activity form, and the accuracy of teachers' judgments of sociometric status.

SUMMARY

An analysis of the data has revealed the extent to which teachers are accurate in judging the sociometric status of sixth-grade boys and girls on the criteria of work companion, play companion, and seating companion.

The findings indicated no difference in the accuracy of the teachers' judgments of boys and girls. Their judgments on the play companion criterion were slightly less accurate than on the criteria of work companion and seating companion.

The ability to make accurate judgments of sociometric status varied widely among the forty teachers. This variation could not be accounted for by the general training and experience of the teacher, size of class, marital status of teacher, length of time the teacher had been in contact with the class, or the freedom pupils felt they had in class. The data revealed more accurate judgments by those teachers who had taken a course in Child Development.

There was a tendency for teachers to over-judge the sociometric status of those pupils they most preferred, and to under-judge the sociometric status of those pupils they least preferred. The amount of bias in this direction was negatively related to the accuracy of their judgments.

CHAPTER V

SUMMARY OF THE STUDY, CONCLUSIONS, AND SUGGESTIONS FOR FURTHER RESEARCH
THE PROBLEM AND THE METHOD OF STUDY

The problem defined in the first chapter was that of determining the accuracy of teachers' judgments concerning the degree to which sixth-grade pupils are accepted by their classmates, and the relationship of certain variables to the accuracy of these judgments. The acceptance of sixth-grade pupils by their classmates was determined by the administration of a sociometric test. The number of choices a pupil received on this test was referred to as his sociometric status. Various specific questions were raised concerning the accuracy with which teachers could judge this sociometric status. A review of the related literature revealed that these questions had not previously been answered.

The method of investigating the problem was discussed in the third chapter. It consisted of the following procedures. A sociometric test was administered to forty sixth-grade classes. On this test each pupil was requested to choose the five classmates with whom he would most prefer to work, the five classmates with whom he would most prefer to play, and the five classmates near whom he would most prefer to sit. In addition, each pupil was requested to respond to eight questions concerning the freedom he had in carrying out routine class activities.

Each teacher, in the same forty classes, made judgments concerning the sociometric status of her pupils on the criteria of work companion, play companion, and seating companion. In addition, each teacher indicated which three boys and three girls she most preferred as pupils in her

623

class, and which three boys and three girls she least preferred as pupils in her class. Personal data information concerning the teachers' training and experience were obtained from the school records wherever possible. Where the school records were not available, the teachers provided the desired information on a personal-data sheet.

The forty sixth-grade classes used in this study ranged in size from fifteen to forty-three pupils per class, with an average of thirty-two. There were 1,258 pupils in all, of whom 632 were boys and 626 were girls. The average age of the boys was 11.8 years, while the average age of the girls was 11.5 years. All except five of the 1,258 pupils were white.

The teachers included in this study consisted of forty women, all of whom were white. The personal-data variables describing the experience and training of these teachers were spread over a wide range. The average teachers, representing this group, was described as approximately forty-seven years of age, with twenty years of teaching experience, thirteen of which were spent in her present position. She was described as having 114 semester hours of college credit, with twenty-two of these in education courses, and nine of them in psychology. Half of her college training was earned before 1932. In addition to the above description of the teacher population, it was found that eighteen of the teachers were single, in comparison with twenty-two married. Sixteen of the forty teachers had been with their classes only one semester and the remaining twenty-four had been with their classes for one school year. Fifteen had taken a course in Child Development and twenty-five had not taken such a course.

The data used in this study were collected during the last three weeks of May, 1949, just before the close of the school year. In collection of the data the investigator contacted each class personally, and used standardized directions for the administration of the sociometric test. The teachers' judgments and preferences were recorded on previously prepared forms and mailed to the investigator within a short time after the sociometric testing. Code numbers were used on these forms so that the teachers' responses would be anonymous to everyone but the investigator. The adequacy of the above procedure was revealed by the quick return and completeness of the responses to all forms.

The teachers' judgments were separate for boys and girls, in the form of continuous ranks, on each of the three criteria. These ranks were converted into standard scores with a mean of zero and standard deviation of one. The relationship between these teachers' judgments of sociometric status and sociometric status as measured by the sociometric test was determined by Pearson product-moment coefficients of correlation. The degree of relationship expressed by these coefficients was referred to as the accuracy of the teachers' judgments.

It was decided that the questions raised in the first chapter, concerning the accuracy of these teachers' judgments, could best be answered by placing them in the form of null hypotheses and determining the consistency of the data with each hypothesis. This was done in the last chapter. The results revealed the data to be consistent with each of the conclusions listed below.

MAIN CONCLUSIONS AND THEIR INTERPRETATIONS

1. There is a difference between teachers in the accuracy of their judgments of the sociometric status of sixth-grade pupils in the classroom. Correlation coefficients representing the average accuracy of each teacher's judgments ranged from .268 to .838, with a mean of .595.

This finding should have some value for teacher training and selection. If the teacher is to be effective in the social adjustment of pupils she must be able to recognize the pupil's present status. From the above findings it is apparent that the ability to do this varies rather widely among teachers. Would it not be wise, then, to take this ability into account in the training and selection of teacher candidates? It is true that much more needs to be known about this area before positive recommendations can be made, but teacher training institutions would do well to make explorations of this ability among their student teachers.

2. There is *no* difference in the accuracy of teachers' judgments of the sociometric status of boys and girls in the classroom.

It is often said that women teachers do not understand boys as well as they do girls. Since all of the teachers in this study were women it is apparent that these data are not consistent with that belief, in so far as judging the sociometric status of pupils is concerned.

3. There is a difference in the accuracy of teachers' judgments of the sociometric status of pupils in the classroom among the criteria of work companion, play companion, and seating companion. This difference was accounted for to a major extent by the lower accuracy of the teachers' judgments on the play companion criterion. This tendency was greater for girls than for boys.

This finding was not surprising since a majority of the teachers stated they had not had the opportunity to observe the pupils as much on this criterion as on the other two.

4. There is *no* relationship between the average accuracy of the teach-

ers' judgments of the sociometric status of pupils in the classroom and each of the following variables: age of teacher, years of teaching experience, length of time in present position, semester hours of college training, recency of college training, semester hours in education courses, semester hours in psychology courses, and size of class.

Apparently the ability required in making judgments of sociometric status is not dependent upon the general training and experience revealed in the first seven variables. Since this is a specific type of judgment based on insight into group life it is possible that training of a specific nature is required.

The lack of relationship between the size of class and the accuracy of the teachers' judgments may be partly explained by the restricted range in class size. The number of pupils per class ranged from fifteen to forty-three. Apparently the accuracy of teachers' judgments of sociometric status is not affected by class size within this range.

5. There is *no* difference in the accuracy of teachers' judgments of the sociometric status of pupils in the classroom between: those teachers who are single and those teachers who are married; those teachers who were with the class two semesters and those who were with the class one semester.

There is a difference in the accuracy of teachers' judgments between those teachers who had taken a course in Child Development and those who had not taken such a course. This difference was in favor of more accurate judgments by those teachers who had taken the course.

The course taken by these teachers was described as one concerned with the development of the whole child, in which emphasis was given to social adjustment and the application of the sociometric technique. In light of the above course description it appears possible that these teachers may have become more aware of social adjustment, and more conscious of overt signs of choice behavior in the classroom, thus increasing the accuracy of their judgments. On the other hand, it may be that those teachers who elected to take such a course were more accurate judges of sociometric status to begin with.

The data in this study have merely revealed a relationship between taking a course in Child Development, as described above, and greater accuracy in teachers' judgments of sociometric status. However, this provides a fruitful area for further research. The cause of this relationship may provide a valuable lead in the training of teachers to make such judgments.

6. There is a tendency for teachers to *over-judge* the sociometric status of the three boys and three girls they *most* prefer as pupils in class, and to *under-judge* the sociometric status of the three boys and three girls they *least* prefer as pupils in class. This systematic bias in teachers' judgments appeared to a marked degree with all four groups of pupils.

This phenomenon is consistent with a study mentioned in the related literature, concerned with the judgment of group opinion. It also supports the statement that teachers tend to confuse the social adjustment between children with the social adjustment between adults and children.

7. There is a relationship between the degree to which teachers' judgments of sociometric status are biased in the direction of the three boys and three girls they most and least prefer as pupils in class, and the accuracy of their judgments of the sociometric status of all pupils in the classroom.

This relationship revealed a tendency for a larger bias in teachers' judgments to be associated with less accurate judgments. This accounts in part for the difference between teachers in the accuracy of their judgments of sociometric status.

8. There is *no* relationship between the freedom pupils have in class, as determined by their responses to eight items on a pupil-activity form, and the accuracy of teachers' judgments of sociometric status. This finding was surprising since it was assumed that pupils would exhibit more overt choice behavior, observable to the teacher, where they were given greater freedom in class. It was believed that this would provide a better basis for the teacher's judgments of sociometric status, resulting in more accurate judgments.

The lack of relationship found in this study reveals that the amount of freedom which pupils were allowed in choosing their own companions, moving around in class, and associating with their classmates, cannot account for the difference between teachers in the accuracy of their judgments of sociometric status.

IMPLICATIONS AND SUGGESTIONS FOR FURTHER RESEARCH

The conclusions just listed have at least provided tentative answers to the questions raised in the first chapter. They have helped to clarify a special ability desirable in teachers, and suggest some modifications in the training and selection of teacher candidates. In addition, they have shown some light on the extent to which adults have insight into childhood and adolescent groups. The implications of these conclusions as well as problems they suggest for further research will now be considered.

The social adjustment of pupils has received much emphasis in education. The majority of the teacher's efforts in this area has been dependent upon her judgment of the social adjustment of the pupils in her classroom. This study has shown that the ability of teachers to make such judgments, in a special area, varies widely among teachers. Some teachers are so inaccurate in their judgments that it is hard to believe that their efforts in this area can be effective at all. On the other hand, some teachers' judgments are quite accurate. The investigator will admit that accurate judgments of social adjustment are not necessarily followed by proper ameliorative practices. It is only emphasized here that accurate judgments are a prime prerequisite. However, this does raise the question of the relationship between the ability of teachers to make such judgments and indices of teaching efficiency. Research in this area may provide an improvement in the selection of teacher candidates.

It has been shown that teachers with the ability to make accurate judgments in this area cannot be selected in terms of general training and experience. Therefore, some specific training has been suggested. The more accurate judgments made by teachers who had taken a course in Child Development has revealed an important lead in this direction. Before any recommendations can be made concerning the value of such training, in this respect, further research would be necessary. This may be done with a group of teachers making judgments before and after taking such a course.

In addition to the above suggested researches, it would appear valuable to determine the comparative accuracy of teachers' judgments at different grade levels. One of the research studies discussed earlier has shown a declining accuracy from the kindergarten to the seventh grade. This should be substantiated with a larger number of teachers at each grade level.

The tendency for teachers to over-judge those pupils they most prefer and under-judge those pupils they least prefer would appear to handicap their efforts in the area of social adjustment. This phenomenon may be so deeply seated in human nature that it cannot be eradicated entirely. However, it calls for increased emphasis, in teacher training institutions, on the teacher's awareness of the pupil's role to his classmates in relation to the pupil's role to herself.

BIBLIOGRAPHY

1. Bonney, Merl E. "The Relative Stability of Social, Intellectual, and Academic Status in Grades II to IV, and the Inter-Relationships between These Various Forms of Growth," *Journal of Educational Psychology*, 34 (January, 1943), 88-102.

2. Bonney, Merl E. "Personality Traits of Socially Successful and Socially Unsuccessful Children," *Journal of Educational Psychology,* 34 (November, 1943), 449-472.

3. Bonney, Merl E. "The Constancy of Sociometric Scores and Their Relationship to Teacher Judgments of Social Success, and to Personality Self-Ratings," SOCIOMETRY, 6 (November, 1943), 409-424.

4. Bonney, Merl E. "Sex Differences in Social Success and Personality Traits," *Child Development,* 15 (March, 1944), 63-79.

5. Bonney, Merl E. "Sociometric Study of Agreement between Teacher Judgments and Student Choices," SOCIOMETRY, 10 (May, 1947), 133-146.

6. Bronfenbrenner, Urie. "A Constant Frame of Reference for Sociometric Research: Part I, Theory and Techniques," SOCIOMETRY, 6 (November, 1943), 363-397.

7. Bronfenbrenner, Urie. "A Constant Frame of Reference for Sociometric Research: Part II, Experiment and Inference," SOCIOMETRY, 7 (February, 1944), 40-75.

8. Fisher, Ronald A., and Yates, Frank. *Statistical Tables for Biological, Agricultural, and Medical Research.* Edinburgh: Oliver and Boyd Ltd., 1948. Pp. 112.

9. Jennings, Helen H. *Leadership and Isolation.* New York: Longmans Green and Co., 1943. Pp. 240.

10. Kelley, Ida B., and Perkins, Keith J. *An Investigation of Teachers: Knowledge of and Attitudes toward Child Adolescent Behavior in Every Day School Situations,* Purdue University Studies in Higher Education, 42. Lafayette, Indiana: Purdue University, 1941. Pp. 101.

11. Kuhlen, Raymond G., and Lee, Beatrice J. "Personality Characteristics and Social Acceptability in Adolescence," *Journal of Educational Psychology,* 34 (September, 1943), 321-340.

12. Kuhlen, Raymond G., and Bretsch, Howard S. "Sociometric Status and Personal Problems of Adolescents," SOCIOMETRY, 10 (May, 1947), 122-128.

13. Moreno, Jacob L. *Who Shall Survive?* Washington, D. C.; Beacon House, 1934. Pp. 440.

14. Newstetter, Wilber I., Feldstein, Mark J., and Newcomb, Theodore M. *Group Adjustment: A Study in Experimental Sociology.* Cleveland: School of Applied Social Sciences, Western Reserve University, 1938. Pp. 154.

15. Northway, Mary L. "A Study of the Personality Patterns of Children Least Acceptable to Their Age Mates," SOCIOMETRY, 7 (February, 1944), 10-25.

16. Northway, Mary, and Potashin, Reva. "Instructions for Using the Sociometric Test," SOCIOMETRY, 9 (May-August, 1946), 242-247.

17. Olson, Willard C. *Child Development.* Boston: D. C. Heath and Company, 1949. Pp. 417.

18. Stoke, Stuart. *The Social Analysis of the Classroom.* Division on Child Development and Teacher Personnel, American Council on Education, January, 1940. Pp. 13.

19. Travers, Robert M. W. *A Study in Judging the Opinions of Groups.* Archives of Psychology, No. 266. New York: Bureau of Publications, Columbia University, 1941. Pp. 73.

20. Tryon, Caroline M. *Evaluations of Adolescent Personality by Adolescents.* Monographs of the Society for Research in Child Development, IV. Washington, D. C.: National Research Council, 1939. Pp. 83.

21. Zeleny, Leslie D. "Sociometry of Morale," *American Sociological Review,* IV (December, 1939), 799-808.

APPENDIX

Instruments Used in Study:
Sociometric Test
Pupil Activity Form
Teacher Judgment Forms
General Instructions to Teachers
Procedures in Making Judgments
Teacher Judgment—Boys
Teacher Judgment—Girls
Teacher Preference Form
Personal Data Form

SOCIOMETRIC TEST

Name.................................... School...............................
Are you a boy or girl?.................... How old are you?.................
We would like to know which children *in this room* you prefer to work and play with.
Write the names of those whom you would choose; choose anyone *in this room* you
wish; your choices will not be mentioned to anyone else. Give both first and last
names. Spell them the best you can.

I would choose to *work* with these children:

1. ....
2. ....
3. ....
4. ....
5. ....

I would choose to *play* with these children:

1. ....
2. ....
3. ....
4. ....
5. ....

I would choose to have these children *sit near* me:

1. ....
2. ....
3. ....
4. ....
5. ....

PUPIL-ACTIVITY FORM
What I Do in This Class

Please read the following questions, and *underline* the answer which you think
best answers the question.

1. How many different pupils did you study or work with in class last week?

1	5	9	13
2	6	10	14
3	7	11	15
4	8	12	

2. Do you usually choose your own study or work companions in this class, or does the teacher choose them for you?

   (a) Choose them myself
   (b) Teacher chooses them for me

3. Do you usually move around in class when studying with other pupils, or working on group projects?

   (a) Yes
   (b) No

4. Do you usually visit with other pupils in class when studying with others, or working on group projects?

   (a) Yes
   (b) No

5. Did you choose the seat you are now sitting in, or did the teacher ask you to sit there?

   (a) Chose it myself
   (b) Teacher asked me to sit here

6. Do you ever play games in this class?

   (a) Yes
   (b) No

7. If you play games, do you usually choose your own play companions, or does the teacher choose them for you?

   (a) Choose them myself
   (b) Teacher chooses them for me

8. Do you usually raise your hand before talking out loud to your neighbor, in class?

   (a) Yes
   (b) No

GENERAL INSTRUCTIONS TO TEACHERS

The students in your class will be asked to name the five children with whom they would *prefer to work* the five children with whom they would *prefer to play,* and the five children near whom they would *prefer to sit.* The total number of choices each child receives on each of the above, will indicate his (her) acceptability to his (her) classmates as *work companion, play companion,* and *seating companion.* On each of these three criteria, some children will be highly accepted, receiving many choices; some will remain unchosen; the remainder will fall in betweeen these extremes. Consequently, the children can be ranked in the order of their relative acceptability from the most accepted to the least accepted.

The Accuracy of Teachers' Judgments

We are interested in determining the extent to which teachers can judge the relative acceptability of each child to his (her) classmates as work companion, play companion, and seating companion. As you know, boys and girls at the sixth grade level seldom choose members of the opposite sex as companions. Therefore we are asking you to judge the boys and girls in your class separately.

SPECIFIC INSTRUCTIONS

On the following page, entitled TEACHER JUDGMENT—*Boys,* please write the names of the boys, in your class, in alphabetical order (Place last names first).

On the following page, entitled TEACHER JUDGMENT—*Girls,* please write the names of the girls, in your class, in alphabetical order (Place last names first).

PROCEDURES IN MAKING JUDGMENTS

Turn to the page entitled TEACHER JUDGMENT—*Boys.* In each column, you are to rank all of the *boys* in the order in which you think they are *accepted by their classmates.* Use the following procedure:

A. *In the work companion Column:*

   (1) Place a *1* after the boy who you think is most *accepted by his classmates* as work companion.

   (2) Place a *100* after the boy who you think is *least accepted by his classmates* as work companion.

   (3) Place a *2* after the boy who you think is *next most accepted.*

   (4) Place a *99* after the boy who you think is *next least accepted.*

   (5) *Continue this procedure* until each boy is ranked in the work companion column.

   (6) *Now,* place a circle around the rank number of those boys, who you think will receive *no choices* from their classmates as work companion.

   (7) *Next,* fold the work companion column back underneath the page so it is not visible to you.

B. *In the play companion column,* repeat the above procedure for each boy's acceptance as play companion.

C. *In the seating companion column,* repeat the above procedure for each boy's acceptance as seating companion.

When you have completed the ranking in all three columns for boys, and have indicated those in each column who you think will receive no choices, turn to the page entitled TEACHER JUDGMENT—*Girls* and repeat the same procedure.

632

The Accuracy of Teachers' Judgments

Code No. ....

TEACHER JUDGMENT—*Boys*

Boys Names (Last, First)	Seating Companion	Play Companion	Work Companion
1.			
2.			
3.			
4.			
5.			
6.			
7.			
8.			
9.			
10.			
11.			
12.			
13.			
14.			
15.			
16.			
17.			
18.			
19.			
20.			
21.			
22.			
23.			
24.			
25.			

Code No. ....

TEACHER JUDGMENT—*Girls*

Girls Names (Last, First)	Seating Companion	Play Companion	Work Companion
1.			
2.			
3.			
4.			
5.			
6.			
7.			
8.			
9.			
10.			
11.			
12.			
13.			
14.			
15.			
16.			
17.			
18.			
19.			
20.			
21.			
22.			
23.			
24.			
25.			

TEACHER-PREFERENCE FORM   Code No. ....

Assume that your class is to be divided into two sections, only one of which you will teach. List below the names of the three boys and the three girls whom you would most prefer as pupils in your section. Also list below the names of the three boys and the three girls whom you would least prefer as pupils in your section. Make your selections only on the basis of how much you would, or would not, enjoy having them as pupils in your section.

Most Prefer	*Least Prefer*
Boys	*Boys*
1.	1. ....
2.	2. ....
3.	3. ....
Girls	*Girls*
1.	1. ....
2.	2. ....
3.	3. ....

Code No. ....

PERSONAL-DATA SHEET

Name................................ School................................

Number of years of teaching experience.............. Age............ Sex..........

Record of the college or University training you have had:

Institution Attended	Dates Attended	Semester Hours Credit	Degrees Awarded
1.	....	....	....
2.	....	....	....
3.	....	....	....
4.	....	....	....

Major study in undergraduate training...

Major study in graduate training...

Length of time in present position...

Indicate how many semester hours of credit you have in each of the following fields:

Education   Psychology
............Education Psychology   ....General
............Child Growth and Development ....Mental Hygiene
............Guidance   ....Child
............Other   ....Other

List the specific teaching positions you have held:

Location	Grades Taught	Years
1.	....	....
2.	....	....
3.	....	....
4.	....	....
5.	....	....

Are you: Single.......... Married.......... Widowed.......... Divorced........

SOME INTRAPERSONAL AND INTERPERSONAL DETERMINANTS OF INDIVIDUAL DIFFERENCES IN SOCIEMPATHIC ABILITY AMONG ADOLESCENTS

By David P. Ausubel and Herbert M. Schiff

The Problem

In an earlier paper (2), the writers introduced the term "sociempathy" to describe a particular variety of social perception—"an individual's awareness of his own and others' sociometric status in a given group of which he is a member." It was postulated that as children grow older they become increasingly able to perceive sociometric relationships involving themselves and others, and that this ability is basic to group organization, to social behavior in the group, and to individual adjustment to and effectiveness in group situations (2). Preliminary evidence of developmental trends in sociempathy, based on rough measures of sociempathic ability (the correlation within a given age group between sets of sociometric ratings and predictions of same), was presented.

In the present study a refined measure of individual, rather than group, sociempathic ability was used. Individual discrepancy scores were obtained which took into account the deviation of each *particular* prediction of a sociometric rating from the corresponding rating. Similar scores have been used by Dymond (7, 8) in the measurement of empathic ability.

Once we ascertain that subjective factors play an important role in the evolution of interpersonal perceptions, the next relevant question relates to the influence which various dimensions of these perceptions (e.g., accuracy, "assumed similarity") exert on social behavior and effectiveness. Gage (10) reviewed the inconsistent results in various studies of the relationship between (*a*) differential ability to predict the attitudes of others, and (*b*) sociometric status and leadership ability. Perhaps the crucial factor in the relationship lies in the relevance of the predicted attitudes to the purposes of the particular group under discussion. That is, superior perceptual acuity enhances social effectiveness only when the perceptual superiority is manifested in those specific areas impinging upon the structural or functional properties of a particular group (4). The positive aspect of this factor of relevance was strikingly illustrated in a study by Fiedler, Hartmann, and Rudin (9) on another dimension of social perception (i.e., "assumed similarity"). These investigators showed that basketball teams which were task-oriented (i.e., whose members

636

tended to perceive dissimilarity between team-mates with whom they could and could not co-operate) also tended to be more successful in inter-team competition.

The purpose of the present study was to identify some of the factors making for individual variability in sociempathic ability. What variables significantly affect the accuracy of perception of own and others' sociometric status? To what extent does "projection" (the tendency to predict that another will rate oneself as one rated him) contribute to perceptual error? Do we perceive more accurately the sociometric ratings or standings of our own or of the opposite sex group? What effect does social distance between rater and ratee have on accuracy of sociempathy, i.e., do we perceive more accurately persons whom we accept or reject? To what extent is the direction of the error of perception (under or over-estimate) related to social distance?

METHOD

1. Population

The population consisted of 44 students comprising (with the exception of a few absentees) the junior class of University High School in Urbana, Illinois. The mean age of these students was 15.8 years. The sex distribution was 19 boys and 25 girls. Socio-economic status for the group as a whole was decidedly above average. The parents of our students are largely professional persons, mostly holding academic appointments at the University. Entrance into the school, however, is not restricted to the children of faculty members of the University.

2. Procedure

The raw sociometric data for this study were obtained by requiring each student to rate all of his classmates on a five-point scale in terms of acceptability as friends, and to predict how each of his classmates would rate him and be rated by the group on the same basis. The details of this procedure have been described in a previous publication (2).

RESULTS AND INTERPRETATION

1. Sociempathic Ability (Self)

Ability to perceive own sociometric status was expressed in two different ways: (*a*) as a total discrepancy score for each individual, representing the

637

sum of the deviations of his predictions of how others would rate him from the actual ratings given him by these persons; (*b*) as a "right" score, representing the total number of times an individual predicted *exactly* how another person rated him. The distribution of both types of scores did not deviate significantly from the normal.

The discrepancy scores ranged from 13 to 52, a difference of 39. The theoretical range of deviation scores runs from 0 to 172, since each individual can be as much as four points in error in each of 43 predictions. Thus, the mean discrepancy score of 28.2 (with a sigma of 8.3) was about one-third as large as the mean deviation score of 86 anticipated on the basis of chance. Similarly the obtained mean "right" score of 17.7 (with a sigma of 5.4) was approximately twice the mean of right predictions that could be anticipated on the basis of chance (8.6 or one-fifth of 43). In both cases, the differences between obtained and expected means was significant beyond the per cent level. We can feel confident, therefore, that this index of sociempathic ability was measuring some ability other than chance to predict own sociometric status.

a. Reliability. The reliability of the sociempathy discrepancy score was determined by correlating mean odd discrepancy scores against mean even discrepancy scores. The corrected reliability coefficient was .796, which is relatively high for this type of function.

b. Sex Differences. Girls manifested better sociempathic ability than boys for both types of scores. In neither case, however, was the difference significant at the 5 per cent level. Some significant differences, however, *did* appear when the data were analyzed in terms of predictions of ratings of like and opposite sex groups.[1] Thus, boys were able to predict ratings given them by girls better than they were able to predict ratings given them by their own sex (P < .01); whereas girls were better able to predict the ratings given them by girls than by boys (almost significant at 5 per cent level). Hence, the sociometric feelings of girls were perceived more accurately by both sexes than those of boys. Dymond (8) obtained similar results in her study where individuals predicted the ratings given them by others on various personality traits.

Boys were superior to girls in predicting the sociometric ratings of the opposite sex, but unreliably so. Girls were significantly superior to boys in predicting the ratings of their like sex group (P < .01).

It would seem, therefore, that the sociometric attitudes of adolescent girls are more perceptible to both sexes than those of boys, and that the sociempathic

---

[1] From this point on, when we refer to "accuracy scores," we mean accuracy of sociempathic prediction expressed as a discrepancy score.

superiority of girls is definitely limited to perceiving the sociometric behavior of their own sex group.

c. Projection. What effect does "projection" (the tendency for an individual to predict that other persons will rate him sociometrically in the same way as he rated these other persons) have on accuracy of predicting own sociometric status? A projection score was determined for Individual *A* by subtracting the ratings he gave to *B, C, D, E,* etc., from the corresponding predictions he made of the ratings that *B, C, D,* and *E* would give him, and by then summing the deviations thus obtained. A low score, therefore, is indicative of a *high* tendency toward projection and *vice versa.* There was no sex difference in the magnitude of projection scores.

When projection scores were correlated with accuracy scores, the resulting coefficient of correlation was .41 [.27 for boys (p > .05) and .56 (p < .01)] for girls. This positive correlation could not occur were there not a tendency for individuals to rate each other reciprocally. Hence, predicting that another will rate oneself as one rated him tends to increase the accuracy of the prediction. Since girls' accuracy scores are more highly correlated with projection than boys', girls evidently have a greater tendency toward reciprocal sociometric rating.

d. Mutuality of expectations. Casual inspection of the data, suggested the hypothesis that there was a positive relationship between the mean rating which an individual predicted he would receive from other persons in the group and the mean rating which the group predicted it would receive from the individual. This hypothesis was tested by correlating these two sets of scores. For the entire group the coefficient of correlation was only .21, but significantly enough, it was .02 for boys, but .41 for girls (P < .05).

A psychological explanation for this mutuality of expectation in the case of girls is not readily available. Apparently, however, girls tend partly to expect the same degree of acceptance from others that the latter expect from them.

e. Effect of "social distance" (degree of acceptance of another) on sociempathic ability. In terms of interpersonal relations, this relationship is highly significant. Are we more or less accurate in predicting how others will accept us if we accept them, reject them, or are neutral in our feelings toward them? How does the direction of the error of estimate (under- or over-estimate) vary with degree of acceptance? To answer these questions, all of the discrepancy scores corresponding to instances where individuals rated others as "5" were segregated. The same procedure was followed for the 4, 3, 2, and 1 ratings. Two types of means were then obtained—a *mean total error* where positive and

639

negative signs of deviation scores were *not* taken into account, and *mean average error* where signs were taken into account in determining the mean. The first type of mean indicates merely *degree* of error; the second type of mean indicates *direction* of error.

When the mean total error corresponding to various categories of acceptance was compared, the differences between all possible combinations of categories were found to be significant beyond the 1 per cent level except for the following combinations: 5 — 1 (P < .05), 4 — 1 (P > .05), 3 — 1 (P > .05), 2 — 1 (P > .05). We are justified, therefore, in concluding that the greater the acceptance one individual extends another the more accurately he can predict how the latter accepts him (see Figure 1). The simplest explanation for this phenomenon is that generally speaking we have most social contact with

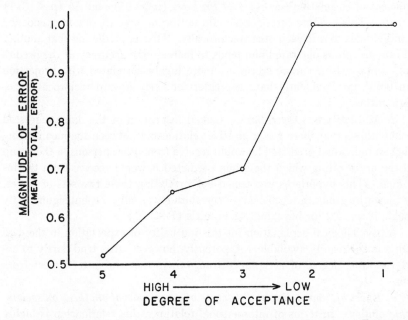

Fig. 1 Magnitude of Error in Predicting Own Sociometric Status as a Function of "Social Distance," i.e., Degree of Acceptance of Others

those individuals in the group whom we most accept; and as a result of this greater contact, we have more opportunity to perceive their attitudes toward us.

From Figure 2 we see that, in general, degree of acceptance varies positively with the direction of error, or more specifically, that the more one pupil accepts another the less he tends to underestimate the rating he receives from him. This, too, is understandable since we would normally expect greater acceptance at the hands of those whom we in turn accept more completely. The differences between means are all significant beyond the 1 per cent level except at the extremes of the scale, i.e., 5 — 4, and 2 — 1 (P > .05), and for the 3 — 1 comparison (P < .05).

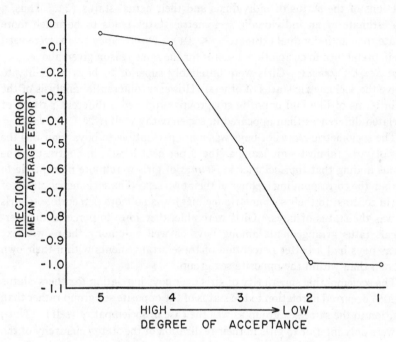

FIG. 2   DIRECTION OF ERROR IN PREDICTING OWN SOCIOMETRIC STATUS AS A FUNCTION
OF "SOCIAL DISTANCE," I.E., DEGREE OF ACCEPTANCE OF OTHERS

2. Sociempathic Ability (Others)

Only one measure of ability to perceive the sociometric status of others was used—the total discrepancy between all of the individual predictions made by a subject of the sociometric status of others and the actual sociometric status scores of the latter. An individual's sociometric status was determined by taking the mean of all the sociometric ratings he received from his classmates.

The discrepancy scores ranged from 21 to 49 and their distribution did not differ significantly from the normal. The obtained mean discrepancy score of 31.1 (with a sigma of 6.5) was somewhat more than a third as large as the mean discrepancy score of 86 that could be anticipated on the basis of chance. This difference was significant beyond the 1 per cent level, demonstrating that these scores were not reflective of a chance ability.

The average correlation between an *individuals'* predictions of the sociometric status of others and their actual status was .48 (p < .01). This was considerably lower than the correlation of .94 found between the group's *mean* predictions of the status of individuals and their actual status (2). Thus, a group estimate of an individual's sociometric status tends to be much more accurate than an individual estimate (p < .01). Discrepancy scores were used again in preference to correlational scores for the same reason given above.

a. Sex differences. Girls were unreliably superior to boys in ability to perceive the sociometric status of others. However, differential analysis of the data in terms of like and opposite sex groups produced a different pattern of sex-related differences than appeared in sociempathy (self).

The sociometric *status* of boys was more perceptible to boys than was the status of girls (almost significant at the 5 per cent level), in contrast to the previous finding that the sociometric *feelings* of girls were more perceptible to boys than the corresponding feelings of their own sex. The sociometric status of girls (in contrast to their sociometric feelings) was no more perceptible to girls than was the status of boys. Girls were able, therefore, to perceive the hierarchical status arrangements among boys as well as among their own sex; whereas boys had a better perception of these arrangements within their own sex group than within the opposite sex group.

The sociempathic superiority of girls over boys in relation to others' status (p < .05) occurred in relation to the status of the opposite sex group rather than in relation to the same sex group as was the case in sociempathy (self). Thus, boys were only inferior to girls in their realization of the status hierarchy of the opposite sex, not of the same sex.

The important points of difference between the two varieties of sociempathy are: (*a*) that the sociometric *attitudes* of girls are more perceptible to both sexes than the sociometric attitudes of boys; and (*b*) that boys are better aware of the *status hierarchy* within their own than in the opposite sex group, whereas girls are equally well aware of the status hierarchy in either sex group.

b. Projection. Individual measures of projection (the mean of the discrepancies between individual ratings given *to* others and individual predictions of their sociometric status) were calculated in the same manner as were comparable measures relating to prediction of own status. No sex differences occurred in mean degree of projection. Projection scores correlated 0 with accuracy scores in both sexes indicating that (in contrast to sociempathic ability relative to own status) it could account for no part of the accuracy of perception of others' status.

Interestingly enough, projection in predicting the status of others was significantly less than in predicting own status (p < .01). This could possibly be explained by the absence of the factor of reciprocity of rating in predicting the status of others. Presumably, individuals are aware that reciprocity holds to some extent in the mutual ratings they give each other, thereby making projection a more realistic basis or prediction of own status than the status which others earn from the group.

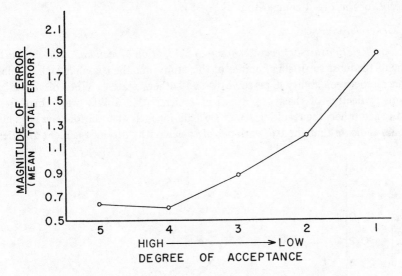

FIG. 3 MAGNITUDE OF ERROR IN PREDICTING OTHERS' SOCIOMETRIC STATUS AS A FUNCTION OF "SOCIAL DISTANCE," I.E., DEGREE OF ACCEPTANCE OF OTHERS

c. Effect of degree of acceptance of another on sociempathic ability. The same type of relationship in general held here as in accuracy of perception of own status (see Figure 3): The more one pupil accepted another the more accurately he was able to perceive how the latter was accepted by the group. Again this may be explained on the basis of differential sensitivity to the status positions of persons one likes better and with whom social contact is presumably greater. All differences between means were significant beyond the 1 per cent level.

From Figure 4 we see that, just as in estimation of own sociometric status, the direction of the error in predicting others' sociometric status is positively related to degree of acceptance. Thus, the more favorably disposed we feel toward an individual the greater our tendency to predict that the group will accept him favorably. These results are in agreement with Gronlund's findings that teachers overjudge the status of preferred pupils and underjudge the status of nonpreferred pupils (11).

This tendency to attribute to the group our own feelings about a person is certainly indicative of projection, and presents a contrast to the situation described above in which projection was not reported as a factor influencing accuracy (as opposed to direction) of prediction of others' sociometric status. The differences between all means were significant beyond the 1 per cent level except for the 2 — 1 comparison (P > .05).

3. General Findings

a. Relationship between accuracy of perception of own and others' status. One of the most surprising findings of this study was the complete lack of relationship between ability to perceive own and others' status. When discrepancy scores reflective of these two types of sociempathic ability were correlated with each other, the resulting *r* was .06 (.08 for girls and .05 for boys). This would indicate that the two varieties of sociempathy are independent abilities

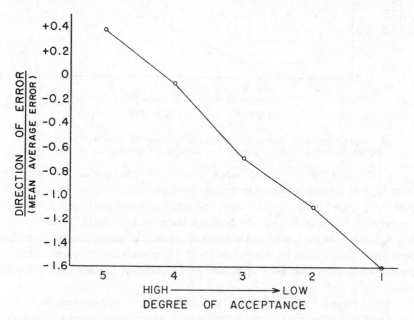

Fig. 4 Direction of Error in Predicting Others' Sociometric Status as a Function of "Social Distance," i.e., Degree of Acceptance of Others

at least insofar as this particular sample of this age group is concerned. The type of sensitivity that enables Individual A to perceive accurately how Individual B accepts him (A) is apparently unrelated to the type of sensitivity that enables him to perceive accurately how the entire group accepts B. Adams (1) found a very low correlation between the abilities to rate self and others. Singer (14) obtained a negative relationship between perception of own status and perception of preferred as opposed to non-preferred persons. Dymond (8), on the other hand, found a significant positive relationship between empathic ability and insight (the ability of an individual to rate himself as others rate him).

Although this lack of relationship held true generally, it is obvious that at least four important combinations of these two abilities exist: (a) individuals who are high on both, (b) individuals who are low on both, (c) and (d) individuals who are high on one and low on the other. A study is now in progress to determine the personality correlates of these four types.

b. Relationship between sociempathic ability and sociometric status. Ability to predict own status was correlated .26 with sociometric status itself ($P > .05$). For boys the r was .10 ($P > .05$), for girls it was .42 ($P < .05$). In the case of the girls, therefore, ability to perceive own sociometric status seems to be positively related to sociometric standing in the class. This result conflicts with Singer's finding that a negative, almost significant relationship prevails between popularity and ability to perceive own status (14), but is in agreement with Gage's finding that a correlation of .40 prevails between sociometric rank and accuracy of social perception of others (10). It is also in agreement with Chowdry and Newcomb's finding that:

> Leaders of a group are significantly superior to non-leaders and isolates in their ability to judge group opinion on familiar and relevant issues. . . . This differential ability on the part of leaders . . . is, however, not evident in unfamiliar or less familiar or less relevant issues (5).

These investigators reach the important conclusion that:

> The ability to function as an effective group member would also seem to be related to the ability to perceive the opinions and attitudes of the group. . . . Each individual adjusts to the situation according to the way he perceives it and not as it "really" is. Since the leaders' perceptions of the prevailing attitude trends tend to be more realistic than those of non-leaders and isolates, the chances of their adequate adjustment are greater than those of non-leaders and isolates (5).

In our study, however, it is important to note that the relationship between sociometric standing and ability to predict accurately one's own sociometric status was significant only in the case of girls. This finding is in accord with the popular notion that women are more sensitive than men to interpersonal attitudes and are able to utilize this sensitivity to further their social effectiveness in group situations. We also tend to agree with Gage in believing that sensitivity to interpersonal attitudes leads to social effectiveness, rather than that interpersonal effectiveness puts persons in a more "strategic position" to develop "superior accuracy of social perception" (10). An alternative explanation, however, suggested by findings in several studies (5, 6, 13) is that individuals who are superior in a given trait tend to be superior in estimating the occurrence of that trait in themselves and others. Here the explanation of superior sociempathic ability would rest upon the possession of superior sociometric status, which would render the individual less defensive in evaluating this phenomenon as it related to himself.

In sharp contrast to these results was the finding that for both boys and girls there was zero relationship between sociometric status and ability to forecast *others'* sociometric status.

c. Relationship between sociempathic ability and teachers' ratings. Available to us in this study were ratings of our subjects by teachers on the following items: personal adjustment, scholastic competitiveness, magnitude of academic aspiration, and persistence. The ratings of five teachers were averaged and the mean ratings were then converted into standard scores. The coefficients of correlation between ability to perceive own sociometric status and mean teachers' ratings were all in the neighborhood of zero. The same was true for the r's between ability to perceive others' sociometric status and teachers' ratings.

As expected, the correlations between these teachers' ratings and sociometric status were all low and positive. In the order given above, they were .55, .45, .39, and .50.

Summary and Conclusions

The ability of a class of 44 high school juniors (*a*) to predict the sociometric ratings given them by their classmates, and (*b*) to predict the sociometric standing of their classmates was measured by means of discrepancy scores representing degree of divergence from actual sociometric ratings. Each student rated every other student on a five-point social distance (acceptance-rejection) scale, predicted how every other student would rate him on the same scale, and forecasted the sociometric status each of his classmates would earn on the basis of this same scale. From these data two discrepancy scores were computed for each individual: sociempathic ability (self) and sociempathic ability (others).

1. Sociempathic Ability (Self)

a. The discrepancy scores did not deviate significantly from the normal in distribution, and were reflective of an ability other than chance beyond the 1 per cent level of significance. The corrected odd-even reliability coefficient was .80. A subject's perceptions of the *individual* sociometric attitudes of others toward him tended to be significantly less accurate than his *mean* prediction of his own sociometric status.

b. Boys were able to predict more accurately the ratings given them by the opposite sex rather than by the like sex group. Girls, on the other hand, could perceive more accurately the ratings given them by the like sex group. Hence the sociometric attitudes of girls were *perceived* more accurately than those of boys by both sexes.

c. Girls were significantly superior to boys in predicting the ratings of their like sex group.

d. Individual measures of "projection" (the tendency for *A* to predict that *B* will rate him as he himself, *A*, rated *B*) were significantly correlated with discrepancy scores in girls, demonstrating that for this sex group "projection" enhanced accuracy of sociopathy because of a tendency toward reciprocity of sociometric ratings. Girls also showed a significant tendency to expect the same degree of acceptance from others as the latter in turn expected from them (mutuality of expectations).

e. "Social distance" exerted a significant influence on sociempathic ability. The more completely one individual accepted another the more accurate he was in perceiving the latter's sociometric attitude in relation to himself, and the more he tended to overestimate the favorableness of same.

2. Sociempathic Ability (Others)

a. The distribution of the discrepancy scores was not significantly different from the normal. These scores were indicative of an ability other than chance which was significant beyond the 1 per cent level. The corrected odd-even reliability coefficient was .76. *Individual* estimates of the sociometric status of others were significantly less accurate than were *means* of group estimates.

b. Boys were able to perceive the sociometric status of members of their own sex group better than that of the opposite sex group. Girls were equally well aware of the status hierarchies within either sex group.

c. Girls were significantly superior to boys in perceiving the status of their opposite sex group.

d. Projection was not a factor in either sex group in enhancing the *accuracy* of perception, but did influence the *direction* of the error of estimate. The subjects tended to overestimate the sociometric status of individuals they accepted and to underestimate the status of individuals they rejected.

e. The subjects perceived most accurately the status of individuals toward whom they were favorably disposed and *vice versa*.

3. General Findings

a. The ability to perceive own sociometric status and the ability to perceive others' sociometric status were completely unrelated in our sample.

b. Ability to perceive own sociometric status was significantly related to social effectiveness in girls as measured by sociometric status.

c. Sociempathic ability was unrelated to teachers' ratings of personal adjustment, scholastic competitiveness, magnitude of academic aspirations, and persistence. These latter ratings showed a low positive correlation with sociometric status.

d. The generality of these findings is open to question since our sample was obviously unrepresentative of mankind in general or even of adolescents in our culture. However, there is no *a priori* reason for believing that the relationships under investigation were in any way a function of the unique characteristics of our sample. It is entirely possible, of course, that these relationships are partly a function of developmental status, and this possibility will be investigated by analysis of comparable data gathered from a variety of age groups.

REFERENCES

1. Adams, H. F. "The Good Judge of Personality," *Journal of Abnormal and Social Psychology*, XXII (1927), 172–82.
2. Ausubel, D. P., Schiff, H. M., and Gasser, E. B. "A Preliminary Study of Developmental Trends in Sociempathy: Accuracy of Perception of Own and Others' Sociometric Status," *Child Development*, XXIII (1952), 111–28.
3. Bender, I. E., and Hastorf, A. H. "The Perception of Persons: Forecasting Another Person's Responses on Three Personality Scales," *Journal of Abnormal and Social Psychology*, XLV (1950), 556–61.
4. Chowdry, K., and Newcomb, T. M. "The Relative Abilities of Leaders and Non-Leaders to Estimate Opinions of Their Own Groups," *Journal of Abnormal and Social Psychology*, XLVII (1952), 51–57.

5. Cogan, L., Conklin, A., and Hollingworth, H. L. "An Experimental Study of Self-Analysis," *School and Society*, II (1915), 171–79.
6. Dudycha, G. J. "Self-Estimates and Dependability," *Journal of Social Psychology*, XII (1940), 39–53.
7. Dymond, R. F. "A Scale for the Measurement of Empathic Ability," *Journal of Consulting Psychology*, XIII (1949), 127–33.
8. ————. "Personality and Empathy," *Journal of Consulting Psychology*, XIV (1950), 343–50.
9. Fiedler, F. E., Hartmann, W., and Rudin, S. "The Relationship of Interpersonal Perception to Effectiveness in Basketball Teams." Urbana, Ill.: Bureau of Research and Service, University of Illinois, mimeographed, 1952.
10. Gage, N. L. "Explorations in the Understanding of Others," *Purdue University Studies in Higher Education*, LXXIX (1951), 86–96.
11. Gronlund, N. E. "The Accuracy of Teachers' Judgments Concerning the Sociometric Status of Sixth-grade Pupils," *Sociometry*, XIII (1950), 329–57.
12. Isaacs, K. S., Fiedler, F. E., and Fiske, W. E . "Some Factors Involved in the Understanding of Patients by Clinicians." Chicago: University of Chicago, mimeographed, 1950.

THE THREE-DIMENSIONAL BASIS OF EMOTIONAL INTERACTIONS IN SMALL GROUPS, PART I

By F. Kräupl Taylor

The Basic Emotional Variates Considered

The essential data necessary for the evaluation of emotional interactions among group members are of two kinds:

1) The feelings a subject entertains towards each of his group partners. These feelings will range from affection through indifference or ambivalence to hostility. They will be designated by the term "love-hate feelings" to indicate the polar extremes of this emotional variate.

2) The feelings a subject assumes that the various group partners entertain towards him. These assumptions appear to be guesses rather than observations—guesses, inspired by the subject's hopes and fears concerning the emotional appeal he has for others, and not firmly based observations of the feelings he has actually aroused in others. This emotional variate will be designated by the term "guessed self-appeal."

Love-hate feelings which are intense and positive are comparable to the sociometric choices elicited by means of Moreno's sociometric test (1951).

I must emphasize, however, that there are essential differences between Moreno's concept of sociometric choice and the concept of love-hate feelings which I am using. Love-hate feelings indicate an emotional variate ranging from strongly positive to strongly negative interpersonal effects. The sociometric choice of an associate, on the other hand, refers to only a limited range of positive feelings.

The second emotional variate with which I am concerned, the guessed self-appeal, ranges through the whole gamut of positive and negative feelings that a subject may assume to have aroused in his various group partners. The positive extreme of this emotional variate indicates the subject's conviction that he is loved by a group companion; its negative extreme reveals the subject's belief that a particular group member is his determined enemy who pursues him with intense hatred. In general, guessed self-appeal will, of course, refer to feelings of less extreme intensity.

A Three-Dimensional Frame of Reference for Emotional Interactions in Small Groups

It is possible to distinguish in a group three kinds of norms or standards which determine the distribution of group variables along three distinct dimensions: (a) a public dimension of variables which have reference to events in the whole group; (b) a dyadic dimension of variables which have reference to events in person-to-person interactions; and (c) an autistic dimension of variables which have reference to events in the intra-psychic sphere.

Public Dimension. Any activity by a group member which is performed in front of the group is a public activity and can be likened to the performance of an actor before an audience.

Dyadic Dimension. The attitude and qualities that characterize the dyadic relations of an individual are independent of the attitudes and qualities that characterize his public relations, and therefore independent of the various forms of public status that he acquires. In his dyadic interactions with different partners, a group member may, or may not, display his preferences and aversions, and he may, or may not, be sensitively aware of the differences of feelings which he arouses in his partners.

It must be mentioned that the distribution of dyadic variables in a group depends not only on the particular personalities of the group members, but also on the opportunity which the general group situation provides for making person-to-person contacts, and on the length of time the group has been in existence. Thus, in comparing dyadic variables in different groups, one has to take these two factors—the opportunity for dyadic contact, and the life span of the group—into account. Most of the groups examined in this paper were therapeutic groups, tested at a fairly early stage of their existence. The investigation, however, includes also some student groups which had offered to their members a better and more prolonged opportunity for person-to-person contact than had been the case in therapeutic groups. As expected, the student groups showed a greater degree of mutuality of love-hate feelings.

Autistic Dimension. A person who is required to assess his interpersonal feelings by introspective observation will inevitably be biased by very private and personal tendencies, desires, hopes, fears, and fantasies. A very important role in this respect will be played by his self-estimate of the kind of person he is, wishes to be, or fears himself to be. There will be a similar difference in the totals of the scores of guessed self-appeal between a person who believes, desires, or hopes to be popular, lovable, and loved in the group, and another person who feels or fears that he is criticized, unloved, and rejected.

Another autistic bias that will receive some attention is a bias that takes account of both the global biases mentioned above. This second-order variable relates to the tendency to assume (or to deny) that one's global emotional attitude towards the whole group is reciprocated by the whole group. This global reciprocity bias is of theoretical interest, as it seems to have some of its roots in certain naricissistic fantasies, such as the narcissistic fear of not receiving sufficient libidinal supplies from the group in spite of a liberal cathexis of libido in the group.

Not all autistic bias variables refer to the global relations between ego and total group. An autistic reciprocity bias can also be discerned in the dyadic relations between ego and individual partners; namely, the tendency to assume (or to deny) that the degree of love-hate feelings which is entertained towards different partners is reciprocated by these partners.

The Group Population Investigated

The reported results refer to the following groups: 16 therapeutic groups with a total membership of 112 persons (51 men and 61 women), and 4 student groups with a total membership of 39 persons (16 men and 23 women).

The members of the therapeutic groups were neurotic out-patients who attended group sessions once a week. These groups had a membership varying from 6 to 10. They differed with regard to sex composition; some contained only members of one sex, others of both. *Table 1* shows the different sex compositions of therapeutic groups.

TABLE 1   *SEX COMPOSITION OF THERAPEUTIC GROUPS*

Type of Groups	Males	Females	Total
3 all-male	22		22
5 all-female		32	32
8 male/female	29	29	58
16 therapeutic groups	51	61	112

Two of the student groups were University Extension Classes, and two were student classes of clinical psychologists and psychiatric social workers, respectively. These groups varied in size from 9 to 11. They were all mixed male/female in composition.

THE PUBLIC DIMENSION

In order to obtain an estimate of the hierarchies associated with the concepts of popularity and dominance, the group members can be asked to rank their companions with regard to them. From their rank scores it is possible to obtain variables which are then operationally defined, and which will be characterized by capital initials as Public Popularity and Public Dominance to distinguish them from the more vague and general concepts of popularity and dominance.

If the rank scores of the various group members are arranged horizontally, a matrix of a special kind is obtained which may be labelled a "ranked socio-matrix." An entirely fictitious example of such a matrix is illustrated in *Table 2*.

TABLE 2 *RANKED SOCIOMATRIX*

	A	B	C	D	
A		1	2	3	
B	1·5		1·5	3	
C	1	3		2	
D	2	1	3		
a-scale	4·5	5	6·5	8	Sum= 24
α-scale	75·00	66·67	41·67	16·67	Sum=200

The sum of all the rank scores given by any one individual to all his part-ners (i.e., the sum of all the rank scores in any one row) will be the same whether there are tied rankings present or not. This sum will be $\frac{1}{2}n(n-1)$, when n stands for the number of people in the group.

Had the group members been ideally competent in judging the public hier-archy in question, and had they been entirely impartial and unemotional in their estimates, their rank scores would have exhibited the highest possible con-cordance. *Table 3* shows a fictitious example of such a ranked sociomatrix of maximum concordance.

TABLE 3 *RANKED SOCIOMATRIX OF MAXIMUM CONCORDANCE*

	A	B	C	D
A		1	2	3
B	1		2	3
C	1	2		3
D	1	2	3	
a-scale	3	5	7	9
α-scale	100·00	66·67	33·33	0·00

If we add the column-scores in a ranked sociomatrix of maximum con-cordance we obtain a scale—here called an "a-scale"—which, because it is de-rived from hypothetical observers of ideal competence and impartiality, reflects accurately the true hierarchical distribution of the public variable assessed.

653

An analogous a-scale can be obtained by summing the column-scores of the ranked sociomatrix of *Table 2*, in which the concordance was not maximum. This a-scale in *Table 2* can therefore not be accepted as an entirely accurate measure of the true hierarchical distribution. The question then arises, how closely does it resemble the true hierarchy? Or, to use statistical phraseology, is it the "best available estimate" of the true hierarchy?

The Coefficient W' of Concordance

The higher the degree of concordance in a ranked sociomatrix, the greater will be the variance of the a-scale of column-totals. The coefficient W' of concordance is therefore expressed as the ratio between the variance found in a particular a-scale and the highest possible variance an a-scale of the same size can have (i.e., an a-scale derived from a ranked sociomatrix of maximum concordance).

The formula for the coefficient W' of concordance is

$$W' = \frac{S'}{\frac{1}{12}n^3(n^2-1) - n\underset{T'}{\Sigma}T'}$$

In this formula

n = number of group members;

$S' = \dfrac{n^2}{(n-2)^2}$ multiplied by the sum of squared deviations from the average in an a-scale;

$T' = \frac{1}{12} \underset{t}{\Sigma} (t^3 - t)$, where t refers a set of ties in any one row. If, for example, a row contained two sets of ties, of two and three items respectively, T' would be $\frac{1}{12}(6+24) = 2\frac{1}{2}$. Summing T' over all rows yields $\underset{T'}{\Sigma T'}$ in the above formula for W'.

The coefficient W' can range from zero (no concordance) to one (maximum concordance).

In almost all the twenty groups I examined (therapeutic and non-therapeutic), the group members were satisfactorily concordant in their estimates of the Public-Popularity status of their companions, and even more concordant in their estimates of Public-Dominance status. The average value (and standard error) of W' in estimating Public Popularity was ·57 ± ·03, and in estimating Public Dominance ·72 ± ·04. With one exception (concerning a Public-Popularity estimate), the concordance was always statistically significant and often very highly so. The aggregate significance of the average

W'-values is therefore extremely high, and there is no doubt that, in general, the a-scales of Public Popularity and Public Dominance can be regarded as the best available estimates of the true hierarchical distribution of these public phenomena.

A coefficient of concordance may be regarded as an indicator of "observer reliability."

We may therefore regard the average W'-values of ·57 and ·72 as measures of the average reliability of group members in judging Public Popularity and Public Dominance, respectively. The observer-reliability which is thus indicated, is not very impressive. The average observer-reliability, which we found, is only good enough to allow us to accept the general trends of the a-scales of Public Popularity and Public Dominance as practically satisfactory estimates of the true general trends of these hierarchies.

One may make it an arbitrary rule to accept as practically satisfactory only those a-scales of public phenomena which yield a coefficient W' of concordance of at least ·50.

A Method of Rendering a-scales Independent of Group Size

The scores of an a-scale depend, in part, on the size of the group from which they are derived. *Table 3,* for instance, shows that, in a group of four people, the smallest possible a-score is 3, and the highest possible a-score 9. In general, in a group of n people, the maximum range of a-scores extends from $(n - 1)$ to $(n - 1)^2$.

In order to free a-scores from their dependence on group size and to make them comparable, even if they have been derived from groups with widely different memberships, one can utilize the fact that the maximum range of a-scores is uniquely defined by n [the maximum range is $(n - 1)^2 - (n - 1) = (n - 1)(n - 2)$]. If we measure a-scores as deviations from the lowest possible value, and express these deviations as percentages of the maximum range, we obtain scores which are of comparable magnitude in groups of any size, and which have a maximum range from 0 to 100. These A-scores, as I shall call them, suffer, however, from a handicap which is due to their derivation from rank scores: the magnitude of a-scores and the magnitude of the status, indicated by them, are inversely related so that the lower the value of the a-score the higher is the status to which it refers, and *vice versa.*

It is, however, not difficult to eliminate this handicap. As the maximum range of A-scores is 100, it is merely necessary to subtract A-scores from 100 in order to obtain what will be called α-scores whose magnitude is directly related to the status they indicate.

The formulae transforming a-scores into α-scores are:

$$\alpha = 100 - A$$

$$A = 100 \frac{a - (n-1)}{(n-1)(n-2)}$$

α-scores can range from 0 to 100. Their average value in groups of any size is always 50.

Assessing One's Own Public Status

In order to obtain the necessary data, the group members were asked, after they had ranked their group companions with regard to Public Popularity and Public Dominance, to indicate which position they believed they themselves occupied in these hierarchies.

Our task was to compare these self-assessments with the corresponding a-scores. For this purpose the device was employed of converting the a-scale into a rank scale (ranging from ɪ to n) and of transforming the self-assessments into a rank scale of the same range. The rank-correlation coefficient between these two rank scales was then used to indicate how well the members of a group were aware of their own public status.

With regard to Public Dominance, the average rank-correlation coefficient was found to be + ·76 ± ·05, and in the case of Public Popularity it was + ·33 ± ·09. Both these average values are more than three times their standard errors, and therefore highly significant statistically.

The difference between these two average values is also highly significant (t = 4·314, D.F. = 26, P < ·001). If we regard these values as indicators of the average degree of insight group members have into their public status, we come to the conclusion that they are far better aware of their own dominance than of their popularity.

If we compare the average rank-correlation of the self-assessments of Public Dominance (i.e. ·76) with the average W'-value (which is comparable to the value of an average rank correlation) when the Public Dominance of others is assessed (i.e. ·72), we notice the close similarity of the two values. This suggests that group members have approximately the same knowledge of the dominance status of others as of their own.

With regard to Public Popularity, the analogous values are ·33 and ·57. The difference between these two average values is significant at the ·01 level (t = 2·831, D.F. = 32). It appears therefore that group members are, in general, less well aware of their own popularity than of that of others.

The Relationship between Public Popularity and Public Dominance

The respective α-scores of these two public variables were found to correlate + ·51. This correlation, though statistically highly significant, demonstrates only a moderate linkage between the variables. It indicates that a person who is very dominant will, more often than not, be also rather popular.

There will, of course, be many exceptions from this moderate tendency. Some group members, for instance, are very popular, though they take little part in group activities and are therefore non-dominant. Many of these members have been found to be women with a strong autistic desire for narcissistic supplies who constantly exert themselves to solicit affection even from people with whom they have only a tenuous social relation.

Of great clinical interest also are some of those group members who are highly dominant and yet unpopular. These members have, as I described in previous papers (1950a, 1951, 1952), a tendency to leave the group prematurely, giving very plausible reasons for their desertion. It also seemed that these dominant, yet unpopular members tended to occupy a particular position in the group which one might call the position of deputy leader, i.e. they tended to be second in dominance status and to compete for the first place.

The Relationship between a Member's Public-Popularity Status and the Love-Hate Feelings He Receives from His Partners

It is now necessary to investigate what relationship, if any, exists between public variables and the network of interpersonal love-hate feelings. The most important problem in this field concerns the variable of Public Popularity. We have seen that the group members have some knowledge of the Public-Popularity status of their companions, and we may therefore frame our question like this: To what extent are the interpersonal love-hate feelings of group members influenced by the status of Public Popularity which their companions occupy?

In order to elicit the love-hate feelings of group members two tests have been applied which have been termed, respectively, the primary ranking test of love-hate feelings and the questionnaire test.

The *primary ranking test of love-hate feelings* is analogous to the test by which the hierarchy of Public Popularity had been elicited. The group members were requested to rank their subjective preferences for their partners in the group. Their rank scores were arranged in the form of a sociomatrix ("primary rank matrix of love-hate feelings").

As these matrices contain the scores of subjective preferences, we shall expect them to have a smaller degree of concordance than the matrices of Public Popularity which contain estimates of an objective phenomenon. This expectation is indeed borne out. The average W'-value in 20 such primary rank matrices is ·37, compared with the average W'-value of ·57 in the Public-Popularity matrices. The difference is highly significant (t = 3·855, D.F. = 38, P = ·0001). This is proof that the group members understood and obeyed the different test instructions, and were able to distinguish between the introspective assessment of their own interpersonal feelings towards group partners and their objective estimate of the public status of these partners.

In the *questionnaire test* the group members were not asked to rank their preferences for different group partners, but to consider each partner in turn. They were therefore given (n − 1) questionnaire forms and on each form they answered four questions which referred to their love-hate feelings towards a particular partner.

The questionnaire replies were scored as follows: a reply indicating positive feelings (or the absence of negative ones) was given the score of + 1, a reply indicating negative feelings (or the absence of positive ones) the score − 1, and a reply indicating indecision or ambivalence the score zero.

The scores were arranged in matrix form as illustrated in *Table 4a*.

TABLE 4   (a) *MATRIX OF LOVE-HATE FEELINGS*

	A	B	C	D	E	Row-Totals
A		+2	+4	+4	−1	+ 9
B	+2		+2	−4	−1	− 1
C	+4	+4		+2	0	+10
D	+4	+2	0		−4	+ 2
E	+3	+3	−1	−2		+ 3
Column-Totals	+13	+11	+5	0	−6	+23

(b) *SECONDARY RANK MATRIX OF LOVE-HATE FEELINGS*

	A	B	C	D	E
A		3	1·5	1·5	4
B	1·5		1·5	4	3
C	1·5	1·5		3	4
D	1	2	3		4
E	1·5	1·5	3	4	
a–scale	5·5	8	9	12·5	15
α–scale	87·50	66·67	58·33	29·17	8·33

The rows of the matrix of love-hate feelings consist of absolute scores which can range from + 4 to − 4. The sum of these row-scores varies from person to person (as shown in the right-hand marginal column of *Table 4a*), according to their different autistic bias in introspective self-assessments.

The simplest way to eliminate this effect of the autistic variable is to transform the absolute row-scores into secondary rank scores and thus to equalize all the row-totals. This transformation leads to a secondary rank matrix of love-hate feelings (*Table 4b*).

The average W'-coefficient of concordance in these secondary rank matrices of love-hate feelings was found to be ·35; that is, it was of the same size as that found in the primary rank matrices of these feelings.

The column-totals in both the primary and the secondary rank matrices indicate the popularity which group members enjoy in direct interpersonal relations. We may therefore speak of a variable of Interpersonal Popularity.

We have two estimates of this variable in the α-scales derived, respectively, from primary and from secondary rank matrices. If we assume that the tests by which these two estimates were obtained are of approximately equal power as measuring instruments of Interpersonal Popularity, we shall expect a high correlation between the two α-scales. The correlation is, in fact, + ·88.

This indicates a fairly high test reliability. By adding the two α-scales we could further improve it to the very satisfactory value of + ·94 (attributing equal weight to the primary ranking test and the questionnaire test, and applying the Spearman-Brown prophecy formula). However, instead of merely adding the two α-scales, I have preferred the more exact way of adding, in each group, the primary and secondary rank matrices. In the resulting matrix the row-scores were re-converted into rank scores. This final matrix may be termed a combined rank matrix of love-hate feelings. The average W'-value in these matrices was ·37. The α-scale derived from them will be used as the best available estimate of the distribution of Interpersonal Popularity.

By correlating Interpersonal Popularity and Public Popularity we can obtain an answer to our original question, namely, the extent to which the interpersonal feelings of group members are influenced by the Public-Popularity status of their partners.

The correlation coefficient was found to be + ·81 (N = 115). This indicates that group members are influenced in their feelings for group companions by their conscious or unconscious awareness of the popularity which these companions publicly enjoy in the group, and that this influence is so marked that it almost completely obscures the fact that genuinely personal feelings, unaffected by the partners' public status, do exist in many dyadic relationships.

Indeed these personal dyadic feelings must be regarded as mainly responsible for the rather low average W'-value of ·37 in the rank matrices of love-hate feelings.

It seems that the influence which Public Popularity exerts on the network of interpersonal love-hate feelings is not the same in all-male and in all-female therapeutic groups. In three all-male groups with a total membership of 22 the correlation coefficient between Public and Interpersonal Popularity was only + ·62; whereas in three all-female groups with a total membership of 19 it was as high as + ·93. The difference between these coefficients is significant at the ·01 level of confidence.

This finding suggests that women, when in groups composed of members of their own sex only, model their interpersonal love-hate feelings to a much greater extent on the Public-Popularity status of their partners than is the case with men in all-male groups.

The fairly close parallelism between the distributions of Interpersonal and of Public Popularity in male/female groups brings with it a practical advantage. In these groups it is sometimes of interest to discriminate between the public popularity which group members enjoy with their own and with the opposite sex. These two types of popularity we shall distinguish by the adjectives "homo-social" and "hetero-social"—terms which were introduced by Flugel (1927) to indicate the social aspects of homo- and hetero-sexual relationships.

We cannot, however, obtain measures of homo-social and hetero-social popularity from matrices of Public Popularity as these deal exclusively with the status achieved in the whole group audience of both men and women. But some measure of these sex-linked popularities can be derived from combined rank matrices of love-hate feelings as it is possible to subdivide them into sections containing only homo-social or hetero-social relationships.

The average α-score of homo-social popularity in all the 74 group members was 55·07 ± 2·83, and the average α-score of hetero-social popularity 45·97 ± 2·70. The difference between these averages is significant at the ·03 level ($t = 2·298$, D.F. = 146). If the differences between the corresponding homo- and hetero-social α-scores of the individual members are considered, and a single-sample t-test applied, a significance level of almost ·001 is attained ($t = 3·024$, D.F. = 73).

We may conclude therefore that a slight, but distinct tendency exists in small groups which renders members, whether male or female, more popular with their own than with the opposite sex.

The correlation between homo- and hetero-social popularity was found to be $+ \cdot 41$ (N $= 74$). This is highly significant statistically, but does not indicate a close correspondence between the degrees of popularity which members achieve with the male and female sections of their groups.

Guessed Self-appeals and the Variable of Attributed Interpersonal Friendliness

So far I have only considered love-hate feelings. A subject's guessed self-appeals (i.e., his estimates of the feelings or preferences he believes himself to have aroused in his partners) can be elicited by means of a primary ranking test and a questionnaire test.

The primary ranking test yields primary rank matrices of guessed self-appeals. The columns of these matrices indicate the degree of interpersonal friendliness which is attributed to individual members by the group members generally. The a-scores of column-totals in these matrices thus correspond to the distribution of a variable which one may call the variable of Attributed Interpersonal Friendliness. These a-scores can be transformed into α-scores to make their values independent of group size.

The questionnaire test yields a matrix of guessed self-appeals (comparable with the matrix of *Table 4a*) which can be transformed into a secondary rank matrix of guessed self-appeals (comparable with the matrix of *Table 4b*) by converting the absolute row-scores into rank scores.

The α-scales of Attributed Interpersonal Friendliness derived, respectively, from primary and secondary rank matrices of guessed self-appeals, have a correlation coefficient of $+ \cdot 77$, indicating a test reliability of $\cdot 87$ in a combined scale. By adding the primary and secondary rank matrices, and re-ranking the resulting row-scores, combined rank matrices of guessed self-appeals are obtained. The α-scale derived from them will be used as the best available estimate of the distribution of Attributed Interpersonal Friendliness.

One might expect that this variable of Attributed Interpersonal Friendliness is related to a public phenomenon, namely, the degree of general friendliness publicly exhibited by the various group members. There are, however, some indications that such an expectation is likely to be disappointed and that the relationship between Attributed Interpersonal Friendliness and publicly exhibited friendliness will not be found to be as close as the relationship between Interpersonal and Public Popularity.

One such indication is that the average coefficient W' of concordance is only $\cdot 27$ in the combined rank matrices of guessed self-appeals. This is significantly lower than the corresponding W' of $\cdot 37$ in the combined rank matrices of love-hate feelings (t $= 2 \cdot 46$, D.F. $= 38$, P $= \cdot 02$). The fact that the concordance of guessed self-appeals is so low suggests that group members base their guesses chiefly on considerations of their dyadic relations and fail to take adequate account of any public phenomenon which—as in the case of love-hate feelings—might have introduced some semblance of agreement into the divergencies of their dyadic scores. Whatever general friendliness a partner exhibited to the group as a whole, seems to have impressed his companions less than the emotions he displayed—or was felt to have displayed—in his private dyadic dealings.

The correlation coefficient of Attributed Interpersonal Friendliness with Public Popularity is + ·62 (N = 115), and with Interpersonal Popularity + ·63 (N = 151). As we do not know to what extent Attributed Interpersonal Friendliness represents a public phenomenon of overtly expressed friendliness, we cannot interpret the first of the above coefficients as indicating either that people who are overtly friendly gain public popularity, or that people who are publicly popular are regarded as friendly towards everybody. But the second of the above coefficients refers to interpersonal—or more exactly, dyadic—data, and this suggests the possibility that the marked positive correlation is due to the working of an autistic influence, namely, of a bias to assume reciprocity of love-hate feelings in dyadic relations. Such a bias, which would tend to equalize the scores of a person's love-hate feelings and guessed self-appeals, undoubtedly exists, but its detailed consideration will be reserved for a later publication.

Homo- and hetero-social α-scales of Attributed Interpersonal Friendliness can be obtained by a procedure similar to that employed in the case of Interpersonal Popularity. The average homo-social α-score for the 41 men and 50 women in these groups was 57·25 ± 2·29; the average hetero-social α-score was 44·41 ± 1·94. The difference between these averages is highly significant (t = 4·282, D.F. = 180, P < ·0001).

There is, therefore, a slight but definite tendency among both the male and female members of male/female groups to attribute a greater degree of friendliness to members of their own sex.

THE THREE-DIMENSIONAL BASIS OF EMOTIONAL INTER-
ACTIONS IN SMALL GROUPS, PART II*

By F. Kräupl Taylor

The Autistic Dimension

In this section I shall be mainly concerned with two autistic variables which refer respectively to two global biases. The variables will be operationally defined and designated "Love-Hate Bias" and "Self-Appeal Bias," and they refer respectively to the bias to profess a particular degree of love-hate feelings towards the group as a whole, and the bias to profess a belief in arousing a particular degree of love-hate feelings in the group as a whole.

To arrive at an estimate of such an autistic variable we can utilize only the absolute scores of the questionnaire test. These scores yield matrices of love-hate feelings or of guessed self-appeals (cf. the matrix of *Table 4a*). In such matrices the row-scores add up to different totals as is shown in the right-hand marginal column of *Table 4a*.

In order to eliminate the potentially distorting effect of the variable column-totals on the row-totals (a distortion which owes its origin to the blank principal diagonal in a sociomatrix), we shall use the same procedure as that by which we obtained secondary rank matrices; but this time it is the scores in the columns which have to be transformed into secondary rank scores, thus equalizing all the column-totals.

In this way the matrix of *Table 4a* is converted into a matrix of Love-Hate Bias which is shown in *Table 5*.

A matrix of Self-Appeal Bias is similarly derived from a matrix of guessed self-appeals.

In such a bias matrix all the column-totals are the same and equal $\frac{1}{2}n(n-1)$.

The a-scores of row-totals in the right-hand column can be rendered largely independent of group size by converting them into α-scores, using the formulae shown on page 454, *Human Relations*, 1954.

The coefficient W', when applied in bias matrices, is, of course, not a criterion of concordance; on the contrary, in these matrices it is a criterion of the discordance and diversity which exists among the global bias attitudes of

* I am greatly indebted to the Board of Governors of the Bethlem Royal and the Maudsley Hospital for a grant from the Research Fund for the purpose of this study.

663

TABLE 5   *MATRIX OF LOVE-HATE BIAS*

	A	B	C	D	E	a-scale	α-scale
A		3·5	1	1	2·5	8	66·67
B	4		2	4	2·5	12·5	29·17
C	1·5	1		2	1	5·5	87·50
D	1·5	3·5	3		4	12	33·33
E	3	2	4	3		12	33·33
						50	250

group members. The higher the W'-value, the greater are the differences of global bias among individual members of that group.

The average W'-values (and their standard errors) in our 20 groups were:

	Average W'
Matrices of Love-Hate Bias	·26±·03
,, ,, Self-Appeal Bias	·35±·03

The difference between these average W'-values is significant at the ·05 level (t=2·1, D.F.=38). When a single-sample t-test is applied to the mean of differences between the W'-values, the level of significance is raised to almost ·01 (Mean Difference=·09, t=2·82, D. F.=19).

This result indicates that when group members assess the kind of appeal they have for others they may be governed by autistic motives far more than when they assess their love-hate feelings towards others.

Homo- and Hetero-Social Scores of Love-Hate Bias

In groups containing both sexes the Love-Hate Bias of group members towards their own and the opposite sex can be separately assessed.

The average homo-social value of Love-Hate Bias in the 11 male/female groups with a total membership of 91, in which homo- and hetero-social scores could be assessed, was found to be 51·92±2·04; and the average hetero-social value 48·31±2·02. The difference between these values is not significant.

The correlation coefficient between homo- and hetero-social scores of Love-Hate Bias was +·28 (N=91) which, though significant statistically, indicates only a relatively minor correspondence between the average person's Love-Hate Bias towards the same and the opposite sex in his group.

Homo- and Hetero-Social Scores of Self-Appeal Bias

The average homo-social value of Self-Appeal Bias was 53·37±2·20, and the average hetero-social value 47·33±2·12. The difference between these values is too small to be statistically significant. Yet the application of a single-sample t-test to the differences between individual homo- and hetero-social scores reveals that there is a significant tendency to assume greater popularity in global relations with the same than with the opposite sex (Mean of Differences=6·03, t=2·95, D.F.=90, P=·01).

The correlation coefficient between homo- and hetero-social scores of Self-Appeal Bias is +·42 (N=91), which is very highly significant and suggests that, in some persons at least, fantasies concerning narcissistic supplies from others apply equally to male and female companions.

Global Reciprocity Bias

It is plausible to expect that the autistic scales of Love-Hate Bias and Self-Appeal Bias are not independent. There may be a general bias among group members to assume that their global feelings for or against the group are reciprocated by the group. One may term this bias a "Global Reciprocity Bias" to distinguish it from a "Dyadic Reciprocity Bias," which refers to the assumption that the *individual* group partners reciprocate the feelings directed towards them. (The Dyadic Reciprocity Bias need not to be the same as the Global Reciprocity Bias.)

The existence and degree of a Global Reciprocity Bias can be easily assessed by calculating the correlation coefficient between α-scales of Love-Hate Bias and Self-Appeal Bias in our 20 groups. This coefficient was found to be +·37 (N=151). It indicates a significant, but not a very marked tendency on the part of group members in general to expect that their global love-hate feelings are requited.

It is, however, likely that a distinction should be made between the Global Reciprocity Bias in men and in women. There is some evidence that the two sexes differ in their readiness to assume a reciprocity of feeling, at least as far as their global homo-social relations (in both one- and two-sex groups) are concerned. The relevant correlation coefficient for men is + ·57 (N=63), and for women +·29 (N=82). The difference between these coefficients is significant at the ·05 level.

Does Love-Hate Bias Influence Public Behavior in Small Groups?

The specific problem is this: Is the overt and public behavior of group members influenced by their Love-Hate Bias or Self-Appeal Bias? As a criterion of overt and public behavior the status of Public Popularity will be used. I shall therefore deal with the questions, whether and to what extent global love-hate feelings towards the group, or the assumptions of being popular (or unpopular) in the group, tend to determine manifest behavior so distinctly that the positions of popularity are thereby affected.

If we want to examine the influence of Love-Hate Bias and of Self-Appeal Bias separately, we have to keep the effect of one of the bias scales constant by partial correlation. The partial correlation coefficients between Love-Hate Bias or Self-Appeal Bias and Public Popularity are presented in *Table 6*.

TABLE 6   *PARTIAL CORRELATION COEFFICIENTS BETWEEN LOVE-HATE BIAS OR SELF-APPEAL BIAS AND PUBLIC POPULARITY*

Groups	N	Love-Hate Bias	Self-Appeal Bias
All-male	22	− ·41	+ ·37
All-female	19	+ ·34	+ ·28
Male/female:			
Male homo–social	34	+ ·07	**+ ·45**
Male hetero–social		+ ·04	+ ·05
Female homo–social	40	**+ ·38**	+ ·17
Female hetero–social		**+ ·38**	+ ·27
One- and Two-sex:			
Male homo–social	56	− ·13	**+ ·43**
Female homo–social	59	**+ ·36**	+ ·20

Significant coefficients are in heavy type.

The results of this table had not been anticipated. It had been tacitly expected—in accordance with the stereotyped concepts of masculine and feminine qualities in our culture—that men would be true to their own feelings towards the group and that, in so far as public behavior was influenced by global bias, the behavior of men would candidly reveal their Love-Hate Bias; whereas women had been supposed to depend more on the impression they believed to have made, and thus to reflect in their public behavior their Self-Appeal Bias rather than their love-hate feelings for the group.

The partial correlation coefficients in *Table 6* do, if anything, contradict this stereotyped assumption. If we jointly consider global homo-social relations of men in both one- and two-sex groups we find that the difference between the partial correlation coefficients is significant beyond the ·01 level. There can therefore be little doubt that men in our groups have, in their homo-social relations, not lived up to expectations based on the social stereotype of masculinity; their public homo-social behavior has not been true to their real global feelings towards other men, but has been influenced rather by autistic fantasies of their homo-social appeal, so that men who believed themselves popular with their male companions tended to adopt a public role which made them popular with those companions, whereas men who thought they were disliked by other men behaved towards them in such a way that they tended to become unpopular.

The women in our groups also tended to belie their social stereotype. In their global homo-social relations in both one- and two-sex groups they had a certain tendency to act in accordance with the Love-Hate Bias they professed to entertain towards their female groups companions. The relevant partial correlation coefficient of $+{\cdot}36$ is significantly different at the $\cdot01$ level from the corresponding male homo-social coefficient of $-{\cdot}13$.

In their global hetero-social relations, women had a similar tendency to reveal their love-hate feelings in overt behavior. Self-Appeal Bias also seems to have had some influence on the homo- and hetero-social public behavior of women, though it was less marked than the influence of Love-Hate Bias.

AWARENESS OF ONE'S SOCIAL APPEAL

By F. Kräupl Taylor*

In this paper it is proposed to examine the degree to which group members become aware of the love-hate feelings they arouse in their dyadic relationships (i.e., the "awareness of dyadic self-appeal").

THE PRESENT INVESTIGATION

An individual's awareness of his dyadic self-appeal is expressed in β-scores.

If an individual were fully aware of all his dyadic self-appeals in a group, his β-score would be 100, the highest possible score. The lowest β-score will generally be zero, but an occasional negative score is not impossible under freak conditions. The chance average of random β-scores would be 50.

Among the 158 patients in our 23 therapeutic groups, the average β-score of awareness of self-appeal was found to be 63·73 and the standard deviation was 17·54. The median was 64·72, which indicates that the distribution of β-scores has a slight negative skew. The distribution is shown in *Figure 1*.

The deviation of this distribution from the normal curve is not marked enough to be statistically significant.

Approximately three-quarters of all β-scores are above the chance level of 50 ($Q_1 = 49·42$). The average β-score of 62·73 $\pm$ 1·40 is very significantly higher than the chance β-value of 50. There can, therefore, be no doubt that the therapeutic group members have some awareness of their self-appeal in dyadic relations.

But the degree of awareness indicated by these β-scores in therapeutic groups falls very far short of anything approaching accuracy. The result merely demonstrates that a sufficient number of group patients had enough inkling of the kind of feelings they had evoked in some of their partners for, in the aggregate, a significant statistical result to ensue.

The average β-score in our five student groups was 73·83 $\pm$ 2·02 ($N = 47$), i.e. it was 11·10 points higher than the average β-score in therapeutic groups. This difference is highly significant ($t = 3·9$; d.f. $= 203$; $P = ·0001$).

The difference in the β-scores in the two kinds of group is most likely due to the fact that the students had known each other longer than the members

* I am greatly indebted to the Board of Governors of the Bethlem Royal and the Maudsley Hospital for a grant from the Research Fund for the purpose of this study.

FREQUENCIES

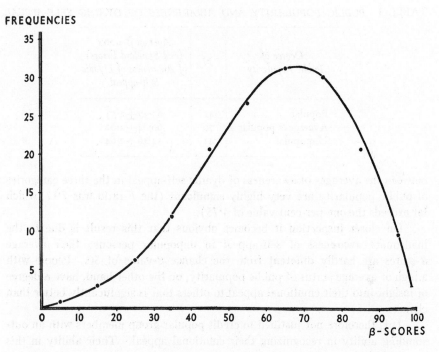

FIG. 1 β-SCORES OF AWARENESS OF SELF-APPEAL IN 23 THERAPEUTIC GROUPS
(Smoothed Distribution)

of therapeutic groups, and had had a better opportunity of becoming acquainted with each other.

An interesting question was the relation between awareness of self-appeal and the status of public popularity. Are popular group members more sensitive to, or more skilled in perceiving, the emotions they have aroused in others than unpopular group members?

Public popularity has been measured in α-scores (7), which are independent of group size, and extend from zero (lowest popularity) to 100 (highest popularity), with an average value of 50.

Let us designate as popular all group members who have α-scores of public popularity of 70 or more; as unpopular all group members with α-scores of 30 or less; and as averagely popular those with α-scores between 30 and 70. The average degree (and standard error) attained by persons in these three categories of public popularity is shown in *Table 1*.

An analysis of variance of the data in *Table 1* shows that the differences

TABLE 1   *PUBLIC POPULARITY AND AWARENESS OF DYADIC SELF-APPEAL*

Degree of Public Popularity	N	Average β-scores (and Standard Errors) of Awareness of Dyadic Self-appeal
Popular	41	63·37±2·53
Averagely popular	76	66·84±2·02
Unpopular	41	54·46±2·64

between the averages of awareness of dyadic self-appeal in the three categories of public popularity are very highly significant (the *F*-ratio was 7·17, which far exceeds the one-per-cent value of 4·75).

On closer inspection it becomes obvious that this result is due to the inadequate awareness of self-appeal in unpopular persons; their average β-scores are hardly different from the chance β-value of 50. People with a high or average status of public popularity, on the other hand, have a degree of insight into their emotional appeal to others that is significantly better than chance.

It is therefore not justified to credit popular group members with an out-standing ability in recognizing their emotional appeal. Their ability in this respect is, in fact, no better than that of group members whose popularity is no more than average. It is more correct to say that unpopular persons differ from other group members in that they are rather obtuse in recognizing the feelings other persons entertain towards them.

DISCUSSION

In order to avoid the possibility of misunderstanding and confused think-ing, it seems advisable to make a distinction between the recognition of emo-tions in others generally, and the recognition of those emotions that are directed at us very personally. This paper deals only with the second kind of emotion. It is at least theoretically possible that some people are good judges of those emotions in others that do not concern them, but bad judges of feelings of which they are the direct recipients.

Another potential source of misunderstanding lies in the disregard of the difference between global and dyadic judgments. For example, it might be said that a paranoid person does not recognize the feelings other people entertain towards him because he assumes that everybody is against him, that he is generally disliked and unpopular. But such a statement merely refers to the global bias of certain paranoid individuals who have a low score when assessed with regard to the autistic variable of global "self-appeal bias." Yet in spite of this constant and indiscriminate misjudgment, paranoid persons may still be correct in assessing the variability of feelings towards them in their dyadic partners. In other words, people with a low score of "self-appeal bias" might still have a high score of "awareness of dyadic self-appeal." This particular combination of scores did, in fact, occur in some members of our therapeutic groups, but it was by no means frequent. In general, the two variables—the global self-appeal bias and the awareness of dyadic self-appeal—were found to be independent.

It was found that unpopular persons tended to be quite ignorant of their dyadic appeal. It may be that the unpopularity of these people was caused by their obtuse misjudgment of the feelings of others towards them, and by the gauche and ill-adapted behavior to which their misjudgment may have given rise. But it may also be that both unpopularity and ignorance of dyadic self-appeal had their origin in the fact that the person concerned had been unable, for one reason or another, to establish sufficiently close and congenial relations with his group companions.

THE TRANSPARENCY OF INTERPERSONAL CHOICE[1]

By Renato Tagiuri, Nathan Kogan, Jerome S. Bruner

The organization of behavior within a group is necessarily dependent upon a certain level of knowledge by its members of their preferences for one another. Are the preferences of the members of a group for each other known to their companions? Does preference involve a distinctive kind of behavior that is visible to the other members of the group? What are some of the factors that determine the degree to which the sociometric choices of a particular member will be known? These are the questions with which this investigation is concerned.

The more usual approach to the problem of whether and to what degree the preferences of people in groups are known to each other is to study the accuracy of social perception (8). Here, rather than asking about the characteristics of the perceiver, we turn the problem around and ask about the characteristics of those whose preferences are to be perceived. In particular, our interest is in the *transparency* of people, the ease with which others can spot their preferences.

Subjects and Procedure

Five groups of Navy enlisted personnel with 12, 12, 15, 16 and 22 men respectively were used as subjects (cf. Table 1). In each case the groups had been working and living together for at least two months on board ship as members of CIC teams.

The following group procedure was used. *First,* the subjects were requested to indicate those of the crew with whom they would like to spend a 72 hours liberty ("choices"). *Second,* they were asked to guess who would choose them as companions for a 72 hour liberty ("guesses"). Following these two questions, the members were instructed to underline the three persons they preferred most among their choices and guesses, or if they had made fewer than three choices (or guesses) to add enough names to bring the list up to three. Thus, the procedure made available data obtained under both free and fixed conditions. In the *third* question, the subjects were asked to put themselves in the other fellow's place and try to figure

---

[1] This work was done in the Laboratory of Social Relations, Harvard University. The project was sponsored by the United States Navy under ONR Contract No. N5ori-07646. This is one of a series of studies of interpersonal perception carried through as part of the development of a method—relational analysis—described fully elsewhere (1).

out which three men he would choose to go with him on liberty. The *fourth* question was of the same type as the third, but subjects were asked to identify individuals whom each of the other members would feel chosen by.[2]

A more detailed description of the procedure can be found elsewhere (1, 7, 9). The information provided here is sufficient, however, for a discussion of the issue in question.

THE TRANSPARENCY SCORE

Consider now how the transparency score of a subject is obtained. Recall that a subject S_i chooses three of the N-1 members and omits the rest. Similarly, another subject S_j is asked to make three choices on behalf of S_i. We can represent this as follows:

Member	1	2	3	4	5	6	7	8	9	10	11
S_i's choices	x			x		x					
S_j's choices for S_i				x		x					x

S_i chooses members 1, 4, and 6, and S_j thinks that S_i chooses members 4, 6, and 11. The transparency of S_i for S_j is measured in terms of the number of matches out of the 11 possible ones existing between S_i's allotments of choices and omissions and S_j's corresponding allotments on S_i's behalf. In the above example, the number of matches equals nine. Next, the scores of all the other members with respect to S_i are added to obtain what we have called the subject's (S_i) transparency score. Thus, a subject's maximum possible transparency is $(N-1)(N-1)$, in this case 121, and his minimum transparency equals $(N-1)(N-1-6)$ or 55.

The above considerations specify the range within which the transparency scores will fall. If, however, we are interested in whether an individual's transparency is above chance, we have to determine whether his score deviates from what it would be if the others were guessing blindly.[3] Since this is a case of the "matching problem", it is possible to compute the expected number of matches and its variance (5).

---

[2] In the present paper we shall not be concerned with data obtained from the fourth question.

[3] Several chance models are conceivable. The one we choose corresponds to the case where the members are regarded as automata allocating their selections at random. The assumptions inherent in the model are these. First, independence is assumed between the different choices made by any single individual, and between his choices and his guesses. Second, the choices and guesses of any subject are taken to be independent from those of any other subject. Finally, there is the restriction that a subject may not choose or guess the same other person more than once.

First, we obtain the extent to which, on the average, the choices of a member will be known by any other member of the group on the basis of chance performance. In the case where the number of choices permitted is three, the expression for this expected mean is

$$E = \frac{(3)^2 + (N-4)^2}{N-1}$$

Since a transparency score is based upon the judgments of each of the $N-1$ other members, we multiply the above expression for E by $N-1$ to obtain a member's expected transparency score. For the 12 man group, then, a member's expected transparency is $(N-1)E = 73$. E has a variance of

$$Var_E = \frac{1}{N-2} \left\{ E(E + N - 1) - \frac{2}{N-1} \left[(N-4)^3 + (3)^3 \right] \right\}$$

Again, this must be multiplied by $N-1$ to obtain the expected variance of the mean transparency score based on chance expectancy. The resulting SD for the 12 man group is 4.6.

COMPARISON OF OBSERVED AND EXPECTED TRANSPARENCY

Table 1 contains the basic transparency data for the five groups comprising a total of 77 subjects. In every group the mean observed transparency scores are significantly above chance expectancy. In addition, the great majority of *individual* transparency scores (75%) are more than 2 SD's above the expected mean. Just four out of the 77 subjects have trans-

TABLE 1

DATA ON TRANSPARENCY OF CHOICE

		Chance Expectancy		Mean	Observed Distribution in SD Units Relative to Chance Expectancy					
Group	N	Mean	S.D.	Observed	−2 and below	−2 to −1	−1 to 0	0 to +1	+1 to +2	+2 and above
H	22	333	5.28	368.3	1	0	0	0	3	18
B	16	153	4.97	177.0	0	0	0	2	1	13
F	14	130	4.73	146.8	0	1	0	1	2	11
S	12	73	4.58	85.5	0	0	1	1	2	8
M	12	73	4.58	86.2	0	1	0	0	3	8
	77				1	2	1	4	11	58

parency scores below chance expectancy, and of these only one is significantly below chance.

That the distribution of transparency scores lies almost entirely two standard deviations above chance expectancy, however, does not imply that we are dealing with a narrow range of transparency scores. In the following section we investigate factors that determine individual differences in transparency.

DETERMINANTS OF TRANSPARENCY

We shall start by assuming that the extent to which a member's preferences are known to the rest of the group is a function of the cue qualities of his interpersonal behavior. Thus, excessive reserve or excessive friendliness on the part of a member may make it difficult for others to identify his choices. Similarly there may be cues provided by the behavior of others toward the member. It may, for example, be particularly difficult to identify the choices of a member who is not chosen by anyone. Finally some cues may emerge from the very nature of the interaction between the member and the others.

Reciprocation

Analysis discloses that the extent to which a member's choices are known depends upon the number of mutual relationships in which he is involved. There is a significant rank-order correlation between a member's transparency score and the number of his *fixed* choices that are reciprocated by a *fixed* choice (Table 2). When no distinction is made as to whether the *reciprocating* choice is free or mixed, the correlations are still positive but smaller in every case.

TABLE 2

RANK ORDER CORRELATION BETWEEN TRANSPARENCY AND NUMBER OF RECIPROCATED CHOICES

Group	N	Reciprocation of fixed choices by	
		fixed choices only	both fixed and free choices
H	22	.58**	.47*
B	16	.59*	.34
F	15	.66**	.42
S	12	.84**	.64*
M	12	.65*	.57

* Significant at the .05 level.
** Significant at the .01 level.

What cannot be shown in terms of these correlations, however, is whether transparency is a function of the reciprocated relationship itself, or of the personality of the individual who tends to be found in mutual dyads. The transparency of a man's choices may well be a function of the type of person he is, rather than of the particular phenomenal saliency of his mutual relationships. If, however, the mutuality of the choice, rather than the style of the chooser were the source of cues revealing the object of the choice, then it should follow that, for any specific individual, his reciprocated choices should be consistently more transparent than his unreciprocated choices.

To inquire into this matter, those individuals who were involved in both reciprocated and non-reciprocated relationships were subjected to further analysis. The frequency with which members recognized the subject's reciprocated choices was compared with the frequency with which they recognized his unreciprocated choices. In order to give as clear an answer to this question as possible, *fixed* choices reciprocated by a *free* choice were not included in this analysis. Only members who had one or two reciprocated choices could be used, cases with no reciprocated choices or with three reciprocated choices clearly not lending themselves to this form of analysis. This left 34 cases in all—ten from group H, eleven from B, four from F, six from S and three from M (Table 1).

Transparency of reciprocated choices exceeds transparency of non-reciprocated choices made by the same individual, in all but three of the 34 cases. According to the Dixon and Mood sign test (5) these results are significant beyond the .01 level. Transparency is clearly a function of mutuality of choice when "personality" is held constant. This finding does not, of course, exclude the possibility of certain personal qualities influencing transparency, when mutuality is held constant. We shall turn to this question in a later section.

So far the analysis of transparency has been carried out exclusively on the data obtained under fixed conditions. This was done to make possible a stringent comparison with chance levels of transparency. While this form of analysis is in keeping with the instructions given to the subjects—to put themselves in the other fellow's shoes and guess which *three* men he would choose—the reader may well have wondered about the effect which other than fixed choices may have had upon transparency.

It will be recalled (cf. Table 2) that the correlation between transparency and reciprocation decreased for every group when choices could be reciprocated by either a fixed or a free choice, as compared to the case in which reciprocation by fixed choices only was considered. We wondered whether this difference might be related to the fact that the fixed choices are the ones subjects declare to be their strongest (cf. instructions to subjects). Pairs made up of mutual fixed choices might involve a more intimate association between the members than mutual relationships composed of a fixed choice on the part of one member and a fourth, fifth, or nth choice on the part of the other. We speculated, then, that mutual relationships composed of high priority choices would provide more salient cues as to a member's preferences than would the less intense relationships. The lower correlation when reciprocation by either free or fixed choices is considered may, however, be due to the fact that under these conditions the range of reciprocated choices is narrower. For, while members cannot have more than three reciprocated fixed choices, inclusion of free choices boosts the number of reciprocations of members who had fewer than three.

Fortunately we are in a position to test the relative contribution to transparency of free and fixed reciprocating choices. Table 3 shows the mean transparency of members who have zero, one, two, and three choices reciprocated by fixed choices (cf. over-all means). Each level of fixed reciprocation is further differentiated according to how many among a member's fixed choices are reciprocated by a free choice. By reading down each column it can be seen that additional reciprocations by *free* choices do not raise transparency. It is clear, then, that a fixed choice reciprocated by a free choice does not provide as perceptible a cue about whom a subject is choosing as does a fixed choice reciprocated by another fixed choice. This is a rather important finding, because it indicates that the first few choices (which in our case happen to be the fixed choices) correspond most closely to distinguishable behavior.

While we find that a subject's transparency is not materially affected as a result of reciprocation by free choices, we cannot maintain that reciprocations involving free choices have no effect whatsoever upon transparency, until we examine the influence exerted by the reciprocation of a member's own free choices. If free choices play any role in transparency, we should find that reciprocations occurring outside a subject's three fixed choices have the effect of misleading observers as to the identity of his three fixed choices, thereby lowering the transparency of that subject. The larger the number of such extra reciprocations, the greater should be the amount of interfering cues. Our hypothesis, then, is that if the manifestations of free choices are perceptible, there will be an inverse relationship between transparency and such extra reciprocations. This hypothesis can be tested by computing the correlation between these two variables *within* the cells of Table 3, thus holding constant both the number of fixed choices reciprocated by *fixed* choices and the number of fixed choices reciprocated by *free* choices. The rank order coefficients vary from .76 to —.36, with an approximate

TABLE 3

TRANSPARENCY AS A FUNCTION OF FIXED CHOICES RECIPROCATED BY FIXED AND FREE CHOICES, AND OF RECIPROCATED FREE CHOICES

Number of fixed choices reciprocated by a free choice	Fixed choices reciprocated by a fixed choice			
	0	1	2	3
0	32.3	47.0	59.0	75.6
	.76* 6†	—.19 8	—.36 10	.10 9
1	20.6	47.6	62.0	
	.02 9	—.01 16	.43 6	
2	21.0	45.0		
	.40 6	.31 7		
3	—— 0			
Over-all means	24.0	46.8	60.1	75.6
Frequency	21	31	16	9

Note.—This table is based on percentile rank scores. The raw transparency scores of members are a function of group size. In order to make members of groups of various sizes comparable, these raw transparency scores were converted into percentile rank units. This involves a rank-ordering of the raw transparency scores of members, and dividing the member's rank by N. If this value is subtracted from 100, high percentile rank scores refer to high transparency.

* Correlation (rho) between extra reciprocations and transparency.

† Cell frequency.

average of .16. Clearly, then, there is no evidence in favor of an inverse relationship between the transparency of a subject and his number of extra reciprocations. As a result, we feel quite confident in claiming that given our procedure, reciprocations containing free choices have a negligible influence on a subject's transparency.

It was also shown that reciprocation is an important determinant of the transparency of a choice. Different choices made by the same member differ in transparency, and his reciprocated choices are more transparent than his non-reciprocated ones. This can be taken to mean that when we consider a member's preferences for other group members, we utilize his behavior toward others as well as others' behavior toward him. If one develops an hypothesis that a given member likes another member on the basis of the first member's behavioral manifestations of choice, that hypothesis is further confirmed by the second member manifesting reciprocation. *It is the interaction between two persons that is evaluated.*

The correlation between reciprocation and transparency hovers somewhat over .6. Reciprocation, therefore, can account for only part of the variance in transparency. Factors other than mutuality affect transparency. Indeed it was shown that with mutuality held constant systematic relationships were found to hold between transparency and four measures of individual difference—i.e., expansiveness, self-confidence, popularity and responsiveness. Thus we inferred that each of these measures also must be related to manifestations that have cue value in revealing a member's preferences.

The fact that group members can be arranged in order of transparency suggests that it may be possible to refine the analysis of studies of accuracy of interpersonal perception by specifying more exactly the difficulty of the perceptual task for the various members of the group. Clearly, the most transparent subject is left to judge a set of less transparent persons. He has the most difficult task in the group. The opposite holds for the least transparent member. In the present study for example, the event to be judged is such that the most popular members are the most transparent. Transparency correlates highly (better than .5) with popularity, a relation mediated by the fact that the popular members' choices are most often reciprocated. So in this case the less popular members have the relatively easier judgments to make and vice versa. It is possible, however, that when the event to be judged is different from the one in this study, other sets of members may be the most transparent.

These considerations may have to be taken into account not only in studies of perception of interpersonal feelings—as illustrated by some of the writers' work (8)—but in any investigation of interpersonal perception where the subjects serve both as judges and as stimulus objects. It is possible that these circumstances may well play a role in some of the investigations such as the well known study by Chowdhry and Newcomb (2), comparing the relative ability of leaders and non-leaders to estimate opinions of members of their own groups.

As we have indicated, results obtained in such studies may be related to factors other than *ability* in judging social events, and the inconsistency of results obtained from investigations (e.g., 3, 6) similar to Chowdhry and Newcomb's may be due to factors such as we have described.

SUMMARY

The present paper examines the problem of transparency, i.e., the extent to which a subject's preferences are known to the other members of a group. We first compared subjects' transparency scores to the level of transparency that would be expected if members judged a subject's choices on a random guessing basis. Approximately seventy-five per cent of the subjects in a group have transparency scores significantly in excess of chance expectancy. The mean observed transparency scores are also significantly above chance in each group.

Next, we explored factors responsible for individual differences in transparency. The most striking relationship discovered was that reciprocated choices are far more transparent than those not reciprocated. Significant rank-order correlations were obtained between a member's transparency score and the extent to which his fixed choices are reciprocated by a fixed choice. It was further shown that the transparency of the reciprocated choices of a member significantly exceeds the transparency of the unreciprocated choices made by that same member. The finding clearly indicates that transparency is predominantly a function of mutuality of choice rather than of personal characteristics of the member involved in reciprocal relationships.

In addition we found that reciprocation by a free choice contributed far less to the recognizability of choice than did reciprocation by a fixed choice.

We next asked whether transparency is related to personal dimensions when the mutuality level is held constant. Expansiveness, self-confidence, popularity, and responsiveness bear a relationship to transparency that depends upon the mutuality level. When the level of mutuality is high (two or three), an inverted U-shaped function is obtained. Transparency achieves maximum values when expansiveness, self-confidence, popularity, and warmth are in the middle range. When the subject has no reciprocated choices, on the other hand, high expansiveness and self-confidence are associated with relatively higher transparency scores. The inverted U-trend does not occur.

The Transparency of Interpersonal Choice

The greater transparency of the reciprocated choices may be understood if we consider reciprocity as providing the perceiver with a double source of choice cues, i.e., the manifestations of the member whose choice is to be identified, and the manifestations of choice on the part of the reciprocating member. While transparency has been shown to be in large part a dyadic phenomenon, we found that personality factors do play a role in transparency over and above the effect of reciprocation.

REFERENCES

1. Bruner, J. S. and Tagiuri, R. Annual Technical Report No. 2, ONR Contract N5ori-07646. Laboratory of Social Relations, Harvard University, March 1, 1953, mimeographed.
2. Chowdhry, Kamla and Newcomb, T. M. The relative abilities of leaders and non-leaders to estimate opinions of their own groups. *J. abnorm. soc. Psychol.*, 1952, 47, 51-57.
3. Hites, R. W. and Campbell, D. T. A test of the ability of fraternity leaders to estimate group opinion. *J. soc. Psychol.*, 1950, 32, 95-100.
4. Jennings, Helen H. *Leadership and isolation.* New York: Longmans Green, 1950.
5. Mosteller, F. and Bush, R. R. Selected quantitative techniques. In G. Lindzey (Ed.) *Handbook of social psychology.* Cambridge, Mass.: Addison-Wesley, 1954. I: 289-334.
6. Sprunger, J. A. Relationships of a test of ability to estimate group opinion to other variables. Unpublished master's thesis, Ohio State Univ., 1949.
7. Tagiuri, R. Relational analysis: An extension of sociometric method with emphasis upon social perception. SOCIOMETRY, 1952, 15, 91-104.
8. Tagiuri, R., Blake, R. R. and Bruner, J. S. Some determinants of the perception of positive and negative feelings in others. *J. abnorm. soc. Psychol.*, 1953, 48, 585-592.
9. Tagiuri, R., Bruner, J. S. and Kogan, N. Estimating the chance expectancies of dyadic relationships within a group. *Psychol. Bull.*, 1955, 52, 122-131.

JUDGMENTAL RESPONSE SETS IN THE PERCEPTION OF SOCIOMETRIC STATUS[1,2]

By Herbert Schiff

THE PROBLEM

In recent years much interest has been manifested in the processes involved in the social perception of one's relative standing in the group in which one holds membership (1, 2, 6, 11, 15, 19). A review of pertinent literature appeared in this journal recently (3a).

Studies of this problem have concerned themselves with relating accuracy of social perception to leadership ability (4), and to clinical (8) and social effectiveness (10). Accuracy of social perception has been operationally defined in these studies as the ability to predict sociometric status, attitudes, traits or self-concepts of others. The findings of these several investigators, however, do not suffice to support the hypothesis that accuracy of social perception is positively related to effectiveness in inter-personal relationships. Other aspects of this perceptual ability, therefore, warrant investigation. Awareness of own and others' status and of others' attitudes or traits may be influenced by tendencies in an individual: (a) to make constant errors of prediction or estimation (i.e., consistent under- or over-estimation of self or others), (b) to reciprocate his own expectations, and (c) to perceive himself as more or less accepting of others than other individuals in the group are. These influences in part will determine an individual's ability to accurately predict the relative degree of acceptance or rejection accorded the component members of the group (including himself) by the other group members.

Since it would be very helpful to have measures of these perceptual-judgmental response sets, a major aim of this study is to evolve such measures. Another purpose is to develop variations of existing methods of research on social perception. A third purpose of the present research is to study the way in which an individual perceives his fellow group members and is in turn

[1] This paper is a condensation of a Ph.D. dissertation submitted to the Graduate College of the University of Illinois, Urbana, Illinois, May, 1953.

[2] Sociometric status is the degree of acceptance-rejection afforded each individual by the members of his group. Perception of sociometric status refers to an individual's awareness of how well each member of the group, including himself, is accepted by all the other group members.

perceived by them, and to ascertain how these perceptual dimensions relate to general adjustment level, status within the group, accuracy of social perception, and feelings of anxiety and self-regard.

Specifically the problems which this study is concerned with are:

1. To investigate perceptual-judgmental sets which are reflected in the sociometric perceptions of individuals. This includes such variables as the tendency: (a) to consistently under- or overestimate in the perception of one's own and others' status; (b) to consistently perceive oneself as reciprocating or not reciprocating the sociometric ratings one expects from others; (c) to consistently perceive oneself as a very accepting or unaccepting individual.
2. To determine the stability and generality of these various perceptual dimensions and their relation to accuracy of perception of own and others' social status.
3. To determine the relationships between these perceptual-judgmental traits and: (a) perceptual judgments in related areas; (b) general adjustment; (c) anxiety; (d) sociometric status; (e) feelings of self-regard; and (f) belongingness in the group.

PROCEDURE

POPULATION

The population consisted of 141 high school students from the University High School in Urbana, Illinois. The entire junior and senior class of 1950-51 and the junior class of 1951-52 were used. Socio-economic status for the group as a whole was above average. The parents of the University High School students are for the most part professional persons, a large percentage of whom hold academic appointments in the University of Illinois. Entrance into the school, however, is unrestricted, except for the payment of a nominal tuition fee. The mean age of these students was 16.2 years. The sex distribution was 55 boys and 86 girls.

METHOD

Several types of instruments were used to obtain measures of sociometric status, sociempathic ability, various perceptual sets used in estimating sociometric status, personality adjustment and level of aspiration. These instruments will be described below.

The sociometric perception scale consisted of space for identification information (e.g., name, age, sex, date, class), and three lists of the names of all the pupils in the class. The texts of the sociometric questions were:

Next to each student's name you are to place a number from one to five. "One" means you do not want this student to be your friend at all.

"Two" means that you would not like to have this student as a friend. "Three" means that you do not care whether or not this student is your friend. "Four" means that you would like to have this student as your friend. "Five" means that you would like to have this student as one of your best friends.

Scale instructions for the second list were comparable to those indicated above but reflective of ratings expected from others, (i.e., "one" means that you think, "This person does not want me as a friend at all").

List three required each student to rate each of his classmates in terms of popularity in the class. The instructions were: "One" means that you think this student is one of the least popular students in the class, that he is one of the students with the fewest friends. The complete scale was described in similar vein, "five" indicating the most popular persons, "three" the average persons, "two" and "four" those of less or more than average popularity but not selected as least or most popular. (For a complete account of the text used and administration of the test see reference 2, pp. 114-115.)

A sociometric status score and six discrepancy scores were derived from this scale.

Sociometric Status. The sociometric status score indicates how each student is actually rated by his classmates. This score was obtained for each student from the data on page two of his classmates' booklets where each student rated every other student in terms of acceptance-rejection on a five-point scale. The sociometric status score is the mean of all the ratings which each student receives from his classmates. A high score indicates high sociometric status or acceptance. A low score indicates low sociometric status or rejection. The sociometric status score pattern shows the general nature of the social structure of the group. It is a function of "tele" (15), a reflection of the mutual attraction between one individual and each of the other members of the group.

Sociempathic Ability. Two measures of sociempathic ability—accuracy in perceiving own and others' sociometric status—were obtained:

(a) *The "self-accuracy"* score was obtained for each individual by summing the discrepancies (without regard to sign) of his predictions of how others would rate him (page three of his sociometric scale) from the actual ratings given him by these persons (page two of the sociometric scale of his classmates). This score is a measure of one aspect of sociempathy—ability to perceive one's own sociometric status within a group in which one holds membership. Low self-accuracy scores indicate accuracy in perceiving one's own status in the group.

(b) *The "other-accuracy" score* was derived for each student by summing the discrepancies (without regard to sign) between all of the individual predictions made by a subject of the sociometric status of the other members of his group (page four of the sociometric scale) and the corresponding sociometric status scores (see above) of the latter. This score is a measure of a second aspect of sociempathy—ability to perceive the sociometric status of other members of one's group. Low other-accuracy scores indicate accuracy in perceiving the status of others.

Perceptual Sets in Estimating Sociometric Status. Four different scores, reflective of different aspects of perceptual set in predicting sociometric status, were obtained:

(a) *The "self-direction" score* is a measure of an individual's tendency to consistently[3] under- or overestimate in predicting his own sociometric status in the group of which he is a member. The self-direction score is a discrepancy score obtained for each student by algebraically summing the differences between the student's predictions of how each of the persons in the class will rate him (this data is taken from page three of the sociometric scale for each pupil) and the actual ratings he receives from his classmates (this data is taken from page two of the sociometric scales of his classmates). A high *positive* self-direction score indicates that an individual consistently tends to overestimate his own sociometric status. A high *negative* self-direction score indicates that an individual consistently tends to underestimate his own sociometric status. Scores approaching zero (low positive or low negative scores) indicate that an individual does not consistently tend to make extreme estimates of his own status in either direction.

(b) *The "other-direction" score* is a discrepancy score obtained for each student by algebraically summing the discrepancies between the student's predictions of the mean sociometric ratings, which his classmates will receive from the group (this data is obtained from page four of his sociometric scale) and their actual sociometric status. The other-direction score is a measure of the tendency for an individual to consistently under- or overestimate in predicting the sociometric status of other members of the group. High *positive* other-direction scores indicate a consistent tendency to over-

---

[3] Consistent under- or overestimation is defined in terms of total discrepancy score. This leaves open the possibility that some individuals could make a high score by just making a few very high estimates in one direction which counteract a larger number of small estimates made by them in the opposite direction. This was true, however, of only 2% of the population. The remainder in each extreme group are those who make a high proportion of estimates in the direction indicated.

estimate the sociometric status of others. High *negative* scores indicate a consistent tendency to underestimate the sociometric status of others. Scores approaching zero indicate no consistent tendency to over- or to underestimate the status of others.

(c) *The "reciprocity" score* is a measure of an individual's tendency to perceive himself as under- or over-reciprocating the acceptance tendered him by other members of the group. The reciprocity score was derived by algebraically summing the differences between the ratings which each student gave to his classmates (page two of the sociometric scale) and his predictions of how each of his classmates would rate him (page three of the sociometric scale). High *positive* reciprocity scores indicate that one consistently gives higher ratings to others than the ratings one expects to receive from others. High *negative* reciprocity scores indicate that one consistently gives lower ratings to others than one in turn expects to receive. Scores approaching zero indicate a tendency to give others the same ratings that one expects to receive from them.

(d) *The "acceptance" score* was derived by algebraically summing the differences between the student's sociometric ratings of his classmates (page two of the sociometric scale) and his predictions of the sociometric status of his classmates. The acceptance score is a measure of an individual's tendency to perceive himself as more or less accepting of others relative to his perception of the group's acceptance of others. High *positive* acceptance scores indicate that one consistently perceives oneself as more accepting of others than the group is. High *negative* acceptance scores indicate that one consistently perceives oneself as less accepting of others than the group is.

MEASURES OF PERSONALITY ADJUSTMENT

The Minnesota Multiphasic Personality Inventory Score. Standard instructions were used for the administration and scoring of the Minnesota Multiphasic Personality Inventory (12).

To derive total adjustment scores from the Minnesota Multiphasic Personality Inventory, raw scores on each of the subscales were first converted into standard scores. Since a positive standard score on a given subscale indicates a degree of deviancy with respect to the trait measured that is greater than the mean of our particular population, we were able to obtain an indication of total personality deviancy for each individual by summing all of his positive standard scores on the various subscales. In the case of the masculinity-femininity scale, since a negative standard score is indicative of inappropriateness relative to sex role, it (rather than a positive standard score) was added to the other subscale standard scores to obtain the M.M.P.I. adjustment score. The higher M.M.P.I. scores, therefore, are indicative of relatively poorer personality adjustment.

Rorschach Adjustment and Anxiety Scores. The administration of the Rorschach Group Test followed the procedure developed by Harrower and Steiner (13). The scoring of the records was in accord with the modified scoring system developed by Klopfer and Kelly (14). Each protocol was systematically surveyed through the use of the comprehensive and relatively objective check-list devised by Munroe (16). This check-list provides criteria for a "normal" range for each type of response determinant. Entries in the checklist are made whenever the subject's performance deviates from the normal range. The sum of these entries provides an adjustment rating score. Hence, a high Rorschach adjustment score is indicative of poor adjustment.

The Rorschach anxiety score was derived by crediting a subject with one point for each anxiety sign[4] manifested in his test booklet. High Rorschach anxiety scores are indicative of a relatively high degree of anxiety, and vice versa.

Teachers' Ratings of Adjustment. The teachers of the junior and senior classes were asked to rate their students on personal adjustment (integration, balance, emotionality, home relationships) on a 5-point scale (excellent to poor). (The mean intercorrelation between the ratings of six teachers was

---

[4] The following Rorschach "signs" were used as a guide in determining the anxiety rating for each subject (3, 7, 14).

1. The total number of card rejections (rej.).
2. The percentage of responses: (a) to the whole card (W) ; (b) of oligophrenic details (O) ; (c) of unusual details (Dd) ; (d) using human movement (M) ; (e) using form as a sole determinant, and the quality of the form (F+, F—).
3. Diffuse shading response (K, KF, kF).
4. The ratio of human detail to complete human figure responses; the ratio of human detail and animal detail to human and animal responses (Hd:H; Hd+Ad:H+A).
5. Content analysis: Threatening, vague, evasive responses, noncommittal comments, etc.
6. Signs of shading shock (Sh. S.) ; Impoverished content, decline in form quality, irregular succession, avoidance of use of texture as a determinant, decrease in ability to see popular (P) responses, etc.
7. Color balance (FC:CF+C).

.64,[5] indicating a fair degree of reliability). The ratings of five teachers on each pupil, were then averaged to give a teachers' adjustment rating score.

Composite Adjustment Score. The M.M.P.I., Rorschach and teachers' adjustment scores, each in the form of standard scores for the population tested, were averaged to provide a composite adjustment rating score for each student.

LEVEL OF ASPIRATION MEASURES

Laboratory Measures. Three paper-and-pencil, level of aspiration tests (speed of reading, arithmetic and digit symbol) were administered individually to each pupil by the investigator. In order to secure ego-involvement, tests presenting tasks with academic connotations were selected, and the importance of the skills involved in these tasks for a wide variety of academic and vocational situations was explained to the subjects.

Speed of reading was measured by the number of sentences a student was able to complete on Form II of the Michigan Speed of Reading Test in a trial of 90 seconds.

The arithmetic test consists of four pages, each of which contains 144 one-place addition and subtraction examples. The subject attempts to complete as many examples as he possibly can on each page (trial) in the course of 60 seconds.

The digit-symbol test requires the subject to substitute geometric symbols for numbers (1-9) in accordance with a code which is presented with the material. The test consists of four pages requiring 100 substitutions. The time limit for each page (trial) is 60 seconds.

The reading, arithmetic and digit symbol tests are all speed rather than power tests. They involve simple tasks of approximately uniform difficulty. Four trials, each with the same time limit, were given for each task. An adequate ceiling, in terms of number of units presented for the stated time limits, was provided so that no individual in the population could complete all units for a given trial.

In each of the three paper-and-pencil tests, level of aspiration for the *first* performance was ascertained after exhibiting the material and explaining the conditions of the test. The subject was asked:

How many sentences (examples, units) like this do you think you could do in 90 (60) seconds? Make the very best estimate you can.

---

[5] Mean intercorrelations were obtained by transforming each r into corresponding Fisher's Z coefficients, finding the arithmetic mean of the Z's and converting the mean Z back to the corresponding r.

After the first performance, the subject was told his score and was asked to predict his score on the second trial. This procedure was repeated until four trials were completed. A prediction for the fifth trial was obtained, but a fifth trial was not administered.

Two types of discrepancy scores were derived from reported performance and level of aspiration: (a) goal discrepancy scores and (b) goal tenacity scores.

(a) *The goal discrepancy score* in each instance was determined by subtracting the reported score on a given trial from level of aspiration for the immediately succeeding trial. Thus, four goal discrepancy scores were available for each type of test material without making use of the initial level of aspiration obtained prior to performance on the first trial. The goal discrepancy scores were converted into standard scores for each type of test material treated separately. These standard scores were then averaged to provide a composite goal discrepancy score or measure of level of aspiration for each individual. A high composite goal discrepancy score indicates that an individual tends to maintain striving at a high level in relation to previous performance or that he is relatively optimistic in predicting future performance on the basis of past performance.

(b) *The goal tenacity score* refers to the relationship between the goal discrepancy score and feelings of success or failure emanating from the previous performance. These feelings are defined operationally in terms of the *performance discrepancy score,* or the difference between actual performance and the prior level of aspiration for it. Four goal tenacity scores were derived. This was done by algebraically subtracting from each goal discrepancy score the preceding attainment discrepancy. This latter discrepancy (indicative of feelings of success or failure in relation to past performance), in turn, was calculated by subtracting from each performance (including the first trial) the preceding level of aspiration for that performance. A high composite goal tenacity score indicates that an individual tends to maintain striving at a high level in relation to previous feelings of intra-serial success or failure, or that he is relatively optimistic in predicting future performance on the basis of previous success and failure experiences.

Academic Goal Discrepancy. Upon the completion of this testing session each student was asked to predict the grade-point average he would receive at the end of the current semester. The discrepancy between this prediction and the student's composite grade-point average prior to the current semester was used as an index of academic level of aspiration.

In addition to the descriptions and definitions of scores given above, the following sub-groups may be defined:

(a) *Self-underestimators* are those individuals who obtain high *negative* self-direction scores. They consistently tend to underestimate their own sociometric status in relation to their actual status.

(b) *Self-overestimators* are those individuals who obtain high *positive* self-direction scores. They consistently overestimate their own sociometric status in relation to their actual status.

(c) *Other-underestimators* are those subjects who obtain high *negative* other-direction scores. They consistently underestimate the sociometric status of others relative to their actual status.

(d) *Other-overestimators* are those subjects who obtain high *positive* other-direction scores. They consistently overestimate the sociometric status of others relative to their actual status.

(e) *Under-reciprocators* are those subjects who obtain high *negative* reciprocity scores. They consistently tend to perceive themselves as less accepting of others than others are of them.

(f) *Over-reciprocators* are those subjects who obtain high *positive* reciprocity scores. They consistently tend to perceive themselves as more accepting of others than others are of them.

(g) *Under-acceptors* are those subjects who obtain high *negative* acceptance scores. They consistently tend to perceive themselves as less accepting of others than the group is.

(h) *Over-acceptors* are those subjects who obtain high *positive* acceptance scores. They consistently tend to perceive themselves as more accepting of others than the group is.

In succeeding portions of this paper we shall refer to the measures of the four different perceptual sets in estimating sociometric status as our *major* independent variables. Measures reflective of sociempathic ability (accuracy in perceiving sociometric status) will be considered as subsidiary independent variables. The major dependent variables are: (a) level of aspiration measures designed to test the generality of perceptual sets in estimating sociometric status in another area of judgment (i.e., the estimation of future performance in relation to the quality of previous performance and in relation to previous feelings of success and failure); (b) measures of personality adjustment; and (c) sociometric status.

692

RESULTS
THE INDEPENDENT VARIABLES
Reliability

The reliability coefficients (split-half method, corrected) of the major independent variables are quite high. For the self-direction score $r = .94$, for the other-direction score .88, for the reciprocity score .97, and for the acceptance score .92. These are of the same order of magnitude as those generally found by previous investigators using similar types of measures (1, 2, 6, 9). These findings indicate that the perceptual personality traits investigated in this study have sufficient stability (i.e., generality over persons) despite their heterogeneous nature, not only for personality research, but also for purposes of prediction in individual cases.

Interrelationships between the Major Independent Variables Eestimation of Own Sociometric Status. The intercorrelations between the major independent variables indicate a significantly better than chance relationship between the self-direction scores and both the reciprocity and acceptance scores. Self-direction correlated negatively with reciprocity (— .32**),[6] and positively with acceptance (.36**). These correlations show that those who consistently *overestimate* their own sociometric status tend to expect that they will receive higher ratings from others than they themselves are willing to give. Such persons also tend to perceive themselves as more accepting of others than other individuals in the group are or as more generous than the group in accepting others. That is, self-overestimators perceive themselves as both highly accepting of others and as highly acceptable to others. This is in line with Sheerer's (18) finding that persons who accept themselves tend more to accept others. On the other hand, those who consistently *underestimate* their own sociometric status tend to expect *lower* ratings from others than they in turn give, and they see themselves as *less* accepting of others than the group. That is, self-underestimators perceive themselves as both not very accepting people and as less acceptable to others, and perceive other group members as more accepting than they really are.

Estimation of Others' Status. The correlations obtained between the other-direction scores and both reciprocity and acceptance were significant but in a direction opposite to those found between the latter variables and estimation of own status. Other-direction scores correlated positively with reciprocity scores (.29**) and negatively with acceptance scores (— .41**).

---

6 ** r significant at the 1% level of confidence or better.

These correlations show that those who consistently *overestimate* the socio-metric status of others have the same pattern of perceptual intercorrela-tions as self-*under*estimators. They tend to have low expectations for self and to perceive themselves as less accepting of others than other individuals in the group are. Other-*underestimators,* on the other hand, have high self-expectations and perceive themselves as more accepting of others, as did the *self-over*estimators.

A reasonable inference that might be drawn from the above findings of similar social perceptual patterns between self-underestimators and other-overestimators might be that feelings of low self-regard are associated with a consistent tendency to both underestimate self and to overestimate others. This inference of low self-regard is made more tenable by the fact that both these groups have low self-expectations, i.e., tend to expect lower ratings of acceptance from others than they give in return. It would seem that rather than reciprocating in actuality the low ratings they expect from others, these individuals project their perception of self as less acceptable to others by perceiving themselves as less accepting than others. The fact that they perceive the group as more accepting than they are might also mean that they perceive the group to be overly accepting in relation to everyone else but themselves.

Those individuals who do not consistently over- or underestimate in predicting either their own or others' status, or who do not do so to any appreciable extent, tend most to give ratings similar to those they expect to receive, and to perceive themselves as neither more nor less accepting of others than the group is. Hence, they seem to differ from the extreme over- or underestimators of self and others' status in being guided more by what they perceive as the group's norms in rating others (including themselves). That is, they use what they perceive as the group norm as a reference frame upon which to base their ratings of others rather than the personal judgments which the two preceding groups use. The individuals in this middle group of the direction score distribution are more influenced in their ratings of self and others by their *perceptions* of how others feel; whereas the two extreme groups of the direction score distribution are guided more in their ratings of self and others by internal aspirational needs, by self-perceptions, and by their own individual affective reactions to people. The extreme groups are presumably more independent and less group-suggestible than the middle group is in their affective responses to associates.

The intercorrelations of the four major independent variables indicate that a different perceptual trait is probably being measured by each of the two direction scores, and that the reciprocity and acceptance scores, too, are independent of each other. The low and not significant correlation between the self-direction and other-direction scores (.12) suggests that an individual's tendency to consistently make relatively high or low predictions in estimating his own sociometric status stems from other source traits or different need patterns than does the tendency to consistently over- or under-predict in estimating the sociometric status of others. This also appears to be true of the determinants underlying perception of self as an accepting (acceptance score) and as an acceptable (reciprocity score) person, since the correlation between reciprocity and acceptance scores (.04) too was low and not significant.

The analysis of these independent traits, by a comparison of the means of the extreme score groups on each variable (Table 1), confirmed the relationships found between the direction scores and both the reciprocity and acceptance scores in the preceding correlational analysis made for the entire population.

Relationships between the Direction Scores and Sociempathic Ability. Low accuracy scores indicate little error in predicting sociometric status or high sociempathic ability. On the other hand, low direction scores indicate consistent underestimation of sociometric status whereas high direction scores indicate consistent overestimation of sociometric status. Thus the significant correlations between the self- and other-accuracy scores and the self- and other-direction scores (.55** and .37**, respectively), mean that those who are most accurate in the perception of own sociometric status tend to underestimate in predicting their own status; and those who are most accurate in the perception of others' status tend to underestimate in predicting the status of others.

Although an explanation of the relationship between over- or under-estimation of others' status and sociempathic ability is not immediately apparent, some conclusions can be drawn with respect to self-under- and over-estimation and sociempathic ability. Self-overestimators, as indicated above, perceived themselves as highly accepting and as highly acceptable persons. In addition, they tend to set higher levels of striving for themselves than did self-underestimators, and they tended to maintain these levels even in the face of failure experiences. In general, therefore, they present a picture of expansiveness in which more is expected than objective reality warrants. Their perceptual or judgmental set is distorted by strong ego needs for success and for acceptance by others.

Self-underestimators, however, perceived themselves not as very accept-

TABLE 1

Significance Levels of the Differences between the High and Low Groups on a Given Independent Variable with Respect to Scores on Other Independent Variables

High and Low Groups on a Given Independent Variable	Self-Direction Scores			Other-Direction Scores			Reciprocity Scores			Acceptance Scores		
	N	M	S.D.	N	M	S.D.	N	M	S.D.	N	M	S.D.
Self-Underestimators	19	−2.12	.42	19	.44	1.44	20	−.73	1.48	20	.78	.86
Self-Underestimators	19	−2.12	.42	19	.14	1.44	21	.31	1.0	21	−.44*	.96
Other-Underestimators	20	.04	1.14	20	−.98	1.08	20	−.14	.92	20	−1.01	.94
Other-Overestimators	20	.42	1.72	20	1.81*	.89	20	−.45	1.51	20	.91*	.91
Under-reciprocators	21	−.84	1.40	21	.13	1.61	23	−1.70	.87	23	−.18	1.22
Over-reciprocators	16	.27*	1.18	16	−.54	.42	17	1.31*	.46	17	.28	.88
Underacceptors	19	.66	1.02	19	−.30	1.13	21	−.27	.90	21	−1.68	.49
Overacceptors	22	−1.15*	1.10	22	.87*	1.36	23	−.26	1.44	23	1.44*	.39

An * placed between two means indicates that their difference is significant at the 1% level of confidence.

ing people and as on the giving end of relatioships. They adjust their aspiration level more readily and realistically in accordance with their performance and their feelings of success or failure. They thus tend to be less euphoric, more realistic and less motivated by ego-enhancement needs in making judgments of their own actual status than self-overestimators are.

Another possible explanation of the finding that self-underestimators make higher accuracy scores than self-overestimators is that it may be quite threatening for a student to admit that others do not accept him (give him a low status rating). Certainly it is easier to admit that one is accepted than not accepted. Hence we would expect that underestimators would not rate themselves as extremely at the low end of the rating scale as overestimators would at the upper. This inclination to minimize one's undesirable sociometric position and to maximize a desirable one could be the explanation of the greater accuracy obtained by the understimators. Cogan and Conklin (5) found that the greatest tendency toward overestimation occurs with respect to the most desirable traits. Therefore, since self-overestimation could be expected to overestimate their popularity (a desirable trait) to a greater extent that self-underestimators would tend to admit to unpopularity, they are understandably less accurate in perceiving and predicting their actual status.

Relationships between the Independent and Dependent Variables Relationships between the Independent Variables and Measures of Level of Aspiration. Evidence for the generality of the consistent self-prediction tendencies measured by the independent variables was sought by comparing the extreme score groups on these variables with respect to level of aspiration and goal tenacity scores. Significant differences between the mean level of aspirations and goal tenacity scores of the extreme groups were only obtained with respect to self-judgments (the self-direction and reciprocity groups.) A significant difference was obtained between the mean composite level of aspiration scores of the high and low self-direction groups ($t = 2.30$) and of the high and low reciprocity groups ($t = 2.94$). The high and low reciprocity groups also obtained significantly different mean goal tenacity scores ($t = 2.27$) (the above t values were each significant at the 1% level of confidence). These findings indicate that those individuals who consistently overestimated in predicting their own sociometric status, also overestimated in predicting their future performance levels on tasks presented to them. In addition, they tended to maintain higher levels of striving (though not significantly so statistically, $p > 10\%$) without much reference to fluctuations in the quality of their preceding performance.

Those who consistently maintained high self-expectations with respect to sociometric status (under-reciprocators), also overestimated their future performance levels on laboratory tasks and maintained their high levels of striving in the face of failure experiences to a significantly greater degree than those whose self-expectations were consistently low (over-reciprocators).

Since the composite level of aspiration scores and the composite goal tenacity scores both measure responses in several different task situations, the above findings may be interpreted as reflective of a generalized personality trend within an individual. Specifically, the personality (judgmental or perceptual trend measured by the self-direction, reciprocity, composite level of aspiration and goal tenacity scores may be conceptualized as a more or less typical or self-consistent way in which an individual tends to respond in making self-judgments based upon his perception of social or task situations.

Relationship between the Independent Variables and Measures of Adjustment. Comparison of the mean adjustment scores obtained by the high and low groups on the independent variables indicate that adjustment is not significantly influenced by an individual's perceptual-judgmental sets with respect to *others'* status and with respect to perceived acceptance tendencies in self and others. On the other hand, *self*-judgments were found to be significantly related to adjustment. Self-underestimators were found to have better adjustment scores than self-overestimators (t = 2.58*) (Table 2).

Self-underestimators might conceivably be better adjusted than self-overestimators despite lower self-regard, because they are more realistic. This finding is in agreement with Chowdry and Newcomb's (4) conclusion that those individuals whose perceptions tend to be more realistic are more likely to achieve adequate adjustment. Since the self-underestimators were also more accurate in predicting their own status than the self-overestimators were, our results are consistent with Sheerer's (18) finding that better adjusted persons' self-estimates are closer to the groups' ratings than those of less well adjusted persons.

Under-reciprocators were found to have better adjustment scores than over-reciprocators (t = 4.12*) (Table 2). This could be interpreted to mean that under-reciprocators have better adjustment despite their less realistic perceptions because of higher feelings of self-regard.

Relationship between the Independent Variables and Sociometric Status.

---

* r significant at the 5% level of confidence or better.

TABLE 2

SIGNIFICANT LEVELS OF THE DIFFERENCES BETWEEN THE HIGH AND LOW GROUPS ON THE
INDEPENDENT VARIABLES WITH RESPECT TO MEASURES OF ADJUSTMENT

High and Low Groups on a Given Independent Variable	Composite Adjustment			Rorschach Adjustment			Rorschach Anxiety		
	N	M	S.D.	N	M	S.D.	N	M	S.D.
Self-Underestimators	20	—.60	1.91	19	—.09	1.04	19	.10	.85
Self-Overestimators	21	.80*	1.43	19	—.02	1.24	20	.07	.90
Other-Understimators	20	.22	1.49	18	.40	.90	18	.10	1.36
Other-Overestima:ors	20	.48	2.25	18	.36	1.03	18	—.01	.94
Under-reciprocators	23	1.47	1.95	22	.59	1.18	23	.37	.92
Over-reciprocators	17	—.87*	1.55	16	—.26*	.75	17	—.15	.72
Underacceptors	21	.42	2.27	21	.14	1.22	21	.48	1.14
Overacceptors	23	—.30	1.49	21	.10	1.02	21	—.13	.87

An * placed between two means indicates that their difference is significant at the 1% level of confidence.

Self-underestimators obtained higher sociometric ratings than did self-overestimators. To an indeterminate extent this finding is partially an artifact. Individuals who have high sociometric status can only make predictions of own status which are either accurate or underestimations since their actual status is at or near the upper ceiling of the scale. On the other hand, those who have low status can be either accurate in their estimations of own status or overestimators since their actual status is at or near the lower ceiling of the scale. It is felt, however, that this finding does suggest a valid relationship when we consider that self-underestimators were also found to be more accurate in predicting their own sociometric status. Since self-underestimators are more realistic in their social perceptions, they are less likely to make unreasonable demands on others. Thus, they may be expected to approach others more successfully without offending them. Wood (20) also found that high school students tend to have higher sociometric status if they are more accurate in estimating their classmates' opinions. On the other hand, the more expansive, demanding self-overestimators, perceiving themselves as highly acceptable and highly accepting individuals, would tend to be more aggressive in their approach, and would, therefore, be more likely to antagonize others.

The high self-expectations of the self-overestimators might also reflect undue concern over the opinions of others and might thus account in part for their relatively lower sociometric status. For as Newstetter and Newcomb (17) have shown, individuals who are least concerned with the opinions people have of them tend to have higher status than those who are highly concerned with their own status.

IMPLICATIONS FOR FURTHER RESEARCH

The results of the present study and of experimental findings by others point up the need for further research into the relationships between social sensitivity and such situational variables as group size and group composition, similarities between rater and ratee with respect to social-class status and social attitudes and the nature and function of the group (i.e., formal or informal, vocational or social, etc.).

The present investigation found consistencies in perception within one administration of the sociometric measures. It would be interesting to know if such consistencies are stable and general enough to be manifested over several administrations on the same group at different times in different activities, and in social, vocational and other types of groups.

The tendency toward extreme perceptual judgments was found to be related to strong motivational bias of a subjective nature. Further study of this problem would require extensive and longitudinal clinical investigation in order to identify the factors in personality development and organization which account for the perceptual differences found.

The finding that accuracy in perceiving own and others' status are unrelated traits suggests study of the perceptual patterns and personality correlates of groups (a) which have high empathic ability with respect to self and others, (b) which have poor ability with respect to both functions, and (c) which have high ability in one function and low ability in the other.

SUMMARY AND CONCLUSION

The general aim of this study was to identify and measure various perceptual-judgmental response sets in the field of social perception. We are interested in evolving measures of characteristic perceptual tendencies reflected in the sociometric ratings of self and others and in determining the relationships between such tendencies and general adjustment, status within the group, perceptual accuracy and feelings of anxiety and self-regard.

The problem of measuring consistent perceptual tendencies was studied by comparing *predicted* sociometric ratings with *actual* sociometric ratings and by deriving indices of perceived "self" and of perceived "other" acceptance-rejection patterns from such comparisons.

Students in two junior and one senior class at a University High School were asked to rate each of their classmates on a five-point scale in terms of acceptability as friends, and to predict how each of their classmates would rate them, and be rated by the group on the same basis.

The discrepancies between each of the predictions made and the corresponding actual ratings were used as indices of tendencies within individuals to perceive themselves or others in more or less self-consistent ways. Four such discrepancy scores were derived, indicating a tendency to consistently: (a) under- or overestimate own status (self-direction score), (b) under- or overestimate the status of others (other-direction score), (c) perceive oneself as a highly acceptable or unacceptable person (reciprocity score), and (d) as a highly accepting or unaccepting person (acceptance score). Sociempathic ability was determined by comparing actual sociometric status with the predictions individuals made of same.

High and low groups were constituted from those subjects scoring one sigma above or below the mean respectively on each of the four perceptual set score distributions. These groups were compared with respect to each other and with respect to sociempathic ability, sociometric status, general adjustment, anxiety, level of aspiration and goal tenacity.

1. The reliability of the independent variables was investigated in terms of internal consistency using an odd-even coefficient corrected by the Spearman-Brown formula. The average reliability of these measures, which ranged from .88 to .97, was .94.

2. The correlations between the two direction scores (.12), between the reciprocity and acceptance scores (.04), and between the two sociempathy scores (.06) were approximately zero and indicated that the paired variables involved in each of these correlations are probably unrelated to each other.

3. The tendency to underestimate own status is related to the tendency to have relatively low self-expectations; and, conversely, self-overestimators tend to have high self-expectations. This is indicated by the significant negative correlation between the self-direction scores and the reciprocity scores (— .32).

4. Self-underestimators tend to perceive group members as more generous than themselves in rating others, whereas self-overestimators perceive group members as less generous than themselves in rating others. This is indicated by the significant correlation between the self-direction score and the acceptance score (.36).

5. Significant differences between self-under- and over-estimators were obtained with respect to level of aspiration, and adjustment. These differences indicate that self-underestimators maintain aspiration levels that correspond

more closely to their levels of performance, and tend to adjust their levels of aspiration more realistically to experiences of success and failure. In addition, they have better general adjustment. Self-overestimators, on the other hand, have less realistic aspiration levels which they modify less appropriately in the face of failure.

6. There is a positive relationship between each of the direction scores and their corresponding accuracy scores (r = .55 and .37 respectively), indicating that both self- and other-underestimators are more accurate than self- and other-overestimators respectively in predicting their own and others' sociometric status.

7. Other-underestimators perceive the group as less generous than themselves in rating others, whereas other-overestimators perceive the group as more generous than themselves in rating others. This is indicated by the significant negative correlation between the other-direction score and the acceptance score (— .41).

8. There is a significant correlation between the other-direction score and the reciprocity score (.29). Those who anticipate low ratings for themselves tend to overestimate the sociometric status of others, whereas those with high self-expectations underestimate others' status.

9. Significant differences were obtained between the extreme reciprocity groups with respect to general adjustment, estimation of own sociometric status, level of aspiration and goal tenacity scores. These results support finding 3 above, indicating that those whose sociometric expectations from others are low tend to underestimate their own status, whereas those with high expectations tend to overestimate their sociometric status. The latter group of subjects also maintains relatively high aspiration levels which are not readily lowered in the face of continued failure experiences.

The four perceptual response set measures derived in this study are sufficiently stable and have sufficient generality over individuals and over related judgmental tasks to warrant their use for purposes of individual prediction. These measures may be interpreted as generalized personality trends within an individual, i.e., as indices of typical, self-consistent modes of perceiving the interpersonal and hierarchical aspects of social situations.

Self-underestimators perceive themselves as neither very accepting nor as very acceptable persons. They tend to be better adjusted than self-overestimators and to modify their aspirations for future performance more readily and realistically in line with objective experience. They are more accurate in perceiving their own sociometric status, but have less self-regard.

Self-overestimators, on the other hand, perceive themselves as highly accepting individuals and as on the receiving end of interpersonal relationships. They set and maintain higher aspiration levels than are warranted by their actual performance ability. They are more strongly motivated by strong needs for success and for acceptance by others; yet despite this fact they are less accurate in their perceptions of others.

Whether perceptual judgments tended to be extreme or in the middle range of the distribution was found to be related to motivational orientation. Extreme judgments appeared to be reflective of strong subjectively oriented needs, whereas non-extreme judgments were more typical of subjects who responded more in terms of group norms.

These conclusions are tempered by an awareness of certain unique aspects of our sample, need for replication and use of somewhat gross methods. However, it is felt that valid evidence of individual differences among students was obtained.

REFERENCES

1. Ausubel, D. P., and Schiff, H. M. Intrapersonal and interpersonal determinants of individual differences in sociempathic ability. *J. Soc. Psychol.*, in press.
2. Ausubel, D. P., Shiff, H. M., and Gasser, E. B. A preliminary study of developmental trends in sociempathy: Accuracy of perception of own and others' sociometric status. *Child Developm.*, June, 1952, 23, No. 2, 111-128.
3. Ausubel, D. P., Schiff, H. M., and Goldman, M. Qualitative characteristics in the learning process associated with anxiety. *J. Abnorm. Soc. Psychol.*, 1953, Vol. 48, No. 4, 537-547.
3a. Borgatta, E. F. Analysis of social interaction and sociometric perception. SOCIOMETRY, 1954 17, N.Y.
4. Chowdry, K., and Newcomb, T. M. The relative abilities of leaders and non-leaders to estimate opinions of their own groups. *J. Abnorm. Soc. Psychol.*, 1952, 47, 51-57.
5. Cogan, L., Conklin, A., and Hollingworth, H. L. An experimental study of self-analysis, *Sch. and Soc.*, 1915, 2, 171-179.
6. Dymond, R. F. Personality and empathy. *J. Consult. Psychol.*, 1950, 14, 343-350.
7. Eichler, R. M. Experimental stress and alleged Rorschach indices of anxiety. *J. Abnorm. Soc. Psychol.*, 1951, 46, 344-355.
8. Fiedler, F. E., and Senior, K. An exploratory study of unconscious feeling reactions in fifteen patient-therapist pairs. *J. Abnorm. Soc. Psychol.*, Vol. 47, No. 2, Supp. April, 1952.
9. Gage, N. L. Explicit forecasting for strangers interests from expressive behavior. *Psychol. Monogr.*, in press.
10. Gage, N. L., and Suci, G. Social perception and teacher-pupil relationships. *J. Educ. Psychol.*, 1951, 42, 144-152.
11. Goodnow, R. E., and Tagiuri, R. Religious ethnocentrism and its recognition among adolescent boys. *J. Abnorm. Soc. Psychol.*, 1952, 47, 316-320.
12. Hathaway, S. R., and McKinley, J. C. The Minnesota Multiphasic Personality Inventory. Minneapolis: Univ. of Minn. Press, 1943.

13. Harrower, M. R., and Steiner, M. E. *Large scale Rorschach techniques; a manual for the Group Rorschach and Multiple-Choice Test.* Springfield, Ill.: Charles C. Thomas, 1945.

14. Klopfer, B., and Kelley, D. M. *The Rorschach Technique.* New York: World Book Co., 1946.

15. Moreno, J. L. *Sociometry in Action.* New York: Beacon House.

15a. Moreno, J. L. *Who shall survive?* rev. Edition, New York: Beacon House, 1953.

16. Munroe, R. Prediction of the adjustment and academic performance of college students by a modification of the Rorschach Method. *Appl. Psychol. Monogr.,* Stanford University Press, 1945, No. 7.

17. Newstetter, W. J., Feldstein, M. J., and Newcomb, T. M. *Group adjustment: A study in experimental sociology.* Cleveland: Western Reserve Univ., 1948.

18. Sheerer, E. T. An analysis of the relationship between acceptance of and respect for self and acceptance of and respect for others in ten counseling cases. *J. Consult. Psychol.,* 1949, 13, 169-175.

19. Tagiuri, R. Relational analysis: an extension of sociometric method with emphasis upon social perception. SOCIOMETRY, 1952, 15, 91-104.

20. Wood, H. G. An analysis of social sensitivity. Unpublished doctor's thesis, Yale Univ., 1948. Reported in Gage, N. L., Accuracy of social perception and effectiveness in interpersonal relationships. Bur. Edu. Res., Univ. of Ill., 1952.

PART IV

History

SOCIOMETRY: DECADES OF GROWTH

By Jiri Nehnevajsa

A. Introduction

In the thirty some years of its existence, sociometry has acquired a rather impressive history. It is a story of men, their ideas, and their activities—a story which might well serve as the best operational definition of the field up to date.

The time has come when it becomes important to look back at the decades of growth of sociometry. Not because the growth of the field, having reached some climax, is about to be arrested but precisely due to the opposite consideration: sociometry has been expanding at an accelerated pace so that, unless we pause to recollect the paths along which the field has travelled thus far, we may lose track of some of them amidst the floods of new achievements. At the same time, sociometry—focused around its Journal for some twenty years—is about to enter an entirely new stage of development—that of international efforts (centering around the forthcoming *International: Sociometry, Group Psychotherapy, Sociodrama*—a journal to be led by Jacob L. Moreno).

Sociometry has been not only identified with the rigorous application of research techniques to specific problems in group and individual behavior—thus pushing back the frontier of methodology as well as content; it has grown also along the lines of social healing—diagnosis and therapy. Simultaneously, sociometry has advanced as a theory of human behavior; on one hand, as a system of propositions rather solidly grounded in research findings, and on the other hand, through its theoretico-speculative growth, capturing the imaginative mind with its poetry of human living.

Criticized by some for its rigor, it has been mocked by others for its expressive desire to aid ailing humanity, while still others have found the poetry of speculative visions incompatible with the scientific rigor. Thus—not unlike all fields and their protagonists—sociometry has failed to please everyone to the same extent.

This combination of science, therapy and philosophy—all intertwined in much of sociometric work—may well be construed as a weakness in science which claims ethical non-involvement. But it has also been sociometry's strength: for it is this combination which permits growth on all "fronts" along all lines which seem promising whether, at the time, they are fashionable or not.

It is rather easy to see that this amalgamation of the three major endeavors—the scientific, the philosophic, and the therapeutic—is explainable in terms of the interests, and capacities, of the man who stands at the roots of sociometry. Jacob L. Moreno, a scientist, a poet, a philosopher, a healer has himself initiated, and pursued, the development of the field along all these lines. Others who have followed (sometimes by verbal non-following) have more-or-less become specialists: some have emphasized methods, some content—both efforts of utmost significance; some have emphasized therapy, others research; some inclined to quench their thirst at the springwells of poetry or else, looking for new springs, others painstakingly awaiting results of research before they dare to utter any generalization. Envisageing sociometry as a blend of research, therapy and theory, emphasizing the balance between the "socius" and the "metric" (etymologically implicit in the concept of sociometry), Moreno has been, perhaps, the only one never to lose sight of the forest for the trees, or the trees for the forest. Yet, in terms of our cultural patterns, Moreno has seemed "guilty" of several rather impressive "crimes". A physician-psychiatrist, he has invaded the domain of the sociologist, the social psychologist and the educator—grounds enough for some union-card minded scholars to reject the man as well as his work (sometimes even without knowing either). A theorist and system-builder, he has opened himself to the (often worthwhile) attacks which are launched against all system-builders and their systems. After attracting, through the development of the sociometric method, the high respect of an empirically minded community of scholars, Moreno has had the daring to come forth, like Comte and Pareto, with a general theoretical construct without always awaiting the outcome of numerous useful (and numerous useless) researches. In a culture which does not seem to favor or nourish the rise of schools of thought, Moreno has openly been encouraging the formation of a sociometric school of thought. And finally—last but not least—the founder of sociometry remained aloof (until very recently*) of institutionalized academic associations (we cannot but think, for example, of the relative coolness of academicians towards a non-affiliated Spinoza). Yet, he has wanted to be heard by academicians. In simple terms, Moreno has not played, or conformed to, the roles expected of him in our particular culture. Hence, some misunderstanding, resentment and even hostility.

---

* Moreno is, since 1952, a member of the faculty of the Graduate Department of Sociology, New York University.

It needs to be emphasized that Moreno's clearcut individualism has not impeded the growth of sociometry but rather fostered it. When one forgets the personal arguments occasionally resulting, a solid body of scholarly discussions remains—a tremendous achievement at a time when it appears fashionable to be "nice to one another" no matter at what cost, and when avoidance of major criticism of one's colleagues in preference to a little bit too much of backslapping is the order of the day.

With these few remarks in mind, we may now look at sociometry, its roots and growth, its present state, its aspirations, and its probable future course. In so doing, we will unavoidably have to be somewhat selective; thus omissions or lack of emphasis given to important contributions to the field are a result of either the ignorance or bias (or both) of this author.

B. Origins of Sociometry

Moreno, indeed, did not "invent" the problems which sociometry was later to deal with. We agree with Florian Znaniecki ("Sociometry and Sociology", Volume 6, Sociometry) when he argues that the issues raised by the new field were old sociological problems but that sociometry merits the credit for enabling the behavioral scientists to study "phenomena which for thousands of years have attracted the social scientists and were rather evaluated than investigated".

Thus we find interest in groups, and in particular smaller groups, in the works of LeBon and Durkheim, Toennies and Simmel—and, of course, at a later date in the classical treatises of Leopold von Wiese and Charles Horton Cooley. But it was certainly Moreno who reduced the problems in question to techniques of measurement and who, subsequently, rephrased their theoretic presentations.

In an article of 1949 ("Three Dimensions of Society", incorporated in Moreno's volume *Sociometry, Experimental Method and Science of Society*), the author says:

> "Sociometry is an axis with two poles. The arm toward one pole is directed toward the discovery of the deeper levels of society's structure. The other is directed toward promoting change of society based upon the dynamic facts found in its structure."

Here then is a clear statement of the research and therapeutic aspirations of sociometry—the difference, sometimes seen with sharp boundaries, between research sociometry and the sociometric movement. As a research field, sociometry has wanted to uncover the underlying social structures, the depth dimension of the society. As a movement, sociometry has aspired at

709

modifying this structure toward betterment, that is, toward alleviation of the conflict which Moreno has seen imbedded in the discrepancy between the institutional (formal) social system and the patterns resulting from the operation of the tele-factor (the flow of affection and disaffection between persons and groups).

The basic roots of role-playing, and with it of group psychotherapy, may be found in the 1919 article "Die Gottheit als Komoediant" (Der Neue Daimon, Vienna). Emphasis on research in situ, in the actual setting of the subjects, originates in the work at Mittendorf, Austria (1916—to be reported for the first time in the 1934 edition of *Who Shall Survive?*) where families select their neighbors in a Government settlement. Suggestions for the use of the laboratory setting for the study, and diagnosis, of individual and group problems comes in 1923 (Stegreiftheater, published in Berlin-Potsdam, 1923).

In this fashion, three important aspects of contemporary activities in social psychology and sociology are more than anticipated: the use of a laboratory, research in situ of small groups, and group psychotherapy.

Modern experimental research in the behavioral sciences has but elaborated upon the basic ideas: that life-like situations, in miniature form, can be reproduced in a setting which is controlled, and controllable, by the researcher.

Research in situ may sacrifice the controls of which the scientist may be capable under laboratory conditions: but it can study the phenomena in question in all their actual intensity, and it may gain, due to potential motivation of subjects, in validity.

Thanks to the versatility of his interests, Moreno arrived at the "small group" focus from three sides at once: the therapy of groups, the experimentation with groups in the laboratory and the role playing techniques in psychodrama. Had he limited himself only to the experiment with laboratory groups, he may have never given "small group" research the big push in the late 20's and early 30's. Had he limited himself to group psychotherapy and psychodrama, in the clinical sense, on a trial-and-error basis, group therapy and psychodrama may not have been on the way towards scientific foundations; but because of his simultaneous interests in all three areas and playing one to fertilize the other, pure research, group psychotherapy and psychodrama have helped each in a different way for "small group" research to come of age.

Group psychotherapy, in its modern sense, cannot be separated from small group research; it may be said to begin here. Former writers had discussed the potential importance of groups in treatment of mental ailments but their notions appear rather vague. In its present sense, group therapy is soundly based on findings about the dynamics of groups, and it is aimed at tackling a patient's problem in its realistic context of *social relations*.

The basic *sociometric techniques* are generated in this era between 1918-23. Role-playing in "Die Gottheit als Komoediant"** (1919), and the sociometric test in "Der Koenigsroman"** (1923) in which children choose new parents (pp. 117-9). Actual psychodrama and sociodrama are reported in the Stegreiftheater (1923). The sociometric test was proposed for Mittendorf (1916); in the theatre of spontaneity (Stegreiftheater)** the actors choose their partners for the production. In this volume, we can also locate the first *interaction diagrams* (pp. 88-95)—to be adopted and further studied by Bales (Interaction Process Analysis, 1949). The first *positional diagrams* (p. 88)—to be adopted later by Kurt Levin (1936)—make their appearance. In these, the location in space and movements with respect to one another, of the psychodrama actors are graphically portrayed.

By 1932, these new concepts, as well as the new research tools, come to be presented to the American public. The National Committee on Prisons and Prison Labor published Moreno's "Application of the Group Method to Classification"; group therapy (p. 60), interaction diagrams and sociograms (p. 102) are here introduced. Sociograms were used during the 57th Annual Session of the American Association on Mental Deficiency (May 29-June 3, 1933) to demonstrate the psychological organization of a community, its depth structure. All this, of course, before the publication of the sociometric classic *Who Shall Survive?* in 1934. It is at this time that research, and therapy, go on in Hudson—with St. Elizabeths Hospital in Washington, D.C. following suit rather soon. By 1936, the first theatre of psychodrama is built in Beacon, New York: a theatre, a school and a mental hospital (in Moreno's own words) have their origin:

> "(The Theatre) was to explore upon its stage various systems of human relations, to arrive at the most productive cultural order. The school was to carry the principles discovered into teaching and learning, the training of sociometrists, group psychotherapists and psychodramatists who could start similar centers elsewhere. The mental hospital which was built around the theatre was to give the most acutely ill representatives of our culture the benefit of antidotes."
>
> (*Who Shall Survive?* 1953, lxvii)

** The author has had a chance to read these publications in the German original. They are available in the Library of Congress, Washington, D.C.

With the appearance of the *Sociometric Review* (1936) to be followed by SOCIOMETRY (1937) under the editorship of Gardner Murphy, sociometry as a field of study, and a technique, was finally "launched" never to be slowed down in its spectacular growth.

Up to, and through, this time all sociometry was what Moreno was later to label "revolutionary" or "hot" sociometry ("Old and New Trends in Sociometry", SOCIOMETRY, Volume 17, May 1954): research was a by-product of the endeavor to better human relationships. Research, diagnosis, therapy and theory remain largely undifferentiated, although specific techniques are applied for the study of relationships (sociometric tests, interaction test), others for diagnosis and therapy (psychodrama, sociodrama) with theory at the foundations of all work.

C. INTERPERSONAL RELATIONS

Moreno's most dramatic definition of interpersonal relations is the one which he put into circulation in spring, 1914:

"Ein Gang zu zwei: Auge vor Auge, Mund vor Mund. Und bift du bei mir, so will ich dir die Augen aus den Höhlen reissen und an Stelle der meinen setzen, und du wirst die meinen ausbrechen und an Stelle der deinen setzen, dann will ich dich mit den deinen und du wirst mich mit meinen Augen anschauen." Translated: "A meeting of two: eye to eye, face to face. And when you are near I will tear your eyes out and place them instead of mine, and you will tear my eyes out and will place them instead of yours, then I will look at you with your eyes and you will look at me with mine."

(J. L. Moreno, *Einladung zu einer Begegnung*, p. 3, Vienna)

In 1918 (*Daimon*, Vol. I, p. 6) he began to use "zwischenmenschliche" Beziehungen, the German phrase for interpersonal relations and from then on systematically in several books, pioneering the modern theory of interpersonal relations which found its concentrated expression in "Interpersonal Therapy and the Psychopathology of Interpersonal Relations", SOCIOMETRY, Vol. I, p. 9-75. The modern versions (Sullivan, Horney and Fromm) of the theory of interpersonal relations are obviously influenced by Moreno's earlier formulations.

He writes in 1923:

"Mit Lage ist nicht nur ein innerer Vorgang, sondern auch eine Beziehung nach aussen gemeint—zur lage einer anderen Person. Aus der Begegnung von zwei verschiedenen Lagen kann der Konflikt hervortreten (Begegnungslage)." Translated: "The personal situation is not only an internal event, it has also a relation outside of himself, to the situation of another person. Out of the interpersonal relation of two different individuals the conflict may arise (interpersonal situation)."

(Das Stegreiftheater, p. 29, Potsdam, Germany)

He writes in 1934:

" 'A' and 'B' are actually two poles of one movement reflecting and changing each other."

(Who Shall Survive?, p. 170, 1st Edition)

Moreno's preeminence in the field of interpersonal relations is summarized by the British psychologist Notcutt:

"The main business of analysis is still a group of two—the patient on the couch and the analyst in the chair. Although Freud's work dealt with the stormiest of human passions, his own attitude was that of a detached, pessimistic observer. The aim of his therapy was the destruction of illusions, the building of a realistic self-image. He had no great hope of making men happier or of seeing a future brotherhood of man, but he thought that he could make men wiser than they had been. A man of this temper is not the one to undertake inspirational work with groups. The fascination of Freud's discoveries was so great, and attracted the best minds in medical psychology to such an extent, that it seems to have been a long time before Moreno's ideas got a hearing in the learned world. Many people may have underrated the intellectual quality of his ideas because of his flamboyant expansive manner. Moreno really believes in brotherly love, and the possibilities of human community. For forty years he has taught that the cure of neurosis lies in the recovery of spontaneity, release from the tyranny of bureaucracy and of the machine, and a restoration of more direct human relations. Many of the ideas later stressed by Fromm and Sullivan can be found earlier in Moreno." (Bernard Notcutt, *The Psychology of Personality*, Philosophical Library, New York, 1953, p. 195.)

D. SOCIOMETRIC SPECIALIZATIONS

Ideally, one might agree with Moreno that a balance should be struck between theory, research and diagnosis. Yet, with the rapid increases in the body of sociometric data, with the unfolding of a theoretical system, with the advancements along methodological lines, specialization within the field was bound to set in. This in part reflects differential interests of men who have become involved in sociometry—as users of its techniques, or as modifiers and innovators, or as teachers. But in part, the absence of an integrated picture in the literature may have been felt rather disturbingly by those interested in all aspects of sociometric effort. At first, sociometric literature consists of the writings of Moreno—in German and in English, and of the articles in the new journal; yet, before anyone could have consumated all that was done up to that point, the number of contributions to the field increased greatly. Relevant bibliographies include today hundreds of titles: Moreno's listing (*Who Shall Survive?*, 1953) incorporates about 1,500 articles and books; the bibliography prepared by Strodtbeck and Hare (SOCIOMETRY, Vol. 17, May 1954) under the sponsorship of the Ford Foundation consists of 1,407 publications; Nehnevajsa's listing (*Koelner Zeitschrift fuer Soziologie,* Vol. 7, March 1955) includes some 500 publications pertaining to sociometric research only. Still, no coherent presentation of the contents of all this literature exists. Moreno's 1953 edition of *Who Shall Survive?* fills the gap in part. In his famed volume on *Social Research* (2nd edition 1942) George A. Lundberg, one of the major contributors to sociometry, presents a brief but rounded picture of the field; in Jahoda, Deutsch and Cook (*Research Methods in Social Relations,* Volume 2, Chapter 17, 1951), Loomis and Proctor come forth with a discussion of sociometric techniques, with Mary Northway (*Primer of Sociometry,* 1949) giving a cursory textbook-like overview of sociometry.

Several articles precede the works of Northway, Loomis and Proctor. Franz gives an early account ("A Survey of Sociometric Techniques", SOCIOMETRY, Volume 2, December 1939), Stuart Chapin reviews trends within the field ("Trends in Sociometrics and Critique", SOCIOMETRY, Volume 3, August 1940), Esther Frankel investigates available materials on friendship configurations ("A Survey of Sociometric and Presociometric Literature on Friendship and Social Acceptance Among Children", SOCIOMETRY, Volume 7, November 1944). A decade of social psychology's growth is reviewed by Leonard S. Cottrell and Ruth Gallagher in the classic "Developments in American Social Psychology", SOCIOMETRY, Vol. 4, No. 2 and 3, 1941; a decade of sociometry's growth is overviewed by Charles Loomis ("Sociometry, 1937-1947", SOCIOMETRY, Vol. 11, 1948) whereas Stuart Chapin, once again, presents some of the salient methodological aspects in his volume on "Experimental Designs in Sociological Research" (Harper and Brothers, 1947, pp. 191-197).

During the past two years, 1954 and 1955, several over-all reviews have appeared. In Germany (Westdeutscher Verlag, Koeln und Opladen) appears Moreno's "Die Grundlagen der Soziometrie" (1954) with an introduction by Leopold von Wiese, a crucial protagonist of sociometry in the country. In France, "Fondements de Sociometrie", Presses Universitaire, launched by Georges Gurvitch, selections from *Who Shall Survive?* are translated and published. In America, Lindzey and Borgatta write an excellent chapter on sociometry in the *Handbook of Social Psychology* (1954, Volume 2). During 1955, two articles surveying research sociometry and sociometric research techniques appear in Germany (Nehnevajsa, "Soziometrische Analyse von Gruppen", *Koelner Zeitschrift fuer Soziologie,* Volume 7, March 1955; and Part II, Volume 7, July 1955). Two outstanding contributions to the literature come from the pen of Mouton, Blake and Fruchter ("The Reliability of Sociometric Measures", SOCIOMETRY, Vol. 18, February 1955), and by the same authors in the August 1955 issue of SOCIOMETRY "The Validity of Sociometric Responses".

Moreno has announced the publication of an atlas of sociograms and psychosocial networks; in Germany, under the editorship of Rene Koenig, Nehnevajsa's survey chapter of sociometric techniques is to appear in a guide to research methods for German social scientists.

Leo Katz to whom sociometric methodology owes a considerable debt, has come forth with a duplicated report on "Recent Advances and Some Unsolved Problems of Sociometric Theory" (Michigan State College Research Memorandum, 1952), supplemented by the author in a paper on "Sociometric Statistics" delivered to the 50th Annual Conference of the American Sociological Society (August 30-September 2, 1955, Washington, D.C.). Another research memorandum was devoted to probability analysis in sociometry by Nehnevajsa ("Probabilistic Analysis in Sociometry", University of Colorado Research Memorandum No. 6, 1954).

Thus, at this time, a complete review of the literature exists in a number of rather scattered sources, but no single source is exhaustive. Sociometrists interested in research have largely ignored theory and therapy; many sociometric therapists have started to view research as an "overintellectualization". In his discussion of trends in the field ("Old and New Trends in Sociometry", SOCIOMETRY, Volume 17, May 1954), Moreno distinguishes between the laboratory, community, and observation approaches on one hand, and between revolutionary, cold, and perceptual sociometry on the other hand. The "introversion of the sociometric test" (whereby the subject expresses his anticipation of choices coming to him, and/or estimates the choice behavior of other members of his group) has added a "new dimension" to sociometric research since Moreno's contribution in "Sociometry in Action" (SOCIOMETRY, Vol. V, 1942). At Harvard, Renato Tagiuri and Robert Bales have continued pioneering work along these lines (a number of reports has been published with others still awaiting publication). In a yet-to-be published study of Miyamoto and Dornbusch at the University of Washington, methodological attempts are made to relate perceptions of subjects to their own choice-behavior in order to get at a more efficient operational clarification of social roles.

Specialization within the field becomes a byproduct of its tremendous growth; very few scientists can call themselves eclectics in sociometry, hence, the emphasis here on research, there on sociodrama and psychodrama —with but occasional attempts to blend the two sociometric branches. Moreno's call for an integrated approach has largely been disregarded, usually under the pressure of the floods of materials available to the scientist today.

Further differentiation sets in with the emerging popularity of the work of Kurt Lewin (whose interest in small groups seems to date back to about 1935 as one may construe from an excellent bibliography published in conjunction with an in memoriam article on Lewin by Ronald Lippitt— SOCIOMETRY, 1947).

Group dynamics emerges as a philosophy of adjustment (quite evidently related to the "other-orientation," in Riesman's terms, of the contemporary American culture, to the rise of the power of the peer-group) as well as a field of research. As a technique for betterment of human relations, the group dynamicists tend to employ role-playing—a sub-form of psycho- and socio-drama. As a research tool, the group dynamicists have used the sociometric test, the sociometric-perception test, but also interaction analysis based on categorization of observed verbal behavior; Moreno had (for example, in "Foundations of Sociometry" (SOCIOMETRY, Volume 4, February 1940) argued that *mere* observation of interaction forms does not, necessarily, reveal the underlying configuration resulting from the flow of tele (along the aversion-affection continuum) which can best be gotten at by the use of the sociometric test and psychodrama. *He argued that research, whether under laboratory or in situ conditions, must appear of consequence to the subjects—thus questioning the validity of data obtained when the subjects are themselves not involved in the outcome of the research. In so many words, one might rephrase his argument as meaning that research data will tend to be valid (with least respondent error) only when the study is seen helpful or potentially helpful to the respondent.* Yet, laboratory experimentation has grown in quantity and importance—the work of Bales and Mills and Tagiuri at Harvard, Swanson and others at Michigan, Rose, Gibb and others at Colorado, and several other centers.

Two newer volumes set out to provide a much needed link between sociometry and group dynamics. The book on *Group Dynamics* by Cartwright and Zander (editors, Row, Peterson and Company, 1953) cuts decisively across both approaches. The trend toward synthesis is even more evident in the Reader edited by Hare, Borgatta and Bales (*Small Groups*, Alfred Knopf, 1955).

The differentiation of emphases in sociometry has, for a while, settled the question of a definition of the field. The broad definitions (though desirable) offered by Moreno, Sorokin, Lundberg and Chapin have been gradually narrowed down in practice to the works of sociometrists who employ the sociometric test, psychodrama and sociodrama, with group dynamics specializing in laboratory observational research, and in "group process" (a concept often used, yet very difficult to pin down).

Within sociometry then, we find scholars with chief interests in *theory;* others who have advanced the frontiers of *group psychotherapy;* others, who have been the providers of *new research techniques*—especially in regard to methods; and still others, who have been predominantly active in *substantive research*—that is research for the sake of its content.

E. SOCIOMETRIC THEORY

Basic to the growth of sociometric theory have been the concepts of "choice", "spontaneity", "creativity", and "the moment". Within the normatively structured social system, functioning through a set of more-or-less well defined social roles, the individual actors make clearcut choices. These choices are socio-emotional in texture; the actors like alters, they dislike other alters; they attach themselves to objects; they relate affectively to symbols. A theoretic system suggested in Leopold von Wiese's associative and dissociative processes and their products is not only envisaged in sociometry but also rendered measurable. Moreno theorizes about, and measures, an underlying depth dimension of our formal social system, a dimension consisting of affective relationships cutting across the institutionally defined structures—sometimes compatible, and often incompatible with them. In many of his writings, the founder of sociometry describes the discrepancy between the official society and its depth dimension as conducive to social conflict, perhaps, crucial to it. Not like in the existential philosophy in which the idea of choice is equated with the notion of a perpetual anguish Moreno sees in the process of choosing a positive force whereby men assert themselves *spontaneously,* wherein they exercise their right to a free society. That is why, to Moreno, choosing does not fill men with anxiety and a feeling of futility but rather, like Frank Lester Ward, choosing is the prime factor in the telic growth of mankind toward its goals.

Giving due credit to Bergson and his notion of "elan vital", Moreno

717

develops his theory of spantaneity. A fascinating discussion of the socialization of the infant ("Spontaneity Theory of Child Development", SOCIOMETRY, Vol. 7, May 1943) goes to point out the "latent genius" of the human baby who is capable to overcome fantastic odds following the trauma of birth. Unless spontaneous, unless there is some measure of the s-factor (as spontaneity comes to be designated), the infant could not even survive; the s-factor is seen topologically located somewhere between the hereditary and environmental factors, yet, different from them.

Socialization of the infant which proceeds, in sociometric theory, through the first universe in which social and psychosomatic roles are blended together to a differentiation between these two sets of roles, and to the suppression of spontaneity by the adoption of stereotype behaviors, paralyzes the human being. It is seen as having a crippling effect upon the latent genius of humanity—hence, Moreno's emphasis on spontaneity training, on the revitalization of the force which promotes inventiveness and creativity most.

Sorokin in his articles on spontaneity and creativity (an assessment of Moreno's theories: "Concept, Tests and Energy of Spontaneity-Creativity", SOCIOMETRY, Vol. 12, August 1949; and "El Supraconsciente", *Revista Internacional de Sociologia,* Vol. 11, January-March 1953) emphasizes creativity as a developed form of spontaneity. The spontaneity test, and spontaneity training, are developed on the psychodrama and sociodrama stages.

> "Spontaneity and creativity are not identical or similar processes. They are different categories, although strategically linked. In the case of Man his s may be diametrically opposite to his c; an individual may have a high degree of spontaneity but be entirely uncreative, a spontaneous idiot." *(Who Shall Survive?,* 1953, p. 39)

Creativity is defined only operationally and pragmatically—by its results. It is an element X (above citation, p. 45); in "order to become effective, it (the sleeping beauty) needs a catalyzer—spontaneity". The indicants of the interaction of spontaneity-creativity are the various forms of the *warming-up process*—the products of the interaction become cultural conserves, that is, products of spontaneous-creative endeavors become accepted as a part of culture.

According to sociometric theory, the moment is a dynamic category of the situation, not a mere time-sequence. It is imbedded in the "philosophy of the moment"—the situational here-and-now. ("The Philosophy of the Moment and the Spontaneity Theatre", SOCIOMETRY, Volume 4, May 1940): hence, in sociometry, one studies in *statu nascendi*—in the state of birth of the situation.

Referring to *psychodrama,* Moreno states in 1923:

"Das gesammte Werk entsteht vor allen Augen, status nascendi". (*Das Stegreiftheater,* p. 23.) Trsl: "The entire production emerges before all eyes, status nascendi."

Moreno writes in 1932:

"Our approach has been that of direct experiment; man in action, man thrown into action, the moment not part of history but *history as part of the moment*—sub species momenti". (*Application of the Group Method to Classification,* New York, 1932, p. 21.)

He writes again in 1933:

"We study individuals just when they enter spontaneously into relationships which lead to the forming of groups, *sub species momenti.* We study these spontaneous reactions in the initial stage of group formation and the organized attitudes developed in the course of such organization. We are *present* during the "trauma" of birth and attempt to foretell the future." (Psychological Organization of Groups in the Community, Proceedings of the American Association on Mental Deficiency, Boston, 1933, p. 24.)

In 1940, writes Kurt Lewin confirming Moreno's position:

"According to field theory, behavior depends neither on the past nor on the future but on the present field." (*Field Theory in Social Science,* 1951, p. 27.)

In this fashion, the philosophy of the moment enters also group dynamics. The psychological past and the psychological (anticipatory) future are, or course, ingredients of the here-and-now, but a situation can meaningfully be investigated when it happens, and as it happens.

F. Role Theory and Role Playing

The two chief exponents of role theory have been George Herbert Mead and J. L. Moreno. There is hardly a greater difference imaginable as between Mead, lecturing at the University of Chicago on the social significance of role taking (1911-1925), and J. L. Moreno, experimenting with groups of role players in the Viennese gardens leading up to the opening of the Stegreiftheater (1911-1924). Mead's primary emphasis was the "role taking process" as it becomes manifest in the shaping of social institutions and organized response, the finished social product. (G. H. Mead: "Mind, Self and Society" 1934, p. 26). Moreno started in contrast to Mead

719

at the opposite end with the critique of the finished product and the "role conserve"; he started with the study of the "status nascendi" of social relations. It is because of the conflict he discovered between the self of the subject and the official roles in which he was cast that he introduced role playing as a potential corrective. ("Die Rolle steht ihm als Individuum *gegenüber*"—*Das Stegreiftheater*, 1923, p. 27. "The roles are alien to him as a private individual". See also "The Spontaneity Theory of Child Development", 1944, Sociometry, Volume VII). Moreno's role theory is therefore closely linked to spontaneity and creativity; the Meadian role theory is linked to social conserves—it would never have led to the invention of role playing and to the experimentation with groups of role players. He did not attempt to "change" the role structure of a given culture but to explain it.

A characteristic phrase of Mead, 1934: "There are, then, whole series of such common responses in the community in which we live, and such reponses are what we term "institutions". The institution represents a common response on the part of all members of the community to a particular situation." (*Mind, Self and Society,* p. 261)

A characteristic phrase of Moreno, 1934:

"Social life has the tendency to attach a definite role to a specific person so that this role becomes the prevailing one into which the individual is folded." "Everybody is expected to live up to his official role in life—a teacher is to act as a teacher, a pupil as a pupil, and so forth. But the individual craves to embody far more roles than those he is allowed to act out in life. It is from the active pressure which these multiple individual units exert upon the manifest official role that a feeling of anxiety is produced." Role playing is then a method of liberating and structuring these unofficial roles. (Pp. 325, 326, *Who Shall Survive?* 1st Edition.)

G. THEORY OF SOCIAL CONFIGURATIONS

The empirically established observation that the choice-relations of individuals do not occur as-if-by-chance, as well as the finding that the discrepancy between the official society and its depth structure does indeed exist, leads to the theory of the tele factor, t-factor. Tele is the flow, to and fro, of affectivity between individuals—an important force to determine the manner in which men relate to each other.

Moreno has differentiated between *projective* and *retrojective* portions of the tele; Loomis and Proctor (in Jahoda, Deutsch and Cook, Volume 2) outlined the six basic types of dyadic relationships between two individuals depending on the direction of each of these tele portions (negative, neutral, positive). Lewis Yablonsky ("A Sociometric Investigation Into the Development of an Experimental Model for Small Group Analysis", SOCIOMETRY, Volume 15, August-November 1952) expands the dyadic types of tele; in his structural patterns, Yablonsky includes also perceptual sociometric relationships interconnecting thus the analysis of the sociometric test data with the data obtained by the use of the intraverted sociometric test in perceptual sociometry.

The tele is not entirely unstructured; in fact, it is defined in terms of different forms of association—it relates to *criteria of choice,* thus varying from one activity to another at least to some extent. The importance accrued (by Moreno, Jennings, Criswell) to specificity of choice-criteria in sociometric research dates back to the observation of differences in tele from activity to activity (the Hudson Project; reported for example by Jennings in *Sociometry of Leadership, Sociometry Monograph; Leadership and Isolation,* 1948; and, of course, by Moreno in *Who Shall Survive?,* 1934).

When both portions of the tele are of the same direction, Moreno speaks of a *simple tele,* whereas *infra-tele* is defined by differential directions; such tele results when one of the subjects misperceives of the other person's feelings toward him.

Tele also varies in intensity. Technically, the tele-intensity may be investigated by the method of ranks (whereby respondents express their first, second . . . nth choices), by the method of paired comparisons (in which all combinatory pairs of individuals in the group are given to each subject for an expression of preference for one of the members of each pair), and by the method of a calibrated scale (thermometer). Several sociometrists have greatly contributed to the development of methods for the measurement of tele intensity: Merle E. Bonney, Leslie D. Zeleny, Vladimir Cervin and others.

Helen H. Jennings has suggestively proposed the differentiation of tele, and of groups subsequently, in terms of *kind*: she distinguishes between the psyche-tele and the socio-tele, one pertaining to private criteria of sociation, the other relevant to collective, or task-oriented sets of criteria. Her theoretical contribution is grounded in research and psyche-tele and socio-tele are concepts coined to describe the systematic difference in configurations when private versus collective criteria are used in the sociometric test. ("Sociometric Differences of the Psychegroup and the Sociogroup", SOCIOMETRY,

10, February 1947). The psychegroups tend to be consistently *smaller*, with the members linked to one another in mutual positive relations, they last longer—that is, endure over a longer period of time; individuals are selected into the psychegroups due to their fitness into the group rather than for their ability to affect the climate of the group. The reverse observations apply to the sociogroup.

An important theory of the tele deals with the referent entity. Moreno discusses tele for *persons* as opposed to tele for *objects*; and finally, tele for *symbols*. Therefrom dates his ideal-type (in the Weberian sense) classification of societies: an emotional panacea (where tele for persons suppresses completely the tele for objects), a technological panacea (where persons are merely carriers of objects and tele relates to objects only), and the Buddhistic panacea—with both the tele for objects and the tele for persons suppressed. ("Organization of the Social Atom", *Sociometric Review*, 1936.) Thus each person is seen by Moreno as having a certain quantity—somewhat variable over time—of tele; this total quantity of available t can be distributed between persons and objects—tele for persons and tele for objects are then complementary.

Each actor is related to numerous individuals under each of the possible criteria of sociation. The fabric of his tele-relations with others has been called in sociometry his *social atom* (first mentioned in 1932 explicitly in Moreno's "Application of the Group Method to Classification" (p. 102) mentioned previously (Section B). The social atom has two perspectives, the *psychological*—the person *and* his relationships with others, and the *collective*—the smallest part of human society. The social atom has a nucleus of consumated mutual (positive and negative) relations—individuals with a considerable number of relationships in the nucleus have been called having a high tele range (by Paul Deutschberger in "Tele Factor: Horizon and Awareness", SOCIOMETRY, Volume 10, August 1947). The next layer of the atom includes the individuals to whom the focal individual feels related; it is separated by a social threshold from the outer layer of the acquaintance volume consisting of persons about whom the subject feels indifferently, and/or who are related to him without his awareness of the fact. An "imbalanced social atom" (Moreno) is typical of individuals with a "low tele range" (Deutschberger). But more so: it is diagnostically typical of individuals with inadequate social relations.

Since the social atom changes over time, considerable interest has been attached to the study of changes in the atom—especially by Moreno ("Social Atom and Death", SOCIOMETRY, Volume 10, February 1947) and Helen

Jennings ("Experimental Evidence on the Social Atom at Two Time Points", SOCIOMETRY, Volume 5, May 1941). Mouton, Blake and Fruchter have overviewed the changing social atom in studies by others from the platform of reliability—consistency of choice-behavior of subjects ("The Reliability of Sociometric Measures", SOCIOMETRY, Volume 18, February 1955).

"Every individual, just as he is the focus of numerous attractions and repulsions, also appears as the focus of numerous roles which are related to the roles of other individuals."

("Psychodrama Treatment of Marriage Problems"—
SOCIOMETRY, Vol. III, 1940)

The conceptual fabric of these role-relations gives rise to the idea of the *cultural atom* the graphic expression of which is the role-diagram (Zerka Toeman, "How To Construct a Role Diagram", *Sociatry,* Volume 2, 1948-9).

The social atom is bounded by specific criteria of association; the cultural atom has a specific culture as its referent, the role-relationships which are reducible to the axio-normative order of a society. The study of these atoms and their interrelations is seen of immense importance in the investigation of psychopathology of interpersonal relations; hence, it is of great significance in any attempt to understand, and modify, personality disorders in as much as they stem from imbalances in the social atom, or poor adjustment between the social atoms and the cultural atom of an individual.

Several social atoms combine into social molecules; these become the more complex socioids and classoids (Moreno). Finally, the *psychosocial network* is defined as the fabric of all sociometric relationships in a community. The riverbeds through which psychological currents flow have initially been charted and discussed in studies of information and rumor spreading by Moreno in his Hudson Experiments (1934), by Charles P. Loomis in "Sociometrics of Rural Communities" (SOCIOMETRY, Vol. II, 1939), in the Revere Project directed by Stuart C. Dodd under a U.S. Air Force contract reported in numerous articles. A typology of communities was suggested in terms of the psychosocial networks prevailing in them; in some cases, numerous relations will link a community with other communities, with the whole nation—with humanity at large. Some individuals within a community will be left outside of the networks—some will belong to but one.

The great contribution to sociology of Emory Bogardus with his measurement and theories of *social distance* is thus placed into a new light. Moreno and Bogardus have provided the basic theoretical concepts as well as techniques of measurement; not unrelated to this development are the exciting mathematical models of communications spreading proposed by Winthrop (in a dissertation at the University of Washington) and mainly by Anatol Rapoport (for example, "Spread of Information Through a Population with Socio-Cultural Bias, Parts I, II and III", *Bulletin of Mathematical Biophysics,* Volume 15, 1953).

Moreno ("Foundations of Sociometry", SOCIOMETRY, Volume 4, February 1940) and Nehnevajsa ("A Sociometrist's Remarks on the Soviet Purges", SOCIOMETRY, Volume 18, August 1955) employed the sociometric network theory to attempt to explain the occurrence of large-scale purges in the Soviet Union; this use of the sociometric theory is still in its infant stage—many problems in international relations may yet be tackled by sociometrists. It should be in part the task of the new journal, *International: Sociometry, Group Psychotherapy and Sociodrama,* to explore the hitherto unexplored areas.

H. SOCIOMETRIC THEORY: ITS MEANING

Many aspects of sociometric theory have been clarified in discussions between various sociometrists. Georges Gurvitch ("Microsociology and Sociometry", SOCIOMETRY, Volume 15, 1-2, 1952), Johnson ("Theology of Interpersonalism", SOCIOMETRY, Volume 12, 1-3, 1949), Margaret Mead ("Some Relations Between Cultural Anthropology and Sociometry", SOCIOMETRY, Volume 10, November 1947), and Rene Zazzo ("Sociometry and Psychology", SOCIOMETRY, Volume 12, 1-3, 1949) have initiated many worthwhile arguments.

In part, sociometric theory is firmly based on research findings. To some extent, it is speculative in character. Thus it has proven to be fertile grounds not only for theoretical dialectics but also for the formation of relevant hypotheses with the testing of which the theory stands and falls.

The theoretical concepts, such as the "social atom", "psychosocial networks" are real to the same extent to which other similar constructs are real; they do describe, mostly with considerable precision, that which they are designed to describe; they are a challenge to imaginativeness of the scientists; a soil for the fermentation of meaningful questions about human behavior.

The major aspiration of sociometry, to study all of humanity due to the fact that the tele-relations link all mankind in some fashion, has, of course, not been fulfilled. In this regard, Margaret Mead's criticism is quite warranted: she is perturbed by the study of *closed social systems* as if it had been established that for the situational analysis of a given social system

724

the relations of the system with other groups, and of other groups with the system, are not fundamental.

While one may agree with this criticism (and Moreno with his visions of *wholeness* would likely be the first one to concur with Mead), it is equally clear that most of our research in the behavioral sciences has been of this nature. The frame of reference, or the level of abstraction, determines the experimental closeness of a system—with numerous external variables of vital importance at work, yet inaccessible for study. When Parsons (*The Social System*, 1953) discusses the differential analytical levels for the study of the personality system, the social system, and the cultural system, he says no more than that it is crucial to clearly define one's closed system of study and that it is disastrous to confuse the different levels. Similarly, we may look at the fabric of formal social roles and come out with sociology of institutions or with stratification analysis (when we cut across the social system vertically); or, we may analyze the depth dimension by sociometric techniques—and, on occasion, the relationship between the two. An advancement in the study of the relationship between the formal and sociometric structures has been made with the proposal for a multi-relational analysis by Massarik, Tannenbaum, Weschler and Kahane ("Sociometric Choice and Organizational Effectiveness: A Multi-Relational Approach", Sociometry, 16, 1953).

I. Sociometric Therapy

For the first time in the history of psychotherapy, the measurement of interpersonal relations is attempted, therapeutic *change* in the behavior of individuals and groups is *measured*. (Sociograms before and after, *Who Shall Survive?* 1934.)

The use of sociometry in social healing can be discussed along several lines. On one hand, their shuffling of groups can be made on the basis of sociometric data (Assignment therapy); on the other hand, the psychodrama and sociodrama stage are the vehicle for diagnosis of individual and social problems, and at the same time, instruments of healing. The acting out of situations by subjects has the effect of mental and social catharsis; it improves the ability of individuals to correctly perceive of their roles with regard to alters—or, as one would say, it trains them toward spontaneity.

In numerous writings, Moreno has explained the advantages of psychodrama over classical psychoanalysis and Gestalt Theory ("Notes on Sociometry, Gestalt Theory, and Psychoanalysis", 1933—in Psychological Organization of Groups in the Community). As to Gestalt Theory: "Sociometry accomplishes the thing which the Gestalt theory does not approach; it studies expression and organization in relation to the act or acts which produces them. We never consider Gestalt separated from the creative act." . . . "The sociometrist does not deal in 'Gestalts'—he is the framer of a Gestalt himself."

As to psychoanalysis: "The role of the analyst changes into the role of a co-actor; the verbal communication supplied by a patient from his couch is supplemented by movement and gesticulation which the acting-out alone permits; interaction replaces one-way communication."

Whatever the pros and cons of sociodrama and psychodrama may have been, one fact remains: since the 1923 days of Stegreiftheater in Vienna, the method has been so generally accepted that, under various names, it is in constant use by psychiatrists, clinicians—private, as well as in hospitals. Before Moreno, the notions of the importance of groups and group relations in healing were generalized observations; what forces were at work in groups escaped the attention of the older writers. In its modern form, group psychotherapy begins with the application of sociometric method to problems. A few years after the opening of the first American theatre of psychodrama in Beacon (1936), some fifty hospitals (with St. Elizabeths Hospital leading the way—where the theatre of psychodrama is now directed by James Enneis, one of psychodrama's outstanding directors) have adopted the techniques. At this time, we may report the opening of the first psychodrama theatre in India, as well as considerable successes of the French psychodramatists—Serge Lebovici, Mireille Monod, Robert Diatkine. Harris has reported the uses of sociometric techniques in selection of British officers during World War II, Ansbacher ("Lasting and Passing aspects of German Military Psychology", SOCIOMETRY, Vol. 12, Dec. 1949) discusses the application in Nazi armies; the report of the Office of Strategic Services ("Assessment of Men") points out the employment of sociodrama in the selection of special personnel during the war in the United States. Sociodrama appears to be an integral part of the program developed by the RAND corporation for crews manning radar stations. A long list of industries might be supplied in which sociometric therapy is playing a part of everincreasing importance.

It is, as already pointed out, not only psychodrama and sociodrama that have been used as instruments of therapy: the sociometric test and sociometric research when applied to groups *in situ* with choice-criteria pertaining to activities in which the subjects are vitally involved has had therapeutic effects as well. We can easily differentiate between sociometric research

726

designed solely for the purposes of hypotheses testing and sociometric research with explicit or implicit therapeutic undertones. While it is quite likely that the administration of a sociometric test always leads to some form of restructuring of a group, that is, has some effect on the respondents, we wish to mention here but the studies more or less explicitly conducted with therapy as their major aim.

Mittendorf (1916) opens the era; Beacon (1932) follows, putting the Mittendorf plan into action: prospective settlers are asked to select their eventual associates. Their selections *matter* (hence expectation of honest responses)—the decision the subjects will make may influence considerably their future. In 1936, Moreno presents a plan for regrouping of communities (*Sociometric Review*, 1936); in the following year, Shepard Wolman reports the use of sociometry in community planning ("Sociometric Planning of a New Community", SOCIOMETRY, Volume 1, 1-2, 1937). In 1938, Loomis and Davidson come with their research-therapeutic work on the community level ("Social Agencies in Planned Rural Communities", SOCIOMETRY, Volume 2, August 1938; "Sociometric Study of New Rural Communities", SOCIOMETRY, Volume 2, February 1938). Great contributions have been made by Henrik Infield—in his "Social Control in a Cooperative Society" (SOCIOMETRY, Volume 5, August 1942), "Cooperative Community at Work" (Dryden Press, 1945), "The Use of the Sociometric Test in Cooperative Community Research" (Proceedings of the 14th Congress of Sociology, Rome, 1950), "Cooperative Community and the Sociometric Test" (*Cooperative Living*, 3, 1951)—and other writings. In 1943, Rose Cologne ("Experimentation With Sociometric Procedures in a Self-Help Community Center", SOCIOMETRY, Volume 6, February 1943) and Muriel Brown ("Some Applications of Sociometric Technics to Community Organization", SOCIOMETRY, Volume 6, February 1943) join the group of scholars interested in therapeutic sociometry; Irwin Sanders offers a plan for effective community action ("The Use of Block Leaders in Effective Community Mobilization", SOCIOMETRY, Volume 12, December 1949).

All these studies have two things in common: *sociometry* is used, and secondly, it is assumed—in the line with the democratic philosophy of life—that communities organized in compatibility with the informal sociometric wishes of the inhabitants, or prospective settlers, will function better.

Numerous sociometrists follow Moreno's early work with children in Vienna, and the Hudson Project of the 30's. Pioneering discussions were initiated by Leslie D. Zeleny ("Sociometry in a Classroom", SOCIOMETRY, Volume 3, February 1939)—with Moreno's explicit discussion of this subject in 1942 (SOCIOMETRY, Volume 6). Daniel Cooper realizes the potentialities of sociometry for school administrators (SOCIOMETRY, Volume 10, May 1947); once again, Nahum Shoobs writes on "Sociometry in the Classroom" (SOCIOMETRY, Volume 10, May 1947). In 1950, Leslie Zeleny ("Adaptation of Research Findings in Social Leadership to College Classroom Procedures", SOCIOMETRY, Volume 13, December 1950), and Levy and Osten ("A Sociometric Approach to Teacher Training", SOCIOMETRY, Volume 13, August 1950) contribute to the growth of applied sociometry; the value of the techniques is outlined by Atkinson ("The Sociogram as an Instrument in Social Studies Teaching and Evaluation", *Elementary School Journal*, 1949-50, 74-85). In France, Goguelin discusses the successes of the sociometric method among apprentices ("Recherches sur les resultants du test sociometrique de Moreno dans un centre d'apprentissage", *Travail Humain*, 1951, 14, 228-242); in America, Frances Todd joins the discussions of Atkinson, Zeleny, Levy and Osten and others ("Democratic Methodology in Physical Education", SOCIOMETRY, Volume 14, May 1951). Merle Bonney who in many ways added to sociometric methodology, substantive research, as well as applied sociometry, has been preparing a major volume on "Sociometry in Education", a work which should be complementary to the book by Robert Haas "Psychodrama and Sociodrama in American Education" (Beacon House, 1948). The relation of "Accident-proneness" to sociometric status has been discussed by Moreno and Blake (Army), Fuller (education) and Speroff (industry).

Problems related to various aspects of the work-situation have similarly attracted both the researchers and the researchers-therapists. Joan Criswell discusses the uses of the technique in personnel departments (SOCIOMETRY, Volume 12, December 1949); Orden Smucker goes into the guidance possibilities of sociometry ("Near-Sociometric Analysis as a Basis for Guidance", SOCIOMETRY, Volume 12, December 1949). The works of John Jacobs (SOCIOMETRY, Volume 8, May 1945), Paul Maucorps in France (*Revue du Travail*, 1950), Moreno and Borgatta (SOCIOMETRY, Volume 14, 1951) and Wechsler, Tannenbaum and Talbot (1952) must be mentioned when one thinks of sociometry applied to industrial settings.

The great promise of sociometry for the organization and functioning of the Armed Forces was clearly envisaged by Leslie Zeleny ("Selection of Compatible Flying Partners", *American Journal of Sociology*, Volume 52, 1947); the interest of the various research organizations within the Armed Forces has been attracted once and for all—to be underscored by the signing of numerous research contracts by the Human Resources Research Institute of the U.S. Air Force and the Office of Naval Research; both of these groups have, indeed, done much to promote the growth of sociometric research, and specifically, research in small groups.

Next, sociometry comes to be applied to problems of social work and social workers. Moreno ("The Sociometric Approach to Social Case Work", SOCIOMETRY, Volume 13, May 1950), Paul Deutschberger ("Sociometry and Social Work", SOCIOMETRY, Volume 13, February 1950) and Helen Green ("Sociometry and Social Integroup Work", SOCIOMETRY, Volume 13, February 1950) have been the pioneers.

Occasionally, rather than employing sociodrama or psychodrama, therapists have utilized the sociometric test among hospitalized patients. Reports come from Newall Kephart ("A Method of Heightening Social Adjustment in an Institutional Group", *American Journal of Orthopsychology*, Volume 8, 1938), Bockman and Hyde ("Application of Sociometric Technics to the Study of Lobotomized Patients", *Journal of Nervous and Mental Disease*, Volume 114, 1951), Kegeles and Hyde ("Sociometric Network on an Acute Psychiatric Ward", *Group Psychotherapy*, Volume 5, 1952), and Benjamin Pope ("Sociometric Structure and Group Values on a Mental Hospital Service for Criminally Insane", *Group Psychotherapy*, Volume 5, 1952).

The story of sociometric therapy is far from complete. We have not mentioned the organization of the Society of Psychodrama and Group Psychotherapy (1942), the growth of the journal *Sociatry*—later to be renamed *Group Psychotherapy* (1947); the numerous psychodrama and group psychotherapy monographs in which Moreno, Zerka Toeman, Fantel, Pratt, Leary and Coffey, Lippitt, MacDonald discuss the uses of the techniques under various conditions; we have not mentioned the development of therapeutic motion pictures; we have hardly touched upon the significant contributions of men like Robert Haas and James Enneis; we have neglected here the outstanding studies of Mary Northway among preschool children (as we intend to mention them explicitly in our discussion of sociometric research). An exhaustive summary of all this effort is clearly beyond the scope of the present paper.

One final comment may be kept in mind quite fruitfully: psychodrama and sociodrama are therapeutic instruments proper; but they have contributed towards research of small groups by supplying them with new research tools, role playing and interaction analysis. The sociometric test is primarily a research tool—but it can be profitably used to obtain data necessary for the restructuring of groups, for the diagnosis of interpersonal conflicts, and for the analysis of imbalances in social atoms of individuals, in social molecules and psychosocial networks.

J. Introduction to Sociometric Research

Research generally is neutral to the welfare of the subjects under study. In an impersonal fashion, the researcher is interested in operationally stating his hypotheses, designing conditions under which these hypotheses can be tested, and in testing them. Whether his findings will, or will not, be used to reconstruct undesirable conditions in individuals, between individuals and groups, the researcher is not interested. In this respect, the designation of pure research sociometry as "cold sociometry" (by Moreno in his 1954 discussion of "Old and New Trends" mentioned previously) seems quite appropriate.

Meaningful results ensue provided that, at least, two conditions are fulfilled: the researcher phrases meaningful questions, and secondly, he has methodological tools available which will help answer such questions. Hence, the development of adequate methodology goes hand in hand with the quest for substantive knowledge.

With little or no knowledge at first, the researcher wants to *describe* the phenomena under study, in our case, the long search for precise describing of sociometric configurations begins. As some knowledge is obtained on the sociometric patterns, the researcher is interested in *relating* these configurations to other, hopefully relevant, variables. Two questions are asked in this regard:

(a) What are the sociometric configurations (of individuals, groups) predictive of?

(b) What (variables) predict(s) the sociometric configurations?

Sociometric research is then a *body of methods* whereby the data is obtained and analyzed, and next and foremost, a *body of findings* in terms of such data. The studies may be best classified by the categories of relationships which they aim to investigate:

(1) Relationships of sociometric configurations under specific criteria to sociometric configurations under other specific criteria.

(2) Relationships of sociometric configurations to personality:
    (a) structural traits—such as sex, age, race
    (b) dynamic traits—such as attitudes, values

(3) Relationships of sociometric configurations to socio-cultural variables—such as income, residence, family size and background, occupation, memberships and participation patterns; social roles and the normative order.

(4) Relationships of sociometric configurations to behavior—such as voting behavior, decision-making, communications, rumor-spreading; and to processes such as cohesiveness, integration, form of leadership.

The sociometric test is the common denominator of all sociometric research; designing of projects then depends on the aims of the investigation with the sociometric test providing basic data on the configurations.

K. THE SOCIOMETRIC TEST

"The sociometric test has a dominant place in this book and is more thoroughly described than the other tests. This should not lead to the conclusion that it answers all questions or that it is most essential. It is only a favorable and strategic *first* (author's italics) step for the more thorough investigation of the depth structure of groups."

(Moreno, *Who Shall Survive?*, 1953, p. 92)

In this volume, as well as in its preceding edition (1934), the reader finds ample information on the sociometric test. The test is described by Stuart Chapin in "Experimental Designs in Sociological Research" (Harper and Brothers, 1947), by Loomis and Proctor in "Research Methods in Social Relations" (Jahoda, Deutsch and Cook), by Borgatta and Lindzey (*Handbook of Social Psychology*, Volume 2, pp. 407-410), by Zerka Toeman ("How to give a Sociometric Test", *Sociatry*, Volume 2, 1948-9), and by Nehnevajsa ("Soziometrische Analyse von Gruppen", *Koelner Zeitschrift*, Volume 7, 1955, pp. 122-124).

In designing a sociometric test, several all-important decisions have to be made. First of all, the researcher asks himself: What criteria am I going to use? Generally, any activity in which subjects engage or potentially engage with other persons may become a test-criterion. Sociometrists have reported the employment of a wide variety of criteria which may, perhaps, be classified into several types:

Communications behavior has been frequently investigated. The criteria employed range from "chatting" with others (Yablonsky, "A Sociometric Investigation into the Development of an Experimental Method for Small Group Analysis", SOCIOMETRY, Volume 15, August-December 1952) to "confiding" in others (for example, in Bassett, "Cliques in a Student Body of Stable Membership", SOCIOMETRY, Volume 7, August 1944). The criteria have been developed to test children (such as reported by Mary Northway), college students (in the above mentioned study of Bassett), as well as adults (county agents and librarians, reported by Loomis and Proctor).

Various activities operationally defining *social proximity and social distance* between subjects have been similarly used. "Sitting together", choice of roommates, choice of companions for meals, "walking together", "playing together", "visiting other families" are typical examples of this class of sociometric test criteria. The studies of Wakely ("Selecting Leaders for Agricultural Programs", SOCIOMETRY, Volume 10, December 1947), Bonney ("A Study of Social Status on the 2nd Grade Level", *Journal of Genetic Psychology*, Volume 60, 1942—and many other studies by the same author published in the *Journal of Educational Psychology, Journal of Social Psychology*, SOCIOMETRY), Kuhlen and Bretch ("Sociometric Status and Personal Problems of Adolescents", SOCIOMETRY, Volume 10, May 1947), and Medalia ("Unit Size and Leadership Perception", SOCIOMETRY, Volume 17, February 1954—as well as other studies resulting from a U.S. Air Force Contract for the so-called Project Air-Sites in which Delbert C. Miller and Nahum Z. Medalia employed sociometric techniques widely), will serve as examples of this approach. The criterion of inter-family visits has usually been connected with investigations of whole communities, George Lundberg's and Steel's famous study ("Social-Attraction Patterns in a Vermont Village", Part I and Part II, SOCIOMETRY, Volume 1, 1-2, 1937 and Volume 2, 3-4, 1937), the works of Loomis and Davidson of rural communities, and of Loomis and Powell in Rural Costa Rica (studies published in SOCIOMETRY, Volume 2, February 1938; and SOCIOMETRY, Volume 12, February-May 1949 respectively) must be mentioned here. An excellent monograph (also published as an article in Volume 9 of SOCIOMETRY) comes from the pen of Charles Loomis on the analysis of political cleavages in a Hannoverian village.

In many studies, *"friendship" configurations* have been studied specifically—on occasions using the somewhat vague description of "Who are your best friends" leaving the interpretation of "friendship" up to the subjects. We find the friendship criterion used by Bonney (in studies which we have already mentioned), Wherry and Fryer ("Buddy Ratings: Popularity Contest or Leadership Criteria?", SOCIOMETRY, Volume 12, February-August, 1949), Orden Smucker ("Dormitory Cliques and Interpersonal Relations", *Autonomous Groups Bulletin*, Volume 6, 1951), Radke, Sutherland and Rosenberg ("Racial Attitudes of Children", SOCIOMETRY, Volume 13, May 1950), Elfrieda Höhn and Christoph Schick ("Das Sociogram", Stuttgart, 1954).

Work-activities of subjects cut clearly across both the formal social structure and the sociometric depth-dimension. The wishes of individuals in terms of their socio-affective relatings are often in conflict with the institutional pattern. Ample attention has been given by sociometrists to the study of configurations by tests designed to investigate forms of association under various criteria of work. Of the researches already mentioned in other contexts, those of Wakely, Bassett, Yablonsky, Bonney and Kuhlen and Bretch need to be mentioned again. Papers of Stogdill ("The Sociometry of Working Relations in Formal Organizations", SOCIOMETRY, Volume 12, November 1949—SOCIOMETRY, Volume 14, November 1951) and Goodacre ("The Use of a Sociometric Test as a Predictor of Combat Unit Effectiveness", SOCIOMETRY, Volume 14, May-August, 1951; "Group Characteristics of Good and Poor Performing Combat Units", SOCIOMETRY, Volume 16, May 1953), as well as the newer works of Speroff ("Job Satisfaction and Interpersonal Desirability Values", SOCIOMETRY, Volume 18, February 1955) and Christner with Hemphill ("Leader Behavior of B-29 Commanders and Changes in Crew Members' Attitudes Toward the Crew", SOCIOMETRY, Volume 18, February 1955) must be added to the list.

The next problem connected with the design of a sociometric test relates to the manner in which the criterion-questions, once the criteria are chosen, will be worded. In this manner, we find studies employing the *level of recall* —that is, asking the respondents to report on their past associations with others. The Vermont study of Lundberg and Steel, the studies by Medalia and Miller and Medalia have been of this type. Next, each criterion-question may be worded on the *actuality level*: it refers to anticipation on the part of the subjects of actual realistic associations. The respondent realizes that his answers to the sociometric test might affect a real situation in the near future. Moreno had, some time ago, designated most other approaches but the one on actuality level as "near-sociometric" or "pseudo-sociometric". Actuality-level questions were asked in all the studies in which therapy was also involved: that is in all researches which were designed to obtain data in order to help restructure the referent population—we mention works of Wolman, Wakely, Loomis and Proctor, Loomis as outstanding examples.

Finally, questions may be *hypothetical*. The respondent is asked to put himself into an imaginary situation, into an as-if setting.

Still another decision must be made. The researcher determines the *number of questions*. He considers the needs of the study, the time available to the respondents, the budget, the willingness of the subjects, the amount of additional types of data which he will need. The pollsters have assembled much material, and acquired much experience, as to optimum lengths of interviews: but the findings vary with some stating that many subjects are willing to be tested for hours, while others react negatively after but several minutes.

Four more decisions remain to be briefly outlined: the researcher decides whether the sociometric test will include the positive direction only, or the negative only, or both. Sociometric literature up-to-date does not provide us with clues about the possible distorting effect*** of negative-direction questions (whom do you like lease to do . . . x . . . with?) on the responses to the test.

Sociometric tests differ also to the extent to which the subjects are expected to react to a preannounced number of other subjects, to an unlimited number of subjects, or to all subjects in the referent population.

A decision must be made regarding intensity-testing. Once the decision is made to test not only the direction of tele (negative, neutral, positive) but also its intensity, the selection of a technique for the investigation of intensities still remains. Bonney in his papers has suggested several equidistant verbal scales, Vladimir Cervin an interesting scale of cooperativeness-to-competitiveness ("A Dimensional Theory of Groups", SOCIOMETRY, Volume 11, 1948).

Finally, we may distinguish (following Moreno) between "horizontal" and "vertical" sociometric tests. The horizontal test does not inquire into the reasons for respective choices; the vertical test does.

In our remarks on the sociometric test, we have avoided mentioning the works of sociometrists who have used practically all the techniques of designing the test. Foremost, Moreno has developed and used all these methods; his relevant writings are far too numerous to be listed here. Helen Jennings and Joan Criswell have similarly employed practically all these methods, as has Mary Northway. With the emergence of *perceptual sociometry* a new issue has necessitated action on the part of the researcher: does one want to invert the sociometric test, regardless of its form, and investigate the anticipations of choices of the subjects? The studies of Tagiuri at Harvard, and Gronlund's report ("Sociometric Status and Sociometric Perception", SOCIOMETRY, Volume 18, May 1955) may be mentioned. In the last two years, quite a few studies of this type have appeared. Edgar Borgatta ("Analysis of Social Interaction and Sociometric Perception", SOCIOMETRY, Volume 17, February 1954), Herbert Schiff ("Judgemental Response Sets in the Perception of Sociometric Status", SOCIOMETRY, Volume 17, August 1954), Erling W. Eng ("An Approach to the Prediction of Sociometric

---

*** See Lundberg in this volume.

Choice", Sociometry, Volume 17, November 1954), and Edward Gottheil ("Changes in Social Perceptions Contingent Upon Competing or Cooperating", Sociometry, Volume 18, May 1955) may be singled out.

This new development in sociometric research appears promising indeed. The relationship between accuracy of perceptions and the sociometric status of an individual accorded to him by others will further refine the theory of psychopathology of social relations, as well as provide additional clues to the understanding of human behavior.

L. Data Collecting, Laboratory and Field

Enrichment of sociometric methodology is also connected with the where, and how, to collect data—once the sociometric instrument has been designed.

Most sociometric projects have been done *in situ*. They are field studies. The researchers approach their populations in actual settings. But laboratory techniques have been used with increasing frequency. The experimenter creates experimental groups as anticipated by Moreno in his Stegreif laboratory (1923) for the sole purpose of studying them so as to maximize his chances of control over many possible intervening variables, as well as to single out particular variables for the study. An excellent treatise by Guy Swanson ("Laboratory Experiments with Small Populations", *American Sociological Review,* June 1951) has served as a guide to a number of small group researchers. Leon Festinger has outlined the problems, and purposes, of laboratory research (in Festinger and Katz, *Research Methods in the Behavioral Sciences,* 1953, Chapter 4). Reva Potashin ("A Sociometric Study of Children's Friendships" Sociometry, Volume 9, February 1946) organized small groupings of children in a laboratory setting; Matilda Riley ("Scales Applied to Dyadic Relationships", Sociometry, Volume 13, February 1950) anticipates the publication of *Sociological Studies in Scale Analysis* (Rutgers University Press, 1954) by Matilda Riley, John Riley and Jackson Toby. Northway's research on "Outsiders" (Sociometry, Volume 7, Februray 1944), Sherif's "An Experimental Approach to the Study of Attitudes" (Sociometry, Volume 1, February-May 1937), and Lewin's and Lippitt's wellknown study of autocratic and democratic leadership ("An Experimental Approach to the Study of Autocracy and Democracy", Sociometry, Volume 1, August-December 1937)—all are conducted under laboratory conditions.

The "where" of sociometric research then presents us with a dichotomous choice: in the field or in a laboratory, each approach having some distinct advantages and some rather distinct disadvantages.

The "how" of data collecting boils down to several techniques: participant observation, or observation, mailed-in questionnaires, telephone interviews, personal interviews, administered questionnaires. Each of these methods has been tried with variable success.

Goodacre (in his military sociometric studies mentioned previously) included observational techniques to supplement data obtained by administration of sociometric questionnaires, as did Medalia in his Air Force studies. Reed Powell ("The Nature and Extent of Group Organization in a Girls' Dormitory—A Sociometric Investigation", SOCIOMETRY, Volume 14, December 1951) used participant observers, again not as primary sources of information but rather for the explicit purpose to gather additional data. Observational methods, of course, play an important role in all interaction process studies by the Harvard group.

Relative success with mailed-in sociometric questionnaires has been reported by Lundberg and Beazley ("Consciousness of Kind in a College Population", SOCIOMETRY, Volume 11, February-May 1948) and Lundberg, Beazley and Dickson ("Attraction Patterns in a University", SOCIOMETRY, Volume 12, February-August 1949). In the previously mentioned report on librarians and county agents ("The Relationship Between Choice Status and Economic Status in Social Systems", SOCIOMETRY, Volume 13, December 1950), Loomis and Proctor mailed their sociometric questionnaires to the respondents.

The telephone-interview was employed in the days of Project Revere, the research on leaflet message diffusion, in the city of Seattle by Dodd and his associates. Personal interviews were conducted in Lundberg's and Steel's study of the Vermont village; in Powell's work in Costa Rica ("A Comparative Analysis of San Juan Sur and Attirro, Costa Rica", SOCIOMETRY, Volume 14, May-August, 1951); in Foa's project among the Yemenite Jews ("Social Change among Yemenite Jews Settled in Jerusalem", SOCIOMETRY, Volume 11, February-May, 1948); and by Loomis and Davidson in their studies of agricultural communities.

In most other sociometric projects, questionnaires have been administered to populations either living together or assembled for the purposes of the test. These studies are most numerous and no specific mentions are thus warranted.

In psychodramatic and role playing research, several methods of acquiring subjects (Ss) and role players have been reported. The classic method is Moreno's training and employment of professional auxiliary egos (SOCIOMETRY, Volume 3, pp. 317—"A Frame of Reference for Testing the Social

Investigator"): the use of clients in need of psychological counselling or vocational adjustment (*Psychodrama*, Volume 1, 1946): the use of voluntary students for temporary role playing tests in the course of interaction analysis.

M. GRAPHIC PRESENTATION

The *sociogram* is, of course, the most famous sociometric chart. In existence since the early days of sociometry as a method of portraying data, the sociogram is, indeed, a widely used instrument. Zerka Toeman has briefly outlined the technique of sociogram construction ("How to Construct a Sociogram", *Sociatry*, Volume 2, 1948-9), following extensive discussions by Moreno in various of his writings (the first somewhat exhaustive presentation in *Who Shall Survive?* 1934, although discussions appeared in his "Application of the Group Methods to Classification" (1932) and the reprint of Moreno's paper for the 57th Annual Session of the American Association on Mental Deficiency in 1933). Borgatta writes "A Diagnostic Note on the Construction of Sociograms and Action Diagrams" (*Group Psychotherapy*, Volume 4, 1951), Bronfenbrenner ("Graphic Presentation of Sociometric Data", SOCIOMETRY, Volume 7, August 1944) discusses the technique, the Horace-Mann-Lincoln Institute publishes a pamphlet on "How to Construct a Sociogram" (1947, Teacher's College, Columbia University).

Rather early, Mary Northway proposes an alternative technique of a modified sociogram—the target diagram ("A Method for Depicting Social Relations Obtained by Sociometric Testing", SOCIOMETRY, Volume 3, May 1940). While no computation is necessary for the construction of sociograms, the target diagram necessitates the evaluation of quartiles in terms of choice receptions by the subjects. The target diagram then consists of concentric circles into which individuals are placed according to their income of choices.

The computation of quartiles, and thus the use of the target diagram, seems particular useful whenever comparisons of sociometrically overchosen and sociometrically underchosen subjects are contemplated. Subjects are then usually taken from the upper quartile and compared with subjects with a sociometric status falling into the lower quartile. Northway and Widgor used the technique in their attempt to find Rorschach responses predictive of high and low sociometric statuses ("Rorschach Patterns Related to the Sociometric Status of School Children", SOCIOMETRY, Volume 10, May 1947).

A further refinement is suggested by Lemann and Solomon ("Group Characteristics as Revealed in Sociometric Patterns and Personality Ratings",

SOCIOMETRY, Volume 15, February-May 1952). The authors give credit to Frederick Mosteller for the development of the *trivariate scatter,* a three-dimensional construct in which individuals are placed in a unique position in terms of their probability standing with regard to reception of positive, negative and neutral choices. A three-dimensional graph was earlier envisaged by Stuart Chapin ("A Three-Dimensional Model for Visual Analysis of Group Structures", *American Journal of Sociology,* Volume 56), while the utility of *graph theory* in sociometric research has been outlined, for the first time, by Horary and Norman ("Graph Theory as a Mathematical Model in Social Sciences", University of Michigan pamphlet, 1953).

Mentioned must be, of course, the *interaction diagrams*—graphs which are an incipient sociomatrix (already in Stegreiftheater, 1923), with subjects heading the rows and time-sequences the columns. These interaction diagrams have been used extensively especially in connection with observational laboratory research. Finally, the *locograms* or *positional diagrams* should be here recalled, as well as the *role diagrams* (Zerka Toeman, "How to Construct a Role Diagram", *Sociatry,* Volume 2, 1948-9; Moreno, Jacob L. in *Who Shall Survive?* 1953, p. 149, *Das Stegreiftheater,* 1923, p. 88—and other writings).

The *sociomatrix* has been, for some purposes, the most fruitful innovation. A modified version of the original interaction diagram, Moreno's, the sociomatrix has been extensively discussed by Dodd ("The Interrelation Matrix", SOCIOMETRY, Volume 3, February 1940; "Analysis of the Interrelation Matrix by Its Surface and Structure", SOCIOMETRY, Volume 3, May 1940; and "Sociomatrices and Levels of Interaction", SOCIOMETRY, Volume 14, May-August, 1951). Dodd has been envisaging multi-dimensional sociomatrices; Tanennbaum, Massarik, Wechsler have proposed a multi-dimensional sociomatrix with interaction patterns recorded on normative, perceived, actual, desired and rejection relationships of the subjects.

Moreno's first interaction diagrams were, indeed, incipient sociomatrices. The columns represented time sequences, whereas the rows were vectors of behavior of the subjects in the respective time periods. The sociomatrix becomes a square matrix wherein the crossections of the row and column vectors indicate the presence, absence and kind of interpersonal relationship between the subject heading the row-vector and the subject at head of the column vector. The sociomatrix makes the evaluation of the number of choices given and choices received very simple: the marginal vectors are used for these purposes. While the sociogram, the target diagram, and even the trivariate scatter become tremendously complex for larger populations so that the difficulty of interpretation increases disproportionately with population size, the sociomatrix remains a simple construct regardless of group size.

N. SOCIOMETRIC INDICES

In elementary analysis of sociometric configurations, the researchers have developed a rather large number of index numbers. These simple ratios have been employed to evaluate the relative position of individuals within a population, the relative position of subgroups within a population, as well as the relative standing of groups.

Who Shall Survive? (1934) initiates the era of index analysis. Since the days of the Index of Positive Expansiveness and Negative Expansiveness, the Index of Choice Status and Rejection Status, numerous new ratios have been proposed and widely utilized. Loomis and Proctor (in Jahoda, Deutsch and Cook, *Research Methods in Social Relations,* 1951) give an excellent survey of Index numbers, preceded by the work of Urie Bronfenbrenner ("The Measurement of Sociometric Status, Structure and Development", *Monograph No.* 6 (1945). In the 1953 edition of *Who Shall Survive?* (p. 453-4), Moreno overviews the various index numbers. Nehnevajsa provides the German reader with an exhaustive survey ("Soziometrische Analyse von Gruppen", Part II, *Koelner Zeitschrift fuer Soziologie,* Volume 7, June 1955). A volume is being prepared for Italian sociometrists, with Moreno's works appearing in French and German translations during 1954.

A combined Choice-Rejection Status index is proposed by Zeleny ("Status, Its Measurement and Control in Education", SOCIOMETRY, Volume 4, May 1941)—as a ratio of choices minus the rejections over the total number of possible choices, further refined by the utilization of the average deviation. Helen Jennings (*Leadership and Isolation,* 1948) has offered her Choice-Rejection Patterns whereby individual index types emerge by referring the standing of each individual to the group mean on his Positive, Negative and Mutual income and output of choices, sixty-four patterns altogether.

The Ratio of Interest and the Ratio of Attraction applicable to group analysis are developed very early by Moreno and Jennings ("Statistics of Social Configurations", SOCIOMETRY, Volume 1, January-April 1938), with Lundberg and Steel working out the Index of Subgroup Cohesion in their research in the Vermont village (SOCIOMETRY, Volume 1, 1938). The Criswell Ratio—comparing the total number of choices expected by a given population subgroup to the actual number of choices received by a subgroup —emerges ("Sociometric Methods of Measuring Group Preferences", So-

CIOMETRY, Volume 6, December 1943). Thanks to the same author, the Index of Group Coherence is developed ("Measurement of Reciprocation Under Multiple Criteria of Choice", SOCIOMETRY, Volume 9, May 1946). In 1947, Zeleny adds an Index of Ingroup Climate ("Selection of the Unprejudiced", SOCIOMETRY, Volume 10, November 1947), elaborated by Loomis and Proctor (in their above mentioned chapter in Jahoda, Deutsch and Cook) in terms of the six types of tele resulting from combinations of positive, neutral and negative portions of tele (projective and retrojective). A set of indeces used by Stogdill ("The Sociometry of Working Relations: 20 Sociometric Indeces", SOCIOMETRY, Volume 14, November 1951) is conceptually similar to the idea of Choice-Rejection Patterns of Jennings (to use a number of ratios for the description of an individual's standing) as well as to the idea of *sociodiagnostic prophiles* whereby a unique graph-line in terms of a preannounced group of index-numbers depicts the standing of a given individual.

A contribution of considerable importance is made by Massarik-Tanennbaum and Wechsler ("Sociometric Choice and Organizational Effectiveness: A Multi-Relational Approach", SOCIOMETRY, Volume 16, 1953); these multi-relational indeces as composite ratios utilizing data on normative, perceived, actual, positive and negative relationships are applicable to both individuals and groups. Bock and Husain ("An Adaptation of Holzinger's B-Coefficient for the Analysis of Sociometric Data", SOCIOMETRY, Volume 13, May 1950) devise a method for the analysis of cliques within a population, an index procedure whereby the researcher can ascertain exactly who does and who does not belong into a given clique. Several innovations come from Paul Maucorps ("Sociometric Inquiry in the French Army", SOCIOMETRY, Volume 12, February-August 1949), while Leo Katz elaborates his Reciprocity Index and a new Status Index in two unpublished research documents ("The Reciprocity Index", Research Memorandum, Michigan State College, 1952; "A New Status Index Derived from Sociometric Analysis", Research Memorandum, Michigan State College, 1952). The Status Index of Katz is theoretically quite interesting, yet, leaves empirically much to be desired. For the first time, however, a sociometric index-number includes not only immediate inter-personal choices but an attempt is made to include the whole *vector* of choices (including contingent ones, that is, involving the notion of the importance of being chosen *through* one, two, . . x, other individuals).

Good discussions of the rationale behind index-numbers are to be found in Lundberg (*Social Research*, 1942) and in the above-mentioned article by Criswell (1949). It is however Paul Lazarsfeld who has delt imaginatively with two major issues in index-analysis: the problem of ambiguity of indeces and the problem of differential sensitivity of indeces ("Some Notes on the Use of Indeces in Social Research", undated mimeographed document of Columbia University). Lazarsfeld not only explains how it is possible that two index-numbers designed to measure the same phenomenon (say group integration) may yield contradictory answers: the seeming contradiction is explainable in terms of an Area of Ambiguity of the performance-lines of such indexes; the author suggests also techniques for determining which index, in such a case, is operationally the more efficient one.

O. Matrix Algebra in Sociometry

The idea that, since sociometric data can be tabulated onto a socio-matrix, matrix algebra, in some of its respects, is analytically useful has been tremendously fruitful. Luce and Perry ("A Method of Matrix Analysis of Group Structures", *Psychometrika,* Volume 14, 1949) develop the basic reasoning of multiplaction of sociomatrices; their technique is employed by Festinger-Schachter and Back in an actual field study ("Social Pressures in Informal Groups", Harper and Brothers, 1950), to be followed by the stimulating discussion of connectivity of sociomatrices by Luce "Connectivity and Generalized Cliques in Sociometric Group Structure", *Psychometrika,* Volume 15, 1950).

The discovery is rather simple: the n-th power of a sociomatrix yields information on n-chains—relationships of one individual with another one through n-1 others. The use of mutual relationships only, that is of the symmetric sociomatrix, will disclose the existence, and size, of cliques non-ambiguously. In many respects, the work of Leo Katz has been pioneering along these lines ("On the Matrix Analysis of Sociometric Data", Sociometry, Volume 10, August 1947; and "Relation of Satisfaction to Reduction of the Choice-Matrix", Research Memorandum, Michigan State College, 1952). Another mimeographed document on the subject comes from Horary and Ross (University of Michigan).

Matrix analysis seems especially useful in any studies of news, rumor, and influence spreading—as it may be meaningfully argued that the position of an individual in his group is not only a function of his direct relationship with others but also of his interrelatedness with others through chains, or k-chains, where k is the number of links in such a configuration. In their joint article, Dodd and Winthrop ("A Dimensional Theory of Social Diffusion", Sociometry, Volume 16, 1953) point out the need for n-dimensional matrix algebra as a possible new area of analytic exploration.

P. PROBABILISTIC ANALYSIS

Paul Lazarsfeld's solution of the mathematical problem presented to him by Moreno and Jennings ("Statistics of Social Configurations", SOCIOMETRY, Volume 1, January-March 1938)—the formulation of the probability of any given individual being chosen by any other specific individual —stands at the roots of probabilistic analysis in the field. The Bernoulli series is used by Moreno and Jennings for a group of 26 with three choices permitted to each individual to evaluate the expectation of choice-income, that is the probability of an individual being chosen 0,1,2 . . . N-1 times. Urie Bronfenbrenner follows with his stimulating articles ("Constant Frame of Reference for Sociometric Research", Part I: SOCIOMETRY, Volume 6, December 1943; Part II: SOCIOMETRY, Volume 7, February 1944). The author evaluates the expectancy of mutual choices—and suggests their expected distribution; expectancies of unreciprocated choices are studied. But foremost, Bronfenbrenner employs shortcut methods to approximate the computationally tedious binomial: the Poisson distribution, the Incomplete Beta Function (tabulated by Pearson, 1934), the Gram-Charlier Series, and the Pearson Type III Function (Tabulated by Salvosa (1930). In their rejoinders, Joan Criswell ("Notes on the Constant Frame of Reference Problem", SOCIOMETRY, Volume 13, May 1950) and Daisy Edwards ("The Constant Frame of Reference Problem in Sociometry", SOCIOMETRY, Volume 11, December 1948) discusses the contributions of Bronfenbrenner; Edwards specifically points out the incorrect solution of the problem of distribution of mutual choices due to the fact that mutualities in sociometric configurations are not statistically independent of each other. As late as 1952, Leo Katz argues the same point ("Recent Advances and Some Unsolved Problems of Sociometric Theory", Research Memorandum, Michigan State College, 1952) to conclude that the issue of mutual choices has yet to be successfully solved by sociometrists.

Leo Katz solves the problem of the distribution of isolated individuals ("The Distribution of Isolates in a Social Group", *Annals of Mathematical Statistics,* Volume 23, 1952), and the problem of expectancy of various k-chains (in the Research Memorandum mentioned above). His work was anticipated by Schutzenberger ("Etudes Statistique d'un probleme du sociometrie", *Acta Gallica Biologica,* Paris, 1948) and Maucorps ("Sociometric Inquiry into the French Army", SOCIOMETRY, Volume 12, February 1949).

Daisy Edwards proposes procedures for evaluating the expectancy of inter-class choice distribution, a technique operationally described later

742

by Nehnevajsa ("Chance Expectancy and Intergroup Choice", Sociometry, Volume 18, May 1955).

Finally, the work of Kephart ("A Quantitative Analysis of Intragroup Relationships", *American Journal of Sociology,* Volume 56, 1950) should be mentioned. The author analyzes mathematically the group structure as a whole, providing clues as to how many various interrelational forms may exist within a group of a given size.

Q. General Statistics

Let finally a few remarks be made about the use of general statistical procedures. Our previous discussions dealt with analytic procedures specifically designed for the study of sociometric configurations. When additional variables are involved, sociometrists have employed general statistical methods. All forms of correlation coefficients have found their way into sociometry—as one may expect. Factor analysis has been utilized (Bock and Husain, "Factors of the Tele: A Preliminary Report", Sociometry, Volume 15, August-December, 1952); Riley ("Scales Applied to Dyadic Relationships", Sociometry, Volume 15, February-May 1952) and Uriel Foa ("Scale and Intensity Analysis in Sociometric Research", Sociometry, Volume 13, December 1950) explore scalograms in sociometric research, primarily leaning on techniques developed by Guttman ("American Soldier", Volume 4).

R. Sociometric Patterns and Personality Traits

The studies relating the tele-configurations to various measures of personality characteristics are far too numerous to deal with exhaustively. But a few more important examples may be usefully mentioned. Basic in these researches are studies of Moreno's group on "cleavages" on the basis of age, sex and race, with a great number of projects following suit. Moreno has reported many findings in both editions of *Who Shall Survive?* (1934 and 1953). Criswell, Loomis, Lundberg and Dickson have studied racial cleavages rather extensively. Reva Potashin studied the relationship between sociometric patterns and mental age; the same author, as well as Bonney, Wakely, Wherry and Fryer (in studies which we have previously referred to) relate intelligence (I.Q.) to tele relationships; Cassell and Saugstadt ("Level of Aspiration and Sociometric Distance", Sociometry, Volume 15, August-November, 1952) employed personality rating scales, French and Mensh ("Some Relationships Between Interpersonal Judgements and Sociometric Status in a College Group", Sociometry, Volume 11, November

1948) and Maucorps use personality self-ratings. Northway and Widgor ("Rorschach Patterns Related to the Sociometric Status of School Children", SOCIOMETRY, Volume 10, May 1947) and Esther Frankel in an unpublished M.A. thesis (University of Chicago, 1948) investigate sociometric patterns in terms of Rorschach inkblots, Borgatta utilizes picture frustration tests, Radke and Sutherland the projective picture tests. ("Racial Attitudes of Children", SOCIOMETRY, Volume 13, May 1950).

S. SOCIOMETRIC PATTERNS AND SOCIO-CULTURAL VARIABLES

Residential proximity was hypothesized conducive to the formation of friendship configurations by Potashin, Lundberg, Beazly and Dickson as well as by Willerman and Swanson ("An Ecologocial Determinant of Differential Amounts of Sociometric Choices within College Sororities", SOCIOMETRY, Volume 15, August-November, 1952). Bonney, Wherry and Fryer and Potashin related academic achievement to sociometric patterns, Longmore investigated differential income levels in a Peruvian communities ("A Matrix Approach to the Analysis of Rank and Status in a Community in Peru", SOCIOMETRY, Volume 11, August 1948). Bonney employed the Dreesy and Mooney Interest Inventory, Lundberg, Beazley and Dickson similarly studied interests of subjects. Seeman ("A Situational Approach to Intragroup Negro Attitudes", SOCIOMETRY, Volume 9, May-August, 1946), Wardlow and Greene ("An Exploratory Sociometric Study of Peer Status Among Adolescent Girls", SOCIOMETRY, Volume 15, August-November, 1952) administered the Ohio Social Acceptance Scale with the latter authors adding the Ohio Social Recognition test. Family background of respondents was related to sociometric configurations in the Vermont study of Lundberg and Steele, in works of Northway, Loomis and Powell. Socio-economic status was measured by Ludberg (Chapin's scale); Wardlow and Greene investigated status and sociometric patterns.

T. SOCIOMETRIC PATTERNS AND BEHAVIOR

The whole issue of *validity* of sociometric data, previously briefly outlined by Pepinsky ("The Meaning of Validity and Reliability as Applied to Sociometric Tests", *Educational Psychology Measurement,* Volume 9, 1949) has been studied recently in an all-out attack by Mouton, Blake and Fruchter ("The Validity of Sociometric Responses", SOCIOMETRY, Volume 18, August 1955), preceded by a 1951 account by Eugene Byrd ("A Study of Validity and Constancy of Choices in a Sociometric Test", SOCIOMETRY, Volume 14, May-August, 1951). An experiment has been reported by Edgar Borgatta ("An Analysis of Three Levels of Response: An Approach to Some Relationships Among Dimensions of Personality", SOCIOMETRY, Volume 14, November 1950); which tries to define a conceptual distance between *actual behavior, role-playing, verbal response behavior* and *written response behavior*.

Robert French ("Sociometric Measures in Relation to Individual Adjustment and Group Performance Among Naval Recruits", *American Psychologist*, 1949), D. M. Goodacre ("The Use of a Sociometric Test as a Predictor of Combat Unit Effectiveness", SOCIOMETRY, Volume 14, May-August 1951), Gough ("Predicting Social Participation", *Journal of Social Psychology*, Volume 35, 1952), Grosser, Polansky and Lippitt ("A Laboratory Study of Behavioral Contagion", *Human Relations*, Volume 1, 1951), Hemphill ("Relations Between the Size of the Group and Behavior of Superior Leaders", *Journal of Social Psychology*, Volume 46, 1951), Nahum Medalia (in his military studies)—all study various aspects of behavior of subjects. Through observational techniques, data is obtained on respondent actions in addition to sociometric testing by Lundberg and Beazley, Potashin, Yablonsky, Gregory, and frequently, by Northway. The Hudson studies, and many subsequent projects of Moreno and Jennings include sociometric measures as well as data on behavior usually assembled by observation.

U. SOCIOMETRIC VISTAS

The growth of sociometry up-to-date is the key to its future development. Sociometric theory, therapeutic methods, research methodology as well as substantive research—all may well be entering a new era. For in spite, and perhaps because, of the numerous achievements, much remains to be done.

Sociometric theory is, at this stage, considerably developed. It provides its student with a systematic analysis of interpersonal relations assuming a social and organic unity of mankind (Moreno, *Who Shall Survive?* 1953). Yet, much careful work must go into relating the theory to the available body of knowledge gathered, in the course of the past three decades, by sociologists and social psychologists. A clearcut presentation, other than hypothetical, of the relationship of sociometric theories to the theories of social roles, for example, or to institutional sociology is still lacking to a large extent. Cross-cultural research in sociometry will help prove, and/or modify, some of the present propositions. The sociometric perspectives of major social processes, such as cooperation, competition, accommodation, conflict, assimilation—while envisaged with lucidity by Moreno and others—are likely to attract the attention of sociometrists.

The further growth of therapy, not unlike that of theory, revolves not only around extended interest in group psychotherapy, the inclusion of the technique in many new practical programs within Universities, in the industry, in Government and in the Armed Forces—in America and abroad, but also around the constant search for new methods. The accumulation of data on results of sociometric therapy will provide the psychodrama director, the sociometrist-therapist with more norms of conduct. Thus on one hand, differences from director to director in analysis may gradually be minimized, while on the other hand, the poetic spontaneity of ad lib productions may yield some way to more formal approaches. A strength, or a weakness— who can tell with definiteness?

Methodological problems center around a few unsolved problems. The main one deals with the probabilistic distribution of mutual choices in a group. The other issues cluster around the analytical imaginativeness of future sociometrists: how far can matrix algebra be exploited for uses by sociometrists? how will the application of scale analysis aid in the study of sociometric patterns? how can probabilistic procedures be modified by the inclusion of additional parameters so that the probability statistics of sociometry may lead to the formation of mathematical models? and, importantly enough, is this a fruitful line of attack at all?

Finally, of potential significance to sociometry are considerations about sampling. Touched upon by Bassett ("Sampling Problems in Influence Studies", SOCIOMETRY, Volume 11, November 1948) and Darrell Bock ("Time Sampling and Sociometric Testing", SOCIOMETRY, Volume 15, August-November, 1952), the issue of sampling *interpersonal relations*—dyadic and larger-sized—remains completely unsolved. With it, the possibility of large-scale generalizations in sociometric research may well stand or fall.

The prospects for substantive research are both bright and gloomy. First of all, an unlimited range of problems exists which having been explored, necessitate retesting and re-retesting. Secondly, many questions have been hardly touched upon by the researcher, specifically the whole set of hypotheses pertaining to the dynamic relationship of sociometric variables and the normative social patterns. Issues of social cohesion, integration, and cleavage await yet a reformulation on some basis which may clarify the presently obscure meaning of the concepts. Hardly any studies have been designed to inquire into possible predictivity of sociometric configurations at some future date provided that data exists on the configurations here-and-now. Nor have the thousands of case-studies of various populations been adequately related to each other—so that predictivity from one population to another is still wanted.

The vistas are gloomy in one sense only: far too many studies are being conducted with little or no coordination between them so that a frontal attack may be launched on some of the burning issues. This, in part, due to the not-too-outstanding communications among contemporary scientists. In part, due to the bias of many scholars for "studiable" and readily accessible populations, projects designed not due to the intrinsic importance of the problem but inadvertently "because a population is available". One aims to fit research problems to available populations rather than locate populations to fit research problems—although many notable exceptions exist. The result: thousands of studies among college and high-school students, with the concluding sentence usually worded somewhat as follows: "The findings are tentative; the need for further research is strongly indicated." But this is not a problem unique to research sociometry.

V. THE SOCIOMETRISTS

We said at the outset that the story of sociometry was one of men, their ideas and activities. In the previous sections of this discussion, we viewed sociometry in terms of several classificatory categories. Thus amidst our remarks, the contributions of a number of sociometrists may have seemed lost scattered over the whole range of their activities. Perhaps this is the right time and place to look at some of these scientists more individually.

While most of the theoretical discussions have come from but a few writers, Moreno, Helen Jennings, Paul Deutschberger, Zerka Toeman, sociometry has benefited greatly by evaluative arguments pertaining to the whole field by a number of outstanding contemporary scientists. We have had an occasion to mention the work of Margaret Mead, Georges Gurvitch and Florian Znaniecki in this context; several such articles have been published by Stuart Chapin ("Trends in Sociometry and Critique", SOCIOMETRY, Volume 3, August 1940; "Relation of Sociometry to Planning in an Expanding Social Universe", SOCIOMETRY, Volume 6, August 1940), Read Bain, George Lundberg (in his *Social Research*), Gardner Murphy (SOCIOMETRY, Volume VI, 1943, pp. 221-2), Gordon W. Allport (*Group Psychotherapy*, Volume VII, 1954, pp. 307-8) and Pitirim Sorokin. In German literature, we find contributions to general sociometry by Leopold von Wiese (also in "Sociometry", SOCIOMETRY, Volume 12, January-August, 1949) and Theodor

Geiger ("Ueber Soziometrik und ihre Grenzen", *Koelner Zeitschrift fuer Soziologie"*, Volume 1, 1948-49). In many respects, the writings of Leslie Zeleny, Merl Bonney, Joan Criswell and Mary Northway have had a direct bearing on the advancement of sociometric theories; Paul Lazarsfeld, one of the early protagonists of sociometric measurement has concerned himself with the affective dimensions of likes, dislikes and indifferences ("Some Properties of the Trichotomy 'Like, No-opinion, Dislike' and Their Psychological Interpretation", SOCIOMETRY, Volume 3, May 1940).

The range of contributions of these scholars varies indeed. Von Wiese and Geiger have been primarily motivated by theoretical interests. Georges Gurvitch has been instrumental in stimulating French social scientists toward an appetite for sociometric research; Zeleny, Bonney, Griswell and Northway have been researchers as well as, implicitly, theorists. In various ways, all four have added to the body of analytical techniques: Zeleny with his sociometric status index, Bonney with his approach to affective-intensity measures, Criswell with her ratio of choices expected by an ingroup as well as in probabilistic analysis, Northway with her target diagrams as well as with her newer cumulative sociometric charts ("A Plan For Sociometric Studies in a Longitudinal Programme of Research in Child Development", SOCIOMETRY, Volume 17, August 1954).

George Lundberg, a philosopher of science in some regards, has been at the same time an innovator in the area of index analysis, as well as in pioneering in new substantive research: whether Wollman or Lundberg were the first ones to study whole communities (preceded by Moreno's Mittendorf studies) seems less important than the fact that both have distinctly added to sociometric work: Wollman in applied sociometry, Lundberg in research sociometry. Nor do we find anywhere but in Northway and her associates such systematic preoccupation with sociometry among children, and in Bonney, systematic attacks on sociometry among adolescents.

As Lundberg and Wollman have pioneered in sociometric community studies, Maucorps, Goodacre, Stogdill, Medalia and Miller have introduced the field in systematic research in the armed forces, while Jacobs ("Application of Sociometry to Industry", SOCIOMETRY, Volume 8, May 1945), James, Maucorps, Massarik, Tannenbaum, Kahane and Wechsler have done the same for the industry. Along these lines, the unpublished contributions of Daniel Katz with Maccoby and Gurin in the area of morale among workers must be at least mentioned.

Nor would it do to omit the numerous works of Loomis, Proctor and Davidson—both pertaining to status relationships in communities as well as to ethnic cleavages with the interests of Henrik Infield concentrated in a similar research area.

Several researchers have been preoccupied with attempts to provide sociometry with a powerful body of analytical techniques. We may think here of the extensive contributions of Leo Katz, Stuart Dodd, Leon Festinger, Urie Bronfenbrenner as well as others such as Ross, Olkin, Horary, Edwards. Some of the exciting newer suggestions have yet to be explored: those related to scale analysis (Uriel Foa, Matilda Riley), and to the uses of symbolic logic (Ake Bjerstedt, "Some Examples of the Possibility of Using Structural Formalizations in Sociometric Analysis", SOCIOMETRY, Volume 16, November 1953).

A new methodological attack upon some crucial sociometric problems has been made by Thrall and Angell under a research contract of the Office of Naval Research. The authors have combined probabilistic considerations with matrix algebra and symbolic logic to arrive at a set of measures whereby community organizations may be analyzed, specifically from the viewpoint of social stratification. ("The Mapping of Community Organizations", Volume 17, SOCIOMETRY, August 1954).

A few cursory observations seem to reveal that the study of psychosocial networks among sociometrists would be of some importance: how has creativity been related to the positions of respective scientists in this network? How does this network cut across the configurations among behavioral scientists in general? The sociometrists, as a group of interrelated individuals, have helped their field grow—and grow out of all proportions and beyond all expectations. Though somewhat indirectly, many other scientists have been instrumental to this growth—perhaps, by their mere support and friendship. In this regard, the contributions of men like Gardner Murphy, Theodore Newcomb, Ernest Burgess, George Murdock, Paul Lazarsfeld may have been tangential to the field; but it is hard to say that without their interest sociometry would have fared as well as it has. Nor have men like Georges Gurvitch and Roger Bastide in France, Leopold von Wiese and Rene Koenig in Germany, Corrado Gini in Italy, done themselves sociometric research or acted as therapists: yet, their "presence" in the sociometric network of sociometrists has, indeed, been vividly felt.

W. MAJOR TRENDS IN SOCIOMETRY

We have already argued that sociometry, up to about 1935 or 1936, is a blend of theory, research and therapy. As a theory, it is a challenge to the psychoanalytic theorizing of Freud and the Freudians; as a research technique, it provides suggestive methods of measurement of phenomena otherwise difficult (if not impossible) to measure; as a therapeutic instrument it falls in line with the democratic ideology on one hand, and, on the other hand, it leads to the growth of therapy which revolves around the social reality of the individual patient as well as around his inner self. As a theory, sociometry has revised the notions of Toennies and Cooley on primary groups by demonstrating theoretically *and* empirically that sociometric networks are different from, and supplementary to, face-to-face configurations of the "Gemeinschaft" and the "primary" type. As a research technique, it has been experimental but also survey-centered: both the laboratory *and* the field have played an immense role in sociometric work. As a method of therapy, it has unleashed individual behavior toward all-inclusive catharsis by capitalizing on his verbal, as well as muscular behavior—not forgetting the crucial influence of the physical-object environment around the subject (when on the psychodrama stage the subject "reconstructs" conceptually the *locus* of a situation and not only the situation itself), and of alters.

Theorizing about small groups as well as studies of processes by the assessment of the verbal interaction has separated out the field of group dynamics from the larger field of Sociometry. Its origins date back to the late 'thirties—at least, as we know group dynamics today. Scholarly arguments, as well as tele-relations among various scientists have tended to increase the seeming gap between sociometry and group dynamics. But both developmental tracks have, simultaneously, helped bridge the gap between psychology and sociology giving rise to the increased emphasis on, and interest in, social psychology. Social psychology borrowed from sociometry the analytic framework of reciprocity of relationships, approaching closer and closer the study of *groups*.

Mathematical sociometry originated in the womb of the field as soon as it became obvious that substantive knowledge will be improved when rigorous analytic procedures are developed. Today, sociometry is equipped with many powerful tools—sometimes even unaware of all their potentialities and ramifications since many scholars who have not been particularly mathematically minded, have found it difficult to keep up with the development of sociometric statistics.

Substantively, sociometry has been primarily devoted to the uncovering of relationships: what variables are, and are not, related to homogeneity of sociometric choice? how are homogeneous variables related to sociometric choice? That is, do people of similar intelligence, sex, race, residence, socioeconomic status form specific sociometric patterns (such as mutualities)?

And, do people of similar sociometric patterns belong to groups homogeneous in terms of intelligence, sex, race, residence, socio-economic status and such?

Thus, several lines of attack upon phenomena in question have been opened in the past fifteen years or so. The promise lies in the integration of all these trends, in a synthesis of the theories, methods and findings. The time seems ripe for such an integration.

What is it that we know today? The numerous case-studies show undoubtedly that sociometric patterns are real—as much as the "atom" of the physicist is real. They show that discrepancies between the affective structures and the formal systems are similarly real, and that, consequently, many social problems can be brought closer to a solution if the discrepancy could be removed. Without sociometric considerations, studies in social stratification, communication, and social institutions become somewhat lifeless; problems of morale, cohesion, integration, leadership, isolation are, indeed, proper sociometric issues, but they are also questions in role—relationships. We know also, from many studies, that an "individual"—an abstraction anyway—moves through his life in, and with, a cluster of changing relationships around him. We guess that the moves toward equilibration, that is toward maximizing his adjustment in the world around him—toward sociostasis. Sociometry, medical sociology, the studies of social problems find their convergence herein.

It is not exaggerated to say that, around sociometry, contemporary sociology and social psychology have widened their scope and enriched their methods—to foreshadow the rise of a *behavioral science,* or a science of man.

X. Ask a Question

Ask a question, today, of a social scientist: What are your major interests in the field? More often than not, the answer will be: I am interested in small groups.

Let a few notes be made about this. Small group research is, indeed, the fad of the day. In America, the climax is approaching rapidly; in many other countries, the interest is but awakening. Is it then a "fad" which, having had its day, shall have disappeared to be replaced by some new fashion? We doubt this strongly.

It is true, that in some cases, small group research is a byproduct of simple considerations: one is expected to do research; one is expected to publish its results; hence, by the principle of least effort, one does that which *appears* "easiest" to do. A small group can readily be assembled. Budgets for small group research *generally* tend to be relatively low. A design can be worked out with relative facility.

But it is equally correct to say that there is much more to the current interest in small groups than this; fortunately, there is much more to it. The researchers have come to realize that small groups perform two major functions in contemporary scientific endeavors: on one hand, they are miniature societies where, weaker though they may be reproduced, social phenomena can be structured with considerable accuracy. The laboratory which has led to so many advances in the natural sciences is becoming common in behavioral research because it is susceptible of controls. On the other hand, small groups are not mere miniatures of larger social fabrics: they are themselves configurations which "really" exist in our societies and which "really" matter. Relationships among members of a particular governing elite might well be more important to provide clues to international problems than the classical formalized diplomatic relationships. Decision-making behavior, in Government, in the military, in industry—wherever we look, occurs in small groups whose pattern is a likely fundamental codeterminant of the outcome of any deliberation. "Powers behind the throne" are merely sociometric "powers"—channels of influence an individual may wield upon a group although he need not be a "formal leader". In fact, we shall assert that small groups are the *basic real referents* for each individual, with "societies", "cultures", "symbols" being referred to only through small groups.

Small group research was not started by Moreno but it cannot be denied that he and the sociometrists were the first to *recognize* its great importance and that they began to develop the field systematically with greater energy than anyone else before them.

"The organization of the Viennese Stegreif laboratory in 1923 (and its many successors in the USA) was one force, Gardner Murphy's "Experimental Social Psychology" (1931) and his fatherly, all embracing support and understanding of all the ego- and production-involved talents throughout the decade of 1930 was a second force; this was followed by the appearance of *Who Shall Survive?* (1934). But the high point of crystallization for all concerned was probably the foundation of Sociometry, *A Journal of Interpersonal Relations* (1937; first published as *Sociometric Review* in 1936), with Gardner Murphy as its first editor. This journal was of crucial importance for the spread of small group research. Between 1936 and 1941 it published seventy-five articles (about 65% of the printed production during that period) dealing with sociometric and near-sociometric small group research. Among the participants in this early production were most of the promising talents in this area, in alphabetic order: S. Chapin, L. Cottrell, S. Dodd, M. Hagen, E. Hartley, H. Infield, H. Jennings, J. Kephart, P. Lazarsfeld, K. Lewin, R. Lippitt, C. Loomis, G. Lundberg, J. L. Moreno, T. Newcomb, M. Northway, I. Sanders, M. Sherif, L. Zeleny. They became, in small group research, the chain leaders of the growing flood of productivity between 1941 and 1953." ("Old and New Trends in Sociometry: Turning Points in Small Group Research", Sociometry, Volume XVII, 1954, p. 186.)

In a similar vein, our societies tell us (or we construe they do) which values are to be cherished and which goals need be achieved. We are told, implicitly, that adjustment is to be preferred to maladjustment. We are told that sanity is to be preferred to personality disorders and mental disease. We are told that social problems need be solved. For the successful discharge of all these tasks, and tasks related to them, our societies look to the social scientists. If we know that functioning in small groups is vital to an individual—to all individuals in such groups—it follows that it is equally vital to malfunctioning. Group therapy does not deal with questions like: "Are these goals desirable?" But it assumes that the goals are desirable, if our society labels them as such, and it aims at their achievement.

One may philosophize that maladjustment is more conducive to imaginativeness than adjustment. One may argue that an adjusted society would be a sterile society. Or, one may say that a maladjusted individual wastes much of his creative energy in hopeless efforts to adjust and, were he to be adjusted, his creativity would become free to flow. The researcher may attempt to answer these, and similar, questions. The applier, however, accepts the paramount social values as given.

No matter how we view our problem, small group research is, indeed, a fad. But beyond and above that, it is a lasting must in the behavioral sciences. Small groups are real or they can be made to stand for something which is real.

Sociometry has thus been not only a field of study in its own right. Not only has it directly enriched our modern research methodology and pushed some of the barriers of the unknown. It has, at the same time, been the fertile soil for many related activities—it has permeated all of contemporary behavioral research to some extent. In its youth of thirty some years, sociometry has done more than well, indeed. Yet its growth has just begun.

Appendix

GLOBAL DEVELOPMENTS, 1950–1960

Austria

University of Vienna, Neuropsychiatric Clinic, Vienna, Austria.
Arbeitskreis für Gruppentherapie und Gruppendynamik.

Cuba

Theater of Psychodrama at the Mental Hygiene Clinic (Dr. Frisso Potts), 1958; Theater of Psychodrama at Havana University (Dr. Jose Bustamante), 1960.

Czechoslovakia

Publications: Psychodrama in Czechoslovakia, Harry Buxbaum, M.D. and Hugo Siroky, M.D., Psychiatric Hospital, Opava, Olomoucv, Czechoslovakia.
Congressus Psychiatricus Bohemoslovenicus, 1959.

France

Groupe Français D'Etudes de Sociometrie-Dynamique des Groupes et Psychodrama, Paris, France. The headquarters are at: Siège Social a l'Institut Pedagogique National, 29 rue d'Ulm, Paris (5e). The members of the training staff are: A. Ancelin Schutzenberger, S. Gounod, A. Abraham, M. Dreyfus, A. Moles, R. Amiel.
Publications: J. L. Moreno, La dynamique des groupes et psychodrame, Presses Universitaires de France, Paris, 1960.—I. Chaix-Ruy, Psychologie sociale et sociometrie, Librairie Armand Colin, Paris, 1960.

Greece

Committee on Group Psychotherapy and Psychodrama, Athens, Greece. Director—Dr. A. Potamianou.
Sociometric Study of a Greek School, Calliope Moustaka, Ph.D., London University and University of Athens, Greece.

India

B.M. Institute of Psychology and Child Development, Ahmedabad (Professor H. P. Maiti), 116 boys and 81 girls belonging to six grades of a school were asked to give their choices from among their classmates in the following four activities: sitting, playing, taking home for a visit, and disliking most.
At Saugor University, Miss M. P. Sethna used sociometry in an investigation aimed at discovering the types of inter-personal relationships existing in a student community and also at studying the factors associated with the phenomenon of "popularity-isolateness."
Sethna used sociometry at Jabalpur University in another investigation which concerned preferences of companions among Nursery School children.
Sociometry is being profitably employed by the Psychological Research Wing of the Defence Science Organization, Ministry of Defence, on a project in connection with assessment of leadership in the armed forces.

Appendix

Bishwanath Mukherjee of the Bureau of Educational and Vocational Guidance, Patna, has been engaged upon many sociometric projects.

At the B.M. Institute of Psychology and Child Development of Ahmedabad, role-playing is being utilized as one of the techniques for the purpose of training workers in interviewing skill to be employed in case work, research investigations, etc.

At the All India Institute of Mental Health, Bangalore, its Director, M. V. Govin-daswamy, has set up a Psychodramatic Stage with a view to using it "for sociometric tests, group psychotherapy, psychodramatic tests and psychodrama as an adjunct to individual therapy."

R. M. Loomba has been trying to use sociodramatic techniques in handling personal counseling on students' problems at Lucknow University, in a somewhat novel and inter-esting approach.

Publications: P. H. Probhu, Sociometry, Telugu Encyclopedia. Andhora University, 1958.

Israel

Sociometry and Psychodrama applied at Government Hospitals as Beer Yaacov near Tel Aviv, The Mazra near Haifa, and at Kfar Schaul near Jerusalem.

Japan

In 1950, Moreno's idea of psychodrama was first introduced to Japan as one of the projective techniques by Sotobayashi (23) in his book entitled "Psychodiagnostics of Per-sonality," in which he translated the term "psychodrama" literally into Japanese "shinri-geki."

In 1956, establishing a research center for psychodrama in the Japan School of Social Work, Sotobayashi, Matsumura, Ishii and others began to co-operate to develop this technique further. Having about seventy trained specialists as its members, the center has been publishing the annual journal "shinri-geki Kenkyu" (Japanese Journal of Psycho-drama) since 1957. In this center the members have been studying the psychodrama most actively under the management of Ishii.

Psychodramatic practice in the classroom is one of the most active and also the most promising areas in Japan. Especially, Fukuoka (2, 3) examined the effect of sociodramatic psychodrama on the interpersonal relationship among children in his classroom for the first time in Japan. Thereafter, he (31–33) reported a diagnostic technique of interpersonal relationships between classrooms. Nishi (22) measured the efficacy of psychodrama on human relationship in her class, in combination with sociometric techniques.

Publications: Gosalho Naruse, Hypnodrama and Psychodrama, Seishin Book Co., Tokyo, 1959.

Argentina

Publications: J. L. Moreno Sociometria y Psychodrama, Ed. Deucalion, Buenos Aires, 1954. J. L. Moreno "Who Shall Survive?," translated into Spanish, Editorial Paidos, Buenos Aires, 1959.

U.S.S.R.

Publications: J. L. Moreno, "Sociometry, Experimental Methods and the Science of Society," 1951. Russian translation, Department of Socioeconomic Literature, Moscow, 1958. M. Baxitov, "The Newest New Social Utopia—Critical Notes about Microsociology and Sociometry, published by the Socioeconomic Literature Publishers, Moscow, U.S.S.R.

Experimental School, Psychological Institute, Academy of Science, Moscow, U.S.S.R.

A sociometric study is being planned under the direction of Madame Bojovitch in this experimental school. A sociometric test is to be applied to three collectives, to the living collective—the criterion being "with whom do you like to live and share the same quarters?"—to the working collective—the criterion being "with whom do you like to work together on a *special* task?"—and to the recreational collective—the criterion being "with whom do you like to go out and participate in games and enjoy yourself?" The children are to be regrouped as much as possible according to their choices. It was planned that the study should be applied to children of different age levels so as to make the differences in responses significant. It will be of interest for pedagogues in the U.S.A. to know what the results of the study are and most important to make a careful comparison of the sociograms of the school communities in the U.S.S.R. as they are reflected in the behavior of the children and the school systems in our country in which sociometric investigations have been made. Let us think further what such comparisons may offer to the management of the behavior problems of our teenagers and our high delinquency rate. Only systematic investigations will make it clear whether the separation of the children from the traumatic situations of intimate family life is of benefit or not.

Sociometric study in an electric plant near Leningrad (Prof. E. Kouzmin), Univ. of Leningrad.

West Germany

Universities of Tübingen, Munich, Hamburg, Berlin and Marburg.

Publications: "Gruppenpsychotherapie und Psychodrama—Einleitung in der Theorie und Praxis," J. L. Moreno, M.D., Georg Thieme Verlag, Stuttgart, 1959.

Yugoslavia

Yugoslavia is one of the socialistic countries where experiments *in situ* of the sociometric type have been carried out. A beginning has been made in farms, villages and schools, experiments sponsored by the Yugoslavian government.

Publication: Translation of J. L. Moreno's "Who Shall Survive?" into Serbocroatian, Jugoslovenska Autorska Agencija, Belgrade, Yugoslavia, 1960.

U.S.A.

New publications:

International Journal of Sociometry and Sociatry, 1956–1960, Beacon House, P. O. Box 311, Beacon, N.Y., Gronlund, Norman E., Sociometry in the Classroom, Harper & Brothers, New York, 1959.

New Publications:

Theatre of Psychodrama ("Princess" Theatre), Psychological Laboratory, Harvard University, Cambridge, Mass. Theatre of Psychodrama, St. Louis State Hospital, St. Louis, Miss. New Sociometric Institute (now Moreno Institute), 78th Street and Broadway, New York City, N.Y.

THE SOCIOMETRIC SYSTEM

by J. L. Moreno

1. The Sociometric Test

An instrument to measure the amount of organization shown by social groups is called *sociometric test*. The sociometric test requires an individual to choose his associates for any group of which he is or might become a member. He is expected to make his choices without restraint and whether the individuals chosen are members of the present group or outsiders. The sociometric test is an instrument which examines social structures through the measurement of the attractions and repulsions which take place between the individuals within a group. In the area of interpersonal relations we often use more narrow designations, as "choice" and "rejection." The more comprehensive terms, as attraction and repulsion go beyond the human group and indicate that there are analogous social configurations in nonhuman groups.

This test has been made in respect to home groups, work groups, and school groups. It determined the position of each individual in a group in which he has a function, for instance, in which he lives or works. It revealed that the underlying psychological structure of a group differs widely from its social manifestations; that group structures vary directly in relation to the age level of the members; that different criteria may produce different groupings of the same persons or they may produce the same groupings; that groups of different function, as, for instance, home groups and work groups, tend towards diverse structures; that people would group themselves differently if they could; that these spontaneous groups and the function that individuals act or intend to act within them have a definite bearing upon the conduct of each individual and upon the group as a whole; and that spontaneous groupings and forms of groupings which are superimposed upon the former by some authority provide a potential source of conflict. It was found that chosen relations and actual relations often differ and that the position of an individual cannot be fully realized if not all the individuals and groups to which he is emotionally related are included. It disclosed that the organization of a group cannot be fully studied if all related groups or individuals are not included, that individuals and groups are often to such an extent interlocked that the whole community to which they belong has to become the scope of the sociometric test.

The responses received in the course of sociometric procedure from each individual, however spontaneous and essential they may appear, are materials only and not yet sociometric facts in themselves. We have first to visualize and represent how these responses hang together. A process of charting has been devised, the *sociogram*, which is more than merely a method of presentation. It makes possible the exploration of sociometric facts. The proper placement of every individual and of all interrelations of individuals can be shown on a sociogram. It is still the only available scheme which makes *structural* analysis of a community possible.

2. Sociometric Self Perception

Every individual "intuitively" has some intimation of the position he holds in the group. He comes to know approximately whether the flow of affection and sympathy or antipathy for him is rising or falling. However vague this intuitive feeling may be it makes him feel happy sometimes—or sad. An individual may try to perceive his own relation to the members of his group and their relationship to him by proceeding as follows: he sketches out all the situations in which he is involved at the time and fills in all the individuals who take a part in them and in which role. Then he tries to clarify for himself how he feels towards each of these people. He is taking part in a sociometric self test and chooses or rejects them according to preference and rank, giving his reasons. In a later step he should make a guess what everyone of these people feel towards him and what reasons they might have. After he has finished his own self perception of his social atom he may ask another person familiar with his situation to rate him independently. Self perception is a sociometric test carried out in the mind of the tester himself. It is probable that the more systematic such a self-rating is made, the more helpful an orientation it will provide for the tester. As a compass of interpersonal relations it is primitive but our intuition and sensitivity in this direction is trainable (tele). The validity and reliability of data from sociometric self perception can be determined by giving to a group of individuals an open sociometric test immediately afterwards.

Appendix

3. Three Aspects of the Social Atom

One can look at a social atom from two directions, from an individual towards the community and from the community towards an individual. In the *first* case, the "individual-centered" social atom, one can see how the feelings radiate from him into many directions towards individuals who respond to him by likes, dislikes or indifference and of whom he is aware, or who choose, reject or are neutral towards him without his being aware of their participation in his social atom. This may be called the psychological aspect of the social atom. In the *second* case, the "collective-centered" social atom, one can look at socioatomic formations from the point of view of the community and it is in this way that it has actually been discovered. When one moves from the community into the realm of a particular social atom he is again confronted, as in the psychological version, with the same individuals who are interlocked with a particular, central individual. But he sees now that these individuals are also interlocked with one another and that their feelings also radiate towards individuals who are not directly a part of this particular socioatomic configuration. He is here face to face with a phenomenon which may easily be overlooked in the course of describing an individual-centered social atom. He sees in the new version that the individuals who are interlocked with the central individual A, enter with fragments and portions of their own social atoms, not only into the circle aronud A, but also into each other's circles. The central social atom appears surrounded with planetary social configurations but each of these planetary social atoms themselves are like the central suns, each surrounded with numerous planetary social atoms, and so forth, *ad infinitum*. Thus, instead of centering our attention upon a key individual with a number of individuals revolving around him, we see an interpenetration of various social atoms, of varying sizes and varying configurations, a visual demonstration that they, which represent the smallest social units of human society, are themselves involved in more and more complex social configuration ad infinitum.

In the third aspect, the "perception-centered" social atom, one can look at the internalized formations of the social atom from the point of view of the correct or distorted perceptions one individual has of the other or one collective has of the other.

4. Science of the Actor

Psychodrama is the science of the actor. The sociometric actor and the psychodramatic actor are two aspects of the same process.

A science of action rests upon the fundamental difference between the world of organism and the world of actors, the organism-in-environment versus the actors *in situ*. The organism is an abstraction, an abstraction from the actor, and behavior is an abstraction, an abstraction from the act. We should keep, for methodological reasons, the actorial system of the human group distinct from its behavioral system.

An action theory like Parson's which implies that organism *equals* actor and behavior *equals* action, or does not differentiate the two principles clearly, is a science of action "in name" only. The equalization of actor and organism is not merely a matter of semantics, it is a perversion of significant terms and further a crucial block in the advancement of an experimental methodology in the social sciences.

How does a social experiment start? It does not start with organisms, behaviors and cathexes; such is the view of observers and spectators. It starts with "you" and "me," with meetings and encounters, with actors and counter-actors. It does not start with "he" and "she," with "interpersonal relations" and the world of the "outsiders." A science of action begins with two verbs, *to be* and *to create*, and with three nouns, *actors, spontaneity* and *creativity*. A collective of actors has a meaning different from a collectivity of organisms, it is a "we," not a "they," it is a "creatocracy," not a universe of interacting organisms. It is urgent that the relation between organism and behavior on one hand and between actor and action on the other be clearly differentiated. The actor's "actings out" and the "data" or interpretations of the observer should not be treated as if they were identical—they may be supplementary but they are not identical. *An action matrix registers the live experience of actors, acts and events. A behavior matrix registers "observations" of actors, acts and events.* The actor must become an observer of himself and an actor towards the observer, i.e., the observer must become an actor towards the observed and an observer of himself; one must co-act the other, a meeting is taking place. In an ongoing socio-psychodrama the existential subjective experience of the actor and the objective view of the co-actor are like two sides of a coin. Indeed, as alter, or auxiliary ego to each other on the plane of action the degree of their reciprocal subjectivities and objectivities are continuously in a process of mixture; A acts towards B, B acts towards A; A observes himself as he acts towards B, B observes himself as he acts towards A; A observes A, B observes B; A observes A and B, B observes B and A; A acts towards C, A acts towards B and C, C acts towards B and A, etc. A genuine theory of action and actors deals with actorial categories and interaction potentials like spontaneity, creativity, the warm up, the moment, the meeting, auxiliary ego and other categories which express the coexperiential level of an actor's world on the level of action.

Moreno versus Parsons

The action systems of Moreno and Parsons have two principles in common. 1. Moreno talks of "actor in situ" (1947*); Parsons of "relationship of an actor to a situation. ..." 2. Moreno defines the actor in terms of roles "every individual has a range of roles and faces a range of counterroles. They are in various stages of development. The tangible aspects of what is known as 'ego' are the roles in which he operates. The pattern of role-relations around an individual as their focus, is called his cultural atom" (Sociometry, Volume III, 1940, page 20). Parsons explains that the concept "actor" "is extended to define not only individual personalities in roles but other types of acting units—collectivities, behavioral organisms, and cultural systems," (American Sociological Review, Vol. 25, No. 4, 1960, page 467). Do they mean the same thing by their definitions? Moreno has used these concepts many years before Parsons. In order to recognize the similarities and differences between the two systems we may have to go behind the books, behind the highly confounding texts to the facts and experiments underlying them. Moreno's concrete anchorage in the live experiments of sociometry, interaction research, psychodrama and sociodrama must be confronted with Parsons' psychoanalytically oriented way of conceptualizing data, with his references to near-sociometric findings (R. Bales), and with the contention that his action theory is strictly a conceptual scheme and in no way purports to be an empirical contribution. But an action theory which does not differentiate to start with between actor and organism in situ is faultily constructed.

5. The Sociometric System and Social Revolution

I differentiate two types of social systems: 1. revolutionary systems and 2. conservative systems. 1. Revolutionary systems try to set up a new type of society and a new type of government. Conservative systems try to maintain the status quo. They try to maintain and explain existing types of societies and governments. Illustrations of revolutionary systems are the Communistic systems of Marx, Engels and Lenin, the Utopian systems of Thomas Moore and Charles Fourier and the sociometric system of Moreno. Conservative systems have been formulated by Comte, Durkheim, Spencer and Weber; in our time by Sorokin.

The precipitating cause of revolutionary systems is the crass unreality of the existing societies and the reluctance of the people to live in them, the perennial drive to change and

* *Current Trends in Social Psychology,* Pittsburgh University Press, 1947.

if necessary, to abolish them. By means of sociometric methods the crass unreality of the human societies can be disclosed.

A "macrosociometry" of society does not exist yet—except for tentative hypotheses suggested by microsociometric researches, because the opportunity for an experiment in vivo on a large scale had not offered itself to a team of sociometrists. Only when a social revolution is "in the making" and social structure as well as the forms of government change can a truly satisfactory investigation be made of the "outgoing" and "incoming" social system of a society. As we live in a century of social revolutions such opportunities may offer themselves to the social scientist. Near at hand is, for instance, the Cuban Revolution which may be sociometrically examined and guided before it gets cold.

Index